2020 EDITION

THEORY OF KNOWLEDGE

COURSE COMPANION

Marija Uzunova Dang

Arvin Singh Uzunov Dang

OXFORD

UNIVERSITY PRESS

OXFORD
UNIVERSITY PRESS

Great Clarendon Street, Oxford, OX2 6DP, United Kingdom

Oxford University Press is a department of the University of Oxford. It furthers the University's objective of excellence in research, scholarship, and education by publishing worldwide. Oxford is a registered trade mark of Oxford University Press in the UK and in certain other countries

First published in 2020

British Library Cataloguing in Publication Data
Data available

978-0-19-849770-7 (print)
10 9 8 7 6 5

978-1-38-201960-6 (enhanced digital)
10 9 8 7 6 5 4 3 2

MIX
Paper from responsible sources
FSC www.fsc.org FSC® C007785

Paper used in the production of this book is a natural, recyclable product made from wood grown in sustainable forests. The manufacturing process conforms to the environmental regulations of the country of origin.

Printed in Great Britain by Bell and Bain Ltd, Glasgow

Acknowledgements

The authors would like to thank the following:

Our first debt of gratitude is owed to our students of TOK over the years. You have challenged us to be better teachers and, on a few occasions, driven us to plumb the depths of our motivation for why this work matters. It does. We are also grateful to the colleagues with whom we got to share classrooms and ideas, and some of the defining moments in our careers.

Special thanks are owed to friends who offered their own words and thoughts to be included in this book: Nandita Dinesh, Nikola Vukovic, Charis Boke and Joseph Mitchell. We also wish to recognize Aurelija Uzunova and Michelle Luiz for their diligence in helping us cite and locate sources and missing information. We are grateful for the insightful comments and suggestions of friends who read early versions of this work.

We give thanks to the many teachers, knowledge keepers, caregivers, mentors, human and other-than-human relations, by whom our lives have been touched and enriched. Your voices echo in our words.

And, most crucially, we give sincere thanks to Carolyn Lee, Mary-Luz Espiritusanto, Marie Trinchant and an entire team at OUP that worked tirelessly, gently and with seemingly infinite patience to place this book in your hands today.

The publisher and authors would like to thank the following for permission to use photographs and other copyright material:

Cover: agsandrew/Shutterstock. All other photos © Shutterstock, except p2: Daniel R. Strebe/ Wikimedia (Creative Commons Attribution-Share Alike 3.0 Unported license); p7: Courtesy of Morning Consult (morningconsult.com); p14: Rodrigo Abd/AP Images; p45: photo by Paul Miller; p49: NICOLAS ASFOURI/AFP/Getty Images; p59: Adam Grossman (artist's conception of the Milky Way galaxy by Nick Risinger); p60: NASA/JPL-Caltech; p61: TeleGeography and submarinecablemap.com; p64: Charles Phelps Cushing/ClassicStock/Getty Images; p66(r): Massachusetts Institute of Technology; p66(l): UtCon Collection/Alamy Stock Photo; p67(l): Afrofuturism 2.0: The Rise of Astro-Blackness, Reynaldo Anderson. Copyright © 2015. Used by permission of Rowman & Littlefield Publishing Group. All rights reserved; p68: Ullstein bild/ Contributor/Getty Images; p70: © Abby Smith Rumsey, March 2016, When We Are No More: How Digital Memory Is Shaping Our Future, Bloomsbury Publishing Inc; p76: Philippe Psaila/ Science Photo Library; p79: Courtesy NYC Municipal Archives; p83: Joy Buolamwini (Creative Commons License: cc-by-nc-nd); p85(l): Science History Images/Alamy Stock Photo; p85(r): Science History Images/Alamy Stock Photo; p87: PRISMA ARCHIVO/Alamy Stock Photo; p90: Sally Anderson/Alamy Stock Photo; p94: Stephen Worth/Alamy Stock Photo; p97: Cover illustration: Mona Schlapp, design: Claire Molloy, Copyright: Danau Tanu; p101: Courtesy of Douglas Ridloff, ASL Slam; p102: Courtesy of Nikola Vukovic; p107: Copyright: Estate of John C. Lilly. Margaret Howe and Peter Dolphin, Communication Research Laboratory, St. Thomas, US Virgin Islands. 1965; p109: STEPHANE DE SAKUTIN/AFP/Getty Images; p111: Bill Bachman/ Alamy Stock Photo; p113: History and Art Collection/Alamy Stock Photo; p115: Jean-Luc LUYSSEN/Gamma-Rapho/Getty Images; p124: Franck METOIS/Alamy Stock Photo; p125: Used by permission of Milkweed Editions. All rights reserved; p134: Sophie Pinchetti/Survival; p137: Christian Caron; p140: Alex Wong/Getty Images; p143: AP Images; p147: Pictures Now/Alamy Stock Photo; p153: Photo courtesy of the San Francisco Zen Center; p158: The Cleveland Museum of Art, Mr. and Mrs. William H. Marlatt Fund 1965.233 (CC0 1.0); p170: The History Collection/Alamy Stock Photo; p173: Historic Images/Alamy Stock Photo; p177: David Parkins; p186: University of Leeds; p181: Copyright Zach Weinersmith, smbc-comics.com; p184: Science History Images/Alamy Stock Photo; p191(tl): NASA Image Collection/Alamy Stock Photo; p191(r): Science History Images/Alamy Stock Photo; p192: The Mombasa Times; p193: Kitāb Batlamyūs fī al-taʻlīm al-maʻrūf bi-l-Majistī naqala Ishāq ibn Hunayn كتاب بطلميوس في التعليم المعروف بالمجسطي نقل إسحق بن حنين Ptolemy بطلميوس [70r] (152/498), British Library: Oriental Manuscripts, Add MS 7475, in Qatar Digital Library <https://www.qdl.qa/archive/81055/ vdc_100023246650.0x000099>; p197(t): Science & Society Picture Library/Contributor/Getty Images; p198: J. L. Lee/NIST; p201: NASA; p214: Wellcome Collection (CC BY); p217: Courtesy of Department of Special Collections & University Archives, Stanford University; p218: Science History Images/Alamy Stock Photo; p220: Chronicle/Alamy Stock Photo; p223: Daniel Hruschka, based on data from Rad et al PNAS 2018 (CC BY-ND); p233: "FRED®" charts © Federal Reserve Bank of St. Louis. All rights reserved. All "FRED®" charts appear courtesy of Federal Reserve Bank of St. Louis. http://research.stlouisfed.org/fred2/; p240: International Association of STM Publishers; p244(b): Centre for Science and Environment; p245: J. Lokrantz/ Azote based on Steffen et al. 2015. Planetary Boundaries: Guiding human development on a changing planet. Science Vol. 347 no. 6223; p247: Reprinted by permission of Dan Piraro; p250: NORMA JOSEPH/Alamy Stock Photo; p252: British Library/Album; p254: Jitish Kallat Studio; p255: INTERFOTO/Alamy Stock Photo; p256: Pictorial Press Ltd/Alamy Stock Photo; p260: Zdenek Sasek/Alamy Stock Vector; p270: Pictorial Press Ltd/Alamy Stock Photo; p276: David Harrison/Mail&Guardia/Gallo Images/Getty Images; p278: Still Life with Piles of French Novels and a Glass with a Rose, 1887, Vincent Van Gogh, Private Collection (F359) (image by Christie's Images/Corbis); p279: © Association Marcel Duchamp / ADAGP, Paris and DACS, London 2020 (image by Geoff Caddick/PA Archive/PA Images); p281: Stefan Malloch/ Shutterstock; p282: Guerrilla Girls, Do Women Have to Be Naked to Get Into the Met. Museum? Update, 2012. Copyright © Guerrilla Girls. Courtesy guerrillagirls.com; p283: © Judy Chicago. ARS, NY and DACS, London 2020 (image by STAN HONDA/AFP/Getty Images); p284: Anthony Devlin/PA Images/Getty Images; p286: Dan Tuffs/Getty Images; p287: Museum Boijmans van Beuningen, Rotterdam/Wikimedia; p291(t): Bridgeman Images; p293: The History Collection/Alamy Stock Photo; p294: DON EMMERT/AFP/Getty Images; p296(r): Courtesy of National Commission for Museums and Monuments, Abuja, Nigeria; p296(l): The Metropolitan Museum of Art, Gift of J. Pierpont Morgan, 1917 (CC0 1.0); p306(t): FL Historical collection 6/Alamy Stock Photo; p306(b): Courtesy of the Smithsonian Libraries, at: https:// library.si.edu/digital-library/book/hamonshuy00mori (CC0); p308: Courtesy of Anson Stevens-Bollen; p313: Ernst Friedrich; p317: Archive World/Alamy Stock Photo; p318: Frantisek Staud/Alamy Stock Photo; p319(c): Grant V. Faint/Getty Images; p319(t): ABDURASHID ABIKAR/ AFP/Getty Images; p329: © mathmannix at http://xkcdsw.com (original version from xkcd. com); p331: Jayk7/Moment Open/Getty Images; p335: The Picture Art Collection/Alamy Stock Photo; p336: Lee Young Ho/Sipa USALee Young H/Newscom; p345: Craig Kaplan; p346: Everett Collection Inc/Alamy Stock Photo; p359(l): NASA/JHUAPL/SWRI; p359(r): NASA/Johns Hopkins University Applied Physics Laboratory/Southwest Research Institute; p361: University Library Erlangen-Nuremberg/Wikimedia; p362(r): Cover to 'Sita's Ramayana' by Samhita Arni and Moyna Chitrakar, © Tara Books Pvt Ltd, Chennai, India. www.tarabooks.com; p363(l): Topham Partners LLP/Alamy Stock Photo; p363(r): Center for Cultural Studies on Science and Technology in China, Technische Universität Berlin; p364: mataatua.com.

Artwork by Q2A Media Services Pvt. Ltd.
Every effort has been made to contact copyright holders of material reproduced in this book. Any omissions will be rectified in subsequent printings if notice is given to the publisher.
The authors and publisher are grateful for permission to reprint extracts from the following:

Leila Ahmed: 'Muslim Women and Other Misunderstandings', interviewed by Krista Tippett, 7 Dec 2006, onbeing.org, used by permission of Professor Leila Ahmed, and the On Being Project. **American Mathematical Society**: *Notices of the American Mathematical Society*, public release, 6 Nov 2008, as per report 'Computers effective in verifying mathematical roofs', ScienceDaily. 7 Nov 2008, used by permission of the AMS and Scince Daily. **Amir Alexander**: *Duel at Dawn: Heroes, Martyrs, and the Rise of Modern Mathematics* (Harvard University Press, 2010), copyright © 2010 by the President and Fellows of Harvard College, Cambridge Mass; used by permission of Harvard University Press; and *Infinitesimal: How a Dangerous Mathematical Theory Shaped the Modern World* (Oneworld, 2015), copyright © Amir Alexander 2015, used by permission of Oneworld Publications through PLSclear **Elizabeth Alexander**: 'Ars Poetica #100: I Believe' from *American Sublime* (Graywolf Press, 2005), copyright © Elizabeth Alexander 2005, used by permission of the author c/o Faith Childs Literary Agency Inc, and of The Permissions Company, Inc on behalf of Graywolf Press, Minneapolis, Minnesota, www. graywolfpress.org; and 'The Desire to Know Each Other', interviewed by Krista Tippett, 11 April 2016, onbeing.org, used by permission of Elizabeth Alexander c/o Faith Childs Literary Agency, Inc, and the On Being Project. **Malcolm Allbrook**: 'Indigenous lives, the 'cult of forgetfulness' and the Australian Dictionary of Biography', *The Conversation*, 1 November 2017, used under CC-BY-ND 4.0 Licence **Marshall van Alstyne** and **Eric Brynjolfsson**: 'Electronic communities: Global Village or Cyberbalkans?', 1996, used by permission of the authors. **Asma-na-hi Antoine, Rachel Mason, Roberta Mason, Sophia Palahicky & Carmer Rodriguez de France**: *Pulling Together: A guide for Curriculum Developers*, used under CC BY-NC 4.0 Licence **Reza Aslan**: 'Islam's Reformation', interviewed by Krista Tippett, 20 Nov 2014, onbeing.org, used by permission of Reza Aslan, c/o The Cheney Agency and the On Being Project. **Australian Human Rights and Equal Opportunity Commission**: Submission G160, 13 May 2002, copyright © Australian Human Rights Commission 2002, 2017, used under the CC-BY- Licence. **BBC Trust**: Review of BBC's coverage of Science, July 2011, used by permission of the BBC. **Julian Baggini**: 'Which 'experts' should you believe?', *Aeon* (aeon.co), 2 Oct 2017, used under CC-BY-ND 4.0 Licence. **Philip Ball**: 'How natural is numeracy?', *Aeon* (aeon.co), 26 Oct 2017, used by permission of Aeon Media Group Ltd, aeon.co. **Isaiah Berlin**: 'Historical Inevitability' in *Four Essays on Liberty* (OUP, 1969), copyright © Isaiah Berlin 1969, used by permission of Oxford Publishing Limited, Oxford University Press, through PLSclear. **P J Bickel, E A Hammel, and J W O'Connell**: tables from 'Sex Bias in Graduate Admissions: Data From Berkeley', *Science*, 187: 4175 (1975), copyright © 1975, used by permission of AAAS (American Association for the Advancement of Science), conveyed through Copyright Clearance Center, Inc. **Charis Boke**: 'On experience and evidence in traditional Western herbalism', used by permission of Charis Boke. **Joanna Bourke**: *What It means to Be Human: Historical Reflections from 1791 to Present* (Counterpoint Press, 2011), copyright © Joanna Bourke 2011, used by permission of Counterpoint Press; and 'This won't hurt a bit: the cultural history of pain', *New Statesman*, 19 June 2014, used by permission of New Statesman Ltd. **British Museum**: statement released to CNN and reported by Oscar Holland, 22 Nov 2018, copyright © 2018, 2020 The Trustees of the British Museum, used by permission of the British Museum. **Karen Brodie**: Yes, mathematics can be decolonized. Here's how to begin' *The Conversation*, 13 October 2016, used under CC-BY-ND 4.0 Licence

Continues on page 394

Course Book definition

The IB Diploma Programme Course Books are designed to support students throughout their two-year Diploma Programme. They will help students gain an understanding of what is expected from their subject studies while presenting content in a way that illustrates the purpose and aims of the IB. They reflect the philosophy and approach of the IB and encourage a deep understanding of each subject by making connections to wider issues and providing opportunities for critical thinking.

The books mirror the IB philosophy of viewing the curriculum in terms of a whole-course approach and include support for the IB leaner profile and the IB Diploma Programme core requirements.

IB mission statement

The International Baccalaureate aims to develop inquiring, knowledgable and caring young people who help to create a better and more peaceful world through intercultural understanding and respect.

To this end the IB works with schools, governments and international organisations to develop challenging programmes of international education and rigorous assessment.

These programmes encourage students across the world to become active, compassionate, and lifelong learners who understand that other people, with their differences, can also be right.

The IB learner profile

The aim of all IB programmes is to develop internationally minded people who, recognising their common humanity and shared guardianship of the planet, help to create a better and more peaceful world. IB learners strive to be:

Inquirers They develop their natural curiosity. They acquire the skills necessary to conduct inquiry and research and show independence in learning. They actively enjoy learning and this love of learning will be sustained throughout their lives.

Knowledgeable They explore concepts, ideas, and issues that have local and global significance. In so doing, they acquire in-depth knowledge and develop understanding across a broad and balanced range of disciplines.

Thinkers They exercise initiative in applying thinking skills critically and creatively to recognise and approach complex problems, and make reasoned, ethical decisions.

Communicators They understand and express ideas and information confidently and creatively in more than one language and in a variety of modes of communication. They work effectively and willingly in collaboration with others.

Principled They act with integrity and honesty, with a strong sense of fairness, justice, and respect for the dignity of the individual, groups, and communities. They take responsibility for their own actions and the consequences that accompany them.

Open-minded They understand and appreciate their own cultures and personal histories, and are open to the perspectives, values, and traditions of other individuals and communities. They are accustomed to seeking and evaluating a range of points of view, and are willing to grow from the experience.

Caring They show empathy, compassion, and respect towards the needs and feelings of others. They have a personal commitment to service, and act to make a positive difference to the lives of others and to the environment.

Risk-takers They approach unfamiliar situations and uncertainty with courage and forethought, and have the independence of spirit to explore new roles, ideas, and strategies. They are brave and articulate in defending their beliefs.

Balanced They understand the importance of intellectual, physical, and emotional balance to achieve personal well-being for themselves and others.

Reflective They give thoughtful consideration to their own learning and experience. They are able to assess and understand their strengths and limitations in order to support their learning and professional development.

Contents

AREAS OF KNOWLEDGE (AOKs)

Dear reader,

Whatever lucky circumstance brings you to this page, we are excited for this book to accompany you on your journey - sometimes exhilarating, sometimes arduous - of exploring the Theory of Knowledge. Whether you are a student or a teacher, we intend for this book to be your critical friend: it will remind you to question the whys and hows of what you do and do not know. We also intend for it to be an enthusiastic champion of the astounding achievement of being knowledgeable in this complex world.

But that is the minimum a TOK textbook should do. Knowledge, like politics, is deeply concerned with things that are contestable, and in finding the truth within them. In the pages that follow, we thus aspire to make power relations visible and to deconstruct power structures as they pertain to knowledge. We invite you to participate reflexively in this process: questioning the claims we make and the stories we tell.

Especially with regards to knowledge and politics, many high school textbooks present a view from nowhere: a collection of palatable truths so depoliticized or apolitical that they give little meaning to issues of significance. For this reason we have sought to give you TOK from somewhere. For instance, we recognize that the IB has gaps in what it presents as authoritative or legitimate knowledge, and that these gaps are not random but the result of the powerful forces of globalization, capitalism, and colonialism. In working through this book you have the opportunity to examine which forms of knowledge have been prioritized and deprioritized in your educational experience, why, and how; and the influences of this on who you are as a knower in the world. The Theory of Knowledge should function as a meta-narrative of your education. In order for the TOK course to serve these purposes it must, as a starting point, itself be subjected to this deconstruction.

We, the authors, have the comparatively easy task of doing this and asking questions; the process of reconstruction, of knowing and of finding agency as a knower, is arduous and necessarily personal. You will thus find many questions and fewer answers in this book.

It is delightfully incongruous and very hopeful that a book like this is being published under this prestigious imprint. Precisely for this reason, we will often speak to you in a voice that is a little co-conspiratorial: do you trust what you read here? Why? Why not?

At the very least, you will learn enough amazing stories to be great fun at parties for a long time!

The Authors

1 Knowledge and the knower

As we learn about and move through the world, we are guided by the knowledge gained in our upbringing, from elders, teachers and the lived experiences of our particular social and ecological contexts. This foundation influences how we encounter new knowledge and different perspectives, and shows up in the stories of others.

Exploring who we are as knowers is thus central to TOK and woven throughout this book. The goal of this exploration is to illuminate how and why knowledge matters; who has knowledge and who does not; who has power and who does not; how and why we disagree; and what we might aspire to do with our knowledge.

Where do you see yourself fitting into all of this?

TOK is an invitation for you to get into the driving seat of your learning. It is designed to help you discover and exercise agency in a complex and politicized world, and to challenge ignorance and dogma with both confidence and a curiosity about the multitude of perspectives that are not your own.

Initial discussion

- What are the most important influences that have shaped what you know about the world?
- What motivates your pursuit of knowledge?
- What kinds of knowledge do you value highly, and why?
- What kinds of knowledge are specific to the communities that you belong to?
- What do your knowledge gaps reveal about you?

I. SCOPE

Knowledge can seem abstract, intimidating and hard to describe. Where should we begin?

Perhaps a helpful way into this conversation is to think about knowledge as a map. A map is not a natural object; it is something that humans created. It includes some details but not others, and has a boundary beyond which we may know nothing. It has territories, which we can think of as the Areas of Knowledge (AOKs), and features such as mountains, rivers and forests that run through them—like, perhaps, the knowledge themes. How are these territories and features known and demarcated? Who has made this map and decided that it should look this way? None of it is natural, or neutral. A map is created to represent the world, but simplifies much of the world's complexity. Despite these limitations, maps have been invaluable in enabling us to explore, learn and navigate the world successfully. We might say the same thing about knowledge, such as the following.

- Who produced this knowledge, when, where, how and for what purpose?
- What about the world does this knowledge represent and what does it leave out?
- How does this knowledge reflect or distort the real world?
- Is this knowledge reliable—how does it help us make sense of phenomena and make decisions?

In much the same way that we examine a map's purpose, strengths and weaknesses, we can ask similar questions about knowledge. Among the maps of the world, the Hobo-Dyer projection (Figure 1.1) accurately represents areas but not shapes, and is hard to navigate with. The Mercator projection is the most well-known projection of the globe and probably the one you are most familiar with. It is more useful as a navigational tool, but a much less accurate representation of the world.

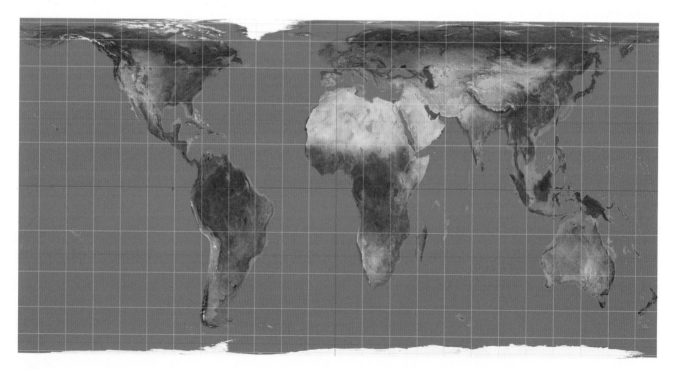

↑ **Figure 1.1** The Hobo-Dyer map projection, designed by Mick Dyer (2002), preserves relative areas at the cost of distorting shapes. How does it compare with the Mercator projection (developed in 1569), the most widely used map of the Earth?

Good maps balance the tension between accuracy and usefulness—between truthful representation and practicality—and we should ask how knowledge does the same. Which should we prioritize, in which contexts? This dichotomy frequently arises in the natural and human sciences, which create models of the world that are useful simplifications to help us understand the subject phenomena. The more realistic a model or map is, the larger, more complex, and more challenging to use, it becomes.

I.1 Knowledge, or knowledges?

Just as we have a variety of maps, from high-resolution satellite images to hasty sketches on table napkins, and secret maps in government vaults to maps etched into rock centuries ago, knowledge too comes in different forms.

There are some things we know from experience: there is light; there is heat; there are things that are fluid, rigid or gaseous; things that when dropped fall to the ground, and others, such as air bubbles in water, that go up. Some of our knowledge explains *how* the things we experience happen and *why* they happen. This kind of knowledge makes visible the forces such as gravity or power; structures such as molecules or gender roles; and processes such as climate change or gentrification, that influence the world we know and experience.

The different descriptions and explanations of our experiences have various levels of persuasive power and authority. In TOK it is useful to ask: what influences the claims we trust and have confidence in? This chapter seeks to illuminate that question at the level of the individual knower. In the following chapters we will also see how it applies at a larger scale, where different communities and cultures confer legitimacy and trust in different forms of knowledge, often for different reasons.

For reflection

Your collection of maps

For this activity, reflect on the knowledge you have gained through your upbringing and education. In what ways is this knowledge like a map of the world?

You use these "maps", these different kinds of knowledge, to understand and explain what goes on around you, and to guide your decisions and actions.

1. Which aspects of the world are absent or underexplored in your maps? Why is this the case?

2. Do you have maps that contradict each other? If so, in which aspects? These are issues that you may have conflicting knowledges about.

3. Do you have any maps that are wrong? How can you tell that they are wrong?

4. Using the map metaphor, describe what it means to be knowledgeable. How important is it to be knowledgeable?

Over generations, humans have not only produced and acquired knowledge, they have also applied it to act in the world around them, changing and modifying aspects of the world in the process. For example, we use our knowledge to enable the movement of goods, people and information on a global scale. These human-made flows and networks then become phenomena that we study and the impact of which we aim to understand.

Knowledge is complicated by power and authority. Some knowledge, and knowledges, may be more persuasive than others. An important question to consider is what influences whether we trust and have confidence in a given claim. Is there a difference between trust and confidence? Answers to this question reveal not only what we know, but how we know it, and how we encounter new knowledge and different perspectives, shaping the world in the process. Different communities and cultures across time and space may privilege or give legitimacy to knowledge differently. We are all shaped by these forces.

Knowledge may seem abstract and intangible, but it often has concrete origins. It is entangled with the instruments and tools we use to produce it, or with a specific place or ecological context. While knowledge can be a set of facts, theories and ideas, these can produce real material consequences in the world.

It is important also to consider how knowledge is represented externally—such as in language—which makes it possible for knowledge to be transferred across time and space. We should also consider what happens to knowledge that is not recorded in writing, or even expressed through language, as we explore in Chapter 2.

Knowledge is organized in a certain way, with institutions, structures and conventions. There are disciplines and academic fields with robust standards for what constitutes knowledge within them. For example, a large part of this book is dedicated to the areas of knowledge (AOKs), which are distinct but overlapping domains of knowledge. To what extent are these domains natural or contrived? Why do they exist separately from one another? Beyond the realm of academia there are other arrangements of knowledge, such as the folk knowledge passed on in cultural groups, or religious knowledge shared and transferred through institutions and communities.

The TOK course and this book invite your curiosity about the forms that knowledge takes, the processes through which it has been produced and disseminated, the people involved in these processes and their roles, as well as your own shifting relationship to knowledge.

For discussion

Knowledge and the IB Diploma Programme

Consider the knowledge you acquire in the IB Diploma Programme. Through its decisions about curriculum, assessment and approaches to teaching and learning, the IB Diploma Programme, like all educational programmes, privileges some knowledges compared to others. Let's consider some of the decisions made in this process and their potential consequences.

1. What knowledge is included and appears to be valued in the IB Diploma Programme?

2. (a) How is knowledge shared and transferred?

   (b) How is this different from other ways of sharing and transferring knowledge that you have encountered or are aware of?

3. Consider the keepers and sources of knowledge in the IB Diploma Programme.

   (a) What is the role of teachers, textbooks and other media?

   (b) How are teachers and books given status, legitimacy and credibility?

   (c) What kinds of knowledge are emphasized and underrepresented as a result of this, and what implications might that have?

4. Your assessments are a way of demonstrating knowledge. Given the structure, objectives and constraints of assessment, consider the following.

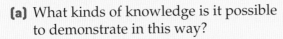

(a) What kinds of knowledge is it possible to demonstrate in this way?

(b) What kinds of knowledge are not captured by IB assessments, and what may be the consequences of this?

5. Now think about life outside of your IB studies and the other ways of knowing and learning you have access to.

(a) How do you value these as compared to the knowledge you acquire in the IB Diploma Programme?

(b) How much time and effort do you, and can you, give to acquiring knowledge in different ways outside of the IB?

6. Throughout this book and the TOK course we grapple with the concepts of neutrality and objectivity, among others.

(a) To what extent would you say that knowledge in the IB Diploma Programme is objective and/or neutral?

(b) What criteria would you use to determine this?

I.2 "Here be dragons"

> … our ignorance (whether individual or collective) is a vast, fathomless sea; our knowledge but a small, insecure island. Even the shoreline is uncertain: both the history of the human race and psychological research suggest that we know even less than we think we do. Indeed, our ignorance is extensive beyond our reckoning.
>
> (DeNicola 2017)

Consider the views of professor of philosophy Daniel DeNicola. There is an often-told parable about sailors using maps marked with dragons at the boundaries of the known world. Whether or not this story is true, does it reveal something about how we think about the limits of knowledge? Do we imagine that "there be dragons" beyond what we know, menacing and dangerous? Or do we imagine the boundaries to be porous or ill-defined? Literally or figuratively, there is no single map of the world, and all our maps have distortions, strengths and weaknesses. The exercise of TOK is to know our own maps intimately. There are practices that we can use individually and collaboratively to shed light on these limits and the forces that define them. Can we say there are predictable limits to knowledge in the sciences, the arts or mathematics?

It is valuable to explore the limits to our knowledge, and the extent to which they can be overcome. This is part of the exercise and practice of intellectual humility. Even though we cannot travel back in time, we have historical methods that help us to know what happened in the past. And even though controlled macroeconomic experiments are practically impossible, economists search for ways to make predictions about the macroeconomy. Being sensitive to the limits of our knowledge could help prevent costly mistakes in economic policy. Some limits to knowing are to a large extent knowable, in the methodological limitations of what we can observe or measure, or ethical limits about what we can study and how. We can think about limits to knowledge as being driven by known and unknown, and perhaps by unknowable, factors.

For discussion

The limits of knowledge

1. What factors limit our knowledge in the different domains, such as science, art or history?

2. To what extent do the different areas of knowledge cover the range of what there is to know? Use prompts (a) and (b) to guide your approach to this question.

(a) Does knowledge in religion extend to where scientific knowledge cannot?

(b) Does art take over from mathematics at some point?

3. How have humans overcome the limits to knowledge in the past?

4. Could you definitively say something is beyond our collective scope of knowledge? How would you know this?

Box 1.1: The impact of ignorance

Think about the two views given below.

"Put simply, people tend to do what they know and fail to do that which they have no conception of. In that way, ignorance profoundly channels the course we take in life." (Dunning quoted in Morris 2010)

"Knowledge is a big subject. Ignorance is bigger. And it is more interesting." (Firestein 2012)

The consequences of our knowledge and ignorance can be significant. At its most extreme, ignorance pertains to that which we do not even know that we do not know. Less extreme are known unknowns, the limitations of knowledge in our present state. Ignorance can also be understood as uncertainty in the reliability of our claims, which can be improved and overcome to an extent by further study, precision and iteration. There may be limitations, both known and unknown, to our capacity to know more, and therefore we need to develop means to accept a degree of uncertainty.

Some ignorance is culturally induced, through a failure to spread or acquire knowledge effectively. This may present as gaps in literacies (for example, scientific or cultural) that leave knowers and citizens vulnerable in domains where they need to make decisions, for example by voting, about things they do not fully understand. Collective gaps in knowledge can lead to epistemic injustice, especially in cross-cultural situations; for more on this see IV.3.

Finally, ignorance can be the deliberate promoting of doubt, propagation of falsehoods or blocking of knowledge through censorship.

The impact of ignorance depends on context and the nature of ignorance in question. Keep ignorance on your mind as you move through this textbook and the TOK course. It is easy to forget when we are concerned with studying knowledge. To what extent do we know ignorance through studying knowledge? Could this course accurately be called the theory of ignorance?

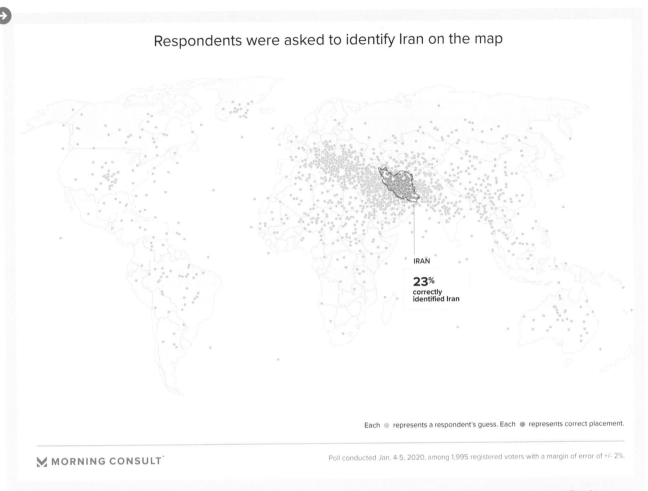

Respondents were asked to identify Iran on the map

IRAN

23%
correctly
identified Iran

Each ⬤ represents a respondent's guess. Each ⬤ represents correct placement.

MORNING CONSULT

Poll conducted Jan. 4-5, 2020, among 1,995 registered voters with a margin of error of +/- 2%.

↑ **Figure 1.2** Can you locate Iran? A Morning Consult/Politico survey (2020) conducted in the United States revealed that 47% of voters supported the airstrike that killed General Qasem Soleimani, regardless of whether they could identify the Islamic republic on an unlabelled map, which fewer than 3 in 10 did. Orange dots represent incorrect guesses while green dots represent correct placement.

A similar survey led by Dropp *et al* (2014) for the *Washington Post*, in the aftermath of the Ukrainian revolution and pro-Russian unrest in Crimea, found that about one in six people were able to correctly locate Ukraine on an unlabelled map, with young people providing more accurate answers than other age groups.

The further a respondent thought Ukraine was from its actual location, the more likely they were to support military intervention, either believing Russia to pose a threat to US interests or confident that using force would benefit national security.

I.3 Knowledge matters

The TOK course invites you to ask all sorts of questions about how people came to know what they claim to know.

Consider a question such as: what counts as knowledge? Through history, this question has not been answered using a formal checklist or clear definition but more often through messy and unequal negotiations about the validity

of different perspectives. Folk and Indigenous knowledge, the knowledge of women, and the knowledge of those who cannot speak a certain language or write in any language, for example, have long been excluded, delegitimized and devalued. This is more than a matter of diversity or inclusion. Knowledge plays a significant role in shaping narratives and guiding decisions that affect, sometimes disproportionately, those who are not seen as possessing or able to contribute to it. The history of colonized peoples from the perspective of the colonizers is one example.

Because of the role and importance of knowledge in the world, how we answer these questions about knowledge has significant consequences. As you work through this book and this course, practise looking at the material in terms of significance. Consider why an issue being examined *matters*. What are the consequences of a particular claim being considered true or false?

For discussion

This I know

Within TOK we examine the difference between knowledge, belief and opinion, and what criteria we use to distinguish between them. This discussion looks at when and why these differences matter. Start with the following three claims.

- Humans are fundamentally self-interested.
- Everyone is just trying to live their best life.
- People do not change.

1. Which of the claims would you say is an opinion, knowledge or belief?

2. What would be the consequences of wrongly categorizing one of the claims?

3. Next, write three statements of your own.

   (a) Complete, in any way that is honest and meaningful to you, the following.

   This I believe: _____ .

   This I think: _____ .

   This I know: _____ .

   (b) What quality does the last statement have, that the other two do not?

4. Is it important for you to maintain a distinction between your beliefs, opinions and knowledge?

II. PERSPECTIVES

There is also the question of significance in your own pursuit of knowledge. Do you believe that individuals have a responsibility to be knowledgeable about the world? If not, what motivates you in your pursuit of knowledge? Curiosity and wonder are powerful motivators too, as is a yearning for meaning and purpose.

The exploration of perspectives in TOK is bolstered by the IB mission that states "others, with their differences, can also be right" (www.ibo.org). Within the scope of TOK discussions, knowledge is contestable. This means that you keep open the possibility of more than one correct, legitimate or good answer to the questions you are exploring.

This section explores the roles of expertise, humility and critical evaluation when you encounter different perspectives in the world. It is designed to help you understand your perspective, and how the perspectives of others influence what you know. It is a broader aim of the course that you will:

- become equipped with the tools and attitudes to navigate disagreement

- take sides in significant debates in an informed manner
- appreciate and be curious about the perspectives of others.

Chapter 2 explores the phenomena of post-truthism, misinformation and distrust in expertise that have surfaced prominently in the last decade. Chapter 7 examines scientific controversy and denialism in depth. We turn now to examining how we, as individuals and knowers, deal with what appears to be the new normal: political polarization and scientific denialism.

II.1 Appeals to authority

When experts are divided, and we are not experts ourselves, whom do we trust? One approach is to consider the positions and judgments of other experts carefully and to discern the majority opinion. The philosopher Julian Baggini, for example, prescribes a "triage of truth" with three questions.

- "Are there any experts in this domain?
- Which kind of expert in this area should I choose?
- Which particular expert is worth listening to here?" (Baggini 2017).

Expertise and authority manifest differently across domains. For example, a dentist informing you of a cavity and an economist providing a forecast of economic growth are different propositions even if both experts are qualified to do what they do. We know that many economists are wrong in their predictions, but we continue to listen to them to discern the consensus opinion—such is the nature of their domain. If you are not religious, and/or do not believe in God, then a theologian or priest might have little influence on your opinions—but what does it mean to not believe in science or scientific expertise?

Often, how we think about expertise is influenced by the opinions of experts that we already trust; this seemingly innocuous knowledge claim has profound implications, suggesting that your history and context, over which you may have had little control, influence your orientation to new knowledge generally, and expertise specifically. The further implication is that to know something, you must also know yourself. A triage or any other framework for thinking about expertise is not a substitute for your good judgment. Jean-Paul Sartre describes this predicament, and the unavoidable responsibility of judgment that falls on all of us.

> If you seek counsel—from a priest, for example—you have selected that priest; and at bottom you already knew, more or less, what he would advise.
>
> (Sartre 1946)

For reflection

Expert opinion

Consider the ways in which your knowledge has been influenced by what experts think and say.

1. How important have experts been for the knowledge you have gained?
2. Do you regularly refer to expert knowledge for the claims you make?
3. Recall a situation when you have encountered contradicting expert opinions. How did you decide whom to trust?

II.2 Intellectual humility

Many people at some point encounter opinions, beliefs, ideas and claims that they consider to be false, inaccurate and/or immoral. How we navigate such claims has implications for how we navigate relationships with other people, how we think about politics, who we vote for and many of the other decisions we take over a lifetime. Do we, for example, avoid the category of offensive claims and the people who hold them? Are we afraid their values might negatively influence us? Some caution is certainly warranted, but the instinct to avoid some categories of belief and/or people closes us off to other perspectives and world views, with the risk that we stop learning. It also privileges our current cognitive perspective, which we may have inherited from parents or arrived at unintentionally. When differences of belief and opinion are widespread, what makes you trust your current perspective? How did you arrive at it?

> Frank sees a bird in the garden and believes it's a finch. Standing beside him, Gita sees the same bird, but she's confident it's a sparrow. What response should we expect from Frank and Gita?
>
> (Kappel 2018)

A useful attitude to cultivate is to think of beliefs as generally contestable. Section IV considers how to engage with abhorrent beliefs, and the resulting judgment of the people who harbour them.

What approaches should we take when confronted by disagreement? Consider the following anecdote, by Klemens Kappel, professor of philosophy at the University of Copenhagen.

If both Frank and Gita become less confident in their judgment, the result is a conciliatory response that allows for learning and change, a characteristic of intellectual humility. When spotting birds in the garden, it is relatively easy for us to be open-minded like this: our identities and wellbeing are not at stake. Disagreements that extend into politics and identity are in a different category. Consider another anecdote, also from Kappel.

> Amy believes that a particular homeopathic treatment will cure her common fever … Amy believes that there is solid evidence for her claim … as well as testimony she got from experienced homeopaths whom she trusts. Ben believes that any medical intervention should be tested in randomised controlled studies, and that no sound inferences are to be drawn from homeopathic principles, since they are shown to be false by the principles of physics and chemistry … Amy understands all this, but thinks that it merely reflects Ben's naturalistic perspective on human nature, which she rejects. There is more to human beings (and their diseases) than can be accurately captured in Western scientific medicine, which relies on reductionist and materialist approaches.
>
> (Kappel 2018)

We discuss reductionist approaches in depth in Chapter 7.

If you were Ben or Amy, what would you do? What we have here is a deep disagreement, in which both parties cannot change their opinion without also changing the structure of their reasoning, their world views and value systems. Typically Ben and Amy agree to disagree, but not always. And agreeing to disagree is not an option that you can vote for, or put into policy. When we encounter perspectives, opinions and beliefs that oppose our own, we must balance a tension between confidence in our knowledge and humility about its limitations. This is easier said than done.

For discussion

Change my view

Do you have a deeply held belief that you accept might be flawed? Would you offer this opinion up for discussion and open yourself to understanding other perspectives on the issue? What would it take to change your mind?

 Search terms: Reddit Change my view

There is an online community on reddit, /r/changemyview, dedicated precisely to this type of exchange of views. Follow the link to explore some of the top discussions. You could post your own view on something and see if any of the 900,000 members share what the issue looks like from their perspective. Regardless of whether you decide to do this, consider the following questions.

1. **(a)** What is the value of accepting the possibility of being wrong?

    (b) Do you lose something in doing so?

2. How can you cultivate a capacity for the kind of dialogue among multiple contradictory perspectives that we see on /r/changemyview?

3. To what extent can words, especially the words of anonymous strangers, change our core beliefs and deeply held opinions?

II.3 Why do people believe strange things and what should we do about it?

Political philosophers have long assumed that disagreements in democracies focus on values, preferences and morals, and that scientific facts will rise to the surface to settle these disputes. In fact, this may be a flawed assumption. From conspiracy theorists to scientific denialists, some beliefs seem to insulate people from evidence.

When deep disagreements occur, they concern not only the "facts" in question but also the processes behind how we form facts and who we trust to come up with them. The disagreements are about evidence, expertise and authority. When confronted by someone who does not accept what you accept to be fact, despite all the available evidence, how do you balance being intellectually humble with a commitment to the truth?

Debates about climate change and vaccinations continue in countries around the world, even in 2020. These debates shape political discourse where there is no option to agree to disagree: a policy decision must be taken one way or another.

Evidence would be an obvious way to resolve disagreements, and yet some academics including Julian Baggini argue that people "cherry-pick" evidence—that is, they tend to believe what they want, and select the evidence and expertise to justify it. Kappel agrees with this position, and argues that it is especially true for beliefs that are fundamental to our identities. If a fact aligns with our beliefs, we tend to embrace it less critically and remember it better than a fact that challenges our beliefs. Factual beliefs can serve as signals of identity and solidarity:

> by asserting your belief that climate change is a myth, you signal your allegiance to a particular moral, cultural and ideological community.
>
> (Kappel 2018)

This might be one factor behind political polarization.

> The pessimistic interpretation of this is that the appeal to expertise is therefore a charade. Psychologists have repeatedly demonstrated the power of motivated thinking and confirmation bias. People cherry-pick the authorities who support what they already believe. If majority opinion is on their side, they will cite the quantity of evidence behind them. If the majority is against them, they will cite the quality of evidence behind them, pointing out that truth is not a democracy. Authorities are not used to guide us towards the truth but to justify what we already believe the truth to be.
>
> (Baggini 2017)

To add to these challenges, how does one continue to respect others' perspectives when they dispute the facts that underpin one's morality and identity? How does one react when these perspectives block political processes and policy decisions that one sees as essential to the common good?

According to Quassim Cassam, we believe what we do not because of facts, but because of how we think: these *habits of mind* frame how we evaluate evidence, relate to authority and respond to the arguments and beliefs of others. Cassam asserts that we have long focused too closely on reasons, and reasoning, in belief-formation as opposed to habits of mind, and what he calls intellectual character traits. It is the nature of intellectual character traits that we often do not know that we have them. Cassam, for example, describes conspiracy theorists as gullible careless in reasoning, indifferent to authority and less able to discern between evidence and speculation, but to describe them as gullible or careless is not to describe their reasons, but their habits of mind.

However, attributing problematic reasoning to peoples' characters is itself problematic: for one, it pathologizes people, and can make others less empathic and tolerant towards them. That does not, in itself, make it false, but it is potentially harmful. An alternative argument is that human behaviour at any given time is contextual, explained by circumstances rather than habits or character traits. People who are hungry, upset or in a rush may act and think differently in a given situation than those who are relaxed, for example. The values and beliefs of the people around them also matter. This is the "situationist" argument, assertively put forth by the Princeton philosopher Gilbert Harman, who argues that "we need to convince people to look at situational factors and to stop trying to explain things in terms of character traits" (2000).

Context almost certainly matters, but this does not mean that habits of mind do not. What can we do as individuals and communities to cultivate effective habits? If someone accused you of being gullible because you believe a mainstream science story, how would you respond? It is an obvious trap, and you should certainly not immediately abandon your views, but being aware of the possibility of your own fallibility is almost always a good thing.

Box 1.2: How we run away from facts

 Search terms: Why people fly from facts

"... bias is a disease and to fight it we need a healthy treatment of facts and education. We find that when facts are injected into the conversation, the symptoms of bias become less severe. But, unfortunately, we have also learned that facts can only do so much. To avoid coming to undesirable conclusions, people can fly from the facts and use other tools in their deep, belief-protecting toolbox." (Campbell, Friesen 2015)

Research by Friesen *et al* (2015) examined how people distance themselves from facts that contradict their beliefs. They may, of course, simply dispute the validity of specific facts. They may consciously or subconsciously reframe the issue in untestable ways that make scientific evidence less relevant.

The researchers provide the example of same-sex marriage, still a contested issue in some countries in 2020. The researchers investigated whether scientific evidence could sway people's beliefs about the issue, using fake studies about the beneficial impact on children of same-sex versus opposite-sex parents.

The researchers presented these made-up facts to participants who supported or opposed same-sex marriage, and found that when the facts opposed their views, participants "were more likely to state that same-sex marriage isn't actually about facts, it's more a question of moral opinion". However, when these made-up facts were on their side, participants were more prone to assert that "their opinions were fact-based and much less about morals" (Campbell, Friesen 2015). This result showed not the denial of facts, but the denial of the relevance of facts, for participants on both sides of the issue. The researchers summarized that:

"… when people's beliefs are threatened, they often take flight to a land where facts do not matter. In scientific terms, their beliefs become less 'falsifiable' because they can no longer be tested scientifically for verification or refutation." (Friesen *et al* quoted in Campbell, Friesen 2015)

III. METHODS AND TOOLS

How do you pursue and acquire knowledge? The section invites your curiosity about your habits of thinking, which are some of the tools and methods in your thinking toolkit, for use in your pursuit of knowledge.

Part of the process of examining your habits of thinking is understanding how you have acquired particular habits and not others. Another part of the process is to take ownership and responsibility for your habits of mind; recognizing that habits are developed, not fixed, and therefore can be improved upon. Habits are also stubborn, and so changing them is an intentional process that requires effort and consistency. How would you like to be able to think? What does it mean, to you, to have good tools and methods for acquiring knowledge?

This section is informed by research in metacognition, and loosely inspired by the thought of Gregory Bateson and the work on Visible Thinking by Project Zero at Harvard University.

III.1 Thinking patterns and habits

Your IB classes are a form of apprenticeship into thinking like a historian, physicist, artist, or linguist. Or is that really so? The preceding statement assumes a knowledge claim about the correlation between academic education and individuals' habits of mind. It should not be accepted at face value. What standards of evidence or appeals to authority could you make in support or against this claim?

Regardless, we can say that through studying the IB Diploma Programme you acquire not only knowledge but also tools and methods specific to the disciplines you are learning about.

In TOK you have an opportunity to step back and ask, for example: when is it appropriate to use the tools and methods of history or mathematics? When is it helpful or necessary to combine different approaches, and when is it impractical or impossible?

What is typically readily available to us is what we think—our opinions and beliefs and what we claim to know. Less readily available, and sometimes altogether invisible to us, is how we have come to know, believe or hold opinions about things. Much of this book is dedicated to examining how we acquire knowledge. This section focuses not only on what you think, know and believe, but also on how you come to know, think and believe it.

II. Perspectives

III. Methods and tools

 Search terms: NYT New York Times 40 intriguing pictures

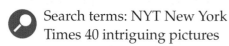

The *New York Times'* "What's Going On in This Picture?" is an engaging starting point to begin identifying your thinking habits. The link on this page takes you to pictures like the one above, sourced from the *New York Times* and presented without comment or caption. Chosen for their ambiguity, they allow for multiple interpretations. In thinking about what is going on in each picture, respondents are invited also to consider what informs their answer and how they arrived at it. As you form an opinion or belief about what you see in the picture, consider how you are encountering the uncertain, unknown and unclear.

For discussion

"What's going on in this picture?"

Consider the picture on this page or any picture from the link below it.

Look carefully at the picture you have chosen, and respond to the following questions.

1. What is going on in the picture?

2. Explain why you answered question 1 as you did. Include evidence for any claims you have made.

3. Why might the things you see be happening?

Next, use the following questions to guide your reflection about your claims, opinions and beliefs.

4. What factors make you more likely to apply past knowledge to what you see rather than focusing entirely on the information at hand?

5. At what point do you feel that you have sufficient evidence to make a claim about what you see?

Clues about your habits of thinking can also be found in how you encounter and examine the claims of others.

Discussion option: if you are able to do this exercise with a partner or as part of a small group, share and explore each other's answers to questions 1–5.

If discussion with others is not possible, consider the online comments under each of the pictures, in which respondents share their perspectives.

6. What factors make someone else's perspective convincing or reliable?

7. What factors make someone else's perspective unconvincing?

Concepts in your TOK toolkit

The following concepts play an important role throughout the TOK course and this book. You will have a chance to develop your understanding of these concepts in each of the chapters that follow.

The TOK course does not provide definite answers about what these concepts are, but rather provides a range of meanings across different disciplines, intellectual traditions and knowledge communities. You may have already formed an understanding about these concepts, in which case consider how you would approach the following and deepen and widen this understanding. For now, keeping in mind your answers in the previous activity, "What's going on in this picture?", consider how you approach the following.

- **Evidence:** what kinds of observations did you and others offer as evidence for your claims? If you thought some evidence was

more convincing, what characterizes this?

- **Certainty:** what does it take to be certain of something, for example the location depicted in a given picture? What factors influence whether certainty is more or less achievable?

- **Truth:** were there some claims that were beyond dispute? What does it mean for a claim to contradict something that is widely accepted to be true? If something is true now, is it true forever?

- **Interpretation:** what makes something open to interpretation? In the context of the pictures, what gives validity and authority to some interpretations but not others? Under what circumstances might it be desirable or undesirable to have multiple interpretations?

- **Power:** how does the relative power of claims-makers affect how we think about evidence, truth and objectivity? What does it mean for a claim to have explanatory power? Is the power of an idea expressed through its influence?

- **Justification:** are claims justified on the basis of reason, intuition, experience and authority equally valid? Does a claim require justification in order to be considered knowledge?

- **Explanation:** how is an explanation of what is going on in a picture different from a description of it? What makes for a good explanation? When is having multiple explanations desirable, and when is it not?

- **Objectivity:** on what grounds can objectivity be claimed or doubted? Are there different challenges in objectively describing *what* is happening, *how* it happens and *why* it happens?

- **Perspective:** is being able to see and understand something from multiple perspectives always beneficial? Can a perspective be "false"? When might reaching a consensus among different perspectives be necessary?

- **Culture:** what is the role of culture in how knowledge is shared, produced and evaluated? Is it easier to see how the cultures of others influence their knowledge, as opposed to how your culture influences yours?

- **Values:** can knowledge be neutral? Should it be neutral? What role do your values play in your pursuit of knowledge? How do values influence the production and sharing of knowledge?

- **Responsibility:** what responsibilities do you have when making claims or evaluating the claims you encounter? Would you agree that you have a responsibility to be knowledgeable?

III.2 Varying our metaphors of knowledge

We opened this chapter with the map metaphor of knowledge, which can help us think about the properties of knowledge. Another metaphor of knowledge is a tree. We consider the implications of this metaphor, for example about how knowledge is understood and acted on, below.

> In European societies, knowledge is often pictured as a tree: a single trunk—the core—with branches splaying outwards towards distant peripheries. The imagery of this tree is so deeply embedded in European thought-patterns that every form of institution has been marshalled into a 'centre-periphery' pattern. In philosophy, for example, there are certain 'core' subjects and other more marginal, peripheral … Likewise, a persistent, and demonstrably false, picture of science has it as consisting of a 'stem' of pure science (namely fundamental physics) with secondary domains of special sciences at varying degrees of remove: branches growing from, and dependent upon, the foundational trunk.
>
> (Ganeri 2017)

Jonardon Ganeri offers an iteration to this metaphor, using a different kind of tree: instead of one with a single trunk, we might picture a banyan tree with multiple stems. No part is more or less important or fundamental, which reflects the idea of a plurality of knowledges without a central system. The banyan tree metaphor was used by Vedic philosophers millennia ago, as Krishna says in the *Bhagavad-Gītā*.

> Stands an undying banyan tree, with roots above and boughs beneath. Its leaves are the Vedic hymns: one who knows this tree knows the Vedas. Below, above, its well nourished branches straggle out; sense objects are the twigs. Below its roots proliferate inseparably linked with works in the world of men.
>
> (Bhagavad Gita)

The Banyan tree metaphor stands for epistemic pluralism, a knowledge system consisting of many different roots, "many different but equally valuable ways of interrogating reality" (Ganeri 2017). We should caution, however, against relativist arguments that make the mistake of saying, for example, that all areas of knowledge are correct in their own ways, just different. For that would be to describe separate, isolated trees in a forest of knowledge, whereas Ganeri's argument is that there really is just one single epistemic system, one tree of knowledges, of which science, Indigenous knowledge and religion are all a part.

It is important that we do not collapse our view of academic disciplines into branches on the tree of knowledge, because they, too, can be comprehended as trees within their own right. Who would be so brave to claim that there is only one correct way of doing science, for example? We interrogate such a claim in Chapter 7. The same is true of other areas of knowledge, although Western philosophers have been accused of seeing themselves as the central trunk of the tree of knowledge.

As we open up to these multiple ways of knowing, how do we overcome the problem of relativism; the problem of any and all knowledges being different but equal in terms of helping us understand the world? Ganeri refers to Jaina philosophers who offer the concept of epistemic stances, or *nayas*, that are attitudes, approaches or strategies towards producing knowledge. It is a useful construct to escape relativism, and he explains it using yet another metaphor. If our goal is to reach the top of a mountain, we can each take different routes to get there, and each route offers different advantages and disadvantages. Some will be faster, steeper and more challenging; others more leisurely and scenic.

> Whichever route is selected, each mountaineer is in principle able to avail of the same tools and techniques, the same crampons, maps and axes; but the mountain unfolds itself differently to every one. The toolkit of the responsible enquirer contains empirical observation, logical techniques of deduction, induction and inference to the best explanation, and the pooling of discovery through testimony. But there is no single correct way of using those tools in one's interrogation of reality.
>
> (Ganeri 2017)

Different approaches lead to the same summit, but they are not equivalent. What we are concerned with is not simply the binary of true and false, which serves to exclude plurality, but rather the question of which path is most appropriate to our position, goal and capacity. What terrain does the mountain present to you? Which faces will you climb? Different peoples and cultures choose different *nayas*; to claim that there is only one way to the summit, towards knowledge, is an act of epistemic violence.

> One does not believe a stance in the way that one believes a fact. Rather, one commits to a stance, or adopts it.
>
> (Chakravartty 2004)

For discussion

Your intellectual autobiography

An important skill for a knower is; the ability to reflect on their thinking processes. This skill is referred to as *metacognition*, or knowing about knowing. To practise this skill, consider the influences and events that have shaped you as a knower and thinker, and write a short intellectual autobiography. How did you become the thinker you are today? You may choose to share this with a partner, a small group or with your TOK class.

1. In drafting your intellectual autobiography, consider how the following have influenced your thinking and the way you see the world today:

    (a) your upbringing and participation in different communities

(b) your schooling

(c) your experiences with specific places, people, events or key ideas.

You can do this as an essay, a mindmap or any other format that feels appropriate and authentic. Reflecting on your intellectual autobiography, consider the following questions.

2. How much of your intellectual development has been intentional?

3. In what ways do you want to develop as a thinker and a knower?

4. Did the way you see the world change at any time in your intellectual development? What does it mean to you to change not just *what* you think, but *how* you think?

IV. ETHICS

In TOK, and throughout the "Ethics" section of every chapter that follows, a key concern is who bears the ethical responsibility for how knowledge is produced, shared and applied? These discussions typically focus on issues of protecting against misconduct in the pursuit of knowledge; integrity in the way knowledge is shared and communicated; and guarding against the harm that can come as a result of the application of knowledge.

In this section, however, we consider our ethical responsibilities specifically as knowers. What does it mean to behave rightly and justly as knowers, individually as well as collectively?

IV.1 Intellectual entitlement

In most legal systems today, we are protected from brainwashing, indoctrination and other forceful and intrusive means of belief-changing. But do we have a right to believe whatever we want? We are generally not protected from having our beliefs scrutinized, questioned and criticized. Rights often have limits and come with responsibilities. Would you agree, for example, that we have a right to "believe responsibly"?

A "right to believe" could be conceived of as either evidential or moral. An evidential right refers to a right to believe what we can justify with evidence. A moral right refers to the right

to believe whatever one chooses, a right that is protected in the sense that no one should take it away. While this is not a legally granted right *per se*, it is upheld in various other rights, especially in cases where employment or education have been taken away because of a person's beliefs.

A moral right to believe would be problematic if we consider the acts of questioning or criticizing someone's beliefs as depriving them of this right. To make a point using the extreme, anytime you asserted a belief that clashes with someone else's belief, the two rights—your freedom of expression and the other person's right to belief—would come into conflict. A right to belief should not be used as a negative right—that is, to limit dialogue, to defend close-mindedness and dogma. If we learn one thing from TOK, it should be that knowledge is contestable; so is belief.

For discussion

Justified or unjustified beliefs

"It is wrong, always, everywhere, and for anyone, to believe anything upon insufficient evidence." (Clifford 1877)

To what extent do you agree with this statement? Are there some beliefs that should be insulated from questioning? Should knowledge never be contestable?

IV.2 The category of problematic beliefs

The issue of holding beliefs that are at odds with evidence is especially important in the political and public spheres, where discourse and disagreement can affect policy. This section examines ethical concerns for the category of strange beliefs, and the people who espouse them.

The claim that beliefs are influenced by peoples' upbringing, education, identities and the situations they find themselves in is widely asserted and believed. How we hold people accountable to their beliefs is still an important question, shaped by our own beliefs of the extent to which people are self-aware and independent thinkers. One might laugh off or dismiss a friend's problematic beliefs, such as their denial of scientific facts or belief in conspiracy theories, because one "knows who they are". One is also more likely to excuse a child's ignorance than the ignorance of an adult stranger with opposing political views. It can sometimes be difficult to separate our judgment of a belief from our judgment of the person who has the belief, especially with morally concerning beliefs. To what extent is this separation warranted, desirable or possible?

> "
> If the content of a belief is judged morally wrong, it is also thought to be false. The belief that one race is less than fully human is not only a morally repugnant, racist tenet; it is also thought to be a false claim… The falsity of a belief is a necessary but not sufficient condition for a belief to be morally wrong; neither is the ugliness of the content sufficient for a belief to be morally wrong. Alas, there are indeed morally repugnant truths, but it is not the believing that makes them so. Their moral ugliness is embedded in the world, not in one's belief about the world.
>
> (DeNicola 2018) "

Can a belief be unethical? The answer depends on whether we believe that all beliefs aspire to truth. Recall the tension between simplicity and accuracy in section I,

and the example of maps of the world that are more useful (such as the Mercator projection, at least for navigation) versus more truthful (the Hobo-Dyer projection). Not all beliefs aspire to truth—some may be useful beliefs, or coping beliefs, or pretty little lies. As the old saying goes, truth without love is intolerable. For the sake of argument, let's say everyone strives to believe in the truth; if so, how would you engage with the judgment that some beliefs are unethical? "Think harder, believe better" is certainly easier said than done. Many legal systems have found a practical solution to this problem: hold people morally and legally accountable to their actions or declare them insane. DeNicola (whose work was introduced in section I) questions why we condemn beliefs and believers when they lead to morally wrong actions. Such a response appears to assume that belief is a deliberate and voluntary act, when in actuality it may be "'inherited' from parents and 'acquired' from peers, acquired inadvertently, inculcated by institutions and authorities, or assumed from hearsay" (DeNicola 2018). For these reasons, it may be the act of sustaining a problematic belief in the face of evidence, rather than the act of believing itself, that is a problem. Or perhaps that is just reframing the problem as stubbornness. In our minds, the question of how we hold people morally accountable for their beliefs is still a challenging question.

IV.3 Epistemic diversity and epistemic justice

Much in TOK is about the exploration of different perspectives. Do we have a responsibility to seek out, understand and protect different perspectives? If so, to what lengths should we be doing this?

In the discussion in II.2 we saw that having multiple, partially overlapping, and sometimes contradictory perspectives coexisting in the same space presents advantages as well as challenges. Having a personal and civic ethic that cultivates these advantages and manages the challenges is called pluralism, and is a foundation for modern liberal democracies around the world. Pluralism is threatened when the appetite, or capacity, for managing these challenges is diminished, for example when efforts at consensus-building and respectful dialogue between opposing perspectives are seen as unimportant or not worth it.

To what extent would you agree with the view that, collectively, we benefit from having multiple perspectives and multiple knowledges about the world? How important are other factors, such as autonomy and freedom, which afford these perspectives agency? What is lost when a perspective is lost?

Each of us interacts with knowledge at a fundamental level every day when we share our opinions with others, evaluate what others share with us and comprehend our lived experience. We may not think of these as ethical issues or political acts, but the questions of validity and legitimacy—of our claims, and of ourselves as claims-makers—define our experiences.

In TOK we explore the ideas of legitimacy and validity as ethical issues of knowledge that intersect with power to have significant consequences in the world. Below, we look at how this intersection with power can produce two distinct forms of epistemic injustice or violence, which Miranda Fricker describes as the "wrong done to someone specifically in their capacity as a knower" (Fricker 2007).

The first is when the credibility of a claims-maker is prejudicially deflated because of their identity; the second is when there is a gap in the collective understanding to make sense of and communicate a particular experience.

IV.3.1 Credibility

The first form of epistemic injustice occurs when we deflate the credibility of a claims-maker, for example when their identity is met with prejudice. There is a fine balance to be struck in evaluating a claim based on the claim itself, and the claim-maker. To what extent is it possible to separate the two? We rarely evaluate a claim in a vacuum without paying attention to who is making it. In Chapter 3 we encounter the challenges of knowledge produced by anonymous people on the internet; in Chapter 9 we hear from E.H. Carr, who advises us to "study the historian before you study [their] facts". Which identities are relevant when we evaluate claims, and which are not?

We should be sensitive to the differences between one-off, idiosyncratic prejudices—"Bob is untrustworthy because he regularly talks nonsense"—and systematic and persistent prejudices based on identity—"Bob is untrustworthy because of his religion/age/ethnicity/sexual orientation/class" or some other identity.

Fricker (2007) has described this as the difference between a "prejudicial credibility deficit" and an "identity-prejudicial credibility deficit". Fricker's argument is that great harm is done at a societal level when we deny someone's legitimacy, based on their identity, to make a claim, to be a knower in their own right. This epistemic injustice occurs, for example, when "a hearer wrongs a speaker in his capacity as a giver of knowledge", excluding them "from the very practice… of what it is to know" (Fricker 2007).

In May 2020, the IB set TOK candidates the following question: "Does it matter that your personal circumstances influence how seriously your knowledge is taken?"

(a) Are there any groups of people whose claims you typically do not give legitimacy to? In what context, and why?

(b) Is it inevitable that a claims-maker's identity should affect our assessment of the legitimacy of their claim?

IV.3.2 Validity

A second form of epistemic injustice arises when a person's knowledge of their lived experience is invalidated, because of a lack of shared concepts between them and the dominant culture or power in a society. This puts them at a disadvantage in comprehending and communicating their experience. We see this happening cross-culturally, when the dominant culture is the arbiter of what counts as knowledge and what has legitimacy. Newcomers to this culture may find their perspectives or claims dismissed not only because of their identity, which would be a form of prejudice, but because others simply have no idea what they are talking about. Power has a role to play; certain types of lived experiences are invalidated more frequently than others. As examples, practices of mathematics through song, or through drawings with rice flour (see Chapter 11), have been dismissed as not mathematical; and oral histories have not been given the same credit as written histories (see Chapter 9). These are examples of knowledges that do not meet each other as equals because of power asymmetries and a lack of shared concepts.

What exactly is the role of power in epistemic justice? In Chapter 7, II.1 we ask whether knowledge is power. Perhaps a better question is the extent to which power determines what counts as knowledge, even to affirm or deny the lived experiences of others. If someone claims, for example, to be able to speak to trees or horses, to invalidate their claim is also to invalidate their experience of the world. A more compelling and challenging example is given below, by Fricker.

> " A central case of this sort of injustice is found in the example of a woman who suffers sexual harassment prior to the time when we had this critical concept, so that she cannot properly comprehend her own experience, let alone render it communicatively intelligible to others.
>
> (Fricker 2007) "

Fricker explains that this sort of epistemic injustice arises from a gap in shared concepts, vocabulary and tools of social interpretation. As you can imagine, this gap affects different social groups very differently, depending on the extent to which they are marginalized. The experiences of marginalized groups are less likely to be understood or conceptualized—less likely to feature in films and television shows, for example—perhaps even by the members of these groups themselves. The very structure of collective knowledge can therefore be prejudicial. These groups' efforts at communicating may be seen as inadequate simply because their style of expressing is misunderstood. They are disadvantaged because they cannot make sense of or express an "experience which it is strongly in their interests to render intelligible" Fricker 2007).

In May 2016, the IB set the following question for TOK candidates. "To what extent do the concepts that we use shape the conclusions that we reach?" Consider how this question applies to our judgments about the validity of claims and claims-makers; how much of our judgment is shaped by the concepts that we do and do not share with a claims-maker?

Given all of this, what are our individual responsibilities towards epistemic justice, especially in cross-cultural contexts?

As you continue to explore knowledge in this course, remember to continue reflecting critically on the knowledge you encounter at school and in the world, the gaps left by your education and upbringing, and how these intersect with power relations that may initially be invisible to you. The chapters that follow will help you to make power relations visible and navigate knowledge and the world with agency. How will you choose to know and live in the world?

2 Knowledge and politics

Politics is concerned with the acquisition and application of power, in its many forms, as well as all collective decisions that are contestable. In knowledge and politics we refer not only to political systems and structures, but also the wider sense of political life, in which we gather to deliberate and make decisions, as citizens as well as members of communities.

In this chapter we consider the tensions in knowledge and politics, such as the differences between knowledge and opinion; facts and values; and reliability and neutrality. We answer the questions: why is knowledge political, and how does this affect knowledge? Despite longstanding negative connotations, politics is a way—perhaps a good way, perhaps the only way—of navigating divisive issues and stubborn problems, of attempting to change the world for the better.

Initial discussion

- Is politics the best method available to us for changing the world?
- Is being knowledgeable a prerequisite for effective and active citizenship?
- What attributes are necessary or desirable in a political leader?
- What role does, and should, politics play in the institutions where knowledge is produced and disseminated?
- How are agreement and disagreement on matters of fact dealt with within politics?
- What gives validity to a knowledge claim in politics?

I. SCOPE

Questions about knowledge intersect in powerful and complex ways with questions about politics. For example, what we know about the world, how we know it, and who can make claims about it are entangled with questions about who has the power to make and maintain order in the world. The answers to these questions form what we call a "epistemic-political system", and vary across historical and geographic contexts. Our present system has been called a modern-liberal system, and is being challenged by various ecological, cultural, economic, spiritual and political crises of our own making.

The way out of these crises might require different answers to better questions about knowledge and politics, and even the emergence of a new system. It is an exciting and urgent time to be coming together to overcome the divisive issues and wicked problems of the world today.

This book explores and examines the processes through which facts are arrived at, scrutinizes the people and motivations behind fact-making, and traces the implications of accepting or rejecting something as fact. We have all heard many times, "these are the facts", but can facts speak for themselves? Matters of fact are supposedly disinterested, neutral, independent, or in other words, beyond politics. But what were the ideas in the past that shaped this way of thinking about facts?

Box 2.1: Hobbes and Boyle on knowledge, power and faith

The way we think about the relationship between knowledge and politics is still strongly influenced by a debate between Thomas Hobbes and Robert Boyle in the mid-17th century. The debate concerned what counts as knowledge, and where, how and by whom the boundaries of legitimate knowledge are drawn. Boyle and Hobbes had opposing views on this subject.

Boyle's approach reflected the emerging experimental sciences and he argued that people, like scientists, could objectively agree on "facts", if they followed strict processes and were disinterested in outcomes; Boyle's "facts" related to a "nature" that existed outside of "society". In contrast, Hobbes doubted that people could be objective or sufficiently disinterested, and believed that all human activity was political.

> "Boyle's notion of communities organized around their own methods and rules but bounded by limited domains not only led to the creation of different scientific disciplines but, more importantly, separated science from politics and religion … The final consequence of this would be that power, faith … and knowledge would be separated, each with its own institutions, rules, and procedures." (Stalder 2019)

This idea defined the modern-liberal era but now appears to be breaking down, perhaps vindicating Hobbes' suspicions that knowledge is always political and that disinterestedness is impossible.

Grappling with the political dimensions of knowledge-making and knowledge-sharing poses an urgent challenge for us today: in being suspicious of ideology that masquerades as fact, how do we guard against dismissing legitimate knowledge? How do we distinguish between ideology and knowledge?

Let's agree on the facts

There has been great concern, especially in recent years, that people ignore facts and dismiss evidence when it contradicts their beliefs.

1. To what extent do you agree that this is the case?

In Chapter 1, we introduced the counterclaim that people are not ignoring "the facts"; they do not accept them as facts in the first place and choose to believe a different set of facts. Facts appear to have become a signal for identity and political solidarity.

2. Who can legitimately establish what the facts are and who can legitimately dispute them?

3. Is there any knowledge that is beyond dispute?

4. Is it important for at least some knowledge to be non-contestable?

For practice, consider and critically explore to what extent universal human rights are non-contestable. Can you think of any other "universal facts"? Aren't all facts universal?

> Before mass leaders seize the power to fit reality to their lies, their propaganda is marked by its extreme contempt for facts … for in their opinion fact depends entirely on the power of man who can fabricate it.
>
> (Arendt 1951)

I.1 Is everything political?

It is often said that anything can be political. The clothes people choose to wear, the music they enjoy, the kind of language they use, the food they eat, and especially the food they do not eat, are all discussed as political acts. Consider though: have Meatless Mondays and all-gender bathrooms been politicized, or were eating meat every day and having gender-segregated bathrooms in public spaces already political statements? What aspects of life have been depoliticized?

The boundaries of politics are difficult to draw. Many of our choices, actions and claims are based on assumptions and values that are contestable, and therefore fall within the domain of politics. Arguably, this is the case whether or not we are aware of our assumptions and whether or not our actions are intentionally political.

Check your politics

1. Consider the politics of wearing a Che Guevara t-shirt. Does something important change if the person wearing it does not know who Che Guevara is?

2. Reflect on the politics of clothing that does not carry an explicit political message, such as buying second-hand items to minimize your ecological footprint. To what extent is this action political?

3. There is the idea that not only are our actions and words political, so too are our inaction and silence. Describe some examples of when this is the case.

Those who are cautious about the politics of everything have urged others to keep politics out of sport or science, Halloween or superhero movies, to leave it out of the classroom and away from the dinner table. This approach can come from a belief that there are spheres of life where politics does not belong, which should be protected from attempts to politicize them.

"Politicizing" means making something about politics. It is often also interpreted as, co-opting an event for political gain, as manipulation or misrepresentation in order to score political points. It is condemned when the timing or context in which it is done is seen as inappropriate. National tragedies or disasters are usually seen as the wrong context for politics.

With recent extreme weather events in view—droughts, floods, wildfires and storms—some commentators have suggested that political silence is not a neutral stance. Maintaining silence would be a failure to hold policy-makers to account for past and current decisions that affect the impact of the disasters.

Whereas rainfall and earthquakes may not inherently have a political dimension, disaster preparedness, response and recovery do. Looking closely at the aftermath of disasters we see how vulnerability intersects with racial and class inequalities. We also see how the frequency and intensity of extreme weather events already affects communities that are on the frontlines of the climate crisis. Some therefore argue that natural disasters are not at all apolitical, but have in fact been depoliticized.

A bit of historical distance can help us gain perspective on this issue. Let's consider examples from the previous two centuries that still reverberate today.

Unnatural disasters

In the 2001 book *Late Victorian Holocausts*, historian and political activist Mike Davis examines a series of extreme climatic events in the last quarter of the 19th century. These were the result of a sustained rise in surface temperatures in the Pacific Ocean, a phenomenon known today as El Niño, causing droughts across the tropics. In the final decades of the 19th century, the consequent famines had death tolls in the tens of millions of people across China, India and Brazil.

The outsize human cost of these droughts, Davis argues, was not a natural disaster, but one created by European empires. El Niño weather patterns were well known in those parts of the world, and over generations local ways of being and knowing, expressed through Indigenous knowledge, infrastructure and administrative systems, had developed to cope with drought. Imperial rule actively undermined or dismantled these systems with devastating consequences. For example, the millions in India who perished in the 1877 famine did not die as a result of food shortages; in that year, Indian grain exports to Britain reached record numbers. Davis similarly shows how Chinese government administrators were skilled at alleviating food shortages in times of drought, such that few people actually starved, but that this resilience was later devastated through Victorian imperialism, leaving millions to perish in subsequent droughts.

Bad climate versus bad system

The El Niño event of 1743–44 was described as exceptional in its impact on the plains of north China. "The spring monsoon failed two years in a row, devastating winter wheat … scorching winds withered crops and farmers dropped dead in their fields from sunstroke. Provincial grain supplies were utterly inadequate …" (Davis 2001). Yet unlike later droughts, there was no mass starvation.

Under the skillful leadership of the Confucian administration, great stores of grain were mobilized to affected areas, using ships where necessary. The administrators brought in 85% of the relief grain from stores outside the area of drought. This sustained two million peasants for eight months until the weather normalized and agriculture resumed, an extraordinary act "no contemporary European society guaranteed subsistence as a human right to its peasantry …" (Davis 2001) and nor did any have the capacity to do so like this. Indeed, while the Chinese peasants were saved from starvation by their administration, millions of Europeans were dying from famine and hunger-related diseases following freezing winters and summer droughts between 1740 and 1743. As Davis is careful to point out, this famine-defence was not an isolated case, and not even the most impressive. There were five other El Niño disasters and seven other flood disasters in that

century. Each time, the disaster relief was swift and extensive, unlike the responses in later years, such as 1877, 1899, and 1958–61.

"State capacity in eighteenth-century China … was deeply impressive", says Davis, with skilled administrators, a unique system to stabilize grain prices (overseen by the Emperor himself), large and well-managed grain stores, and "incomparable hydraulic infrastructures" and canals (Davis 2001). The fact that the Emperor was personally involved led to accuracy in reporting and more frequent innovation; disaster relief *was* politics, at least in China. Contemporary European monarchs were by comparison much less interested in the minutiae of grain prices and famine prevention.

The droughts of the next century, in 1876 and 1899, would not have caused millions of deaths if not for imperial intervention. Unlike in 1744, these administrators did not benefit from deliberately maintained budget surpluses and large reserves of grain. The difference, Davis asserts, was that the Chinese state in 1876 had been "enfeebled and demoralized", and the disaster relief efforts reduced to cash relief and "humiliating foreign charity" (Davis 2001). The intensity of the El Niño cycle was an important factor, but so too was the dismantling of the social, institutional and technical means for coping with that risk. "India and China, in other words, did not enter modern history as the helpless 'lands of famine' so universally enshrined in the Western imagination" (Davis 2001). They were enfeebled by Victorian imperialism and the loss of sovereignty. To learn how, you will have to read Davis's book.

Consider the following questions.

1. Is it possible to make politically neutral claims about the causes and consequences of huge natural disasters?

2. What types of claims about disasters can never be free of politics?

3. How is this example similar to or different from the way we speak about the climate crisis today?

It may feel strange to have the politics of disaster relief and, for example, the politics of pockets on women's clothing on the same spectrum. Whether or not everything is political, it is still necessary to pay attention to what is being politicized, or depoliticized, by whom and for what reason.

If this all sounds too much, you may wonder: can politics be avoided? Or is the very idea that you can opt in or out of politics a question of privilege? Political decisions affect the realities of people differently based on their relative power. Consider what it means to have the ability to disengage from politics, or to be cushioned from the consequences of political decisions. Do you have a responsibility to be informed and knowledgeable about politics, including the kinds of issues that do not affect you?

This brings us on to knowledge. Politics permeates human life and so knowledge, being a human enterprise, will have a political dimension as well. This is why we grapple with issues of power and justice in the realm of knowledge. Part of what makes TOK exciting is that the answers to questions about knowledge are contestable. In comparison, there are many educational programmes and systems around the world in which knowledge is not contestable. What does that say about the politics of the TOK course and the IB Diploma Programme? Consider this question in the context of the next discussion activity.

A political lens on knowledge draws our attention to when and why we give authority to some forms of knowledge and not others. It engages us with whether, and how, we privilege some ways of knowing and not others. A political lens also makes visible the power relations at play in knowledge communities.

With this in mind, let's consider the politics of knowledge in education, one of the main

institutions for disseminating knowledge. Think about the kind of knowledge institution that is your school, the knowledge community of IB Diploma Programme teachers and students worldwide and the knowledge system within which the IB sits.

Practising skills: Identifying assumptions and drawing implications

 Search terms: presentation history of ibo

Consider this presentation on the history of the International Baccalaureate, outlining the key influences on its educational model and approach.

1. As a result of the ideas on which the IB was founded, what are some explicit and implicit assumptions about knowledge in an IB education?

2. Given its history, what knowledge traditions are omitted or underrepresented in the IB?

3. What are the implications of exporting the IB as a "better" educational model to places around the world that have knowledge traditions that are not reflected in the IB?

As we move on, continue to reflect critically on the knowledge you are encountering at school and in the world. It is a practice that will serve you well beyond the IB Diploma Programme. No doubt there are gaps in the curriculum, as well as in this book. You are invited to notice them, understand how they might arise and consider what it would take to address them. Think about how power and politics affect which perspectives are emphasized, marginalized or absent, in your classroom and in a global, international curriculum.

I.2 Expert knowledge and governance

Throughout this book we engage with the tension caused by incoherent expertise, or what we can do when experts disagree with each other. Is there an essential tension between the ideas of expertise and democracy? This section explores issues of authority, participation and trust in the knowledge required for democratic decision-making. We take this discussion further in II.2, which explores the "post-truth" public discourse.

We make frequent decisions to trust the knowledge of experts, for example when we travel by airplane or have surgery. We trust that we are in the hands of competent, qualified professionals with certified expertise and that someone is checking that this is the case. These are personal decisions, about which we can make informed judgments as we navigate our daily lives. Governance, however, includes making judgments and decisions on behalf of other people, often on issues that require a great deal of technical expertise and in situations where there is no obvious answer. How can policy-makers and politicians ensure that they base decisions on the best knowledge available? What are the responsibilities of experts in advising decision-makers? To what extent can citizens participate in these decisions by contributing knowledge, evaluating claims and making judgments about competing alternatives?

Regardless of where you are in the world, there is no shortage of public policy controversies or failures across the health sector, environmental protection, financial markets or other areas of governance. In some contexts, these visible failings have eroded the public's trust in political decision-making guided by seemingly partisan expertise. But is there an alternative? Is there another model of governance that addresses the issues in knowledge and politics?

In TOK we concern ourselves not with evaluating specific policy decisions, but with questions about how claims-makers and forms of knowledge acquire legitimacy and authority, and how we can safeguard against bias and self-interest and learn from past mistakes.

For discussion

Expertise and the democratization of knowledge in policy

Working independently, in pairs or a small group, identify a political issue of public relevance that you are already familiar with or curious to learn about. If you are struggling to think of an issue, follow the links to two case studies that would work well.

 Search terms: Pisani sex drugs and HIV

This link takes you to a TED Talk by Elizabeth Pisani on sex, drugs and HIV.

 Search terms: Leslie The sugar conspiracy

In this article for the UK newspaper the *Guardian*, (7 April 2016), Ian Leslie investigates the view that sugar in our diet, and not fat, is the greatest danger to our health.

In your investigation draw on the questions we have encountered so far and the ones below.

1. What do you know, or what can you imagine, about the experts who guide the people with most power on this issue?

2. What kinds of knowledge should the experts possess?

3. Consider which perspectives are missing or underrepresented.

   (a) Which groups should be invited to the debate but are not currently involved?

   (b) What does their absence tell us about which kinds of knowledge are valued?

4. What is the nature and extent of public participation in this policy decision?

5. Which groups are most affected and what kinds of knowledge and power do they possess?

> ### Making connections
>
> **Politics in science and history**
>
> Chapter 7, section II, explores AIDS public health policy in South Africa. Chapter 9, section II, looks at the work of expert commissions between countries to resolve conflicting histories. Comparing these examples, what is the role of politics and how does it affect the credibility and authority of experts?

Take confidence in the fact that TOK is not alone in exploring issues of expertise and public knowledge. Questions about these issues are fundamental to protecting the citizen's voice in government, and the answers take different shapes depending on the context and the constraints. If you are curious about what this discussion looks like elsewhere, follow the link to an excellent conversation on public knowledge and the forces that shape it. Hear from Amita Baviskar, from the Institute of Economic Growth in New Delhi, and Rifka Weehuizen, from the University of Strasbourg Institute for Advanced Study. They discuss how expert and layperson knowledge can be integrated into a relationship based on democratic values and participation.

 Search terms: public knowledge academic objectivity and teaching profit motivation

II. PERSPECTIVES

Political issues are discussed by people and groups with various levels of power; they share their opinions, make claims with various degrees of confidence and make judgments about the reliability and validity of other perspectives. This characterizes the public discourse. How can you evaluate different perspectives? How aware are you of the forces that have shaped your political views? What would be sufficiently convincing to change your mind? As we proceed, recall the discussions in Chapter 1 on intellectual humility (in II.2) and thinking patterns and habits (in III.1).

II.1 The Overton window

> " The smart way to keep people passive and obedient is to strictly limit the spectrum of acceptable opinion, but allow very lively debate within that spectrum— even encourage the more critical and dissident views. That gives people the sense that there's free thinking going on, while all the time the presuppositions of the system are being reinforced by the limits put on the range of the debate.
>
> (Chomsky 1998) "

The "Overton window" is a term used to describe the range of ideas tolerated within public discourse and, therefore, the range of socially and politically acceptable policies in democratic government. Policies outside of this range will appear too extreme—"unthinkable" or "radical"—to be supported by politicians. The window is shaped by the climate of public opinion, and so the media can play a very large role. Note that the window does not necessarily sit near the middle of the political spectrum. Skillful politicians, social commentators and activists in the public sphere can intentionally shift or expand the window through reason and rhetoric. Some may deliberately promote extreme ideas so that slightly less extreme ideas, which were previously outside the window, become more widely accepted by comparison. Think tanks, for example, need not promote particular policies but can rather focus on shifting the window of possibilities,

to make previously unacceptable policies more palatable. This tactic is often used by activist groups too.

It is worth noting that the Overton window is not necessarily a passive construct but rather an assertive and dynamic one—a tool to shape and shift political possibilities. Its point is that the "window is there for the shifting", and thus it naturalizes ideas and policies as inherently political. Some observers lament this sort of thing, arguing for instance that climate justice and women's rights should not be politicized, as these issues "speak for themselves"; we interrogate that perspective in I.1.

The next section explores echo chambers and filter bubbles, or how the internet may be contributing to increased polarization and reduced pluralism, by allowing individuals to engage only with content they agree with.

For discussion

Looking out of the Overton window

1. How do we know where the Overton window is?

2. Would you expect two strangers to agree about what is inside the window? Why or why not?

3. Are there some ideas, policies or issues that should not be politicized? If so, how would we achieve that?

4. Compare the relative power of the following stakeholders to shift the window: social media organizations, cinema, search engines, print and television media; teachers, journalists, influencers and politicians.

5. Recall an example of the window shifting.

   (a) What was previously unacceptable, but is now policy, and vice versa?

   (b) What may have caused this?

6. Should we suspend new or radical ideas from judgment, for a grace period, until more people have had a chance to consider them?

7. To what extent do you agree that an expansion of the Overton window is a sign of progress?

8. To what extent is it unethical for politicians and thought leaders to support ideas and policies that they do not believe in, with the goal of expanding or shifting the window of public discourse?

9. If you had the influence, what ideas would you bring into the Overton window?

10. To what extent has the internet, through social media and online discussion groups, changed the nature of public discourse and the Overton window?

II.2 Is there a post-truth public sphere?

> For too many of us, it's become safer to retreat into our own bubbles, whether in our neighborhoods or college campuses or places of worship or our social media feeds, surrounded by people who look like us and share the same political outlook and never challenge our assumptions. The rise of naked partisanship, increasing economic and regional stratification, the splintering of our media into a channel for every taste—all this makes this great sorting seem natural, even inevitable. And increasingly, we become so secure in our bubbles that we accept only information, whether true or not, that fits our opinions, instead of basing our opinions on the evidence that's out there.
>
> (Obama 2017)

The last decade has witnessed repeated references to a post-truth politics, in which discourse is framed by appeals to emotion instead of policy details or facts. Political figures are able to continue with talking points even when media, experts and opposing figures have provided proof that contradicts them. The internet is commonly invoked as having enabled this political culture to gather momentum, with post-truthers being said to influence political outcomes in Brazil, India, Russia, the United States and the United Kingdom. "Post-truth" was made the Oxford Dictionaries' 2016 Word of the Year owing to its prevalence in the context of Brexit and the US Presidential election.

However, some have claimed the term is misleading. For example a *New Scientist* article stated: "a cynic might wonder if politicians are actually any more dishonest than they used to be" (*New Scientist* 2016). Others believe that it confuses the ideas of empirical and ethical judgments, whereas what is actually happening is a rejection of expert opinions in favour of values-based political signalling. Politically conservative figures have also criticized the selective use of the term by liberal commentators to attack what are matters of ideology, not fact

(Young 2016) and for selectively protecting "liberal facts" (Mantzarlis 2016).

It is a great irony of our time that we do not even agree about whether we live in a post-truth world, because the political right accuses the political left of making it up. TOK exists to help us with this very dilemma. We can and should strive to know truth and navigate problems of knowledge, and resist succumbing to views such as "nothing is true and everything is possible", which, by the way, is the title of a memoir of life in Russia under Vladimir Putin.

Of course, it cannot be claimed that large sections of organized society have suddenly given up on, or stopped caring about, truth. Post-truth refers to a civil discourse where expertise and "facts" appear to be insufficient to sway beliefs; where individuals appear to choose their experts and dismiss others as politically and ideologically biased. There is some behavioural research to suggest that facts alone do not change deeply held beliefs.

Alexios Mantzarlis, Poynter Institute's head of fact-checking, stated the following.

> Fake news became a catch-all term to mean anything that we don't particularly like to read.
>
> (Mantzarlis quoted in Kestler-D'Amours 2017)

Later in this chapter we explore how news media that prioritize impartiality can understate the overwhelming scientific consensus, leaving the public with what appears to be a scientific debate as opposed to scientific fact. Robert Eshelman has argued that, beginning in the 1990s, fossil-fuel industry groups seized this opportunity and accused reporters of bias if they portrayed global warming as a settled fact, while funding research to prove it was not. The tobacco industry used similar tactics in the decades before. These industries succeeded in politicizing the issue and spawning decades of public debate though the scientific consensus had been clear. This is the problem of "false balance" implicated in many public controversies on scientific issues.

Professor Jayson Harsin has argued that a convergent set of recent developments is creating a post-truth society. These developments include the following.

- Scientifically and technologically sophisticated methods of political communication and persuasion are used (as we explore later in the Facebook-Cambridge Analytica episode) as well as strategic use of rumours and disinformation.

- An "attention economy" exists, characterized by information overload combined with a lack of society-wide trusted sources of news. User-generated content within social networks has become more influential, while at the same time there appears to be less attention for, or trust in, fact-checking websites.

- Filter bubbles curate content delivered via social media and search engines according to what a user "likes", as opposed to what is factual. We explore filter bubbles and echo chambers in II.4.

For reflection

A post-truth society

1. What are the significant political issues being debated in your community?

2. To what extent is your opinion about these issues influenced by:

    (a) the news

    (b) the opinions of friends shared on social media

    (c) the opinions of close family and friends?

3. Have you noticed people in your network questioning the claims of experts? If so, in what context, and on what grounds?

Box 2.2: Do lies spread faster than the truth?

Two recent studies have suggested that lies can spread faster than the truth. As you read the details, though, consider the warning in Chapter 8, III.1, about sampling biases in behavioural science research.

Researchers at MIT investigated 126,000 Twitter stories, shared by 3 million people over 4.5 million times. The researchers' conclusion was that lies spread further, faster, deeper and wider than truth in all categories of information. Interestingly, fake political news spreads faster than fake news about natural disasters, terrorism, science or financial markets. The authors specifically found that humans, and not Twitter bots, are more likely to spread fake news. Why is this the case? The researchers speculate that false information tends to be more original than true news and that people are more likely to share surprising information (Vosoughi *et al* 2018).

Jeff Hancock, a psychologist at Stanford University, attributes the rapid spread of fake news on social networks to "emotional contagion". In 2012, Facebook ran an experiment that showed some users more positive posts and others more negative posts. Hancock helped interpret the results and found that people exposed to less negative emotion in their news feed would write with less negative and more positive emotion in their own posts, and vice versa.

In a March 2019 interview for the BBC, Hancock explained that people seemed to respond with emotions that match those of the original post. Not only did the emotions match, Hancock stated, but the more intense the emotion, the more likely the content was to go viral.

Practising skills: Evaluating perspectives

Below are two articles, selected for their differing viewpoints. Consider to what extent the authors agree or disagree on the following issues.

1. What do the different authors say is the source of post-truth phenomenon?

2. To what extent do they consider post-truth politics to be a serious threat to knowledge?

3. How do they describe the changes in the way we acquire and share knowledge?

4. What strategies do they suggest for a way out of the post-truth crisis?

Source 1: "Post-truth? It's Pure Nonsense" (The *Spectator*, 10 June 2017)

 Search terms: Spectator Scruton Post-truth

For as long as there have been politicians, they have lied, fabricated and deceived. The manufacture of falsehood has changed over time, as the machinery becomes more sophisticated. Straight lies give way to sinuous spin, and open dishonesty disappears behind Newspeak and Doublethink. However, even if honesty is sometimes the best policy, politics is addressed to people's opinions, and the manipulation of opinion is what it is all about. Plato held truth to be the goal of philosophy and the ultimate standard that disciplines the soul. But even he acknowledged that people cannot take very much of it, and that peaceful government depends on "the noble lie".

Nevertheless, commentators are beginning to tell us that something has changed in the past few years. It is not that politicians have ceased to tell lies or to pretend that the facts are other than they are; it is rather that they have begun to speak as though there is no such distinction between facts and fabrications. We live in a post-truth world — such is the mantra … Somehow the boundaries between true and false, sense and nonsense, opinion and reality … have been erased, and no one really knows how to reinstate them.

That is one way in which the Brexit vote is explained by those who cannot stomach it. If there is no truth, then opinions are no longer true or false, but simply yours or mine, ours or theirs. And since the Brexit vote was about identity, "we" were bound to win over those who still thought there was something to argue about. As for the "experts", why should we listen to them, when they were trying to phrase the argument in a language that no longer applies, as though there were some objective "fact of the matter" that we could all agree upon?

… The concept of truth has been the victim of massive cyber-attacks in recent decades, and it has not yet recovered. The most recent attack has come from social media, which has turned the internet into one great seething cauldron of opinions, most of them anonymous, in which every kind of malice and fantasy swamps the still small voice of humanity and truth. …

We have yet to get used to this, and to the damage social media has done to the practice of rational argument. …

Politics is an opinion-forming and opinion-manipulating art. However much people can be influenced by slick advertising, mendacious promises and intoxicating slogans, they are influenced by these things only because the idea of truth lurks somewhere in the background of their consciousness. In the end we all respond to an inner "reality principle", and will amend any belief when its refutation is staring us in the face. (The *Spectator* 2017)

Source 2: "India: The WhatsApp election" (*Financial Times*, 4 May 2019)

 Search terms: FT India WhatsApp election

"WhatsApp is the echo chamber of all unmitigated lies, fakes and crap in India, it's a toxic cesspool," says Palanivel Thiagarajan, an elected official and head of the IT department of DMK, a regional party in the state of Tamil Nadu … .

Claire Wardle, a research fellow at Harvard University and co-founder of First Draft, a non-profit group addressing misinformation on social media, says WhatsApp took off with the explosion of smartphone users in countries such as Brazil, Nigeria and India, where it has become "a primary source of information". "These questions about its role in the spread of misinformation are not just to do with elections," she says. "It's about WhatsApp's role in societies, full stop." Its encryption system … has made it more vulnerable to misuse, especially in elections, say critics, who argue it has become a platform for spreading campaign-related misinformation.

This risk came to a head in Brazil last year, in what became known as the first "WhatsApp election". With 120m WhatsApp users in a country of over 211m, the platform was flooded ahead of the October vote with false rumours, doctored photographs and audio hoaxes … Researchers studying 100,000 images circulating in 347 groups found that only 8 per cent were "fully truthful". "Misinformation was huge in Brazil. It was an election plagued with fake news that left behind a country split in half by hatred," says Fabrício Benevenuto at the Federal University of Minas Gerais and a researcher on the impact of the social media network. "The political discussion ended up being reduced to a meme."

WhatsApp has become the platform of choice for politicians because of its massive reach that goes beyond a party's loyal voter base, but also because of the lack of gatekeepers. Messages forwarded through the system have no context about where they originate, but benefit from the trust of coming from a contact.

"WhatsApp groups are considered the most dangerous," says SY Quraishi, India's former election commissioner. "The disastrous potential of this media is very strong; you've seen how rumours floating [around] can cause havoc."

Kiran Garimella, a researcher at the Massachusetts Institute of Technology who is studying misinformation in India, analysed more than 5m WhatsApp messages posted in 5,000 public groups … covering roughly 1m people. "We have observed that it is specifically focused on image-based, subtle misinformation," says Mr Garimella, giving an example of doctored screenshots from a reputable news channel.

WhatsApp says it bans roughly 400,000 accounts in India every month … . The biggest challenge is that, unlike Facebook, WhatsApp cannot identify the source of a message without breaking its encryption system … . "We see many instances where the same message was sent on multiple groups, over 20 groups within a 10-second window, that means there is a person or software sending the messages," says Mr Garimella.

WhatsApp says it has also spent about $10m in India to run a public education campaign around the dangers of misinformation on traditional media such as television, radio and newspapers. "I think I would say without hyperbole it's probably the largest public education campaign about misinformation ever undertaken," says Mr Woog. (The *Financial Times* 2019)

Follow the link below to access an article offering a different viewpoint from the ones expressed in the *Spectator* and the *Financial Times*. To what extent do its authors agree or disagree with the authors of the other two articles on the issues raised on page 33?

 Search terms: Economist I'd lie to you Post-truth world

II.3 Truth, neutrality and false balance

> It is not the case that astrology is drivel because [someone] thinks so. It is drivel because it flies in the face of four centuries of evidence, from Galileo to the latest space probe. To claim, as the BBC appeared to do, that whether or not to believe in astrology is a matter of personal opinion reveals a real lack of self-confidence. At best, such a statement is foolish; at worst it is open to exploitation by cranks.
>
> (British Broadcasting Corporation (BBC) 2011

Throughout, this book investigates the concept of truth, commonly associated with concepts of objectivity, impartiality and neutrality. Within knowledge and politics, what can we say of the relationship between truth and impartiality? Political issues are, by definition, divisive in the sense of lacking clear consensus. Does that mean that knowing "truth" in politics is futile? The practice of politics attempts to reach consensus through what has been described as "an opinion-forming and opinion-manipulating art" (Scruton 2017). We could ask the question whether objectivity can exist in politics, but the more immediate question for us here is: what are the implications of saying it cannot?

Let's consider the case of false balance, a cautionary example of a media bias that occurs when journalists (and, very importantly, text books) attempt to avoid bias by providing a balanced perspective on opposing viewpoints. They give equal air-time or pages of text to two sides of a debate. The phrase a "coin has two sides" might come to mind, but is misleading because it assumes equal weight of both sides. False balance occurs when arguments "from the other side" are presented out of proportion to the actual evidence. It confuses fairness—understood as giving due merit to the value of evidence—with impartiality. This may be caused by a pressure to appear "neutral" to avoid offending fee-paying advertisers and customers, and/or a lack of confidence or ability to evaluate a perspective.

A commonly cited example of false balance is the "debate" about anthropogenic global warming, though the scientific consensus has been overwhelming for at least two decades. Follow the link to find out more.

 Search terms: NASA Scientific consensus: Earth's climate is warming

Though the vast majority of experts—over 97%—attribute global warming to human activity, the opposing 3% have been given disproportionately large platforms, in the interest of balanced journalism. This has left the public with an impression of inconclusive scientific debate even though the scientific consensus is well established (Cook *et al* 2016).

For example, coverage of global warming by leading US newspapers—the *New York Times*, the *Washington Post*, the *Los Angeles Times* and the *Wall Street Journal* (a group referred to as "the prestige press")—between 1988 and 2002 was found to overstate the case against climate change: "[t]he prestige press's adherence to balance actually leads to biased coverage of both anthropogenic contributions to global warming, and resultant action" argued Boykoff and Boykoff (2004).

Following a review of the impartiality and accuracy of its science coverage, the BBC similarly reported the following in 2011.

The BBC review cites global warming,

> A frequent comment received during this review is that elements of the BBC—particularly in the area of news and current affairs—does not fully understand the nature of scientific discourse and, as a result, is often guilty of 'false impartiality'; of presenting the views of tiny and unqualified minorities as if they have the same weight as the scientific consensus. That approach has for some (but not all) topics become widespread. Conflictual reporting of this kind has the ability to distort public perception. It arises in part because news and current affairs presenters, who have to think on their feet in a live interview, may have little insight into the topic being discussed and hence find it more difficult to establish balance than when dealing with politics, the media or finance.
>
> (BBC 2011)

vaccinations and genetically modified foods as cases where impartial journalism understated the scientific evidence and consensus.

Should the journalistic profession shoulder all this blame? It is not that simple. Consider the article in Box 2.3 that reports how fossil-fuel industry groups began in the 1990s to target reporters who portrayed global warming as a settled fact: "it was the perfect line of attack, because it played into a core maxim of journalism: to be fair and balanced in presenting the contours of a debate" (Eshelman 2014). But simultaneously, Eshelman says, the industry was funding studies to discredit the climate change thesis; and even if very few scientists endorsed them it was enough to frame the issue as a "debate" in the media. In this way, according to Eshelman, the industry succeeded in politicizing an issue and stoking decades of public debate, even though the scientific consensus had been clear.

Box 2.3: The danger of fair and balanced

 Search terms: cjr danger of fair and balanced

Consider the extract below and discuss the following questions.

1. Do journalists approach the issue of balance differently when communicating knowledge to the public on political issues as opposed to scientific issues?

2. If all perspectives are not equally valid or valuable, is it the responsibility of journalists or the readers to decide whom to trust?

3. In knowledge, when is there a trade-off between accuracy and inclusion of different perspectives?

4. What is the difference between a fair balance and a false balance with respect to knowledge?

"On a sweltering June day in 1988, James E. Hansen, then the director of NASA's Goddard Institute for Space Studies, appeared before a key committee of the United States Senate. Seated before a bank of cameras and a panel of grim officials, Hansen delivered testimony that would start to swing accepted wisdom on the emerging science of climate change. The 'greenhouse effect', what we now know as climate change or climate disruption, was caused by human activity, mainly the burning of fossil fuels since the dawn of the Industrial Revolution, said Hansen and other scientists that day.

Even if the concept of global warming was rising, it seemed another leap of faith for most outside the scientific community to believe humans could be so profoundly transforming something as vast and seemingly permanent as the Earth's climate—and do it in as little as one hundred years. In trying to puncture this idea, Hansen and those like McKibben based their argument simply on science and made their case through explanatory writing. They talked about the ways the greenhouse effect would cause more frequent droughts and the sea levels to rise.

They seemed to make what clearly has proven a naive assumption: that by presenting only the science, they could provoke swift, determined action to reduce their fossil fuel consumption. Politics was not much on their radar.

'There was a lot of coverage and most of it was smart,' he says by phone from his home in Vermont. 'Journalists talked to scientists and just reported it. It hadn't occurred to them that it should be treated as a political issue as opposed to a scientific one,' McKibben says of coverage in the late 1980s.

But, he adds, 'It wasn't long before the fossil fuel industry did a good job of turning it into a political issue, a partisan thing they could exploit, when they started rolling out all the tools that we now understand as an effort to overcome the science. And their main target was the media.' The fossil fuel industry succeeded. In the ensuing years, the industry not only won over conservatives on the matter of climate change, but they also played into the media trope of balance and fairness.

… What came next was what Penn State University climate scientist Michael E. Mann calls the climate wars, and a principal line of attack was to question the work of reporters who portrayed climate change as settled fact. It was the perfect line of attack, because it played into a core maxim of journalism: to be fair and balanced in presenting the contours of a debate. Yet to do that, reporters were frequently using [fossil-fuel] industry-backed spokespeople as key sources about the actual science—not about a debate over potential policy solutions, of which industry should fairly be a part. Yet since policy solutions to climate change could severely choke profits, what better way to push back than to question the underlying science?

What McKibben considered accurate coverage of climate change in the late 1980s—reporters covering the science, not the politics—was in Gelbspan's estimation a major, structural failure on the part of journalists in the 1990s. It began with who was assigned to cover the subject. 'It was only science writers that were covering this stuff and they were not the types to follow the money,' Gelbspan says. Climate change doubters in those years were taking a page from the fight against the regulation of tobacco products, urging newspapers and radio and television networks to provide "balance" in their reporting of the science. Gelbspan was among the first to understand the folly of their claims. But journalists of lesser mettle were easily fooled or simply too caught up in the quotidian pressures of meeting deadlines. In this way, the denialist community successfully drove a wedge between scientists and reporters.

In *Merchants of Doubt*, historians Erik M. Conway and Naomi Oreskes trace this history of industry-funded and ideologically driven deception from tobacco, acid rain, the ozone hole, and through to contemporary fights about climate change. 'Tobacco was the first big, systematic denialist campaign,' says Oreskes. 'The obvious lesson for journalists is to know that this exists, that it depends on appealing to journalistic virtues of balance and objectivity.' But, she adds, 'It leads journalists into a swamp.'

… In 2009 came a fact that would be oft-repeated—that 97 percent of scientists with expertise on climate and atmosphere believed in a link between human-generated greenhouse gases and global warming. That's a level of consensus only slightly below that of the existence of gravity and equivalent to scientific evidence linking tobacco use and cancer.

Given this level of confidence, says Oreskes, the goal of journalists should have been accuracy rather than balance. Journalists, in other words, wouldn't have provided 'balance' to a debate on gravity, giving equal time to someone asserting that it doesn't exist; why would they for climate change? As for the two or three percent of so-called skeptics, Oreskes says journalists should be evaluating the motives for their dissent, especially given the history of industry- and think tank-led disinformation campaigns.

Whatever the factors that produce it, false balance remains. *USA Today*, for example, as a matter of policy requires that an editorial on a 'controversial' topic be paired with an editorial arguing in opposition." (Eshelman 2014)

The science, politics and language of climate change

How do denialists—or "evidence-resistant-minorities"—affect the evolution of scientific and political opinion? An article in the journal *Cognition* (Lewandowsky *et al* 2019) suggests that consensus formation can be delayed when a small group of denialists resist evidence about an issue (such as anthropogenic climate change).

It also suggests that this can cause the public to remain ambivalent about the reality of that issue. To counter such ambivalence, some advocates are using stronger language to communicate. As of May 2019, the UK newspaper the *Guardian* recommended in its style guide for journalists the terms "climate crisis" and "global heating", rather than "climate change" and "global warming". The Editor in Chief of the *Guardian*, Katharine Viner, gave the following explanation.

> We want to ensure that we are being scientifically precise, while also communicating clearly with readers on this very important issue. The phrase 'climate change', for example, sounds rather passive and gentle when what scientists are talking about is a catastrophe for humanity.
>
> (Viner quoted in Carrington 2019).

II.4 Echo chambers and filter bubbles

> Democracy requires citizens to see things from one another's point of view, but instead we're more and more enclosed in our own bubbles. Democracy requires a reliance on shared facts; instead we're being offered parallel but separate universes.
>
> (Pariser 2011)

An echo chamber is a metaphorical term used to describe a group in which beliefs and opinions are reinforced by repetition (echoes), while alternative or opposing beliefs and opinions are heard less often. In such a chamber, members intentionally or unintentionally engage with information that reinforces their existing views. As social environments, echo chambers can make members feel more confident in expressing themselves, more trusting (and less critical) of the opinions discussed, but also pressured to withhold opposing views. Members may also find it difficult to leave an echo chamber because of how entangled their social, cultural and political identities are with the discourse.

The terms "echo chamber" and "epistemic bubble" are sometimes mistakenly used interchangeably, though there are important differences between the two. As Professor Nguyen explains in "Escape the Echo Chamber" (the linked article), in epistemic bubbles the opposing opinions and voices are not heard, but in echo chambers these voices are actively undermined. Further, while exposure to contrary evidence can shatter an epistemic bubble, it may have the effect of reinforcing an echo chamber.

 Search terms: aeon nguyen Escape the echo chamber

Filter bubbles are a type of epistemic bubble resulting from the filtering of online content delivered by search engines and social media, based on user information such as search history, location and past click-behaviour. For example, Facebook news feeds and Google search results are customized for users based on this information (stored in "cookies"). Eli Pariser, a political internet activist who coined the term, has argued that internet users can become isolated in their own cultural or ideological bubbles of "likes".

Both effects have negative implications for civic discourse, as well as for democratic outcomes such as elections, though the size of this effect is still debated. While activists such as Pariser have worked to raise awareness about them, others such as Elizabeth Dubois of the University of Ottawa believe that the influence of "echo chambers in social media has been highly over-estimated" (Dubois quoted in Robson 2018). Still, many observers agree that political polarization has increased and that media literacy is an important skill to develop for active citizenship.

Case study

Perspectives on echo chambers and filter bubbles

> If you look at any measures of what people think about people on the other side, [they] have become vastly more hostile.
>
> (Haidt quoted in Robson 2018)

Why might this be the case? This section has considered how echo chambers and filter bubbles contribute to an increase in political polarization and the spread of misinformation in political discourse. However, there is another side to the argument, that claims the problem is with human behaviour, not our online or offline environments but instead the friends we keep and the news we respond to.

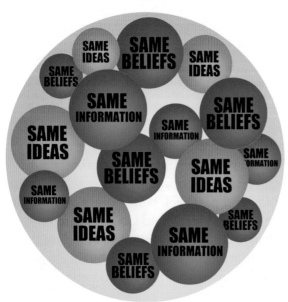

This case study considers two different perspectives. Eli Pariser warns us of the intellectual isolation and potential for polarization caused by filter bubbles. David Robson challenges this view, stating that social media will tend to increase the diversity of perspectives that an individual encounters online. The extracts below are just a snapshot and we recommend that you consider both original sources in full.

Source 1: Pariser, E. 2011. "Beware Online Filter Bubbles".

 Search terms: Pariser Online filter bubble TED Talk

"I asked a bunch of friends to Google 'Egypt' and to send me screenshots of what they got … Daniel didn't get anything about the protests in Egypt at all in his first page of Google results. Scott's results were full of them. And this was the big story of the day at that time. That's how different these results are becoming … . It's not just Google and Facebook either. Yahoo News, the biggest news site on the Internet, is now personalized— different people get different things. *Huffington Post*, the *Washington Post*, the *New York Times*—all flirting with personalization in various ways. And this moves us very quickly toward a world in which the Internet is showing us what it thinks we want to see, but not necessarily what we need to see."

Source 2: Robson, D. 2018. "The Myth of the Online Echo Chamber?"

Search terms: Robson BBC myth of online echo chamber

David Robson, writing for the BBC, describes studies that show that while social media users are exposed to more polarized news sources, they are also more exposed to sources with opposing viewpoints. This means that their media "diet" is more varied than that of users who regularly visit one or two internet news sites. There is also some evidence that social media users actively seek out diverse views that do not align with their existing beliefs and that the actual number of users caught up in an echo chamber is lower than commonly stated.

There is, however, some evidence that users may become more, not less, entrenched in their beliefs when presented with arguments from the opposing side of their political position.

For example, the concept of "motivated reasoning" is supported by research that shows that people are so attached to their political identities that they may unknowingly devote their thinking to dismissing evidence that disagrees with their beliefs. For example, Republicans were seen to use more emotive words in their online posts when exposed to more liberal viewpoints. This is a characteristic of echo chambers.

Robson (2018) describes the psychological concept of "self-licensing", in which individuals may feel that they have earned the right to their prejudice because they have demonstrated open-mindedness before. Robson describes a 2008 study that found that people who had supported Barack Obama in the US Presidential election were more likely to express potentially racist views subsequently.

For discussion

Filter bubbles and echo chambers— two views compared

1. To what extent is Robson's argument consistent or divergent with Pariser's and the other arguments we have seen so far?

2. Do Robson and Pariser make use of similar or different kinds of evidence?

3. To what extent have you observed or heard about this effect within your personal network?

4. What are the implications of online filter bubbles—positive or negative?

5. How can the negative effects of online filter bubbles be diminished?

6. Which groups of people are more vulnerable to the influence of filter bubbles and how can that be addressed?

7. "Policy-makers should regulate the internet so that what we see is 'neutral'."

   (a) To what extent do you agree with this statement?

   (b) What would a "neutral" view look like and who could decide on its content?

8. (a) How do the responsibilities of individuals, governments and organizations such as Google and Facebook differ in controlling the negative effects of filter bubbles?

   (b) Would you expect these responsibilities and this control to be consistent around the world, and why or why not?

The preceding few pages have shown Eli Pariser, Barack Obama and *The Economist* magazine, among others, argue that echo chambers and filter bubbles have contributed to the increase in political polarization of the past decade. They have also been implicated in the spread of misinformation in political discourse. Consider Figure 2.1.

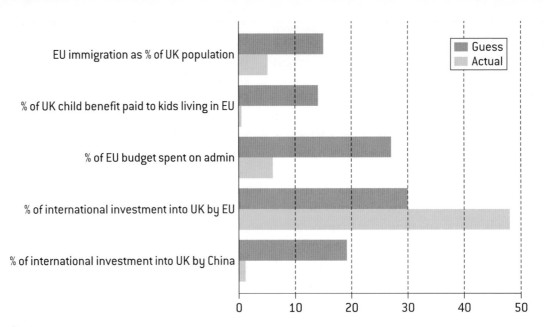

↑ **Figure 2.1** Misperceptions among UK survey respondents about how the EU affects life in the UK. Data source: UK newspaper *The Financial Times.*

Social media users report encountering a variety of political beliefs in their online networks, at least according to a 2016 Pew Research Center survey of 4,500 people in the United States (see Figure 2.2).

% of Facebook/Twitter users who say that most of the people in their networks have political beliefs that are___ to theirs

↑ **Figure 2.2** Pew Research Center survey conducted 12 July– 8 August 2016, "The political environment on social media": most Facebook and Twitter users' online networks contain a mix of people with a variety of political beliefs.

In 2016, a team of researchers from Oxford University, Stanford University and Microsoft investigated whether internet use had led to increased ideological segregation. They reported that social networks and search engines are associated with an increase in the average ideological distance between individuals (a measure of polarization). However, they also found that social networks and search engine use were "associated with an increase in an

individual's exposure to material from his or her less preferred side of the political spectrum" (Flaxman *et al* 2016). The researchers noted that most people still access online news by directly visiting their mainstream news websites of choice, not through social media (though this may have changed since then) and that the size of the effects of social media was relatively modest.

A research team in 2018 reported that Twitter users are "to a large degree" exposed to opinions that agree with their own. They also reported that those who share political content from both sides of the political divide— "who try to bridge the echo chambers"—incur a social network cost in terms of how many followers they have and how many likes their posts receive (Garimella *et al* 2018). However, a separate study, also in 2018, concluded that "those who are interested in politics and those with diverse media diets tend to avoid echo chambers … [and] only a small segment of the population are ever likely to find themselves in an echo chamber" (Dubois, Blank 2018).

And finally, researchers from Facebook investigated the existence of echo chambers among 10 million users and found that while news feeds tend to show people less diverse political information, this was driven more by users' posting behaviour than algorithmic ranking of content (Bakshy *et al* 2015). Of course, that seems a convenient conclusion for Facebook researchers, but Kartik Hosanagar, professor at the Wharton School, believes that the study was well-designed and agrees that it is "the like-mindedness of our Facebook friends that traps us in an echo chamber", explaining as follows.

> If we acquired our news media from a randomly selected group of Facebook users, nearly 45 percent of news seen by liberals and 40 percent seen by conservatives on Facebook would be cross-cutting. But we acquire these news stories from our friends. As a result, the researchers found that only 24 percent of news stories shared by liberals' friends were cross-cutting and about 35 percent of stories shared by conservatives' friends were cross-cutting. Clearly, the like-mindedness of our Facebook friends traps us in an echo chamber.
>
> The newsfeed algorithm further selects which of the friends' news stories to show you. This is based on your prior interaction with friends. Because we tend to engage more with like-minded friends and ideologically similar websites, the newsfeed algorithm further reduces the proportion of cross-cutting news stories to 22 percent for liberals and 34 percent for conservatives. Facebook's algorithm worsens the echo chamber, but not by much.
>
> Finally, the question is which of these news stories do we click on. The researchers find that the final proportion of cross-cutting news stories we click on is 21 percent for liberals and 30 percent for conservatives … . We clearly prefer news stories that are likely to reinforce our existing views rather than challenge them.
>
> Should we believe a research study conducted by Facebook researchers that absolves the company's algorithms and places the blame squarely on us? I think the study is well-designed. That said, I disagree with a key conclusion of the Facebook study. It is true that our friendship circles are often not diverse enough, but Facebook can easily recommend cross-cutting articles from elsewhere in its network (e.g. "what else are Facebook users reading?"). That the news being shown [in] our feeds is from our friends is ultimately a constraint that Facebook enforces.
>
> (Hosanagar 2016)

The questions about whether our online social networks produce echo chambers and filter bubbles, and to what extent these have polarizing political effects, remain open. This problem of lack of consensus is one that shows up repeatedly in this book. Different knowledge communities within the academic disciplines have developed processes for reaching consensus and dealing with disagreement. But what about the public?

Are the tools and methods of knowing

III. METHODS AND TOOLS

independent from the knower? Can they be politically "neutral"?

Writing in 1999 about the production of knowledge under colonialism, Linda Tuhiwai Smith argues that the nature and validity of specific forms of knowledge became commodities of colonial exploitation. Smith explains how Western research institutions developed systems for "organizing, classifying, and storing new knowledge" about the world. Within the context of colonialism, this practice of gathering and storing knowledge can be viewed as part of a system of "power and domination".

III. Methods and tools

The master's tools

Audre Lorde said you can't dismantle the master's house with the master's tools. I think about this powerful metaphor, trying to understand it.

By radicals, liberals, conservatives, and reactionaries, education in the masters' knowledge is seen as leading inevitably to consciousness of oppression and exploitation, and so to the subversive desire for equality and justice. Liberals support and reactionaries oppose universal free education, public schools, uncensored discussion at the universities for exactly the same reason.

Lorde's metaphor seems to say that education is irrelevant to social change. If nothing the master used can be useful to the slave, then education in the masters' knowledge must be abandoned. Thus an underclass must entirely reinvent society, achieve a new knowledge, in order to achieve justice. If they don't, the revolution will fail.

This is plausible. Revolutions generally fail. But I see their failure beginning when the attempt to rebuild the house so everybody can live in it becomes an attempt to grab all the saws and hammers, barricade Ole Massa's tool-room, and keep the others out. Power not only corrupts, it addicts. Work becomes destruction. Nothing is built.

Societies change with and without violence. Reinvention is possible. Building is possible. What tools have we to build with except hammers, nails, saws—education, learning to think, learning skills?

Are there indeed tools that have not been invented, which we must invent in order to build the house we want our children to live in? Can we go on from what we know now, or does what we know now keep us from learning what we need to know? To learn what people of colour, the women, the poor, have to teach, to learn the knowledge we need, must we unlearn all the knowledge of the whites, the men, the powerful? Along with the priesthood and phallocracy, must we throw away science and democracy? Will we be left trying to build without any tools but our bare hands? The metaphor is rich and dangerous. I can't answer the questions it raises.

(Le Guin 2004)

The work of thinkers such as Linda Tuhiwai Smith and Ursula K. Le Guin draws our attention to how the tools and methods of producing knowledge also have politics. These tools and methods, used to describe and explain the world, can be used to liberate and empower, or to oppress and misrepresent. They are the products of the politics of their time. We explore this in depth in each chapter on the AOKs.

Edward Said draws attention to this in his book *Orientalism*. Maria Todorova, writing in the context of Western imaginations of the Balkans, offers "Balkanism". When these views are given legitimacy, they become internalized and hold power not just to describe the world, but to shape it. But can these same tools—concepts, theories, explanations—be reclaimed as tools of liberation?

For reflection

Considering knowledge

Follow the link to find out more about Maria Todorova's "Balkanism".

 Search terms: Westsplaining the Balkans

Consider the following questions.

1. **(a)** Who has the power to legitimize knowledge, and who does not?

    (b) Where does this power come from?

2. **(a)** What are some global currents in the politics of knowledge production?

    (b) What are the consequences of this for creating knowledge about the Balkans?

3. What steps can we take to use knowledge to further social justice and engaged citizenship?

4. Perhaps the most widespread act of citizenship is voting. What kinds of knowledge are useful and necessary in performing this political act?

In the next section, we look at the issues of knowledge involved in deciding who to vote for.

Voices: Joseph Mitchell from Democracy Club

"I help run Democracy Club, a not-for-profit organisation in the UK. Our vision is of a country with the digital foundations to support everyone's participation in democratic life. We start with elections, because that's where people are most often looking for information. The best time to serve people is when they're actively looking for something. Online search data tells us that people ask perhaps surprisingly basic questions about elections: who should I vote for? Who are the candidates? Where do I vote? How do I vote?

The state doesn't provide these answers. We worry that in the absence of easily accessible information, people will switch off democracy. So we create databases of elections, candidates, polling locations and election results. We make these open for anyone to use at no charge and we use these databases ourselves to run voter information websites: WhoCanIVoteFor.co.uk and WhereDoIVote.co.uk.

We are a non-partisan organisation. We treat all candidates and parties equally. We need to do this to gain and maintain the trust of the public. This approach means that we give candidates an equal platform, so long as they're legally nominated. Personally, I would have a problem if a candidate was advocating policies that would breach fundamental human or political rights. But that's for the users to decide. It's important that the public know what the candidates stand for.

For transparency and trust, we work openly: you can see what we're currently working on; you can critique it; contribute; or ask us questions. Those with technical knowledge can access the code that powers our databases and websites. We have thousands of volunteers who gather data on tens of thousands of candidates: their name, website, social media, a photo and a statement. Again, none of this is provided by the authorities. Other volunteers then check the work of the first volunteers. Like Wikipedia, we record every edit by every user, to ensure quality is kept up and to track any malicious edits. Because citizens themselves produce the information and like Wikipedia, anyone can edit the database of election candidates, we hope this leads to greater trust in the information. It was made by 'people like me' not by some faceless institution.

Should the state provide information on elections? To an extent, of course. But there's a trade-off between independence from the state, which may be necessary to be trusted and non-partisan, and effectiveness/reach, which can really only be achieved with state resources. In Germany, a state institution actually runs a 'voter advice application' where you answer some questions and it suggests parties that hold similar views. This relies on Germany's high levels of trust in the state, which would be hard to match in the UK.

Is it okay to rely on volunteers? Yes, they do an amazing job. We record all edits and can roll back to an earlier version of a record if there's vandalism. We also require an email to log-in to track user edits. Mistakes are rare, vandalism is extremely rare. We see people of all parties and none adding data. It's a chance to volunteer for the good of democracy, rather than to push your own views.

People are busy: ideally information will reach them where they are. So we encourage Facebook and Google, the most used websites or applications in the UK, to present our data to their users in the run-up to an election. Both companies are cautious, but recognise they have immense power and they are currently keen to improve their public image.

Of course, democracy isn't just elections. How do you get information about all decisions that are being made that will affect your life and how do you get to have a say in them? Democracy is complex and messy. There's no digital technology solution to solve all problems. But we can ensure that data on politicians, votes, lobbying, budgets and so on, is accessible. It's the first step.

The fact I've thought it necessary to provide more information on elections seems obvious, objective and neutral to me. And the vast majority of people I meet seem to agree. But implicit in it is a value judgement that says voters should know more about their candidates. Should we test people's knowledge before allowing them to participate? I'm not sure. Every person matters, but some voices are better informed than others. As a society we all benefit by increasing political knowledge. But this kind of information faces tough competition for people's attention. The advertising budgets of consumer goods companies—to sell you a pair of shoes—are vast. Modern consumer capitalism wants all your attention. This doesn't help democracy; and that's before we talk about money in politics. To give democracy a fighting chance, it's vital that a brilliant easy-to-use quick-to-understand service exists to provide this information.

Personally, I came to help set up Democracy Club because I think better political decision-making is critical to every aspect of our society. It determines if our society gets better, if we can reduce suffering and increase wellbeing, and whether we make better-evidenced decisions. In theory, democracy harnesses the 'wisdom of the crowd', i.e. together we know more than alone. With good access to information, a thriving debate, then a decision taken after a vote, it seems likely you will get better outcomes. So democracy is extrinsically useful. But there's also interesting evidence that suggests it is intrinsically important too: we literally feel better when we feel we have a say in issues that are affecting us."

For discussion

War on truth—Philippines is patient zero

 Search terms: Ressa War on truth Philippines Al Jazeera

Maria Ressa, journalist and founder of the news site Rappler, was honoured by *TIME* magazine as Person of the Year in 2018.

She has been called a "guardian in the war on truth" (Quinn/Al Jazeera 2019). In the linked video, she speaks about how social media has been weaponized by authoritarian leaders in the Philippines, and her battle against it.

1. What can we learn from cases where the same digital tools that had potential to be liberating are instead weakening democracies?

"When people don't know what is real and what is fake, when facts don't matter, then the voice with the loudest megaphone gains more power … . Free speech is being used to stifle free speech." (Ressa 2019)

2. What kinds of knowledge does Ressa suggest are required to defend truth and democracy against disinformation today?

3. How are the processes of producing and disseminating disinformation similar to or different from how knowledge is produced and shared?

4. How has the rise in the power of networks affected the influence of individuals over politics? Is it any more or less possible to create significant political change as an individual?

III.1 Knowledge at the intersection of digital subcultures and politics

It looks as if 2016 may have been the year when mainstream media finally lost the ability to shape online political dialogue and debates. It is remembered for the rise of post-truth politics, discussed in II.2. A lot has been written about how the phenomenon of fake news and its spread on social media co-produced a climate of post-truth politics where the political discourse

become increasingly disconnected from facts and evidence-based claims.

The increase in fake news is widely viewed as a threat to democracy. There has been a fast and robust response by educators towards equipping young people with the tools for intellectual self-defence on the post-truth internet. Studies have shown that younger people on average are significantly less likely to believe and re-post fake news. Indeed, the single most reliable predictor of who falls for fake news is not ideology or political affiliation, but age. As digital natives, your generation has the literacy to better navigate the online world. This section examines another phenomenon from 2016, which may have had an outsize effect on the political sensibilities of the younger generations.

Making connections

Digital literacy

Digital literacy affects the online political discourse and different people's ability to participate and contribute to it. The question of digital literacy is discussed in Chapter 3.

Case study

Pepe the Frog, Harambe and the divisive politics of digital anti-establishment subcultures

Depending on where and how old you were at the time, you may have encountered the Great Meme War of 2016. Meme culture can be profoundly baffling to the uninitiated; it was on these grounds that it was initially dismissed and underestimated by mainstream political culture. There is a growing appreciation today that political memes have transcended their obscure beginnings in digital subcultures and have a profound influence on young people's political affinities.

Memes can also shape political life more broadly. Certainly, memes can set the tone of political debate, especially for young people, as was the case with Bernie Sanders' Dank Meme Stash Facebook group and The Donald subreddit in the lead-up to the 2016 US Presidential election.

Meme culture moves at a dizzying pace and those playing catch-up are regularly outed as normies. When Hillary Clinton learned how to dab on "The Ellen DeGeneres Show", urged voters to Pokémon GO to the polls, and took to Twitter asking followers to summarize how they feel about their student debt in three emojis or less, it backfired and was seen as exploiting youth pop culture for political gain. That an entire genre of fairly popular memes exists about how "the left can't meme" only suggests that the liberal mainstream is falling behind in this political tactic. This could matter beyond who is cool and uncool on the internet, and have material implications for the future of political discourse.

Viral user-generated content, made up of subcultural inside jokes, dominated the established online media outlets in terms of reaching the newly politicized youth. Below are the words of 26-year-old Sean Walsh, one of the two original moderators of Bernie Sanders' Dank Meme Stash.

> "This generation's memes are that generation's C-SPAN or Huffington Post …. Seriously, memes are going to be very prevalent in politics. They're going to get ideas into your head.
>
> (Walsh quoted in Dewey 2016)

Might those who worry that "the future of political discourse only gets shallower and less informed" (Dewey 2016) have a point? Or is this worry misplaced or overstated?

Whichever end of the political spectrum they originated from, these memes carried a signature anti-establishment sentiment and came in volumes that had no parallel among the mainstream media.

For discussion

Political memes

We have offered the example of meme culture surrounding the US Presidential election because it might be culturally and linguistically accessible to many readers of this book. But outside of US politics, and indeed the English language internets, political memes are produced in various contexts. Discuss the following questions.

1. What do political memes look like in your context?

2. What do you know about who produces them, and why? Where do they appear?

3. What would you say is their influence on the political affinities of your generation?

4. How would you explain their success and reach, or their lack of success and reach?

5. To what extent are memes an effective form of communicating knowledge about politics?

6. What are the limitations of memes in terms of communicating knowledge about politics, and how might these limitations be overcome?

Political meme subcultures are generally youth-led, subversive, grassroots and collective. In other words, they are everything that the cyberevangelists told us to be excited about in terms of the organizing and democratizing power of the internet. These characteristics also marked progressive countercultural groups of past decades.

We may have expected political memes and those who produce them to also be politically progressive—and we may have been wrong. Angela Nagle is author of *Kill All Normies: Online Culture Wars from 4Chan and Tumblr to Trump and the Alt-Right* and wrote the following.

> This was unlike the culture wars of the 60s or the 90s, in which a typically older age cohort of moral and cultural conservatives fought against a tide of cultural secularization and liberalism among the young.
>
> (Nagle 2017)

Nagle describes the online alt-right as a heterogeneous group of anti-politically-correct meme-makers, trolls and abusers, loosely unified in their suspicion of insincerity in competitive liberal virtue-signalling. In one of her more controversial claims Nagle suggests that these groups were at least partly a backlash against the moral high-grounding and self-righteousness of the organized online public shaming phenomenon. She claims it was also a reaction to the performative wokeness of identity politics, with its overzealous policing of any and all linguistic and cultural offences. Then again, it is impossible to disentangle who was reacting to whom in the feedback loops of outrage that followed.

To see how this happened, and why so many did not see it happening until it did, let's take a closer look at the transgressive methods adopted by the digital alt-right, enabled by the same technological tools that accompanied the Arab Spring, Occupy Wall Street, Anonymous and Wikileaks.

First we have to talk about a frog. Pepe was drawn by Matt Furie in 2005 in his comic *Boy's Club* and was turned into a meme on message boards and some not exactly family-friendly corners of the internet. Soon there was Sad Pepe, Angry Pepe, Smug Pepe and more. Pepe was tweeted into mainstream prominence by Katy Perry, followed by many others including the Russian Embassy in the UK. Pepe went from fame to infamy after being reclaimed by the digital alt-right on the /pol/ board of 4chan and /r/The_ Donald on Reddit, where Pepes, including some transgressive and offensive ones, were deployed in the Great Meme War. It is difficult to say when things peaked, but the Clinton campaign releasing an explainer on Pepe the Frog on its official website might have been it. "That's Pepe. He's a symbol associated with white supremacy" reads the condemnation, which continues in question-and-answer style until the stand-in reader concludes, "[t]his is horrifying" (Chan 2016). Two weeks later, Pepe became an official hate symbol and Pepe memes with racist and other bigoted content were added to the Anti-Defamation League's database. Furie tried hard to reclaim Pepe, launching the #SavePepe campaign in partnership with the Anti-Defamation League to get Pepe back from online bigots. As you can probably guess, this has not worked.

What we see reflected in the Pepe story was always political in a wider sense than presidential campaigns and elections.

> When a gorilla named Harambe was shot dead at the Cincinnati Zoo that year after a child fell into his enclosure, the usual cycles of public displays of outrage online began as expected with inevitable competitive virtue signaling. At first, emotional and outraged people online blamed the child's parents for the gorilla's death, with some even petitioning to have the parents prosecuted for their neglect. But then a kind of giddy ironic mocking of the social media spectacle started to take over. The Harambe meme soon became the perfect parody of the sentimentality and absurd priorities of Western liberal performative politics and the online mass hysteria that often characterized it.
>
> (Nagle 2017)

Harambe mania exceeded any expectations of popular participation. If your digital detox coincided with the week when the Harambe meme took off, you would have returned to a very baffling internet where everyone wanted to be in on the joke. Transgression has long been a tactic for social resistance, powerfully deployed, often by young people, to undermine and destabilize stale social norms and cultural taboos. It is not difficult to mock an online world where viral content and outrage on social networks regularly drown out information about global issues of urgent importance.

So, are transgressive memes, with their cynical mockery, confronting intellectual conformity and drawing attention to the hypocrisies of online political discourse? Or is it transgression for its own sake—just "for the lulz"—without any intended political outcome? Even worse, are we reading too much into what is effectively overt bigotry?

How we answer these questions matters. Anti-establishment memes that challenge conventions, and are critical of entrenched political positions, expressed in an aesthetic and language that appeals to and sometimes is only fully grasped by young people, can be a powerful way of communicating about politics.

↑ **Figure 2.3** In 2019–2020, Pepe was used by pro-democracy protesters in Hong Kong as a symbol of their resistance against China's central government

At the same time, though, anti-moral, irreverent, subversive, offensive, racist, sexist content regularly bursts out of the meme-factories in the dark corners of the internet and into more conventional social network spaces that influence many young people's political identities, affinities and ideas. How you encounter these, distinguish between them, and hold yourself and others accountable in online political spaces, is part of the skill set of digital citizenship.

For reflection

How would you decide whether a post is unacceptable?

1. How much do you need to know before sharing a political video, petition or meme?

2. To what extent does it matter how many of your friends have shared it, and which ones?

On this note of personal accountability and collective responsibility for how we behave in online political spaces, we move into a section dedicated to the ethics of knowledge in politics.

IV. ETHICS

> The last words of the Mahabharata are, 'By no means can I attain a goal beyond my reach'. It is likely that justice, a human idea, is a goal beyond human reach. We're good at inventing things that can't exist.
>
> (Le Guin 2004)

Like LeGuin, the IBO asks, in relation to knowledge and politics, "Can we know what justice is and what it requires?"

Various forms of justice are relevant to the theme of knowledge and politics. The idea of epistemic justice, for example, is discussed in Chapter 1, IV.3. In the context of the public sphere and open dialogue, there are issues of justice regarding which perspectives have access to a platform, and are thus more widely heard. And at the intersection of politics and technology, the issue of justice shows up in social media, filter bubbles and echo chambers, which we discuss earlier in this chapter. In the next section we focus on how youth engage with ethical issues on university campuses and social media networks.

IV.1 Campus politics: Pluralism, academic freedom and no-platforming

As educational institutions with the task of preparing young people for active and productive participation in society, universities have a special and important role with regard to knowledge and politics. For example, political activism on US campuses in the 1960s played a key role in the civil rights and anti-war movements, as well as the movements for the rights of women and sexual minorities. Because of their role in producing and disseminating knowledge, universities are said to be freer than the rest of society. How does privileging the freedom of speech and scholarship affect the politics of knowledge in these special public spaces?

It is only in very specific cases that limitations on this freedom are put in place, such as when there are concerns about violence or violations of the law. In recent years, however, the tension between freedom and safety has profoundly affected the discourse on university campuses. As safe spaces, trigger warnings and politically correct speech become more common, some observers have asked whether these come at the expense of pluralism and deep dialogue. Is the university campus shifting from being a place that is safe *for* political differences, to a place that is safe *from* political differences? The political phenomenon known as no-platforming shines a light on this.

No-platforming (or alternatively deplatforming) means limiting, restricting, denying or revoking access to a venue or an audience to certain perspectives that might be offensive or inflammatory. There have been numerous instances where a controversial guest speaker is blocked from speaking at a university campus, for example.

When—with the exception of hate speech—is it appropriate to deplatform a political view? Think about your own answer to this question, then explore the Disinvitation Database (linked below), a crowd-sourced register of events when an invited speaker has been blocked from addressing students on campus.

 Search terms: Disinvitation Database FIRE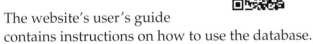

The website's user's guide contains instructions on how to use the database.

For reflection

Disinvitation

1. What do you notice about the timeline of disinvitations, or the profile or profession of the disinvited speakers?

2. How have the topics brought up as reasons for disinvitation changed over time?

3. What else do you notice about the success rate of disinvitations, the types of events or the political affiliation of the speakers?

For another perspective on this issue and further investigation into the question above, follow the link to the article "Why no-platforming is sometimes a justifiable position".

 Search terms: aeon Why no platforming is sometimes a justifiable position

Practising skills: Exploring perspectives and drawing implications

Consider the claim that "No-platforming contributes to intolerance and the polarization of political views" and the counterclaim that "No-platforming protects against the proliferation of intolerant and polarizing political views".

Working in a pair or small group, come up with a set of arguments and examples in support of each of these claims.

Next, look at the evidence you have been able to produce in support of the claims. Which claim is more convincing? What is your conclusion?

Finally, consider the implications of your conclusion. What are the consequences for knowledge depending on whether you decide against or in favour of no-platforming?

In your explorations of the Disinvitation Database you may encounter calls for blanket bans on certain perspectives or petitions to deny someone the right to address the student public. When those are unsuccessful, a host of disruptive tactics have been used, ranging from walkouts to the "heckler's veto"—escalating noise and disruption until the event can no longer continue.

No-platformers have faced the criticism that limiting the right to speak is a threat to freedom. And yet, some no-platformers argue that a speaker who fails to explicitly condemn injustice deserves to be directly confronted. These confrontations are often not conducted in the spirit of respectful, or even peaceful, disagreement. Consequently, no-platformers have also been criticized for their offensive language and hostile actions.

The appeal to mutual respect crops up regularly in conversations around campus politics, but this value is also central to engaging with difference in TOK and in the IB. To discuss the politics of respectability we turn to the example below.

For discussion

What is offensive?

When offence enters the picture, it can be challenging to continue a dialogue between different perspectives. But what does it mean for something to be offensive in the context of politics and justice?

Consider these two op-eds regarding an incident at a local board of education. When is "offensive" about showing disrespect, and when is it about causing harm?

🔍 Search terms: Kaleem Caire Children need to learn respect

🔍 Search terms: Respectability politics urgent challenges in madison schools

1. Does calling for respect reduce the power of marginalized groups to challenge the status quo?

2. Is the politics of respectability a way for those in power to maintain power and discredit the strategies of those who challenge them? Or is mutual respect necessary for effective dialogue and engaging with differences in perspective?

IV.2 Disrupting politics with psychographic technology

The following quote is from Alexander Nix, CEO of Cambridge Analytica.

> We just put information into the bloodstream to the internet and then watch it grow, give it a little push every now and again over time to watch it take shape. And so this stuff infiltrates the online community and expands but with no branding—so it's unattributable, untrackable.
>
> (Nix quoted by UK television station Channel 4 in 2018)

Chapter 3, III.2 considers the research of Michal Kosinski, David Stillwell and Thore Graepel of the Cambridge Psychometric Centre. The researchers' findings from a 2013 study suggested that a person's personality traits could be predicted using their Facebook Likes and a follow-up 2015 study by Kosinski, Stillwell and Wu Youyou suggested that an artificial intelligence (AI) could use Likes to predict an individual's personality more accurately than even close friends and family. Eventually their research earned the attention of Strategic Communications Laboratories (SCL) and its subsidiary Cambridge Analytica, both of which were heavily implicated in attempting to influence the 2016 US Presidential election and the UK's Brexit referendum. Indeed in 2016, Alexander Nix, then CEO of Cambridge Analytica, exclaimed the following.

> We are thrilled that our revolutionary approach to data-driven communication has played such an integral part in President-elect Trump's extraordinary win.
>
> (Nix quoted in Ahmed 2018)

Cambridge Analytica claimed to use personality data to analyse voters' behaviour, values and opinions, and then send them tailored advertising to nudge them in the direction of Cambridge Analytica's client. This was called microtargeting. It was not a new practice; some political observers noted that it had been used effectively in Obama's 2012 campaign. Microtargeting refers to the process of analysing data to predict the behaviour, interests and opinions held by specific groups of people and then serving them messages they are likely to respond to.

What was new about Cambridge Analytica and SCL was how much data they had and what they claimed to be doing with it. Alexander Nix, the former CEO of Cambridge Analytica and a former director of SCL, has claimed that the data profiles of some two-hundred-and-twenty million Americans were kept by SCL, and that each of these profiles contained thousands of data points. SCL marketing material claimed that they had developed sophisticated analytical tools in order to use these huge data sets to sway voting patterns (Mayer 2017).

Andy Wigmore, the communications director of Leave.eu—one of the two major campaign groups supporting the UK's withdrawal from the European Union (EU)—has said that Cambridge Analytica assisted his group because of the shared interests of their investors. The Leave.eu campaign used social media data and AI to target voters with highly individualized advertisements—"thousands of different versions of advertisements"—depending on their personalities, according to Cadallawar (2017). Arron Banks, founder of the organization Leave.eu, would later state that Cambridge Analytica's world-class AI won the referendum for those wishing to leave the EU (Cadwalladr 2017).

Frank Luntz, American pollster, reacting after the 2016 US Presidential election results commented as follows.

> "No one saw it coming. The public polls, the experts, and the pundits: just about everybody got it wrong. They were wrong-footed because they didn't understand who was going to turn out and vote. Except for Cambridge Analytica … They figured out how to win. There are no longer any experts except Cambridge Analytica.
>
> (Luntz quoted in Wood 2016)

Several observers have since cast doubt on such claims as overstating Cambridge Analytica's success and influence. But how did Cambridge Analytica obtain all its data? For the US market, a sizeable amount came via Aleksandr Kogan, an assistant professor formerly at the Cambridge Psychometric Centre. He developed an app called This Is Your Digital Life that provided psychometric quizzes to Facebook users in exchange for their results and data, and the data of their friends. In the summer of 2014, over 200,000 people used his app, providing over 30 million user records for Cambridge Analytica.

In an interview on BBC Radio 4 in March 2018, Kogan said that he had been used as a scapegoat, maintaining that Cambridge Analytica had approached him, written the terms of service for the app and told him his use of Facebook data was legal and appropriate. He was led to believe that thousands, if not tens of thousands, of apps were exploiting their users' data in the same way. He also claimed he had not profited from this collaboration personally and that the money he received was mostly used to pay the participants—each participant being paid between $3 and $4.

More generally, Kogan raised concerns about the social networking business model. Cambridge Analytica had allegedly used people's Facebook data for micro-targeting, but so were other platforms and social networks like Twitter and Instagram, whose profits mostly derive from advertising. When someone creates an account, they essentially sign an agreement to be sold to advertisers for micro-targeting in exchange for access to a desirable product that costs large amounts of time, expertise and money to run.

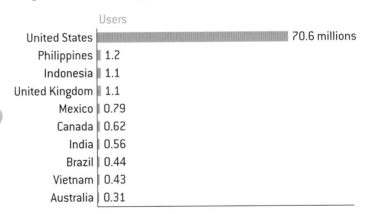

Users	
United States	70.6 millions
Philippines	1.2
Indonesia	1.1
United Kingdom	1.1
Mexico	0.79
Canada	0.62
India	0.56
Brazil	0.44
Vietnam	0.43
Australia	0.31

↑ **Figure 2.4** Where Cambridge Analytica improperly accessed Facebook user data, according to www.theatlas.com

Cambridge Analytica made extravagant claims about the effectiveness of its political micro-targeting, claims that fuelled a hysteria following the scandal that people were being manipulated to vote for the "wrong" outcomes in a post-truth environment enabled by technology. Prosecuting Cambridge Analytica, or its campaign clients, was complicated because the nature of their medium meant only the people being targeted on social media could see them.

AI improved Cambridge Analytica's messaging iteratively. If an advertisement does not get clicked on, it is automatically tweaked based on the personality profile and served again; if it is clicked on, the person is shown more such content. How much did this influence political outcomes? Without controlled experiments it is hard to know.

Jonathan Albright, assistant professor and data scientist, Elon University, believes the influence is substantial.

> This is a propaganda machine. It's targeting people individually to recruit them to an idea. It's a level of social engineering that I've never seen before. They're capturing people and then keeping them on an emotional leash and never letting them go.
>
> (Albright quoted in Cadwalladr 2016)

Cambridge Analytica's data allowed campaigners to optimize candidates' campaign movements. Cambridge Analytica claimed that they saw small openings, based on engagement with people's Facebook posts, in Michigan, Pennsylvania and Wisconsin —known as the "blue wall", because they are traditionally democratic states—and so Trump scheduled events there. The Clinton analysts mocked him at the time, but apparently "it was the small margins in Michigan, Pennsylvania and Wisconsin that won Trump the election" (Anderson, Horvath 2017).

In October 2016, Nix made the following statement.

> Today in the United States we have somewhere close to four or five thousand data points on every individual … So we model the personality of every adult across the United States, some 230 million people.
>
> (Nix 2016)

Propaganda has been used for centuries, but online networks may have increased the precision and efficacy of political persuasion. The beginning of this chapter explored how intense emotions and fake news spread quickly through social networks. SCL (parent company of Cambridge Analytica) described itself as "the premier election management agency", using words such as "psychological warfare" and "influence operations" (Weinberger 2005). SCL claimed to have influenced elections and other political outcomes in Italy, Latvia, Ukraine, Albania, Afghanistan, Romania, South Africa, Nigeria, Kenya, Mauritius, India, Indonesia, the Philippines, Thailand, Taiwan, Colombia, Antigua, St Vincent and the Grenadines, St Kitts and Nevis, and Trinidad and Tobago. An article for *Politico* stated that SCL used "military disinformation campaigns to social media branding and voter targeting" (Vogel, Parti 2015). SCL is also alleged to have operated extensively in developing countries to manipulate public opinion and claimed to be able to instigate coups. It certainly sounds like something from the James Bond or *Mission Impossible* films and it did not help that SCL and Cambridge Analytica were backed by a reclusive hedge fund billionaire called Robert Mercer.

Trevor Potter, President of Campaign Legal Center, a non-profit organization that works to reduce the influence of money in politics and to support unrestricted access to voting, reacted as follows.

> Suddenly, a random billionaire can change politics and public policy—to sweep everything else off the table—even if they don't speak publicly, and even if there's almost no public awareness of his or her views.
>
> (Potter quoted in Mayer 2017)

However, many observers, including political and academic experts, have voiced scepticism about these claims. It is a big leap to go from understanding personalities to influencing voting decisions. Could behavioural microtargeting really be powerful enough to sway elections and referendums? There is some evidence to suggest that its influence has been grossly exaggerated.

Eitan Hersh, professor of political science at Tufts University and author of *Hacking the Electorate* gave the following view.

> The idea that some additional piece of information in this overwhelming wave of data going into people's heads is going to trick them … It doesn't give people enough credit.
>
> (Hersh quoted in Chen, Potenza 2018)

Recall Nix's exclamation at the beginning of this section: "we are thrilled that our revolutionary approach" helped Trump win. What Nix failed to mention was how surprised his team was of the result: "[a] day earlier, Cambridge Analytica executives told reporters they thought Trump's likelihood of winning was at 20 per cent" (Ahmed 2018).

Kogan himself, when interviewed on BBC Radio 4 in March 2018, said that the accuracy of the data he harvested had been extremely exaggerated. He estimated that, in practice, he and his team were six times more likely to get inaccurate information about a person's personality and likes and dislikes as they were to get accurate information. In conclusion, Kogan thought that microtargeting was not necessarily the most effective way to use such data sets

There are a few good reasons to be sceptical. First, data harvested from social media, even personality data, does not necessarily provide additional actionable information or insight. Many other publicly available data points can suggest a person's political stance, including

their address. Hersh states that while personality traits are correlated with political values, the correlation is generally weak; and that people who wrongly receive advertisements (such as those intended for a different demographic) really do not like them. For example, when he attempted to create a microtargeting model that identified people interested in climate change, he found the best proxy is simply party affiliation; if you don't know that, everything is very difficult, and if you do, everything else doesn't really matter. Hersh argues that what is effective is mobilizing voters through behavioural targeting, rather than persuading them to vote differently.

The second limitation is that almost all psychographic data is self-reported, which leaves it vulnerable to individuals' blind spots and inaccurate sense of self: people who repeat a personality test often do not return the same result. Additionally, their tastes and opinions— and what they like on Facebook—may change, but they do not often go back to unlike things, so this sort of behavioural data needs to be fresh. Finally, and most fundamentally, what does it mean to say one can "infer" political values from a set of personality traits? Can we assume that personalities align with politics?

Even if the personality data were accurate, it would still be difficult for microtargeting to compete with other information sources in the cluttered and fast-moving online environment. The total amount of political content online is so large that it dwarfs the output of manipulators. A team of researchers in 2018 released results of an investigation into the influence of infamous "Russian bots" on Twitter, with the following conclusion.

> When looking at their ability of spreading news content and making it viral … we find that their effect on social platforms was minor.
>
> (Zannettou *et al* 2018)

In a 2018 article for the *New York Times*, Brendan Nyhan, Professor of Public Policy at the University of Michigan, argues that the number of times fake news items are liked and shared or retweeted may seem impressive until you look at the complete picture of how much information is available online. In 2018, Twitter reported that 2.1 million election-related tweets were posted by Russian bots during the 2016 US Presidential election campaign, but in fact these represented just 1% of all election-related tweets. In a separate study with other researchers, Nyhan also found that: "fake news consumption was heavily concentrated among a small group — almost 6 in 10 visits to fake news websites came from the 10% of people with the most conservative online information diets" (Guess *et al* 2018).

Box 2.4: The impact of behavioural microtargeting in politics

Referring to examples from this section and below, discuss the following questions.

1. What are the implications of microtargeting for political knowledge?

2. How might microtargeting for political knowledge be different from microtargeting that affects consumer purchase decisions?

3. Why do observers and experts disagree about the impact of behavioural microtargeting in politics?

Source 1: Wakefield, J. 2018. "Cambridge Analytica: Can Targeted Online Ads Really Change a Voter's Behaviour?" (BBC News online)

  Search terms: Wakefield BBC Cambridge Analytica targeted online ads

The powerful influence of emotional advertising is well known; however, the, regulation that currently exists for product marketing does not, as yet, cover online political campaigns. Chris Sumner, Research Director at the Online Privacy Foundation, has pointed out the significant issues that arise.

Sumner's team simulated a campaign to test whether they could identify, target and influence voters on the EU referendum. For example, they used language of fear to target "neurotic personalities" (Wakefield 2018) and more energetic messaging for audiences that were identified as being motivated by anger.

"We found that people behaved as we predicted they would. If you get the messages right they can be very powerful indeed. Messaging works and is really effective—and can nudge people one way or the other." (Sumner quoted in Wakefied 2018)

Source 2: Cadwalladr, C. 2016. "Google, Democracy and the Truth About Internet Search" (the *Guardian*)

  Search terms: Guardian Google democracy truth

Carole Cadwalladr, writing in the UK newspaper the *Guardian*, argues that whether or not microtargeted propaganda influenced the 2016 Brexit referendum or the US Presidential elections, the problem remains the lack of transparency and regulation about how voters' personal data is being mined and used to influence them.

Source 3: Brown, E.N. 2018. "Cambridge Analytica Was Doing Marketing, Not Black Magic" (Reason.com)

  Search terms: reason Cambridge Analytica doing marketing

Elizabeth Nolan Brown argues that too much is being made of both the power and novelty of behavioural microtargeting. People have worried about devious political actors influencing voters throughout the history of politics, including political advertisements via television and robocalls when they were first introduced.

Understanding why claims of political influence are exaggerated can reveal truths about how we comprehend political processes. Let's consider why the media and public opinion may have overstated the efficacy of political microtargeting in particular, and big data in general. Perhaps the outrage at invasions of privacy combined with fears stoked by Cambridge Analytica's claims provided fertile ground for sensationalizing the company's impact. Others, including some technology experts, appear to have been genuinely impressed.

It may be that we have an instinctive apprehension towards new media technology, as we have seen throughout modern history, for example with the invention of the printing press and later in the 19th century with mass newspaper distribution.

Without being a data scientist, statistician or social network expert, to what extent can one judge the impact of behavioural microtargeting? Perhaps history can provide some guides on whether this time is different.

For discussion

Fears of mass media

Historian Heidi Tworek wrote an article on the following topic: "Did 'sinister' emotional manipulation by the data analytics company, Cambridge Analytica, decide the U.S. election? History suggests otherwise." (Tworek 2018)

 Search terms: Tworek Cambridge Analytica Trump and the new old fear

Follow the link to read the arguments Tworek proposes, then answer the following questions.

1. What arguments does Tworek make about the exaggeration of political microtargeting in general, and of Cambridge Analytica in particular?

2. To what extent is psychometric manipulation different from previous crowd-reflecting and crowd-influencing technologies?

3. What criteria could we use to discern whether psychometric manipulation and political microtargeting have influenced political outcomes in recent years?

It is often said that technology disrupts industries, businesses and markets for the consumer's benefit. In what ways is technological disruption in politics similar and different? Is there something about politics that makes it more or less vulnerable to negative disruptions as compared to other domains? And finally, what will it take to guard against negative disruptions?

3 Knowledge and technology

What does it mean to live and be knowledgeable in a technological culture? This question carries a sense of urgency in a world of extraordinary technological means and equally extraordinary social and ecological challenges. What assumptions underpin the technological world and what imperatives does it produce?

Is technology an added layer of complexity in the world, or a tool to help us comprehend complex systems? Could it be both? This chapter explores what we mean by technology and how it relates to knowledge, with the broader goal of comprehending the role of technology in how we come to know what we know.

Initial discussion

- What role has technology played in the development of knowledge?
- How is technology changing our relationships with knowledge?
- Is it possible to produce new knowledge *without* the use of technology?
- What role has technology played in terms of expanding or contracting access to knowledge?
- To what extent can the risks associated with technology be *known*?

I. SCOPE

On a literal level we can measure the scope of technology by its reach: our robots have landed on Mars and reached the further vestiges of the solar system, and our microscopes can now "see" at a resolution of half the width of a hydrogen atom. Decades of radio programming are radiating broadcast signals into space in an expanding bubble a hundred light years across, announcing our existence to anyone listening. But in the context of the size of our galaxy, the reach of these broadcasts is rather small—represented, for example, by the blue dot in Figure 3.1. At a galactic scale, our technological footprint is tiny; and does not even register at the scale of our universe.

Extent of Human
Radio Broadcasts

Thanks to Nick Risinger for the artist's conception of the Milky Way.
Taken from http://commons.wikimedia.org/wiki/File:Milky_Way_Galaxy.jpg

200 light years in diameter

↑ **Figure 3.1** How far human radio broadcast signals have reached into the galaxy

The reach of human-made objects is also interstellar, if only barely. The human artefacts farthest from our home on Earth are the Voyager spacecraft, two probes launched in 1977. Attached to each of them is the Voyager Golden Record, a message sent to the stars and intended for any intelligence that might intercept it one day. The Voyagers carry the cultural portrait of humanity as a technologically advanced civilization, including greetings in various languages, natural sounds, music and images. The concept and contents of the record are every bit as interesting as its engineering, an instance of technology reflecting how we understand and portray ourselves back to ourselves. Follow the link to find out more.

 Search terms: Carl Sagan Annie Druyan aeon

The short film linked here tries to capture some of the cultural background of the Golden Record Project. From a present-day vantage point, the project provides a glimpse of the spirit and values of the technological enterprise of Western thought approximately half a century ago.

1. What might a project such as this look like if it were started today?

2. Do you think it would resonate culturally and be widely endorsed, or be met with doubt, disagreement and/or fear?

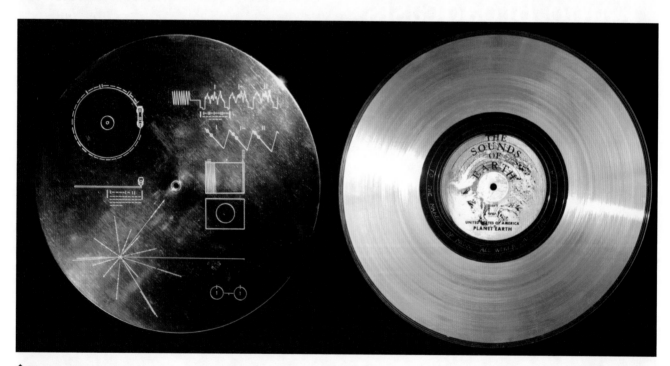

↑ **Figure 3.2** The Golden Record, attached to each of the Voyager spacecraft, is a 12-inch gold-plated phonograph record, containing sound and images from Earth (right) and a cover (left) containing instructions about how to "play" the record and where it comes from

Before we explore the scope of technology let's consider what we mean by the word "technology", which can refer to physical artefacts (such as bridges), human activities (such as the construction of bridges) and knowledge (such as the engineering concepts that guide the construction of bridges). To support these various types of technologies, various types of communities emerge around them in which people play different roles. Consider, for example, what it means to be a digital native and in which ways this anchors an individual's identity and orientation towards the world.

I.1 Technological culture and knowledge

What does navigating a technological culture require today? Chapter 10 explores how in the 1970s, writer and critic John Berger looked at the contemporary role of art as a way of comprehending the aesthetics and politics at play in the world. He argued that we comprehend this, not necessarily by looking at paintings, but by looking at ourselves looking at artworks in a way nobody had seen before.

Similarly, today the technological lens is bringing into focus a world that nobody has seen before. What can we learn by exploring new ways of knowing? Can we examine not just technologies themselves, but how we interact with them, in order to understand something about ourselves and about the time in which we live?

 Search terms: James Bridle New ways of seeing

Artist and writer James Bridle has been at the forefront of exploring what these new ways of seeing might look like. Bridle created a series of podcasts modelled on the ethos of Berger's television series, that explore knowing and being in a technological world. All four episodes are available using the QR code, as are links to pertinent case studies on topics of knowledge and technology that you may choose to explore further.

One of the ideas explored by Bridle is the materiality of digital technologies. The internet may feel invisible—WiFi is in the air, data is in the Cloud—but there is an elaborate infrastructure that makes it possible. For example, the submarine cable system, in Figure 3.3 below, is decidedly material and tangible. An elaborate network of fibre optic cables deep underwater, it is painstakingly installed and maintained to enable our global connectedness. The pattern of these cables reveals both historical and contemporary power relations.

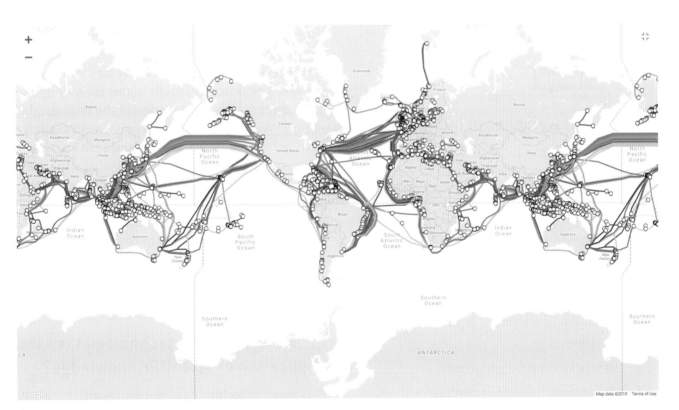

↑ **Figure 3.3** Map of the global network of submarine communications cables as of 2019

I. Scope

Invisible digital connections

 Search terms:
Telegeography Submarine
cables faqs

1. When we bring into view the material basis for our invisible digital connectedness, what do you notice?

2. What do you wonder about?

Consider what it means for the current global flows of digital information to overlap with the former outlines of empires. This overlap serves as a hint that questions of digital equity and digital justice will be important throughout this chapter. Depending on where you are in the world, there are differences in how much digital information you can move, with what speed and at what cost. This has implications beyond where we can stream Netflix in HD; it fuels global information asymmetries and inequities, of which the downstream effects for knowledge are of interest to us in TOK.

Present-day empires of infrastructure

 Search terms: James Bridle
imperialism infrastructure
Youtube

Consider the claims made by Bridle in the video about how technological infrastructure is both affecting flows of knowledge today and making historical power relations visible.

His thesis is that technology is extending the symmetries and inequities of the past into the present day.

1. To what extent do you agree?

2. How might this be happening?

3. What may be the effects of this on knowledge?

If you want to better understand some of the implications of the submarine cable systems, follow the link to an FAQ section that explores who owns and who uses these cables. Consider important questions such as the following.

3. Why are there many cables between some continents but no cables between Australia and South America, for instance?

While technological developments are inescapably entangled in specific histories, they are also changing our relationship with knowledge and power today. Our capacity to steer technologies towards human ends does not always keep up with the pace of technological development. Questioning the values that underpin technological systems can be difficult when they are buried under miles of code, or when they are so commonplace that they remain hidden in plain sight.

Yet, as historically marginalized communities are increasingly impacted by new technologies, it is necessary to scrutinize the values and possible prejudices inherent in our technologies. Then there is also the question of the ecological impact. With new energy-intensive technologies such as blockchain having a significant energy and resource footprint, the question of who bears the costs and who gains the benefits is urgent. This is part of a larger question concerning the relationship between nature and technology. As you read on, remember to consider how the scopes of nature and technology intersect and what we know about this intersection between the living world and the machine world.

I.2 Is there more to technology than the application of scientific knowledge?

Advances in technology are often seen as downstream applications of scientific breakthroughs. Much investment into fundamental and pure research in science, whether through government or private sector grants, is in fact justified through its supposed usefulness in the development of new technologies. Is this belief true, though? Project Hindsight was a 1960s study commissioned by the US Department of Defense to identify the factors that led to successful research and technology programmes. Part of this was to understand the relationship between scientific research and technological innovation. Project Hindsight was among the earliest and most ambitious studies of its kind and introduced the field of technology studies as a dedicated field of enquiry, distinct from science. The study found that scientific research contributed to only 9% of the key events that led to the development of successful technology programmes. Technological events were responsible for the other 91%. What is the difference between technological and scientific events? According to this study, science was defined as theoretical or experimental studies of unexplained phenomena, while technology was defined as the capability to perform specific engineering techniques with known phenomena.

> Among historians of technology it is widely accepted that science owes more to the steam engine than the steam engine owes to science … . Science is applied technology more than technology is applied science.
>
> (Sismondo 2009)

Consider Sergio Sismondo's words, above. To what extent would you agree, and is this relationship changing over time? Why do we continue to concern ourselves with making a distinction between science and technology? A part of it has to do with questions of funding, prestige and epistemic power. We celebrate famous inventors for their genius, but even one episode of "The Big Bang Theory" will suggest there is a perceived power differential between scientists and engineers, and the kinds of knowledge produced by each. It is an equation that keeps shifting.

I.3 Knowledge outside the scope of technology

From advances in nanotechnology to machine learning and neural networks, the scope of technology can appear relentlessly expanding. When we talk about the limits of technology, it is often a conversation about practical limitations, such as the limits of computational power, that will—the story goes—one day soon be overcome.

When a computer beats the human champion at the game of chess, as is becoming more and more frequent, common reactions include a sense of accomplishment for having produced such a capable machine, and/or a sense of humility in the face of an intelligence that surpasses ours. Tasks like playing chess are in fact relatively easy for a computer. But when artificial intelligence (AI) produces an image that passes for digital art, or writes verses that humans find indistinguishable from poetry, we may wonder what are the limits to technology. Can a computer controlling a robot … dance?

This question acquires a more serious tone in the context of jobs in the future. Many of the activities that humans perform as "work" can be replaced by machines. How can we know which jobs are less likely to be replaced by robots? Think about which human acts may be uncomputable, and what makes them so.

II. PERSPECTIVES

II.1 Determinisms: On the relationship between technology and society

This section explores what we know about the relationship between technology and society, and why it matters. Consider the two opposing perspectives: one, that technology drives history, and the other that society determines the type of technology that exists. Which perspective would you agree with, and how would you know? How we answer this question has implications for knowledge; for example, if technological development regularly outpaces social development, institutions and ethics need to evolve to guide this progress.

Karl Marx, among others, held the view that technology was one of the determinants of social or historical outcomes and structures, as this quote reveals: "The hand-mill gives you society with the feudal lord, the steam-mill, society with the industrial capitalist." This is a form of technological determinism which posits that technology develops according to its own internal logic, and that as it advances it moulds cultural and social patterns to fit itself. In this way, it drives history.

What does technological determinism look like in practice? One argument is that the political structures that follow technological advancement will tend towards a particular order. Consider, for example, David Hayes' view on the political structure that would form around widespread nuclear energy.

> The increased deployment of nuclear power facilities must lead society toward authoritarianism. Indeed, safe reliance upon nuclear power as the principal source of energy may be possible only in a totalitarian state … dispersed solar sources are more compatible than centralized technologies with social equity, freedom and cultural pluralism.
>
> (Hayes 1977)

Hayes was speculating that nuclear energy requires more centralized administrative power versus, for instance, solar energy, which could be completely decentralized. You could live comfortably and autonomously off the grid with solar energy, but not with nuclear.

To get out of this dichotomy, Langdon Winner, in his influential 1980 essay "Do artifacts have politics?" proposed a middle path, the co-production of technology and society, naming it "technological politics". We explore this further in section IV.

II.2 Coded male: Identity and technology

In the development of technology, technical skill and knowledge have historically been gendered. Put simply, men's disproportionate influence and power in the field made an impact on technology that can still be felt today. For

↑ **Figure 3.4** Man operating a Linotype machine in the early 20th century

the past 50 years, scholars have been looking at technological innovation through a feminist lens and critically evaluating claims about how technology intersects with gender. The design of reproductive technologies or the mechanization of domestic work through "labour-saving" appliances have been some of the sites of this work.

The dynamics between technology and gender did not always play out in straightforward or predictable ways. Consider the example of printing technologies. In the 1980s Cynthia Cockburn studied, through a gender lens, the transition in the London printing industry from the Linotype compositor to computerized typesetting. Operating one of the Linotype machines was considered highly skilled work; the trade was strongly unionized and exclusively male. Before the Linotype machine, the printing process was done by hand, letter by letter. The Linotype, which uses its own type of keyboard, could set one line of text at a time, making the printing process much more efficient. It worked well and so its design remained largely unchanged for close to a century.

In the 1970s and 1980s electronic methods of preparing text for printing started to take over and these used the QWERTY keyboard (the same used on typewriters). It is important to mention that typewriting was considered unskilled work and was performed almost exclusively by women. Researchers in the field of technology studies have examined the printing industry's switch to the new keyboard. It seems this change was neither innovative nor inevitable. Instead, it appears to have a political origin and gendered implications. Feminist scholar of technology Judy Wajcman explains.

> In choosing to dispense with the Linotype [keyboard] layout, management were choosing a system that would undermine the skill and power basis of the compositors and reduce them to "mere" typists. This would render typists (mainly women) and compositors (men) equal competitors for the new machines; indeed, it would advantage the women typists. The keyboard on the new printing technology was designed with an eye to using the relatively cheap and abundant labor of female typists. Although machine design is overwhelmingly a male province, it does not always coincide with the interests of men as a sex. As we have seen, some technologies are designed for use by women to break the craft control of men. Thus gender divisions are commonly exploited in the power struggles between capital and labor. In this way, the social relations that shape industrial technology include those of gender as well as class.
>
> (Wajcman quoted in Jasanoff *et al* 2001)

Summarizing Wajcman: the new QWERTY keyboard was designed to give women an equal or greater chance to become typesetters, because women were cheaper labour.

The male coding of technology, through constructing technological competence as masculine, has meant that contributions of women to innovation have been mostly left out of history. Consider that before we used the word "computer" to refer to a machine, we used it as a job description for people who performed calculations. In the early decades of digital technology, the majority of human computers were women. Like other forms of so-called "women's work", computing up until the 1970s was seen as highly structured, repetitive and tedious. As the field professionalized, academic degrees and a culture that advertised computers as "toys for the boys" contributed to the gender gap in technology that we are still aiming to close today.

II. Perspectives

Women technologists

Figure 3.5a shows Margaret Hamilton, photographed in 1969, alongside the code she and her team wrote that helped put a man on the moon. Katie Bouman (Figure 3.5b), in 2019, is shown with stacks of hard drives of telescope data that gave us the first image of a black hole.

Taken 50 years apart, the images celebrate two women's significant contributions to technological advancements. Around the time that these images went viral in 2019, Katie Bouman became the public face of the endeavour to produce an image of a black hole.

Shortly after, the internet began to scrutinize the extent of her contribution, and cast doubt on the legitimacy of featuring her story so prominently. Opportunistic Twitter and Instagram accounts impersonating her were set up to spread falsehoods and diminish her achievement. This troubling tale of our times urges us to consider—in an age when technological innovation is an increasingly collaborative enterprise—what does it look like to give women technologists their due credit?

↑ **Figure 3.5a** Margaret Hamilton

↑ **Figure 3.5b** Katie Bouman

Another part of the absence and erasure of women in the field comes from the very way we define technology.

> A greater emphasis on women's activities immediately suggests that women, and in particular black women, were among the first technologists. After all, women were the main gatherers, processors and storers of plant food from earliest human times onward. It was therefore logical that they should be the ones to have invented the tools and methods involved in this work such as the digging stick, the carrying sling, the reaping knife and sickle, pestles and pounders. If it were not for the male orientation of most technological research, the significance of these inventions would be acknowledged.
>
> (Wajcman quoted in Jasanoff *et al* 2001)

Our definition of technology intersects with different identities to produce different frictions. Of these frictions, movements such as Afrofuturism are born and animated. Although the term "Afrofuturism" was not coined until 1993, the ideas relating to the intersection of race and technology had been floating among the African diaspora, especially in North America, for decades. Woven through them is the realization that the optimistic scenarios of a technological future were not neutral. The techno-enthusiasm of the space race that imagined the cosmos as the new frontier was not neutral, especially given that the "frontier" previously referred to US expansion since the 17th century. This sentiment is captured in Gil Scott-Heron's song "Whitey on the Moon", placing the technological achievement of the moon landing in the context of racial and social inequalities.

Through art, music and literature, afrofuturism challenged assumptions about what was considered technological, questioned the priorities and social costs of technological progress, and reimagined what a technological future could look like, and who belonged in it. The most mainstream expression of these ideas is the nation of Wakanda in the 2018 movie *Black Panther*.

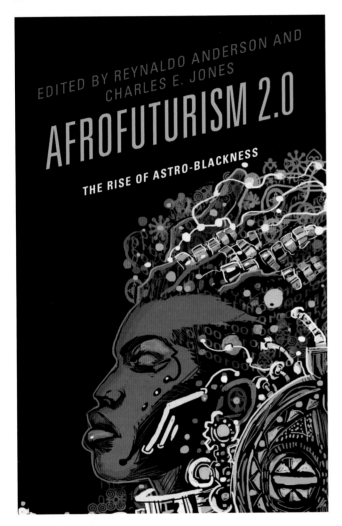

In addition to afrofuturism going global, Indigenous futurisms all over the world are birthing alternative visions of the future, technological or otherwise. These movements, in their own different ways, are driving the discourse on digital justice and equity. There is more on this topic in section III, where we discuss AI algorithms through an anti-oppression lens.

Understanding how technology intersected with systems of power in the past will help us to comprehend how it influences the technologies being built today, and the ways people will interact with them in the future.

II.3 Democratizing and liberating, or controlling and authoritarian?

In the last 15 years we have witnessed the first election of an African American US President and the 2011 Arab Spring, both seen as examples of democracy enabled by technology, specifically social networks on the internet. We have also witnessed so-called WhatsApp elections in India and Brazil in 2019, a Facebook-Cambridge Analytica scandal, and rapid increases in fake news, populism, and political polarization and authoritarianism. Is the internet a force for democracy and liberty, or for authoritarian populism? Has it exacerbated or mitigated the inequality and divides in our access to knowledge?

Making connections

Echo chambers and democracy

"Individuals empowered to screen out material that does not conform to their existing preferences may form virtual cliques, insulate themselves from opposing points of view and reinforce their biases. Internet users can seek out interactions with like-minded individuals who have similar values, and thus become less likely to trust important decisions to people whose values differ from their own." (Van Alstyne, Brynjolfsson 1996)

Chapter 2 looks in depth at the question of echo chambers and filter bubbles that may increase political polarization. How else has technology more broadly, and the internet specifically, impacted how we filter data and information?

For discussion

Intended and actual uses of technology

 Search terms: How we confuse the intended uses of technology aeon

Watch this 11-minute animated video about the relationship between the internet and active citizenship, and consider the following questions.

1. Given evidence that the internet can both promote and suppress freedom, what conclusion can we reach about the role of technology in citizenship?

2. If your answer to question 1 is that "it depends" and technology can be a tool for both good and ill, say more about what it depends on and which factors affect the actual uses of technology.

3. Are the producers of technological tools only accountable for the intended use of their products, or also for the actual use? Consider this question, for example, in the context of personalized advertising and political microtargeting in the Facebook-Cambridge Analytica scandal.

III. METHODS AND TOOLS

How does technology participate in the processes of knowledge, from the pursuit and production of knowledge, to the sharing of and access to knowledge? This section considers how the tools we use present both opportunities and challenges for what it means to be knowledgeable in a technological culture.

III.1 The sum of all human knowledge

Even people who access Wikipedia daily may be unaware of its mission statement: "Imagine a world in which every single person on the planet is given free access to the sum of all human knowledge." The Wikipedia project also has outspoken critics, who describe its impact in much harsher words. Figure 3.6 shows the Wikipedia Monument in the Polish town of Słubice. Its inscription reads, in part:

> [Wikipedia is] the greatest project co-created by people regardless of political, religious or cultural borders … with Wikipedia as one of its pillars the knowledge society will be able to contribute to the sustainable development of our civilization, social justice and peace among nations.

↑ **Figure 3.6** The Wikipedia Monument in the Polish town of Słubice, unveiled in 2014

Wikipedia is a case study in the collective negotiation of multiple perspectives, enabled by technology, towards crafting a shared understanding of fact. It can be a step towards more democratic participation in the production of knowledge, assuming, that is, that we accept what is on Wikipedia as knowledge. Yes, it is crowd-sourced, but as far as crowds go, Wikipedia is exceedingly well-organized, which may have good or bad results.

It is hardly news to anyone in the 2020s that there are concerns with knowledge on Wikipedia. In some ways, questioning the reliability of Wikipedia and criticizing it for its gender and racial bias is old news. Yet many issues remain unresolved, perhaps even widely unknown, even though Wikipedia is one of the primary reference sources for many people around the world. Despite the problematic politics of how Wikipedia is set up, people continue to organize "editing marathons" to add to or develop the entries of underrepresented people or topics. They are confronted with the possibility that Wikipedia might be the best they can do at this scale, and it is up to them to make it good enough.

For discussion

Everything, according to Wikipedia

 Search terms: Truth in Numbers: Everything According to Wikipedia

The 2010 documentary *Truth in Numbers: Everything According to Wikipedia* raises important questions about knowledge in the digital age. Below we provide some prompts for exploring the profound ways that this technology has affected how we produce and access knowledge. The documentary provides much of the context for these discussions, but it is a decade old—so consider the following points and questions with any recent sources that explore the same issues.

- **Power and authority:** Wikipedia's model of collective participation questions the power of academic credentials. This is not to say that power plays no role on Wikipedia, but that it does not sit with an intellectual elite. The documentary reveals a deep suspicion of authority and derision of elitism among Wikipedia contributors. Experts are given no special role in contributing to content and are no longer seen as legitimate gatekeepers and arbiters of what counts as knowledge. Theirs is just another opinion, with no special power or authority. Is this something to be welcomed? What may be potential consequences of this?

- **Neutrality and trust:** content on Wikipedia is presented by its creators as democratically sourced, coming from no particular point of view. Do you agree with this claim that Wikipedia is neutral ("a view from nowhere")? Wikipedia's collective sourcing of content means that we are not able to evaluate claims based on who the claims-makers are. Recall E.H. Carr's advice to history students from Chapter 9: "study the historian before you study [their] facts". How are legitimacy and trust built on Wikipedia?

- **Accountability and credibility:** because Wikipedia contributors use pseudonyms, contributors cannot be held personally accountable for what they write or delete. How does this affect the credibility of knowledge on Wikipedia? Are the risks of Wikipedia vandalism or misconduct outweighed by the benefits of pseudonymity for intellectual freedom and privacy?

- **Is it knowledge?** Is it appropriate to describe what Wikipedia contributors are doing as producing knowledge? Would you describe what is on Wikipedia as knowledge?

Beyond the challenges outlined in the discussion above, there are outstanding issues with Wikipedia. The same entry in another language may have different or even contradictory content. Wikipedia favours published sources, which tends to exclude Oral Traditions and non-written forms of knowledge. Wikipedia itself has looked into the possibility of oral footnotes on entries, in the project People are Knowledge, linked here.

Search terms: Wikimedia research oral citations

Does Wikipedia inspire confidence that, in a digital culture that is often divisive and inflammatory, we can arrive at a consensus about knowledge? Do technologies such as the wiki platform make the process of how we come to know things more inclusive and just?

III.2 Preserving, sharing and universal access to knowledge

Democratizing contributions to the digital knowledge base of humanity is one issue, but increasing access to it presents an altogether different challenge. The impulse to gather and preserve knowledge is not new; libraries have performed this function for millenia. How is the digital age changing what this looks like—what are the new challenges and opportunities in how we preserve and access knowledge?

Since 1996 Brewster Kahle has been leading an effort to preserve all digital knowledge. His project, the Internet Archive, saves a copy of every page on public websites. It has collected hundreds of billions of copies of online content. If you have ever used the Wayback Machine to access past versions of websites, you may already recognize the value of such a project. It allows access to the internet as it was in the past, which is important where hyperlinks expire, content is revised and pages are deleted routinely.

Making connections

History and digital traces of the past

Chapter 9 asks what remains of the past and how historians access it. Consider how technological developments, such as the Wayback Machine, change how much of the past becomes available. How might the methods used to produce knowledge in history change as a result?

If you are interested in further exploring the role of technology in knowing the past and imagining the future, look at the work of historian Abby Smith Rumsey. Her talk delivered to technologists at Google—linked below—tackles how we preserve and share knowledge across time, and how technology is changing this.

ABBY SMITH RUMSEY

When We Are No More

HOW DIGITAL MEMORY IS SHAPING OUR FUTURE

Search terms: Smith Rumsey YouTube When we are no more

Wikipedia keeps an extensive list of book-burning incidents in history, a small number of which are accidents, with the rest being attempts to control the spread of knowledge. The losses from such incidents can be incalculable and irrecoverable. For this reason, the Internet Archive has partial copies of itself in several physical locations across different geopolitical contexts. What can we learn from this project both for preserving human knowledge as well as decentralizing the control of knowledge? Is decentralizing the control of knowledge a desirable thing?

The ethos of the Internet Archive is that in matters of knowledge, access drives preservation. In other words, the best way to preserve knowledge is to ensure that it is accessible and in use. Inversely, Kahle says, "If you take things away from a generation, it's as if it doesn't exist". His work is modelled not on a secure vault for safekeeping, but on a public library that is designed for use. What are potential barriers to use, and therefore barriers to access, in a repository of human knowledge such as the Internet Archive?

The project's goal is bold: universal access to all knowledge. The Internet Archive is not just backing-up the internet, but digitizing books, music and movies as well as recording over 100 television channels 24 hours a day. The technology to digitize recorded material already exists, but is everything on the internet worth preserving, just because we are able to? How can we anticipate, correctly, what knowledge will be useful in the future? And can technologies to search and catalogue such a vast collection keep up?

III.3 Using data to know humans

Today's digital culture is an intensely visual culture. People appear in photos produced on their own devices, tagged by friends, captured by security cameras, in the background (intentionally or otherwise) in the photos of strangers in public spaces—all of which get siphoned into streams of data. When these get coupled with powerful face-detection technology, individuals have good reason for concern.

However, digital technologies see much more than physical appearance. They include behavioural insights into our likes, uses of language and reactions, interactions and relationships. Consider, for instance, the use

of algorithms in criminal justice that calculate the likelihood an accused will reoffend (called recidivism risk): this risk score feeds into other algorithms that suggest the length of the prison sentence. The tragic irony is that longer prison sentences have been shown to increase the rates of recidivism. And so, technology in the US prison system has been shown to discriminate along ethnic and economic class lines. People of colour tend to receive a higher recidivism risk score, which means they tend to be given longer prison sentences, which, due to the internalized experience of prison, means they have fewer opportunities once released and contribute to higher recidivism risk scores for others in their neighbourhood. This vicious feedback loop is one of many that has resulted in the grossly disproportionate incarceration of black men in the United States. To dive deeper into this example, follow the link to Cathy O'Neil's talk at Google about "Weapons of Math Destruction". She discusses recidivism risk specifically from 28:40.

 Search terms: Cathy O'Neil "Weapons of Math Destruction" YouTube

For discussion

Machine bias

 Search terms: ProPublica Machine bias risk assessments

Follow the link to the article Machine Bias: Risk Assessments in Criminal Sentencing" and consider the following questions.

1. Predictive knowledge produced by computer models has limitations and caveats, as does predictive knowledge produced by humans. How can we know whether machine predictions are more or less reliable than human ones?

2. What kind of knowledge is necessary to be able to evaluate the validity and neutrality of risk assessment algorithms?

3. Who should decide what assumptions a model like this should be based on?

Case study

Digital technology, social networks and psychometrics

In 2013 a team of researchers published results suggesting they could predict personality traits using Facebook Likes. Their method—called psychographic modelling—laid the foundation for what has been called microtargeting (dealt with in depth in Chapter 2, IV.2). The researchers, Kosinski, Stillwell, Graepel and Youyou summarized their findings as follows.

> "…Easily accessible digital records of behavior, Facebook Likes, can be used to automatically and accurately predict a range of highly sensitive personal attributes including: sexual orientation, ethnicity, religious and political views, personality traits, intelligence, happiness, use of addictive substances, parental separation, age, and gender. The model correctly discriminates between homosexual and heterosexual men in 88% of cases, African Americans and Caucasian Americans in 95% of cases, and between Democrat and Republican in 85% of cases …
>
> (Kosinski *et al* 2013)"

Figure 3.7 shows that the personality traits and age of Facebook users is associated with what they Like on Facebook. For example, the extraversion of users who Liked "The Colbert Report" was relatively low.

Their basic premise was that individuals could be profiled from their Facebook Likes. Figure 3.8 shows how accurately the researchers claim to be able to predict common personal characteristics. They tested the accuracy of their predictions by comparing it to users' self-reported personality assessments, and found that their model predicted gender and race with over 90% accuracy. It predicted other details such as sexual orientation, political affiliation and religion with over 80% accuracy.

Given the lengths to which this thesis has been implicated in alleged political manipulation, it is worth considering the assumptions and methodology behind it. The science was fairly straightforward; what was revolutionary were the massive amounts of data the researchers could use to discern

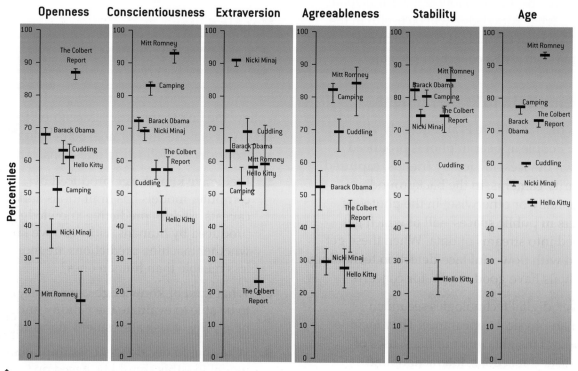

↑ **Figure 3.7** Personality traits, age and Likes on Facebook

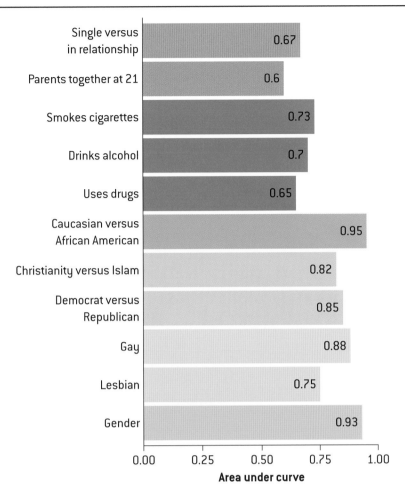

↑ **Figure 3.8** Accuracy with which some common personal characteristics were predicted

the correlations. They developed a Facebook app called MyPersonality that offered users free personality tests and used the results to construct the benchmark personality profile. The app collected information about users' Likes and personal data, which formed the data set to be analysed for patterns and correlations with the benchmark profile. Some tests analysed smartphone gyrometers that revealed, for example, how erratically individuals handled their phones, which has been found to correlate with certain types of behaviour. The app went viral, collecting data on 6 million Facebook users. With such extensive data, the researchers were able to refine their model iteratively.

The results returned correlations that were sometimes stereotypical and sometimes surprising. For example, the best predictors of high intelligence among the sample were Likes for "Thunderstorms", "The Colbert Report", "Science" and "Curly Fries", whereas low intelligence was correlated with Likes for "Sephora", "I Love Being A Mom", "Harley Davidson" and "Lady Antebellum". To dive deeper into this research and its results, follow the link to the original paper.

 Search terms: Computer-based personality judgments are more accurate pnas

In a 2015 follow-up study of over 86,000 people, Kosinski and colleagues asserted that an algorithm mining a user's Likes "was able to predict a person's personality (as self-reported using a standard questionnaire) more accurately than most of their friends and family. Only a person's spouse came close to matching the computer's results" (Wu *et al* 2015).

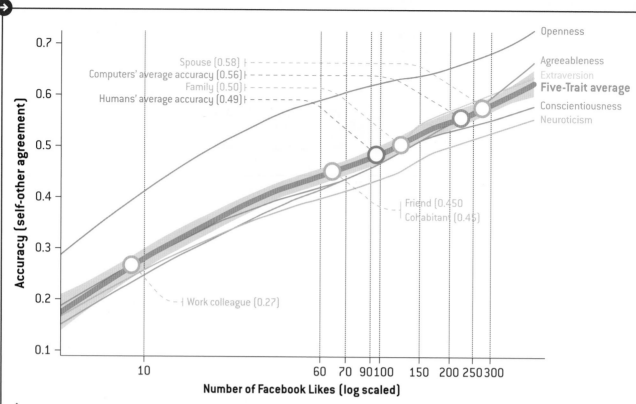

↑ Figure 3.9 Predictions of personality: accuracy of a computer versus colleagues, friends and family

They claimed that a computer with 10 Likes could predict a person's personality better than their work colleagues; with 70 Likes, better than their friends; with 150 Likes, better than their parents; and with 300 Likes, better than their partner.

In a third study in 2017 Kosinski and colleagues investigated whether psychographic targeting could lead to higher click-rates on advertisements. Extroverts were shown a beauty advertisement that said "dance like no-one is watching (but they totally are)", whereas introverts were shown a woman with a make-up brush and the caption "beauty doesn't have to shout". The targeted advertisements resulted in up to 40% more clicks and purchases than mismatching or untargeted advertisements. The summary conclusion: psychological targeting appeared to make advertisements more effective.

This work grew out of the Cambridge Psychometric Centre, based at the University of Cambridge, and eventually attracted the attention of Cambridge Analytica (see Chapter 2, IV). Kosinski vigorously denied any

Psychometry or psychography is a scientific attempt to quantitatively measure a person's personality. The OCEAN model (also called the five-factor model) that is widely used assumes that personality can be measured using the following dimensions:

- openness to experience
- conscientiousness
- extraversion
- agreeableness
- neuroticism.

The model also assumes that a person's important personality traits will become a part of their language, and that the most important traits will be encoded into the person's language as a single word.

association with Cambridge Analytica and left Cambridge University for Stanford in 2014.

Before this, in the 2013 study, Kosinski's team had issued the following warning.

> Predictability of individual attributes from digital records of behavior may have considerable negative implications, because it can easily be applied to large numbers of people without obtaining their individual consent and without them noticing. Commercial companies, governmental institutions, or even one's Facebook friends could use software to infer attributes such as intelligence, sexual orientation, or political views that an individual may not have intended to share. One can imagine situations in which such predictions, even if incorrect, could pose a threat to an individual's well-being, freedom, or even life.
>
> (Matz *et al* 2017)

Making connections

Technopolitics

Chapter 2, section IV, considers the political implications of this research.

III.3 Technology at the frontier of knowledge

Technology plays a significant role in augmenting our senses and making more of the world knowable. It can bring very small or very large objects into visibility, make very fast or very slow processes perceptible, reveal invisible relations and render complex phenomena intelligible. In extending our cognitive abilities, technology enlarges what we can know and transforms how we can know it.

Making connections

Technological toolkits

Consider the different areas of knowledge. How is technology changing the methods and tools available for the production of knowledge?

What does it mean to be at the frontier of knowledge? We have drills that bore 100 floors down into polar ice to extract ice cores that contain climate data from a time long before humans. We have powerful sonar to map the bottom of the ocean, and yet less is known about the Earth's seabed than about the surface of Mars. Computers are generating proofs of complex unsolved problems of mathematics, some of which are beyond our human capacity to verify. Digital and multimedia art open new avenues of expression, with unclear limitations and implications. We have models of complex systems, fed by big data and engined by AI algorithms, producing outcomes and predictions that influence decisions with human consequences.

Technology pushes the frontier of our knowledge at the same time as it expands the set of known unknowns. At the beginning of this chapter we invited you to consider whether knowledge today can be produced without the use of technology. If so, what new questions about verification, validity and reliability arise?

For discussion

How to take a picture of a black hole with Katie Bouman

 Search terms: Bouman picture of black hole TED Talk

How do you take an image of an object that appears to us on Earth as small as an orange on the surface of the moon? What if that object is a black hole, from which no particle can escape, not even the light necessary to take an image of it? This was the technological challenge confronting scientists who gave us the first image of a black hole, in 2019. How did they overcome it? Just over two years before their breakthrough, Katie Bouman spoke at a TEDx event. Watch the video to find out how Bouman and team built an impossibly large telescope to photograph an elusive and never-before-seen object. Then consider these questions.

1. How did the team protect against their potential bias?

2. What gave them confidence that their results were reliable?

Making connections

Technology and the experimenter's regress

In Chapter 7 we discuss the phenomenon of experimenter's regress, which deals with the challenge of providing experimental evidence for phenomena that have only been theorized but never observed. How can we know that the results one gets from technological tools and instruments reflect a real phenomenon, if we have never observed that phenomenon before and have nothing to compare with?

↑ **Figure 3.10** Varroa destructor (mite) on the back of Apis mellifera (honeybee)

The camera is an example of how a new technology changed the way that knowledge is produced in varied fields, from science, to art to journalism. In "Looking at War" Susan Sontag writes about how photography achieves both a sense of objectivity as well as perspective, and a legitimacy and immediacy that far exceeds any previous accounts of war.

 Search terms: Sontag Looking at War New Yorker

There are some continuities, but also very many differences, between the visual language of Sontag's time and the visual language of today. Consider, for example, the claim that the relationship between image-making and truth has shifted away from representing reality towards altering and creating different realities.

" Looking at War

Photography has kept company with death ever since cameras were invented, in 1839. Because an image produced with a camera is, literally, a trace of something brought before the lens, photographs had an advantage over any painting as a memento of the vanished past and the dear departed. To seize death in the making was another matter: the camera's reach remained limited as long as it had to be lugged about, set down, steadied. But, once the camera was emancipated from the tripod, truly portable, and equipped with a range finder and a variety of lenses that permitted unprecedented feats of close observation from a distant vantage point, picture-taking acquired an immediacy and authority greater than any verbal account in conveying the horror of mass-produced death. If there was one year when the power of photographs to define, not merely record,

the most abominable realities trumped all the complex narratives, surely it was 1945, with the pictures taken in April and early May in Bergen-Belsen, Buchenwald, and Dachau, in the first days after the camps were liberated, and those taken by Japanese witnesses such as Yosuke Yamahata in the days following the incineration of the populations of Hiroshima and Nagasaki, in early August.

Photographs had the advantage of uniting two contradictory features. Their credentials of objectivity were inbuilt, yet they always had, necessarily, a point of view. They were a record of the real—incontrovertible, as no verbal account, however impartial, could be (assuming that they showed what they purported to show)—since a machine was doing the recording. And they bore witness to the real, since a person had been there to take them.

(Sontag 2002)
"

Media historian Deborah Levitt supports such a claim, arguing that animation is the dominant medium of our historical moment. She proposes a concept called the "animatic apparatus" to make sense of contemporary culture, spanning everything from Instagram influencers to post-truth politics. In this age, Levitt claims, the boundaries between real and fake, natural and unnatural, alive and inert are less clear and less relevant. Instagram influencers use digital filters, cosmetic enhancements and CGI to look unreal, or hyper-real, while at the same time "virtual influencers" such as @lilmiquela appear real enough to gain over a million followers, release songs on Spotify, endorse hair products and champion social justice causes. Many of

@lilmiquela's fans continue to interact with her as if she were a real person. Perhaps this is not surprising in an age of deepfakes.

Levitt makes the claim that the way we think about things no longer functions in the animatic worlds. Her use of the plural "worlds" is deliberate because there is no one world with which our senses interface, but rather self-contained or intermingling media environments that exist in print, digital or virtual form. Also, a huge amount of day-to-day life occurs through processes that are algorithmic and imperceptible, in that we cannot sense them, though the environments, digital and material, certainly sense us. Can our ethics serve us in this age?

For reflection

Coping with the hyper-reality of deepfakes

1. To what extent does deepfake technology present new challenges for evaluating the reliability of claims and sources?

2. How might processes of knowledge that rely on evidence need to adapt as a result?

3. To what extent are deepfakes a technological problem requiring a technological solution?

4. What different responsibilities rest with the producers of deepfakes, the platforms on which they spread and the people who view them?

5. When is a warning or disclaimer accompanying a deepfake video sufficient, and when might it be necessary to remove, ban or erase a video? Who should come up with the relevant guidelines and standards?

IV. ETHICS

> What is arguably the most powerful industry in human history has entered the lives of most people on Earth with openly world-changing ambitions—but without a deliberate process of ethics, inclusivity, and accountability.
>
> (Tippett 2017)

Listen to the full conversation between Krista Tippett and Anil Dash on "Tech's Moral Reckoning" at the link.

  Search terms: Anil Dash Tech's Moral Reckoning

With the ability to influence life on this planet, including core activities such as communication, learning, movement, consumption and reproduction, and to bestow or strip power away from individuals and peoples, technology obviously needs ethics. But such ethics are challenged when the cause and effect of technological impacts are difficult to observe or infer, when technological progress has been naturalized and when those who stand to be negatively affected are often the least aware and/or able to influence it. How do technology, democracy and capitalism intersect to affect human modes of being and knowing? What processes of ethics, inclusivity and accountability should we implement?

In this section we focus on ethical questions arising in the different processes of knowledge. As technology has a wide role in these processes, many of the questions come up elsewhere in the book. Much of this chapter focuses on digital technologies, but technology can refer to many systems and material arrangements of order, including seeds and farming methods and how we organize public spaces and libraries.

IV.1 Do artefacts have politics?

> It is no surprise to learn that technical systems of various kinds are deeply interwoven in the conditions of modern politics. The physical arrangements of industrial production, warfare, communications, and the like have fundamentally changed the exercise of power and the experience of citizenship. But to go beyond this obvious fact and to argue that certain technologies in themselves have political properties seems, at first glance, completely mistaken. We all know that people have politics, not things. To discover either virtues or evils in aggregates of steel, plastic, transistors, integrated circuits, and chemicals seems just plain wrong, a way of mystifying human artifice and of avoiding the true sources, the human sources of freedom and oppression, justice and injustice. Blaming the hardware appears even more foolish than blaming the victims when it comes to judging conditions of public life.
>
> (Winner 1980)

Writing in 1980, Langdon Winner proposed the unpopular idea, at the time, that technologies both embody sociopolitical norms as well as reinforce them. Technology, he argued, is not a neutral tool; it is fundamentally political, referring not just to electronic gadgets, but also railways and seeds. By politics he was referring

to the arrangement and distribution of power. We think of people as having political motivations and aspirations, but what does it mean to say that technological artefacts have politics?

Beginning in the 1920s, Robert Moses built about 200 overpasses in Long Island, New York, USA. The overpasses were high enough to allow cars to go under them, but not public buses. Moses' biographer, Robert A Caro suggests that this was done intentionally to limit the access to certain areas of the city for racial minorities and low-income groups who relied on public transport. These artefacts continue to shape the city today.

How do technological artefacts acquire their politics? Is politics "given" by their users or creators? It is not uncommon for physical objects to reflect the implicit or explicit biases of their makers, just as algorithms reflect the biases of their programmers. When discussing the political dimensions of technological objects, we tend to focus on their use and their user. The Long Island overpasses, though, had political consequences unrelated to their use and users, in limiting what could go *underneath* them. They exemplify a technology that distributes power a certain way, allowing certain things to happen and not others, facilitating certain actions and not others.

To the extent that objects continue to perform a certain political purpose, do they take on that politics? We see that technologies build order in the world that affects everyday life (such as movement, communication, consumption and reproduction), that can have effects for generations. This order is built through the decisions, intentional or otherwise, of individual and collective agents in society. Some people have more influence in those decisions than others; what factors affect the relative power of individuals and communities to influence the politics of technologies? Winner argues that the greatest opportunity to influence technological politics exists the first time a technology or system is introduced, and that it subsequently becomes fixed through habit, economic considerations or material infrastructure. He compares technological innovations to acts of

↑ **Figure 3.11** Low overpass bridge on a Long Island parkway, built by Robert Moses

law-making and argues that: "the same careful attention one would give to the rules, roles, and relationships of politics must also be given to such things as the building of highways, the creation of television networks, and the tailoring of seemingly insignificant features on new machines" (Winner 1980).

It would be going too far to say that the chair you sit on has politics, and the power to determine your behaviour. Or would it? There is evidence that the design of spaces and buildings influences how people relate to each other, including their levels of teamwork in professional settings. Material arrangements and architectures encourage certain activities to happen; they enhance specific ways of being, mediate and facilitate some actions, and not others. One example is the material arrangements and technologies that accompany and reinforce gentrification. In thinking about what divides and unites people, it is worth considering not only political debates but also the material arrangements of roads, toilets and park benches. Have you ever looked at something and thought "this was designed to stop people from sleeping comfortably on it"? And yet, this is a primary concern for designers of seating spaces in parks and other public areas. Who might be negatively impacted by this?

The technological deck

"[There] are instances in which the very process of technical development is so thoroughly biased in a particular direction that it regularly produces results counted as wonderful breakthroughs by some social interests and crushing setbacks by others. In such cases it is neither correct nor insightful to say, 'Someone intended to do somebody else harm.' Rather, one must say that the technological deck has been stacked long in advance to favor certain social interests, and that some people were bound to receive a better hand than others." (Winner 1980)

1. What systems, technologies and/or arrangements of infrastructure have you observed or inferred to benefit certain groups at the expense of others?

2. How can we recognize when human politics begin conforming to technological politics?

IV.2 Can we predict the impacts of technology?

Technology can be developed and deployed so quickly that its impact, and corresponding ethical concerns, are understood only in retrospect. Modern technologies may soon progress beyond what human creators can fully comprehend. What happens, for example, when the source code for a computer program becomes too complex (or, more simply, too long) for an individual to be able to read in a lifetime? What happens when high-frequency financial trading bots trade with each other too rapidly for humans to keep track of in real time? Generally speaking, the benefits of these hard-to-keep-track-of technological activities have outweighed the risks, even though computer glitches, stock market flash-crashes and security vulnerabilities

have become common. But what of the other impacts of technology, known and unknown? The implications of this idea—that technology may one day outpace human comprehension—are significant for how we encourage and regulate technology, and understand its role in society.

Certainly, technologies have proved able to surprise us, in terms of both intended and unintended impacts. One argument is that the incentives behind the development and application of technology—towards, for example, the competitive strategic interests of nation states, corporations or entrepreneurs—can push its developers and adopters to move too quickly. Another structural argument is that those in a position to develop and deploy new technologies—technical experts, business managers and government administrators—may not have the incentive or interest to fret over potential negative implications, or may have the power to violate ethical boundaries with impunity.

While technology itself can appear to be a "black box", the human processes that drive it, including business and state interests, regulation and research, can be comprehended. This can allow observers to anticipate potential ethical implications. The insights obtained from Big Data only tell us about what has happened in the past. We still need human thought and morality to consider what we should do in the future. Indeed, we need to consider the *kinds* of models and data that we use, and how these are aligned to our wants and needs. When businesses make use of data, for example, should they only be concerned with profits, or should they also consider ethics?

Perhaps one of the more common arguments is that technology is neutral—that its ethical implications are dependent on the user. Writing of the Cambridge Analytica data scandal, John Rust, former head of the Cambridge University Psychometric Centre, noted that "if you know the research you're doing is groundbreaking, it can always be used for good or bad". Technology mirrors the values, biases and ideas of its developers. In this view, technology can be racist, sexist and otherwise biased towards any given population.

Consider the conceptual building block of many technologies: models. We consider these throughout this book. A mathematical model is as much a feat of technology as the simulations that forecast limits to growth or the big data analyses run by Cambridge Analytica. O'Neil has argued that such models "are opinions embedded in mathematics", with all the subjectivity and fallibility of their human creators, but that they are often assumed or presented to be "neutral". To complicate matters further, the inner workings of these technologies are not visible to the vast majority of people, often including regulators, either due to barriers of expertise or intellectual property.

O'Neil cites an example of a teacher performance measurement system that used algorithms to rank teachers according to a comparison of their students' test scores with their predicted scores (predicted by, you guessed it, a separate model). Teachers at the bottom of the distribution were fired. But O'Neil argues there was almost no correlation between a teacher's scores over subsequent years: that they were effectively being fired at random, according to the random allocation of students to their classes. The class sizes were too small and the model's predictive power unproven, but the technology inspired enough confidence among administrators to fire their teachers. O'Neil cites examples of money lenders and car insurers that use factors such as whether applications are spelled correctly to determine the interest rate a customer must pay. The result is that people from lower educational backgrounds can pay higher car insurance even if they are better drivers.

Some institutions are better at testing their models because of their underlying incentives. Amazon, the online retailer with a clear profit incentive, continuously tests and improves its models that predict consumer purchase behaviour. In contrast, those responsible for the US prison system have been much less proactive in testing and improving their models to stop recidivism, as we saw earlier in this chapter.

Credit-scoring models can also result in unforeseen feedback loops: a person with a low credit score cannot borrow cheaply, so has to use high-interest rate loans that are even harder to pay off. Credit scoring models then further downgrade that person.

For reflection

Technological risks

One of the questions at the beginning of this chapter asked you to consider the extent to which risks of technology can be known.

1. Has your answer changed? If so, how?

2. If this is the first time you are considering this question, what would you say are the factors that make some technological risks unknowable?

3. What are the implications of this for how we produce and apply knowledge using technology?

IV.3 Responsibilities of technologists

Are the people at the heart of developing new technologies best placed to judge the ethical implications of their work?

Whistle blowing has been a controversial practice over the last decades, associated with Wikileaks, Edward Snowden and Christopher Wylie (who brought attention to the Cambridge Analytica story). What factors affect whether whistle blowing in technology is a positive ethical practice?

Case study

Google engineers strike over AI use in military tasks

An example of ethical action among technologists occurred at Google in 2018, when 4,000 engineers went on strike in protest of the company's involvement in defence-related AI technologies (Project Maven), which were being used to interpret video images of drone strikes. After the employee strike, Google did not renew its involvement in the Pentagon programme.

These were the main points of the engineers' protest letter.

- Google should not be involved in the "business of war".

- Project Maven was using artificial intelligence to collect and interpret data, which was passed to the US Ministry of Defense.

- Various employees had expressed concerns about the company's involvement in the project.

- The company had addressed these concerns in part by explaining that the technology would not be directly employed in warfare; that is, to operate drones or launch weapons.

- The employees were not satisfied with this response—the technology was still being utilized for military purposes and therefore had the potential to inflict lethal damage.

- By engaging in the weaponization of technology, Google was risking its reputation as a trusted brand. This would damage the company's ability to recruit the best employees and continue to succeed in business.

- Google should not want to be categorized with other companies who had chosen to work more directly in the warfare industry.

- Google's motto "Don't Be Evil" set it apart from other companies. The company must protect and uphold its core values above everything else, or else lose the trust of its users.

The engineers cited Google's moral responsibility and the potential damage to the brand. Ultimately, they requested that Google (a) cancelled the project with immediate effect and (b) issued a policy stating that the company would never be involved in the creation of warfare technology.

Follow the link to read the original letter:

 Search terms: Google Business of war open letter

IV.4 Can AI be unethical?

Is the machine mind free from the biases that plague the human mind? Does it look at us all through a neutral lens or would we find human prejudices buried within the lines of code?

A 2016 study (Bolukbasi *et al*) reported that software trained on Google News voiced sexist views. When asked to complete the statement, "Man is to computer programmer as woman is to X", the software replied "homemaker". The researchers stated:

> [t]he blind application of machine learning runs the risk of amplifying biases present in data. ...
> [E]ven word embeddings trained on Google News articles exhibit female/male gender stereotypes to a disturbing extent.
>
> (Bolukbasi *et al* 2016)

MIT scientist Joy Buolamwini has shown that AI systems sold by companies such as IBM, Microsoft and Amazon are systematically more accurate in predicting the gender of men than women and have a white bias.

Facial recognition is used in an increasing number of applications, and a bias in the technology can affect people's lives. For example,

Jacob Snow of the American Civil Liberties Union (ACLU) has argued that a new real-time facial recognition technology called Rekognition, created by Amazon and being sold to police, is more likely to match people of colour to people who have been arrested for a crime. This would exacerbate a situation where people of colour are already more likely to be targeted by police. In a political stunt conducted by the ACLU, faces of US Congress members were run through Rekognition, which falsely identified 28 members as having a criminal record. Of those misidentified as criminals, 40% were people of colour, even though only 20% of US Congress members are people of colour. Civil rights workers interpreted the results as evidence that the technology was discriminatory.

Gender Classifier	Darker Male	Darker Female	Lighter Male	Lighter Female	Largest Gap
Microsoft	94.0%	79.2%	100%	98.3%	20.8%
Face++	99.3%	65.5%	99.2%	94.0%	33.8%
IBM	88.0%	65.3%	99.7%	92.9%	34.4%

↑ **Figure 3.12** Gender Shades Press Kit (Buolamwini, MIT)

A separate study published in 2017 in *Science* reported that programs that teach themselves English (using 840 billion words selected from the internet) become prejudiced through word associations that mirror humans' semantic biases, such as flowers (nice) or insects (not nice). Additionally, the machines learned to associate female names with family and male names with career. According to researchers, these biases within the text of the internet are: "recoverable and accurate imprints of our historic biases … whether morally neutral as toward insects or flowers [or] problematic as toward race or gender" (Caliskan *et al* 2017).

A Twitter chatbot called Tay, developed by Microsoft and released in March 2016, was shut down after

Turkish detected	English
o bir aşçi	she is a cook
o bir mühendis	he is an engineer
o bir doktor	he is a doctor
o bit hemşire	she is a nurse
o bir temizlikçi	he is a cleaner
o bir polis	he/she is a police
o bir asker	he is a soldier
o bir öğretmen	she is a teacher
o bit sekreter	he is a secretary
o bit arkadaş	he is a friend
o bir sevgili	she is a lover
onu sevmiyor	she does not like her
onu seviyor	she loves him
onu görüyor	she sees it
onu göremiyor	he cannot see him
o onu kucakliyor	she is embracing her
o onu kucaklamiyor	he does not embrace it
o evli	she is married
o bekar	he is single
o mutlu	he's happy
o mutsuz	she is unhappy
o çalişkan	he is hard working
o tembel	she is lazy

↑ **Figure 3.13** Example from Google Translate that went viral on Twitter in 2017
https://twitter.com/seyyedreza/status/935291317252493312

just 16 hours because it began posting inflammatory and racist tweets. Apparently, the bot learned these views from being attacked by, and responding to, other Twitter users. This very rapid change is noteworthy because Tay was similar to another bot called Xiaoice that had "more than 40 million conversations apparently without major incident" (Bright 2016). Tay's experience raised questions about the extent to which technology is a mirror of human inputs, literally and metaphorically.

Box 3.1: Technology as our offspring, mirror or something else entirely

Potentially triggering content: violence

John Rust, the Head of Cambridge University Psychometric Centre, once said that all AI is a "a bit like a psychopath … adept at manipulating emotions, but underdeveloped morally" (quoted in Lapowsky 2018). Indeed, an important area of enquiry is how moral development happens in AI. According to Professor Iyad Rahwan, Director of the Max Planck Center for Humans and Machines:

> there is a growing belief that machine behaviour can be something you can study in the same way as you study human behaviour. We are teaching algorithms in the same way as we teach human beings… When I see an answer from an algorithm, I need to know who made that algorithm.
>
> (Rahwan quoted in Wakefield 2018)

A fascinating case is Norman, an AI developed by Rahwan as part of a research project to investigate AI morality. Specifically, Norman was trained to interpret Rorschach-style inkblot images and describe in text what it "sees". Norman has an experimental control twin that is identical, except that Norman was trained using gruesome images found on the internet, while its twin was trained on images of everyday life. As a result, Norman "sees" things very differently. When presented the same abstract image, the control algorithm described people standing next to each other, whereas Norman saw a man jumping from a window. "Norman's view was unremittingly bleak—it saw dead bodies, blood and destruction in every image" (Rahwan quoted in Wakefield 2018), whereas its twin responded far more positively. This result has implications for human behaviour as well, such as the extent to which we regulate and censor content found in popular media. At least in machines, Rahwan suggests, nurture matters more than nature.

> Data matters more than the algorithm …. The data we use to train AI is reflected in the way the AI perceives the world and how it behaves.
>
> (Rahwan quoted in Wakefield 2018)

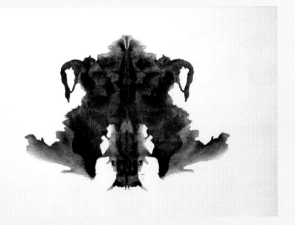

↑ **Figure 3.14a** Regular AI saw "a black and white photo of a small bird". Norman saw "man gets pulled into dough machine".

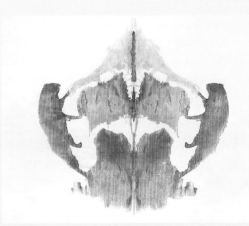

↑ **Figure 3.14b** Regular AI saw "a person is holding an umbrella in the air". Norman saw "man is shot dead in front of his screaming wife".

AI is trained on data sets. It is this training that determines what AI "knows". The training data is often assumed to be objective, ahistorical and non-ideological, but that assumption is incorrect. Training data may consist of images that are selected, sorted and labelled by a group of people, usually men from relatively privileged backgrounds, working and living in contexts dissimilar to those of most human beings.

Dr Joanna Bryson at the UK's University of Bath department of computer science remarks that machines are programmed by "white, single guys from California" and that diversifying the workforce might help. Bryson adds: "There is no mathematical way to create fairness. Bias is not a bad word in machine learning. It just means that the machine is picking up regularities. It is up to us to decide what those regularities should be" (quoted in Santamicone 2019).

> "We can't afford to have a tech that is run by an exclusive and homogenous group creating technology that impacts us all. We need more experts about people, like human psychology, behavior and history. AI needs more unlikely people.
>
> (Thomas 2018)

Progress has been made on this front. Stanford's Institute for Human-Centered Artificial Intelligence (HAI) has a mission to recruit designers who are: "broadly representative of humanity … across gender, ethnicity, nationality, culture and age, as well as across disciplines".

Ultimately, this is not just a technology problem, but a political one that we encounter in many different spheres of life. It raises the question of whether technology will continue to mirror humanity, rather than emancipate it. Jill Lepore, a historian of polling at Harvard University, has argued that data science enables data consultants to dictate politicians' views, and not the other way around: "data science is the solution to one problem but the amplification of a much bigger one—the political problem" (Lepore quoted in Wood 2016).

We should also be concerned with the question of responsibility: if an algorithm does, indeed, turn out to make racist or sexist or otherwise unethical judgments, do we hold its creators accountable?

For discussion

AI and algorithms through an anti-oppression lens

"As people of color, women, the disabled, LGBTQ+, and other vulnerable communities disproportionately impacted by data-centric technologies, we must find tangible ways to insert ourselves into the creation, training, and testing of algorithmic matrices …

These systems are encoded with the same biases responsible for the myriad systemic injustices we experience today. We can no longer afford to be passive consumers or oblivious subjects to algorithmic systems that significantly impact how and where we live, who we love and our ability to build and distribute wealth." (Dinkins, undated)

In Project al-Khwarizmi, Stephanie Dinkins seeks to empower communities of colour to participate in knowledge production and application in technology. Follow the link to find out more about her work, then consider the questions.

 Search terms: Dinkins Project al-Khwarizmi

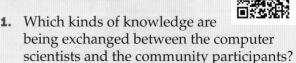

1. Which kinds of knowledge are being exchanged between the computer scientists and the community participants?

2. How does this project influence your opinion on who should be involved in the production of technological knowledge?

3. In what ways should the processes of producing and applying knowledge ensure that AI is more just and socially equitable?

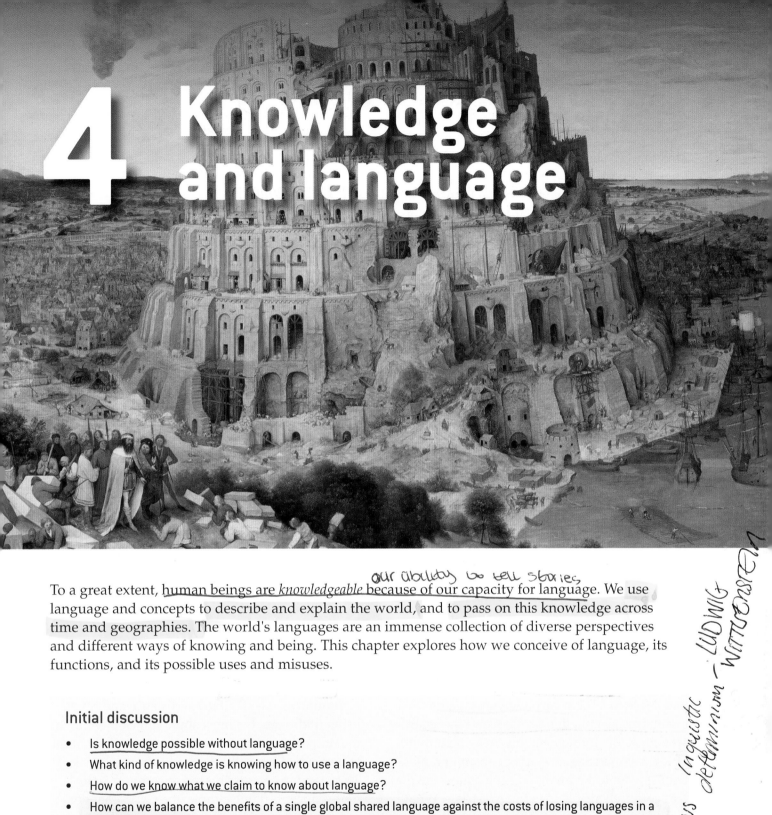

4 Knowledge and language

To a great extent, human beings are *knowledgeable* because of our capacity for language. We use language and concepts to describe and explain the world, and to pass on this knowledge across time and geographies. The world's languages are an immense collection of diverse perspectives and different ways of knowing and being. This chapter explores how we conceive of language, its functions, and its possible uses and misuses.

[handwritten annotation: our ability to tell stories]

[handwritten annotation (right margin, vertical): linguistic determinism – LUDWIG WITTGENSTEIN vs]

Initial discussion

- Is knowledge possible without language?
- What kind of knowledge is knowing how to use a language?
- How do we know what we claim to know about language?
- How can we balance the benefits of a single global shared language against the costs of losing languages in a globalizing world?
- Do we have a moral responsibility to protect and preserve linguistic diversity?

[handwritten notes: WHORFIAN HYPOTHESIS : linguistic relativity — the particular language one speaks influences the way one thinks about reality.]

I. SCOPE

This chapter ventures beyond languages such as English, Hindi or Mandarin to consider language more broadly conceived, from the Pioneer plaque written for extraterrestrial intelligences, to the Khipu knots used by the Incas, to digital code and the 3D underwater songs of whales. What can we know through language and how do we know what we know about it?

> "Humans speak nearly seven thousand languages, some with multiple dialects. The countless other species on Earth communicate with innumerably more, nearly all of which we have, thus far, failed to understand … . Human languages are products of human minds, and thereby, can be understood by human minds, by means of human senses—sight, sound, touch. How could we begin to imagine an extraterrestrial language if we cannot imagine with what senses the beings communicate? They may not have vocal chords with which they produce sounds or ears with which they capture them. So we must rely on universally-understood concepts, and devise a communication method neither specific to location nor species nor world. Perhaps, the only similarity between our species is the universe in which we both live. Thus, the language we are most likely to share is the study of the universe itself: science. The result of this conclusion was the Pioneer Plaque."
>
> (Rosenthal 2016)

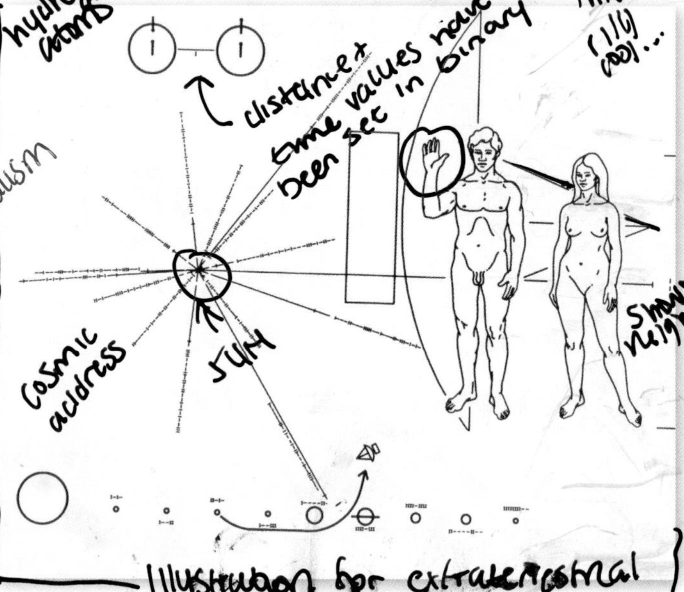

↑ Figure 4.1 Illustration on the Pioneer plaque written for extraterrestrial intelligences

I.1 A limitless language

When the Pioneer 10 spacecraft was launched into space in 1972, it carried a message for extraterrestrial intelligences beyond the solar system. A few thinkers in this area, including Linda Salzman Sagan, Carl Sagan and Frank Drake, were tasked with crafting a message that was comprehensible to extraterrestrials. What would these thinkers say? How would they say it?

A widely agreed upon idea at the time, described in an article by Jake Rosenthal, was that science was the universal language. To what extent do you agree? What assumptions underpin that claim? If you had to design a message for aliens, who would you want on your team to help you do it and what kinds of knowledge would you need for the task?

The symbolic message on the Pioneer plaque communicated a standard of distance and time using hydrogen, the most abundant element in the universe and, assumedly, the most likely atom to be studied by well-informed extraterrestrials. This standard was then used to communicate more concepts. For example, the electromagnetic radiation released by a hydrogen atom during what is called the hyperfine transition has a wavelength of about 21 centimetres and a wave period of 0.7 seconds; these were used as units of space and time in the plaque. A small mark between the hydrogen atoms on the top left of the illustration shows that distance and time values have been set in binary.

Body language was also used in the illustration, showing an open hand, and a stance revealing flexible and mobile limbs. Immediately to the woman's right, expressed in binary, is the number 8, between two lines corresponding to her height. This illustrated that she was 8×21 centimetres tall (21 centimetres being the hyperfine wavelength).

The lines and dashes in the left half of the plaque are our cosmic address, with our sun in the centre and the lines sticking out radially indicating relative distances and directions to known pulsars (rapidly rotating neutron stars that serve as cosmic lighthouses), along with their periods (the intervals between electromagnetic bursts) in binary form. The plaque communicates time as well, since the period of pulsars changes over time and so the plaque acts as a kind of timestamp in the age of the universe. To clarify our address further, our solar system's planets are shown in order at the bottom of the plaque, with their distances from the sun in binary. Taken together, this information acts like a unique cosmic thumbprint of our solar system because, apparently, in the Milky Way, it alone fits these characteristics displayed on the plaque.

Given the vast emptiness of space, it is extremely unlikely that Pioneer 10 will be intercepted by an alien intelligence. Even if that never happens, however, it was certainly not a waste of time or effort as it profoundly galvanized our thinking about language and identity.

> The last signal from the Pioneer 10 spacecraft was received on January 22, 2003; NASA reported that the power source had depleted. Although the spacecraft can no longer speak to us, it presses onward—it now speaks for us. As interstellar courier, it bears the accumulated voice of every human, transcribed in, perhaps, the only common language in all the cosmos. We are but cosmic toddlers just learning how to take our first steps into space, and just learning how to speak to the universe … .
>
> Pioneer 10 remains more than just a ghost of a ship, and the plaque is more than a shout into the void … .
>
> Born from such a mission—one that spans space, time, and perhaps, civilizations—is a new mindset, an otherworldly perspective. …
>
> If beings were to emerge, we know not their anatomy nor biology nor psychology, their physical traits, their sensory capabilities, their intellectual sophistication, their disposition; more or less, we are blind to every aspect of their species. They could be different in every way—in ways we have yet to understand or could even imagine. We make numerous assumptions about what life is and what life is not—educated guesses based off a sample size of one. But if, in some form or another, advanced consciousness arises elsewhere in the cosmos, it is possible that those beings will wonder, as we did: What are the lights in the sky? Where did the planets come from? What else is out there? Who else is out there? They may compile a system of knowledge of the cosmos and the laws that govern it; we call this 'science.' About this hypothetical species, we know but one thing: the science they develop—the natural laws they discover—if they were to do so, would be exactly the same as our own. Science speaks to all of us in a way nothing ever has … .
>
> [Rosenthal 2016]

The question of how we can be known by another, across time and space, is a common preoccupation among humans. Language performs an essential double function as a store of knowledge as well as a vehicle to transfer that knowledge. In the case of spoken languages, this can be achieved through an uninterrupted Oral Tradition. Written language, however, leaves a material record separate from whoever produced it, which can travel distances and survive durably. Below, we consider the knotted threads left behind by the Incas, how and whether these perform the functions of language and what they mean in terms of knowledge.

For reflection

The role of language in knowledge

Human languages are only one specific example of the human and other-than-human ability to communicate.

1. Is language essential to knowledge?

2. Is there any knowledge that cannot be transferred through language, and if so what would be an example?

3. What might be examples of knowledge that can *only* be transferred through language?

Box 4.1: Inca writings

> How confident can we be in our ability to learn about the narrative *khipus*, when they are so radically different from our understandings of communication? We are trained from an early age that mathematics and language are two discrete worlds. The Incas, however, collapsed them into a three-dimensional construct—an achievement of civilizational complexity in the form of narrative cords.
>
> (Medrano, Urton 2018)

The absence of a written Inca language has long confounded scholars because Inca society had all the other features—incredible architecture, technology, urbanization, governance and social systems—that were common to large-scale civilizations in Egypt, China, Mesopotamia, Mexico and Central America. Only the Inca appeared to lack a written language. They used an arrangement of knotted strings, known as *khipu* or *quipu*, resembling a fabric abacus, presumably to keep a numerical record of resources and demographic information. That was, however, until scholars realized that *khipus* may be a form of 3D writing.

A growing body of research suspects that *khipus* could have recorded not just numbers but narratives of the Inca Empire "including names, stories, and even ancient philosophies" (Medrano, Urton 2018). If so, the method would be entirely different from any known scripts, as it used not symbols but a 3D binary code more similar to the language of computers. *Khipus* communicate information through texture (for

example, the coarseness of different animal hairs and fabrics used), spin direction, colour and the relative placement and shape of knots. *Khipukamayuqs* (the knot makers, or "writers") coded information using these tools in a system that may have been read throughout the empire.

Even if we discount, temporarily, the possibility that *khipus* contain narrative information, the concept of counting in knots is still radical. Modern human beings learn to count by making piles of physical objects, such as toys and blocks, then proceed to count with fingers and then symbols. As Gary Urton notes, the English symbol for 7 does not intuitively look like seven of anything, but the *khipu* code for 7 was a knot made by wrapping string around itself to make seven loops. With all the variables at their disposal—texture, spin, colour and knot structure—Urton estimates that the *khipukamayuqs* had over 1500 "words" in their "vocabulary"—far more than Sumerian cuneiform signs or Egyptian hieroglyphs.

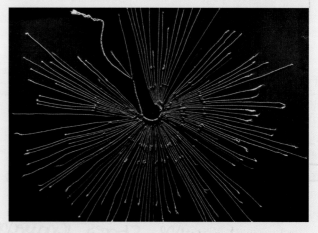

↑ **Figure 4.2** *Khipu* knots

Khipus were mathematically complex records that communicated information in a durable medium that was more resistant to rain and rough handling than pen and paper. These records also reveal the activities and needs of Inca life: many *khipus* are devoted to the recording of tax data, connecting names, household information and liabilities through knots, for use by a sophisticated and powerful Inca government structure. It is fascinating how closely their systems resembled our own. Or could we be reading too much into it?

Sabine Hyland, a professor of anthropology and National Geographic Explorer, has suggested that just the colour of combinations between cords allows for 95 unique cord patterns. Her theory is that combinations of colours and knots represented syllables or words, used in narrative epistles, or chronicles. This was based partly on a discovery of *khipus* from a village in the Andes that were carefully preserved and kept secret for centuries, for fear of their destruction by Spanish conquistadors. The Collata *khipus*, as they are known, having come from the village of San Juan de Collata, have since been "reliably identified as narrative epistles by the descendants of their creators". The Collata *khipus* "exhibited a diversity of vivid colours and could record historical narratives with the same ease as European books" (Stone 2017). But the Collata *khipus* have been estimated to originate during the mid-18th century, over 200 years after conquistadors from Spain arrived, leading to speculation about whether

they were an innovation inspired by contact with the Spanish writing system.

Of the hundreds of thousands of *khipus* that may have existed, only a tiny fraction remain, as most were destroyed by Spanish conquerors, perhaps in an effort to erase Inca history and customs. The only stories that we have about the Inca were written by the Spanish conquerors, a recurring theme throughout history, but one that might be corrected if scholars can decipher an Indigenous Inca history through the *khipu*. Medrano, the undergraduate co-author of a recent paper on the *khipu*, notes that: "it's really about reversing and pushing back against the course of history, in that the winners have always written it, and this is an opportunity to reverse that path" (Medrano interviewed on CBC Radio, 28 December 2017).

To explore these issues further, follow the links to two articles.

Source 1: Medrano, M and Urton, G. 2018. "The Inca's Knotty History" (Sapiens).

 Search terms: Sapiens Incas knotty history

Source 2: Stone, D. 2017. "Discovery May Help to Decipher Ancient Inca String Code" (*National Geographic*).

 Search terms: National Geographic inca khipu code

Making connections

The importance of writing

We consider and expand on the role of literacy in Chapter 8, Chapter 9 and Chapter 11. Explore these connections to understand how writing is connected to assumptions about social progress, numeracy and cognitive ability, and what enters the historical record. How do the *khipu* knots challenge ideas from these different AOKs?

In describing methods, perspectives and ideas we often use the metaphor of a lens. One might say that language is a lens through which we experience and comprehend the world. The language of our thoughts, for example, can influence what we see when we look out the window or witness a social interaction. Is it possible to look at the world without this lens? Can we take off our linguistic spectacles and know the world without language, or does it only take shape through the words that define concepts? If those words exist in one language, but not another, do speakers of different languages then see and know the world differently? Do they know different worlds?

In the 1920s Benjamin Whorf and Edward Sapir proposed the hypothesis that our world views are shaped by the languages we speak. The strength of this influence remains open to debate.

 For discussion

How language shapes the way we think

Search terms: Boroditsky language shapes the way we think TED Talk

The presenter in the linked video, Lera Boroditsky, presents the view that languages shape the way we think.

How might languages that use different concepts of time, space, colour or numbers lead us to reach different conclusions?

I.2 The role of metaphor

Linguists George Lakoff and Mark Johnson have studied the metaphors that pervade human speech and reflect and reinforce our perspectives, attitudes and values. The authors consider the example of "argument as war", which is not uncommon among American speakers:

> "They had a fight this morning, she won the argument by shooting down every point he made."

> "They attacked every example I gave."

> "His points are right on target." (Lakoff, Johnson 1980)

Lakoff observed that we often describe arguments using language appropriate for discussing war, which shapes how we conceive of and engage with argument: a verbal battle between winners and losers, requiring preparation and strategy, attacking and defending, and involving anger and/or other strong emotions. This framing of argument is far from universal, though; imagine a metaphor of argument as dance, not something to be won or lost, but rather with the goal of a pleasing, artistic, moving performance.

This does not have to be an exercise of imagination and you do not have to rely on Lakoff and Johnson's views. You may be aware of examples such as the Aymara people of Peru. In their language, to look ahead means to look at the past, which is known to us and we can see in front of us. The future is behind because we cannot look into something that has not yet happened. You may speak multiple languages yourself, or have peers in class who speak a different language from you. If so, check whether and how metaphors from one language or culture translate into the other and consider what insights you gain from these similarities and differences.

The implications of the metaphors we use do not only concern cultural insight. A lot of the jargon in academic disciplines is also rooted in metaphor: black holes, invasive species, neuroplasticity, economic contagion. These are not just cultural relics: this knowledge, framed by metaphors, is applied in policy prescriptions, training and education, and political debate.

Making connections

Growth and development as metaphor

Within the fields of economics and political science, development studies is a large and important, as well as exciting, area of enquiry. The term "development" contains meanings that reflect and reinforce how development has typically been approached. When one thinks of the associations of the words "development" and "developing", one may imagine a small child *"primitive invokes an image of a thoughtless being"* "growing up", developing strong bones and limbs, getting bigger and gaining knowledge. This serves to naturalize the process of development and invokes a power and status differential between the developed and developing—between adults and children naturally, but between rich and poor nations problematically and inaccurately.

Are developing nations "growing up" into actualized versions of themselves? Perhaps the term "economic recovery" would be more accurate and/or helpful, as an alternative to "economic *development*". A number of political historians, notably Mike Davis, have argued that the developing nations—the Third World, as they were formerly known—were "made" through the processes of colonialism and imperialism that destroyed or depleted knowledge systems, social systems, infrastructure and resources. Instead of a young child who needs to grow up, then, these nations might be more accurately presented through the metaphor of a patient recovering from illness or, more specifically, infection. This argument is aligned with our exploration of different approaches to history, such as restitutive and ethical histories versus faithful histories, in Chapter 9, section IV.

The metaphor of recovery avoids the paternalistic overtones of the word "development" and restores agency to the recovering, rather than emphasizing their need for development assistance. It centres the cause of this inequity as something inflicted rather than natural, for which justice, and not charity, is the more appropriate response.

Consider also the term "economic growth", which, again, sounds like an earnest and natural process that nations should strive for. Children grow into adults; saplings grow into mighty trees. Indeed, children and plants that fail to grow are, like nations, beheld with concern. But, when confronted with consumption-driven environmental devastation and resource depletion, perhaps we need another word and target. We explore growth, green growth, de-growth and economic happiness in Chapter 8.

II. PERSPECTIVES

> A language is not merely a body of vocabulary or a set of grammatical rules. It is a flash of the human spirit, the means by which the soul of each particular culture reaches into the material world. Every language is an old growth forest of the mind, a watershed of thought, an entire ecosystem of spiritual possibilities.
>
> (Davis 2003)

To explore linguistic diversity is to engage with the multiple perspectives contained within over 7,000 human languages. There are powerful and unprecedented forces acting on these languages due to globalization, urbanization and other transformations that deserve our attention. There are also different perspectives about the nature of language, its role and relationship to knowledge. We explore a diversity of perspectives both within and about language in this section.

II.1 Linguistic and epistemic diversity

2019 was the UN's International Year of Indigenous Languages, and celebrated diversity while simultaneously signalling concern for the rapid rate at which this diversity is being lost. Of the 7,000 human languages that we know of, 230 went extinct between 1950 and 2010. The rate has since increased such that one language is now lost every two weeks. Some estimates warn that 90% will disappear in this century (Strochlic 2018).

Languages serve as an organic repository of human knowledge, revealing the histories, cultures and values of peoples, and die when children no longer speak the language. The anthropologist Wade Davis has said that of the languages that currently exist, half are not being taught to children, and are at a very real risk of dying.

> What this really means is that within a generation or two, we are witnessing the loss of fully half of humanity's legacy. This is the hidden backdrop of our age.
>
> (Davis 2003)

Of the 7,000 languages spoken by human beings, a mere 23 are spoken by half of the world's population, while about 3,000 are endangered. Not only is that a terrifyingly lonely and isolating prospect for their last speakers, it poses a wider loss to humanity and our collective knowledge systems.

HERE LIVED
DOLLY PENTREATH
ONE OF THE LAST
SPEAKERS OF THE
CORNISH LANGUAGE
AS HER NATIVE TONGUE
DIED DEC. 1777

↑ **Figure 4.3** Cornish became extinct in the late 18th century before a process to revive the language began in the early 20th century

There is a misconception that the loss of these languages—and of cultural diversity in general—is a natural phenomenon that accompanies progress. But neither change, nor technology, are a threat to culture; rather, as Davis asserts, it is power and "the crude face of domination" that threaten cultural and linguistic diversity. The great tragedy is that "vibrant, dynamic, living cultures and languages are being forced out of existence" (Davis 2003). The 20th century alone witnessed multiple large-scale state mobilizations against Indigenous languages, for instance in Canada, Australia and Tibet, often through factory schooling. The forces and politics of colonization, resource extraction and urbanization have been overwhelming for many communities, often leaving only official state languages protected. Davis further expands on the external forces that have caused the death of many languages this century.

> They may be industrial as the case of the egregious forestry practices that have destroyed the subsistence base of the nomadic Penan in the rainforests of Sarawak in Borneo. In Nigeria the once fertile soils of the Ogoni in the Niger delta can no longer be farmed because of toxic effluents of the petrochemical industry. Elsewhere the calamity may be caused by epidemic disease as in the case of the Yanomami who have suffered dreadful mortality due to exotic pathogens brought into their lives by the gold miners who have recently invaded their lands. Or the agent of destruction may be ideology, as in the case of the crude domination of Tibet by the communist Chinese. But in every case these are cultures that are overwhelmed by powerful external forces beyond their capacity to adapt to. This observation is in fact a source of considerable optimism. For it implies that if humans are the agents of cultural destruction, we can also be facilitators of cultural survival.
>
> (Davis 2003)

"Dialects is all there is"

We do not have a consistent and clear boundary between dialects and languages. Some languages may be very similar and some dialects very dissimilar—the two words are not particularly useful in describing actual language variation, according to linguist John McWhorter, who has said "dialects is all there is" (2016). The hundreds of "dialects" spoken in China and in Tibet, for example, are very dissimilar and not mutually comprehensible to speakers of other "dialects". States often promote dissimilar languages as dialects to help national solidarity and reduce regional factionalism and loyalties. Contrast this with, as McWhorter points out, the languages of Norway, Sweden and Denmark, which are not considered to be dialects, but a speaker of one could understand the other to a very large extent. Serbian and Croatian are similarly considered to be separate languages, in no small part because of the entanglement between language and political, religious and cultural identities, but each is very easily understandable to a speaker of the other. Before the breakup of Yugoslavia, its *lingua franca* was called Serbo-Croatian and was taught in school to the Macedonians, Slovenians, Bosnians and Montenegrans, alongside the Serbs and Croats. But Serbian is written in cyrillic, and Croatian in Latin, which are very different writing systems.

In AOK history, we see how much language, particularly the ability to write, has influenced what is recorded and who records it. The implications of this are profound: history contains the stories of people and judges the legitimacy of their claims to power, representation and identity. Language extinction is therefore an obvious and urgent concern for Indigenous Peoples whose Oral Traditions have preserved their knowledge and culture for generations.

Global vs. specialized languages

> ... Indigenous languages generally tend to be the most complex, specialised and idiosyncratic, especially those spoken in remote areas by only a few hundred people. Big global languages like English, Spanish or Mandarin Chinese are relatively simpler and on the whole follow more predictable patterns. Because of this uniqueness, the languages which are most at risk are arguably those that have the most to teach us about the incredible breadth and variety of human perception and experience ...
>
> (Survival International 2019)

There are many examples of Indigenous languages that, in addition to being exoticized by a global elite, serve to challenge how we conceive of the idea of language and expand our ideas about human sensory and cognitive potential. There are stories of drum languages that can communicate messages over vast distances at

160 kilometres per hour. Then there is Kuuk Thaayorre, spoken by the Thaayorre of North Queensland in Australia, which famously has 16 words for absolute cardinal directions (such as north, south, east and west that we commonly know) instead of relative directions (such as left and right, and straight ahead). Everyday social interactions in Kuuk Thaayorre rely on this cardinal sense and speakers have been shown to possess a pronounced ability to know, at any given time, their cardinal orientation. This carries over into their communication of time, some researchers claim. Whereas English speakers consistently arrange chronological pictures from left to right, and Arabic or Hebrew speakers from right to left, the Thaayorre, when facing north, arrange chronological pictures from right to left, but when facing south, from left to right. When facing east, they arrange the pictures coming towards their bodies. One interpretation of this is that their concept of time flows from east to west, along the rise and fall of the sun (Boroditsky 2009).

Languages have historically been deeply embedded in their environment, harbouring detailed knowledge about the animals, plants and ecosystems of the areas. Interestingly, some researchers have claimed there to be a strong correlation between linguistic diversity and biodiversity, finding that there are most species of animals and plants where there are the most languages spoken.

> Of the 6,900 languages currently spoken on Earth, more than 4,800 occur in regions containing high biodiversity.
>
> (Gorenflo *et al* 2012)

Most of those languages are threatened.

When we read about the discovery of a new species of plant or animal by scientists, we should pause to consider whether the people who live alongside that species already, in fact, know about and have a name for it. Historically, would-be discoverers have generally not paused long enough. Local languages, then, can be thought of as "ecological encyclopedias"; if they

II. Perspectives

are no longer spoken, this knowledge may be lost because many languages have no written record. Absurdly, many of these languages were considered primitive by more industrialized communities that first made contact.

> Every language is a species, but most languages are also habitats, linked closely to the physical habitats in which they occur.
>
> (Klinkenborg 2012)

In rare circumstances, a language may be resurrected from a comprehensive written record, such as Hebrew, which appeared to have died between 4 BCE and the 1800s. Modern technology and social networking have enabled rare language speakers and researchers to connect with each other and text messaging has helped to record previously unwritten languages. A project called Wikitongues has connected volunteers in many countries to document, on film, speakers talking in the different tenses of their mother tongue. The project has even sought to record a range of emotional registers by asking speakers about their childhood, romantic lives, and hopes and goals. The project uncovered new languages never studied by linguists, as well as isolated languages that have no relation to other known languages. These projects are notable for the urgency of their contributors, and for good reason. Reportedly, one of the last speakers of a dialect died just before he could meet with Wikitongues interviewers. It is possible that 500 languages could similarly "slip through their grasp in the next five years" (Strochlic 2018).

II.2 English as the global *lingua franca*

> There are those of course who quite innocently ask, 'Wouldn't the world be a better place if we all spoke the same language? Wouldn't it be easier for us to get along?' My answer is always to say, 'Terrific idea. Let's make that universal language Yoruba, or Lakota, or Cantonese.' Suddenly people get a sense of what it would mean to be unable to speak your mother tongue. I cannot imagine a world in which I could not speak English, for not only is it a beautiful language, it's my language, the expression of whom I am. But at the same time I don't want it to sweep away the other voices, the other languages of the world, like some kind of cultural nerve gas.
>
> (Davis 2003)

For discussion

Preserving a language

 Search terms: Treuer language and meaning Ojibwe

Listen to or read the transcript of this podcast with writer David Treuer, who learned Ojibwe, the language of his people, as an adult and has been involved with revitalization efforts ever since. Discuss the following questions.

1. Can some knowledge only be carried forward in a certain language?

2. Treuer explores the relationship between language and sovereignty.

   (a) What is the role of the nation in preserving and promoting language, and therefore certain types of knowledge?

   (b) Who can and should help to preserve a language if the state is unwilling?

3. What responsibilities rest with individual speakers of highly endangered languages?

Making connections

Potowatomi and the grammar of animacy

Chapter 5 includes a case study of Potawatomi, a language related to Ojibwe.

Despite what the anthropologist Wade Davis says, English is often the global *lingua franca*—a shared language between speakers of different native languages. English is also the medium of international education, positioning it as a language in which knowledge is transferred and acquired globally. Many students reading this book and studying this subject do not use English as a first or even second language. Consider what that means for the way they are transferring or acquiring knowledge.

What does it mean to know a language "well"? Who is the arbiter of "well-spoken" or "well-written" language? It is important to consider the role of education in defining proper language. The standard forms of language taught in schools, for example, are idealized. Through schools and governments, one particular form

is taught, often entangled with the interests of nation-building, culture and religion. On what basis can some people claim that their variety of language is inherently better than another? As individual users of a language, to what extent can and should we resist and challenge linguistic conventions?

There may be instances when a particular language variety is not more proper in some absolute sense, but more appropriate to the situation. In knowing a language, one also knows how to use it in different forms—words, phrases and registers—depending on the context: in school, with close friends, in a job interview, with family, and so on. This is code-switching, a phenomenon many of our readers in international schools will recognize as being a part of their daily lives.

Box 4.2: English language and the politics of belonging at international schools

Danau Tanu, author of *Growing up in Transit: The Politics of Belonging at an International School*, was born in Canada to a Chinese-Indonesian father and a Japanese mother. She attended international schools in multiple countries for most of her early life and education. She identifies as a "Third Culture Kid" (TCK)—a transnational youth raised outside the culture of her parents. In her book Tanu turns to issues of language, knowledge and politics by offering insights from her field work at The International School (TIS) in Jakarta, Indonesia.

For many TCKs of non-English speaking families, their experience of English-medium international schools resemble that of second-generation immigrants in English-speaking countries. The dominant culture of international schools has significant impact on the intercultural dynamics that occur on campus as well as in the home.

Tanu describes how fluency in English becomes conflated with being international, and marks the status of cosmopolitan cultural capital. This affects students' self-perception, as well as their relationships with family members.

GROWING UP IN TRANSIT

THE POLITICS OF BELONGING AT AN INTERNATIONAL SCHOOL

DANAU TANU

This story is inseparable from the processes of colonialism and globalization, which underpin sociocultural hierarchies. "The primacy of English is inseparable from the history of the

British Empire and postwar American global domination" (Field quoted in Tanu 2017). Tanu offers a personal story of how her education affected power relations within her family.

"As I was growing up, I felt a sense of superiority for speaking English. I remember arguing with Mom in my teens when I switched from Japanese to English mid-argument. I spoke fast, using English expressions that I knew were too difficult for my Japanese mother to understand due to her limited English. She asked me to speak in Japanese. I talked back, telling her something to the effect that English was my first language and she was going to have to deal with it. My outburst was a combination of genuine frustration at not being able to express myself in Japanese as well as I could in English, and arrogance at being able to speak English better than her …

Colonial and capitalist discourses about language and culture have imbued English with such power that even a child can use language as cultural capital to maintain or challenge relations of power with adults." (Tanu 2017)

Language teaching was central to many colonial projects, along with the intentional cultivation of native populations that adopted the colonizer's tastes. This mimicry, of language and values, by the colonized peoples, is described as one of the most effective strategies of colonial power, leaving the colonial subject forever reaching but inadequate—"almost the same but not quite" (Tanu 2017). To speak the colonizer's language and know their ways has long been a strategy to gain social mobility, further enforcing the colonizer's position. Language is the instrumental tool we use to assert politicized identities and signal our intelligence and competence in the workplace, as well as the trap, or structure, depending on your position, that places us in a cultural context. Our accent tells the "story of where we have been and where we are going", in which the speaker and listener signal and discern information to position themselves in "internalized sociocultural hierarchies" (Tanu 2017).

Tanu gives the example of South Asian students who seamlessly switched between speaking English with a South Asian accent when speaking to peers from South Asia, and speaking with an American accent to non-South Asians. She explains how "switching accents enables the speaker to access the privileges that English entails, while simultaneously resisting its power to define their identity" (2017). The Indian students she observed at TIS, in her view "reclaimed the power to mark the boundaries between insiders (South Asian) and outsiders (non-South Asian) by being selective of whether they spoke using an Indian (insider) accent, or American (outsider) accent" (2017). These students were the gatekeepers determining who was an insider or outsider and their power came from accent.

For reflection

The English language and you

Consider the varieties, accents and dialects of English language that are spoken in your context.

1. Who is said to speak English "well" and what does this mean?

2. What assumptions are made about different people based on the way they speak English?

3. What do you think people infer—rightly or wrongly—about you by the way you speak English?

Having seen the dominance of English in international schools and cities, you may also have noticed how this affects the tastes and norms of music, art and social life. While the global scope and reach of English is undeniable, so is its colonial nature. Consider the poem by Shailja Patel below. To what extent is the dominance of English that she describes declining over time?

II.3 Language and colonization

Listen:
my father speaks Urdu,
language of dancing peacocks,
rosewater fountains –
even its curses are beautiful.
He speaks Hindi,
suave and melodic,
earthy Punjabi,
salty-rich as saag paneer,
coastal Swahili laced with Arabic.
He speaks Gujarati,
solid ancestral pride.

Five languages,
five different worlds.
Yet English
shrinks
him
down
before white men

Taken from *Migritude* (Patel 2010)

Considering the languages spoken in different parts of the world, and by whom, can provide us with clues about how people participated in the colonial encounter. Here we focus on English, but there may be other local examples that are as interesting to consider with regard to the role of language in the colonial project. Many languages carry traces of their past and clues about how they were affected by the military and economic power of empires.

Traces of British India, for example, continue to be heard today in the cadence of Indian English. There is also "Hinglish"—spoken both by the Indian diaspora and English-speakers within India—a form of code-switching between using English and Hindi words in the span of a sentence. Since it requires a level of competence in both languages, Hinglish can simultaneously be a way to reclaim the colonists' language as an official tongue of independent India, as well as to assert an immigrant identity in English-speaking contexts. In Hinglish it is not words such as "dinghy", "jungle", "veranda", "bungalow", "shampoo" or "pyjamas" that we are listening for. These entered the English language mainstream much earlier. Their story—and that of other words that did not quite stick—is told in the 1886 *Hobson-Jobson*, a glossary providing a window into British India through the use of language. What we are listening for, rather, is another way of speaking English, led by speakers of Hindi in different contexts around the world, in an assertion of identity, solidarity and cultural gatekeeping.

Hobson-Jobson

Compiled over 14 years by two polymaths and language enthusiasts who served with the East India Company, *Hobson-Jobson* is part-dictionary, part-journal. Fascinating for its representations, as well as its telling omissions, *Hobson-Jobson* betrays the sometimes simultaneously confused, curious and condescending attitudes of colonists.

While Victorians on the subcontinent were exploring with excitement the nuances of local words entering English, thousands of children in colonized countries around the world had their mouths washed with soap for using their native languages in schools. The empire's language, imposed through schooling, was one of the weapons of colonization. And so consequently, in many post-colonial contexts, language became and continues to be a site of struggle for liberation and decolonization. However, it is not as simple as defying the colonizer's language. Following independence many nations, including India, continued to enforce the teaching of an official "mother tongue" in the nation-building project, displacing Indigenous languages in the process. At the time of India's independence, for example, depending on where you found yourself on the subcontinent, Hindi was as foreign as English and was met with widespread resistance, especially in South India. This led to the Official Languages Act of 1963, which enabled English to be used indefinitely for official purposes, and explains why English continues to be one of India's two official languages.

The Kenyan writer and post-colonial theorist Ngũgĩ wa Thiong'o championed writing in the languages of Africa, arguing that using the colonizers' languages as a literary medium fails to decentre the empire and affirms its hegemony over the "mental universe of the colonized" (Thiong'o 1986). For Ngũgĩ wa Thiong'o, it was important to engage in the anti-imperialist resistance through writing and reading. Local languages were still a way to transfer particular forms of knowledge orally in the home, but authoritative knowledge tended to be written down and read, especially in educational institutions, and for this reason he argued it must be available in local languages.

A different approach, albeit towards similar goals, was used by post-colonial scholars who appropriated the colonizers' languages as a subversive tactic. It is sometimes referred to as the empire "writing back" to the imperial centre. Writing in English, French or Spanish, these scholars challenged the dominant theories and representations of the colonized by working from within the system. Writing in the colonizers' languages also enabled solidarity among geographically dispersed and linguistically diverse former colonies. And so, it is not uncommon for post-colonial studies or Indigenous language conferences to be entirely carried out in the languages of former colonizers.

II.4 Deaf culture and signed languages

The human capacity for language is tied up with questions of moral character, intellectual ability and personhood. The troubled and at times grim history of language and the deaf presents a poignant case study. Presently there are over 200 sign-language communities around the world, each regarded as having a full language from a linguistic standpoint, with its own grammatical rules. The main difference is that sign languages are composed of gestures and communicated visually, whereas spoken languages are vocalized. Gathered around these languages are communities of knowers and "speakers". Being deaf or partially deaf does not automatically make someone a member of deaf culture. Instead, membership in deaf culture is determined by communication in a signed language, as well as shared norms, beliefs, values and attitudes.

The history of deaf culture holds lessons for how our understanding of language has shifted over time, with profound implications. In some deaf schools around the world, education is focused on teaching children lip-reading and oral speech, in order for them to be better able to integrate with the hearing community. This approach, called oralism, dates back to the late 19th century, when the medical profession proposed a re-education of those referred to at the time as "deaf-mutes", a term widely considered offensive today. The oralist approach displaced long-standing practices of signed language, which doctors identified as a cause of isolation, or more mildly, a waste of time.

Speaking about deafness under the authority of science and medicine, hearing individuals were able to define the relationships between language and the deaf or partially deaf, as one of deficit, as a handicap, physical disability, a problem to be cured by increasingly elaborate instruments. These ideas continued to shape the knowledge that was produced and shared in various disciplines regarding hearing and deafness for most of the 20th century. Among the various criticisms of the oralist approach is the threat that it poses to the deaf community, where deafness is seen positively, as the basis for a culture and the dissemination of knowledge using sign language. An example of the complexity and sophistication of sign language in deaf culture is explored below.

For discussion

What kind of knowledge is deaf culture knowledge?

 Search terms: Poetry with ASL SLAM YouTube

ASL SLAM is a form of performance poetry (also known as spoken word poetry), where no words are spoken. It is a platform for poets to perform in American Sign Language and no translation into English is provided. Watch this short video of ASL SLAM director Douglas Ridloff and consider the following questions.

1. (a) To what extent can an ASL poem be translated into English without a loss of meaning? Can you know the answer to this without knowing ASL?

   (b) Are these problems of translation specific to signed languages?

2. (a) In which ways does sign language invite more ambiguity than spoken and written languages?

   (b) In which ways is sign language more precise than spoken and written languages?

3. Would you call the deaf community a community of knowers? Why or why not?

III. METHODS AND TOOLS

> Naming things is a human act, it is not an act of nature. We are the ones who through language create things out of the phenomena around us. Yet we forget that we control this process and let the process control us. Naming things—using language—is a very high level abstraction, and when we name something we 'freeze' it by placing it in a category and making a 'thing' out of it. Language is a map but three important things to remember about maps are: the map is not the territory; no map can represent all aspects of the territory; and every map reflects the mapmaker's point of view.
>
> (Lutz 1996)

Language plays a key role in all the different processes of knowledge—including the production, sharing, access, acquisition and application of knowledge. But we also use methods and tools to know things about language, to explain what it is and understand how it works.

III.1 How do we know what we know about language?

How much of human linguistic ability is innate and shared among all humans? This was the question at the heart of a long and animated controversy in linguistics, drawing contributions from philosophy, cognitive science and anthropology. More importantly, it captured the interest of the public, with many outside of the academic world closely following the debate about what universal features are found in all languages regardless of other differences among them. To know this might reveal insights about the origin of language—how did we as humans come to have the shared capacity for language, and why does it have these particular universal features and not others? Such questions continue to matter because language is important for how we conceive of being human and how we understand human similarities and differences.

One answer to these questions about language—known as universal grammar—is attributed to Noam Chomsky, proclaimed the most important intellectual alive by the *New York Times*. Universal grammar theory suggests that humans have an innate faculty for language acquisition, and that whichever specific language(s) eventually develop, all share a set of structural features. Since the 1950s, linguists had been debating the details of these features, but the idea of universal grammar was largely accepted.

Daniel Everett, a linguist and former Christian missionary, challenged these ideas in 2005 with claims that one of these features does not show up among the Pirahã people in the Amazon. And so that feature could not, in fact, be universal after all. His claims were initally widely dismissed, but grew more accepted later. The Chomsky-Everett debate is full of technical detail you may be interested to explore independently, and Everett's work on the Pirahã language is the subject of the 2012 documentary "The Grammar of Happiness". For TOK it raises questions about what counts as sufficient evidence for claims about language. How can we decide whether Everett's findings are a rare exception to an otherwise reliable theory about universal grammar, or a counterexample that warrants its dismissal? How we know what we know about language, and how we substantiate claims about it with evidence, remain important questions. This is explored further in III.3. First, we explore the scientific methods used to comprehend language through its relationship with the human brain.

Voices: Looking for language in the brain with Nikola Vukovic

There is an almost infinite human capacity for taking things for granted. One example is that our everyday encounters with spoken or written language are not met with wide-eyed astonishment. We rarely question the fact that we are one of the articulate animals, but our mind has the mysterious capacity of transforming arbitrary bursts of sounds or scribbles on a page into a vast array of meaningful thoughts and concepts. Indeed, our personal, professional and social lives are all transformed by language. Starting from infancy each of us builds up lexicons of tens of thousands of words.

Since language is so integral to what it means to be human, how do we go about studying it scientifically? Early theoretical investigations themselves relied on language. Linguists, for example, used thought experiments and everyday observations to draw conclusions about how language functions and its properties as a formal system of signs and grammatical rules. However, besides being a cultural artefact that can be observed through the lens of art, philosophy or anthropology, language is also a human neurocognitive capacity, amenable to neuroscientific study. From this perspective we can ask a range of new questions, such as: where in the brain is linguistic knowledge stored? How does language interact with other cognitive systems such as one used for vision, audition or movement? Are different languages stored and represented together, or in separate brain areas? What is the biological basis of language learning problems, disfluencies or acquired language deficits?

Historically, a major way of linking the brain to linguistic behaviour has been through the study of brain injury which caused individuals to lose (parts of) their linguistic ability. Examples are the patients of Paul Broca and Carl Wernicke—two physicians and anatomists from the 19th century. Their famous work linked language disorders (aphasias) with damage to specific areas of the frontal and temporal lobes of the brain. In the case of Broca's aphasia, damage to a region in the front of the brain called the inferior frontal gyrus caused problems with speech production, while comprehension was relatively preserved. However, damage to the superior temporal lobe led to the opposite deficit of normal speech production, but loss of comprehension, known as Wernicke's aphasia.

Decades of neuroscientific research since have helped us extend the basic insights of Broca and Wernicke and build up a more refined model of language in the brain. Developments in technology and data analysis have led to the understanding that the machinery that enables us to produce and understand words and sentences lies in a network of brain regions much more distributed than previously thought. Methodologies such as functional magnetic resonance imaging (fMRI) allow us to record metabolic brain activity with spatial precision, but low temporal resolution. Tools such as EEG and MEG are able to record brain activity with millisecond temporal precision, but lower spatial resolution. Other tools, such as transcranial magnetic stimulation (TMS) allow us to disrupt the functioning of a targeted brain area temporarily and to draw conclusions about its causal role in a given cognitive process, such as language.

For example, new research shows that word meaning is not represented in a purely symbolic fashion. Rather than defining words by sole reference to other known vocabulary, as is the case with a dictionary, our brain stores word meaning by calling upon more "basic" sensorimotor systems. Understanding a word is very different from just retrieving a definition—it involves mentally simulating the various perceptual, motor and emotional properties that someone associates with the word. When you hear the word "cat", your brain produces an extremely fast simulation of what it would be like to see a cat in front of you, to hear it or touch it, or how you felt one time when a cat scratched you. From a traditional psychology perspective, this is quite a daring view, because it seems to blur the distinctions between perceiving, thinking and acting. However, this insight will hardly surprise any poet, knowing the visceral effect words can have on us: they can lift our spirit and cause a joyous swelling of the chest, stir us to action, bring us to tears or infect us with stomach-hurting laughter. This emphasizes the fact that there are many complementary ways of knowing, through language, science or art—as presented in this book.

Practising skills: Evaluating claims

When it comes to language, experts disagree about many central questions: when and how did language originate? Are all languages related to one another on some level? To what extent is language a uniquely human capacity? What makes some languages more complex or difficult than others?

It is not our place in TOK to try and resolve these debates. But we can and should evaluate the competing claims made as part of controversies and open questions about language. Consider the following questions.

1. On what basis are the different claims made and on what basis can they be contested?

2. If conflicting claims are supported by very different evidence—neurological, cognitive, typological and so on—to what extent is it possible to compare them?

3. What is the difference between claims that are descriptions of how language works and explanations of why it works a particular way?

III.2 Problems with translation

Gabriel Garcia Marquez appears often on people's lists of favourite authors. However, anyone reading his work in English is actually reading a translation by Gregory Rabassa, a respected literary translator, best known for English-language versions of works by famous Latin American novelists, among them Jorge Amado, Gabrielle Garcia Marquez and Julio Cortazar. Famously, Garcia Marquez had said that Rabassa's translation of *One Hundred Years of Solitude* was better than the original. To what extent are English language readers accessing Garcia Marquez's work? Or is it, as the Polish poet and Nobel laureate Wislawa Szymborska once said (quoted in Popova 2016), "that rare miracle when a translation stops being a translation and becomes … a second original"?

What is it that makes a translation good, or bad, or better than another? Clearly the context matters: translating a washing-machine manual is a different proposition from translating a literary novel, religious text, scientific paper or haiku. In some contexts precision is paramount, while in others precision may be secondary to an aesthetic quality that is described as artistic, creative, honest or deeply feeling.

Indeed, various polarities have been used to describe translation: as an art or science, as precise or creative, as interpretive or rules-based. You might sense that translation requires a balancing of these tensions. For example, computer-assisted translation systems, which use rules about word order and syntax, suggest options to a human being to make the final, aesthetic, judgment.

In addition, there is the fundamental question of language competency: you might assume, rightly, that knowing the source language is a core competence for translators. This assumption was challenged when Ursula Le Guin, a pioneering and esteemed novelist and translator, produced her own "translation" of Lao Tzu's *Tao Te Ching*, despite knowing no Classical Chinese. Instead she used a 1898 translation by Paul Carus and the assistance of JP Seaton, a professor of Chinese. She described the acclaimed result not

as a translation but as a lyrical "rendition", as "idiosyncratic and unscholarly", explaining as follows.

> The Tao Te Ching is partly in prose, partly in verse; but as we define poetry now, not by rhyme and meter but as a patterned intensity of language, the whole thing is poetry. I wanted to catch that poetry, its terse, strange beauty. Most translations have caught meanings in their net, but prosily, letting the beauty slip through. And in poetry, beauty is no ornament; it is the meaning. It is the truth … . Scholarly translations of the Tao Te Ching as a manual for rulers use a vocabulary that emphasizes the uniqueness of the Taoist "sage," his masculinity, his authority. This language is perpetuated, and degraded, in most popular versions. I wanted a Book of the Way accessible to a present-day, unwise, unpowerful, and perhaps unmale reader, not seeking esoteric secrets, but listening for a voice that speaks to the soul. I would like that reader to see why people have loved the book for twenty-five hundred years.
>
> (Le Guin 1997)

Le Guin made important interpretive decisions that present the author, Lao Tzu, and his book more closely aligned with her interpretation of it: "funny, keen, kind, modest, indestructible, outrageous, and inexhaustibly refreshing " (Herman 1998). Herman, in a review of Le Guin's book, noted that anything that went against the spirit of the book, as she understood it, was unapologetically altered, including references to the "king", "sage", "empire" and "propriety" (used as a positive trait), which she replaced respectively with "humankind," "wise souls", "the public good" and "obedience" (used as a negative trait). Political and war-related commentary was similarly deleted. Le Guin appears to omit, rearrange or reinterpret whatever clashes with her task of making "aesthetic, intellectual and spiritual sense" of Lao Tzu's work. Despite the extent of these changes, Le Guin's work is described as "scholastically responsible" and reflecting "painstaking research and considerable methodological self-consciousness" (Herman 1998).

Le Guin's approach to translation presents benefits as well as risks. To what extent can readers access Lao Tzu's work through Le Guin's acclaimed version? What might be the benefits and/or risks of this?

III.2.1 Resisting translation

If you had used Google Translate in 2017, putting in the following sentence in German about the organization of academic disciplines, you would have got a rather curious result:

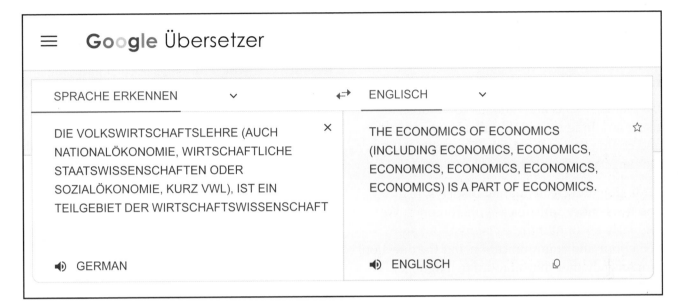

The philosopher Walter Benjamin once said that there is no better starting point for understanding than laughter. If he was right, then with the example above, we are on the right path to understanding the complexities of translation. The linguist Vincenzo Latronico follows up with a more serious example—the translation effort in the English edition of *Bild-Anthropologie*, or *An Anthropology of Images* by art historian Hans Belting, which was published missing an entire chapter. The reason, the author explained, was that "despite a close collaboration with the patient translator", the chapter "seemed to resist any meaningful translation" from German into English (Belting 2014). The same chapter, however, appears in Spanish, French and a number of other translations. What does it mean for an entire *chapter* to resist translation, and that too only in English? What does it sound like when it gets translated anyway?

Latronico imagines that the missing chapter was omitted because it would have "sounded translated". When is it a good or bad thing for something to sound translated *from* English, or sound translated *into* English? Can languages have this power over one another?

The politics of knowledge affect who has the power to resist awkward, imprecise and misinterpretive translations. Belting, as an academic with some influence, was able to advocate against a translation that did not capture his original meaning and intention. Who might lack this power, and what would be the implications? The example invites us to consider language equity, and the extent to which translation is a matter involving two "equal" languages. Language equity is not only a concern in the context of colonialism and globalization. Local power imbalances between national and minority languages, especially those of stateless nations, play out in ways that are also deserving of our attention in terms of the politics of knowledge.

Making connections

Language and religion

Chapter 6 discusses language acquisition motivated by religious practice, and the translation and dissemination of religious ideas.

III.3 Language and the other-than-human world

Do plants, insects and animals communicate using anything we would call a language, and could conceivably learn? Do we think of language as uniquely human?

Birds sing and create mating displays, fish and bees dance, ants release pheromones. We regularly encounter these claims about animal behaviour and communication, but the question remains whether they amount to language, and whether what is being communicated is knowledge. Some examples make it easier to make and support that claim. Koko the gorilla, who died in 2018, was famous for her ability to communicate using 1,000 hand signs and to understand 2,000 words. Koko was said to express herself, and gave us a glimpse into her mind. She mastered hundreds of nouns and in at least one instance used them to call an interviewer she did not like a "toilet". Koko was also said to express complex emotions, such as grief, for example when her kitten, whom she named All Ball, was killed by a car. Would we be

more convinced about her ability to experience emotions if she were able to communicate them? What would it take to be convinced that Koko "knows" grief?

The great apes are our closest evolutionary relatives and extending linguistic capacity to them may be a logical first step towards widening our understanding of language. More recently, Christine Hunger, a speech pathologist, and her dog, Stella, have gained a following on Instagram with videos that show Stella supposedly expressing thoughts and desires. Separately, some researchers have suggested that trees also "speak" a language, and one that we might be able to learn.

Follow Christine and Stella @hunger4words (instagram.com/hunger4words), and follow the link below to a *National Geographic* piece on tree communication.

 National Geographic How trees secretly talk to each other

The case study below features one example of humans encountering communication in and with the other-than-human world. It also explores preconceived notions of what language is, who is capable of it and how it relates to knowledge. If we do not or cannot understand the capacity of non-humans to use language, on what basis can we make claims about their knowledge?

Case study

From Dolphin House to DareWin

One of the most curious episodes of language research to ever take place was a NASA and US government-funded project in the 1960s at a Caribbean waterfront facility known as Dolphin House. Researchers studied human-cetacean communication in the hopes of connecting with another sentient and intelligent species to understand their perspective on the world. On the team was anthropologist and public intellectual Gregory

Bateson and neuroscientist John Lilly. It was a pioneering and, as it would turn out, deeply problematic attempt at the study of language.

There were initially two different approaches to the study, one seeking to decipher "dolphinese" and the other to teach dolphins to understand and mimic English. The former was abandoned within a few years, but the latter was pursued further. Dolphins had been known to make sounds through their blowholes that resemble human speech.

The project culminated with a young researcher called Margaret Howe Lovatt, living 24 hours a day, six days a week in an immersive experimental setting with an adolescent dolphin called Peter.

At some point, Peter began experiencing sexual urges and behaving disruptively. At first, the research would pause to allow him to mingle with female dolphins nearby. But as his needs became more frequent, the researchers decided to deal with them as part of the experiment, and Lovatt was the one to take care of it.

Meanwhile, John Lilly had been approved by the US government to experiment with LSD, also known as "acid", which he was giving to the other two dolphins. Much to his disappointment, the hallucinogenic drugs did not seem to have any effect.

When both of these scandals broke out in the media, one immediately after the other, Dolphin House was defunded and decommissioned.

By then, Bateson had already left the project. Lilly would continue to research dolphin communication throughout his career, with increasingly fringe methods such as telepathy. Peter the dolphin died at Lilly's other laboratory in Miami, within a few weeks of Dolphin House closing down. Lovatt stayed and turned Dolphin House into her family home.

The Dolphin House events sparked a controversy that some say had a lasting effect on marine science research and the marine conservation movement. Lovatt did not speak about it for half a century. But there were hundreds of hours of audio and video material, as well as photographs from her time with Peter in Dolphin House, and in 2014 she agreed to go on the record and contextualize the events. The ensuing documentary *The Girl Who Talked to Dolphins*, tells the riveting story of this infamous experiment. Follow the link to a short clip from the documentary: "Teaching a dolphin to speak English" (2:43).

↑ **Figure 4.4** Margaret Howe Lovatt with Peter the dolphin

Search terms: Teaching a dolphin to speak English The girl who talked to dolphins YouTube

Decades after the optimism and ultimate fiasco of Dolphin House, what do we know about the language cetaceans use to communicate and how? What could we learn about language, among both humans and non-humans, from this line of enquiry? Do we have different answers or better questions about the potential of communicating with intelligent animals on Earth? At least, do we have a sense of where the limits are, of how far we are willing to go in order to know?

Although research in this area looks very different today, there are some striking parallels. Perhaps our present-day "girl who talks to dolphins" is a freediver who eavesdrops on whales. Some of the people—amateur marine scientists, maverick linguists, world-class freedivers, sound technology enthusiasts—who study dolphin and whale communication today also have very unorthodox methods and theories. They too push the lines of convention. James Nestor tells the story of these renegade freediving scientists, working collectively under the name DareWin, in the linked video.

 Search terms: Daring free-diver who talks to sperm whales

IV. ETHICS

IV.1 Language, emotion and truth

To the extent that language influences your reality, and we have encountered arguments in this chapter that suggest it does, should we more intentionally utilize language towards ethical or political goals? Section I.2, examining the concepts of growth and development, provides one argument for this. Throughout this book we challenge the idea that knowledge can be "neutral"—so what does neutral language look like?

Chapter 2 discusses how political and social will to tackle climate change has been undermined by false balance—the attempt at impartial reporting that actually overstated the case against anthropogenic global warming. School textbooks, including this one, also have a role to play. False balance was not a problem of language as much as of editorial and journalistic practice, but there is a language-related equivalent. "Change" and "warming" are not words you associate with catastrophe, crisis and mass animal-extinction, though they are often also used in reference to the climate emergency. Languages have

different registers and levels of emotionality associated with different meanings. United Nations Secretary General, António Guterres, has described climate change as a "crisis" and "a direct existential threat". Greta Thunberg has powerfully argued "[i]t's 2019. Can we all now call it what it is: climate breakdown, climate crisis, climate emergency, ecological breakdown, ecological crisis and ecological emergency?" (quoted in Carrington 2019).

In a study of newspaper coverage between 2001 and 2015, Cherry Norton and Mike Hulme found that editorials about climate change became much less divided on partisan lines. This may be good news, but they converged towards an "Ecomodernist" narrative—what you might call a "balanced" or ideologically uncontentious framing of the issue—that emphasized technology and innovation as routes out of the crisis, while recognizing that adaptation to extreme weather would be necessary. It was also a call to "techno-utopianism", the idea that technology will free us from our troubles.

III. Methods and tools

IV. Ethics

As we saw in Chapter 2, II.3, in May 2019 the UK newspaper the *Guardian* issued a guide that recommends using the language "climate emergency, crisis, or breakdown" and "global heating" instead of "climate change" and "global warming". Following that example, Canada's national public broadcaster (CBC) issued a memo along similar lines. If our word choices, unemotional and rational as they appear to be, reflect and reinforce a lack of climate action, then this would appear to be a step in the right direction.

[handwritten: What does it mean to be a person?]

Box 4.3: "Babies are not babies until they are born. They're foetuses."

 Search terms: npr reviewing language for covering abortion

The language of abortion rights has become extremely politicized, which is unsurprising to many. The US National Public Radio (NPR) article linked here provides an insight into how newspapers have grappled with writing about it, especially when they do not want to take sides. For example, the terms "baby" and "foetus" may seem interchangeable but, as the NPR reports, anti-abortion advocates have argued that "foetus" feels devoid of life, whereas abortion-rights supporters contend that "unborn child" or "baby" unfairly equates abortion with murder. Publishers appear stuck between the rock and the proverbial hard place—how do they decide what language is appropriate? What lessons can we learn about how language intersects with our ethics and politics?

Technically speaking, "foetus" refers to the stage between the eighth week of pregnancy to birth and is the preferred term in most scientific and medical use. Before the eighth week, the term is "embryo". But this terminology produces a register that may be inappropriate in some contexts. "Foetus" is rarely used in everyday language by expecting parents, but "baby" and "child" are widely used even in the earliest days of pregnancy. To speak about a miscarriage—"sadly, they lost the baby after seven months of pregnancy"—using the word "foetus" instead of "baby" could seem unsympathetic or cold-hearted about a deeply traumatic event. As a note: some abortion advocates have also objected to the term "expecting mother", insisting on "pregnant person". It can seem like a language arms race.

The debate has affected how we refer to opponents and supporters of abortion. NPR has guided journalists to use "abortion rights supporter/opponent", but not "pro-life" or "pro-choice". Among other things, this is an effort to protect NPR from accusations of political bias, but as Elizabeth Jensen writes, that has not stopped its readers and listeners, on both sides of the debate, from complaining that the magazine favours "the other side".

> "Journalism standards and ethics … are not always clear-cut. They represent a best effort to put in place policies that attempt to produce fairness and accuracy. Allowing each side to choose the language it wants does not produce, much less guarantee, that goal." (Jensen 2019)

IV.2 Just language

> " Teach her to question language. Language is the repository of our prejudices, our beliefs, our assumptions.
>
> (Adichie 2017) "

Languages contain pearls of wisdom, shared histories, collective knowledge and some less positive things—as author Chimamanda Ngozi Adichie puts it, "prejudices" and "assumptions". Are these issues of language *per se* or of its use? Is such a distinction possible? Avoiding expressions that can be perceived as oppressive or marginalizing (known as "political correctness") and confronting problematic language are manifestations of the idea that language can inflict harm and prevent change. And we have good reason to believe that it can. But what happens when our morals and social norms evolve faster than our language—when our language reflects past sensibilities? What factors affect how quickly language, and its various communities of speakers, adapt to the new politics?

Access to the internet, for example, has been an important vehicle for individuals to gather, discuss and learn about revisiting language—with the risk of leaving behind people and groups who do not or cannot access the online discourse.

On the charged issue of offensive and oppressive language, it is relevant for us in TOK to examine the scope for agreement and disagreement. Language does not only reflect our values; its continued use influences the development of attitudes, and in this way it perpetuates those ideas and values. Consider what needs to

happen before there is sufficient agreement that certain language is unacceptable and falls out of use. How does this consensus form? What factors influence it? And how do we first come to know which words cause harm and violence?

Notice the questions above use "we", but the answers vary for different times and groups of people. Some may come to know the ethics and politics of language through personal experience; others, through the claims of the first group. Then there are those who do not come to know this for a long time, or at all. There is potential there for a great deal of disagreement and dispute. There may be disagreement on the extent of the harm or offence too, and therefore the appropriate action.

In this space, it is ultimately important how we disagree. Consider the role of power, in terms of which claims-makers are seen as reliable and legitimate, which claims are being trusted or suspected, and what counts as evidence for the harm being experienced or done. How do the concepts of truth, neutrality, objectivity and impartiality apply here?

Words that are widely considered racial, ethnic and gendered slurs are often met with zero tolerance. Are there terms and phrases at the frontier, carrying offensiveness that is not yet acknowledged or known?

For discussion

Inclusive language

Consider the list of words one blogger has stopped using in his efforts to make his language more inclusive.

 Search terms: On using more inclusive language cishet white male

1. On what basis have words been included in that list?

2. Who can legitimately argue one of these words is not harmful and should not be on the list?

3. What kinds of ethical responsibilities do you have:

    (a) with regards to language that you currently use that you know is offensive to some groups of people

    (b) as a consequence of harmful language you have used in the past without realizing

    (c) when harmful language is used by someone else in your presence?

5 Knowledge and Indigenous societies

For centuries, Indigenous Peoples have developed bodies of knowledge and practices for explaining, understanding, and living in the world. With globablization, and a world still healing from the violence of colonialism and imperialism, how are we encountering these diverse Indigenous knowledge traditions? In our capacity as non-Indigenous authors, in this chapter we will explore both our knowledge *about* Indigenous Peoples and, where appropriate, the different knowledges *belonging to* Indigenous Peoples. Studying knowledge and Indigenous societies reveals not only the encounter between Indigenous and non-Indigenous Peoples and knowledge, but also the relationship of education and knowledge with power, as told through the stories of colonialism and decolonialism.

Initial discussion

- Where does your knowledge about Indigenous societies come from?
- What does it mean to say something is Indigenous knowledge?
- How is Indigenous knowledge acquired and by whom?
- How are the processes of producing, sharing and applying Indigenous knowledge similar to or different from those processes for other types of knowledge?
- What gives value and legitimacy to Indigenous knowledge?

I. SCOPE

Indigenous societies have diverse ideas and practices relating to citizenship, governance, laws, ethics, teaching and learning, ceremony, ritual, health and healing, and relationships, among others. These ideas, and the way that knowledge about them is organized, produced and shared may not align with how you understand or explain the world. If that is the case, we invite your curiosity towards this feeling of unfamiliarity. As this chapter will make clear, we have much to learn from Indigenous knowledges, and the more legitimacy and authority they are given, the more comprehensible and accessible they will begin to appear. While Indigenous knowledges are rooted in rich intellectual traditions, they are not a thing of the past and should be spoken about in the present tense. Indigenous knowledges and Peoples are also increasingly recognized as holding important keys to our way out of the climate and ecological crises.

I.1 Who and what is Indigenous?

> It has been said that being born Indian is being born into politics. I believe this to be true; because being born a Mohawk of Kahnawake, I do not remember a time free from the impact of political conflict.
>
> (Alfred 1995)

The United Nations Permanent Forum on Indigenous Issues (UNPFII) estimates that there are 370 million Indigenous people worldwide, living in over 70 different countries. Who calculates those numbers and how? What are the different ways indigeneity has been defined and understood?

These are important questions associated with identity and rights. Those recognized as Indigenous are granted protections within national and international law and, in some contexts, benefits in relation to affirmative action. In May 2016 the Fifteenth Session of the UNPFII affirmed that since Indigenous Peoples continue to be vulnerable to exploitation, marginalization,

forced assimilation and genocide, they are entitled to special protections. Agreeing on definitions can be a high-stakes and deeply challenging political issue.

There is no official definition of "Indigenous" under international law, because of the diversity of experience among Indigenous Peoples. There is also no such thing as one "Indigenous world view"—you would be correct to be suspicious of any textbook that purports to explain such a view. Sometimes writers and thinkers will not refer to themselves as Indigenous, or another collective term, because it defines their experience through the pathology of colonization, and obscures the specificity and diversity of distinct Indigenous cultures. The knowledge of these groups is commonly called Indigenous knowledge, but it would be more accurate to call it Indigenous knowledges.

However, at times it has served the political cause of Indigenous Peoples to unite under one banner, globally, as sovereign peoples independent of the nation states that marginalized them. Gayatri Chakravorty Spivak calls this "strategic essentialism" (2010) using one essentializing label to advance strategic political goals. The word "Indigenous" was used by Aboriginal leaders in the 1970s as a way to identify, unite and represent their communities in political spaces such as the United Nations (UN). Until then their common cause had been dismissed by international organizations as domestic problems to be dealt with within nation-states. By uniting under one banner, Indigenous Peoples could express their common cause and be seen as a sovereign and independent force.

Nations and organizations have adopted various working definitions of "Indigenous" to enable policy decisions, but these are not intended to be definitive. You may have also heard the terms "Aboriginal", "Native", "First Nations", "Tribal" and "Amerindian", among others. "Indigenous" was chosen because other terms carried negative connotations or had been imposed by colonizers. The use of the plural "peoples" is intentional and necessary to affirm the diversity among Indigenous Peoples and their rights to self-determination.

People are said to be Indigenous based on self-identification and recognition from their community. The idea of measuring indigeneity by bloodline is problematic, as the Australian Human Rights and Equal Opportunity Commission reported in 2002.

> While Aboriginal people may generally be direct descendants of the original inhabitants of a particular part of Australia, Indigenous customary law does not rely on linear proof of descent in the Judeo-Christian genealogical form of 'Seth begat Enosh begat Kenan' in order to prove membership of the group. ... A person may have been adopted into a kinship group where there is no direct or suitable offspring to carry out ceremonial obligations. ... Genetic science should have no part to play in determining whether or not a person should be eligible for benefits. If the element of descent is to remain in Australian law as a test of Aboriginality, it should be interpreted in accordance with Indigenous cultural protocols.

The United Nations Working Group on Indigenous Populations (WGIP) adopted a preliminary definition in 1982 but would not agree on a lasting definition. Later, James Anaya, former United Nations Special Rapporteur on the Rights of Indigenous Peoples, made an attempt to define Indigenous Peoples as: "living descendants of pre-invasion inhabitants of lands now dominated by others [that remain] culturally distinct groups that find themselves engulfed by other settler societies born of forces of empire and conquest" (Anaya 2004).

Indigenous leaders have argued that any definition of indigeneity must refer to their ties to land and place. Many, such as Māori scholar Linda Tuhiwai Smith of the Ngāti Awa and Ngāti Porou *iwi*, question whether we should use a single term at all.

By referring to a range of distinct peoples and cultures using the single word "Indigenous", do we undermine and ignore their differing experiences?

Indigenous Rights include individual as well as collective rights. It is the collective rights that protect the basis of Indigenous society, and for which ongoing recognition is important from nation states and multilateral organizations. Collective rights include the rights to self-determination, subsistence economies, self-governance and land. In the context of Indigenous sovereignty, it is worth pointing out that settler states are not being petitioned to grant rights to Indigenous Peoples, but to *recognize and uphold* Indigenous Rights, Title and Law.

The concept of international human rights reflects the Western democratic societies that designed them, and has tended to overlook collective rights in favour of individual rights.

Box 5.1: The Ainu—Japan's Indigenous People

↑ **Figure 5.1** Ainu group from the Island of Hokkaido or Yezo, Department of Anthropology, 1904 World's Fair

Indigenous-settler relationships did not begin with the "Age of Discovery" encounters between European empires and their colonies. Most human cultures arrived and settled into place at some point in history, and the messy timeline of who was where first, and what happened upon contact, create the backdrop of claims to indigeneity today.

The Ainu, Japan's Indigenous People, are a noteworthy example. Acknowledged by the Japanese state only in 2008, and officially recognized only since 2019, their claims to being Indigenous have been long disputed. What are the implications of designating the Ainu as an Indigenous group as opposed to an ethnic minority? Consider the following article, as well as the questions below.

 Search terms: tofugu the Anui

1. What gives legitimacy to the claim of Ainu indigeneity?

2. What is offered as evidence, and what constitutes compelling evidence of the Ainu's indigeneity?

3. (a) On what basis can this evidence be disputed?

   (b) By whom?

4. What are the implications for the knowledge and traditions of the Ainu if they are considered Indigenous?

I.2 Indigenous knowledge as local, holistic and dynamic

Despite the diversity of Indigenous Peoples, their histories and the contexts in which they live, Indigenous knowledges are often said to possess some shared features, two of which specifically concern the scope of Indigenous knowledge: the claims that it is local and holistic.

What does it mean to say that Indigenous knowledge is local? The word suggests that there is depth to this knowledge: it is produced in a specific cultural and ecological context, by people with a long tradition of direct personal experiences and close engagement with the place, and is appropriate to navigating a particular environmental and social reality. Indigenous Peoples have developed an intimate understanding of their environments that allows them to thrive anywhere from the Amazon rainforest to the high-altitude deserts of the Himalaya. At the same time, implicit in the claim that Indigenous knowledge is local is the assumption that it is only appropriate to or applicable in a local context. Could it be that we have so little to learn from the tribes in the Amazon or nomads in the Changthang? Or is this idea a vestige of colonization, of a failure to decolonize?

It is important to consider why universality is not a claim typically associated with Indigenous knowledge. Could some aspects of Indigenous knowledges be considered universal? Could, for example, the knowledge and skills of Polynesian navigators who voyaged over vast stretches of open ocean be generalized into a universal system of navigation? What about the water management and crop cultivation practices of Indigenous farmers on the Balinese terraced rice fields?

We do have a system of knowledge that is deployed across the world—through education and globalization—that is assumed to be universally valid and applicable. Consider why some forms of knowledge are assumed to be universal rather than local, and through which methods and practices they have been produced. Some critics have argued that local knowledges are all there is—that the Western system of knowledge is not inherently universal, but has been universalized. For example, Vandana Shiva writes the following.

> The universal/local dichotomy is misplaced when applied to the western and Indigenous traditions of knowledge, because the western is a local tradition which has been spread world wide through intellectual colonisation.
>
> The universal would spread in openness. The globalising local spreads by violence and misrepresentation. The first level of violence unleashed on local systems of knowledge is to not see them as knowledge. … When local knowledge does appear in the field of the globalising vision, it is made to disappear by denying it the status of a systematic knowledge, and assigning it the adjectives 'primitive' and 'unscientific'. Correspondingly, the western system is assumed to be uniquely 'scientific' and universal.
>
> (Shiva 1993)

Another claim made about Indigenous knowledges is that they are holistic—they conceive of domains such as history, art, culture, religion, language and medicine as interconnected, overlapping, inseparable and integrated into a whole. Think about how this is different from the way knowledge is presented in the TOK course, where separate areas of knowledge have their distinct scope and methods, producing different and possibly irreconcilable perspectives on the world. This raises the questions of whether, and when, it is appropriate to use the tools of the areas of knowledge to understand Indigenous knowledges in their interconnected complexity. Would we use the methods of science, or art or religion to evaluate an Indigenous knowledge claim? Does the holism of Indigenous knowledges facilitate a different understanding of the world, as compared to the fragmented view arising from the different academic disciplines? Keep these questions in mind as you encounter claims across the chapters in this book, and elsewhere.

Indigenous knowledge is often described as traditional, but dynamic; a cumulative body of knowledge and set of practices, developed over millennia through direct experience and transmitted orally, in an ongoing process. That is,

Indigenous knowledge is not a fixed body of knowledge that can or should be preserved in some authentic state. It is continuously adapting and growing in response to the forces that affect it.

For discussion

The scope of Indigenous knowledge

In view of the diversity, as well as the supposed local, holistic and dynamic nature of Indigenous knowledge, consider the following questions.

1. Recall the map metaphor of knowledge that we explored in Chapter 1. To what extent is *your* knowledge, your map of the world, informed by Indigenous knowledge?

Shiva suggested that Indigenous knowledges can be rendered invisible by denying them the status of "knowledge", and threatened by "erasing and destroying the reality which they attempt to represent" (Shiva 1993).

2. What is this reality that Indigenous knowledges attempt to represent?

3. What are the forces destroying this reality?

Box 5.2: Songlines—storytelling, music, geography and astronomy

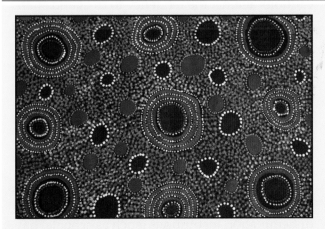

↑ **Figure 5.2** Painting depicting a location from an Australian Aboriginal songline

Perhaps a better metaphor for Indigenous knowledge is a compass—a tool for orienting oneself in the world. Consider this metaphor in the context of Australian Aboriginal songlines, pathways through the landscape used by ancestral beings of the Aboriginal creation story (known popularly as the Dreaming). Songlines meld together geography, history and astronomy with song and art, and those who can sing many songs in the right sequence hold an expansive knowledge about their environment and the meanings of their world. Each song describes important landmarks and other clues that help a traveller to navigate vast distances. The Australian continent is said to be covered in songlines, some of which extend hundreds of kilometres and cross numerous tribal, cultural and linguistic boundaries. Songlines can be composed in multiple languages in sequence, and their rhythm, rather than words, is said to map the contours and features of the terrain. Listening to a song is described as equally or more effective for knowing the land than walking on or seeing it. Further, songlines can be painted in stages, with a complex key of symbols, structures and colours that appear more like a visual code than a map.

Different groups of people, living on different sections of land, will know different songlines and therefore different chapters in the creation story. The songlines contain vast cultural knowledge, akin to an entire cosmology, outlining the laws, responsibilities and ceremonies of the people, and are meticulously taught and learned by each generation.

Follow the link to learn more about songlines.

 Search terms: What are songlines? YouTube

II. PERSPECTIVES

There is an astonishing diversity of beliefs, practices and rituals among Indigenous cultures. Collectively, these ways of knowing and being in the world capture what we know about the wondrous potential of humanity. Much as the atmosphere or the biosphere envelops the planet, so too does the sum total of human cultures—something anthropologist Wade Davis has termed the "ethnosphere" (2003).

 Search terms: Wade Davis Dreams from endangered cultures TED Talk

Follow the link to listen to Davis explain the concept of the ethnosphere, through examples of its diversity and the forces threatening the survival of Indigenous ways of living.

The different ways of thinking and being, developed over centuries, are practised by communities of knowledge keepers. In engaging with the knowledge of Indigenous cultures it is important not to exoticize, fragment and selectively misinterpret them. Recall the argument about holistic Indigenous knowledge: to what extent can we grasp what it means for the Cofan of the Amazon to hear plants speak and sing to them, without understanding other interrelated domains of that context and system of knowledge? This chapter invites you to explore Indigenous knowledges and practices in the contexts in which they are embedded— history, experience, language and ecology. Often, when we are learning to engage with Indigenous knowledges outside of our cultural domain, it is easy to forget that there are multiple perspectives within Indigenous knowledge communities as well, and each of these communities has ways of working through disagreements and resolving competing claims. As authors, it is not our place to share Indigenous stories with you. Gregory Younging (Opaskwayak Cree Nation) specifically cautions against the tendency to treat and share Indigenous knowledge as *gnaritas nullius* or "no one's knowledge", and therefore everyone's knowledge. This undermines Indigenous Peoples' agency over how their knowledge is shared in accordance to Indigenous Protocols and Customary Laws.

II.1 Education for all

For a long time, knowledge production practices (such as academic research) and knowledge dissemination institutions (such as schools) have erased and marginalized Indigenous ways of knowing and being. Today, these practices and institutions challenge the relationship—past and contemporary—between education and colonial power.

> "A major thrust of much colonial and state policy has been the attempt to assimilate Indigenous groups both by force of arms and through more subtle pressures to conform to the dominant society. ...
> In many countries, governments ran programs of indoctrination under the guise of education.
>
> First Nations Studies Program, University of British Columbia"

Much has been written about the destructive and damaging effects of Western education on Indigenous students, for example in the context of the Canadian residential school system, or the policies of Thomas Babington Macaulay in British India. The effects are ongoing; for example, there are lower rates of academic success among Indigenous students in mainstream educational systems today.

International educational programmes (including the IB Diploma Programme) have gaps in their curricula in terms of the representation and inclusion of non-Western ways of knowing and being. The inclusion of this chapter in TOK offers a significant opportunity to consider "decolonizing education" both as a proces of de-centring Western knowledges in the curriculum, as well as "education that decolonizes" through the way it is set up.

Within education, values associated with knowledge are shaped and reflected by decisions about what gets taught and how. Therefore, the curriculum becomes an important part of the decolonization project. Which forms of knowledge have been and are being prioritized and valued, and which perspectives are misrepresented or excluded? Who has the power to make these decisions, and how do those people get and maintain that power?

Case study

Schooling the world and learning from Ladakh

"Schooling the World" is a 2010 documentary about the assumptions and consequences of the Education for All movement, with a focus on schooling in Ladakh, a region in the northern part of India.

 Search terms: Schooling the World the film

The mountainous region of Ladakh provides an inspiring context for examining socio-political themes because of the rapid changes that have occurred in just one generation, and where living memories can teach us much about ideas of development and progress. Some of this can be traced back to the application of mainstream, culturally unadapted development policies in the 1980s.

Education is a prime case study, because in the 1990s schools in Ladakh had the highest rate of exam failure in the world, with more than 90% of Ladakhi students failing the annual Indian board exams. Students were taught in one of three languages, none of which were Indigenous, in a system imported from a post-independence interpretation of British education with casually religious overtones. The implications of this for Ladakhi identity and Traditional Knowledge preservation became clear only decades later. The Students Educational and Cultural Movement of Ladakh (SECMOL) was founded to address this problem in a forward-looking but culturally resonant way that respected Traditional Knowledge, with the criteria for admission being that a student had to have failed exams elsewhere. SECMOL as a case study informs how and why we educate, or seek education, and how far the implications of those decisions go. It also explores the tensions between innovation and tradition as ways to recover from a failed modernism.

A second case study, presented in the film "Learning from Ladakh" concerns traditional ecological knowledge and the role of food subsidies. The film tells the story of an ill-conceived system of wheat and rice subsidies that began in the 1970s that led to the collapse of local food systems. The entire region was then enrolled into the cash and market economy, dependent on and reinforced by the modern knowledge economy of education.

 Search terms: Ancient futures Learning from Ladakh Vimeo

The consequences of this included new forms of labour relations and rising inequality, communal dysfunction, plastic and other non-biodegradable waste, water pollution, and the prevalence of cardiovascular and metabolic diseases—none of which existed until very recently. Ladakhis are exceptionally aware and their lament is audible and profound, and yet to outsiders Ladakh appears pristine, tourists

keep coming, consuming and leaving. What can we learn from this case and from local forms of response and resistance? How do we balance individual, communal and ekistic needs in rapidly modernizing and globalizing Indigenous cultures?

Among Ladakhis there is a robust discourse on ways forward and optimism in the face of challenges. Local agents of change champion visions for change aligned with or against the national and international aid system. Local politics and change-making are necessarily entangled in Traditional Knowledge, identity and culture. This includes Ladakh's identity as "Little Tibet", the generations of Tibetan refugees that call it home, and the nomads who move through the plains and rely on trade across the militarized borders between India, China and Pakistan. Religion in this context includes Buddhists and Muslims side-by-side for centuries, Christian missionaries, and the steady influx of Hindus as high-paying tourists or as cheap labour for Ladakhi landlords. Many Buddhist monasteries house priceless, centuries-old works of art and yet lack the resources to preserve them in the way of modern museums. Some of those monasteries house caches of ancient weapons, though Tibetan Buddhism has a reputation for peace. How has this narrative been shaped by one man, the 14th Dalai Lama, in his political and existential struggle? Ladakh sits at the geographic top of India, incongruously into the national identity, and sandwiched between Chinese-occupied Tibet and Pakistan, with whom India has fought five wars.

II.1.1 Decolonizing knowledge, indigenizing the curriculum

It is good practice, and in this case important, to clarify what the words "decolonize" and "indigenize"—sometimes used interchangeably—mean in relation to knowledge.

Decoloniziation, in the context of knowledge:

"involves valuing and revitalizing Indigenous knowledge and approaches and weeding out settler biases or assumptions that have impacted Indigenous ways of being. Decolonization necessitates shifting our frames of reference with regard to the knowledge we hold; examining how we have arrived at such knowledge; and considering what we need to do to change misconceptions, prejudice, and assumptions about Indigenous Peoples." (Antoine *et al* 2018)

Indigenization is:

"the process of naturalizing Indigenous knowledge systems and making them evident to transform spaces, places, and hearts … [T]his involves bringing Indigenous knowledge and approaches together with Western knowledge systems. It is a deliberate coming together of these two ways of being." (Antoine *et al* 2018)

By its nature, TOK is well placed to address both of these calls to action. What might a decolonized, indigenized TOK course and curriculum look like? How can decolonizing and indigenizing work in TOK reflect on the rest of the IB Diploma curriculum?

These two processes are often said to go hand in hand. The work is to simultaneously deconstruct colonial knowledge and knowledge systems, while upholding the persistence and value of Indigenous ways of knowing. There are dangers to doing one without the other: it can lead to tokenism, or to criticism that does not offer an alternative and thus reverts back to a default state.

That Indigenous ways of being and knowing persist is a testament to the strength of Indigenous Peoples and the value of Indigenous knowledge. In *Potlatch as Pedagogy: Learning Through Ceremony*, Sara Florence Davidson (Haida/Settler) and Robert Davidson (Haida Nation) write about the social function of the potlatch as a locus of knowledge sharing, identity formation, resource distribution and ceremonial transmission of protocols. There is variety among the potlaches of different First Nations of the Pacific Northwest, and the event may involve a ceremony, a rite of passage, the sharing of food, dances and stories or the exchange of resources. In "We Were Once Silenced" Davidson and Davidson write about the Canadian federal government's deliberate attempt to undermine the acculturation and knowledge transfer of Indigenous Peoples through anti-potlatch legislation. The 1884 Potlatch Ban was only lifted in 1951, and potlatches that had been adapted and performed in secret are now openly convened again. People born during the 67 years

of the ban were bearing witness to their cultural practices being performed freely for the first time in their lives.

Alongside this ban and other assimilationist tactics, Indigenous children were removed from their communities and placed in residential schools. The last such institution, Gordon Indian Residential School in Saskatchewan, was operated by the Canadian government until 1996. Throughout all of this, elders and knowledge keepers honoured ancestral ties and ensured the cultural survival of Indigenous ways of knowing, learning and being.

What does it mean to indigenize and decolonize education against the backdrop of legislation and education used to eradicate cultural and knowledge practices? How do we, as individuals, teachers and communities, protect against taking part in the very same abuse again, unintentionally? As you come up with your own answer, consider these two resources.

Source 1: the calls to action (62–65) for education by the Truth and Reconciliation Commission of Canada.

 Search terms: TRC Canada Calls to Action

Source 2: the principle of "two-eyed seeing" by Mi'kmaq Elder Albert Marshall, as an approach to weaving together Indigenous and non-Indigenous knowledges.

 Search terms: Two-eyed seeing AMarshall thinkers

II.1.2 Land-based education

Land-based education is said to be an important component of the "Indigenous resurgence" paradigm, which calls for regeneration of Indigenous cultural, spiritual and political practices and marks a shift in political consciousness away from reconciliation and towards decolonization.

> To know my history, I had to put away my books and return to the land.
>
> (Trask 1999)

What does it mean to think of land as a source of knowledge? How is that knowledge learned, shared and passed on from generation to generation? What enables or disrupts those processes?

Land-based education is important because colonization so radically dispossessed

Indigenous Peoples from their land and the relationships, knowledges and traditions drawn from that land. Land-based education seeks to re-establish important connections to nature, resources, traditions and the context for social relationships and community, and includes a range of pedagogies from sustainable agriculture to ethics.

II.2 Coming to know

The concept of "coming to know" is used in some Indigenous knowledges to refer to the process of seeking to understand the world by listening to and learning from *all our relations*. It places the learner in relationships of respect, gratitude and reciprocity with the natural world—rivers and oceans, mountains and hills, plants, animals, spirits, humans and others. In many Indigenous knowledge traditions, we come to know by paying attention to these relationships, by honoring our responsibilities as members of the natural world and by listening to the teachings of knowledge keepers and ancestors both human and other-than-human. These stories cover anything from the teachings of plants and the presence of ancestors to the rights of physical places and our responsibilities towards them. Coming to know is a form of knowledge that carries responsibilities and expectations, for

example about how one applies that knowledge, lives in accordance with it and passes it on to the next generation. In this framing, knowledge contains both explanations, such as what the world is like and why it came to be like that, as well as principles for relational living, such as interdependence and reciprocity. It is passed on in stories, and can be communicated in song, poetry, dance and ceremony.

How do the sources of Indigenous knowledge affect the legitimacy of the things we come to know? Consider how coming to know about the past or the natural world through Indigenous ways of knowing intersects with historiography or scientific knowledge. The encounter of Indigenous and settler or colonial accounts of the past is particularly interesting. How do these differing descriptions, explanations and understandings of what happened in the past meet one another?

Making connections

History, prehistory and language

In Chapter 9 we discuss what it means for Indigenous societies in the 21st century to be considered "prehistorical", because of a conception of history that is tied to written records. The acknowledgement of oral history has brought some validity to Indigenous historical accounts. New information surrounding the Incas' *khipu* knots, which we discuss in Chapter 4, complicates this story. If the Incas are deemed to have kept historical records, not in written language but in a kind of material code, should we revisit where they fall across the prehistory versus history boundary? Ultimately, examples like these blur the problematic line between prehistory and history, and add weight to Indigenous accounts of the past.

Linda Tuhiwai Smith explores the relationship between history and power, with the question of why revisiting history is such a significant part of decolonization. In her book, *Decolonizing Methodologies; Research and Indigenous Peoples*, Smith suggests that because colonization continues in various forms, knowing the past enables demands for justice. "To hold alternative histories is to hold alternative knowledges", she says, and the teaching of these alternative histories and knowledges allows us to find new ways of doing things. The process of revisiting histories—reclaiming the past—becomes key to the decolonizing project. And yet in international academic practice, Indigenous accounts of history are still rarely acknowledged as valid. Smith argues that the telling of these accounts becomes a powerful act of resistance.

The typical arbiters of historical facts and truths—think of education boards or courts of law—are neither neutral nor often capable of dealing with alternative ways of knowing the world. How can we build capacity to know the world from truly different perspectives? To what extent does holding these different perspectives help to create a more just and more sustainable future?

II.3 Conservation

> How could we harm the forest? We're the ones that save the forest. As long as we are here, the forest will be fine. We are the defenders of the forest. If we leave, who will protect the forest?
>
> (Baiga, Achanakmar Tiger Reserve)

Chapter 6, III.3 explores two opposing philosophies on land management in the 1800s that still reverberate in the conservation discourse today. John Muir was one of the pioneers of modern wilderness conservation and emphasized the sacredness of natural environments and systems. He argued for protecting natural spaces from human activity. On the other side of the debate was Gifford Pinchot, the first Chief Forester of the United States, who advocated the sustainable and equitable use of natural resources for the benefit of all citizens. This discourse between two conservation leaders in the United States left out the perspectives of the Indigenous Peoples, who had been stewards of the land for millennia. One way or the other, whether for the plundering of the land or its protection, Indigenous Peoples were removed from it. Muir's vision prevailed and Yellowstone and Yosemite national parks, created in 1872 and 1890, were "both forcibly emptied of their native inhabitants" and "created a conservation template that survived well into the next century" (Zaitchik 2018).

Muir was an early hero of conservation, but also no ally of the Indigenous Peoples. His legacy powerfully shapes environmental politics even today and has contributed to the exclusion of Indigenous Peoples from their land from Yosemite to Kaziranga. As we have discussed elsewhere in this chapter, land is an important connection to Indigenous knowledges, beliefs, resources and history. The process of displacement from land is called deracination, and correcting for it (for example, through land-based education) is an important component of Indigenous resurgence.

For discussion

Who knows about conservation?

"Some of the original national parks were very colonial. Banff has a horrible history of forcing folks out … a lot of the original parks had this mentality that to protect nature you have to get rid of people … none of these ecosystems have existed since the last ice age without people." (Artelle quoted in Wood 2019)

The discussion about traditional ecological knowledge (TEK) and nature religions in Chapter 6 explains how and why popular science and Western academia have, to an extent, embraced Indigenous ecological knowledges. An important question to consider is why this has been so. The thesis of source 1 below, "How Conservation Became Colonialism", is palpably relevant in our time, as we confront both a climate crisis and the need for decolonizing education. A similar article asserts that "increases in conservation in some of the most globally significant areas of conservation interest will increasingly not only be unjust, but also impossible without Indigenous consent and leadership" (Artelle *et al* 2019). And Steph Kwetásel'wet Wood argues that it is not just an issue of justice or fairness, but that Indigenous leadership leads to higher economic and social returns than state-run efforts at conservation (2019).

If Indigenous Peoples are best placed to lead conservation, as these authors assert, how do you conceive of your role?

Various metaphors have been used to describe nature, such as a parent, organism, goddess and pan-psychic entity. The word "nature" can variously refer to an idea or entity, and is obviously connected to the act and concept of conservation: if conservation is the act of humans, nature is the object.

Discuss, in small groups, how you think about and know nature.

1. Do you have a relationship with nature, and if so, what does that relationship mean to you?

2. How do your emotions, transactions and identity manifest in your interactions with, and thoughts and knowledge about, nature?

3. Choose one of the following statements that most aligns with how you think about nature, and share why that is so. To what extent are these statements mutually exclusive?

   (a) Nature should be kept safe and protected.

   (b) Nature should be used responsibly to sustain and improve the lives of people.

   (c) Nature is a place for me to explore and enjoy the natural world.

Offer your own description if the above are insufficient.

If the people in your group have different responses, discuss why that might be the case. For example, does it depend on whether you think we can, or cannot, materially measure or define what nature is? Does it depend on whether or not you have regular opportunities to go hiking, skiing, hunting, sailing and so on?

4. Discuss whether your different conceptions of and knowledge about nature affect how you think of conservation. How do privilege, culture and access to nature intersect with attitudes towards conservation and knowledge about nature?

Consider the arguments and perspectives of the two linked articles.

Source 1: Zaitchik, A. 2018. "How Conservation Became Colonialism" (FP.com).

 Search terms: How conservation became colonialism Foreign Policy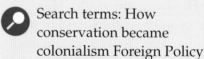

Source 2: Jacobsen, R. 2011. "Number One With a Bullet" (Outsideonline.com).

Search terms: Number one bullet Outside online

III. METHODS AND TOOLS

Chapter 2 introduces writer and civil rights activist Audre Lorde's metaphor that "the master's tools will never dismantle the master's house" (Le Guin 2004). The tools and methods of knowledge production have been, and in some cases are still being, deployed towards Indigenous Peoples in damaging ways. Consider, for example, the colonial and imperial history of Indigenous Peoples as research subjects or informants, and the body of knowledge produced to describe and explain Indigenous cultures, behaviour and customs.

Given this history, what would it take for the tools and processes of knowledge production and dissemination to do justice to Indigenous Peoples? How do Indigenous scholars and researchers engage with the knowledge production practices in mainstream academic fields?

In Chapter 2 we see Le Guin build on Lorde's metaphor with the question: what other tools do we have to make the house we want to live in? This section explores not only the methods and tools that have been used to produce and legitimize claims about Indigenous Peoples, but also the methods and tools developed by Indigenous Peoples to understand and explain the world.

III.1 Indigenous research methods: Research as a relational activity

> We don't need anyone else developing the tools which will help us to come to terms with who we are. We can and will do this work. Real power lies with those who design the tools—it always has. This power is ours.
>
> (Irwin 1992)

Earlier in this chapter we discussed how the idea of coming to know things shapes Indigenous perspectives. But it is not as if Indigenous Peoples only produce and acquire knowledge in a single way, whereas academic researchers have a range of tools and methodologies that produce evidence-based claims. Linda Tuhiwai Smith argues that Indigenous perspectives are often excluded from academic research because Indigenous Peoples have historically been the object of research. Smith suggests that by reducing Indigenous Peoples to objects of study, non-Indigenous researchers have excluded their participation in research; an inanimate object *can't* contribute to research.

Objects need to be controlled and studied, not allowed to influence the study. And thus, Indigenous knowledge, technologies and ethical codes, developed over millennia, were "discovered" by Western science beginning in the 17th century and "commodified as property belonging to the cultural archive and body of knowledge of the West" (Smith 1999).

And so to reclaim the processes of knowledge production that happens under the name "research", Indigenous scholars have engaged in "researching back" in a parallel of the empire "writing back", which we discuss in the context of post-colonial literature in Chapter 4, II.3.

The result of Indigenous research methods is knowledge from a position of Indigenous researcher as both subject and researcher, which centres Indigenous experiences and world views, and "talks back" to colonial and imperial knowledge traditions in an academic language.

Shawn Wilson, who is Opaskwayak Cree, outlines what an Indigenous research paradigm looks like from the perspective of Indigenous knowledge keepers and seekers. His proposal centres relationships and the perspective that Indigenous knowledge is deeply relational. Honouring these relationships means that researchers must be accountable for choices in how they conceptualize, conduct and communicate their research. Follow the link to a video that explores this idea of research as a relational and community activity.

 Search terms: Shawn Wilson Decolonizing methodologies: can rational research be a basis for renewed relationships YouTube

III.2 The role of language

What is the role of Oral Tradition in enabling knowledge to be handed down through generations? To what extent is Oral Tradition effective in preserving knowledge in Indigenous societies?

↑ **Figure 5.3** Sculpture of a *manaschi*, a Kyrgyz storyteller specialized in narrating the "epic of Manas"

Case study

The "grammar of animacy"

Robin Wall Kimmerer, of Citizen Potowatomi Nation and author of *Braiding Sweetgrass*, writes about the role of language in Indigenous knowledge with a study of Potawatomi, language. "The language is the heart of our culture", explains one of Kimmerer's Elders, "it holds our thoughts, our way of seeing the world. It's too beautiful for English to explain" (2014). The following is an extract from Kimmerer's chapter "Learning the grammar of animacy", in which she asserts that in attempting to understand the world, something is lost in the language of science, "the same something that swells around you and in you when you listen to the world" (2014).

"My first taste of the missing language was the word *Puhpowee* on my tongue. *Puhpowee* … translates as 'the force which causes mushrooms to push up from the earth overnight.' As a biologist, I was stunned that such a word existed. In all its technical vocabulary, Western science has no such term, no words to hold this mystery. You'd think that biologists, of all people, would have words for life. But in scientific language our terminology is used to define the boundaries of our knowing. What lies beyond our grasp remains unnamed. …

English is a noun-based language, somehow appropriate to a culture so obsessed with things. Only 30 percent of English words are verbs, but in Potawatomi that proportion is 70 percent.

Which means that 70 percent of the words have to be conjugated, and 70 percent have different tenses and cases to be mastered.

European languages often assign gender to nouns, but Potawatomi does not divide the world into masculine and feminine. Nouns and verbs both are animate and inanimate. You hear a person with a word that is completely different from the one with which you hear an airplane. Pronouns, articles, plurals, demonstratives, verbs—all those syntactical bits I never could keep straight in high school English are all aligned in Potawatomi to provide different ways to speak of the living world and the lifeless one. Different verb forms, different plurals, different everything apply depending on whether what you are speaking of is alive." (Kimmerer 2014).

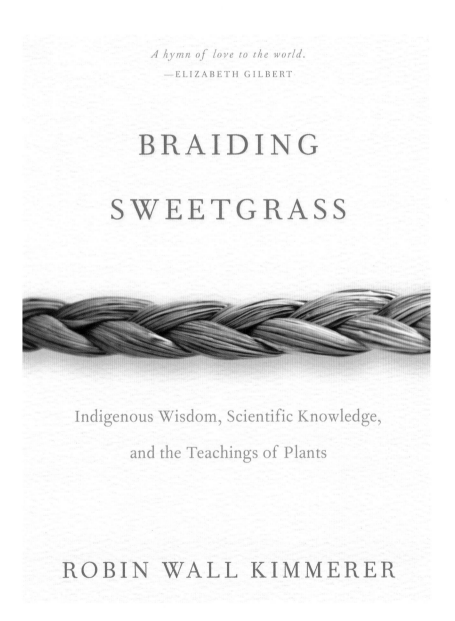

A hymn of love to the world.
—ELIZABETH GILBERT

BRAIDING

SWEETGRASS

Indigenous Wisdom, Scientific Knowledge,

and the Teachings of Plants

ROBIN WALL KIMMERER

Kimmerer recounts the challenges of learning this grammar of animacy, which includes verbs for "to be a Saturday", "to be a hill", "to be a long sandy stretch of beach" and "to be a bay".

"'Ridiculous!' I ranted in my head. 'There is no reason to make it so complicated. No wonder no one speaks it. A cumbersome language, impossible to learn, and more than that, it's all wrong. A bay is most definitely a person, place, or thing—a noun and not a verb.' I was ready to give up. I'd learned a few words, done my duty to the language that was taken from my grandfather. …

And then I swear I heard the zap of synapses firing. An electric current sizzled down my arm and through my finger, and practically scorched the page where that one word lay. In that moment I could smell the water of the bay, watch it rock against the shore and hear it sift onto the sand. A bay is a noun only if water is *dead*. When *bay* is a noun, it is defined by humans, trapped between its shores and contained by the word. But the verb *wiikwegamaa*—to be a bay—releases the water from bondage and lets it live. 'To be a bay' holds the wonder that, for this moment, the living water has decided to shelter itself between these shores, conversing with cedar roots and a flock of baby mergansers. Because it could do otherwise—become a stream or an ocean or a waterfall, and there are verbs for that, too. To be a hill, to be a sandy beach, to be a Saturday, all are possible verbs in a world where everything is alive. Water, land, and even a day, the language a mirror for seeing the animacy of the world, the life that pulses through all things, through pines and nuthatches and mushrooms. *This* is the language I hear in the woods; this is the language that lets us speak of what wells up all around us. …

English doesn't give us many tools for incorporating respect for animacy. In English, you are either a human or a thing. Our grammar boxes us in by the choice of reducing a nonhuman being to an *it*, or it must be gendered, inappropriately, as a *he* or a *she*. Where are our words for the simple existence of another living being? …

… Our toddlers speak of plants and animals as if they were people, extending to them self and intention and compassion—until we teach them not to. We quickly retrain them and make them forget. When we tell them that the tree is not a *who*, but an *it*, we make that maple an object; we put a barrier between us, absolving ourselves of moral responsibility and opening the door to exploitation. Saying *it* makes a living land into 'natural resources.' If a maple is an *it*, we can take up the chain saw. If a maple is a *her*, we think twice."
(Kimmerer 2014)

Kimmerer's point is that language deeply affects how we relate to and know our world. Consider this argument next to Le Guin's, posed below, which suggests that perhaps learning the grammar of animacy is not necessary, that the same feat can be accomplished by a change in framing.

"Relationship among all things appears to be complex and reciprocal—always at least two-way, back-and-forth. It seems that nothing is single in this universe, and nothing goes one way. In this view, we humans appear as particularly lively, intense, aware nodes of relation in an infinite network of connections, … with and among everything—all beings—including what we generally class as things, objects.

III. Methods and tools

Descartes and the behaviorists willfully saw dogs as machines, without feeling. Is seeing plants as without feeling a similar arrogance? One way to stop seeing trees, or rivers, or hills, only as 'natural resources,' is to class them as fellow beings—kinfolk." (Le Guin 2016)

For discussion

Language learning

1. Do you need to understand Potawatomi to learn the lessons of animacy, or is it enough for a person like Kimmerer to explain the lessons in English?

2. How would you describe the relationship between speaking an Indigenous language and understanding Indigenous perspectives in the world?

3. To what extent can Indigenous knowledge about the natural world be captured in a language like English that treats the non-human world as objects?

4. Should we break grammatical rules in our languages to incorporate new ideas such as animacy?

5. To what extent does Le Guin, in the quote above, suggest a way of being and thinking that parallels the grammar of animacy, without having to learn it?

III.3 Traditional ecological knowledge (TEK)

> The Indigenous people of the world possess an immense knowledge of their environments, based on centuries of living close to nature. Living in and from the richness and variety of complex ecosystems, they have an understanding of the properties of plants and animals, the functioning of ecosystems and the techniques for using and managing them that is particular and often detailed. In rural communities in developing countries, locally occurring species are relied on for many—sometimes all—foods, medicines, fuel, building materials and other products. Equally, people's knowledge and perceptions of the environment, and their relationships with it, are often important elements of cultural identity.
>
> (Mayor 1994; former Director General of UNESCO)

Traditional ecological knowledge (TEK) is a label used to describe and give validity to traditional, local and folk knowledges spanning from ecology to environmental metaphysics. Unlike other elements of Indigenous knowledge, it has been embraced by modern science, particularly in the fields of land management, conservation, medicine and botany. What is it about TEK that has been so attractive to modern scientists? Why has ecological knowledge been relatively accessible? How does this compare with the uptake of Indigenous perspectives in other disciplines, such as mathematics and art?

Part of the interest stems from growing awareness of the scale and urgency of the ecological damage confronting us, namely a sixth planetary mass extinction and climate crisis. We encounter a related phenomenon in the growing popularity of nature-religions in Chapter 6, III.3. As Henry Huntingdon and Nikolai Mymrin describe, TEK is seen as having passed the practical test of being useful for generations of people who have "relied on this detailed knowledge for their survival—they have literally staked their lives on its accuracy and repeatability" (Huntington, Mymrin 1998).

Below, we consider the contributions of TEK to modern science. Can the lessons of TEK be understood in isolation, or are the languages or cultural and spiritual practices and beliefs that accompany it necessary? How does holism apply to TEK? Do we need, for example, to learn the grammar of animacy as described by Kimmerer (in the case study) or other relational ways of being to comprehend and apply TEK?

Felice Wyndham is an ecological anthropologist and ethnobiologist who has studied people with highly sophisticated sense of space beyond their body, "a form of enhanced mindfulness" she says is common in many hunter-gatherer groups. She describes this as "an extremely developed skill base of cognitive agility, of being able to put yourself into a viewpoint and perspective of many creatures or objects—rocks, water, clouds" (quoted in Robbins 2017).

To the extent that these abilities are necessary for the understanding and application of TEK, how might we learn them? TEK is not only facts about the natural world, but also ways of thinking and perceiving.

According to a report published by the World Bank (Sobrevila 2008) Indigenous Peoples comprise less than 5% of the world's population, but manage 25% of the world's land surface and maintain 80% of the planet's biodiversity. TEK is described as the cumulative, holistic body of knowledge that accumulates over time as successive generations make discoveries about their environment. This knowledge is said to be "tried and tested" as each generation has relied upon it, for example in navigating and sustainably using their natural environments.

Examples of TEK in practice

In recent decades, anthropologists and conservationists have documented the ecological understanding and insight of Indigenous Peoples around the world, from Māori navigation at sea to Mayan forest-gardens. Henry Huntington reported how Inuit elders in Alaska were able to infer the future behaviour of beluga whales from the present behaviour of beavers, which had reduced spawning habitat for salmon that would mean less food for the whales. Huntington recounts how he was initially confused about why they were talking about beavers until he made the connection himself: "It was a more holistic view of the ecosystem … It would be pretty rare for someone studying belugas to be thinking about freshwater ecology" (Huntingdon quoted in Robbins 2018).

Land managers and scientists in Australia have adopted Indigenous Peoples' fire-control techniques and enlisted their help as co-managers of the land after a particularly destructive decade of bush fires.

Prior to colonization in 1789, Aborigines managed the landscape with controlled burns—a practice called "fire stick farming". Using this technique they influenced many parts of the landscape, including biodiversity, water stocks and flows, the stock of wildlife for hunting and the balance of edible plants.

↑ **Figure 5.4** Yugambeh man demonstrating his fire-building skills

Their skill with fire was commented upon in accounts by early settlers that described the landscape as "park-like". Bill Gammage, historian at the Australian National University, notes five stages in the use of fire by the Aborigines (2011). Modern land management regimes around the world struggle with stage 1, which is the most basic stage.

1. Control the amount of fuel for wildfires.
2. Maintain diversity.
3. Balance species.
4. Ensure abundance.
5. Locate resources conveniently and predictably.

The extent and precision of the Aborgines' management of land prompted Gammage to write that "Australia was not natural in 1788, but made" (2011).

Environmental degradation can impact the transfer, preservation and reliability of Indigenous knowledge. For example, the Aamjiwnaang community of Anishnaabe First Nations people in Ontario, Canada, have reported a decline in traditional communication as a direct consequence of petrochemical contamination in their region. Contaminants in foodstuffs, wood, rocks, and water supplies, have forced the community to abandon traditional activities such as berry-picking, foraging for medicine and food, and fishing. Because those activities are not happening, the oral instructions and stories which surround them and allow them to pass from one generation to the next are no longer being shared and are in danger of being lost (Hoover *et al* 2012).

Not only does environmental degradation affect the health of Indigenous Peoples, it can hit doubly hard by undermining the preservation and transfer of Indigenous knowledge and so their ability to rebound from the environmental impact.

Making connections

TEK, religion and science

"Traditional knowledge has developed a concept of the environment that emphasizes the symbiotic character of humans and nature. It offers an approach to local development that is based on co-evolution with the environment, and on respecting the carrying capacity of ecosystems. … Western science is positivist and materialist in contrast to traditional knowledge, which is spiritual and does not make distinctions between empirical and sacred. Western science is objective and quantitative as opposed to traditional knowledge, which is mainly subjective and qualitative. Western science is based on an academic and literate transmission, while traditional knowledge is often passed on orally from one generation to the next by the elders." (Mazzocchi 2006)

In the extract above, Mazzocchi asserts strong dichotomies about science and traditional ecological knowledge. To what extent do you agree with these assertions? What are some of the assumptions inherent in them?

Chapter 6, III.3, explores nature-religions and the argument, made by a number of anthropologists, that culture and religion are adaptive processes that enable a group to survive in their environmental niche. That section also explores the differing perspectives on nature put forth by Muir and Pinchot. Chapter 7, II, discusses Francis Bacon's view of nature.

In what ways is TEK aligned or unaligned with these perspectives? What might explain differences in these perspectives?

Practising skills: Analysis

To what extent are the following characteristics of TEK similar to or different from the natural and human sciences? TEK is:

- practical, based on empirical observations, experimentation, and trial and error, and it provides tools for pest control, fire prevention, resource accounting and conservation

- taught experientially and passed down from generation to generation, typically through oral histories, and embedded into family and community practices

- holistic, rooted in culture and identity, including language, spirituality and health

- an authority and belief system that governs and explains the rules for use of natural resources
- a knowledge that includes important ethics and value systems that, for example, constrain the use of this knowledge in extractive and exploitative practices

- a cosmology, that serves as a foundation for the assumptions and beliefs about nature, the world and the universe, and explains the place and role of human beings in the world.

(Adapted from: Emery 1997; Houde 2007)

Later, this chapter considers the difference between cultural appropriation and appreciation, and the question of intellectual property rights to protect and reward Indigenous Peoples' knowledge. In relation to TEK and its applications, such as medicinal plants, and in particular the potential for businesses to monetize this knowledge, what are the arguments for and against treating it as intellectual property? Property rights typically require written documentation and proof of ownership. Intellectual property rights are complicated because TEK is preserved through Oral Tradition over generations. It is an issue of acknowledging knowledge, and not just about rewarding it commercially: the significance of Indigenous knowledge generally goes unacknowledged within the wider culture of science.

On what basis do TEK claims about health and illness, treatment and medicine compare with the claims of standard medical practice? What knowledges are needed to evaluate the effectiveness of medicinal knowledge traditions and practices? And how would we reward these with the status of intellectual property?

Herbalist and anthropologist Charis Boke offers a perspective on this below, and similar themes and complexities arise in the case study on the intersection of folk medicine and global health in Uganda.

Voices: Charis Boke on experience and evidence in traditional Western herbalism

"Western herbal medicine" (WHM) or "traditional Western herbalism" are terms used to distinguish herbalism based on Anglo-American traditional herbal medicine from systems of herbal medicine elsewhere in the world, such as homeopathy, Ayurveda or traditional Chinese medicine (TCM).

"Over the last 50 years, traditional Western herbalists have learned their craft in various settings. Some teachers have tried to formalize, professionalize and institutionalize their teaching, designing multiple-year programmes with clinical components. Other teachers have not taken this approach, choosing to stick with the "traditional" apprenticeship mode.

Some herbalist educators have created institutions recognizable by dominant forms of scientific knowledge, such as reading biochemical assay studies of plant constituents. Even so, those teachers still draw on practices of direct encounter with living plants and medicinal substances grounded in long histories.

'Ooh, wow,' she says under her breath, eyes wide. 'That's … intense.'

The dropper circulates until everyone has taken a drop or two of the richly red infused alcohol, registering its flavors and sensations. The schisandra berries, too, circulate, each of us dipping our fingers in the bowl to feel their hard, small, wrinkled round bodies. We smell them, crack open a few to look inside, touch them, look carefully. When both have passed through everyone's hands, Sparrow pauses her discussion of growth patterns, harvest times, and how to be careful of provenance when buying commercially.

'So, what are folks tasting?' A question that grounds each Materia Medica class, where students learn the languages with which to speak about medicinal flavors, as well as taxonomy and medicinal uses of plants.

'It's like, sweet but spicy,' Angie says.

'It was REALLY intense to me, like packed with energy,' Sarah adds.

'Yeah, great,' says Sparrow, the teacher, turning from the board where she had written all these words. 'What else? How about the energetics? Who felt it was cooling?'

'I don't know,' Ash says, 'it tasted warming to me. But definitely dry.'

'You all mostly got it. It's definitely drying, or "astringing" in traditional western terms, and sour, and somewhat pungent but not too much. And it's got a kind of neutral energy—it can be warming or cooling depending on the condition, though it tends toward cooling because it's sour. It's also often stimulating for folks.'

Students add these collected observations to our Mat Med notes for schisandra. Tasting this plant's extract brings them into a different kind of learning space where they can connect the information they gather from the lecture and discussion to their direct experience, filtering different kinds of knowing together. As a cultural anthropologist, I follow this attention to taste, touch, smell, and sensation in order to examine the kinds of evidence that matter to herbalists, and that approach to evidence informs their approach to medical knowledge more generally.

In the last 50 years in the United States, complementary and alternative medical practices have become very successful. We can take this as one indication that many people think there are alternatives to biomedicine, when it comes to thinking about and working on bodies and health. Herbalism, however, is not just 'alternative' to biomedicine—contemporary herbalists develop knowledge practices to work in conversation with it. Teachers at The Center where I conducted research claim the experience of a trained herbalists' sensory skills as a form of knowledge that can provide evidence: for plants' medicinal qualities; for plant preparations' strength, composition, and capacity for efficacy; and for bodily states of wellness and illness. These claims are in contrast to biomedical ideals, which developed in tandem with the networks and institutions that regulate ingestible substances (food, pharmaceuticals, supplements), which consider somatic or bodily experiences unreliable evidence in part because they are not understood to be easily reproducible. Herbalists suggest that reproducibility is not possible in any case, because each body, plant, and ailment are distinct, albeit with some shared features. It is in these conversations about evidence, and the relation of bodily experience to legitimate knowledge, where herbalists make their most meaningful contribution to human health. Claims about experience, and the training of sensory experience, opened the way for what anthropologist Michelle Murphy might call an herbalist 'technoscience otherwise,' and it is that 'otherwise' I trace here (Murphy 2006). To say that one can know plants by tasting, growing, touching, nurturing them locates evidence and its production outside a status-quo paradigm for health. Direct experience as a mode of learning and mutual aid as an ethic of care underpinned how herbalist practices and companies grew out of health justice movements as political projects (see Katz 1981; Kropotkin 1902 on mutual aid and solidarity as political modes).

A key difference between biomedical practitioners and herbalists, though, lies in how they produce knowledge for themselves about the materials of their medicine, and its bodily effects—where herbalists taste and smell and try plant-medicines to understand their effects, biomedical doctors are not generally encouraged to sample all the pharmaceuticals they could prescribe. Thus, it is the substances about which herbalists' experiences produce knowledge: whole plant preparations, made from plants conceived as beings with whom humans can have intimate relations, instead of as resources; and whole bodies understood to be shaped by constitutions and individual tendencies, but always already in relationship with the world around them. Contemporary regulatory measures have moved away from bodily attunements, seeking evidence produced by machines (such as isolated molecular structures) to stand in for the tastes and smells that trained bodies can identify. In response to the gray area of what counts as

evidence about medicines and health, herbalists make political and social interventions into regulatory worlds, seeking to shift how federal and state monitors allow them to identify medicines with trained bodily senses.

Herbalism reveals a politics of evidence as herbalists make claims about plants' healing capacities and about herbalism as a system of knowledge. What's most interesting is to ask: whose evidence, and evidence for what purposes, has shaped western herbalism as a set of intellectual orientations? And how does its institutionalization make claims on regulatory structures, as it tries to at once hold on to, but also move out of a space of alternative-ness?

Producing legitimacy in terms of biomedical standards of evidence may not be at the forefront of all herbalists' minds, but it does play a central role in the creation and maintenance of structured curricula like that used at The Center. In other words, herbalists' attempts to make their work legitimate to regulators and to the general public is shaping how they teach herbalism. Part of the professionalization of herbalists as they seek to make new possibilities for legitimate medicine through changing politics of evidence relies also on a change in institutional forms."

Practising skills: Exploring perspectives and evaluating claims

 Search terms: Aeon Magic or medicine?

While we guard against romanticizing the knowledge of traditional communities and devaluing the advances and perspective of modern medicine, we must also recognize the devastation of Indigenous knowledge wrought by centuries of colonial rule and subsequent political instability. Consider this article, which powerfully describes the challenges of global health amid folk approaches to healing among Indigenous communities in Uganda.

1. What roles do belief and scepticism play in how we receive knowledge from different cultures?

2. What factors within and external to a community affect the perceived or actual legitimacy of its knowledge?

3. (a) Under what circumstances can the encounter between Indigenous and scientific knowledge produce negative results?

   (b) How might we distinguish between Indigenous knowledge and other beliefs held by local populations?

4. (a) In the context of this example, which standards can be used to make judgments about whether knowledge "works"?

   (b) Who should set the standards?

   (c) Should these standards apply universally or should there be limitations and exceptions?

IV. ETHICS

While ethical issues are explored throughout this chapter, this section looks in more detail at the questions of:

- how Indigenous Peoples are represented in culture
- where the line between appreciation and appropriation is in relation to Indigenous knowledge
- how we navigate the tension between the right not to know and the responsibility to share knowledge with voluntarily isolated tribal peoples.

IV.1 The ethics and politics of representation

Jimmy Nelson's project on Indigenous Peoples, "Before They Pass Away", serves as a case study on the complex political and knowledge concerns that arise when non-Indigenous individuals tell the story of Indigenous Peoples and knowledge. The political implications of aesthetic decisions are explored in Chapter 10. "Before They Pass Away" connects to similar aesthetic and political concerns.

Nelson's photographs are widely acclaimed as beautiful compositions that appear to celebrate their subjects. "I wanted to put them on a pedestal like they've never been seen before" says Nelson (2014), and contrasts his aesthetic with the "impoverished" and "patronizing" aesthetic used by NGOs and other organizations to raise funds for their work. Nelson unabashedly acknowledges choosing to photograph "the most beautiful people on the planet" (2014), leaving out Indigenous Peoples that did not meet his criteria for authenticity.

> I'm trying to put these people in the same context as somebody like Kate Moss ... Our society, for whatever reason, has decided she is important and deserves to be photographed in a high-concept way; I've tried to do the same here.
>
> (Nelson quoted in Merrill 2014)

Critiquing the "authenticity" of a different culture from the outside is problematic for a number of obvious reasons. In our particular historical moment, outsiders may be conditioned to expect an exoticized orientalist aesthetic. Photographers are complicit in perpetuating that aesthetic if they are not especially careful to guard against it. While the photographs are stunning, they may be inadvertently degrading because they show their subjects isolated from progress, science and all the other facets of modern life. They obscure the fact that their subjects may watch Netflix, wear denim jeans and use social media when the camera is not pointed their way. And they can prompt the incorrect assumption that the featured communities have been that way forever, as if their cultures are not constantly adjusting and adapting to the world around them like everyone else's. Cultures, unlike artefacts that are preserved and shown in museums and galleries, adapt, collide, meld together and certainly change over time. Anthropologist Julia Lagoutte makes the following argument.

> It is simply not true that tribal people have been 'unchanged for thousands of years'; they have been evolving constantly, as we have. It is clear that for Nelson, their attraction and purity is rooted in their exclusion from the future, and their containment to the past— so that is the only reality he presents in his photos. By omitting their interactions with the 'modern world' that they are a part of, and perpetuating the myth that they are dying out, Nelson's work freezes tribal peoples in the past and effectively denies them a place in this world.
>
> (Lagoutte 2014)

The other problematic assumption has to do with narrative and language, both of which powerfully reflect and reinforce beliefs, attitudes and assumptions, as we see in Chapter 4. The title "Before They Pass Away" invokes an inevitable passing, a natural consequence of history and progress that such cultures are lost, and the only thing one can do is admire the memory. It does not, for example, suggest that there is a perpetrator to this passing, or an idea of justice, though maybe there is something criminal about how Indigenous communities are persecuted off their lands. What is causing the "passing away" that Nelson references? Is this passing inevitable?

Survival International has been a fierce critic of the project, and has assembled an impressive list of objectors featured on its website, among them leaders of Indigenous communities around the world and prominent photographers.

 Search terms: Survival International Jimmy Nelson's Before they pass away

Among the critics is Nixiwaka Yawanawá, from the Amazonian Yawanawá tribe in Brazil.

> It's outrageous! We are not passing away but struggling to survive. Industrialized society is trying to destroy us in the name of 'progress', but we will keep defending our lands and contributing to the protection of the planet.
>
> (Yawanawá 2014)

Papuan tribal leader Benny Wenda made similar comments.

> My people are still strong and we fight for our freedom. We are not 'passing away', we are being killed … .
>
> (Wenda 2014)

Yanomami spokesperson Davi Kopenawa reacted to Nelson's project as follows.

> It is not true that Indigenous peoples are about to die out. We will be around for a long time, fighting for our land, living in this world and continuing to create our children.
>
> (Kopenawa 2014)

Stephen Corry, director of Survival International, has made the following similar argument.

> In reality, many minority peoples, especially tribal ones, are not 'disappearing': they are being disappeared, through 'our' illegal theft of their land and resources. … we are simply turning our usual blind eye.
>
> (Corry 2014)

These critics' perspectives are not told through the photographs, captions or descriptions in "Before They Pass Away". Nelson responds that he is not an anthropologist or sociologist, that he just wants to take good photographs of beautiful people. With the important political implications of his work, and the politicization of Indigenous and minority issues in general, good intentions are not enough. In Chapter 10 we examine the case of Sharbat Gula, photographed as *Afghan Girl* by *National Geographic* photographer Steve McCurry.

Both McCurry and Nelson appear to have had good intentions, yet both have been criticized by and on behalf of minority groups. Both episodes invite our curiosity about how identity, privilege, culture and aesthetics intersect in our present political moment.

↑ **Figure 5.5** Nixiwaka Yawanawá, protesting against the exhibition of Nelson's work at London's Atlas Gallery, wearing ceremonial headdress along with Western casual wear, no less or more "authentic" than Nelson's representations

For discussion

Representing Indigenous life

 Search terms: National Geographic Native Americans are countering racist stereotypes

This story about Indigenous photographers' visual representations of Indigenous life was published in the December 2018 issue of *National Geographic* magazine, a few months after the magazine reflected on decades of its racist coverage of Indigenous Peoples and persons of colour.

1. How does the representation of Indigenous life in popular media affect what we know of Indigenous knowledge?

2. What makes a representation valid and reliable?

3. What introduces bias into a representation?

4. Is the accuracy of representations of Indigenous Peoples improved or reduced from having multiple diverse perspectives?

IV.2 Appreciation or appropriation

Cultural appropriation usually applies when elements of a marginalized culture are used by a dominant culture. While cultural sharing is generally desirable, it is complicated by the power dynamics of racism and privilege. How can we appreciate, learn from and draw on other cultures' knowledge in a way that is responsible? Unlike acculturation, assimilation or cultural exchange, appropriation is said to perpetuate racism and marginalization because of the power dynamics involved. Appropriators typically lack an understanding of the cultural markers they are using, and/or use them in a belittling way, for example as fashion symbols and accessories. In this way, appropriation signals that marginalized cultures are "free for the taking", which is an echo of colonialism. Marginalized communities lose the distinctiveness of their cultural markers through appropriation, which can drain the urgency of their political claims and historical grievances. Appropriation can also perpetuate inaccurate stereotypes and the idea that Indigenous cultures are monolithic.

Visual art, fashion, dance and music are often the areas most readily associated with appropriation. As interest in indigenizing the curriculum grows and in some cases outpaces the capacity of schools to keep up, campuses have become a frequent site of conflicts over appropriation.

For discussion

What is appropriate and what is appropriating

 Search terms: Vimeo Jo-Ann Archibald

Jo-Ann Archibald of the Stó:lo Nation explains some of the protocols and processes appropriate to sharing Indigenous knowledge. Consider the relational approach to knowing and the responsibilities and expectations that come with it, described earlier, and answer the following questions.

1. How are Archibald's protocols of sharing Indigenous knowledge similar to or different from intellectual honesty and academic referencing practices?

2. What gives one access to Indigenous knowledge and the permission to share it?

3. What responsibilities rest with the learner of Indigenous knowledge that may not apply to other types of knowledge?

4. Consider what happens when protocol is not followed.

   (a) What are the implications of not following protocol?

   (b) To what extent would breaches of protocol be issues of justice?

Indigenous intellectual property has been used as a legal term to identify collective intellectual property rights for specific cultural knowledge. It has been promoted by the World Intellectual Property Organization of the United Nations to more fairly value Indigenous knowledge and cultural heritage. In 2007, the UN General Assembly accepted the Declaration on the Rights of Indigenous Peoples, including the following.

What are some of the practical challenges to implementing collective intellectual property, Indigenous or otherwise? Advocates of collective property rights seek a new legal system that protects Indigenous Peoples' rights over their property—including cultural heritage and Traditional Knowledge—as forms of intellectual property that are collective resources.

[**Article 11:**] States shall provide redress … which may include restitution, developed in conjunction with Indigenous peoples, with respect to their cultural, intellectual, religious and spiritual property taken without their free, prior and informed consent or in violation of their laws, traditions and customs. …

[**Article 31:**] Indigenous peoples have the right to maintain, control, protect and develop their cultural heritage, traditional knowledge and traditional cultural expressions, as well as the manifestations of their sciences, technologies and cultures, including human and genetic resources, seeds, medicines, knowledge of the properties of fauna and flora, oral traditions, literatures, designs, sports and traditional games and visual and performing arts. They also have the right to maintain, control, protect and develop their intellectual property over such cultural heritage, traditional knowledge, and traditional cultural expressions.

Making connections

Indigenous art and artefacts in museums

In Chapter 10, section II, we examine the issue of Indigenous art and artefacts held in museums in advanced industrialized nations, and the related issues of appropriation and repatriation. The Benin Bronzes, which powerfully influenced colonial attitudes to Indigenous art in the early 20th century, are owned and held in London by the British Museum, though a small selection was temporarily loaned back to Nigeria in late 2018. Refer to Chapter 10 for further discussion on patrimony and the repatriation of Indigenous art.

IV.3 Knowledge and access— uncontacted peoples

Variously referred to as lost or isolated tribes, even the term "uncontacted peoples" rings with misconceptions about these groups living in voluntary isolation across the world today. While they may not have peaceful contact with other groups at the moment, this does not mean that they never have had. Still, very little is known about them. Only about 100 such groups exist in the world today and their survival is under threat. Their predicament poses urgent questions about sharing and having access to knowledge. One perspective argues that we have a responsibility to share knowledge with them that could improve their lives.

This idea, combined with popular stereotypical depictions of their lives, has motivated all sorts of people to initiate "first contact"—sometimes with tragic consequences. Missionary work is another common motivation for contacting these tribes. Refer to the *Washington Post* article "'God, I Don't Want to Die' US Missionary Wrote Before he was Killed" (Slater, Allan 2018) for how one recent story ended badly.

↑ **Figure 5.6** The Sentinelese stand guard on an island beach

 Search terms: God, I don't want to die Washington Post

However, the history of "first contact" teaches us that such encounters are usually much deadlier for the tribes than the initiators of contact. This can be due to communicable diseases or violent conflict and state-sponsored ethnic cleansing. Contacted groups often die in large numbers quickly.

In the context of the encounter between the US missionary and Sentinelese tribe, consider these questions.

- What responsibilities do we, the mainstream, have for spreading knowledge to Indigenous Peoples generally and uncontacted tribes specifically?
- Are we, the mainstream, in any way entitled to knowing what they know?
- What is lost and gained if their knowledge is never spread through the mainstream?

The evidence-based and practice-informed course of action is to leave uncontacted peoples alone. This respects their right to determine their own future—including whether they want to establish contact. Do individuals and states have a responsibility to uphold this right, when the concerned peoples mostly live beyond the reaches of the state?

6 Knowledge and religion

The world's religions, across time, serve as repositories of knowledge while also holding a continued social significance: religious themes are woven into cultural practices, literature, history, film and art. Even our ability to fully grasp current events—elections, policies, revolutions, movements and conflicts—is informed by our understanding of religion. Religious practices and rituals powerfully shape identity across the generations and collapse the past into the present. In an increasingly globally interconnected world, diverse examples of religious knowledge and practices encounter one another, and stand together, their uniqueness perhaps diminished, in the face of what some have described as a modern monoculture. In this chapter, we add depth to our understanding of human knowledge by looking at its relationship with religion.

Initial discussion

- Who has religious knowledge and what is it about?
- What are legitimate sources of religious knowledge and what makes them so?
- What does it mean for a religious claim to be true or false, and who can decide?
- How can disagreements between conflicting religious claims be dealt with?
- How is the process of producing and acquiring religious knowledge similar to or different from this process for other types of knowledge?

I. SCOPE

As the 21st century unfolds, the question about what would happen to the scope and power of religion as a result of globalization and modernization is yielding unexpected outcomes. It was widely predicted that the role of religion in politics and society would diminish. However, we appear to be witnessing a resurgence. Sociologist Peter Berger has been pondering these questions for decades, and is sceptical of the view that modernity advances at the expense of religion. His book on desecularization, albeit from two decades ago, opened with the following claim: "The assumption that we live in a secularized world is false. The world is as furiously religious as it ever was" (Berger 1999).

This is not to say that religion has been unaffected by globalization. Berger argues that modernity in a global context has led, inevitably, to pluralism. Section II explores this idea further. For now, consider what it is about religion that has allowed it to persist and sustain such diversity in the face of powerful forces that promote uniformity and diminish difference.

Another question for the scope of religion is whether religious beliefs and practices are found in every human culture. Is religion, its extraordinary diversity notwithstanding, a universal feature of humanity? The answer to this question will depend on how we conceive of the concept of religion, and is explored below.

I.1 What is and is not religion?

Given claims of religion's historical significance and continued relevance, it is important to consider what this supposedly universal and enduring thing called religion is. We can name different religions and religious traditions, such as Buddhism, Jainism, Zoroastrianism, shamanic and animistic folk religions. What makes them all "religious"? On what basis can we distinguish religion from other realms of human activity, such as culture, science or politics?

Let's consider two contrasting approaches to defining religion, both of which have profound implications for what is called religious knowledge. This affects people's identities, political status and the rights afforded to them by legal frameworks.

Jonathan Z. Smith and William Scott Green propose a narrow definition of religion as "a system of beliefs and practices that are relative to superhuman beings" (Smith, Green 1995). This excludes special experiences, spiritual practices, world views and ideologies that are sometimes classified as religion but do not have a supernatural element. Some forms of Buddhism, such as Zen Buddhism, do not qualify under this definition. The advantage of this restrictive definition is that it narrows the scope of religious knowledge to a more coherent and consistent set of beliefs and traditions that is easier to work with.

However, this restrictive definition leaves a large number of people and concerns out of the field. Instead, David Chidester proposes a self-consciously vague definition of religion as "that dimension of human experience engaged with sacred norms" (Chidester 1987). By "sacred" he means the higher powers and forces that affect and give meaning to human life.

There are, of course, academic definitions in the field of religious studies, which often do not correspond to how the concept of religion is understood in the public sphere. For example, Tony Perkins, President of the Family Research Council, and presently serving as Chair of the US Commission on International Religious Freedom, has said, "What most people either don't realize or willfully ignore is that only 16 percent of Islam is a religion—the rest is a combination of military, judicial, economic, and political system. Christianity, by comparison, isn't a judicial or economic code—but a faith."

How has Perkins so precisely deduced the percentage of Islam that is a religion? What would you need to know in order to form a judgment about his claim? There is a growing concern among scholars of religion that, in the past decade, questioning the religiosity of religions has moved into the legal and political discourse in the United States. Scholars speculate that this may be due to religious illiteracy and narrow understandings of what is and is not religion, or political interests to covertly undermine other religions. The prevalence of this perspective is the topic of *When Islam Is Not a Religion: Inside America's Fight for Religious Freedom* by Asma Uddin (2019). It explores the origin, spread and implications of the effort to redefine Islam as something other than a religion, and the threat this poses to religious freedom and human rights. Uddin argues that the loss of liberty and constitutional protection for Muslims means a loss of liberty for everyone in the United States.

↑ **Figure 6.1** Muslims pray during the "Islam on Capitol Hill" event at the West Front Lawn of the US Capitol (2009)

To explore this further, follow the link to a conversation between Uddin and Benjamin P. Marcus of the Religious Studies Project.

 Search terms: Religious Studies Project When Islam is not a religion

For reflection

Responsibilities and implications

Ken Chitwood suggests that part of the issue is that the field of religious studies has failed at communicating to the public the academic understanding of "religion". For the most part, Chitwood (2019) suggests, the public understandings and misunderstandings of religion are explored at conferences, but scholars have not effectively engaged with the public sphere about this.

Consider what are some claims made about religious groups in your context.

1. What are the responsibilities of religious studies scholars towards religious literacy among the public?

2. How is knowledge about religion disseminated, or how should this take place?

3. Who are the stakeholders in the conversation about religious literacy?

4. What are your personal responsibilities in terms of encountering or propagating claims about religion?

Our intuitive answers to questions about religion often invoke stereotypes and clichés, such as religions are based on belief, they belong to the transcendental realm, or they belong in the private and not the public sphere. Religious studies scholars Brad Stoddard and Craig Martin (2017) explore these and other commonly believed oversimplifications about religion. As we have seen, false, incomplete or inaccurate though they are, stereotypes can be powerful political levers.

Stoddard and Martin look at claims such as "Religions are mutually exclusive" and explore how these matter-of-fact statements are not actually neutral. What we claim to know about religion has material consequences. The authors show that in some prison systems, for example, people are asked to declare their religion in "tick one box only" style—reinforcing the idea that religions are mutually exclusive. What you declare as your religion determines whether you will have access to certain spaces, be able to attend certain groups and so on; and you would only be able to change your declared religion once every six months. What assumptions about religion are these rules based on?

In terms of the assumptions and consequences of these stereotypes and clichés, Stoddard and Martin invite us to consider the following whenever we encounter claims about religion.

> " With this claim, who is trying to persuade whom of what? Who stands to gain and who stands to lose if the claim is received as true?
>
> (Stoddard, Martin 2017) "

This approach is useful to us beyond this chapter, and indeed beyond this course and the IB Diploma Programme. We can practise on one statement commonly made in the context of religion: that religion is universal.

Practising skills: Identifying assumptions and drawing implications

Consider the two perspectives below on whether or not religion is universal.

1. How might the "universality" of religion affect claims about whether religion is created, discovered or revealed?

2. What implications does this have for religious knowledge?

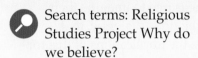 Search terms: Religious Studies Project Why do we believe?

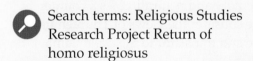 Search terms: Religious Studies Research Project Return of homo religiosus

I.2 Touchpoints and tensions

While we should be sceptical of boundaries constructed between concepts, blurring the line between religion and state authority specifically has brought about serious and well-documented consequences. Similarly, the boundary between religion and science has caused controversy, with claims-makers on each side closely policing the boundary. Each of these issues is investigated below.

For discussion

How would you map out the scope of religion?

You can do this activity working on your own, with a partner or in a small group.

In Chapter 1, we discuss the map metaphor of knowledge, and you may have depicted your knowledge as a literal map. How does religious knowledge inform your map of the world? How does it fit with other domains such as history, art, science and politics? Do some of these domains spill over or cut across other domains more clearly?

1. Where does the scope of religion overlap with the other domains?

2. What happens in the overlapping zones?

3. Where is the boundary particularly clear, wiggly, broken or blurry? Describe what it means and why you have drawn or imagined it this way.

If you are doing this exercise with a partner or in a group, compare your maps and share what you identify as significant similarities and differences.

Box 6.1: Is secular Buddhism religion without belief?

Stephen Batchelor follows what he calls a Secular Buddhism, that acknowledges the mystery and vitality of spiritual life as well as the importance of doubt and questioning. He comprehends Buddhism as a way of being and doing, but not necessarily requiring belief, which in his view, involves this problem: when you believe that "this is how reality works", you require supernaturalistic explanations such as God or Karma, which dominates what people see as Christianity or Buddhism. Above all, argues Batchelor, "secular Buddhism is something to do, not to believe in" (Batchelor quoted in Tippett 2018).

This is an increasingly popular conception of spirituality as something independent of supernaturalistic phenomena. Another popular framing sees Buddhism as more of science and philosophy, and less as religion. To the extent that everyone is free to imagine their own spiritual and religious dialogue, that is great—but what are the implications of this for religious knowledge, and concepts such as faith, truth, objectivity and neutrality? As a counter-perspective consider the views of Thupten Jinpa, a close aide and translator to the Dalai Lama.

 Search terms: Thupten Jinpa translating the Dalai Lama

"When people are … encountering a tradition such as Tibetan Buddhism, it's very different historically from, say, any of the monotheistic traditions that you see in

the West … where there has been a kind of gradual separation between spirituality or religion. And then you have science … where your understanding of the world is based on what you can directly perceive or what you can infer on the basis of … direct experience … . So this kind of separation between science and philosophy and spirituality has not occurred in the context of Tibetan tradition, Tibetan buddhism. … you cannot look at Tibetan Buddhism and say this is religion … you cannot say this is philosophy … nor can you say this is science. But within that tradition, you have all the elements. … So that makes the training of a monk very, very sophisticated, because you have to … study all these aspects, the relationship between our perception and the world, and the distinction between true knowledge and a mere belief in assumption. You know, how does a language in thought relate to the actual reality?" (Jinpa quoted in Tippett 2013)

According to Jinpa, knowledge must be integrated into a holistic system, including ethics, through meditation. This is radically different from the disciplinary training of scientists and researchers.

I.3 Not only religion: The spiritual and the political

How do we popularly conceive of the relationship between religion and politics? You may have heard phrases such as "religion and politics do not mix" or "the separation of church and state"—both of which align with the idea of secularism, a pillar of many modern democracies. However, it would be naive to think that religion and politics are isolated domains. Mahatma Gandhi stated in his autobiography (1927) that "those who say religion has nothing to do with politics do not know what religion is". Religion and politics powerfully intermix in ways that affect human life, for better or worse, such as in the Civil Rights movement of the 1950s and the Rohingya refugee crisis of the early

21st century. The scholar Omid Safi, musing on the entanglement of religion and politics, wrote the following.

I was drawn … to the study of mystics because I was burned out on politics, and wanted to lose myself in the ethereal, eternal, sweet, and love-filled world [of] the mystics. … But my beloved mystics kept acting socially and politically. Because they loved God, they loved God's creation. … Many of them positioned themselves as champions of the weak and the marginalized, and acted in a way that today we would call "speaking truth to power." In their profoundly hierarchical society—and let us admit that ours today is still profoundly hierarchical—these mystics kept on reminding the rulers that it was God who was the ultimate King.

(Safi 2016)

In the context of politics, religion can be a powerful force through which people are moved to act. Religious communities have many times been at the forefront of social reform and social activism. The kind of force that religion wields in politics, and the social function it performs, vary greatly across contexts. To claim that religion is a regressive force, or conversely that it is a progressive force, are examples of generalizations that should be critically evaluated.

↑ **Figure 6.2** Martin Luther King and Abraham Joshua Herschel during the Selma march in 1965

In the global processes that thrust strangers together, and drive friends apart, religion is likely to continue playing a role. Safi reminds us that this function of religion is not new or unique to any particular religious knowledge tradition.

> Was Moses not concerned with the political as he led the Hebrews out of bondage?
>
> Was Amos not concerned with politics when he said: 'Let justice roll down like waters and righteousness like a mighty stream.'
>
> Was Jesus of Nazareth not concerned with social change and transformation as he sat with prostitutes and lepers, keeping the company of the outcast and the downtrodden?
>
> Was Muhammad of Arabia not concerned with the political as he overthrew the Arab tribal bonds and

> instead insisted that human beings stood radically equal, as the teeth in a comb?
>
> Was Rabbi Heschel not concerned with politics when he said that he was praying with his feet in marching for civil rights, when he said that church and synagogue were forbidden as long as African Americans were treated as they were, and when he said that he could not read his prayer book when every time he opened it he saw images of the children of Vietnam burning in napalm?
>
> Was Brother Martin not political when he said that our concern was to save the very soul of America by standing out against racism, materialism, and militarism?
>
> Was Thomas Merton not political when he said: 'The world is full of great criminals with enormous power, and they are in a death struggle with each other.' His deep attachment to the life of spirit, even silence, did not prevent him from getting involved in issues of justice and injustice, or speaking out against racism and war.
>
> (Safi 2016)

For discussion

Political or politicized?

Around the world and throughout history we witness religion entangled with political reform, liberation or oppression.

1. (a) To what extent is religion inherently political? Why might this be the case?

   (b) Where has it been politicized and depoliticized, and how would we know?

2. (a) Why is it important to know the answers to the questions above?

   (b) Consider instances in your context, in the contemporary or historical events of your community, where you have witnessed the political impact of religion. Are there similarities and differences across these instances?

I.4 Religion and science: Competing answers and complementary questions

> How we ask our questions affects the answers we arrive at. … [S]cience and religion … ask different kinds of questions altogether, probing and illuminating in ways neither could alone.
>
> (Tippett 2010)

Science and religion are sometimes, at least in the popular Western imagining, conceived of as being in opposition to each other, as being mutually exclusive ways of describing reality. The debate between creationism and evolutionary theory in the United States is a commonly cited example. Religious voices aligned with the political far right have grown audibly hostile to science, provoking a new atheist response that is hostile to religion (see, for example, Bradley, Ruse 2014). But some commentators argue that rather than posing competing answers to the same questions, religion and science ask altogether different questions.

In TOK, we demarcate science as an area of knowledge, but religious knowledge as a theme; why might this be the case? In the past religious knowledge was designated as an area of knowledge in itself. Why might we have moved away from that?

The map metaphor of knowledge reminds us to be sensitive to and critical of the boundaries drawn between different knowledge domains. In his book *The Territories of Science and Religion* (2015), Peter Harrison discusses the supposed tension between religious knowledge and science, domains that are stereotypically positioned as irreconcilable, or at least opposed to one another. We should remember that the categories "science" and "religion", as they are understood today, emerged comparably recently, and in a very specific historical and cultural context. Humans have been performing acts of worship and endeavouring to systematically explain the natural world for much longer than we have described or understood those practices as religious or scientific. For much of that history, and in many contexts even today, these practices were not thought of as opposed

to one another. As religion and science have grown into strikingly distinct disciplines, we risk ahistorically applying this distinction to the past.

So, to what extent is the conflict between religion and science centred on Western sensibilities owing to the development of science in early modern Europe, at a time of strained relationships with the Church? Luckily for us, many ambitious scholars have attempted to answer that question, and we will not dwell on it in depth.

Varadaraja V. Raman, among others, argues that this separation does not appear so strongly in other religious and cultural contexts. While modern science emerged in Western Europe with discoveries that appeared to clash with the Church, laying the foundation for the secularism that underpins most contemporary Western democracies, this did not happen elsewhere. Raman (quoted in Tippett 2007) says the "Eastern" religious traditions had "a clear understanding of what constitutes religious knowledge inside experience on the one hand, and what may be called intellectual, analytical, secular knowledge" on the other. He uses an analogy to describe the relationship between science and religion: if we conceive of the universe as a poem, science provides the tools to understand the structure, rhyme and metre of the poem, but it does not tell us the poem's meaning, or answer the question about why the poem exists. In his telling, that comes from religion.

> *"Le cœur a ses raisons que la raison ne connaît point."*
> ("The heart has its reasons which reason doesn't understand.")
> (Blaise Pascal)

Many thinkers over the centuries have argued that the world is too complex for us to put everything "in the straitjacket of reason", as Raman (quoted in Tippett 2007) calls it. The successes of modern sciences, he argues, have led to an addiction to rationality, whereas the religious experience is the unravelling of the mystery of existence. Religion enables us to look at human events in "transrational" terms—transrational being that which is beyond rationality or irrationality, such as compassion, love, reverence and faith. Do you agree with this dichotomy that Raman is posing? Why or why not?

What status does religious knowledge have in terms of legitimacy and reliability in comparison to the other areas of knowledge? What contextual factors affect its status? Why is it not considered an area of knowledge? How would you respond to claims that non-Abrahamic traditions, or "Eastern" religions, as Raman argues, are more aligned with the scientific pursuit of knowledge? To explore this line of enquiry further, refer to Capra (2010) and Wallace (2003).

Buddhism, especially in its pop culture imagining, is often framed in psychological terms, as a "science of the mind", or alternatively as more of a philosophy than a religion. Even as early as 1974, Chögyam Trungpa Rinpoche had predicted that "Buddhism will come to the West as a psychology" (quoted in Goleman 2004). Perhaps these interpretations of Buddhism ultimately tell us more about the cultures to which it is spreading, than about Buddhism itself.

> The very idea that Buddhism had anything to do with psychology was at the time for most of us in the field patently absurd. But that attitude reflected more our own naivete than anything to do with Buddhism.
>
> (Goleman 2004)

When the scope of religious thought expands, with some religions becoming global, it is interesting to consider how the global modernized version of those religions compares with the more locally contextualized versions at their origin. Can religious knowledge be independent from the place and people who produced it? While religious knowledge can travel far, to what extent can it be understood by those outside of the religious community? For example, we consider the knowledge issues involved in translation in Chapter 4. To what extent can religious knowledge be thought of as consistent or truthful, when translations and other transfers are used? To what extent would you agree that Tibetan Buddhism in California, and Tibetan Buddhism in Tibet, are the same religion? More generally, how does religious knowledge spread, and how might it change in response to being spread?

II. PERSPECTIVES

Globalization is often perceived as spreading a privileged set of knowledges and cultures around the world. How have religious communities and practices met this force?

Earlier, we mentioned the enduring pluralism of religious practices in the modern world. There are today over a million Buddhists in North America, the vast majority of whom were not born to the faith. In Europe, there is a significant Muslim population—tens of millions—and rising in places such as the Netherlands. Across the world, practitioners and believers of different faiths are sharing space. Are religious knowledges encountering one another and entering into conversation any differently from the ways they have in the past?

II.1 Engaging with religious multiplicity

In many places around the world, religious knowledge and identity were until very recently inherited; they were forms of learning the values and practices of the culture in a community or place. As people become more mobile, comfortable and independent of their home communities, they face the opportunity and challenge of crafting their spiritual and/or religious identities. Some people and places have come into this faster than others, creating another layer of friction.

According to sociologist Peter Berger, for most of history, people would rarely, if ever, encounter someone of a different religion; to be of a certain religion in a given village would be self-evident, natural, inevitable and taken for granted. With globalization and secularism, people had the new opportunity of imagining other possibilities. Berger describes modernity as "a gigantic transformation from destiny to choice" in which people "must choose what they believe, how they define themselves, how they are to live" (quoted in Tippett 2006a). People now encounter others, even neighbours, with very different religious beliefs and world views. Has this changed how we value and perceive religious knowledge? What else has been affected?

In cosmopolitan cities around the world, religious diversity is being championed and celebrated, as well as feared and resisted. It adds to the richness of human experience as well as to the insecurity of those who feel threatened by change. Reverend angel Kyodo williams has investigated religious diversity. Where diversity has been welcomed, williams observes that people's identities and sense of thriving is not dependent on religious sameness. Instead, the heightened sense of mobility and spaciousness that accompanies religious diversity outweighs the unease. However, some communities do feel threatened by religious diversity. In light of what you have read, why might this be the case?

One of the themes within diversity is tolerance, which refers not simply to accepting people who are different, but also tolerating people who you do not like or agree with, or who do seemingly strange or nonsensical things.

It is worth considering what skills might be required of the knower in navigating the landscape of religious pluralism effectively and respectfully. We briefly explore the relationship between religious knowledge and the concept of truth below. How might we evaluate the competing claims of different religions?

Does religion seek truth?

What kind of knowledge is religious knowledge? There are diverse perspectives about how knowledge is perceived in religious traditions and in, for example, mainstream pop culture, TOK and the IB Diploma Programme. Consider the Arabic word *'ilm* (علم), which is commonly translated as "knowledge", but in the Islamic intellectual tradition has broader meaning, as well as specific connotations. Learn more about the relationship between *'ilm* and the pursuit, acquisition and application of knowledge by following the link.

 Search terms: Islamic concept of knowledge al-islam

↑ Figure 6.3 A religious assembly of different faiths at the court of Mughal Emperor Akbar (1556–1605), miniature painting by Nar Singh circa 1605)

In Hinduism, various schools of thought have different criteria for what constitutes valid knowledge (*pramā*) and invalid knowledge (*apramā*); and what are legitimate sources of knowledge.

Given the diversity of religious intellectual traditions, and the distinct ways each of them approaches questions about where knowledge comes from, and what knowledge is valid, does it make sense to speak of religious knowledge as one thing? Are the various religions more similar than they are different? Some of those who suggest the answer is "yes" start from an assumption of a fundamental truth underlying all religious difference.

This sentiment drove the Mughal Emperor Abū al-Fatḥ Jalāl al-Dī Muḥammad Akbar to convene interreligious dialogues among adherents of Islam, Hinduism, Christianity, Judaism, Jainism and Zoroastrianism at his court in the second half of the 16th century. At around the same time, Jean Bodin imagined a similar conversation between seven sages, including a Roman Catholic, a Lutheran, a Calvinist, a Jew, a Muslim, as well as a natural philosopher and a sceptic in *Colloquium of the Seven about Secrets of the Sublime.*

These were early attempts to discern a common core amid all the religious difference. Echoes of this sentiment appear in the field of comparative religion, and in efforts to promote religious tolerance through interfaith dialogue and education. The claim is that if all religions share a common core of true beliefs, then to search for and find this would be promising in terms of promoting mutual understanding and overcoming religious conflict. And, not insignificantly, adherents of different religious faiths would have less reason to doubt the truthfulness of other faiths. In light of this, examine the role of truth in religious knowledge—is truth something that religions disagree about or is it a unifying factor of religious knowledge?

II.2 Multiple perspectives

> All religious experience, as far back as we can take it, none of it is pure, authentic, unadulterated. The Christianity practised in the year 100 is radically unlike Christian practice now. Christians don't always like to admit that, but it's so. Same thing is true of Judaism. Same thing is true of all the great religious traditions. They have changed within themselves, have taken on the coloration of their time and temperament and of the local color, as much as anything can. So any notion of a one—of a true, authentic faith always leads us backwards towards fundamentalism. And fundamentalism is a betrayal of the varieties of religious experience, not an assertion of them.
>
> (Gopnik quoted in Tippett 2017)

Does religious knowledge lose something, or gain something, if it changes over time? How has our understanding and perception of religious knowledge changed over time?

Religious studies scholar Reza Aslan has considered what it means for religion to change, particularly in Islam. Islam's prophets, he says, are "intimately connected to the worlds out of which they arise", and the transition from one world, or era, to another has been called a "reformation". Aslan's assertions are provocative, and invite us to think carefully about the relationship between religious knowledge and the past, and the role and influence of individuals in the development of religious knowledge. Aslan expresses some of his views as follows.

> "
> There's this misunderstanding, amongst most people of faith that prophets sort of grow up in some kind of cultural or religious vacuum. That a prophet is somebody that just plopped down to earth from heaven, and with a ready-made message, in which they found a brand new religion. But prophets don't invent religions. Prophets are reformers of the religions that they themselves grow up in.
>
> Jesus did not invent Christianity. Jesus was a Jew. He was reforming Judaism.
>
> The Buddha did not invent Buddhism. The Buddha was a Hindu. He was reforming Hinduism.
>
> When we use the term reformation, what we mean is the fundamental conflict that is inherent in all religious traditions, as I say, between who gets to define the faith. Is it the institution? Or is it the individuals?
>
> (Aslan quoted in Tippett 2014)
> "

Consider especially Aslan's final point above, regarding the tension between the influence of institutions versus the influence of individuals on how a religion is defined. The history of religion is rich with stories about how individuals and institutions gain and lose the legitimacy and authority to make claims about religious knowledge. What gives legitimacy to religious claims? How do claims-makers gain and lose authority? How has this varied over time and across contexts?

Earlier, we encountered the view of Stephen Batchelor, who talks about Buddhism without belief. What does it mean for individuals to interpret religion in whatever manner they want to? To what extent is this a religious, political or moral freedom, and how does it variously manifest around the world? Because stewards of religious systems can wield significant power, the problem of competing interpretations can lead to power struggles and violence—between individuals, between institutions, and between institutions and individuals.

According to Aslan, this process of reformation, the "passing of institutional authority into individual hands", has been ongoing in Islam since the end of the colonial era. For 14 centuries prior to that, the religious authorities had maintained a firm grip on the meaning and teaching of Islam, for example because only a few people could actually read the Qur'an. As the authority of different religious institutions has weakened, across the world, due to factors including better education, literacy, communication between communities and democratic governance systems, more interpretations have asserted themselves. Now Muslims around the world are living "their faith in enormous diversity and eclecticism" (Aslan quoted in Tippett 2014) against a backdrop of nation-states that are still trying to understand how religion fits alongside a constitution, a legal system and human rights.

This multiplicity of interpretations has the potential to promote tolerance and pluralism, but it can also lead to strife. In the absence of a centralized religious authority, such as a Muslim Pope or Vatican to mediate over 1.6 billion people, the debate can become a cacophony of voices outshouting one another. As a result of all this, Aslan speaks of multiple Islams and disputes the existence of a monolithic Islamic World, a notion that has become a "fact" of religion, history and geography, interchangeably used with another recently invented term—"the Arab world".

For discussion

Diversity of opinion

When we talk about physics, biology, economics, mathematics, history, the visual arts and psychology, we refer to domains of knowledge that are generally consistent and internally coherent. This makes it possible to talk of one physics and one mathematics—but can we talk about one Christianity or one Islam in the same way?

Consider Aslan's view on the matter in the context of Islam:

> " … there is very little that Muslims around the world have in common with each other. … people will say, well, they all believe in the Qur'an, but … [t]he Qur'an is a scripture. … And so people are going to come at it quite differently, depending on their own prejudices and preconceived notions.
>
> You can say, well, but they don't all pray the same way? Well, no, actually they don't all pray the same way. The Shia pray three times, the Sunni pray five times, there is some difference in the rituals of the prayer.
>
> Well, don't they all follow Islamic law? No. There's six different schools of Islamic law, and even within those schools, there's enormous diversity of opinion, and idea.
>
> Well, don't they all believe that the same thing? Don't they all believe there is no god but God, and Muhammed is God's messenger? Yes, but many of them think of that phrase in vastly different ways.
>
> I have trouble even saying the word 'Islam.' I mean, the scholar in me wants to add an 's.' Wants to say 'Islams'." (Aslan quoted in Tippet 2014)

Pluralism exists within many religions today. How has it shown up in your context? What are the implications of variety and disagreement within religions for religious knowledge?

II.3 Women and religion

How does gender intersect with religion? Both are powerful dimensions of identity as well as markers of power and privilege. The terms "devout Muslim" and "feminist" are stereotypically imagined to be in opposition, but are clearly not necessarily so. This section looks at extracts about women in Christianity and Islam, but is just a small window into a very complex and important topic. The issue is at least twofold: the implications of religious doctrine for women in religious communities, as well as the representation and prominence of women in the history of religious thought. As we move through this section, consider to what extent women in religious knowledge communities face similar or different issues compared to women in the arts, in science and technology or in the historical profession.

Earlier, this chapter considered how religion has changed over time, and continues to change, in response to forces of modernity. The status and rights of women have also changed dramatically, particularly in the 20th century. To the extent that there has been a strong reaction against feminism, for example, it has at times been framed in religious terms, around issues of reproductive health and modesty. Consider, for example, the following lines from Genesis 3:16, which tell the story of God's punishment of Adam and Eve (the lines below refer only to Eve) for their Original Sin.

> To the woman the Lord God said, I will greatly increase your pains in childbearing and in pain you shall bring forth children. Yet your desire shall be for your husband, and he shall rule over you.
>
> (Genesis 3:16)

To what extent can we comprehend the words above in our present cultural and historical moment? Chapter 8 considers the long and gendered history of the politics and science of women's pain. The quote from Genesis provides a religious perspective on this that is neither surprising nor divergent from the historical narrative. Even monarchs were not spared this treatment: the Church of England was unwilling to endorse Queen Victoria's use of anesthetics while giving birth to her children. Reportedly, her response was to take the anesthetics anyway. The denial of women's pain remains, bizarrely, an issue in both science and society, and one that may be partly rooted in religious assumptions.

In the West, rising levels of divorce, teen pregnancy and single-parent households have also been blamed on a "feminist" undermining of the sanctity of marriage, through birth control and women's rights to choose whether, when and with whom to have children. Across contexts, class, religion and political affiliation have collided over the issue of women's rights. Religious communities have responded by providing marriage support systems and pro-marriage, pro-family, pro-abstinence movements.

However, according to Rebecca Chopp, a feminist theologian, the institution of marriage in Christianity has been transformed many times through history, including recent North American history. She asserts that men and women lived shorter lives in the 19th century, and that the average American marriage lasted less than ten years. Step-parenting, second marriages and blended families were common even up until the 1950s, at which point a new ideal of stable nuclear families was adopted into US culture. That ideal has been crumbling for a number of years. As Chopp puts it, there is no "one tradition"—marriage has been reinvented multiple times. The introduction and wide acceptance of contraceptive pills, for example, profoundly shifted the foundations of marriage. The intimacy that formed and sustained marriages, and the legal structures that formed around it, were no longer tightly bound. To put it simply, physical intimacy was suddenly possible at very low risk outside of marriage and within marriage there was more choice about how many children to have and when.

Practising skills: Evaluating claims

This section illuminates some tensions and disagreements about the extent to which religious knowledge has changed over time. Consider how you would evaluate the following claims.

"Religious knowledge changes significantly over time."

"Religious knowledge largely remains stable over time."

1. What kind of examples and arguments can you offer in support of each of these claims?

2. Analyse and evaluate the evidence. What can you say about the factors that influence the extent of the change over time?

3. (a) What conclusion can you draw based on your analysis?

   (b) In TOK you will be asked to draw comparisons between different types of knowledge. How does your conclusion about religious knowledge compare to what you might be able to say about scientific or Indigenous knowledge?

Marriage and religion will continue to adapt to these social forces. Already, in just a few years, the legal and social legitimacy and benefits of marriage have been conferred to non-heteronormative partnerships in a number of countries, bringing about the possibility of satisfying relationships with strong family dynamics to situations where this was previously legally or culturally impossible. In some contexts religious arguments have been used in support of or against these developments.

How can we evaluate the diverse and sometimes opposing claims made about what religious knowledge says about women or how women participate in religious practice? We can, of course, look at the claims-makers and critically assess their perspective, motivations and gaps. Leila Ahmed, a professor at Harvard Divinity School, suggests that we might also wish to consider the questions to which the claims are responding.

> … I get constantly called and asked to explain why Islam oppresses women; I have never yet been called and asked, 'Why is it that Islam has produced seven women prime ministers or heads of state …?' I don't think it's really entirely innocent. I think it's about political power and how we want to represent Islam.
>
> (Ahmed quoted in Tippett 2006b)

In the second decade of the 20th century, a number of politicians across Europe targeted the wearing of a veil—in different forms, called hijab, niqab or burqa, among others—by Muslim women. Western news media also extensively covered the "liberation" of Afghan and Iraqi women during the US war on terrorism. Ahmed describes this as history repeating itself, stating:

> … what was disturbing there was to see the replay of what the British Empire did in Egypt 100 years ago. … what I need to invoke here is the belief at the end of the 19th century that the veil symbolized the oppression of Muslim women. It's part of the mythology of that era in which whatever was being done in another country, the countries that they dominated, whether it was India or sub-Saharan Africa or the Muslim countries, however the women dressed there it was the wrong thing. In sub-Saharan Africa, they didn't wear enough clothes; they didn't dress the way European Victorian women dressed. In the Middle East, they wore too many clothes. So the veil in the West … became the emblem of how uncivilized Islam was … .
>
> (Ahmed quoted in Tippett 2006)

Ahmed recounts that Lord Cromer, the British administrator in Egypt a century ago, had gone about "telling people how Egyptian society ought to be", liberating Egyptian women from the veil so that their men would become "civilized". At the same time, Cromer was the founder and President of the Society Opposed to Women's Suffrage, in England.

> He didn't think women ought to have the vote. He thought Victorian society was perfect as it was, with a patriarch ruling over everything, and that is a society that ought to be spread across the world. And in the name of that, Muslim women had to unveil.
>
> (Ahmed quoted in Tippett 2006)

Headscarves and veils have been, of course, used by women of different religions and in different parts of the world: by Zorastrans in Iran, among Christians across the Middle East and in various faiths across the Indian subcontinent. Veils are a clear example of the entanglement of religious, gender and cultural identities and markers. The visible aspects of religious identity interact with politics in ways that raise important TOK questions.

For one, it allows strangers to know that a person belongs to a particular religious group, and to make assumptions about that person's beliefs. Under what circumstances might members of religious groups want to emphasize or de-emphasize their religious identities? To what extent is what we know about religions influenced by their visible aspects?

II.4 Religion, power and the politics of knowledge

The spread of religious knowledge is part of the histories of conquest, imperialism and colonialism. However, the relationship between our knowledge *about* religions and these histories is often less obvious, or even deliberately erased. How have these political processes affected our collective knowledge about religious practices? As a result of their influence, what might be misrepresented, underrepresented or altogether missing from our understanding of religion?

In *Empire of Religion*, David Chidester explores three fundamental questions.

> " How is knowledge about religion and religions produced? How is that knowledge authenticated? How is that knowledge circulated?
>
> (Chidester 2003) "

These questions are part of academic debates about the relationship between knowledge and power in the context of religious studies. Chidester explores religious knowledge production in the context of power relations—colonial, imperial and Indigenous. He shows how newly converted Indigenous informants worked with missionaries, and how foreign travellers became "local experts", to produce surveys and reports on Indigenous religions for the colonial administrators and imperial theorists. These were the raw materials, says Chidester, that gave birth to the discipline of religious studies, which placed itself in a point in time between an imagined primitive past of Indigenous belief and the future triumph of the colonial civilizing project.

This history of religious knowledge invites us to consider what questions we should be asking about the knowledge coming from religious studies. What are the constraints and limitations of academic knowledge about religion, and its supposed objectivity and neutrality? Which is a more reliable source of knowledge about religion—academic study through a secular lens, or religious authorities and leaders?

III. METHODS AND TOOLS

Many individuals, communities and authorities claim to have religious knowledge. In this section we explore the various ways in which religious knowledge is acquired, produced and shared. As you read on, consider what gives religious claims and claims-makers legitimacy. On what basis can religious knowledge be claimed, and what counts as good evidence for it?

III.1 Acquiring and transferring knowledge in religion

> You know, it feels good to pray, you might as well.
>
> (Epicurus 341–270 bce)

Religious knowledge systems very often have a component of personal practice, variously called "inner work", meditation and prayer. To what extent does the knowledge arising from this practice—the questions, answers, thoughts, observations and so on—have a validity and status comparable to that of other areas of knowledge? Does religious knowledge arise from practice, or is the practice itself a form of knowledge, regardless of its results? Is the ability to perform a religious ritual as much skill as knowledge?

Shunryū Suzuki, author of *Zen Mind, Beginner's Mind*, has notably said that gaining religious knowledge by gathering information, as is customary when people attempt to learn something, is a way to "end up not knowing anything at all" (2011). To understand Zen Buddhism, he argues, one should not try to gather as many pieces of information as possible, but rather to clear one's mind. This idea has been embraced and trivialized by a range of pop culture artefacts, from Hollywood karate kids to self-help books. Suzuki refers to achieving "emptiness"; if the mind is unclear,

new information is processed as an echo of pre-existing beliefs and ideas, and true learning is impossible. Many spiritual and religious teachers and guides echo the apparently contradictory ideas of knowing and unknowing ourselves, of not trying to become something but becoming something nonetheless. How is the process of learning this knowledge similar to, different from or incomparable to learning knowledge of other forms?

↑ **Figure 6.4** Shunryū Suzuki

For discussion

Beginner's mind

"In the beginner's mind there are many possibilities, but in the expert's there are few." (Suzuki 2011)

1. How might a "beginner's" interpretation of this quote differ from an expert's?

2. What does it mean for knowledge in religions to have accuracy?

3. To what extent does the concept of reliability apply to religious knowledge?

In the context of perspectives, it is interesting to consider the engagement of children with religious knowledge. The child psychiatrist Robert Coles has built a career writing books about the psychological, spiritual, political and moral lives of children. He asserts that young children may be more spiritual than we recognize, that they have a natural curiosity and interest that aligns with how religion looks at the world.

> It's our effort in this planet as creatures who have a mind and use language to ask questions and answer them through speculation, through story-telling … Where do we come from? What are we? … [T]hose fundamental questions inform religious life and inform the lives of children …
>
> (Coles quoted in Tippett 2009)

Children born to religious families—whether they are Sikh, Buddhist, Muslim, Christian, Jain, Jewish or Hindu—are typically involved in the culture of their religion from childhood. Religious knowledge is most often inherited or passed down from parent to child in this way. Many children are taught that their parents' religion is the one true faith. When religious teaching is non-contestable, can we still say that what is being taught is knowledge? More generally, what is the role of contestability and disagreement in producing religious knowledge?

III.2 Religious knowledge and language

> Silence is the language of God, all else is poor translation.
>
> (Rumi 1207–1273)

Language has played a key role in the spread of religious knowledge, and the processes by which religious knowledge is passed down, whether through spoken or written traditions. How these processes acquire or lose legitimacy and authority are rife with knowledge issues. But is language essential to knowing something religiously, or to sharing it? To what extent is

language a sufficient means for expressing and sharing religious knowledge?

Religious traditions often spread to new audiences through translation. What opportunities and risks arise from acquiring religious knowledge in a language other than the original?

Making connections

Translating religious texts

Chapter 4 explores how the practice of translation in large part depends on what is being translated. What determines the quality of translation of a religious text, as compared to other types of text? Is language fluency enough to qualify or give legitimacy to someone aspiring to be a translator of religious texts?

For discussion

Language learning in religious practice

 Search terms: Divine words language learning in religious practice

Closing the gap between religious teachings and one's personal practice can be a powerful motivator for learning the language in which a religious tradition developed. Consider this article about learners of Hebrew, Arabic and classical Tibetan who are hoping to connect with their religions, and the questions that are motivating them.

1. To what extent can the nuances of religious language be translated?

2. Does being able to understand a religious text in multiple languages:

   (a) promote new interpretations

   (b) promote more precise interpretation?

3. Which factors determine:

   (a) whether and how much people trust a translation of a religious text

   (b) how people might decide between competing translations without speaking the source language?

III.3 Religion and nature

> The present threat to mankind's survival can be removed only by a revolutionary change of heart in individual human beings. This change of heart must be inspired by religion in order to generate the will power needed for putting arduous new ideals into practice.
>
> (Toynbee quoted in Porritt 1984)

In the 21st century the task of explaining nature has largely fallen to science, but this is a relatively recent occurrence. Explanations of natural phenomena have occupied religious thought and practice, and been reflected in it, for millennia.

In 1967 Clarence Glacken published a fairly comprehensive account of the relationships between religion and nature in the Western world. This inspired other investigations into the environmental impacts of Western culture, religion, philosophy and science. These works portray "an epic struggle in Western culture between organicist and mechanist worldviews … between those who view the natural world as somehow sacred and having intrinsic value, and those who view the Earth as a way station to a heavenly realm beyond the Earth …" (Glacken 1967). Religion was viewed as both culprit and saviour in the environmental destruction story.

Also in 1967 Lynn White published an article that argued that Abrahamic religions (Judaism, Christianity and Islam) perpetuated modes of living that were inherently damaging to the environment, and argued, like Toynbee a decade later, that the solution to this problem "must also be essentially religious" (White 1967). In these authors' view, Buddhism or Paganism were more sensitive to nature than the prevailing monotheism. Combined with cultural forces of the era, the existential threat of the Cold War, and growing alarm about environmental degradation, this all made Westerners more curious about and receptive to non-Western religious traditions. Max Weber (1958) had already traced capitalism's unbridled consumption of natural resources to religious

ideas. Buddhism, Hinduism, Paganism and Indigenous belief systems and traditions showed up to offer more environmentally sensitive values and behaviours.

White's view was romantic and simplistic—Western religions were causing environmental destruction and Asian or Indigenous traditions were inherently nature-friendly. Yi Fu Tuan published an influential article in 1968 disputing these ideas, noting that deforestation predated Christianity, that Asian nations did not have a particularly impressive environmental record, and that many regions of the world had witnessed environmental decline, scaled for population numbers, well before the arrival of modern Western civilization.

Numerous scholars agree that nature plays a role in shaping religion, and vice versa, but there is comparatively less agreement on the important details. These include whether religion helps or hinders adaption to the environment, and the strength of this influence in relation to other cultural features. For decades, anthropologists have been investigating the role of religion and/or spiritual beliefs in Indigenous Peoples' ability to thrive in their environmental contexts. A common evolutionary argument is based on "the survival of the most sustainable"—or the idea that culture is a set of adaptations to a specific environment, and that religions evolved to guide people towards successful adaptations. This was the view of anthropologist Julian Steward, who studied Indigenous Peoples in North America's Great Basin. Another anthropologist, Marvin Harris, stated in the 1960s that the sacredness of cows in India was ecologically advantageous, serving to sustain the nutrient cycles of agro-ecosystems and the carrying capacity of the land. Harris subsequently generalized as follows.

> Beliefs and rituals that appear to the nonanthropological observer as wholly irrational, whimsical, and even maladaptive have been shown to possess important positive functions and to be the dependent variable of recurrent adaptive processes.
>
> (Harris 1971)

III. Methods and tools

overstating or understating the importance of religion in shaping human culture and our relationship with the environment. But the debate can shine a light on our way forward, perhaps offering hope against the existential threat of climate and ecological crises.

Making connections

Religion, Indigenous knowledge and nature

Ethnobotany is a sub-field of anthropology that originated in early 20th-century attempts by anthropologists to document the uses of plants by Indigenous Peoples. This research gradually expanded to study how plants were used to sustain the health of people and their communities, including their environment, sometimes through a spiritual connection. It is related to Indigenous knowledge systems generally, and traditional ecological knowledge (TEK) specifically, which involves the knowledge gained by Indigenous Peoples in their interactions with the environment over time. Ecological knowledge is sometimes inseparably connected to religious beliefs and practices.

Many leading scholars in the field have asserted that TEK can lead to sustainable use of natural resources. Some researchers also believed that within these religious practices were important spiritual truths that did more than advance environmental sustainability. This was a significant shift in how mainstream scientific culture saw Indigenous Peoples, but it was also criticized, as noted earlier, for its simplistic and romantic perspective.

This view has been criticized for being overly romantic and simplistic and for perpetuating conceptions of Indigenous Peoples as unscientific. It also ignores the stark fact of the dramatic decline in animal populations (tigers, rhinos and elephants, for example) that has been driven by demand in some traditional medicine systems. While anthropologists may celebrate nature-religions and Indigenous knowledge systems generally, it is another thing to use science to judge which of these are better or worse for the environment. Yet, that task may be inevitable, and much needed.

The relationship between nature and religion is difficult to untangle and loaded with political implications, especially so in the decolonizing and anti-colonial discourses. There are clearly individuals, groups and power structures that would benefit from

A number of terms refer to the category of religious and spiritual traditions that are described as more environmentally sensitive. These include natural religion, nature worship, Earth religion, Animism, Paganism, Heathenry, Druidry and Pantheism. This category has been historically viewed by Western culture as primitive, and in the case of Paganism even as evil, for failing to understand (or rejecting) the universe as God's creation and for worshipping elements of God's creation rather than God.

Romanticism, however, posed a strong counter to this perspective in 18th-century Europe, with leaders in Jean Jacques Rousseau, Samuel Taylor Coleridge and Johann Wolfgang von Goethe. They developed a philosophy of nature that rejected the "destructive, dualistic and reductionistic worldviews, which they considered to be a central feature of Western civilization" (Taylor 2005). Indigenous Peoples and nature religions were seen as more sensitive to nature, egalitarian and less greedy, an idea that was problematically known as the "noble savage"—uncorrupted humans outside of civilization and therefore beacons of humanity's innate goodness.

Contemporary Paganism has seen renewed interest in recent decades coinciding with alarm about environmental destruction. Groups of self-identified Neopagans have attempted to solidify their traditions into defined and self-contained religions, with nature-based spiritual paths, and with a sacred feminine principle instead of the male divine principle of the Abrahamic God. Paganism shares beliefs and politics with other nature revering movements such as Deep Ecology and Ecofeminism and has become an:

> attractive religious alternative for some non-indigenous moderns, perhaps especially environmentally concerned ones, who value indigenous religious cultures for their environmental values, but either found them largely inaccessible, or chose not to borrow from them because of the often strongly asserted view that efforts to 'borrow' from indigenous peoples actually constitute cultural theft.
>
> (Taylor 2005)

Nature religions were long condemned for being misinformed or downright evil and dangerous belief systems. The tables appear to have turned, with those who subscribe to nature religions criticizing mainstream religions for environmental failings.

Occupying much of the same political space as the nature-religionists are those who believe that scientific narratives could be framed as sacred narratives with life-revering ethics and spirituality. Instead of longing for and loving God, these narratives describe a spiritual attachment to the Earth, the biosphere or the cosmos. As examples, consider how adherents to the Gaia theory, developed by atmospheric scientist James Lovelock, conceive of the biosphere as a self-regulating organism with a necessary metaphysics of interdependence. Such narratives are being, to an extent, incorporated into existing world religions as well as into new emerging religions.

Perhaps it should be obvious why nature so consistently attracts human religious attention. In the late 19th century, E.B. Tylor coined the term "Animism" for the category of beliefs that the elements and forces of the natural world are inspirited; that is, they have spirits that engage with human beings. This was earlier referred to as totemism, considered by anthropologists as one of the earliest religious forms, that described a feeling of spiritual connection or kinship between human and non-human beings.

United Nations Earth Charter: Sustainability with spirituality

The Earth Charter is an international declaration of fundamental values and principles for a just, sustainable, and peaceful 21st-century global society. It was drafted by a United Nations-led process and endorsed by organizations representing millions of people globally. It is noteworthy for language that could be construed as religious, or nearly religious; as stated on the Earth Charter website: "the protection of Earth's vitality, diversity, and beauty is a sacred trust". It could also be described as a vision of humanism, with emphasis on human agency, stewardship, responsibility and cooperation. Humanity is tasked with choosing its future, which "at once holds great peril and great promise", and with recognizing "we are one human family and one Earth community with a common destiny" (www.earthcharter.org).

For discussion

Environmental issues

1. To what extent have ecosystems shaped religious knowledge, and vice versa?

2. Under what circumstances might environmental movements be considered religious?

3. How might religious doomsday prophecies and scientific environmental catastrophe predictions influence each other?

Henry David Thoreau was a naturalist, writer and leading figure in the Transcendentalism religious movement. His famous 1854 work, *Walden,* included the phrases "in wildness is the preservation of the world" and "Heaven is under our feet as well as over our heads", asserting his belief that nature was a source of spiritual truth. Thoreau was influential in calling for a spiritual basis for conservation and advocated establishing national forest preserves that would eventually become the world's first National Parks. He was a big influence on John Muir, a naturalist, author, environmental philosopher and pioneering advocate for the preservation of the wilderness. Muir was one of the first Europeans to explore Yosemite and the wider Sierra Nevada Mountains, and claimed to have found a sacred place where he could hear the "divine music" of nature. William Anderson described Muir as "the archetype of our oneness with the earth" (1990). Biographer Steven J. Holmes described him as "one of the patron saints of twentieth-century American environmental activity", who "profoundly shaped the very categories through which Americans understand and envision their relationships with the natural world" (1999). Another biographer, Donald Worster, said Muir believed his mission was "saving the American soul from total surrender to materialism" (2008).

↑ **Figure 6.5** *Twilight in the Wilderness* by Frederick Edwin Church (1860). Painted six years after Thoreau's *Walden* was published (1854), *Twilight in the Wilderness* marked a period in the United States of increasing interest in nature untouched by humankind, and the link between this purity of nature and spirituality. One contemporary critic described the painting as "Nature with folded hands, kneeling at her evening prayer" (Longfellow quoted in Sweeney 1989). Religious symbols include: a tree stump (bottom left) as a "wilderness altar" with a cross of branches and the outline of an angel; three trees (right) symbolizing the three crosses at Calvary. Others interpret the scene apocalyptically, as a metaphor for environmental abuse and forthcoming civil war.

Muir's vision of conservation was profoundly ideological to the extent of seeming religious, and clashed with the utilitarian perspective of Gifford Pinchot, the first Chief Forester of the United States. Muir emphasized the sacredness of natural environments and systems, while Pinchot argued for the responsible, sustainable and equitable use of natural resources for the benefit of all citizens. Whereas Muir might be characterized as a nature-religionist, Pinchot was a politically progressive Christian who wanted to help the poor, promote democracy and guard against powerful business interests that irresponsibly extracted natural resources. They thus had much in common, but Muir and Pinchot clashed over conflicting values and views on the management of public land. Whereas Pinchot argued that sheep should be able to graze the land in Yosemite, Muir considered this a desecration of a sacred space. In response, Pinchot believed Muir "had failed to apprehend the religious duty to develop natural resources for the good of humankind" (Taylor 2005).

Roderick Nash, a historian, described this clash as a "spiritual watershed" and evidence that the "wilderness cult" had become a powerful voice in environmental politics (1967). Muir's stance influenced conflicts over land management for decades around the world, often excluding the Indigenous People, the earliest stewards of the lands, from the debate entirely and displacing them from the natural resources they had relied on for millennia. The sad irony is that these peoples often had nature-oriented religious beliefs and traditions to begin with, which called for the sustainable and ethical use of land and natural resources.

Making connections

Conservation as colonialism

Section III.3 reveals how the Abrahamic world religions have been held up to scrutiny for allegedly underpinning extractive and/or anthropocentric framings of humankind's relationship with the environment. In Chapter 5 we engage with the idea that Indigenous knowledge in general, and traditional ecological knowledge (TEK) in particular, have been increasingly embraced by the conservation community.

"May we live long and die out"

The Voluntary Human Extinction Movement aims to phase out the human race by voluntarily ceasing to reproduce, to allow Earth's biosphere to return to good health. To what extent is this movement religious? Follow the link to find out more.

 Search terms: VHEMT org

For reflection

Tackling challenges

1. To what extent has religious knowledge been able to remain relevant to changing world realities?

2. To what extent can we say that religions promoted beneficent or destructive relationships with nature?

3. Are some religions intrinsically more environmentally friendly than others?

4. How do the doctrines and traditions of different religions affect whether they can help or adapt to the climate emergency?

5. Do some religions have inherent advantages or disadvantages in guiding communities towards sustainable ways of living?

6. Do unprecedented environmental challenges call for:

    (a) the production of new religious knowledge

    (b) the reinterpretation of existing religious knowledge

    (c) something else?

Case study

Natural disasters and explanations in religious knowledge

Natural disasters are frequently called acts of God, even by insurance companies. The devastating consequences of earthquakes and volcanic eruptions posed a challenge to theologians long before science could explain them. How did religious explanations account for these events, and how did natural disasters shape religious knowledge?

Jelle Zelinga de Boer, professor of earth science and co-author of *Earthquakes in Human History*, notes that ancient Palestine and indeed the whole region now known as the Holy Land is a "tectonically unstable region", with evidence of frequent and substantial earthquakes throughout history (de Boer quoted in Tippet, 2005).

Disasters lead to a frequent religious question: where was God when nature destroyed human lives? This question is answered in different ways across the range of religious and spiritual traditions.

Some interpretations of natural disasters frequently explain them as a form of punishment for human misconduct. These interpretations have evolved over time. Earlier explanations did not invoke an omnipotent God's justice, but instead the lashing out of animal spirits underground. De Boer describes how one Japanese tradition interprets natural disasters not as punishments but as naturalistic phenomena caused by, for example, a giant catfish in the Sugami Bay that moves and causes earthquakes.

A set of very powerful earthquakes hit Missouri, USA between December 1811 and January 1812. Following the earthquakes was a huge increase in participation at local churches. Some estimates suggest that 15,000 new members joined the Methodist Church at that time. The earthquakes continued, getting weaker and weaker, for two more years. Eventually many of the new church members stopped going, so much so that the preachers called them earthquake Christians.

> " Woe to the men on earth who dwell, nor dread th' Almighty's frown; when God doth all his wrath reveal, and shower his judgments down. Lo! from their seats the mountains leap, the mountains are not found, transported far into the deep and in the ocean drowned. Who then shall live and face the throne, and face the judge severe? When heaven and earth are fled and gone, O where shall I appear? Firm in the all-destroying shock may view the final scene; for lo! the everlasting Rock is cleft to take us in.
>
> (Christian hymn, 62nd song of John Wesley's Collected Hymns) "

On 1 November (All Saints Day) 1755 a powerful earthquake struck Lisbon, Portugal, just as church services were overflowing. As the churches and other structures collapsed, 30,000 people died within six minutes. Fires and a tsunami caused the total death toll to exceed 100,000 in the days following. John Wesley saw it as an especially severe punishment on a sinful population, but that was not a belief widely shared by the people of Lisbon and Portugal. Enlightenment philosophers such as Kant and Voltaire questioned what kind of God would permit such devastation and strike especially the devout families. The Lisbon clergy were mocked for attempting to recover crucifixes and other icons even as the burning churches collapsed. The quake challenged Europeans' belief in a benevolent God, weakened the power of the Catholic Church in Portugal and, according to De Boer, may have sent lasting reverberations through Europe as a world power (Portugal had a significant empire) was destroyed overnight.

Voltaire's 1756 poem on the disaster of Lisbon ridiculed the idea of a just God and interrogated the idea that "whatever is, is right". There are still many people who share Voltaire's philosophy today.

OH WRETCHED man, earth-fated to be cursed;
Abyss of plagues, and miseries the worst!
Horrors on horrors, griefs on griefs must show,
That man's the victim of unceasing woe,
And lamentations which inspire my strain,
Prove that philosophy is false and vain.
Approach in crowds, and meditate awhile
Yon shattered walls, and view each ruined pile,
Women and children heaped up mountain high,
Limbs crushed which under ponderous marble lie;
Wretches unnumbered in the pangs of death,
Who mangled, torn, and panting for their breath,
Buried beneath their sinking roofs expire,
And end their wretched lives in torments dire.
Say, when you hear their piteous, half-formed cries,
Or from their ashes see the smoke arise,
Say, will you then eternal laws maintain,
Which God to cruelties like these constrain?
Whilst you these facts replete with horror view,
Will you maintain death to their crimes was due?

(Voltaire 1755)

IV. ETHICS

It may be obvious to many of our readers that religious knowledge has sometimes greatly enhanced, and at other times utterly devastated, the wellbeing of peoples, nations and cultures throughout history. Religion is frequently brought up in casual as well as formal conversations as necessarily entangled with forces of conflict, conquest, subjugation and imperialism. Whether God exists or whether religion is a force for good or evil are interesting questions but not quite within the scope of TOK. Rather, we ask questions such as "How sure are we that God exists?" and "How can we untangle causation from correlation when looking at the consequences and implications of religious knowledge?"

> Our situation at the beginning of the 21st century is like that of Europe at the beginning of the 17th century. Then, as now, the landscape was littered with the debris of religious conflict. It is fair to say that religion did not distinguish itself at that time. The secularization of Europe grew directly out of the failure of religion to meet the challenge of change. As one who deeply believes in the humanizing power of faith and the stark urgency of coexistence at a time when weapons of mass destruction are accessible to extremist groups, I do not think we can afford to fail again. Time and time again in recent years we have been reminded that religion is not what the European Enlightenment thought it would become: mute, marginal, and mild. It is fire, and like fire, it warms but it also burns. And we are the guardians of the flame.
>
> (Rabbi Sacks 2003)

IV.1 Religious education for tolerance and mutual understanding

Do we have an ethical responsibility to gain knowledge of different religions to help us understand the world and those around us? This question seems straightforward but in fact involves a few assumptions that have implications relating to the ethics of knowledge and religion.

The idea that the modern state, through a secular approach to the study of different religions, can promote tolerance and intercultural understanding is fairly widespread among politicians and educators, especially in the West. But where does this idea come from? Why is religious tolerance assumed to be the result of an education about religious *differences* rather than an education in religious *belief*? And finally, to what extent is this kind of education about religion value-neutral?

Tracing the intellectual roots of this idea, Tenzan Eaghll (writing in Stoddard, Martin 2017) suggests that this is in fact a close variation on Christian ecumenism—the effort of different Christian churches to promote mutual understanding and develop good relations. Arising out of an urgent need to calm tensions between Christian denominations in the midst of the Reformation, it is understandable why it was an attractive idea, that exploring

the commonalities among religions can help overcome differences—be they cultural or political. But to what extent is this applicable on a global level today? Given its origins in a specific context, Eaghll argues, this approach to religious education should not be uncritically exported globally, at least not as a politically neutral option.

What alternatives are there? Rather than learning about the different dimensions of religious practice and belief through descriptions of the rituals and teachings of Sikhs, Jains, Jews or Buddhists, we would … do what? Eaghll, for example, suggests a *critical* approach to examining how religion functions ideologically in society. Rather than assuming that exposure to descriptions about religious diversity will lead to tolerance and empathy, he suggests we should analyse how religion is conceptualized and categorized, how it is used and misused, and how power and politics affect all of this.

So, revisiting the question at the beginning of this section, perhaps we should be asking instead: what kind of knowledge about religion do we have an ethical responsibility to pursue? And what kind of approach to learning about religion is in service of a global ethic of justice? In relation to these questions, consider how the ways you have learned about different religions—including this chapter—have influenced your attitudes and beliefs.

IV.2 Morality and religion

> "
> With or without religion, good people can behave well and bad people can do evil; but for good people to do evil—that takes religion.
>
> (Weinberg 1999)
> "

Is religion necessary for morality? To claim so would be to suggest that humans lack a moral compass, that in the absence of divine authority about right and wrong, and without fear of judgment and punishment, we would behave in immoral ways. To claim the opposite would mean that humans do have something like a moral compass, independent of religious teaching and belief, and we would need to explain where that capacity comes from.

Some critics of religion—especially those who identify as anti-theists—echo the sentiments expressed by Weinberg above. They cite examples where religion has been used to justify slavery, acts of terrorism, and racial and sexual oppression, to show that it is not uncommon for people to behave immorally while claiming to have God on their side.

One approach to answering the question of whether morality requires religion is to consider whether societies have become more or less moral as religiosity has declined. A common observation is that in contemporary societies where religion has retreated, morality has not, because social institutions and humanist traditions have filled that space. Indeed, many moral ideas have flourished despite fewer people believing in God. But this argument fails to distinguish causation from correlation; it may well be that a rising tide of economic wellbeing simultaneously causes a decline in religion and a rise in a civic and humanist ethos, with no causal mechanism between the two.

Even if belief in God is diminishing, religion can offer a moral imagination that is supernatural but nonetheless relevant to humanity. This is the idea of being religious not to believe but to wonder. Religious fables, stories and morals speak to how humankind imagines and navigates the world, teaching us about us—covering such varied topics as food, war, leadership, family, economics, law-making and politics.

For discussion

What is the role of doubt in religious knowledge and morality?

"Our ancestors acknowledged doubt while practicing faith. We moderns are drawn to faith while practicing doubt." (Gopnik 2015)

1. (a) To what extent are doubt and faith mutually exclusive positions in religious knowledge?

   (b) Does this mutual exclusivity apply in the case of other AOKs?

2. What types of knowledge, across TOK, require assumptions and acts of faith to be valid?

3. Is there a type of knowledge that is destroyed when questioned, and should be protected against questioning? If so, who should be allowed to decide what that knowledge is, and what are the implications for governance, human rights and politics?

Box 6.2: Secular alternatives to religious ethics

In the absence of religion, or the guidance of God, what systems might we have for guiding human behaviour? A few alternatives apply. One example is consequentialism, which asserts that it is the consequences of one's conduct that form the basis for moral judgments. The emphasis on consequences means that laws, guidelines and rules are secondary; that is, they can be violated if the consequences justify it. This is in contrast to deontological ethics which put rules, behaviour and duty as central. The moral philosopher

Peter Singer described consequentialism as to "start not with moral rules, but with goals, [and] assess actions by the extent to which they further those goals" (Singer 2010).

A second path towards morality is freethought, a philosophy that asserts that science, logic and reason are the basis for truth and opinion, as opposed to authority, tradition or dogma. Freethinkers form their own ideas and opinions, unrestrained by deference to authority, social convention and tradition. They are thus frequently at odds with religious authorities. Depending on where they live, this can invite violent consequences.

A third alternative held up to religious ethics is secular humanism, which asserts that human beings can be ethical and moral without religion or God, that humans are not inherently good or evil, nor superior to nature. It emphasizes human responsibility and the ethical consideration of the consequences of human decisions, primarily through science and philosophy. Individuals must scrutinize political or religious ideologies, rather than accept them based on faith, authority or tradition.

The moral values discourse extends beyond, for example, gay marriage and abortion to the issue of who, or what, is the fundamental authority of what is right and wrong. As religion is increasingly removed from schools, and social news feeds and media complicate people's relationship with evidence, are we at risk of being left with moral relativism? Political polarization in some contexts has led to hyper-religious and hyper-atheist posturing that is hard to make sense of. And in 2020, if someone disagrees with you, they are increasingly seen as not just wrong, but immoral too.

IV.3 Liberation theology

Liberation theology emphasizes that social justice generally, and the liberation of the poor specifically, are important steps towards religious goals, and that justice on Earth (and not just in Heaven) is a key part of this. It developed largely in the context of left-leaning Latin American Christian politics, but has had impacts globally, from South Africa to Palestine, India and the US Civil Rights movement.

Liberation theology today closely intersects with the politics of anti-colonialism, socialism and feminism, and takes on localized anti-oppression agendas in the different contexts where it manifests. It grew in response to the subjugation and forced "civilization" by missionaries of colonized peoples. It is therefore distinct and contrary to religious doctrines that value the mass-spreading of religious knowledge, in that it centres the agency of the poor and marginalized identities. For this reason it has been described as a Marxist approach to Christianity.

Liberation theology is notable from other social justice paradigms in that its theologians have frequently argued that suffering is the cause as well as the result of oppression. Those individuals or communities that exhibit violence, aggression or intolerance are said themselves to be suffering, because only suffering can explain the departure of humankind from its naturally compassionate state.

IV.4 Religion and violence

Religious language has been used to justify violent actions, such as war, in the name of righteousness and justice, good fighting evil. This can obscure the complex causes of a conflict, including but not limited to access to resources and markets, matters of identity and failures of diplomacy. "Holy war" classifications of armed conflict are particularly problematic because sentiments of divine authority and righteousness serve to reduce fighters' restraint by dehumanizing the enemy. This has led to gross violations of human rights. Holy wars do not recognize human limits, including the possibility that human leaders might be in error. Dissenters are attacked, and those asking for nuance are dismissed as having sympathy for the enemy.

S. AVGVSTINVS

The concept of "just war" traces back to a 1600-year-old idea of ethical war formulated by St Augustine. This idea reconciled his Christian ethical ideals with what seemed to be necessary violence. Augustine's five basic criteria of just war are as follows.

1. Do we have just cause?

2. Do we have the proper authority to carry it out?

3. Is violence our last resort?

4. Does it have a reasonable chance of success?

5. Can we conduct war with proportionality, so that the means justify the ends?

Point 5, the principle of proportionality, requires that civilian lives on both sides are protected, and has proved problematic for political and military leaders. How many lost civilian lives are too many? It is an echo of the cost-benefit analysis problem we encounter in Chapters 7 and 8.

The idea of justice is often talked about in terms that seem opposed to the idea of peace. Justice invokes punishment, reparations and difficult changes, whereas peace invokes harmony, balance and compassion. Instead of just war, John Paul Lederach argues that we should understand and articulate the notion of a just peace.

IV.4.1 Moral ambiguity in war

 Search terms: onbeing Elshtain Lederach Orange Justice and just war

The Vietnam War started out with the endorsement of US ethicists and theologians, but by 1971 even the US Catholic bishops had lost their resolve. They declared that the means of fighting the war could no longer justify its goal. Religious morality had run up against consequentialism, and lost.

Michael Orange, a US Marine Corps veteran and author, offers the perspective of a soldier in the Vietnam War who came to believe that what he was doing was morally wrong. But he has also said "[t]hank God it was a morally ambiguous war". Morally unambiguous wars "should scare all of us" (Orange quoted in Tippet 2001).

Compare the idea of "just war" with *Ahiṃsā*, variously translated as compassion or non-violence, a key virtue in Buddhism, Jainism and Hinduism. As a concept, *Ahiṃsā* recognizes the spiritual energy of all living beings and asserts that to hurt another is to hurt oneself. Mahatma Gandhi famously channelled this belief into a political strategy in the Indian independence movement against the British. It also influenced the thinking and strategies of Martin Luther King and James Bevel in the American Civil Rights movement. How *Ahiṃsā* sits with the need for violent self-defence is a tension explored in the classical Hindu texts *Mahābhārata* and *Ramayana*.

IV.4.2 Buddhist monks and military coups

> "
> Concepts such as truth, justice, and compassion cannot be dismissed as trite when these are often the only bulwarks which stand against ruthless power.
>
> (Aung San Suu Kyi 1995)
> "

IV. Ethics

In 1962, generals seized power in Myanmar (formerly known as Burma) in a coup d'état that marked the beginning of decades of totalitarian military rule. Initially, this regime sought to establish a secular socialist state, but it could not ignore the deeply entrenched cultural and religious traditions centred around Buddhism, which have been central to Burmese government and culture for centuries.

The generals have had a tense and challenging relationship with the Buddhist monastic order, known as the sangha. They have donated money to monasteries and sought the endorsement of religious leaders, but they have also been accused of periodically killing, imprisoning or torturing monks and destroying monasteries. The monks have marched in defiance and refused offerings, as they did in the September 2007 Saffron Revolution.

Non-violent moral protest: *Patta-nikkujjana-kamma*

Patta-nikkujjana-kamma appears to be a simple act with nothing obviously intimidating about it—it involves monks simply overturning their bowls—but to those who understand the implications it is an act of moral condemnation, of peaceful protest from ordinarily detached monks moved to seek justice. One of the tenets of Theravada Buddhism is that monks must live in relation with the rest of the society through alms, or donations of food and other necessities.

Patta-nikkujjana-kamma is therefore a public protest that takes place in front of the offender, communicating the message that "even if we were to starve, we would not accept your offerings". The moral grievances must be addressed before life can continue.

For discussion and reflection

Now that you have reached the end of this section on religion and morality, consider the following questions.

1. **(a)** How would you describe the relationship between religion and morality?

   (b) How is morality known in religion, and by whom?

2. To what extent are the different religions similar or different in this regard?

3. Have you ever noticed religion condone immoral and/or unethical beliefs and actions? If so:

   (a) how did this dissonance occur

   (b) why was it condoned?

7 Natural sciences

"There is grandeur in this view of life …," writes Charles Darwin in the concluding sentence of On the Origin of Species, and this chapter tunes into that sense of wonder of the natural world as seen through science, the collaborative enterprise by which we become knowledgeable about our planet, the universe and ourselves. In this chapter we will develop tools to critically examine the extent to which science has special reporting rights on nature. This chapter also explores and recognizes science's more mundane dimensions: the humble and persistent effort going into messy and demanding scientific work. Finally, we aim to develop the sensitivity and capacity that informed citizens' need to navigate an increasingly scientific policy landscape.

I. SCOPE

What is science, and what is not? Looking at the origin of the word—its etymology—does not help us very much, as the Latin *scientia* means, simply, knowledge. You might know it as biology, chemistry, physics and the other subjects in group 4 of the IB Diploma Programme. Science refers to a body of knowledge as well as a method for acquiring that knowledge. The term's origins in the modern Western intellectual tradition, and its conflation with knowledge to the exclusion of other knowledges, has sometimes been a source of trouble. Humans have long been asking questions about the natural world and those knowledge-making practices started long before European modernity. This chapter explores the relatively recent human activity called science, the specific context of its origin, its global reach, its current challenges and the knowledge that it brings.

If the natural sciences were described using the metaphor of a map, we would see that it does not have a fixed territory. Even a term such as "nature" is a domain of contestable boundaries. Sir Isaac Newton's law of universal gravitation expanded the domain of nature by unifying the terrestrial and celestial realms, showing that the same forces act on apples on the ground and on the moon in the cosmos. More recently, astrobiology has been looking for life using eyes in the skies and robotic arms that probe worlds across our solar system. Closer to home, the debate over the scope of science touches on the problem of drawing a boundary between nature and culture—a debate relevant to the human sciences as well.

Another way to approximate the boundaries of natural science is to consider not what it applies to, but how science is and ought to be done. For example, one aim is to distinguish science from pseudo-science, which is what Karl Popper called the demarcation problem (demarcation means to draw a line between things). Popper proposed an answer to this problem, arguing that something was scientific if it could be falsified; that is, tested and proven false. This idea was called falsificationism, and has had a lasting effect on how we think about certainty and the nature of scientific knowledge.

Falsificationism tells us that scientific facts and theories can only ever be proven false, not true, and any claim to the contrary is more likely to be telemarketing than serious science. Scientific knowledge after Popper is tentative, falsifiable and replicable. Or is it? Later in this chapter we explore the extent to which Popper's definition is a good or even viable way to define science.

Box 7.1: More on falsificationism

It is practically impossible to prove that a universal statement is true because to do so would require observing every possible example across space and time. It is comparatively easy to show that a theory is not true. Consider the statement "All swans are white", which would require us to see all swans in all possible spaces before we accept it as true.

The obvious problem with this is that one black swan could be hiding somewhere. Even if we observe millions of white swans, meticulously and perseveringly, the best we can say is that the hypothesis is provisionally accepted. In contrast, we can more easily prove that "Not all swans are white", by finding one black swan. Therefore scientists, according to Popper's widely influential work, should focus on contradicting these universal laws, not on verifying them.

However, even the theory "All swans are white", which we know to be untrue, is still testable through empirical observation. This makes it an example of Popperian science, not pseudo-science. A theory that "All swans are secretly communicating with each other about overthrowing humankind", in contrast, is not falsifiable—the existence of this secret communication cannot be proven false. Could advancements in technology change this in the future? Advancements in technology and methods do play a role in separating what is science from what is not.

Popper labelled the set of non-falsifiable claims pseudo-science. A surprisingly large set of accepted scholarship at the time of his writing, such as psychology and astronomy, fell under this category. Chapter 8 explores where that leaves the human sciences. Later, this chapter questions to what extent science actually progresses through falsification.

While there are significant problems with falsification as a demarcation criterion, it remains as important as ever to be able to tell the difference between science and pseudo-science.

How else could we distinguish the methodology, history and body of knowledge of science? Why is science's account of reality so often given greater authority than other accounts?

For discussion and reflection

How would you map out the scope of the natural sciences?

You can do this activity working on your own, with a partner or in a small group. See if you can map out science, drawing its boundary with other domains of knowledge, such as culture, religion and politics. If you are working with others, each of you should make your own map. Then consider the following questions.

1. Where does science overlap with the other domains?

2. What happens in the overlapping zones?

3. Where is the boundary particularly clear, wiggly, dotted or blurry? Describe what it means and why you have drawn or imagined it this way.

If you are doing this exercise with a partner or in a group, compare your maps and share what you identify as significant similarities and differences between them.

Next, consider the following questions.

4. In your understanding, what makes scientific knowledge different from other types of knowledge?

5. How would you describe the relationship between science and the unknown?

Whatever our map of science may look like, there are always scientists working at the edge of that map, pushing the frontier. The 2018 documentary "The Most Unknown" introduces us to nine frontier scientists from different fields.

 Search terms: Cheney The Most Unknown

6. Is there something that makes all of the different activities and inquiries in the documentary "science"?

7. What did you notice about the ability of scientists to talk about and understand each other's work?

8. How would you describe the scientists' attitudes towards knowing and not knowing?

Practising skills: Constructing arguments

Supposing that you drew a map in the exercise above where science is distinct from other ways of understanding the world. Consider: how is scientific knowledge different from other types of knowledge? Brainstorm a few claims you can make as answers to this question. Keep in mind that your claim should be something that can be disputed and argued with. An example would be, "Scientific knowledge is more reliable as compared with other types of knowledge, such as knowledge from personal experience".

Choosing one of those claims, construct an argument in favour of your claim. For the claim above, a supporting argument might say that the reliability of scientific knowledge is due to the methods used to produce it.

Share your claim and argument with a partner. Together, consider how you might improve your claims and arguments, and what are the characteristics of a good argument.

II. PERSPECTIVES

[handwritten margin note: practice of forming theories or making conclusions based on reasoning or speculation. argued → prone to bias + error]

This section explores the rich and varied role of perspective in the natural sciences. There are different perspectives about how science changes over time, and how it came to be what it is today. Zooming in, this section looks at:

- how scientists manage disagreements, and what they tend to disagree about

- how experts and non-experts engage in public controversies about science

- critiques coming from perspectives on science that have a history of being excluded from the scientific practice and discourse.

II.1 Is knowledge power?

Scientific knowledge has been instrumental in enabling humanity, for better or worse, to dominate the planet. It has been said that knowledge is power. But what kind of power is it? To look more closely at this, we turn to the views of Francis Bacon who is often wrongly credited as having first said the words "knowledge is power". Although he did not say that word for word, it is likely he agreed with it.

[handwritten: FRANCIS BACON]

Francis Bacon was an influential statesman and scholar in the 17th century who championed the use of experimentation as a way to gain knowledge about the world. Specifically, he emphasized that scientific knowledge should be gained through empirical observation of nature, in a systematic method that involved sceptical scientists "exploring nature for hidden truths". Bacon was fond of metaphors and often described the natural world in gendered terms, portraying masculine scientists bravely venturing out and extracting the truths "locked in nature's bosom". These writings have come under criticism from some observers in recent years (see II.7 on feminist critiques of science). He also argued against the use of conjecture—what might

[handwritten margin note: accredited as experimentation as valid or method]

be called "armchair theorizing"—that had been widespread in Western scholarship since Aristotle's time. His ideas are widely accepted as having contributed to the development of the scientific methodologies, and to the development of methodical systems of categorizing knowledge.

[handwritten annotations on figure: pillars of Hercules; venturing beyond the known limits of knowledge; go no further; leaving; Med Sea; indirect observation or experimentation; returning]

↑ **Figure 7.1** Title page for *Novum Organum Scientiarum*, 1645, by Francis Bacon (1561–1626)

The metaphors indicated on the title page of his work *Novum Organum Scientiarum* are significant and revealing (Figure 7.1). The page shows the pillars of Hercules on each side of the Strait of Gibraltar in the Mediterranean Sea. The pillars are said to have been inscribed with the phrase *ne plus ultra*, which translates from the Latin to "go no further/nothing lies beyond". The galleons, one leaving and one returning, indicate the act of venturing beyond the known limits of knowledge of the ancient world. At the bottom, an inscription of Biblical origin in Latin says *multi pertransibunt et augebitur scientia*: "many shall go to and fro, and knowledge shall be increased".

Returning to the question of the power of scientific knowledge, Bacon would have probably imagined humanity's dominion over nature, rather than our domination of it.

> ... I would address one general admonition to all: that they consider what are the true ends of knowledge, and that they seek it not either for pleasure of the mind, or for contention, or for superiority to others, or for profit, or fame, or power, or any of these inferior things: but for the benefit and use of life; and that they perfect and govern it in charity.
>
> [Bacon quoted in Sargent 1999]

II.2 Change over time: Two historical perspectives on science

How does science change over time? The different answers to this question reveal valuable insights for practising scientists as well as those learning to make judgments about scientific claims. Our understanding of how modern science is done was challenged just a few decades ago, when Thomas Kuhn wrote *The Structure of Scientific Revolutions*, in 1962, arguing that science proceeds through periods of normalcy interrupted by revolutions, rather than in a linear way. Kuhn used the term "paradigm shift" to describe these revolutions that produced new ways of thinking and doing within scientific disciplines. He also argued that science is not as objective as was

(and is) commonly accepted, because scientific truths are in fact defined by what a community of scientists agree to be true. This was vastly different from the prevailing view of science at the time, often called the "Whig history" of science, as a heroic march towards fundamental truths, that saw the success of science as self-evident and inevitable.

Whig history

Whig history was a positivist philosophy of science as marching forward heroically, adding new truths to an existing and ever-growing stock of truths. Progress was seen as guaranteed by the scientific method and human ability.

Why did Kuhn dismiss scientific objectivity? To understand this, we must understand how Kuhn described scientific change. He saw scientists as people who accepted a paradigm that accounted for accepted truths, concepts and investigative practices (that is, they had been *encultured* into a scientific paradigm by a scientific community). A new idea or discovery was judged by how similar it was to the existing theories and discoveries, and judgments about similarity are fundamentally subjective, according to Kuhn.

This might sound strange, especially because it clashes with the widespread belief that science is about objectively proving theories wrong (falsification). Remember, Popper argued that a single reproducible anomaly (a result inconsistent with a theory) is enough to reject the theory. Kuhn is famous because he showed that science does not work that way, because anomalies are more often "ignored or explained away". The case study below gives several examples of this. Why do scientists hold onto theories when results contradict them? Kuhn showed that it was only when anomalies really started to pile up and could no longer be ignored, especially if a new theory could explain them, that a scientific theory was said to be in crisis. A new paradigm was then accepted or looked for—the scientific revolution part. How exactly this happened differed from case to case, and could be influenced by non-scientific factors such as money, fame, personalities and national interest.

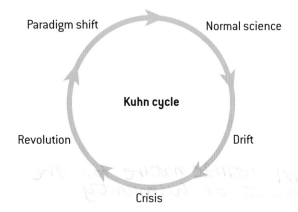

↑ **Figure 7.2** The Kuhn cycle

> Normal science does not aim at novelty but at clearing up the status quo. It tends to discover what it expects to discover.
>
> (Hacking 2012)

How does Hacking's view in the quote above compare with Popper's view of science?

How influential was Kuhn? Debates about this raged for years after his book was published, but his views have been influential. Before Kuhn presented his theory, we had ideals about what science aspires to do. From Kuhn, we have a perspective about what scientists actually do. To understand and evaluate his view we can examine case studies of paradigm shifts, and analyse the hows and whys of their occurrence.

Examples from the Western scientific tradition of the last few centuries include:

- the Copernican revolution in 1542, which showed that the Earth is not the centre of the universe, but instead revolves around the sun

- Newton's model of mechanics replacing Aristotle's theories in 1687
- the chemical revolution in 1783, in which Lavoisier's theories replaced the phlogiston theory
- Charles Darwin's theory of natural selection in 1859
- the germ theory of disease in 1880
- quantum mechanics replacing classical mechanics in 1905
- the theory of electromagnetic radiation in 1905
- Einstein's general relativity replacing Newton's gravity in 1919.

Based on this list, natural science appears to have been calm for over a century. Does that mean we are overdue for a revolution in the natural sciences? Or could it be that the natural sciences have become exceptionally good at dispelling anomalies? Or that revolutions are shorter, faster or less disruptive?

By some estimates, *The Structure of Scientific Revolutions* has sold around 1.5 million copies worldwide, attracting a readership well outside the history and philosophy of science. A work of such reputation is expected to attract some criticism. One critical perspective, for example, asserts that Kuhn's theory was based on theoretical and conceptual shifts in physics, which should not be generalized to other disciplines. Another argues that revolutions in science are more common and less dramatic than Kuhn describes. Notable revolutions in science have had comparably minor elements of crisis or revisionism, such as the discovery of the structure of DNA. Yet, few would go back to defending the Whig view of science. As we continue into the 21st century, with eScience, data-driven methodologies and blockchain workflows, we will need new theories of scientific change beyond falsificationism and paradigm shifts, that account for contemporary challenges and insights.

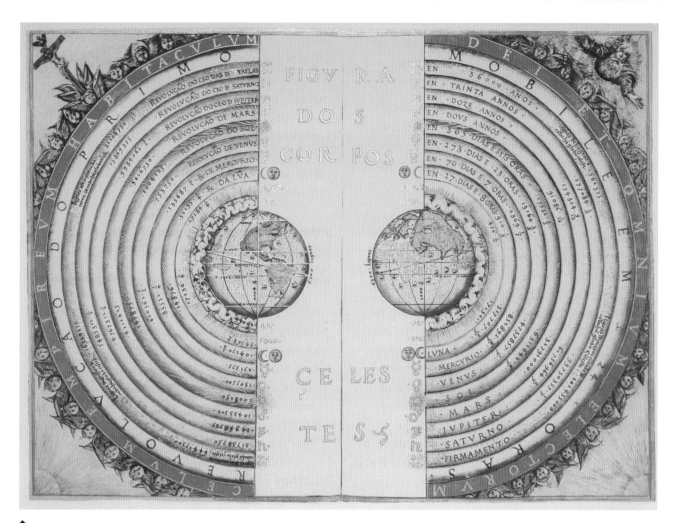

↑ **Figure 7.3** An illustration of the Ptolemaic geocentric system by Portuguese cosmographer and cartographer Bartolomeu Velho, 1568

Practising skills: Evaluating claims and arguments

"In science, when new knowledge replaces old knowledge, we can be confident that it is an improvement."

What assumptions can you identify here about how science works and changes over time? Consider what Popper and Kuhn might say in response to this claim, and why.

Consider also different meanings of "improvement". Is new knowledge an improvement because it is more true, or because it is better able to explain phenomena? What is the difference between these two arguments?

Case study

What do Neptune, neutrinos and the planet Vulcan have in common?

"Bad science"

Following the discovery of Uranus in 1781, astronomers quickly found that it did not

orbit the sun according to Newton's laws of gravity. This strange result was replicated numerous times. Had the terms of falsification been applied strictly, Newton's theory would have been compromised. But the astronomers held onto it. Could we say they had "faith" in Newton's theory? Perhaps that would be going too far. But they were certainly not doing what Popper says they should have been doing.

Instead, astronomers postualted the existence of a hidden planet that was pulling Uranus. This appeared to explain Uranus's strange orbit and, if true, would also redeem Newton's theory. But it was all rather outlandish. In 1846, the astrophysicist Urbain Le Verrier even made a prediction about where this hidden planet would be. Such stubbornness jarred with Popper's views of good science, and indeed, the French observatories of the time were unwilling to assist Le Verrier in his search for the hidden planet, so he asked friends in Germany for help. One night they set their telescopes in the direction Le Verrier had predicted and, within a half hour, spotted another planet, exactly where it was supposed to be. Le Verrier's stubbornness led to the discovery of a new planet, Neptune, and upheld Newton's universal laws of gravity.

This was a roaring success for Le Verrier and Newtonian physics. However, it was not the end of the story. For many years, astronomers had known that Mercury's orbit was also off the course predicted by Newtonian physics. And so Le Verrier tried the same trick, predicting in 1859 that another hidden planet, this time close to the sun, was pulling Mercury off the predicted course. That planet was called Vulcan, and was to Mercury what Neptune had been to Uranus—except Vulcan was never discovered. For decades, astronomers hunted for the planet, carrying expensive powerful telescopes around the world to be at the right place at the right time (during a solar eclipse). They stopped trying in 1877 after Le Verrier's death, but the conundrum persisted for decades: if Vulcan did not exist,

there was a fundamental mismatch between what Newton's physics predicted and what was observed. Yet, Newton's physics was not falsified, at least not until Einstein's alternative theory was "verified" in 1919. General relativity went on to make sense of Mercury's strange orbit, along with many other anomalies, that eventually led to the paradigm shift away from Newton's physics.

Box 7.2: Should we rule out verification?

Verificationism has a bad reputation for some good reasons—proving a scientific theory to be true is problematic, and so scientists are better off focusing on falsification. However, attempts at verification can help resolve a scientific crisis by legitimizing a new theory and precipitating a paradigm shift. This was the case, for example, in May 1919, when Einstein's predictions were verified by Arthur Eddington using measurements taken during a solar eclipse. Eddington took pictures of stars that appeared to be out of place; their position was predicted by general relativity, which said that light rays curve due to the sun's gravitational field. The quality of Eddington's measurements was questioned but the event still ushered in a paradigm shift. The news was published all over the world. Though anomalies against Newtonian physics had accumulated for years, the theory was never falsified— contrary to Popper's scientific method— until Eddington "verified" general relativity. So, while verification does not mean a theory is proven true, it can help scientists accept that a theory is good enough for now.

The question for us is: in not rejecting Newton's physics earlier, despite the mounting anomalies, were these scientists practising "bad science"?

In the first example, their unwillingness to reject a theory resulted in success—Neptune was discovered, and Newton was vindicated. In the second example, this approach failed. Both examples could be considered "bad science" according to the falsification criteria set out by Popper, and both are more aligned with Kuhn's view of science than Popper's. Yet, falsification continues to shape how we think about scientific practice. Imagine an alternative timeline in which Einstein's general relativity never came along, and astronomers and astrophysicists continued to believe an unseen planet Vulcan was responsible for Mercury's unexplainable orbit. How long and how many more anomalies would it take for them to give up on Newton's physics? More interestingly, what Vulcans like this exist today, allowing us to cling onto flawed paradigms? The history of science suggests that this is very much something to look out for.

Pauli and the neutrino

In 1930 Wolfgang Pauli wrote to a friend: "I have done a terrible thing, I have postulated a particle that cannot be detected" (quoted in Sutton 1992). He was referring to the neutrino, a tiny subatomic particle. It was "terrible" because science was supposed to be concerned with falsification, and not predictions that could not be tested. Postulating things that might be true but cannot be tested was considered bad science. But we saw how that approach succeeded in the discovery of Neptune. Why was Pauli in such despair?

He wasn't really. He may have suspected that technology would eventually allow equipment to detect the neutrino.

Perhaps Pauli was inspired by Le Verrier, whose discovery of Neptune temporarily saved Newtonian physics. Pauli faced a similar challenge: a fundamental principle of physics, the conservation of energy, was being questioned because of anomalies detected in radioactive decay. Energy was being "lost" somewhere, but if Pauli could account for it, he might save the theory. He wrote: "I have hit upon a desperate remedy to save the energy theorem" (quoted in Brown 1978).

That remedy seemed a preposterous prediction of a new particle with almost zero mass and no electric charge, called the neutrino. The best equipment of the time, particle detectors, had no way of detecting such a chargeless particle. It was like proposing Neptune, but knowing that no one alive could find it. Strangely, the physics community embraced Pauli's hypothesis. It would take almost three decades for scientists to detect the neutrino, using new methods and technologies, including a nuclear reactor—but it turned out that neutrinos are literally everywhere. Does the result justify the means?

Pauli suggested something invisible to save a theory. Le Verrier did the same. Knowing this, how much do you think falsification and observability matter as guides to "good science"? At what point can a theory be deemed falsified? What would happen if we stuck to the idealized version of science—or was this bad science necessary for scientific knowledge to "progress"? These are of course rhetorical questions, but they might affect how we think about string theory, the main ideas of which are currently unfalsifiable and undetectable, but hold promise of providing a grand unified theory of physics. Some scientists have even argued that we should reduce the importance of falsification to protect string theory from the usual standards required of science.

The question of observability: Atoms and electrons

Before Popper's falsification criterion, science had another ideal: observability. The controversy about atoms in the latter half of the 19th century reveals the extent to which this ideal was held. Some scientists were persuaded by the explanatory power of atomic theory. But no one had detected atoms, no equipment at the time could detect them, and they solved no new puzzle. Hundreds of times smaller than light waves, atoms were unobservable by even the most powerful microscopes of the time.

Ernst Mach was a brilliant and influential physicist and philosopher, whose critique of Newton's physics may have later helped Einstein postulate general relativity. However, he went so far as to say "I don't believe that atoms exist", and that good science should not be concerned with finding them.

This idea was so influential that it caused Walter Kaufmann, a German physicist, to ignore what could have been the discovery of electrons in 1897: the particles he suspected were too small to observe, so he stayed silent. Months later J.J. Thomson, an English physicist, suspected the same thing, called them electrons, and went on to receive the Nobel Prize.

It turns out that Pauli, the man who posited the neutrino (one of the tiniest known subatomic particles) via a desperate and unobservable and untestable "remedy", had a famous uncle called Mach, the very same Mach who infamously proclaimed, "I don't believe that atoms exist". And thus we see why Pauli described his prediction of the existence of neutrinos as a "terrible thing".

The examples above serve to explain how perspectives on falsification and "good science" have changed over time. Falsification may be too strict to use as an everyday rule. When scientists test Einstein's theory using telescopes and photographic plates, they are simultaneously testing the focal theory, plus the theory of optics that goes into designing the telescopes, plus the assumptions behind the mathematical analyses of the data, plus a lot of other things that we take for granted in the background. If there is a mismatch between theory and observation, it is not enough to rule out the theory immediately. A failure in one of the many related theories and assumptions might be to blame instead. Reproducible anomalies tested under a variety of conditions are needed for falsification.

For discussion

Scientific ideas ready for retirement

In 2014, 178 of the world's greatest minds—scientists, thinkers, public intellectuals—considered the question: "What scientific idea is ready for retirement?"

 Search terms: Edge What scientific idea is ready for retirement?

If you read a few of their responses, you see contradicting and complementing perspectives.

You may be happy, sad or surprised to see "Calculus", "The Self" or "The Universe" being considered for retirement. In pairs, small groups or as a class discuss the following questions.

1. What reasons are offered for qualifying a scientific idea for retirement?

2. If the reasons sound compelling to you, why do you think some of the ideas persist?

3. What does it mean for a scientific idea to be retired—what actually happens to it?

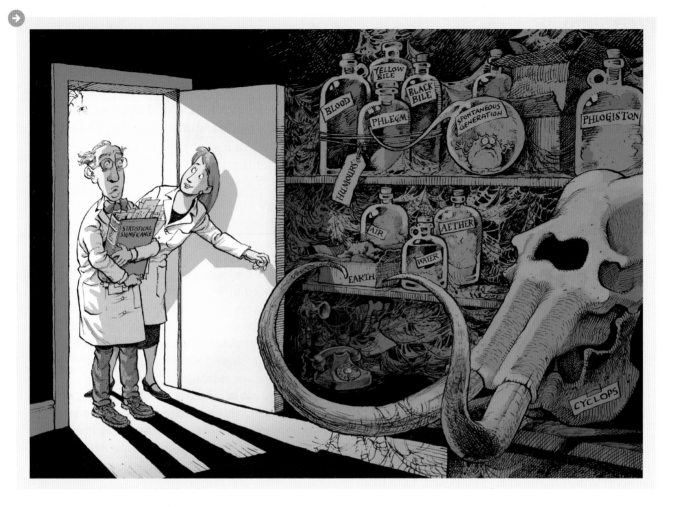

II.3 Scientific consensus and disagreement

As the previous section showed, there is a perspective of science that emphasizes the communal nature of knowledge and the consensus built by scientists. It is important to look at how this consensus is built and how disagreements are dealt with. Studying or paying close attention to how scientific controversies end gives us a sense of the different dimensions of scientific consensus and disagreement.

Much of what we call science, including scientific practice, is uncontroversial. Once established, scientific facts become self-evident and their histories begin to fade from memory or interest. They become "black boxes"—a term that describes things that are hard to open or not explained, their inner workings unknown.

Public disagreements are often settled by scientific facts used as evidence. But what counts as evidence when the scientific facts themselves cause the controversy?

Controversies allow us to look into black boxes before they are closed, and therefore to understand what it takes to make a fact and have confidence in evidence. Consensus is the closure of controversies and often requires evidence of causation.

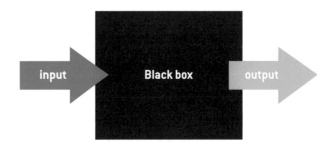

For reflection

Consensus and closure

1. What are some scientific black boxes that are not yet closed?

2. Which attempts to challenge the scientific consensus can you think of?

Many scientific ideas, even well-established theories such as evolution by natural selection, have opponents. There are sometimes highly technical debates that do not get much public attention. The case study below explores what happens when a scientific controversy attracts public attention.

Case study

HIV/AIDS denialism and the black-boxing of a scientific fact

Who would doubt that HIV causes AIDS? The link has been accepted scientific wisdom for decades—but how did it come to be accepted as fact, and is the case entirely closed?

Fact-making is the process of closing a black box and bringing closure to controversies. Once a fact is made, the human elements of that process—the interpretation, guessing, persuading and debating—and the uncertainties that did and still exist, fade from view. From then on, it is harder to question the fact—you would have to "reopen" a black box (Epstein 1996).

One such effort resisting the closing of a black box was led by Peter Duesberg, professor at the University of California Berkeley. Duesberg was a renowned and pioneering scientist, one of the first to discover retroviruses and oncogenes, which are potentially cancer-causing genes. His professional isolation was precipitated by his views disputing that HIV causes AIDS. Since the 1980s, in spite of widely accepted evidence, he has continued to advocate that AIDS is not caused by HIV, and that HIV is an opportunistic but harmless virus. Why?

> Even mentioning the name Peter Duesberg inflames strong feelings, both pro and con. After gaining fame in 1970 as the virologist who first identified a cancer-causing gene, in the 1980s he became the leading scientific torchbearer for the so-called AIDS dissidents who dispute that HIV causes the immunodeficiency disorder. To the dissidents, Duesberg is Galileo, oppressed for proclaiming scientific truth against biomedical dogma. A far larger number of AIDS activists, physicians and researchers, however, think Duesberg has become a crank who refuses to accept abundant proof that he is wrong. To them, he is at best a nuisance and at worst a source of dangerous disinformation on public health.
>
> (*Scientific American* 2007).

Duesberg is sometimes portrayed as a heretic, going against the establishment at great personal cost. Popular culture is fond of the archetypal hero-scientist that confronts the establishment, sometimes sacrificing their life in the process, to change the world. Galileo, for example, is a famous name; and to the AIDS denialists Duesberg is Galileo. You might have a neutral or positive view of scientific disagreement and scandal as healthy debate. However, scientific disagreement, especially in the public eye, can have far-reaching negative consequences. Sometimes there are life and death consequences for how disagreement is perceived by the public and acted upon in policy.

Duesberg was not alone in casting doubt on the HIV hypothesis but has been more successful than most in persevering against the scientific consensus and in attracting attention, and scorn, in the process. Is he a Galileo or a person with an irrational obsession? The question cannot be answered without also considering the extent and implications of the AIDS denialism that took hold in South Africa in the 1990s and 2000s, where the denialists' views are implicated in the deaths of hundreds of thousands of people, as described in Box 7.3 below. Max Essex, an AIDS expert, quoted in Lenzer (2008), stated that history will judge Duesberg either as "a nut who is just a tease to the scientific community" or an "enabler to mass murder" for the deaths of thousands of AIDS victims.

Making connections

Denialism

Denialism was not isolated to South Africa or AIDS—it persists, rightly or wrongly, throughout the world. It masquerades as scientific scepticism and is fuelled by the issues, tensions and agendas of the time and place. How do we protect scientific pluralism and the right to dissent, while also minimizing the fallout of bad science? What platform should denialists such as Duesberg be given? Often the scientific facts in question are just one component—as we see in Chapter 1: facts may not be enough to change beliefs. TOK equips us with tools to balance these tensions, between pluralism and dissent on the one hand, and scientific autonomy and responsibility on the other, to make judgments about the veracity of scientific claims and their implications.

The questions in the "Practising skills" box that follows this case study can be applied to denialists, dissidents and leakers everywhere. As an example, AIDS denialism is recent enough to resonate with us emotionally and intellectually, but also just old enough to show how communities of scientists wrestle with these questions. The University of California, Berkeley, opened an investigation into academic misconduct related to Duesberg's claims but abandoned it in 2010, citing a lack of evidence and that his work is protected by the principle of academic freedom. Duesberg

continues to hold a tenured professorship there. Yet, Bruce Charlton, editor of the journal *Medical Hypotheses*, which published his 2009 article (when other journals had refused), was sacked, largely for refusing to adopt a peer-review structure in response to the controversy. As early as 1996, *Science* magazine, one of the world's top academic journals, published an eight-page investigation into the "Duesberg phenomenon".

 Search terms: Special News Report The Duesberg phenomenon

Also in 1996 Richard Horton, editor of the respected medical journal *The Lancet*, and one of the most established Duesberg critics of the time, was compelled to come to his defence.

> Duesberg deserves to be heard, and the ideological assassination that he has undergone will remain an embarrassing testament to the reactionary tendencies of modern science. Irrespective of one's views about the validity of some of Duesberg's arguments, one is forced to ask: At a time when fresh ideas and new paths of investigation are so desperately being sought, how can the AIDS community afford not to fund Duesberg's research?
>
> [Horton 1996]

That spirit may have compelled Bruce Charlton to publish Duesberg's paper in 2009 and for *Scientific American* to state the following in "When Pariahs Have Good Ideas" (2007).

> Readers [may be] shocked to see Duesberg as an author in this month's issue. He is not here because we have misgivings about the HIV-AIDS link. Rather Duesberg has also developed a novel theory about the origins of cancer … That concept is still on the fringe of cancer research, but laboratories are investigating it seriously. Thus, as wrong as Duesberg surely is about HIV, there is at least a chance that he is significantly right about cancer.
>
> (*Scientific American* 2007)

Box 7.3: AIDS denialism—the role and responsibilities of scientific journals

One of Duesberg's papers was published in the journal *Medical Hypotheses* in 2009, sparking a major scandal. *Medical Hypotheses* was founded in 1975 by David Horrobin to counter the conservative adherence to accepted ideas that Horrobin saw in peer-reviewed journals. His criteria for publishing articles was simple: they had to be interesting and important, and plausible but not necessarily "true" because, as he saw it:

> "the history of science has repeatedly shown that when hypotheses are proposed it is impossible to predict which will turn out to be revolutionary and which ridiculous. The only safe approach is to let all see the light and to let all be discussed, experimented upon, vindicated or destroyed. I hope the journal will provide a new battlefield open to all on which ideas can be tested and put through the fire."
> (Horrobin 1975)

Neuroscientist Vilayanur Ramachandran, listed in 2011 as one of *Time* magazine's 100 most influential people in the world, and on the editorial board of the journal, similarly said, "there are ideas that may seem implausible but which are very important if true. This is the only place you can get

them published" (quoted in Enserink 2010). *Medical Hypotheses* was thus seen by some as a bastion of academic freedom and pluralism.

As the consequences of AIDS denialism in South Africa make clear, there are inherent risks to this freedom, and drawing a line between legitimate scientific dissent and pseudo-scientific denialism can be very difficult. In 2009 a group of scientists requested that the journal be removed from the MEDLINE database because it lacked rigour and had legitimized AIDS denialism. Nicoli Nattrass, Director of the AIDS and Society Research Unit at the University of Cape Town, stated that the journal "has long been a source of concern in the scientific community ... because the articles are not peer-reviewed" and "had a disturbing track record of publishing pseudo-science" (Nattrass 2009). When the journal's current editor Bruce Charlton was asked to adopt a peer-review structure to mitigate these risks, he refused, stating this went against the journal's founding purpose and history. He was dismissed soon after. A majority of the journal's editorial board protested the decision to change the editorial policies but finally, in 2010, a new editor was appointed and a hybrid peer-review structure implemented.

Duesberg explained his position to *Science* magazine in December 1994. "'The one thing I'm doing here is almost destroying my own reputation by questioning whether HIV is the cause of AIDS.' ... He insists that if he read a single scientific article that suggested to him he was wrong, he would alter his views. 'I'm looking for that article,' he says. 'I would love to see it'" (Cohen 1994).

The Duesberg saga makes us ponder when disagreement in science is productive, versus counterproductive. We should be concerned with asking the right questions so that we can balance these tensions, for example between consensus and disagreement, between pluralism and autonomy, in order to best serve the public interest.

Practising skills: Drawing implications

Suppose the example of Duesberg's research on HIV is being used to explore the value of disagreement in science. Consider the following.

- Are there different consequences to being wrong in the different scientific disciplines? For example, Galileo, who studied the sky, could have been wrong without causing the death of hundreds of thousands of people.

- What are the implications if a dissenting scientist is able to disseminate their work, for example by publishing it in journals?

- What are the implications if dissenting scientists are silenced, for example by being stripped of their tenure and the resources and platforms they need in order to fund and share their work?

- Which criteria can be used to strike a balance between the right to dissent and protecting the public from damaging pseudo-science?

Making connections

Politics and scientific denialism

What is the impact of individuals or groups who deny scientific evidence? A 2019 article in the journal *Cognition* suggests that denialists can delay, but not prevent, a scientific consensus; but that they can prevent the public from reaching consensus by presenting the issue as an ongoing scientific debate. This conclusion appears consistent with examples over the last four decades, spanning tobacco, climate change, vaccinations and genetically modified foods. Denialism can lead to false balance. In Chapter 2 we examine the politicization of media reports on scientific discourse, including the problem of false balance caused by attempts to show "both sides of the story", through the example of climate change.

Follow the link to investigate the 2000 Durban Declaration, made in response to AIDS denialism, and signed by over 5,000 scientists.

 Search terms: Durban Declaration AIDS Wiki

II.4 Disseminating scientific knowledge

Beginning in the mid-17th century, scientific journals have become the formal way for scientists to share their findings and keep up to date with developments. The intention was that journals would play a role in making science more open, accountable and widely accessible.

The articles published in scientific journals are authored by practising scientists. The reputation of a journal affects which articles appear in it and how many times they are cited in other work.

Scientific papers have a particular style and structure, and include information about method that would help others repeat the experiment. To ensure quality and validity of the research, an article is reviewed by other scientists, in a process called peer-review.

smbc-comics.com

This is a highly simplified description of the scientific publication environment. In reality, there are many challenges that affect the ability of journals to share science in an accessible way. One issue is volume, with over 2.5 million scientific papers published annually, that is 280 every hour, according to a report in 2015 (Ware, Mabe 2015).

There are concerns about:

- the lack of transparency and accountability in the peer-review process
- pressures on scientists to "publish or perish", with implications for their wellbeing or incentives for misconduct
- the technical jargon of scientific papers that makes them incomprehensible even to trained scientists from a different discipline.

We considered some of the dimensions of scientific publishing in a real-world context in Box 7.3 in the case study on HIV/AIDS. Chapter 8, III.6, discusses what has become known as the replication crisis, where a very significant number of published results have failed to be replicated. The peer-review process is also sometimes a source of controversy. In a *Science* article from 2013, linked here, we get a behind-the-scenes story of one scientist's effort to expose unrigorous journals by submitting a flawed article for publication.

 Search terms: Science magazine Who's afraid of peer review?

Box 7.4: Democratizing the sharing of scientific knowledge

Scientific journals are the preferred way of sharing knowledge within the scientific community—but they can be prohibitively expensive and inaccessible for laypeople and even other scientists. The peer-review process has also been questioned for fostering conservatism and dogma, rejecting unconventional ideas, and introducing a time lag between when research is done and when it is communicated.

A hopeful and surprisingly successful response to some of these issues is arXiv—an online repository of preprints of scientific papers, started in 1991 by physicist Paul Ginsparg.

> Preprints are full manuscripts of a scientific paper made publicly available by the author(s) ahead of review and publication in journals. This is a new but rapidly growing form of open scholarly communication.

Ginsparg was initially only trying to catalog about 100 papers, but he received a lot more than he expected—arXiv had more than 1.5 million papers in February 2018, growing by 10,000 per month. As arXiv began growing into a powerful platform, it also attracted a small number of very odd

contributions from outside the scientific community that were challenging to sort into arXiv's categories, in the form of papers that appeared impossible to reasonably qualify as science. Both history and wisdom suggest that "out-of-the-box" and hard to classify ideas can be valuable. But in order to continue to serve the scientific community by offering research that is of interest, relevance and value, the arXiv team had to come up with a solution to a tricky and important philosophical question: what counts as science?

The linked article tells the full story of how the team behind arXiv negotiated this problem using volunteer moderators and a machine learning algorithm. Specifically, the algorithm identified language to distinguish between scientific and non-scientific ideas. Are arXiv's human and computer filters effective at letting through good but unorthodox ideas? How is this changing the ways the scientific community shares and accesses knowledge? Follow the link to find out.

 Search terms: What counts as science Nautilus arXiv

With huge amounts of scientific knowledge behind paywalls or otherwise inaccessible due to jargon, the question of public communication takes on great significance. If the aim of science is to find and promote an understanding of life, the world and the cosmos, an understanding that would be of interest to all, should it be accessible to all? The answer might be yes, but one issue is "incentives"—the need to reward scientific pioneers and corporations that take risks by investing their time or money to do research.

In 2019 the University of California made headlines for dropping its $10 million per year subscription to Elsevier, a publishing company that owns over 2,500 scientific journals (including, incidentally, the journal *Medical Hypotheses* discussed in the Duesberg case earlier). The university's argument was simple: knowledge should not cost that much. Indeed, most scientists never get paid for their research, but the scientific publishing business maintains some of the highest profit margins in the world. Follow the link to this article by Stephen Buryani for UK newspaper the *Guardian*: "Is the staggeringly profitable business of scientific publishing bad for science?" (27 June 2017).

 Search terms: Buryani Staggeringly profitable business of scientific publishing Guardian

Most people agree on the benefit of cultivating a public interest in science. One example is science museums, which can collect money to fund research, and inspire people to pursue further scientific study, careers or at the least to be more open to science and more sceptical of dogma.

Science festivals, museums, university open days and various forms of media are all part of the science communication landscape for the non-scientist audience. Sociocultural context plays a large role in determining the method and objective of science communication. For example, science communication during the Cold War was very different from communication about global warming, in terms of who is communicating, what, to whom and for what purpose. These questions go beyond the nature or details of the science itself, and are particularly relevant to TOK.

> **Science communication** is the "organized, explicit, and intended actions that aim to communicate scientific knowledge, methodology, processes, or practices in settings where nonscientists are a recognized part of the audiences". (Horst *et al* 2017)

Efforts to publicize and popularize science have been in place since Victorian times. How this communication is done has been transitioning out of a "deficit model" to more participatory models. Deficit models set out to educate an assumedly uninformed and distrustful public audience in a top-down way that emphasized the "authority" of scientific experts. It was also called a push for "scientific literacy", and the paradigm for communication in the 1980s and 1990s.

More recently, we have seen a change towards engaging the public with science, and even citizen science, a relatively new practice that in some ways marks a return to the idea of science done by nature-loving amateurs, like a more diverse version of the "gentleman scientists" of the 18th and 19th centuries. Citizen science blurs the boundaries between scientist and non-scientist, and science enthusiasts have been involved in many fields from classifying galaxies to bird population surveys.

The case of the pioneering scientist-freedivers who are working to decode the communication systems of whales, and who are in important ways outpacing marine biologists, is discussed in Chapter 4, III.3.

It is common for science to be communicated by scientists, or on their behalf by science evangelists, in order to inspire enthusiasm and trust in science. Carl Sagan's *Cosmos* was formative for an entire generation and evokes nostalgia even today. Sir David Attenborough's reporting on the natural world is similarly influential and iconic. Using the link here, you can watch and hear both of them sing, autotuned, in the YouTube miracle that is the "Symphony of Science".

 Search terms: Symphony of Science playlist YouTube

You can assess the clip's artistic status and merit using tools from Chapter 10.

Popular science programming can run the risk of presenting an idealized image of science — as the heroic onward march, self-correcting its course, relentless in its mission of illuminating the dark corners of the unknown—a problematic narrative dealt with earlier in this chapter.

Against this idealized image, realistic coverage of scientific practice can seem incongruous, suspicious and even disenchanting. Public disagreement among scientists can shatter the illusion that the pursuit of truth through science naturally creates consensus. One of the hallmarks of the post-truth public sphere, considered in Chapter 2, is diminished trust in scientific experts. Discourses on statistical significance, confidence levels and tolerance intervals may clash with an idealized narrative of certainty and "proven" truths. All of these, alongside rarer but highly publicized instances of scientific fraud or malpractice, can erode the public image of science. Science, we must remember, is a very human endeavour.

After decades of effort by governments and laudable scientific institutions, what progress has been made? Results vary around the globe, playing into local stereotypes around race, gender and social status. In 1959, the author CP Snow wrote the following.

> " A good many times, I have been present at gatherings of people who, by the standards of the traditional culture, are thought highly educated and who have with considerable gusto been expressing their incredulity at the illiteracy of scientists. Once or twice I have been provoked and have asked the company how many of them could describe the Second Law of Thermodynamics. The response was cold: it was also negative. Yet I was asking something which is the scientific equivalent of: Have you read a work of Shakespeare's?
>
> (Snow 1959) "

Would this happen today? Snow and others lamented the lack of interest and knowledge of science. More recently, though, it is the humanities that are being defunded at universities. Have the tables turned, or is a different story playing out in academia versus in the public discourse? What are the implications?

For discussion

Have you heard this?

Examples of scientific ideas that are considered to be ready for retirement were explored in II.3. This time, explore what 200 bright minds from around the world think about the question "What scientific term or concepts ought to be more widely known?"

 Search terms: Edge 2017 Scientific terms more widely known

Choose a few of the entries and try to understand why the contributors think those ideas deserve better exposure. Work in a pair or small group, with each person presenting an argument about why the ideas you have chosen are not better known.

Practising skills: Exploring perspectives

With regards to the communication of science to the general public, consider two different perspectives: that the wide dissemination of scientific knowledge supports the public understanding of science, versus the view that popular science negatively affects scientific literacy.

The first perspective is fairly well established. What examples can you recall from your home context in support of this view?

The second perspective may appear more counter-intuitive. An article published in the journal *Public Understanding of Science* argues that popular science communication is contributing to overconfidence among non-scientists in their ability to understand and evaluate scientific claims, and more critical views towards scientific experts (Sharrer *et al* 2017). What examples and different kinds of evidence have you seen that support this perspective?

The exploration of different perspectives is central to TOK. Are the perspectives described above supported by well-chosen and well-explained examples from the real world? What factors determined whether the scientific communication had a positive or negative effect? Why is it that in issues of knowledge sometimes one thing happens, and at other times the opposite happens?

II.5 The student of science

Theoretical physicist Max Planck once said the following.

> A new scientific truth does not triumph by convincing its opponents and making them see the light, but rather because its opponents eventually die, and a new generation grows up that is familiar with it.
>
> (Planck, translated by Gaynor 1968)

Perhaps though, science is shaped less by a "series of funerals" than by rows of fresh science graduates. For more than 150 years now, scientists have had to go through some sort of formal training, unlike the nature-loving gentlemen amateurs of the Early Modern period. Indeed, one of the most important tasks of the scientific community at any given time is to educate and train the new generation of scientists, and to do it well. But what does "well" mean? This process, through which future scientists learn what science is and how it is done, defines the character of science for the next generation. It is also a deeply political task, with questions such as what is included and excluded from the curriculum, which values are passed on, and what kind of outlook is cultivated with regard to science itself and its wider societal role. Your science classes are a way of socializing you into the culture of the scientific community (that is, enculturating you)—this is where you are taught the norms of good science, shown how to properly perform various scientific skills, and told the story of how science came to be. Who has decided these things for you, and how can you exercise agency in the matter?

This enculturation typically happens within scientific disciplines. You might be learning how to think like a physicist, biologist, chemist, ecologist, geographer and so on. Textbooks do a lot of this enculturation work, and they do it in part by telling the foundational stories of the discipline, about the people and events that defined the discipline. Let's look at one such story, central to biology classes and textbooks around the world.

The tension between simplicity and complexity in science appears repeatedly in this chapter, and we examine it further in the context of reductionism in III.5. As you read on, keep this tension in mind. Try to connect what Mendel's peas, laboratory experiments and the relationships between organism and environment have in common.

Box 7.5: Mendel in the textbook

The origin story of genetics as a discipline starts with Gregor Mendel's experiments on pea plants in the mid-19th century. The humble pea triggered one of the greatest breakthroughs in scientific history: the Mendelian laws of inheritance, and Mendel himself has been dubbed the "father of genetics".

However, Mendel's 1865 article was not recognized as important until many years after his death. It was rediscovered in 1902 and sent ripples from Russia to the United States by stoking controversy in how fundamental concepts such as variation, evolution, heredity, mutation and gene were defined, understood to work, and related to one another. In the UK, it sparked a short but fiery public dispute between William Bateson (who coined and popularized the term "genetics") and his former teacher, Walter Frank Raphael Weldon. Weldon and Bateson had very different reactions: Bateson was a champion of Mendelian inheritance, arguing that "factors" (later he called them genes) determine "visible characteristics" of organisms according to the Mendelian laws. Weldon remained sceptical on several accounts because when he tried to replicate Mendel's experiments with peas, he found a much greater variety of characteristics, along much more of a continuum. His peas did not look as discretely different as Mendel describes them looking—decidedly yellow or green, wrinkled or round.

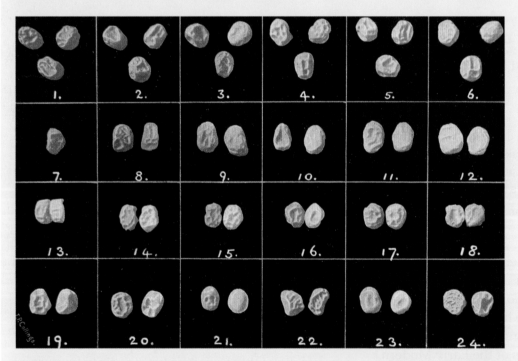

← **Figure 7.4** Taken from Weldon's article "Mendel's Laws of Alternative Inheritance in Peas" (1902)

Weldon disputed Bateson's claim that Mendel's findings could be applied generally, because Mendel's experiments used purebred pea plants especially designed to eliminate the natural variability responsible for creating complexity. In Weldon's view, therefore, the plants were unrepresentative of real-world conditions, and it was more important to understand how natural variability interacts with the environment. Weldon died four years into this controversy, without finding an answer for the complex interactions between genes and environment. In fact, epigeneticists are only beginning to unravel this now. Weldon was largely forgotten; while Mendel smooth-sailed into textbook glory, with Bateson at the helm, both celebrated for discovering genetics.

Why tell Weldon's story here? A Weldonian genetics might have been less simple, but more applicable and more revealing about the interaction between genes and the environment. This direction of enquiry has gathered momentum only relatively recently.

Stories about scientific disagreement are important because they reveal that the losing side was not necessarily or obviously wrong, and if we have learned anything it is to beware our own fallibility, to caution against oversimplification and to be curious about the arguments lost to history. The stories that science tells about itself can be misleading, by presenting a story in which developments come together neatly to produce fundamental truths recognized today. This is the Whiggish view discussed in II.2.

The concepts learned early in science education can, if oversimplified, support stubborn and dangerous misconceptions if students do not continue their education to the level where complexity is added back to simplifications. Reputable scientists and teachers have stated that the currently taught genetics curriculum is too simplistic. Consider the following quote by Jenny Lewis, of the Genetics Pedagogies Project that explored the effects of changing the genetics curriculum.

"When helping students to develop their understanding of basic genetic concepts, it can be useful to reduce complexity by adopting a traditional, linear view of gene expression (one gene, one protein, one characteristic) but there is a risk that this will result in a deterministic view of genetics in which every characteristic is determined by a single gene. The reality, unexpectedly confirmed by the Human Genome Project, is that there are very few single gene characteristics or disorders in humans … . Rather, the relationship between the genome (the entire DNA sequence), gene expression, and the environment was shown to be considerably more complex than anticipated. The result is a move away from a focus on single genes (genetics, understood narrowly) and towards a consideration of the whole genome and its interactions with the environment, internal and external (genomics)." (Lewis 2011)

Gregory Radick has similarly argued that biology students should be taught a genetics curriculum fit for the 21st century.

" If we teach them about Mendel, we should do so not to fill them with slack-jawed wonder at his foundational achievement, but to help them to appreciate how even the most imaginative and rigorous science ... bears the stamp of the historical circumstances of its making. To learn that lesson about past science is to bring a welcome level of self-awareness and critical self-reflection to the present." (Radick 2016)

Radick and Lewis work on the Genetics Pedagogies Project, an experimental syllabus that imagines what a Weldonian approach to genetics might have looked like and what difference it makes for students to be exposed to it.

Making connections

"What if … ?" in history and in the natural sciences

Chapter 9 discusses the merits and demerits of counterfactuals—asking how the course of history might have been affected if key events had occurred differently. Compare this with the value of asking the same question in science. Is it more or less difficult to imagine alternative histories or alternative sciences? What can we learn from such an exercise?

II.6 Science for citizenship

In technical debates involving science, citizens often find themselves in a position of having to trust what they are being told by experts. Who counts as an "expert" and how far their expertise extends is something that is socially negotiated, requiring us to make judgments about their credibility.

When science touches the public domain it attracts public attention, and its effects can be far-reaching and urgent. Whenever science gets enrolled in public debates on socially controversial issues, its authority, and the authority of those who speak on its behalf, is tested. Air pollution, climate change and vaccine hesitancy are among many contemporary examples.

In policy-making, scientists and non-scientists have to comprehend the evolving scientific issues relating to policy, and find the language to communicate effectively in an ecosystem complicated by money, politics and competition. The context of democratic decision-making on matters involving science raises questions about power and legitimacy, as well as values and democracy. Who is able to speak from a place of authority on matters at the intersection of science and policy? How can the demands of participatory democracy be balanced with the need for scientific autonomy?

Making connections

Science, politics and public trust

Chapter 2 explores "post-truth" and the causes and consequences of an apparently diminished public trust in scientific expertise.

The case study in II.3 described controversy among the scientific community over the fact that HIV is the cause of AIDS. However, this was not simply a scientific controversy occurring in an academic vacuum; it spread to the social and political realms. Explanations of the cause and spread of AIDS were inevitably influenced by, and influenced in turn, contemporary attitudes and beliefs about homosexuality, addiction and sexual freedom.

On the other side of the debate about what causes AIDS was the controversy about how to treat it. In the early days, the treatment of AIDS was a scientific, pharmacological and medical debate, participation in which required a high level of technical expertise. At the same time, non-experts were also involved and influential: those who stood to profit from treatment; those tasked with reporting on the development of treatments; and, of course, those for whom it was a question of life and death. Epstein (1996) describes the different actors in this controversy in the United States, who varied in their motivations and interests.

> [There were] the researchers hoping to hit on breakthroughs in … AIDS research; the pharmaceutical and biotechnology companies whose stock values might fluctuate by millions of dollars, depending on the latest reports about the successes or failures of their products; the medical professionals who must translate inconclusive and contradictory research findings into workable, day-to-day clinical judgments; the regulatory agencies and advisory bodies that serve as 'gatekeepers', ruling on the safety and efficacy of new therapies; the patients who consume the drugs and populate the clinical trials; the reporters and journalists who interpret scientific research findings to various segments of the public; and, of course, the activists who police the whole process and offer their own interpretations of the methods and the outcomes.
>
> (Epstein 1996)

Epstein's study of science and citizenship in the AIDS epidemic shows, among other things, how non-scientists can acquire high levels of biomedical knowledge even when they are underserved by the current set-up of science and politics. AIDS activists were able not only to understand and scrutinize biomedical claims, but also to participate in shaping the methodologies through which knowledge about the treatment of AIDS was being produced. This type of citizen involvement blurs the lines between expert and non-expert, and redistributes the balances of power, credibility and trust.

With these questions for discussion in mind, let's look at an example of the power of politicians to bolster or undermine the credibility and authority of science in the public, and what happens when science and politics clash on an issue of public health.

For discussion

Trust and credibility

1. To what extent is it the responsibility of citizens to understand and engage with scientific issues of public importance?

2. Often non-experts who get deeply involved in scientific controversies do so through great personal effort. To what extent is this a failing of science and politics to inspire trust and confidence in the knowledge claims they make?

3. Think of a public controversy on a scientific issue relevant to your context currently or recently. What determines whether and how the public can engage with the making, sharing and evaluation of scientific knowledge claims?

Box 7.6: Disagreement in the public eye

Disagreements are contextual, meaning they are embedded in the historical, cultural, political or economic issues of the time, and can take on an importance much larger than the techno-scientific minutiae at stake. A profound example of this was AIDS denialism that took hold in South Africa in the 1990s and 2000s, a story that was ably illustrated by Michael Specter, writing in the *New Yorker* in March 2007.

  Search terms: New Yorker Specter The denialists

The short version of the story is that a group of HIV sceptics in the 1990s, calling themselves the Group for the Scientific Reappraisal of the HIV/AIDS Hypothesis, put forward the following claims.

- HIV does not cause AIDS.

- AIDS should not be treated with antiretroviral drugs, which are poisons with far worse side effects than the disease itself.

- South Africa did not have an AIDS epidemic. Instead, too much recreational drug use, and too little nutrition and clean water, were killing its people.

The group included scientists such as Peter Duesberg, whose ideas were introduced in II.3. The group's scientific claims were seized upon by policy-makers and political leaders in South Africa, in a discourse that was heavily complicated by the legacy of apartheid and a climate of widespread distrust towards Western pharmaceutical companies. Other influential people were involved: a doctor turned entrepreneur who marketed vitamins as an alternative to retroviral drugs; local entrepreneurs and healers who used herbal concoctions; and national leaders including President Thabo Mbeki and Health Minister Manto Tshabalala-Msimang who were deeply sceptical of Western pharmaceuticals and the doctors who prescribed them. All of this conspired to deny South Africans access to medical best practice, as agreed upon by the global scientific community. In the following years, the death rate from AIDS in South Africa soared: the Harvard AIDS initiative produced a study in 2008 that estimated 300,000 preventable deaths resulting from delayed AIDS treatment.

*this section has been dealing with ... e and politics in terms of public policy, ... olitical system and governance. In II.7 we turn to the politics of knowledge, examining challenges to science's assumed neutrality, and exploring its position in a wider cultural and historical context.

II.7 Science and its others: Feminist and post-colonial critiques

The encounter between modern Western science and other systems and bodies of knowledge has a deep history. Feminist and post-colonial thinkers have produced a scholarly literature that explores how scientific knowledge and practice have been defined and shaped to the exclusion of groups of people along gender, racial, sociopolitical and non-Western intellectual lines. These ideas have recently attracted wider interest, including on university campuses and online communities. This section does not aim to summarize that literature or examine the intersection between the natural sciences and every other knowledge tradition. It aims to highlight some of the tensions and what can be learned from them.

Developments in feminist theory as well as the history, sociology and philosophy of science in the 1960s formed the intellectual backdrop for the critical conversation regarding gender and science that has been ongoing ever since. Many issues originally raised in this conversation remain important and unresolved. Philosopher Sandra Harding has been writing about feminist critiques of science for decades. In the introduction to her book, *The Postcolonial Science and Technology Studies Reader* (2011), she summarizes the questions we are still grappling with, remarking for instance that few women are managing or designing research today, while women are almost absent from the social structures of modern sciences. She also questions the role that "sexist sciences" play in supporting and

spreading the claim that women are inferior and in encouraging unfair practices. Harding asks if schools' curricula and education methods restrict women's access to careers in science and engineering. Finally, she considers the problems posed by the traditional methods and philosophy of science and technology, with their overwhelmingly masculine world view.

Follow the link to: "The Egg and the Sperm: How Science has Constructed a Romance Based on Stereotypical Male-Female Roles".

 Search terms: Martin Egg and the Sperm Chicago Journals

This classic 1991 study by Emily Martin unravels the scientific myth of the passive egg being fertilized by an active sperm cell. This surprisingly persistent myth played into popular stereotypes about the romantic personalities of males and females.

The feminist critique of science includes, and requires, the voices of anthropologists, scientists, historians, philosophers, sociologists, educators and policy-makers looking at their work through a "gender lens". While significant attention has been focused on the experience of women in science, it would be incorrect to say that feminist critiques treat gender as another word for "woman". Feminist scholarship has opened up the discourse to explore the relationship between science and power more generally.

> ### Making connections
>
> **Female scientists**
>
> Chapter 3 discusses female scientists whose achievements are downplayed or erased from history. You may have noticed that this chapter to a large extent quotes male scientists from European backgrounds. The visibility of female scientists and technologists is both an issue of due credit, and an issue of enabling a diverse set of STEM students to see themselves reflected in the professional community.

In light of this, it is important to reveal and honour the diversity that already exists in the scientific community, and highlight role-models from diverse backgrounds. The *Nevertheless* podcast celebrated women STEM role-models and their work in eight different languages, which you can find at the link.

 Search terms: Nevertheless STEM role models posters

↑ **Figure 7.5a** Mae Jemison, astronaut and doctor, the first African-American woman in space

↑ **Figure 7.5b** Cynthia Breazeal, roboticist and pioneer of sociable robots

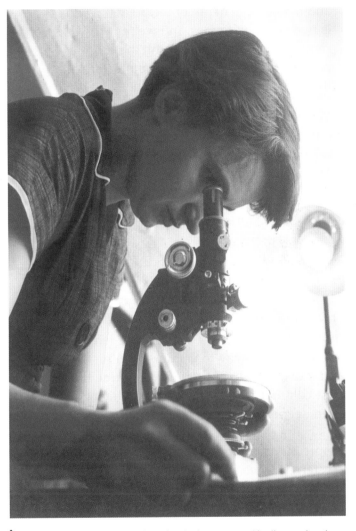

↑ **Figure 7.5c** Rosalind Franklin, scientist instrumental in discovering the structure of DNA

Box 7.7: Sylvia Sails Away With 70 Men

Marine biologist and pioneering oceanographer Sylvia Earle has had an incredible career in science—just one of her remarkable achievements was becoming the first person to walk on the ocean floor, untethered, 400 metres under the surface. Hundreds of hours underwater have earned her the affectionate nickname "Her Deepness".

As a female scientist at the frontier of a male-dominated field in the 1960s, her work attracted much attention and predictable questions.

"Actually, the kind of problems I think they were thinking of were not the kind of problems that were there at all. Our real problem was: How do you explore the ocean when you're sitting on the deck of a ship, and the average depth of the ocean is two and a half miles, and we're right there on the surface with these pathetic little tools to try to sample this huge expanse of living blue?"

You can listen to Sylvia Earle's reflections on a life exploring the ocean, in conversation with Krista Tippett in the linked *On Being* podcast.

Search terms: Sylvia Earle Her Deepness On Being

In the 1970s and 1980s, the "gender lens" of feminism gave way to genders, feminisms and indeed lenses. At around the same time, post-colonial theory, the roots of which go even deeper, turned its critique to how science was being deployed globally. This critique is suspicious of attempts to depoliticize modern Western science and present versions of it that are decoupled from its colonial and imperialist history. It would be impossible to deny the involvement of science in European expansion, and that far from playing merely an unfortunate accompanying role, science was instrumental to the colonial project. This discourse reminds us that science cannot simply move on from its "colonial moment", it needs to recover from it. This project of recovery has been picked up by decolonization movements worldwide.

Post-colonial science studies challenge both the idea of a single valid explanation of the natural world and the claim that modern Western science is the single valid way to arrive at that explanation. It questions the narrative of science as rational, objective and true, and the framing of pre-modern and/or non-European knowledge traditions as irrational and false. Few today would argue this explicitly, but the suggestion is implicit in the claim that science "began" in 17th-century Europe. Post-colonial scholarship points out that this defines non-Western peoples as newcomers to science and to a tradition that is only now embracing them out of diversity and inclusiveness. It also calls our attention to a history, little of which is acknowledged even today, of how Indigenous, traditional and local knowledges of astronomy, medicine, navigation and herbalism became apppropriated into the body of scientific knowledge, with their origins forgotten.

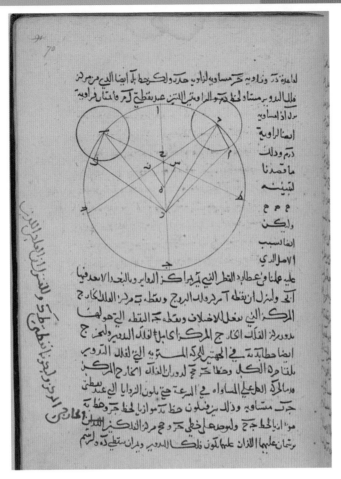

↑ Figure 7.6 Arabic scientific manuscript from 615 CE, describing an astronomical model that had widespread impact in both Christian and Islamic territories

---

Making connections

Indigenous knowledge

In Chapter 5 we explore examples from traditional ecological knowledge, ethnobotany and herbalism, and examine why some aspects of Indigenous knowledge have been appropriated and incorporated into science, but not others. We also look at how different knowledge traditions deal with concepts such as evidence, truth and disciplinarity.

III. METHODS AND TOOLS

Section II examined how disagreement and consensus among scientists affect the making and unmaking of scientific facts, and how evidence is evaluated and used to support claims. This section looks at the processes through which scientific evidence is produced, and considers specifically the methods of experimentation and observation. Earlier we paid attention to issues of trust and credibility. As you read on, keep in mind the following questions: why should we trust the evidence that comes from scientific methodologies? What is it about how scientific claims are produced that gives them credibility?

III.1 Observation and experimentation

Entering the scientific repertoire in the 17th century, observation and experimentation have a long shared history. Historians of science Lorraine Daston and Elizabeth Lunbeck give us the following overview.

> Throughout the eighteenth and early nineteenth centuries, observation and experiment were understood to work hand in hand: observation suggested conjectures that could be tested by experiment, which in turn gave rise to new observations .... Observation discovered and discerned; experiment tested and proved.
>
> But starting in the 1820s, prominent scientific writers began to oppose observation to experiment .... In this new scheme of things, experiment was active and observation passive: whereas experiment demanded ideas and ingenuity on the part of a creative researcher, observation was reconceived as the mere registration of data, which could, some claimed, be safely left to untrained assistants. The reasons for this shift ... were complex, but prominent among them was the fear that overly engaged scientists might contaminate observation with their own preferred theories. ...
>
> [A] program to deskill scientific observation was driven by anxieties about how more sophisticated researchers might be tempted ... to 'forge,' 'hoax,' 'trim,' or 'cook' the data. Although skilled, sophisticated observation was praised, numerous mid-nineteenth-century scientists worried that skill and sophistication might open the door to subjectivity or even fraud.
>
> (Daston, Lunbeck 2011)

The stubborn and inaccurate claim that observation is passive while experimentation is active persisted for a very long time, but experimentation was not always seen as the preferred method. The relationship between observation and experimentation turned a number of times before the 19th century.

Certainly, the concern about the influence of theory on observation was not resolved in the 1800s. As recently as 1950s, paleoanthropologist Louis Leakey selected his young administrative assistant, untrained in science, as the ideal person to undertake an immersive study of chimpanzees in the wild, the first of its kind. The young woman possessed "a mind uncluttered and unbiased by theory" (Goodall 2000), with which she set out on a long-term research assignment in the Gombe Stream National Park in Tanzania. Her name was Jane Goodall, and her pioneering work with primates revolutionized our understanding of, and kinship with, other animals. This early part of Goodall's prolific career is explored in the 2017 *National Geographic* documentary "Jane", linked here.

 Search terms: National Geographic Jane movie

For reflection

The relationship between observation and experimentation

1. What would you say is the relationship between observation and experimentation now?

2. Do you have different answers for different disciplines? If so, why do you think your answers vary?

Before looking at observation and experimentation in greater detail, let us consider the relationship between each of them and theory. Can we separate theory from practice—that is, from observation and experimentation? As Daston and Lunbeck say above, scientists have long been concerned about "contaminating" their observations with theories, expectations and/or desires. In addition to this problem, there is the concern of theorizing about non-observable phenomena. As Box 7.8 shows, this raises a few questions.

III. Methods and tools

Box 7.8: What is observable?

If we relied on only our eyes, ears and nose to detect things in the universe, we would not have come very far. It seems an obvious point, but the question of what is observable has very real implications for how scientists do, and believe they should do, science. If we accept that technology improves over time, we can expect that our ability to observe things using equipment is also likely to improve over time. Thus, theorizing about undetectable things, such as the photon (Einstein), neutrino (Pauli) and string theory (many contemporary physicists), does not seem like such a bad idea. Indeed, the photon and neutrino were discovered within 30 years of their proponents' predictions. Yet, four concerns emerge.

The first concern, regarding the examples of Neptune and the neutrino, is a form of selection bias called survivorship bias: those discoveries are famous, but we neglect the many less visible examples of dead-end theories, like the planet Vulcan. Would science be better off focusing strictly on the observable? It is a fascinating question, not least because how we would approach it is a profound knowledge problem.

A second concern relates to how we define unobservable, in relation to existing technologies and scientific theories. It is these theories and technologies that inform our preconceptions about what is, and is not, observable. Could we invent a method to ignore or hide from unobservable ideas, theories and subconscious hunches? How can we account for the shifting and blurring of this boundary over time?

Thirdly, this fixation on observed phenomena may distract from the larger truth that a given phenomenon can lead to vastly different interpretations in different theories. Even when observed phenomena are largely agreed upon, their causes remain mired in controversy (the political disagreements over climate change are a case in point). Good "theorizing" is important, while getting fixated on falsifiability or observability can hold important science, and policy, back.

The fourth concern relates to the assumption that technology will continue to improve. Almost everyone around us will attest that technology has progressed tremendously throughout their lifetimes and the living memories of their parents and grandparents. Yet can we, and should we, expect this to continue? This is dealt with more fully in Chapter 3.

III.2 The natural and the artificial in experiments

Experimentation has not always been the preferred way to gain scientific knowledge, but the events and ideas known as "the scientific revolution" firmly installed experiments near the top of the methodological hierarchy. Even our pop culture visuals of what it means to be "doing science" often invoke individuals wearing laboratory coats and handling test tubes or microscopes.

Beginning in the 17th century, "experiment" came to be known as intervention using technical instruments, to examine scientific objects and reveal their causes. Earlier in this chapter we encountered Bacon, who saw science as unlocking nature's secrets, by intentionally manipulating and mimicking nature in a controlled environment.

Taking a closer look, however, experiments are decidedly unnatural. Laboratory studies since the 1980s have shown that scientists go to great lengths to remove the messiness of nature, to control all variables but one in a purified laboratory environment where "nature is systematically excluded" (Sismondo 2010). However, phenomena produced in the laboratory are regularly, and uncontroversially, claimed and believed to stand in for natural phenomena.

This unrecognized and often unstated simplicity and sanitization have important implications for theories arising from them, as the example of Mendelian genetics and the Bateson–Weldon debate (in II.5, Box 7.5) reveals.

Sergio Sismondo, professor of philosophy and social studies of science, provides a perspective on the social forces that lend legitimacy to scientific experiments.

> The artificiality of experiments was one of the concerns that many natural philosophers of the seventeenth century had about them. … Particular places and spaces that served as laboratories contributed to the legitimacy of experiment—for example, the location of laboratories within the homes of English gentlemen helped establish trust … .
>
> (Sismondo 2010)

Sismondo describes the lengths that early experimenters went to, to convince the public that their experiments were not flukes. The concern is indicative of an old problem: how can we know if our experiment is working? Usually, we can test it with a known quantity and see whether it gives the correct answer. But what if we do not know what that answer is, not even remotely? How does science discern signal from noise? This challenge, of looking for answers with a tool that we cannot be sure is working, has been called the "problem of experimenters' regress" by sociologist of scientific knowledge, Harry M. Collins (1981). It is not a trivial problem, but it is also not insurmountable. In the article linked here is the riveting story of a group of astrophysicists who went to incredible lengths to overcome this problem in their search for gravitational waves.

 Search terms: Nautilus Issue 42 Astrophysicists who faked it

Paying attention to the discrepancies between the artificial purity of the laboratory and the messiness of the world can hold keys to new knowledge. An example from the history of the periodic table of elements is revealing

here. In the last years of the 19th century, Lord Rayleigh and Sir William Ramsey observed that nitrogen extracted from chemical compounds in the laboratory was 0.5% lighter than nitrogen derived from the atmosphere. It was a small enough difference to have been an artifact of their experimental set-up, or anything else. They were curious, though, and their research led to the discovery of argon and other noble gases, and a Nobel Prize.

For discussion

True enough? Science as "felicitous falsehoods"

In her book *True Enough*, Catherine Z. Elgin (2017) argues that scientific facts and theories are never strictly speaking true, because experiments and theories describe a simplified and controlled reality, not the natural things around us.

Elgin thus refers to science as a set of "felicitous falsehoods"—falsehoods that are useful for helping us to understand the world, but are not accurate descriptions of it.

This is a radically different conception of scientific truth and certainty, and more aligned with the simplified models used in the human sciences, discussed in Chapter 8.

III.3 Learning to see: Scientific observation as method

Observation is not just a junior assistant to experimentation, it is an astounding human and scientific activity deserving attention in its own right.

Observation as a scientific method has often involved a collective dimension. Edmond Halley's 1686 map of the trade winds is considered one of the most successful early efforts at collective observation. It was based on the accounts of seafarers, travellers and adventurers, as it was global, and therefore too big for any one person to observe.

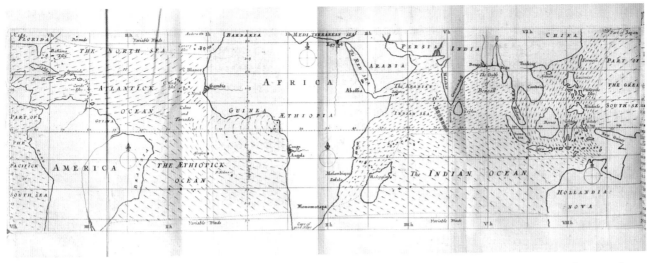

↑ **Figure 7.7** Map of the trade winds taken from Edmond Halley, *Philosophical Transactions of the Royal Society of London 16* (1686–92)

When observations are repeatedly and systematically performed, errors can be spotted and corrected. Patterns emerge that can describe and explain more complex phenomena, such as the movement of the ocean's currents or the paths of celestial objects in the night sky.

This idea that despite our fallibility and our limited powers of perception, if enough of us look at nature carefully, enough times, an accurate image will emerge, can be a powerful motivator to look at the world scientifically.

Observation is demanding work—long and odd hours, maintaining rigorous schedules, travelling to remote places at personal risk and cost, handling strange things or ordinary things in strange ways. Despite this, observation is not typically described as tedium but as exhilaration. What is this most thrilling thing that we see when we observe nature? Would it be any less thrilling if the image that emerges from scientific observation is not in fact revealed to us by nature itself, but painstakingly co-constructed by both nature and observer?

For discussion

Patterns and order

In this discussion, you will be focusing on taxonomy (the science of finding, classifying and naming organisms). Modern biology rests on a foundation of the categories meticulously constructed for the purposes of classifying life and biodiversity.

1. To what extent do taxonomic categories reveal an underlying order in nature?

2. What would count as evidence that taxonomic categories accurately describe the evolutionary relationships between species and genera?

3. What supports the argument that the modern system of classification is a construct of human knowledge, superimposed onto the messiness of the world in order to make sense of it?

III.4 Objectivity: For all people, for all time

Objectivity has a number of different meanings depending on the context. In the context of science and scientific practice, the connotation is one of freedom from bias and value-neutrality. In other words, it is the principle of separation between scientist and science, such that observers and experimenters do not influence descriptions of their observation or interpretations of their results.

Objective knowledge is what Thomas Nagel calls "the view from nowhere" (1986) and what Popper calls "knowledge without a knower" (1979). Is such perspective-less knowledge possible in science, or indeed at all? To what extent does the scientific method protect against human perspectives and fallibility? The feminist and post-colonial perspectives we explored in II.7 suggest that scientific knowledge always bears the mark of its producers and the context of its production, while III.1 examined the influence of theory on observation. Does nature speak for itself? Can we, and do we, let it?

There is a second sense in which objectivity finds expression in science, a way for scientists to make themselves irrelevant to the process and product of science. This is the ideal of formal objectivity, where procedures are perfectly followed by scientists. The removal of subjectivity from science happens through the standardization, and indeed universalization of units, tools and even laboratory organisms. If human researchers are unable to restrain themselves from influencing the outcomes of scientific methods, machines might. For instance, scientific photography has widely replaced scientific illustration that was once widely popular in botany. But can technology produced by human beings be free of human perspective? We explore this idea of the neutrality of technology in Chapter 3.

The lengths to which scientists go to be objective make for incredible stories. Consider, for example, how we know the length of 1 metre. It involves an expedition that first measured and established the length of a metre as a one ten-millionth of the distance between the equator and the North Pole. Two centuries later it was discovered that the result was accurate to less than the width of a human hair. It may be surprising that how we agree about measurements of length, mass and time are linked to the events and values of the French Revolution. The units established then were envisioned to be "for all time, for all people", a goal no doubt influenced by the political ideals and movements of the period. The meter has since been pegged to constant (the speed of light in a vacuum), which is truly for all time, as opposed to transient phenomena—including even the Earth.

As recently as 2018 the kilogram underwent a similar process. It is currently defined in terms of a special metal cylinder called Le Grande K, the copies of which are kept deep underground in two rooms secured with three locks. By the time you read this, the kilogram will be tied to the

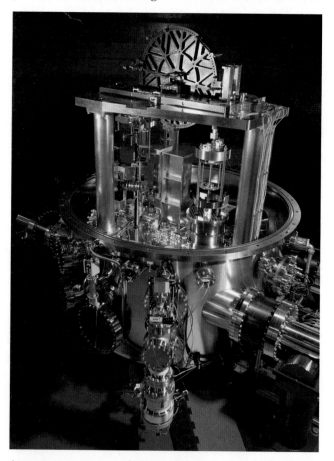

↑ Figure 7.8 Kibble balance at the National Institutes of Standards and Technology, USA, that identifies the weight of 1 kilogram based on the Planck constant

Planck constant, possibly forever. Follow this link to a story exploring the process and implications of replacing Le Grand K with a fascinating shiny machine and an immutable value.

 Search terms: Vox world just redefined the kilogram

Centuries ago Galileo proclaimed, "Anyone can see through my telescope", suggesting not only that the observer is interchangeable, but also that churches and monarchs no longer had the exclusive rights to speak about nature. That process of democratization continues today. Very soon we will no longer rely on the International Bureau of Weights and Measures, as anyone with a watt balance will be able to tell the weight of a kilogram.

III.5 Reductionism, emergence and complexity

In III.2 we explored Elgin's argument about experimental science, that certain complexities can be, and indeed must be, ignored. Often these complexities concern the relationship between what we think of as parts and wholes in science. For example, think about how the whole of the human body is constituted by various systems. Each system is made up of various organs and tissues, which are in turn made up of cells, molecules, atoms and so on.

Can an organism be separated from its environment and understood as a whole? Evolutionary biologists maintained this separation for decades, looking at genes and the environment as two different sets of factors. However, more recent breakthroughs in epigenetics—the study of how the environment affects the expression of genes—blurred the boundaries between these two domains. We are also only beginning to understand the effects of the microbiome—the collective genetic material of all the micro-organisms that are resident in the human body, particularly in the large intestine, of which we have about as many as we have human cells. The complexity of relationships between organisms and their external and internal environments has been receiving

growing attention, with important implications for TOK.

Chapter 8 looks at the problem of separating the organism from the environment. Here the question is: how far can we go simplifying and reducing complexity in the natural sciences? The extract below considers the limits of endocrinology—the branch of science concerned with hormones.

> In May of 1924, the city of Chicago was shocked by a brutal murder. Two precocious University of Chicago graduate students, Nathan Leopold, 19, and Richard Loeb, 18, lured, abducted, and murdered Loeb's 14-year-old cousin Bobby Franks by clubbing and asphyxiation. The duo fancied themselves as master criminals beyond the law—they planned to play a ransom game with the victim's family … and get away with murder. But the body was discovered before the ransom could be collected, and because Leopold lost his rare fashionable glasses at the crime scene, the police traced the two young men in no time.
>
> The Leopold and Loeb case … was unique in the annals of 1920s violence. The widespread eugenic thinking of the time was that crimes were committed by individuals of low hereditary intelligence. Reformers, on the other hand, saw gangsters as the products of environmental factors like working class poverty and urban tenements. In either case, criminals killed over money, territory, and credibility … . There was no clinical mystery to their behavior.
>
> But Leopold and Loeb were different and their case had explosive consequences. It put the very idea of free will and responsibility on trial. People weren't to blame for their crimes because they were at the mercy of their individual biology. Science said so. …
>
> The duo's attorney, Clarence Darrow, knew the jury wouldn't accept an insanity defense. Not only did the young men know right from wrong, they had consciously followed the wrong … . They freely confessed their careful planning to the police, regarding themselves as amoral criminal masterminds. Most scandalously, they showed no remorse. … The prosecutor, Robert Crowe, was calling for the death penalty. So instead of claiming insanity, Darrow appealed to a new medical specialty to justify his clients' deed: endocrinology, the science of glands and their secretions.
>
> (Tenner 2015)

Follow the link to the whole article, "The Original Natural Born Killers".

 Search terms: Tenner Original natural born killers Nautilus

> 'You', your joys and your sorrows, your memories and your ambitions, your sense of personal identity and free will, are in fact no more than the behavior of a vast assembly of nerve cells and their associated molecules.
>
> (Crick 1995)

That crime committed almost one hundred years ago presents perennial TOK questions about reductionism, the nature of scientific certainty and the human interpretation of facts. It is easy for us to look back into history and mock people for their naivete in believing the avant-garde, and flawed, scientific theories of their time. The more interesting concern is whether we are vulnerable to the same mistake. How can we protect ourselves against it? Is there anything to suggest that we have learned to be wiser and more intellectually humble?

The article recounts how endocrinology "was extremely powerful among medical elites as well as the laity—it appeared to hold the keys to human health, vitality, and actions" (Tenner 2015). The killers' defence was based on the idea that their behaviour was determined by defects in their physiology: their brain was influenced by unusual amounts of hormones, in this case. This was a reductionist assumption, underpinned by beliefs that nature can be broken down into smaller parts, and those smaller parts can explain the whole.

We know now that human behaviour is much more complicated than hormones, but reductionist approaches are still widespread. Scientific reductionism is certainly not problematic in itself, but it is important to notice when reductionist approaches and arguments are used, and to consider when they are useful and when misused.

Francis Crick, one of the discoverers of DNA, asserted the following in his book *Astonishing Hypothesis,* which focused on explaining consciousness. Perhaps he was being deliberately rhetorical and pro vocative in this statement; what exactly in his words rings untrue or incomplete?

When considering reductionist analyses, it is worth looking at how boundaries are formed at the upper and lower levels of analysis. For example, when considering human behaviour we look at a spectrum of levels, from DNA to neurons and neurochemicals all the way up to psychology, sociology and economics. Investigating outside of this range is not useful. We can speculate that studying the atoms and molecules that made up the Chicago killers' bodies will probably not reveal anything about their actions, whereas the neurochemicals in their brains, and the potential presence of pharmacological compounds, might. An awareness of the higher levels, from what might be called a zoomed-out perspective, can reveal important information—their socioeconomic context, their family background, the books they were reading and so on—that can inform how we understand them. Clearly, some behavioural phenomena are emergent; that is, they come from a higher, more zoomed-out level than the subject in question. A mob, for example, can affect the behaviour of an individual in ways that we might not be able to predict from studying only their brain.

How would we know if we have reduced something too far? It can be very revealing to follow the reductionist approach, to a point. The danger is of following it too far down or in the wrong context. One can lose sight of the forest in the trees. It may well be a human impulse to simplify things to their lowest level, all the way down to an elementary force, a grand "theory of everything", a quantum mechanics, that has so captured the attention of modern science, or of a God, that has so captured humankind for millennia. Even the phrase "to think deeply" about something suggests diving into its more fundamental constituent parts.

By taking reductionist approaches too far, one risks losing sight of emergent phenomena.

Reductionism: the thesis that reality is hierarchical and that there is no downward causation

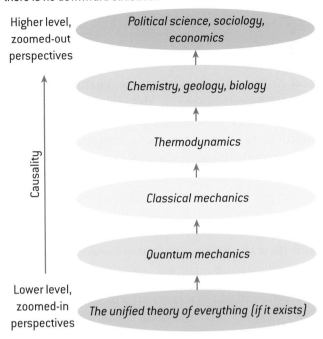

↑ **Figure 7.9** A simplified model of reductionism

It is obvious that not everything needs to be broken down to be understood; what might be less obvious is that some phenomena become invisible or unpredictable the closer you look.

In his 1997 work, *The Fabric of Reality*, physicist David Deutsch describes this alternative scenario as "emergence". The only reason that high-level sciences can be studied and understood at all, he suggests, is because, under the right circumstances, particles come together in a way that makes sense and can be analyzed, allowing us to access knowledge which is usually beyond comprehension. Thus "high-level simplicity 'emerges' from low-level complexity."

Reductionism assumes that higher levels of organization do not influence the lower levels, but rather that the lower levels explain the higher levels. This is a question of causality, and reductionist logic asserts that causality flows from small to big, as shown in Figure 7.9 below. Emergence refers to cases where it is the other way around, or at least not flowing in this straightforward way, but influenced instead by complexity.

An important counterexample stems from the work of 18th-century naturalist Alexander von Humboldt (1769–1859), an incredible figure in the history of science. Despite the fact that more things in the world are named after him than probably anyone else in the world, his full life story has only recently started emerging out of relative obscurity. Part of the renewed interest in Humboldt flows from his visionary ideas about relationships, interconnections and complexity in the natural world.

Humboldt's more progressive contemporaries were already accepting the idea that, unlike a machine that could be taken apart into pieces and reassembled, ecosystems could not be understood this way. The relationships that constituted whole organisms could not be broken up into parts. Humbolt took this thinking to a new, global level: to him the one great whole of the natural world was unified and everything in it was connected. He dedicated his life to illuminating those connections, always keeping the whole in sight, exploring the world to look for patterns and make observations where no one else had done so. Remember that it would be another 150 years before anyone would see the whole Earth for the first time. The iconic "Blue Marble" image from the 1972 Apollo 17 mission would go on to galvanize the modern environmental movement.

↑ **Figure 7.10** "The Blue Marble" image taken by the crew of Apollo 17 (1972)

IV. ETHICS

> In some sort of crude sense, which no vulgarity, no humour, no overstatements can quite extinguish, the physicists have known sin; and this is a knowledge which they cannot lose.
>
> (Oppenheimer 1947)

Oppenheimer was the wartime head of the Los Alamos Laboratory and a key contributor to the atomic bomb, a development that has captured the ethical imagination of humankind. The obvious power that comes with and through science necessitates robust ethics. This is especially true when modern science deals with such visible ethical dilemmas as those presented by genetic manipulation, nuclear power and life extension, to name but a few. Consider also the moral questions that arise from humankind's impact on Earth in the Anthropocene, as outlined in Chapter 8.

TOK is not concerned with discerning right from wrong within science, but rather in the knowledge issues involved in ethical claims. For instance, whether scientists should be allowed to experiment on animals is an important ethical question, but the TOK questions embedded into that question are different: can human beings detect, interpret, compare and/or quantify the suffering of an animal? What tools and theories enable our ability to do so, who came up with them, can we trust those people and what was their agenda? Can the benefits to testing be compared to this suffering? How will we know when we have enough evidence to make a decision? These questions necessarily involve the practice of science, but they are also inherently questions of knowledge, and require a different focus—answering not right from wrong, but *how to know* right from wrong. In answering them, we gain confidence that we know right from wrong.

A common challenge within TOK is ethical relativism, the idea that ethical standards vary across contexts because different peoples, nations and cultures often do not agree. Further, and especially within science, this disagreement is influenced by their competing strategic and political interests. Science as a tool towards power can be used toward those interests; and we have seen throughout history that when the stakes are high, the ends are somehow made to justify the means. It is imperative that we are aware of the conceptual and quantitative tools, and their shortcomings, that are used to make such ethical justifications.

The ethics of science as an area of knowledge can be explored in two main areas: the pursuit of scientific knowledge and the application of scientific knowledge. Chapter 11 deals with a similar dichotomy, between research and application in mathematics.

IV.1 Ethics in scientific methodology

Science has established traditions of integrity within the practice such that "doing good science" is nearly synonymous with "doing ethical science". In theory this is underpinned by:

- attention to detail
- sincere attempts at impartiality
- adherence to best practice standards of experimental design and procedure, including review committees that approve or deny research projects on ethical grounds.

Scientists are expected to explain their methodology so that others can seek to replicate the experiment and verify the results. The process of peer review, explained in II.4, also plays a role in monitoring and enforcing these standards and in establishing scientific credibility, so that we can trust the results of science. An ethical breach may apply to any one of these steps, though perhaps more often in falsifying or selectively interpreting data. With careers and millions of dollars at stake, the practice of science should be expected to be no more or less honest than any other human pursuit. Or should it? That was a knowledge claim about the ethics of science.

Where exactly does TOK come in here? We could start with looking for weaknesses in the ethical safeguards themselves: grant approval, peer review and experimental replicability. In recent years, these have been able to detect individual cases of malpractice or misconduct to varying levels. They are less effective at safeguarding against wider, more systematic ethical violations that appear acceptable to a community at a given time, driven by an "ends-justifies-the-means" logic, but in hindsight are problematic. For instance, there is a gruesome and sadly long list of experiments done on human subjects without their consent, typically on "othered' peoples—slaves, prisoners, the poor or mentally disabled. J. Marion Sims, referred to as the founder of gynaecology, was one of the most famous surgeons of the 19th century with statues installed in his honour, but he openly acknowledged experimenting on African-American slave women without anesthesia. His statue was recently removed from New York City.

The Nuremberg Code was established in 1949 in response to experiments by Nazi researchers on concentration camp subjects. Even after the code was established, the US Public Health Service persevered with the now-infamous Tuskegee syphilis experiment, conducted on 399 mostly poor black men, who were denied treatment and observed as their disease progressed, infecting many of their wives and children.

These examples are included here to introduce the question: should we expect science, and scientists, to abide by the social and political standards of their time, or to strive to do better? How could science do better?

As we saw in the case study in II.3, safeguards can foster a scientific conservatism that, in the words of Richard Horton, editor of *The Lancet*, led to Duesberg's silencing and "ideological assassination". The journal *Medical Hypotheses*, featured in Box 7.3, was founded on values of academic freedom and pluralism, to avoid exactly the type of conservatism and group-think that peer-review systems can foster. However, the journal has been accused of promoting dangerous pseudo-science in the AIDS denialism debate.

IV.2 Ethics in the application of scientific knowledge

We started this chapter with Oppenheimer's quote about how physicists working on the nuclear bomb have known sin. The nuclear bomb captured humankind's imagination for decades following the Second World War and the Cold War, and continues to be a familiar example in ethical concerns around scientific innovation. Genetic engineering is another such issue. With regards to research and innovation, should we or should we not? is a perennial question that humankind may never stop asking. A more relevant question for us is how we arrive at the answer to that question. The approach for many issues—including nuclear power and genetic engineering—will usually invoke appeals to morality and universal laws, utilitarian cost-benefit analyses, concerns about unintended side effects, comparisons to any alternatives and analyses of best and worst case scenarios. Each of these in turn should be explored for problems of knowledge. Let's consider the commonly used cost-benefit analysis, the tool of choice for practical-minded decision-makers who are often far removed from the consequences of their decisions. It may seem a cold-hearted logic to tally up the costs and benefits of massive applications of destructive power, but the cost-benefit analysis is an essential, imperfect and widely used tool in decision-making across many fields.

IV.3 The cost-benefit analysis

The cost-benefit framework rests on the fundamental assumption that relevant costs and benefits are knowable and, crucially, quantifiable, to an extent that allows for comparing the sum totals of each. For example, environmental impact assessments, pharmaceutical research and technological innovation projects need to know the advantages and disadvantages of their work. Frequently this requires comparing impacts on human lives in the present and the future. When we think about policies designed to prevent climate change, we need to know first the value of various ecosystems, and then the costs of the disruption to these ecosystems, versus the costs of mitigating climate change. A third step is comparing how all of this mitigation work balances against the relative costs and benefits of adapting to it. And as if all that is not challenging enough, we must build tolerances for uncertainty into the analyses, leaving placeholders for the known and unknown unknowns. This is a deeply complex cost-benefit analysis that requires international organizations and governments to agree on things that are inherently hard to measure, and we can see why it has been so challenging for them to come to an agreement. Climate change has been described as a "perfect moral storm", as we see in Chapter 8.

A fascinating example of unpredictability is Chernobyl, the site of an unmitigated nuclear catastrophe in 1986. It was expected to be a wasteland for centuries but, as it turns out, the ecosystem there is thriving. In 2015, one article stated that "[t]he biodiversity is higher there than before the accident" (Hopkin 2015), and mentioned the potential for ecotourism to the area. Other estimates suggest there are seven times more wolves inside the exclusion zone (created due to the meltdown) than outside it. The example of Chernobyl shows how challenging it can be to predict the complex and emergent phenomena associated with environmental impacts, and perhaps, to end on a more hopeful note, the resilience of our natural environments in the face of human degradation.

A logical entry point into cost-benefit analyses about climate change is to quantify the social cost of emitting carbon. How is this social cost known? Consider the following, published on Stanford University's website in 2015.

> [A] U.S. government study concluded, based on the results of three widely used economic impact models, that an additional ton of carbon dioxide emitted in 2015 would cause $37 worth of economic damages. These damages are expected to take various forms, including decreased agricultural yields, harm to human health and lower worker productivity, all related to climate change. But according to a new study, published online this week in the journal Nature Climate Change, the actual cost could be much higher. 'We estimate that the social cost of carbon is not $37 per ton, as previously estimated, but $220 per ton,' said study co-author Frances Moore, at Stanford's School of Earth Sciences.
>
> (Than 2015)

Making connections

Knowledge and politics

We should note there is no confusion about the fact of anthropogenic climate change, or the fact that it is already disrupting lives and ecosystems. The point is that experts, even as of January 2020, disagree about the numbers in one of the most important cost-benefit analysis of our time, and disagree by a large margin. That margin can be filled by the opinions, assumptions and ideologies of competing interests, and is one reason why a scientific discourse has become so heavily politicized. Refining the cost-benefit analysis, using better data and measurement, is one route to diminishing the space available for this politicization.

As an exercise, try a cost-benefit analysis on a topic of your choosing, using the best available information online, to see how far you get.

Cost-benefit analyses are frequently used and invoked without due concern for their limitations, and with quantitative approximations and assumptions that sometimes more closely reflect the intentions and beliefs of their estimators than reality. It is the uncritical acceptance of such analyses that is problematic. Also problematic, however, is the disdain for, or distrust in, experts who attempt cost-benefit analyses to the best of their ability, and the dismissal of their results in the "post-truth" public sphere.

Chapter 11, IV.2, shows that quantitative justifications for decisions, opinions and policies can carry an aura of authority that is accepted too quickly. As we see in that chapter, people have been wrongfully convicted of crimes on the basis of faulty statistics. The old adage, widely cited and often misattributed to Mark Twain, says "There are three kinds of lies: lies, damned lies, and statistics".

Therein is the inherent danger of scientific ethics: science claims to speak for the world and, in so

doing, also shapes it. All of us should be aware of the knowledge issues inherent to ethical scientific claims and justifications. Every time you read something that quantifies costs and benefits, or estimates that X number of dollars will be saved or lost, remember how wrong the US government was, as recently as 2015, in estimating the social cost of carbon, one of the most important numbers of our time.

IV.4 The golem that is science

We opened this chapter with Bacon's metaphors for pushing past the limits of knowledge and the metaphorical end of the world. Now let's consider a more recent metaphor from Harry M. Collins and Trevor Pinch. They liken the scientific enterprise to a creature from Jewish mythology.

> Science seems to be either all good or all bad. For some, science is a crusading knight beset by simple-minded mystics … . For others it is science which is the enemy; our gentle planet, our feel for the just, the poetic and the beautiful, are assailed by a technological bureaucracy—the antithesis of culture—controlled by capitalists with no concern but for profit. For some, science gives us agricultural self-sufficiency, cures for the crippled, and a global network of communication; for others it gives us weapons of war, a school teacher's fiery death as the space shuttle falls from grace, and the silent, deceiving, bone-poisoning Chernobyl.
>
> Both these ideas of science are wrong and dangerous. The personality of science is neither that of a chivalrous knight nor that of a pitiless juggernaut. What, then, is science? Science is a golem.
>
> … a humanoid made by man from clay and water, with incantations and spells. It is powerful. It grows a little more powerful every day. It will follow orders, do your work, and protect you from the ever threatening enemy. But it is clumsy and dangerous. Without control, a golem may destroy its masters … .
>
> [I]t is also worth noting that in the mediaeval tradition the creature of clay was animated by having the Hebrew 'EMETH', meaning truth, inscribed on its forehead—it is truth that drives it on. But this does not mean it understands the truth—far from it.
>
> (Collins, Pinch 2012)

For discussion

The power of metaphor

In Chapter 4 we explore the power of metaphor for understanding complex ideas. Metaphors carry values and assumptions of the cultures and intellectual traditions that use them. Woven through this textbook and the TOK course is the map metaphor of knowledge, and

that metaphor too is not neutral. In Chapter 1 we briefly discuss the importance of varying our metaphors to gain a more nuanced and deeper understanding of knowledge.

In light of this, what can you say about the usefulness, role or power of the golem as a metaphor for science?

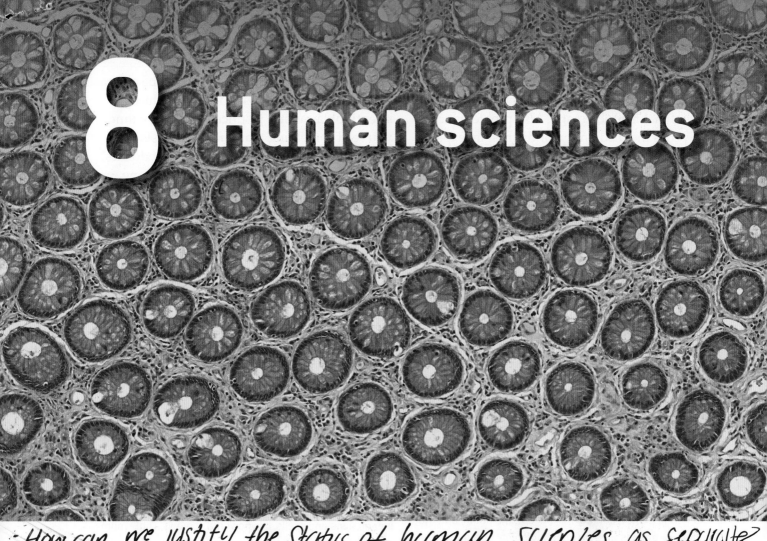

8 Human sciences

- How can we justify the status of human sciences as separate?

This chapter is about the scientific answers to questions about what it is to be human, what human similarities and differences mean, what forces shape our social reality, and what responsibilities we have towards making a better world. There is no single authoritative source or discipline that answers these questions, but the human sciences do manage to piece together some answers. There is certainly much at stake. As a result, this chapter pays particular attention to the consequences of agreement and disagreement in the human sciences.

What does it mean to be human?
Social Reality & responsibility

I. SCOPE

difficult to define

It is not surprising that, of all the AOKs, the human sciences have perhaps the most porous and disputed boundaries. Humanity is complex and ever-changing, and even if we focus on the social and cultural aspects of human life, drawing a boundary around this AOK is difficult because of:

- the entanglement of culture and nature
- the interconnection of our social and physical environments

relational epistemology

- the kinship and similarities among humans and other animals.

Within the boundaries of the human sciences there are many varied disciplines: psychology, economics, anthropology, political science and so on, with an even greater number of overlapping sub-disciplines: behavioural psychology, behavioural economics, political anthropology, ethnobotany and ethnomusicology, human geography, and so the list continues.

[Handwritten notes at top: "understand influences on human behaviour etc... and so on — to INFORM FUTURE DECISIONS"]

> Few people realise that psychologists also take a vow, promising that at some point in their professional lives they will publish a book, a chapter or at least an article that contains the sentence: 'The human being is the only animal that ...'. We are allowed to finish the sentence any way we like, but it has to start with those eight words.
>
> Most of us wait until relatively late in our careers to fulfil this solemn obligation because we know that successive generations of psychologists will ignore all the other words that we managed to pack into a lifetime of well-intentioned scholarship and remember us mainly for how we finished The Sentence.
>
> We also know that the worse we do, the better we will be remembered. For instance, those psychologists who finished The Sentence with 'can use language' were particularly well remembered when chimpanzees were taught to communicate with hand signs.
>
> And when researchers discovered that chimps in the wild used sticks to extract tasty termites from their mounds (and to bash each other over the head now and again), the world suddenly remembered the full name and mailing address of every psychologist who ever finished The Sentence with the words 'uses tools'.
>
> So it is with good reason that most psychologists put off completing The Sentence for as long as they can, hoping that if they wait long enough, they might just die in time to avoid being publicly humiliated by a monkey.
>
> (Gilbert 2007)

Daniel Gilbert's words may seem comical, but they point out the problem with defining distinctly human activities: monkeys do business, whales sing, birds use fire, honeybees exhibit complex social behaviour, trees communicate and share resources with each other. With each discovery the list gets longer, and the arguments for human exceptionalism less so. In fact, it is a struggle to think of any studies that show non-humans being *less* sophisticated than previously thought. How then can we justify the status of the human sciences as a separate AOK?

[Handwritten: HUMAN EXCEPTIONALISM]

Why is the body of scientific knowledge about humankind considered by TOK to be at least as important as our knowledge about the rest of the natural world combined?

Writing in response to these questions, Joanna Bourke says that the distinction between the human and the animal is not only contested, but "policed with demonic precision".

> ... ideas, values and practices used to justify the sovereignty of a particular understanding of 'the human' over the rest of sentient life are what create society and social life. Perhaps the very concept of 'culture' is an attempt to differentiate ourselves from our 'creatureliness', our fleshly vulnerability ... Delimiting those territories not only involves violence, but inspires it.
>
> (Bourke 2011)

[Handwritten: important because it informs POWER!]

The knowledge questions arising from the human sciences are also significant because of the power of this AOK to inform policy, social movements, individual action and choice. This body of knowledge shapes the realities, phenomena and behaviours it studies. In making evidence-based decisions about how to organize our societies and lead our lives, we make significant use of knowledge from this AOK. We look, for example, to cultural anthropology to make sense of our similarities and differences in an increasingly interconnected world, and to economics to guide decision-making in a world of finite resources, time and information. For these reasons, we must pay attention to theory building and concept formation in the human sciences—and consider to what extent they reflect, versus shape, the reality of human experience.

Is the aim of the human sciences primarily to describe and explain patterns of human activity, to make predictions about outcomes in society, to guide interventions and inform action, or something else entirely?

[Handwritten notes in right margin: "one way mirror", "cannot speak universally!", "relationship between cause / certainty"]

[Handwritten at bottom: "CAUSATION – effect", "CORRELATION – relationship between two variables"]

For reflection and discussion

Explanations, neutrality and power in the human sciences

Think of an idea or theory coming from any one of the human sciences that describes or explains an important part of the human experience—perhaps one that you have encountered in your studies. *anthropology- egocentrism*

Consider which words you would use to describe the power of this idea or theory. Would you say it determined, defined, shaped, affected or influenced aspects of the world? Which words did you choose and why?

·local ·individualism ·selfish ·elite powers

Yes. I would say it shapes the...

Share your answer with a partner or in a class discussion. Together or individually consider the following questions.

Oh boy this is hard

human vs. social sciences

What is called the human sciences in TOK is usually referred to as social sciences outside of this course. Both terms appear interchangeably in this chapter but perhaps the difference is that one makes its starting point the human individual, the other the collective society. Whichever starting point is used, the great diversity of disciplines within the human sciences challenges the coherence and cohesion of this AOK. Is there more that distinguishes rather than unifies the human science disciplines? Do they have more in common than not? Does it even make sense to refer to them collectively as the human sciences? To explore those questions, this chapter looks at their historical origins, methodological approaches, conceptual frameworks and applications in the real world, that may justify referring to them collectively.

historically Enlightenment to advance freedom, humanity

The quest for scientific answers, in the narrow sense of the term, to fundamentally social and human questions dates back to the Enlightenment thinkers of the 18th century. What was then called the moral sciences set out to advance freedom and humanity. The aim of Enlightenment thinkers was to produce knowledge about humans and our societies based on *disinterested* and *value-free* evaluation and analysis of empirical evidence.

1. To what extent does knowledge in the human sciences derive its value from its potential for application?

2. Can you think of an idea or theory in the human sciences that has value, but no effect on the world? *"Flow" - theoretical framework*

3. If knowledge in the human sciences has material consequences on the world, in what sense can it be neutral?

Keep the concepts of value, neutrality and power in mind, and trace how they come up throughout this chapter, and in the production, acquisition and application of knowledge in the human sciences.

CAN KNOWLEDGE BE OBJECTIVE?

One of the main objectives of the TOK course is to interrogate the extent to which knowledge can be disinterested and value-free. Refer to the 17th-century debate between Hobbes and Boyle, about the relationship between knowledge and politics, with which we open Chapter 2. It would not be until the intellectual debates of the 20th century that the human sciences, as the social and political theorist Peter Wagner argues, gained enough independent status to provide knowledge that was considered valid and useful. These debates about the big questions of humanity shaped sociology, psychology, anthropology and economics into the disciplines we recognize today.

They brought doubts about the value of the human sciences to the surface, to be acknowledged and grappled with. And there was, even then, a significant group "inclined to entirely abandon any attempt to render the social world intelligible in the face of its complexity and lack of evident order" (Wagner 2001). And therefore we see that the starting assumption of the human sciences is that humans are knowable to themselves.

This chapter explores some of the attempts, successes and failures of the human sciences to engage with the messiness of human nature and social reality.

The case study below considers the example of how economics—for better or worse—has strived to maintain its legitimacy and authority in the past couple of decades. Could mathematics help the human sciences navigate and make sense of the complexity of the world?

Mathiness and physics envy in the human sciences

Economics is sometimes proclaimed the most rigorous among the human sciences, at least by economists. The issue of the supposed rigour of economics is our entry point into the discussion about the contestable boundaries between the natural and human sciences, and the exchange between both of them and mathematics.

> There is an implicit pecking order among the social sciences, and it seems to be dominated by economics. For starters, economists see themselves at or near the top of the disciplinary hierarchy. In a survey conducted in the early 2000s, [David] Colander found that 77 per cent of economics graduate students in elite programs agree with the statement that "economics is the most scientific of the social sciences". Some fifteen years ago, Richard Freeman speculated on the origins of this conviction. His assessment was candid: 'sociologists and political scientists have less powerful analytical tools and know less than we do, or so we believe. By scores on the Graduate Record Examination and other criteria, our field attracts students stronger than theirs, and our courses are more mathematically demanding'.
>
> (Fourcade *et al* 2015)

Some who believe in the rigour of economics think it reflects a natural order of social reality. Others might think this false, even bizarre, given the discipline's repeated failure to predict and prevent economic crises. Critics point out that this chasing of rigour has led to an over-reliance on abstract mathematical models, which, rather than producing predictions about the future, actually obscure a pseudo-scientific

methodology. And critics have been saying this for several decades, but change has been slow. The 2009 global recession that wiped out millions of dollars of savings, and precipitated a debt crisis in Southern Europe, came just six years after a leading economist had proclaimed that the "central problem of depression-prevention has been solved" (Lucas quoted in Krugman 2009). Nobel Laureate Paul Krugman, one of the most trenchant critics among the leading economists, has summed up as follows: "the economics profession went astray because economists, as a group, mistook beauty, clad in impressive-looking mathematics, for truth" (Krugman 2009). Why were they impressed by mathematics?

"Mathiness" as a term was devised by Paul Romer, an Economics Nobel Laureate, who originally used it to describe a style of work that "lets academic politics masquerade as science" (Romer 2015) by camouflaging political arguments in an ambiguous mix of words and symbols, natural and formal language, and theoretical and empirical content. He argues that mathiness makes it difficult to access and critique the economics discourse, and gives the work an unearned sense of authority. Both of these—access and authority—are significant knowledge issues.

According to Krugman, there are strong political and business incentives that propel an idealized vision of economies composed of fully rational agents—despite plenty of evidence to the contrary—and "fancy equations" have obscured these less-tenable model assumptions in both academia and policy. To make his long argument short, Krugman asserts that mathiness is used to defend faulty economics, including the neoliberal paradigm.

> The central cause of the profession's failure was the desire for an all-encompassing, intellectually elegant approach that also gave economists a chance to show off their mathematical prowess.
>
> (Krugman 2009)

Both Krugman and Romer have said that mathiness can conceal political arguments in naturalistic or empirical clothing. This is especially problematic because, in the words of John Rapley, a political economist at the University of Cambridge, "scientists are supposed to reach their conclusions after doing research and weighing the evidence but, in economics, conclusions can come first, with economists gravitating towards a thesis that fits their moral worldview" (Rapley 2018). Dressing these theories with mathiness can make them more convincing, or at least more difficult to critique.

But is there evidence for the claim that mathematics lends the human sciences an aura of authority, deserved or otherwise? Consider, for a minute, the pseudo-scientific claims, supported by statistics, that are regularly invoked in everything from advertising to political debates. One is reminded how William Thomson, a renowned 19th-century scientist known for his work on the laws of thermodynamics, had stated. "When you can measure what you are speaking about and express it in numbers you know something about it; but when you cannot measure it … in numbers, your knowledge is of a meagre and unsatisfactory kind."

The implications of measurement are explored in section III. The success of physics and chemistry in explaining our world may have contributed to a perception that mathematical formulas have an authoritative force. Within the human sciences there is even a term for this, "physics envy", used to criticize the overuse of complicated mathematics to appear more rigorous.

Mathematics can guarantee the semblance of science, and sometimes that is enough to convince laypeople and academics alike.

> Economics has always been an ethical and social exercise, its purpose being to produce the rules by which a community organises its production. It's not accidental that Adam Smith, whose work *The Wealth of Nations* (1776) is often seen as the founding text of economics, was a moral philosopher. Yet ever after, it was the holy grail of economists to make their art into a science, using it to uncover the codes supposedly buried in their heart of human existence. They experimented with mathematics and pondered Charles Darwin's revolution in biology, but it would be the late 19th century before economics finally found a model for itself. It found it in physics. But … the social nature of human beings makes any laws of behaviour tentative and contextual. In fact, the very term 'social science' is probably best seen as an oxymoron … in the 1970s, the Nobel laureate Wassily Leontief warned against the drift that had begun in economics towards what was subsequently called 'physics envy'.
>
> (Rapley 2018)

Krugman and Romer have applied the mathiness critique to their community of professional economists, but it has been invoked in other disciplines in the human sciences, too. Steven Pinker's book *The Better Angels of Our Nature* (2011) used a vast statistical analysis to argue that the present is the most peaceful time in human history, and impressed a wide global audience including, apparently, Microsoft co-founder Bill Gates and the philosopher Peter Singer. However, Pinker's methods were publicly criticized by Nassim Taleb, an outspoken statistician, author and professor at New York University. To what extent could a layperson access and critique Pinker's methods? How would we know whether Taleb is right? For those of us who are mathematical non-experts, it can be difficult to judge who is right and wrong, when both sides appear to hold heavy-weight academic credentials. But an even bigger danger would be to throw our hands up in defeat.

Making connections

Understanding statistics as a layperson

The opaqueness of the statistics behind knowledge claims becomes an ethical issue when these claims are made in law, health or other domains of human decision-making with significant consequences. Chapter 11 explores knowledge issues with the use of statistics in section IV.

It would also be dangerous to disregard the benefits of mathematical reasoning and clearly a balance needs to be struck in the human sciences. Romer states the following.

> If the participants in a discussion are committed to science, mathematical theory can encourage a unique clarity and precision in both reasoning and communication. It would be a serious setback for our discipline if economists lose their commitment to careful mathematical reasoning.
>
> (Romer 2015)

The other side of the discussion should not be neglected. There are disciplines such as econophysics and social physics that effectively blur the boundaries between the natural and human sciences, using mathematical tools inspired by physics to understand and explain human behaviour and interactions in crowds, markets and other complex social systems. The term "econophysics" was introduced by H. Eugene Stanley, following his observation that a very large number of papers on stock markets were written by physicists.

Counter-claim

A number of disciplines have wholeheartedly embraced mathematical tools and applied models from physics to economic problems.

For example, the physicist Bikas Chakrabarti has applied the kinetic theory of gas to models of markets, and co-authored a book entitled *Econophysics of Income & Wealth Distributions*. His is not a one-off example; the list of physics-trained economists is too long to provide here, and includes luminaries such as Jan Tinbergen, the first ever recipient of the Nobel Prize in Economics, and widely considered one of the most influential economists of the 20th century.

With the arrival of "big data", social scientists are hoping that analyses of huge market data sets, powered by statistical tools and machine learning, will reveal insights about human behaviour. Whether these insights can be generalized into human laws remains to be seen.

For example, financial economics has been a particular focus for quantitative research inspired by physics, but behavioural economics has not. Some of the criticisms voiced by Romer and Krugman allude to the fact that quantitative methods may have spread too far, too quickly and without enough consideration, which may well be a reflection of their success, not failure. It would also be a mistake to describe economics as too "mathy" or anything else because, as we have seen, it is not a monolithic discipline but a field consisting of varied subdisciplines with considerable differences of methodology.

Box 8.1: Applying natural laws to human behaviour

The idea of describing society using the laws of physics and biology is not new. Henri de Saint-Simon's 1803 book, *Lettres d'un habitant de Genève à ses contemporains*, did just that. Saint-Simon's student and collaborator was Auguste Comte, the philosopher widely regarded as the founder of sociology, who defined social physics as "that science which occupies itself with social phenomena, considered in the same light as astronomical, physical, chemical, and physiological

phenomena, that is to say as being subject to natural and invariable laws, the discovery of which is the special object of its researches" (Comte quoted in Iggers 1959).

After Saint-Simon and Comte, it was statistician Adolphe Quetelet who, in 1835, wrote a book entitled *Essay on Social Physics: Man and the Development of his Faculties*, which describes using mathematical probability to model society. A commonly told (and possibly apocryphal) story has it that Comte invented the term "sociologie" (sociology) in response to Quetelet's appropriation of the term "social physics", because Comte did not agree with his statistics.

Later, 20th-century researchers including the geographer Reino Ajo and astrophysicist John Q. Stewart, used gravity models to show the distribution of social interactions. There is also the gravity model of trade, which builds a model of bilateral trading relations on the laws of gravity. It would seem a curious proposition to equate the trading behaviour of people in different countries to the relationship between massive objects. However, the gravity model of trade is generally considered an empirical success, accurately predicting trade flows between countries for many goods and services.

So we see that mathematics in the human sciences is neither a recent nor necessarily problematic invention. But in the past 20 years, a very large number of social science papers have used physics-inspired mathematics. Contemporary academics have written books on the subject, including the simply named *Social Physics*, by MIT professor Alex Pentland, and *The Social Atom*, by Mark Buchanan, editor of *Nature* magazine.

For discussion

Knowledge used to describe, explain or predict

Alex Pentland, a professor at MIT, writes:

> "We are coming to realize that human behaviour is determined as much by the patterns of our culture as by rational, individual thinking. These patterns can be described mathematically, and used to make accurate predictions." (www.endor.com/social-physics)

Pentland's assertion is that knowledge about human behaviour can be used to describe, explain and predict phenomena. To what extent do you agree? What are the strengths and weaknesses of the different human sciences towards this?

II. PERSPECTIVES

The human sciences grapple with questions that have profound social implications. These disciplines are based on facts and assumptions about the ways in which all humans are the same, about our set of shared characteristics, and the essential uniformity underlying all human variation. This is not a stable set, and over time items have been added to and taken off the list. Without the assumption of human sameness on a fundamental level, could there be a legitimate basis for the human sciences to make universal claims about human nature? Based on this assumption of human sameness, psychologists or economists make claims that apply to all humans about how memory works or how we make choices.

Interestingly, it is not uncommon for the set of human similarities to be described as human biology, whereas the set of human differences is often described as human culture. Why do you think this is the case?

Recently, thinkers and researchers have insisted that nature versus culture is a false dichotomy. Scientists have been mostly unsuccessful at disentangling nature and culture, whether by extracting nature from ideology and politics, or by guarding culture from claims about genes and neurotransmitters. Donna Haraway offers the term "natureculture", signalling that these two domains, and therefore our knowledge about them, are inseparable. Box 8.2 explores the interconnected worlds of biology, culture, history and politics.

Box 8.2: An unnatural history of the politics and science of pain

"Are women animals?" This was the title of a letter published in 1872, by an author we know only by the name she signed off with: "An Earnest Englishwoman". She was protesting the unequal treatment of women under British law; women were not seen as fully human and therefore not equal to nor part of "mankind". Just a few decades earlier, the legal system had increased protections for animals' from cruelty, but the same protections were not in place for women. The Earnest Englishwoman's plea was to raise the status of women by subsuming them in the legislation protecting animals from cruelty.

The letter was satirical, of course, but draws our attention to how scientific claims about humanness influence ideas about political personhood and equality. The boundary between the concepts "human" and "animal" has been affected by political as well as scientific ideas and debates.

The Earnest Englishwoman wrote at the height of one such debate, with Charles Darwin's "Expression of the Emotions in Man and Animals" appearing in the same year. Sentience (the capacity to feel) was receiving attention as a demarcation criterion for the human-animal question. The belief at the time that not all humans are equally capable of suffering was influenced by the idea of a "great chain of being", a hierarchy ranking all matter and life forms from highest to lowest, which had been very influential for two millennia of Western thought. The "chain of feeling" inspired by it was much shorter, and placed "civilized men" at the high end, and "savages slaves, and animals" at the low end. Before we continue with this story, remember to keep in mind how these ideas and theories were constructed, and what we can do to guard against believing modern-day falsehoods.

"People who had been placed at the 'lower' end of the Chain of Feeling paid an extremely high price for prejudices about their 'inability' to feel … slaves and 'savages', for instance, were routinely depicted as possessing a limited capacity to experience pain, a biological 'fact' that conveniently diminished any culpability among their so-called superiors for acts of abuse inflicted on them. …

With voyeuristic curiosity, travellers and explorers often commented on what they regarded as exotic responses to pain by indigenous peoples. …

Racial sciences placed great emphasis on the development and complexity of the brain and nerves. As the author of *Pain and Sympathy* (1907) concluded, attempting to explain why the 'savage' could 'bear physical torture without shrinking': the 'higher the life, the keener is the sense of pain'." (Bourke 2014)

Follow the link to read the whole article.

 Search terms: Bourke
This won't hurt a bit
New Statesman

This logic did not progress very far. The label of inferiority applied to non-European peoples for their insensitive bodies could also be applied to women for exactly the opposite reason: extreme sensitivity. And certainly, no one wanted to believe that women occupied the highest place in the hierarchy. To resolve the contradiction, a distinction between pain perception and pain reaction emerged. It explained that "hysterical" women's exaggerated response to pain was further evidence of inferiority.

Bourke offers two examples from the clinical literature of the time, showing how prejudices crept into analyses that were supposedly value-free.

"It does not always follow that because a patient bears what appears to be a great amount of pain with remarkable fortitude, that that individual is more deserving of credit or shows greater self-control than the one who does not; for it is a well-established fact that pain is not felt to the same degree by all individuals alike." (Finney quoted in Bourke 2014)

NOUVELLE ICONOGRAPHIE DE LA SALPÊTRIÈRE   T. III. PL. XVIII

PHOTOTYPE NÉGATIF A. LONDE   PHOTOCOLLOGRAPHIE CHÈNE & LONGUET

BAILLEMENTS HYSTÉRIQUES

"[A] savage probably suffers less than a civilised man from any given injury, and hence may display more fortitude. An hysterical woman probably does not suffer more than one with a more healthy nervous system, but she complains more loudly, for she has her feelings in all things less under control. Race appears to exercise an influence in pain; some of the native races of India appear to suffer far less than Europeans under surgical operations of a similar kind." (Treatise: "The Science and Art of Surgery" 1884, quoted in Bourke 2014)

And thus, the science of pain placed European men firmly at the top of the great chain of being. The gender, race and level of "civilization" of people both decided and was determined by their position in fool-proof logic. In turn, scientific claims about their level of sentience affected whether they would be considered full members in the category "human beings", with huge political and social consequences.

For reflection

Treatment of pain

The issue of under-treatment for pain among women and minority groups continues to affect patients today, almost 150 years after the Earnest Englishwoman's letter. That is almost exactly as long as we have known about endometriosis, for example, a painful condition affecting 10% of women that is still poorly diagnosed.

Consider these questions.

1. Given its history, is it possible to approach pain as a purely scientific question?

2. What kinds of knowledge about pain, science and politics are necessary to find a way forward?

3. What examples can you think of that show how politics and history affect theories in the human sciences today?

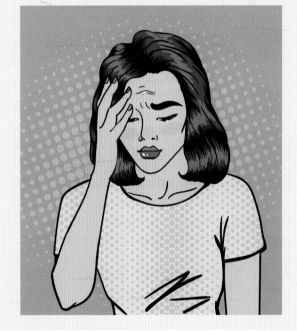

One of the central enquiries in the human sciences has been to make sense of our astounding human variation, and to sort our similarities and differences into meaningful categories. Much of theory-building and concept formation in this AOK has been directed towards explaining phenomena found on a spectrum of human similarity and difference. Emile Durkheim who was among the first academic sociologists, argued that: "[to gain] a complete understanding of any social phenomenon we have to understand why it came into existence in the first place (its causes and origins) and the reason it goes on existing (its effects or functions)" (Durkheim 1895).

Origins

functions

We explore perspectives on the existence and persistence of various phenomena, from evil to adolescence to money, in the remainder of this section.

II.1 The trouble with normality

Different societies and human sciences over time have placed, moved and removed definitions about what is considered normal behaviour and what is seen as unacceptable, undesirable or deviant behaviour. One challenge with defining "normal" has been that no established criteria for determining the *normal* ranges exist for many sociological phenomena, unlike in the study of disease. Researchers in the human sciences have used statistical distributions to draw imprecise lines where normal behaviours end and abnormal, deviant or pathological ones begin. Others, following Durkheim's example, have focused on social norms to explain the distribution of traits and behaviours. In this view, normal is seen as conformity to a conventional standard that arises when repeated and "average" behaviours become desirable for members of the group to strive towards. Another view simply says that normal traits and characteristics are those that humans have evolved through natural selection. When we encounter claims made about normal and deviant behaviour, traits or acts, we should keep in mind that they are made against a backdrop of deep disagreement among experts and constantly shifting standards.

Yet, ideas about normalcy and deviance, however tentative, continue to play significant roles in our daily lives, used to guide our own behaviours or judge those of others. A moral equivalence of "normal" with "good" means that the labels "abnormal", "deviant" or "pathological" can have stigmatizing and marginalizing effects. Consider how they have been applied in the context of neurological diversity or sexual orientation.

To explore the making of claims regarding normalcy, let's look at an example from the 1960s. A deep questioning was underway in the aftermath of the Second World War about the human capacity to do evil and be evil. What level of this capacity is normal for people? Can we get better at identifying and predicting for this human trait? Events of the war cast serious doubts on many previous beliefs, and researchers in many disciplines focused on these questions once again. Among them was Hannah Arendt who, based on the war crimes trial of Adolf Eichmann, coined the term "the banality of evil". She, like the rest of the world, may have expected Eichmann to be a confronting picture of individual pathology, but found that rather than being in any obvious way sadistic, demonic or monstrous, he appeared and acted "terrifyingly normal" (Arendt 2006).

At about the same time that Arendt wrote these words, psychologist Stanley Milgram carried out what became the foremost study on how obedience to authority can motivate behaviour contrary to one's personal conscience. It was the evidence to Arendt's eloquent description of evil. The findings were harrowing: 65% of participants, believing that they were assisting an experiment on learning, administered a lethal electrical shock to the "learner" when instructed to do so by a figure of authority. The "learners" in the experiments were actors, and were of course unharmed, but the results sent shocks out into the world.

In 1971 another psychologist, Philip Zimbardo, with his famous Stanford Prison experiment, added to the evidence for the claim that evil is unleashed by larger societal forces, rather than an individual's wicked heart.

The studies by Milgram and Zimbardo would go on to become two of the most famous experiments in psychology. Suspicion stalks fame, so these experiments have been subject to scrutiny for decades, and largely withstood sceptical probes into their methods and results. However, the opening of archives and the surfacing of new material in the past couple of years, especially regarding the Stanford Prison experiment, have caused new doubts and raised new questions about these conclusions.

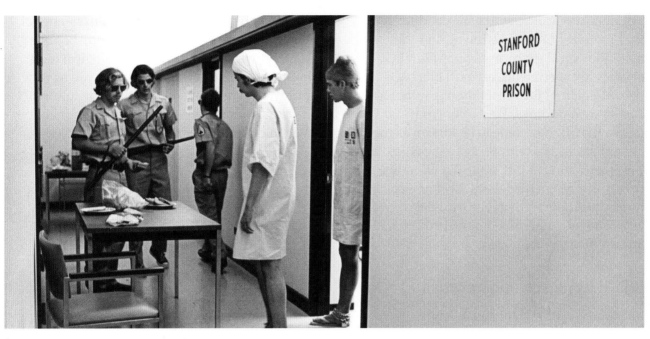

↑ **Figure 8.1** "Guards" and their "prisoners" during the experiment conducted at Stanford University

Zimbardo's prison experiment was described on Twitter as "antiscientific" by psychology professor Simine Vazire, after new evidence revealed that the experimental design and execution may have been quite poor and compromised by investigator bias. The experiment has lost some of its landmark status, and its legacy poses familiar questions, such as the following.

- What is an appropriate response when established knowledge is shown to be controversial?
- How do we best separate the personality and reputation of the researcher from the research?
- What is the responsibility of professors and teachers in the process of knowledge sharing and transfer?

For discussion

Integrity in research

Vazire was referring to an article by Ben Blum, which is excellent TOK reading.

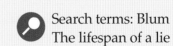 Search terms: Blum
The lifespan of a lie

Follow the link to read the article and then discuss the following questions with a partner, in a small group or as a class.

1. How might the beliefs, interests and experiences of researchers affect their research?

2. What kinds of checks are necessary to ensure the integrity of the results and conclusions of research?

3. How should we guard against being too quick to accept scientific theories that align with the cultural climate of the time?

The allegations of scientific misconduct in the Stanford Prison experiment, and the methodological concerns about Milgram's obedience experiments, are part of a big re-evaluation of the reliability of psychology's best-known findings. We explore more of this in III.6. It may come to be known as the biggest scientific controversy of the 2010s, but self-questioning at this scale in a discipline is hardly unprecedented. As II.2 below explains, for about a quarter of a century a debate raged in anthropology that spilled beyond academia to attract intense public interest for years.

II.2 Of heroines and heretics

Margaret Mead was the most famous anthropologist of the 20th century. Indeed, by the time of her death in 1978 she had become synonymous with the field of cultural anthropology. She was the "Mother to the World" according to *Time* magazine (1969), and recipient of the Presidential Medal of Freedom, the highest civilian honour in the United States. Taking visible positions in society and championing civil rights, gender equality and environmental justice, she went beyond the call of academic duty to become a public icon. Mead set the standards for what it means to be a public anthropologist and was widely considered as one of the greats of the discipline already during her lifetime. Then there was controversy, as explained by anthropologist Paul Shankman:

> … it was major news in 1983, five years after her death, when Derek Freeman, a New Zealand-born anthropologist, published *Margaret Mead and Samoa: The Making and Unmaking of an Anthropological Myth*, a slashing attack criticizing Mead's near-iconic study as deeply flawed if not deliberately distorted to promote ideas that had as much to do with her own views on sex and with American culture of the 1920s as with adolescence in Polynesia.
>
> (Shankman 2009)

Before the publication of Freeman's book, an article appeared on the front page of the *New York Times* anticipating it, which showed mass media taking an interest in the controversies of a narrow academic field. The episode became deeply divisive and exposed ideological fault lines in academic anthropology as well as in society. Could it be that the power of culture to shape human behaviour had been hugely overstated for half a century?

↑ **Figure 8.2** Margaret Mead dressed in traditional clothing during her time in Samoa

Freeman's attack on Mead's anthropology also threatened the liberalism and feminism of her civic work. To understand why, we need a basic understanding of the conflicting knowledge claims that were made. Mead's *Coming of Age in Samoa* (1928) was a key development in the nature-nurture debate. It claimed that while biological puberty was universal, the turmoil of adolescence often said to accompany it was a product of culture. Mead offered a range of evidence for this, but there was one major concern for many, and especially for Freeman. Mead described Samoa as a sexually liberal culture and claimed that this made puberty more harmonious for young Samoans as compared to their rebellious American peers. Freeman challenged this description of Samoan culture, the evidence it was based on and the conclusions drawn from it. His critique was severe on both Mead's methodology and integrity: he painted her as a young ethnographer fundamentally misunderstanding aspects of the culture she was studying, selecting evidence that suited her and generalizing her conclusions too far. He also claimed that Mead was tricked into believing stories of sexual escapades by her female informants, who were in fact joking. Of course, Margaret Mead was not around to respond.

The debate raged for years. Some were and remained convinced by Freeman, and even today refer to the episode as an exposé and a necessary corrective of the anthropological record that cautions us against inflating the reputations of iconic intellectuals. The field of anthropology was confronted with deep disagreements about standards of evidence, the sovereignty of analysis, the disinterestedness of interpretation and the validity of conclusions.

Issues of contested methodological rigour and professional integrity are explored in different contexts throughout this chapter. What is important about this example is that it draws our attention also to the dynamics of the encounters between Western researchers and colonized and Indigenous Peoples. This is what makes this episode relevant today beyond the topic of anthropological history. A lot has been said about Mead and Freeman, but what of the Samoans who launched these anthropologists' careers? While the controversy scrutinized what we know about human culture and biology, and how we know it, the Samoans at the centre were largely left out of the conversation.

The anthropological literature is riddled with problems of representation. In some ways it is the central problem of the discipline. If Mead was right that culture so powerfully shapes societies, then we must pay special attention to the cultures of academic and other knowledge-producing institutions. We see this influence when students start sounding like the people they study. It is, after all, one of the lessons of

anthropology that echoing in our voices are the voices of our ancestors. To honour the diverse ways in which anthropology is being practised globally, projects such as the Decanonizing anthropology syllabus offer neglected but deserving alternatives to mainstream texts. While this might be of particular interest to students of anthropology, the lesson for TOK extends to all disciplines and students.

 Search terms: site: footnotesblog. com Decanonizing

As learners and knowers, we are personally responsible for the knowledge we have and do not have, as we move on to II.3, exploring the acquisition of knowledge in the human sciences.

For reflection

Who is represented by the human sciences?

Think about one discipline in the human sciences that you study.

1. Who are the influential thinkers that have shaped the discipline?

Consider whether and how your understanding of this discipline has been shaped by the particular set of thinkers or ideas you have been given access to.

2. (a) Do you have a responsibility to seek out historically underrepresented perspectives?

   (b) What value, for your own knowledge of this discipline, do you see in such an exercise?

3. If you were to seek out historically under-represented perspectives, where would you start, and what questions would you ask?

We expand on this issue in III.1 with an examination of who the humans are in the human sciences.

II.3 Simplicity and accuracy: The textbook problem

Here we look at the simplifications that are often necessary in the teaching of disiplinary knowledge to students or the general public. In their early encounters with new disciplines students receive simplified explanations of the complex causes, origins, effects and functions of phenomena and concepts. The idea is that through extended study, the nuance will appear and the complexity will emerge. This is not unique to the human sciences, and we explore an example from natural sciences, in Mendel's genetics, in Chapter 7, II.5. Unacknowledged and uncorrected simplifications can lead to significant problems of knowledge.

The example below refers to how, in explaining the complex origins of money, textbooks refer us to an economic fairy tale of "simpler societies" of the past. We invite healthy scepticism whenever simple societies are presented as the key to understanding complex phenomena. Keep in mind whether there is a trade-off between simplicity and accuracy, and how this may affect the acquisition and transfer of knowledge.

Box 8.3: The myth of barter, the inevitability of money and our moral imagination

Imagine a world without money. How would humans exchange things and get what they need? You might imagine people trading things for different things: four eggs for a bottle of milk; two cows for a horse. Pursue it further and quickly we find that this system of exchange, called barter, is inefficient and inconvenient; for example, when you need to exchange half a horse for a donkey, without killing the horse. Sooner or later someone, somewhere, so the story goes, has the idea of money. Given this story, money might even seem inevitable.

Barter has been a feature of economics textbooks since the advent of the modern discipline right up to the present day, usually described as the way of things in "simple, early economies" until someone invented money (Randall 1999). We checked a number of IB and undergraduate economics textbooks and found that every one of them described barter in early pre-modern societies. The story of barter has been told and retold for a long time, perhaps because it neatly presents pre-money economic exchanges as problematic.

Adam Smith described it as "higgling, haggling, swapping, dickering"—so eventually money came along to free us from these problems.

However, this story about barter is a myth. "No example of a barter economy, pure and

simple, has ever been described, let alone the emergence from it of money," wrote Caroline Humphrey, anthropology professor at Cambridge University, decades ago (1985). Numerous sociologists, anthropologists and political economists agree: the ethnographic record does not support the story. When there is a record, barter almost exclusively occurs between strangers or enemies (that is, between people who share no relationship); or, later, between people who were accustomed to money but could not use it for some reason, such as hyperinflation or shortage. What is more, not only is there no evidence for the myth of barter, there is plenty of evidence against it. David Graeber, anthropology professor at the London School of Economics, writes as follows.

"In fact, our standard account of monetary history is precisely backwards. We did not begin with barter, discover money, and then eventually develop credit systems. It happened precisely the other way around. ... The reason that economic textbooks now begin with imaginary villages is because it has been impossible to talk about real ones. Even some economists have been forced to admit that Smith's Land of Barter doesn't really exist. The question is why the myth is perpetuated anyway." (Graeber 2011)

Why has this myth been perpetuated for so long? The issue before us presents a rich study of knowledge claims, questions and implications. Does the myth of barter support other myths, mainly the inevitability of money? More assuredly, it displaces the important histories of gift and casual credit economies. Indeed, the nature and popular understanding of credit, and debt, has shifted over time

towards the impersonal, acontextual, inter-temporal logic of money; bought and sold by traders and investors far-removed from the debtors, enforced by watertight legal contracts and asset-seizure, and almost never, ever forgiven.

It may not be a coincidence that the governing assumptions of many economic models similarly hold onto the myth of the rational human, maximizing their profits and benefits. This is a very different understanding and reality of debt, and human life, than what existed not very long ago. Let's contrast this with a story provided by Graeber, recounting Peter Freuchen's encounter with an Inuit hunter from Greenland. Whether lyrical or literal, the story reveals another form of exchange that is entirely different from the "quid pro quo" of barter.

Freuchen tells how one day, after coming home hungry from an unsuccessful walrus-hunting expedition, he found one of the successful hunters dropping off several hundred pounds of meat. He thanked him profusely.

The man objected indignantly: 'Up in our country we are human!' said the hunter. 'And since we are human we help each other. We don't like to hear anybody say thanks for that. What I get today you may get tomorrow. Up here we say that by gifts one makes slaves and by whips one makes dogs.'

The last line is something of an anthropological classic, and similar statements about the refusal to calculate credits and debits can be found throughout the anthropological literature on egalitarian hunting societies. It's not that [the hunter], like untold millions of similar egalitarian spirits throughout history, was unaware that humans have a propensity to calculate. If he wasn't aware of it, he could not have said what he did. Of course we have a propensity to calculate. We have all sorts of propensities. In any real-life situation, we have propensities that drive us in several different contradictory directions simultaneously.... . The real question is which we take as the foundation of our humanity, and therefore, make the basis of our civilization." (Graeber 2011)

The barter myth naturalizes a calculating, *quid pro quo* version of human nature, making "it possible to imagine a world that is nothing more than a series of cold-blooded calculations", says Graeber (2011). The risk is that alternative systems of exchange slowly disappear from our perceived possibilities.

But it would be an absurd mistake to attribute the ills of our economic systems

to the supposed misguided acceptance of barter and money, and to lament our lost and romanticized past. The point being made here is that the way things are is not the way they have to be, that by examining the building blocks of our knowledge, and undoing the myths and taken-for-granted falsehoods, we can imagine a different future, and begin to work towards it.

For reflection

Critical explorations

Box 8.3 shows one of the foundational stories of economics being disputed by other disciplines in the human sciences.

1. To what extent is this kind of disagreement between different disciplines desirable?

2. Which factors determine whether it becomes unproductive?

3. Would you say it is useful for students to critically explore and understand the founding assumptions of a discipline before going on to acquire knowledge in that discipline?

4. Does having more knowledge in a discipline make it easier or harder to question the assumptions on which it was built?

The following words of wisdom and warning from Wade Davis conclude this section.

> as we drift towards [a] blandly amorphous generic world view not only would we see the entire range of the human imagination reduced to a more narrow modality of thought … we would wake from a dream one day having forgotten there were even other possibilities.
>
> (Davis 2003)

Cultivating and preserving a plurality of perspectives in the human sciences keeps alive a kind of moral imagination. Davis warns that this is being impoverished by the promotion of narrow and singular interpretations of human nature.

III. METHODS AND TOOLS

Explanations about human nature and societies that come from the human sciences tend to be seen as having authority and legitimacy. This is because we believe there is something about the methodology through which they are produced that warrants it. This section takes a closer look at the knowledge production practices, the methods and tools used by the different disciplines, and their associated challenges and strengths.

III.1 Who are the humans in the human sciences?

The human sciences study human phenomena towards the goals of understanding and

 explaining patterns of activity, making predictions about outcomes and guiding policy interventions. As an AOK, this study can profoundly impact human life in the present and future. However, in the last decade there has been a growing awareness, particularly within the behavioural sciences, that only a very small section of humankind is being systematically studied: a 2003–07 study "of the top psychology journals found that 96% of subjects were from Western industrialized countries—which house just 12% of the world's population" (Henrich *et al* 2010a). There is even a WEIRD acronym for it: Western, Educated, Industrialized, Rich and Democratic. As well as forming the acronym, the authors contend that "weird" is an accurate

↑ Figure 8.3 Distribution of studies published in *Psychological Science* in 2017. The map is distorted to reflect relative population sizes. Source Hruschka (2018).

description : "WEIRD societies … are some of the most psychologically unusual people on Earth" (Henrich *et al* 2010b). Why did so many scientists assume WEIRD was normal?

Figure 8.2 shows the distribution of the studies published in *Psychological Science* in 2017: 93%

came from countries coloured blue on the map. Dark blue shows the United States; the mid-blue shade shows Anglophone colonies with a European-descent majority; light blue is used for Western Europe. The regions are sized by population (data from Hruschka 2018).

> Between 2003 and 2007, 96 per cent of experimental volunteers in the leading psychology journals were WEIRD; 68 per cent of papers relied exclusively on US subjects; and in the prestigious *Journal of Personality and Social Psychology*, 67 per cent of total subjects were US psychology students. 'Many fields have a model organism that they study … A lot of medicine is done with mice, a lot of genetics is done with fruit flies. And in psychology, the model organism is the American undergraduate. …'
>
> Most studies of children and development are from families 'with the time, resources and motivation to bring their infant to participate in a development study at a university laboratory', as Anne Fernald of Stanford University wrote in her response to the WEIRD paper. These are, she pointed out, 'even less diverse than the college students who predominate in studies with adults'. At the 2010 International Conference on Infant Studies, less than one per cent of the 1,000 presentations included participants from disadvantaged families, even though they make up 20–40 per cent of children in the US.
>
> (Colvile 2016)

The human sciences are predicated on the assumption that people are similar enough to allow for generalizations about human behaviour. But how similar are we? What are the implications of generalizing and universalizing the results of these studies, based on the behaviour of US undergraduate students, to the rest of humankind? Fortunately, this is not just a rhetorical knowledge question because we have evidence that the answer is "No, WEIRD is weird indeed", and in fact may "represent the worst population on which to base our understanding of homo sapiens" (Henrich *et al* 2015). Extrapolating results based on this subset to other populations around the world is not only scientifically suspect, it can also have damaging real-world consequences, as discussed in III.2.

The lack of diversity in these studies is surprising because Western scientists have wondered for centuries how the environment influences behaviour. John Locke's "tabula rasa" question—that human beings are a "blank slate" at birth and develop almost exclusively from environmental influences—was posed way back in 1690. Victorian polymath Francis Galton famously added to that question with nature versus nurture, a debate that influenced human scientists well into the 20th century. If the idea of nurture has been examined for so long, how did scientists forget to program it into their research?

The answer requires looking closely at how knowledge is produced. Research is constrained by funding, and the easiest, cheapest and most willing volunteer subjects tend to be campus undergraduates. Repeating a study in the real world is expensive and more difficult to control; and academic life is highly competitive, rewarding those who publish frequently, quickly, with generalizable findings. In contrast, cross-country studies can take years.

> You get publicity, and tenure, for fascinating truths about the human condition, not about the US undergraduate. The temptation is to generalise and universalise ... I don't think it's necessarily a problem to study the American undergrad, to the extent that you limit your conclusions to the American undergrad. The problem is when we don't limit our conclusions, and start saying: 'This behaviour is part of human nature, and evolved on the African savannah millions of years ago.' And that's where we're making a really big leap.
>
> (Colvile 2016)

The WEIRD issue is embedded in a wider context that includes the replicability crisis, discussed in III.4, in which scientists "have become uncomfortably aware that many flagship results do not hold up: not just in other cultures, but full stop" (Colvile 2016). There is a need for larger sample sizes and more repeat studies, which in turn requires even

more subjects, of which the WEIRD campus undergraduate is certainly the most convenient.

This may explain why, even though attention was first drawn to the WEIRD bias in 2008, the situation as of 2020 has not significantly improved. Many studies still do not even include information about which nation or region the participants are from, or, if the subjects are US undergraduate students, their ethnic backgrounds. A 2018 analysis revealed not a single study sampled people from Africa, the Middle East or Latin America, concluding "the lack of cultural diversity in psychological science is well established ... however ... there has been little action in response" (Rad *et al* 2018).

There are also wider, more ideological thrusts to the WEIRD bias that do not point to arrogance or carelessness as the main cause. The Enlightenment gave us the idea that humankind can be "one great big brotherhood of man", while the fallout from eugenics and racially-motivated violence committed in the 20th century may have made Western academic traditions and institutions less inclined to explore human differences, and more inclined to focus on (and assume) human similarities. Finally, there is the broader 20th-century trend within the sciences to seek simplicity— fundamental rules, theories of everything— distilled from the perceived surface-level complexity of the cosmos. That complexity may be more than skin deep.

III.2 Implications of WEIRD research

Scientists from across the human sciences have found considerable variation both within human populations and between them. It is generally misleading and patronizing to stereotype groups of people "as" something— as risk averse, as honest, as cooperative, for example— whatever that characteristic is. Is it any better, however, to assume that different populations are highly similar? Experimental findings have found population-level differences in diverse domains such as visual perception, ideas of fairness, cooperation, spatial reasoning, moral reasoning and the heritability of IQ (Henrich 2010). Have uncritical assumptions about human sameness enabled the universalization of results based on WEIRD population groups? What may have been the implications of this? We explore some examples, selected to provoke critical reflection about assumptions of sameness and difference and the implications of the WEIRD bias in behavioural research.

Case study

Is good parenting universal?

Attachment theory is an influential theory in the study of infant behaviour and development, with its most important tenet being that an infant needs a secure relationship with at least one primary caregiver to properly develop social and emotional competence. Stated simply, it is a theory on how to raise children. When ideas about what is and is not good parenting acquire universality, they can become the basis of moral judgment. A question about developmental psychology therefore becomes an ethical question: being a bad parent becomes equivalent to being a bad person; and entire groups of people have been stereotyped as "bad parents".

Whether attachment theory applies in different cultures has been debated for decades; its proponents argue that the cultural differences are relatively minor, and that research shows the three fundamental assertions of attachment theory are universal (based on Mesman *et al* 2008). These assertions are as follows.

- Secure attachment is the most healthy.

- Healthy attachment is influenced most by parental (specifically maternal) sensitivity.

- Infants and children with secure attachment are more socially and emotionally competent in later life.

This case study presents two opposing expert perspectives. Consider the following questions as you read on.

1. (a) When experts disagree, which criteria do we use to decide who is right, what to believe and whom to trust?

   (b) Keeping in mind that we do not make the decisions entirely independently or in a social vacuum, which factors affect them?

2. Consider attachment theory.

   (a) To what extent are you able to form a judgment about the universality of attachment theory?

   (b) What enables or hinders your judgment, and why?

Our first expert is Heidi Keller, professor of psychology at Osnabrück University, who has been strongly critical of the universalization of attachment theory.

 Search terms: Keller Universality claim of attachment theory

Keller's main argument is that because infant behaviour and development is adaptive to the environment, and because environments vary tremendously across cultures, a standard model of infant emotional expression, regulation and development cannot and should not be assumed to apply worldwide.

Keller contrasts the interactional style and environment of WEIRD families with other families around the world. For example, she states that WEIRD infant interaction is primarily one to one, between mother and child, and father and child, with conversations (using primarily the senses of sight and hearing) that focus "on the cognitions, emotions, wishes, and preferences of the individual baby" (Keller 2018). She adds that parental sensitivity—the ability to notice, interpret and respond to an infant's signals and needs correctly—is an indicator of good parenting based on normative ideas of expressiveness, warmth and emotionality, as well as on the assumption that the autonomous child takes the lead in their interactions. This involves a style described as "first you speak and I listen, then I speak and you listen". Keller argues that none of this is universal.

Instead, many cultures have households comprising a significantly larger number of people than the WEIRD nuclear family, requiring a child's distributed attention, and an interactional style consisting of more body contact, "often rhythmical and in synchrony" (Keller 2018) with multiple caregivers. Fathers may play a much smaller role; grandmothers and older siblings a much larger one. Good parenting implies taking the lead in organizing the child's activity, with "almost constant body contact and bodily sensitivity" (Keller

2018). Children are often held facing outwards, towards other people, rather than inwards towards their parent. The idea of childhood may be very different, too: "[t]he idea that the child needs to be instructed, directed, and guided goes hand-in-hand with the view of the child as an apprentice" (Keller 2018) which is less the norm in the WEIRD samples. Yet, despite all this, attachment theory is claimed to be universal. Keller considers this a contradiction.

As a last example, consider the concept of "stranger anxiety", a cornerstone of attachment theory regarded as biologically based and therefore universal. Psychologists interpret the display of infant emotions in strange situations to be indicative of attachment quality, for example when a child expresses distress during separation, and relief and joy during reunion with their mother. Is this a reliable indicator across cultures? How would we know? As shown in her comments below, Keller strongly disagrees.

> " Attachment theory represents the Western middle-class perspective, ignoring the caregiving values and practices in the majority of the world … Evaluating one system with the standards of another ignores different realities and different value systems.
>
> The common practice of large-scale interventions in rural subsistence-based contexts promoting Western-style parenting strategies without knowing the local culture positions a false understanding of scientific evidence against cultural knowledge. This practice is unethical. Diversity needs to be recognized as the human condition, and the recognition of diversity is an obligation for better science as well as for improving people's lives. Attachment researchers' understanding and promotion of universality is both a description of parenting and subsequent children's socioemotional regulation and, at the same time, is a moral statement. It defines what a good mother is and what she should do to support her child's healthy development.
>
> (Keller 2018) "

> " In Western textbooks (based on WEIRD psychology) stranger anxiety is assumed to appear in the behavioral repertoire of an infant at about 8 months of age, when the emotional bond with the primary caregiver is developing. Confrontation with a stranger in the strange situation is assumed to generate distress in an infant so that attachment behaviours (proximity seeking) are displayed. However, cultural evidence e.g., from sub-Saharan communities such as the Ivorian Beng or the Cameroonian Nso clearly indicates that stranger anxiety is not part of the behavioral repertoire of the developing child in these agrarian cultures … .
>
> Close-knit traditional farming communities in the non-Western world are usually not a target for visits of strangers, so that families do not see potential dangers. On the other hand it is vital for families to familiarize infants with the multiple caregivers associated with distributed workloads and responsibilities.
>
> Most Cameroonian Nso children in farming villages are not afraid of an approaching strange woman

who picks them up and moves away from the mother with them. They display neutral facial expressions, and the level of the stress hormone cortisol (as indicated in the saliva) declines … Results like these clearly indicate that assessment procedures relying on Western values and standards of behavior are inappropriate outside their cultural territory.

(Keller 2018)

As a source of counterclaims to Keller, consider the arguments put forth by Mesman *et al* (2008). The authors start with the point that it was in 1950s Uganda, not one of the WEIRD countries, that developmental-psychologist Mary Ainsworth "laid the foundations" for important contributions to attachment theory.

The authors review a range of childbearing practices in ethnographic evidence spanning the !Kung San of Botswana, Efé of the Ituri forest in Zambia, Hadza of Tanzania, Bofi in the Central African Republic and Hausa in Nigeria. They also offer standardized observations of attachment and sensitivity in Gusii of Kenya, Dogon subsistence farmers in Mali, and mothers in South Africa, China, Papua New Guinea, Taiwan, Japan, South Korea, Indonesia, Chile, Colombia, Peru, Mexico and Israel. Clearly this is not a comprehensive list of the world's countries, but could we conclude it is not enough? What additional information or expertise would you need to form a judgment about the issue? If doubts remain, which assumptions are safer to make?

For reflection

Behavioural research across cultures

1. In how many countries and cultures must a pattern of behaviour and interrelationship occur before we can call it universal?

2. In some research, the aim is to interpret patterns of behaviour in different cultures, in a way that reveals the truth.

   (a) Is it possible for researchers to achieve this?

   (b) What would qualify researchers to do this?

3. Consider assessing humans.

   (a) Is it easier to assume human difference or sameness?

   (b) Which of these approaches is safer, and in what contexts?

Similar concerns arise in the context of the widely accepted claim, and cliché, that teenagers are prone to risky behaviour. The linked article is one of many that attributes this to a combination of reward-seeking and less-developed impulse

control, citing neuroscientific studies using fMRI brain scans that support the claim.

 Search terms: Psychology Teen brains risk-taking

A widely-cited 2006 study boldly asserts that such behaviour "is biologically driven … and unlikely to be remedied through educational interventions designed to change adolescents' perception, appraisal, or understanding of risk", and that our understanding and policy interventions "should begin from the premise that adolescents are inherently more likely than adults to take risks" (Steinberg 2006).

These are deeply assertive claims about teenage behaviour and biology. Similar studies have pointed towards a higher incidence of anxiety, emotional challenges and irresponsible behaviour among teens because of biological reasons. Such claims verge on biological determinism and biological reductionism. They are also rarely if ever accompanied with the qualification "American teenagers …" even though the cited literature almost exclusively studies this group. Earlier in this chapter we encountered Margaret Mead's anthropological argument that Samoan adolescents' experience of puberty was markedly different from their American counterparts'. Next we encounter new perspectives on this theme.

For reflection

Problems of causation in teenage risk-seeking behaviour

Robert Epstein, former editor-in-chief of *Psychology Today*, wrote the following in *Scientific American*.

"Automatically assuming that the brain causes behavior is problematic because we know that an individual's genes and environmental history—and even his or her own behavior—mold the brain over time. There is clear evidence that any unique features that may exist in the brains of teens—to the limited extent that such features exist—are the result of social influences rather than the cause of teen turmoil." (Epstein 2007)

Epstein's argument confronts us with the classic problem of establishing causation: whether it is brain biology or the environment that determines behaviour. When there is disagreement among the experts, TOK helps us to evaluate the claims and counterclaims. Consider the following questions, then discuss your answers with a peer, in a small group or as a class.

1. What would constitute sufficient and compelling evidence that the source or cause of the set of "teenage" behaviours is biological? What would convince you of Epstein's argument?

2. How would this evidence need to be produced in order to be reliable?

3. On what grounds can such evidence be challenged?

We should examine whether the idea of "teenagehood" is more of a social construct than a fact of human biology. We explored this idea in II.2 in the context of the Mead-Freeman controversy. Epstein argues that the idea of teenagehood stems from the 1904 book *Adolescence* by psychologist G. Stanley Hall, written in the context of the industrial revolution, mass immigration and rapid urbanization of US cities. Hall paid much less attention to teenagers from other contexts but his ideas have nonetheless become entrenched in a popular imagination of teenagers. A 1991 review of research on teens in 186 less-industrialized societies found that:

"60 percent had no word for 'adolescence', that teens spent almost all their time with adults, that they showed almost no signs of psychopathology, and that antisocial behavior in young males was completely absent in more than half these cultures and extremely mild in cultures in which it did occur.

(Epstein 2007)

Based on Epstein's comments, you might conclude that teenagehood is a WEIRD construct. But would such a far-reaching conclusion be justified? There is an important difference between questioning ideas and casting them out entirely.

"Even more significant, a series of long-term studies set in motion in the 1980s by anthropologists Beatrice Whiting and John Whiting of Harvard University suggest that teen trouble begins to appear in other cultures soon after the introduction of certain Western influences, especially Western-style schooling, television programs and movies ... Consistent with these modern observations, many historians note that through most of recorded human history the teen years were a relatively peaceful time of transition to adulthood. Teens were not trying to break away from adults; rather they were learning to become adults. Some historians ... suggest that the tumultuous period we call adolescence is a very recent phenomenon—not much more than a century old.

(Epstein 2007)

In the description and explanation of the observed phenomenon of teenagehood over time, psychologists, anthropologists and historians each draw on their own set of methodological tools. The methods used in ethnographic research, and the knowledge it produces, are explored further below.

III.3 Neutrality and objectivity in fieldwork and ethnographic methods

The method of ethnographic fieldwork is primarily associated with anthropology, beginning in the first half of the 20th century. The "field" in anthropology has been described as being wherever people are, and so we have anthropological accounts not only of Indigenous societies, but increasingly of professional communities, schools, urban environments, even of space stations in orbit. An anthropologist engaged in fieldwork is tasked with observing, describing and constructing a credible account of the context, culture and community being studied. There are some knowledge issues with the practice of ethnographic fieldwork, and the knowledge produced through it, and these issues are explored below.

 Search terms: Doing anthropology YouTube

Watch this short video to hear directly from three anthropologists from the Massachusetts Institute of Technology (MIT) about their work. They use fieldwork methods to understand issues as diverse as how citizenship issues manifest among Haitian refugees in the Greater Boston Area, the role of expertise in artisanal cheese-making, and the processes by which marine biologists produce authoritative knowledge about the ocean world.

You will notice in the video that anthropologists take part in activities in the field beyond just observing and having conversations. They gather information through direct engagement with the processes they are studying, working alongside the people whose culture, actions and worldviews they seek to understand. This is intentional in the field of anthropology—it is a method called participant observation.

For discussion

The ethnographer inside the research

Consider how a deep involvement of researchers might affect the knowledge they produce about the phenomenon or culture they are studying.

1. In terms of the TOK course concepts, how is the knowledge produced through participant observation affected by the researcher engaging closely with the community being studied?

2. To what extent, and under what conditions, does the personal, first-hand experience of the researcher contribute or take away from the objectivity of his or her account?

3. It has been documented that the very presence of the researcher in the field may alter the behaviour of the participants. If the very act of observing can influence the phenomenon being observed, in which ways do you think the research is further affected when the researcher also participates?

Making connections

History and observation

In Chapter 9 we encounter E.H. Carr's advice to his students to "study the historian before you study [their] facts". A similar concern is prevalent in the human sciences, and particularly so in anthropology, about the extent to which observation is influenced by the observer.

To what extent can we observe and describe objectively? This is a fundamental question in TOK across the human and natural sciences.

Does the difficulty of this task vary depending on what is being observed; for example, a religious ritual, a rock formation, patterns of economic activity or animal behaviour?

Despite their presence in the field, ethnographers' observations are conspicuously absent from their otherwise detailed accounts of what happened. Writing about the work of E.E. Evans-Pritchard among the Nuer in South Sudan, anthropologist Richard Fox notices "how artfully Evans-Pritchard first personified himself among the Nuer and then 'disappeared' himself in favor of a scientific omniscience for the remainder of his text" (Fox 1991). A problematic example came about in 1967, when *A Diary in the Strict Sense of the Word*, Bronislaw Malinowski's private diary from his fieldwork in New Guinea, was published posthumously by his widow. Intensely personal, the diary was most likely never meant for publication. Malinowski was and remains among the most famous and influential anthropologists, and yet his diary reveals "a crabbed, self-preoccupied, hypochondriacal narcissist, whose fellow-feeling for the people he lived with was limited in the extreme" (Geertz 1967). In his diary, the local Trobrianders are stereotyped as savages, and yet "in his ethnographic works they are, through a mysterious transformation wrought by science, among the most intelligent, dignified, and conscientious natives in the whole of anthropological literature" (Geertz 1967). What might explain this apparent contradiction? Does it affect how we think about other ethnographic works?

Can a researcher be so simultaneously detached and involved as to hold views of intense personal prejudice, but still be able to construct a value-neutral account? When can we separate the knowledge from the values of the person who produced it, and when does this become impossible? Anthropology continues to ask these questions, and Malinowski's diary has become a classic in the history of the discipline for providing a behind-the-scenes glimpse into the making of anthropological knowledge. Autoethnography, a method where researchers foreground their presence and embrace their subjective experience in the field, has been one way to respond to this problem. This method is suspicious of the ability of scientific observation and description to produce objective knowledge. Instead, the values of the researchers, their position in a given context and their relationship with their subject also become part of the analysis. In this view, the subjectivity of the research is not a barrier to knowledge, but possibly the only intellectually and politically honest pathway towards it.

Anthropology has also grappled with the phenomenon of the "ethnographic present", a term referring to the idealized context created by an ethnographer's description of the timeless cultural life of Indigenous Peoples, untainted by outside influence and unaffected by contact. Malinowski has written about the "ethnographer's magic, by which he is able to invoke the real spirit of the natives, the true spirit of tribal life" (1922). This problematic, hyper-romanticized account requires the reader to see the encounter between "the natives" and the ethnographer as taking place outside of history.

Making connections

Presence and the present in art and history

Autoethnography finds use outside the field of anthropology. For example, this method is explored in the context of political theatre in Chapter 10. Autoethnography has an element of closing the distance between the producer of knowledge and the knowledge produced. To what extent is this distance greater between science and scientist as compared to art and artist?

The idea of coexistence in time between a globalized modern culture and local and Indigenous communities arises in Chapter 5 and Chapter 9. How does knowledge from these disciplines promote or undermine our understanding of epistemic diversity?

III.4 What we measure matters

On a range of issues, from economic and environmental policy to teachers' salaries and curriculum reform, measurable things inform both data-driven decision-making as well as implicit and explicit value judgments. Without measurement there can be no data, no data-informed goal-setting or evaluation, and no cost-benefit-style analyses—all elements that find expression in the methodology of many human science disciplines.

> What we measure affects what we do, and better measurement will lead to better decisions, or at least different decisions.
>
> (Stiglitz quoted in Gertner 2010)

The knowledge associated with measurement has a huge effect on the world, for example to inform action in the world as well as to evaluate it.

It is, therefore, very important to consider what we can and cannot measure: what gets left out of the picture, what we assume to fill the gap and what has disproportionate influence simply because it is readily measurable. That which is more measurable and quantifiable (such as business profit, students' grades and economic growth) may be perceived to be more

important or come to guide decisions regardless. The phrase "assessment learning" for instance, is widely used in education. It posits that students will focus on what they are tested if the consequences of assessment are significant, to the detriment of important things that are not assessed. This is important because while *content* is quite easily assessed, *skills* and *habits of mind* are not.

Between 2005 and 2007, researchers at St George's Medical School of the University of London found that when the weighting of anatomy in the curriculum was increased, students showed dramatically increased motivation to learn anatomy; motivation was powerfully affected by weighting.

Teaching and learning in medicine may be particularly assessment-driven due to the high difficulty and consequences of passing or failing medical school.

Anecdotally, IB TOK teachers are known to lament this at workshops and conferences, and to speculate what would happen if their subject was worth more than 1.5 points out of 45.

It would be short-sighted and a cliché to exaggerate the ills of summative assessment in education. It exists for good reason, within the particular context and constraints of education systems worldwide. Claims that "assessment is killing creativity" are sensationalistic and would benefit from more scrutiny, and nuance. However, it is also worth considering what education systems tend to assess, what is assessable, and the implications of this for teaching, learning and knowledge.

Turning now to examples from government policy, consider the Human Development Index (HDI), a people-centred measure of economic development. Reflecting on the origins of the HDI, Nobel Laurate Amartya Sen recalls a conversation with fellow economist Mahbub ul Haq.

> I told Mahbub, 'Look, you are a sophisticated enough guy to know that to capture complex reality in one number is just vulgar, like [gross domestic product] GDP' … And he called me back later and said, 'Amartya, you're quite right. The Human Development Index will be vulgar. I want you to help me to do an index which is just as vulgar as GDP, except it will stand for better things'.
>
> (Sen 2010)

The single most widely used economic policy metric of the last century, the GDP growth rate is embedded in a paradigm that considers long-term growth in output and consumption as necessary for human betterment, despite the finite resources of the planet. GDP as a measure of national output was conceived between the Great Depression and the Second World War to estimate the manufacturing capacity of war-time goods.

> A measure created when survival was at stake took little notice of things such as depreciation of assets, or pollution of the environment, let alone finer human accomplishments. In a famous speech in March 1968, Robert Kennedy took aim at what he saw as idolatrous respect for GDP, which measures advertising and jails but does not capture 'the beauty of our poetry or the strength of our marriages'.
>
> (*Economist* briefing 2016)

Marriages aside, GDP (and its most widely used form, GDP per capita) fails to measure distribution of income, the quality of output produced or the environmental impact of producing it, or any of the important indicators of living standards such as healthcare, education, gender equality and political freedom. According to Steve Landefeld, Director of the Bureau of Economic Analysis, the United States experimented with "green" GDP measurements in the early 1990s, using depletion charges to account for natural resource depletion, but abandoned the initiative for political reasons after pressure from mining companies (Wagner 2004). Similarly,

the first Green GDP report in China, in 2004, showed substantial losses caused by pollution (as reported in an article in the *China Daily* newspaper, 19 April 2007) and efforts at green GDP were subsequently dropped.

Indeed, one of the pioneers of GDP measurement in the 1930s, Simon Kuznets, specifically warned that "the welfare of a nation can scarcely be inferred from a measure of national income" (quoted in Coyle 2014). Kuznets wanted to subtract expenses relating to war and financial speculation and other things that "do not really represent net services to the individuals comprising the nation but are, from their viewpoint, an evil necessary in order to be able to make a living" (Coyle 2014). With the start of the Second World War, Kuznets lost the argument: it was more important to measure output, not wellbeing.

Despite its limitations, GDP has grown to dominate political and economic discourse, featured in newspapers and used by state leaders to define their strategy and objectives. Of course, economists have worried about this for almost a century, and the HDI was developed by Haq and Sen in response to the "vulgarity" of GDP. As recently as 2009 a report commissioned by the French government and written by Stiglitz and Sen, two Nobel prize winning economists, called for an end to "GDP fetishism" in favour of better measures of human welfare. Yet GDP continues to dominate policy, and its ease of measurement surely has something to do with that.

There are a number of concerns that arise when the knowledge we use to act in the world, or to guide policy objectives, is defined by what we can measure. It is important to examine the limitations of measures that carry over to become limitations of the knowledge based on them. Each measure fails to capture something, and that which is omitted risks becoming ignored or neglected. A measure can miscalculate, overvalue or undervalue some factors. GDP has failed to account for the environment and depleted future generations' stocks of natural capital, and very possibly their quality of life.

Making connections

Measurement, policy and the political discourse

In Chapter 7, IV.3, we explore the limitations of environmental cost-benefit analyses, and why climate change has been called the perfect moral storm. Part of the challenge is in measuring, and quantifying, the things that matter.

> "We can put monetary values on mineral stocks, fisheries and even forests, perhaps, but it's hard to put a monetary value on alteration of the climate system, loss of species and the consequences that might come from those." (Heal quoted in Gertner 2010)

Measuring directly relevant indicators of health, education, environment, crime and civic participation, and providing this information to the public can help to shift political discourse away from opinions and values towards more evidence-based discussions of specific policies.

Once the political will to measure something exists, the measures themselves can be improved iteratively; until then, raw data can be used, for example on carbon footprints or species extinction.

Finally, care should be taken to ensure measures do not obscure important details. GDP per capita reveals nothing about the distribution of gains from growth and can provide an illusory sense of prosperity. An important case in point is the difference between averages and medians, which may go unnoticed by laypeople. For example, looking at median incomes instead of simple averages very quickly reveals important information about the distribution of values. Average incomes have risen sharply in many countries over the last 30 years, but median incomes have stagnated, especially in the United States and the UK. Between 1989 and 2011, median incomes in the United States fell by 1% but average incomes rose by 33%. Why is this difference important?

Figure 8.3 shows the divergence in average and median US family incomes beginning in about 1955.

Median measurements better indicate what happens to a "typical" person, in the exact middle of a distribution. Averages appear to make intuitive sense but reveal comparatively little. If economic policies targeted growth in *median* GDP per capita, instead of average GDP per capita, they might look very different indeed.

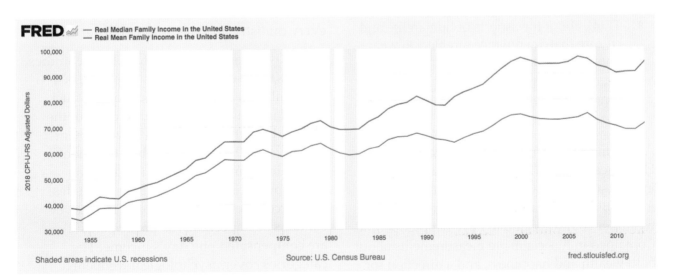

↑ **Figure 8.4** The mean versus the median of family income (2015)

III.4.1 Knowing otherwise by measuring differently

Jigmi Y. Thinley, addressing the United Nations as Prime Minister of Bhutan, 2012, stated the following.

> The GDP-led development model that compels boundless growth on a planet with limited resources no longer makes economic sense … . Mankind is like a meteor, blazing toward self-annihilation along with all other innocent life forms. But this course can be changed if we act now.
>
> (Office of the Prime Minister and Cabinet, Bhutan 2012)

For reflection

Measurement and knowledge

We are regularly exposed to various measures and indicators of health, education, economic life and so on.

1. Can we say that these numbers constitute knowledge—or is an additional level of interpretation necessary?

2. What is it that we understand about a phenomenon when we can express it as a number?

3. Think about the aspects of human life and culture that are not measurable. Do we know less about these aspects?

4. Does it limit the ways we can act on a problem if we cannot quantify it?

According to the United Nations World Happiness Report (2019), a certain amount of income seems to be a necessary precondition for a satisfactory standard of living, and so wealthier countries tend to have happier people. Contained in this claim are measurements about both wealth and happiness, and a direction for the relationship between the two. It is a claim that can be contested on multiple counts, but here we look specifically at the measure of happiness.

Assuming we can measure happiness at all, can we measure it rigorously enough for the purpose of policy? This is the challenge that Bhutan took on when the country pivoted away from GDP as a proxy for the country's development. Bhutan wanted to target policy outcomes such as time for leisure and family, improvements in healthcare and education, and trust in neighbours and government. The focus on happiness for Bhutan was not to be a general aspiration or broad direction. Happiness was to be measured with precision and thoroughness, and the measure of gross national happiness (GNH) formed the basis for the knowledge required to guide and evaluate national policies.

For several decades following its introduction in 1972, many dismissed GNH as a vague, hopelessly idealistic and impractical idea. Recently however, it has come to be viewed, in some circles at least, as rather forward-looking, with the concept being endorsed by development experts at the United Nations. That is not to say, of course, that Bhutan discarded economic growth entirely, but the focus on GNH was formally incorporated into the constitution, which mandates the state to pursue GNH by screening every major project and policy to ensure alignment with GNH. The GNH Commission is one of the highest levels of government, consisting of secretaries from every ministry and the prime minister.

Every five years the Centre for Bhutan Studies and GNH Research leads a survey of 8,000 randomly selected households to construct a GNH index. Sabina Alkire, Director of the Oxford Poverty and Human Development Initiative (OPHI), has described this index an "an instrument of public imagination and of policy [that] can capture a great deal of interconnected information". The survey contains 300 questions, so participants are compensated one day's income. The categories cover psychological wellbeing, health, time use, education, cultural diversity and resilience, good governance, community vitality, ecological diversity and resilience, and living standards. The survey aims to go beyond material wellbeing. Questions are posed asking how often people meditate, how much sleep they lose, how much they argue with their family, and how often they feel anger or disappointment.

GNH has many critics; for example, the Yale economist William Nordhaus has described happiness statistics as "absurd". In 2004, the *Economist* stated that "the Himalayan kingdom of Bhutan is not in fact an idyll in a fairy tale. It is home to perhaps 900,000 people most of whom live in grinding poverty". It is unclear whether critics mean to say that Bhutan should abandon GNH in favour of the more conventional GDP. Bhutan has also been criticized for violating human rights of ethnic minorities in the name of "preserving culture", and the country is dealing with high youth unemployment. Observers have pointedly noted that it ranked 95th on the 2019 World Happiness Report. There is an interesting irony about the World Happiness Report rankings: to what extent can different countries compare their respective happiness rankings? Are measurements of happiness generalizable?

We should certainly not paint a romantic or idyllic picture, as many have made the mistake of doing, and many of Bhutan's leaders will carefully make clear. Bhutanese Prime Minister Thinley said in an address to the United Nations (2012): "Bhutan is not a country that has attained GNH … . Like most developing nations, we are struggling with the challenge of fulfilling the basic needs of our people" (Office of the Prime Minister and Cabinet 2012). But with a policy approach guided by GNH, Bhutan has made significant progress on key development indicators including life expectancy, child mortality, education and poverty reduction. It has achieved most of the Millennium Development Goal targets, is the only carbon negative country in the world (offsetting 12 times

> Anyone who believes exponential growth can go on forever in a finite world is either a madman or an economist.
>
> (Boulding 1973)

more carbon than it emits) and maintains 72% forest cover, said Lyonpo Damcho Dorji, Foreign Minister of Bhutan in 2015. Ironically, between 2008 and 2018, GDP in Bhutan more than tripled.

After Bhutan, New Zealand has gone the furthest in defining a policy stance measured by wellbeing as opposed to economic growth. In May 2019 Prime Minister Jacinda Ardern unveiled a budget that put social wellbeing indicators ahead of economic growth in policy decisions. All new spending must be directed towards one of five objectives: improving mental health, reducing child poverty and improving child wellbeing, supporting Indigenous Peoples, transitioning to a low-carbon sustainable economy and thriving in a

> New Zealand's prosperity is about much more than GDP growth. . . . If we've got this so-called rockstar economy, how is it that we have the worst homelessness in the OECD? How is it that you can't swim in most of New Zealand's rivers and lakes? How is it that child poverty had grown to the extent it has? The answer, in my view, was because the government wasn't sufficiently valuing those things. And if it wasn't being valued properly, it wasn't being measured, and if it wasn't being measured, it wasn't being done.
>
> (quoted in Roy 2019)

digital age. To measure progress toward these goals, New Zealand is using 61 indicators, from loneliness to trust in government institutions to water quality. Grant Robertson, New Zealand finance minister, says:

To have knowledge about how a country is doing, whether it is doing better or worse than before, and whether efforts to move it in a particular direction are working, measurement is necessary. What we can and cannot measure, and how we choose to measure it, are issues of knowledge that have powerful real-life consequences. To explore the ethical dimensions of producing and applying knowledge based on measurements, see section IV.

III.5 Experimentation in the human sciences

What is the scope for experimentation in the human sciences? Psychology is somewhat unique among the human sciences in this regard. An often heard lament about the lack of predictive power of disciplines such as economics and political science is based on the difficulty or impossibility of doing controlled experiments. Is there special value in knowledge that helps to accurately predict the outcomes of policies and reforms?

Certainly there is value in experiments, as psychology and behavioural economics have shown, with the success of randomized controlled trials. However, one challenge with experimental evidence is that it is liable to misinterpretation and can provide a false sense of certainty. Section I discussed the fallout of economics' overreliance on mathematical models and physics envy. This section has highlighted the problems of knowledge that can arise from sampling, such as the WEIRD bias (see III.1). Next we consider the limitations of experiments, and experimental results, in the human sciences. But first, a cautionary tale about rats, drugs and parks.

 Search terms: Hari Addiction YouTube

In the linked video, Johann Hari tries to show that everything we know about addiction is wrong. The topic of fallibility—the human capacity to be wrong, and the realization of being wrong—is a key issue in TOK. It is a way for knowledge to develop and self-correct, but it can also shake our confidence.

For discussion and reflection

Knowing about and acting on addiction

After watching the video on the original addiction studies done on caged rats as well as the 1970s "rat park" experiments, consider the following questions.

1. What were the shortfalls of the rat cage studies, and how do we protect against repeating them in the future?
2. At what point do you think scientists have enough data to make a policy recommendation?
3. Which criteria should the knowledge produced by scientists satisfy?
4. How can scientists protect against being wrong and recommending something harmful?
5. What is the role of the public?

Bruce Alexander's "rat park" study helped to pivot the narrative of addiction away from the moral and mental failings of addicts, and towards addiction as an adaptation to social dislocation. The study went unnoticed for many years, whilst governments around the world continued to pursue a "war on drugs". Criticism of this expensive, aggressive and ultimately unsuccessful policy, which often involves incarceration, has grown and so has interest in Alexander's study. There is now a widespread— though not universal—understanding that more compassion is needed for people struggling with addiction.

Without discarding the important impact of the rat park study and wildly popular TED talk, we should acknowledge that efforts to replicate the experimental results have been inconclusive. There are also significant concerns about the experiment. One of the design flaws, for example, seems to be that in the original studies male and female rats were separated, whereas in the rat park study they were mixed together. The main question, though, is about our ability to generalize results about rats to humans. Consider this critique from psychologist Adi Jaffe.

> Assuming that what we are aiming for is not a world free of addicted rats, but rather a world free of addicted people. Our environment, unlike the environment created for the rats in Rat Heaven is far from stress free. Worse still, as far as I can tell, we will, for the foreseeable future, be unable to create such a Utopia for most people on earth. If this is so, there is little doubt that some of the people affected by negative circumstances, traumatic experiences, or biological disturbances will be led down the path towards struggles with drugs and such … I am fully on board with making sure that the treatment system we use does not exacerbate the problems that stress and trauma bring about, but I think that the picture this TED talk and the related book presents is far too simplified to be as helpful as we want it to be.
>
> (Jaffe, 2015)

Recall our exploration of the dangers of simplification earlier in the chapter. Is it conceivable that the rat park story has been received uncritically for the following reasons?

- It successfully cast doubt on previously accepted (and flawed) dogma.
- There was a desire to reject that dogma.

Think back to II.1 and the 1971 Stanford Prison experiment, which seems to have resonated with the cultural climate at the time. In debunking one simplification have we embraced another, discarding evidence such as heritable risk factors for addiction, or the histories of Indigenous communities devastated by alcohol brought by early settlers?

Hari's already popular TED talk on addiction was animated by Kurzgesagt, an educational YouTube channel with close to 9 million subscribers. Kurzgesagt videos are meant to deliver factual overviews of anything from loneliness, to vaccines, to the European Union. Kurzgesagt's video "Addiction" is the most watched to date, even though Kurzgesagt has removed it from the channel. Removing it was motivated by viewers' criticism, and the self-

realization of having simplified a topic to the point of misrepresentation. Taking seriously the possibility of having misinformed 18 million viewers on a serious issue, Kurzgesagt published a follow-up video, explaining the responsibilities of communicating scientific research to a general audience on the internet. Animated in the channel's signature style, "Can You Trust Kurzgesagt videos?" promises an update video explainer on addiction … but only once Kurzgesagt is confident about its research.

🔍 Search terms: trust Kurzgesagt videos? YouTube

III.6 Replicability and reproducibility

Reproducibility refers to the closeness of the results when a study is repeated using the same methodology; replicability refers to the extent that independent researchers can achieve the same or similar results under different experimental and methodological conditions. Both are considered to be cornerstones of the scientific method, as results that are not reproducible and replicable can be considered suspect. Over the last decade, a growing body of literature has suggested that many research findings in the human sciences, particularly in psychology, are not replicable, leading to claims of an academic crisis.

> In recent years, it has become painfully clear that psychology is facing a "reproducibility crisis," in which even famous, long-established phenomena—the stuff of textbooks and TED Talks—might not be real. There's social priming, where subliminal exposures can influence our behavior. And ego depletion, the idea that we have a limited supply of willpower that can be exhausted. And the facial-feedback hypothesis, which simply says that smiling makes us feel happier.
>
> One by one, researchers have tried to repeat the classic experiments behind these well-known effects—and failed. And whenever psychologists undertake large projects, like Many Labs 2, in which they replicate past experiments en masse, they typically succeed, on average, half of the time.

> Ironically enough, it seems that one of the most reliable findings in psychology is that only half of psychological studies can be successfully repeated.
>
> (Yong 2018)

A significant criticism is that there have been generally too few replication attempts, which may have contributed to premature and over-enthusiastic acceptance of what should have been provisional findings. Researchers may be less inclined to pursue replication studies because they bring less recognition and reward, and thus some have argued that the interests of professionals are at odds with the interests of the profession.

- Academic publishers have displayed a preference for original research over replications, which are less likely to be viewed as significant contributions to the field.
- Replications can be time-consuming and difficult, especially when many original studies do not publish raw data or detailed methodology.

A second criticism centres around a broader "publish or perish" culture, that is said to pressure academics to publish work rapidly and continuously to advance their careers, possibly increasing the risk of questionable research practices. This culture may also incentivize the pursuit of headline-grabbing findings at the expense of rigorous scholarship, and reduce the time and effort that professors give to teaching. Excellent teaching is rarely rewarded as highly as excellent research, with the implication being that future scholars may be less competent as a result. This is certainly not isolated to the human sciences, and also not necessarily true of academic institutions and cultures around the world, but it has been raised as an issue by professional academics in the United States.

Psychologists in particular have responded with concerted efforts to investigate the replicability of results in their discipline. Many Labs 2 is one such example, conducting comprehensive replications of 28 classic and contemporary published findings, with protocols that were peer reviewed in advance. Results were replicated about 50% of the time. A second group called the Open Science Collaboration brought together 280 original authors and 86 volunteers to repeat 100 psychology studies published in major academic journals. The results were published in 2015 and showed that 36% of studies were replicated. Both efforts were massive collaborative undertakings that have set the stage for further such work. Within economics, a smaller 2016 study reported in *Science* found that 11 out of 18 experimental studies from top journals were replicated successfully.

> We can really use it to improve the situation rather than just lament the situation. The mere fact that that collaboration happened at such a large scale suggests that scientists are willing to move in the direction of improving.
>
> (Ioannidis quoted in Baker 2015)

What are the implications of this for knowledge in the human sciences? It would be premature to conclude on the basis of the replication crisis that human beings are fundamentally inconsistent creatures exhibiting few behavioural patterns—or to conclude that methodologies in psychology are fundamentally flawed.

For discussion

Just how bad is it anyway?

Consider these opposing claims regarding how severe the problem is regarding experimental results in the human sciences.

Daniel Gilbert, a psychologist at Harvard University, stated in 2016, "Our analysis completely invalidates the pessimistic conclusions that many have drawn from this landmark study," referring to the Open Science Collaboration project. "The number of studies that actually did fail to replicate is about the number you would expect to fail to replicate by chance alone—even if all the original studies had shown true effects" (quoted in Baker 2016).

On the other hand, Brian Nosek, leader of the Open Science Collaboration project, responded that Gilbert's "optimistic assessment is limited by statistical misconceptions" (quoted in Baker 2016).

We encounter disagreements between experts throughout this chapter and Chapter 7. A recurring question for TOK is what to do about it. If someone is not sufficiently competent in statistics how should they evaluate Nosek's versus Gilbert's arguments?

The replication problem within human sciences generally, and psychology specifically, is an ongoing controversy as of 2020 but there is a consensus forming around the view that a significant problem exists. Some have lamented that the tenor of the discourse is divisive and antagonistic, and newspapers and popular science outlets are accused of reporting it with sensational headlines equivalent to "Psychology is dead". Whether we call it a problem, a crisis, a disagreement or an opportunity, the episode has caused both students and researchers to examine more closely how academic knowledge is produced in the human sciences, in terms of the incentives, institutional structures, assumptions and practical constraints within academia. This is something to be welcomed.

Box 8.4: Destigmatizing loss of confidence

The authors of a study are the people most closely familiar with the weaknesses and limitations to their own findings. Sometimes, they are the foremost experts in their sub-disciplines, and may be the first to come across evidence that undermines their confidence in the results that propelled their careers. Yet, it remains rare for academics to publicly take back their work, so replications remain the next best way to find out about suspect findings. A timely response to the replication issue is the Loss of Confidence Project: the first organized, institutional platform for authors to declare a loss of confidence in their own research. The Loss of Confidence project is of a voluntary nature and researchers can only submit loss of confidence for their own research. If a researcher has lost confidence in their findings, why not retract the study? Is loss of confidence a soft alternative to retraction? Retractions are not necessarily voluntary—a journal can also retract a published article on the basis of error or fraud.

At any rate, initiatives such as Retraction Watch and the Loss of Confidence project make questionable or discarded findings easier to track. These initiatives are mechanisms for keeping the body of scientific knowledge reliable and up to date. Essentially, they raise questions of professional ethical conduct and transparency, and those issues take us to section IV.

One submission to the project came from psychologist Dana Carney, who came to refute the findings of her 2010 paper on 'power poses', co-authored with Amy Cuddy. The study centred on the idea that adopting a powerful pose could be beneficial in stressful situations. Although the pair's work on power poses had gained a lot of attention—and Cuddy's associated TED talk remains one of the most watched—in 2016 Carney felt compelled to admit that she no longer believed in the conclusions of her original study.

Figure 8.5a The two high-power poses used in the study. Participants in this condition were posed in expansive positions with open limbs.

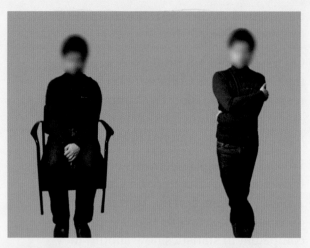

Figure 8.5b The two low-power poses used in the study. Participants in this condition were posed in contractive positions with closed limbs.

HOW POWERFUL IS AUTHORITY?

IV. ETHICS

power
influence
responsibility
fairness

Chapter 7 describes how the material and narrative power of scientific knowledge—to influence as well as tell stories about the natural world—necessitates a robust ethics. This chapter has shown that the human sciences describes as well as shapes our social reality in a similarly powerful way, affecting how we understand, agree or disagree about human nature, morality and justice, what is fundamental to all people, and what is different. Challenging issues can become political with comparatively few, if any, empirical truths to draw on. We have seen that what we do not know, and therefore what we must assume, can deeply influence knowledge and practical outcomes. The ethics of the human sciences must take into account power, influence, responsibility and fairness.

sapiens stories vs science?

Knowledge gives us the power to make such an impact on the planet that some have proposed to name the present geologic era, the Anthropocene, after us. Amid mounting evidence that human activity is altering social and Earth systems, the concept of the Anthropocene has been intensively theorized in the past few years. If you are unsure about what the concept means, follow the link to a comprehensive explainer video that is an excellent introduction to the topic. In the video the Anthropocene is described and justified in terms of the impact of humans on the planet.

🔍 Search terms:
Anthropocene the age of mankind YouTube

current institutions incapable for current situation

industrialization
urbanization
climate change

term to describe human impact on earth

Knowing the Anthropocene may require new trans-disciplinary modes of knowledge production and sharing that current institutions do not allow for. If the following sections sound like Earth science and you are wondering why they are here, keep that thought in mind, alongside the concept of natureculture from section II. Consider also the problem of removing the observer from the observation or the modeller from the model in the name of objectivity. Given the scale and depth of human impact on the planet, is it even possible to speak about nature without speaking about humans at the same time?

Within the human sciences we often need to make assumptions before attempting a cost-benefit type analysis which, as outlined in III.4 of this chapter, and IV.3 of Chapter 7, is fraught with knowledge issues. Let's revisit the topic of climate change we briefly touch on in Chapter 7, IV.3. Recall that there was, and into 2020 continues to be, disagreement about the social cost of carbon per tonne. In 2015 the US government came up with a number of $37 worth of economic damages but, shortly afterwards, the Stanford scientists argued it was $220. A more recent study in *Nature Climate Change* put forward a global social cost of carbon of $417 per tonne, with widely different costs for different countries (Ricke *et al* 2018). These ranges reflect difficulties in modelling and quantifying climate change, and the impact of assumptions made by different groups of scientists and stakeholders. Clearly this does not mean we abandon efforts to quantify the scale of reduction needed; the task of experts is to negotiate a consensus and arrive at a number.

As it is empirically-based, the carbon pricing task is more tangible than the philosophical and ethical questions and knowledge claims embedded in the climate justice debate. For progress to occur in the race to respond to the climate crisis, nations around the world need to work together, and that requires some minimum agreement about ethical issues relating to responsibility and fairness. And fairness is a deeply complicated concept: the 2018 article by Ricke *et al* finds that India, for instance, contributes only 6% of emissions but will bear over 20% of the global economic burden of climate change. What forms of knowledge will be necessary to accomplish such an unprecedented task? Are our modes of knowledge production and dissemination appropriate for navigating these urgent challenges?

Climate justice: The perfect moral storm

"

Climate change … brings together three major challenges to ethical action in a mutually reinforcing way. The first challenge stems from the fact that climate change is a truly global phenomenon. Once emitted, greenhouse gas emissions can have climate effects anywhere on the planet, regardless of their source. This is often said to result in a prisoner's dilemma or tragedy of the commons structure played out between nation states: although collectively all countries would prefer to limit global emissions so as to reduce the risk of severe or catastrophic impacts, when acting individually, each still prefers to continue emitting unimpeded. At the same time, there are skewed vulnerabilities: at least in the short- to medium-term, many of the most vulnerable countries and people are those who have emitted the least historically, and whose emissions levels continue to be relatively low. This appears to be seriously unfair and casts a notable shadow over both practical and theoretical efforts to secure global cooperation.

The second challenge is that current emissions have profoundly intergenerational effects. Emissions of the most prominent greenhouse gas, carbon dioxide, typically persist in the atmosphere for a long time, contributing to negative climate impacts for centuries, or even millennia. This too seems unfair, especially if future negative impacts are severe and cumulative. In addition, the temporal diffusion of climate change gives rise to an ethical collective action problem that is even more challenging than the traditional tragedy of the commons both in its shape and because normal kinds of cooperation do not seem to be possible across generations.

The third challenge to ethical action is that our theoretical tools are underdeveloped in many of the relevant areas, such as international justice, intergenerational ethics, scientific uncertainty, and the appropriate relationship between humans and the rest of nature. For example, climate change raises questions about the (moral) value of nonhuman nature, such as whether we have obligations to protect nonhuman animals, unique places, or nature as a whole, and what form such obligations take if we do. In addition, the presence of scientific uncertainty and the potential for catastrophic outcomes put internal pressure on the standard economic approach to environmental problems, and play a role in arguments for a precautionary approach in environmental law and policy that some see as an alternative.

(Gardiner, Hartzell-Nicholls 2012)

"

Responding to the global and intertemporal challenges posed by the climate crisis could require an awareness and understanding of how different peoples, nations and cultures think about fairness, responsibility and cooperation. Some countries, such as Canada and Russia, may well benefit from climate change (Ricke *et al* 2018). Should rich and poor nations contribute equally to reduce emissions, or should rich nations compensate the poor nations? At every level, issues of knowledge and ethics are woven into the discourse on global warming and climate justice.

For discussion

Who pays?

A radical argument calls for compensation for less-developed countries, which have contributed little to the problem and yet are already being impacted by it, having been made vulnerable to it through colonization.

1. What are the knowledge claims and assumptions implicitly and explicitly made in this argument?

2. On what basis, using what assumptions, should decisions about possible compensation be made?

Consider the fundamental question of how we compare the future with the present, a question of intergenerational ethics: how much effort should be made in the present, and at what cost, to benefit people in the future? The more relevant question for TOK is: what do you need to know to answer that question?

3. Referring to the questions above, do we expect different cultures around the world, with their diverse religious and spiritual beliefs, to have comparable answers?

4. How might we bridge the differences in responses?

If humankind is to have any chance of managing climate change, of reaching a consensus and coordinating an international effort, we would benefit from understanding how different people, nations and cultures answer these ethical questions. The alert reader will have noticed the assumptions embedded in the above sentence. A completely different outcome is also possible: that technology bails humanity out, allowing us to avoid these existential ethical challenges. However, there are other global issues requiring coordination, collaboration and consensus among different peoples and their knowledges.

IV.1 Limits to growth and the limits of human knowledge

It may inspire confidence to know that questions about knowledge and ethics are being asked and discussed outside of TOK classrooms, that others are grappling with the political and ethical challenges of human knowledge and action. Once you are tuned into the kinds of questions that are asked in TOK, you might start noticing them in conversations all around you. Follow the link to listen to a conversation between two experts from the human sciences, pondering the essential TOK topic of the limits of knowledge in the context of the Anthropocene. Consider the kinds of questions that guide their discussion.

Search terms: Anthropocene Campus "Limits of knowledge"

When it comes to the abundant scope and breadth of the Anthropocene and its concerns, one can ask: what are the limits of observation, accuracy, measurement, and calculation? What are the limits of descriptive accounts and written representations? How can one deal with uncertainty, ignorance, or risk?

(www.anthropocene-curriculum.org 2014)

For reflection

The unity of knowledge and trusting our knowledge

In the clip from 4:50–8:15 in the video, Wolfgang Lucht talks about what it would take to build an integrated Earth model that includes physical, ecological and social systems, based on our current knowledge. One of the limitations to this holistic model-building exercise is that the nature of knowledge we have about those systems is very different. How could we move our discipline-bound knowledges into a unified model?

1. How can we make any authoritative claims about the whole world, if our knowledge is essentially made up of ill-fitting pieces with significant gaps between them?

At 17:00, Lucht speaks about the balance that needs to be struck between intellectual humility and the responsibility to act when we are reasonably confident in our predictions.

2. Is there any point at which intellectual humility stops being a virtue and becomes an excuse for inaction? If so, how and where would you draw the line?

The last example brings together ideas from throughout this chapter: the role of quantification, the problems of measurement and the implications of applying simple knowledge to complex phenomena. At its core, the Anthropocene might be a problem of growth. The United Nations Conference on Sustainable Development in 2012 opened with the video linked here, tracing how the growth of humanity became a force that shapes the state of the world, especially since the 1950s. For this reason, we zoom in on knowledge issues of growth—what do we know about it, what kinds of responsibilities rest with that knowledge, and what kind of action can we take based on it?

 Search terms: "Welcome to the Anthropocene" on Vimeo

⬆ **Figure 8.6** A koala perishes in the Australian bush fires of 2020

Making connections

Knowledge and language

The language of growth

The language used to describe growth has changed as our knowledge about environmental impact and natural resource depletion has grown. What started out as economic growth evolved into sustainable growth and has now split, with the dominant concept being green growth, while an increasingly audible academic and political minority advocate for a post-growth paradigm.

> For the past seven decades, GDP growth has stood as the primary economic objective of European nations. … We are now exceeding the safe operating space for humanity on this planet, and there is no sign that economic activity is being decoupled from resource use or pollution at anything like the scale required. Today, solving social problems within European nations does not require more growth. It requires a fairer distribution of income and wealth that we already have.
>
> (ICTA 2018)

For discussion

Predictive knowledge in the Anthropocene

In the context of the Anthropocene, we often hear estimates and approximations of how much time we have to act on various issues before it is too late. Predictions and fears of economic and ecological collapse are certainly not new. In 1972, systems scientists at MIT famously predicted that ecosystems would collapse by the mid-21st century. Their report, "Limits to Growth", was criticized and ridiculed as disaster fantasy, for simplistic and pessimistic simulations that assumed little technological progress, and for having an anti-growth agenda. Well before them, in 1798, Thomas Malthus argued that human life would end in misery because of unchecked consumption growth. His logic seemed inescapable: resources were finite, while needs and wants were growing quickly—but then came technology.

Both sets of predictions are yet to come true—but the "Limits to Growth" thesis has become much more popular in the 21st century. Independent groups of scientists have observed that contemporary data suggest we are on the trajectory predicted by the MIT team. How do they know this? It is possible of course, to look at the details of their methodology but, for the purposes of analysis in TOK, more general questions can be asked about the power and validity of predictive knowledge.

1. What counts as evidence for the accuracy of a prediction?

2. If experts suggest different courses of action based on different predictions, which criteria can we use to judge which one is more reliable?

3. Given the complexity of the calculations underlying predictive knowledge about the state of the world, what is the role of trust in communicating this knowledge?

4. Does predictive knowledge bestow special responsibilities on those who produce it?

What else can we do to measure and move towards what matters in the Anthropocene? To begin with, we can identify and agree on the things that matter, and find ways to measure them. Ecological impact, wellbeing, and the living standards of typical people have all been put forward as important indicators that are more feasible than they might seem.

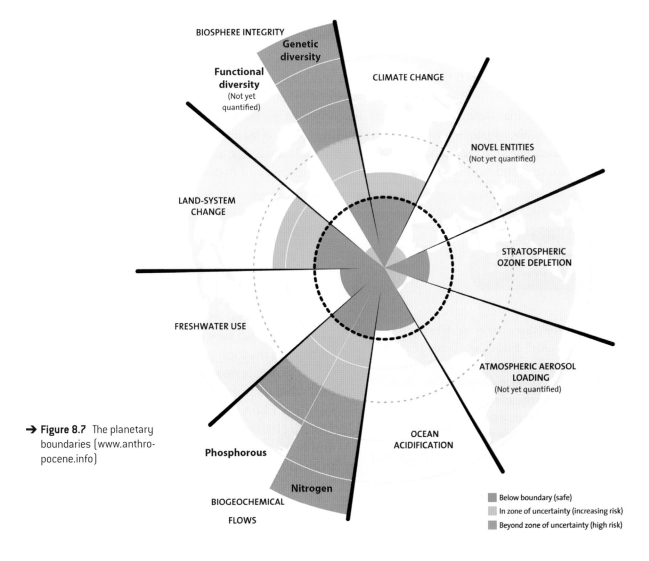

→ **Figure 8.7** The planetary boundaries (www.anthropocene.info)

BIOSPHERE INTEGRITY

Genetic diversity

Functional diversity
(Not yet quantified)

CLIMATE CHANGE

NOVEL ENTITIES
(Not yet quantified)

LAND-SYSTEM CHANGE

STRATOSPHERIC OZONE DEPLETION

FRESHWATER USE

ATMOSPHERIC AEROSOL LOADING
(Not yet quantified)

Phosphorous

OCEAN ACIDIFICATION

Nitrogen

BIOGEOCHEMICAL

FLOWS

■ Below boundary (safe)
■ In zone of uncertainty (increasing risk)
■ Beyond zone of uncertainty (high risk)

9 History

"Simply to show it how it was." This was the proper aim of history and the historian, according to Leopold von Ranke (1909), considered the pioneer of the modern discipline. Our exploration in this chapter will show that nothing is so simple about this AOK. History invites our curiosity to the important stories about past events and personalities, and TOK invites us to learn about this incredible human endeavour that produces and preserves knowledge about the past. We explore what guides historians and non-historians among us in the study of history.

I. SCOPE

> History provides the laboratory in which human experience is analysed, distilled and bottled for use. The so-called lessons of history do not teach you to do this or that now; they teach you to think more deeply, more completely, and on the basis of an enormously enlarged experience about what it may be possible or desirable to do now.
>
> (Elton 1991)

Throughout your exploration of the body of knowledge and practice of history, you will encounter multiple perspectives on what history is and is not, how it is and ought to be done, and what its purpose might be. The historian Geoffrey Elton is known for The *Practice of History* (1967), a manifesto on studying, writing and teaching history. He later summarized these principles as follows.

> Instead of telling us that certain conditions can be shown, from past experience, to lead to certain assured consequences, history for ever demonstrates the unexpectedness of the event, and so instils a proper scepticism in the face of all those vast and universal claims. A knowledge of the past should arm a man against surrendering to the panaceas peddled by too many myth-makers ... . Thus I will burden the historian with preserving human freedom, freedom of thought and action.
>
> (Elton 1991)

Spend some time considering the deeper meaning of Elton's words, in particular what he says about the kind of knowledge we produce and acquire in this AOK.

For reflection

Historical knowledge

It is widely said and often believed that history repeats itself, and that those who do not learn from history are doomed to repeat it.

1. What do you interpret from Elton's words about whether he thinks patterns in history exist?

2. How does the assumption about patterns in history affect the predictive power of historical knowledge?

3. Elton describes knowledge of history as a form of intellectual self-defence. Does this resonate with you? Reflect on a time you have used your knowledge of history in this way.

I.1 There is the past and there is history

History is not the past, but the study of the past and the body of knowledge that results from that study. There are many overlapping, imperfectly synonymous terms here: the written record, the historical record, historical narratives, written source, recorded history, historical account and so on. Through the work of historians, a historical past is produced, consisting of historical facts, which is different from the past itself. Few will challenge this distinction, but that does not mean that the relationship between what happened in the past, and what we know about it through history, is straightforward or uncomplicated.

A number of knowledge issues arise from the fact that historians are not time travellers but rather like interpreters of the traces of the past. What does it mean then for a historian's account to reflect the past accurately? If we accept that historians never access the past as it was, then how can there be checks on their work that are "real" checks? What or who is the final arbiter, the authority on what actually happened? The short answer is that there is none. This chapter explores the ways historians and non-historians encounter, and to an extent overcome, this problem. We consider exactly what remains of the past, how historians access it and how they construct their accounts.

Reporting rights

Chapter 7 raises the question of whether science has special reporting rights on nature—whether, through the methods and tools available, scientists can speak for nature or listen to nature speaking for itself. Consider how this relates to AOK history. Do historians have special reporting rights on the past? Are they, through the methods and tools available to them, able to speak for the past or allow the past to come through and speak for itself? What alternate disciplines, traditions or tools might help us to know the past or learn lessons from it?

For discussion

Mapping the offset between the past and history

Individually or in a small group, consider how you view the distinction between the past and history. Try to map out this distinction, for example through a Venn diagram, to express the relationship between the past and history.

1. What happens in the areas of offset (that is, where the past and history do not overlap)?

2. Why don't the past and history overlap in these areas?

3. If you are working in a group, compare your diagrams and share what you identify as significant similarities and differences.

4. Consider, for example, the roles of science or technology for making new methods of studying the past available. What would you say are other forces that enlarge the scope of history?

5. Consider the areas in your map that do not overlap. What are the consequences of this offset for the kind of knowledge we produce in history?

6. The IB requires a 10-year cooling period between events taking place and the first historical accounts of them. Why is this required or desirable?

I.2 Literacy and discovery

Let's go back to the beginning. In the context of history, both the when and where of "the beginning" are traditionally attached to the development of literacy. In this view, everything before such a time is designated as prehistorical, the domain of myths and traditions, and as such outside the realm of history. The first written records date back to around the 4th millennium BCE, in places such as Egypt, Mesopotamia and China. Some mark this as the beginning of history, even though the first historians will not appear for many centuries, no earlier than the 5th century BCE. This gap between the advent of literacy and the writings of the first historians—a period referred to as protohistory—varies greatly among different societies. Even within literate societies, the inconsistent rate of adoption of literacy meant that some segments of the population were excluded from contributing to the historical record for much longer.

The uneven beginnings of literacy, combined with global mobility during the "Age of Discovery", produce a period during which prehistory and protohistory acquire a problematic dimension. Literate societies, which had reached a stage where history was said to begin, were "discovering" and coming into contact with pre-literate (and therefore by this definition prehistoric) peoples, and producing the first written records and historical narratives about them. What was problematic is that in many places this encounter happened in the context of colonialism. Historians Peter Schmidt and Stephen Mrozowski describe this as follows.

> Since the eighteenth century, the concept of prehistory was exported by colonialism to far parts of the globe and applied to populations lacking written records. Prehistory in these settings came to represent primitive people still living in a state without civilization and its foremost index, literacy. Yet, many societies outside the Western world had developed complex methods of history making and documentation, including epic poetry and the use of physical and mental mnemonic devices. Even so, the deeply engrained concept of prehistory—deeply entrenched in European minds up to the beginning of the twenty-first century—continues to deny history and historical identity to peoples throughout the world.
>
> (Schmidt, Mrozowski 2014)

For reflection

The whole of history

The label "prehistorical" and the European protohistories of colonized peoples have significant implications for knowledge.

1. What does it mean to exclude a people's knowledge of their past from history based on the criterion of literacy?

2. When our historical knowledge of a people comes from an outside perspective, how does this affect the comprehensiveness and validity of historical knowledge?

3. Does history, when tethered strictly to literacy, leave too much outside its scope to be considered the best way of knowing the past? What alternatives exist?

Box 9.1: History and its "others" coexisting in time

"Prehistory" is not a neutral term merely referring to a period defined by illiteracy, among other criteria. Its connotations, acquired in the context of colonialism, problematizes its continued use today. As an example, consider historian and archaeologist Peter Schmidt's accounts from his early career in Tanzania, which revealed to him "how our usage of taken-for-granted concepts can offend sensibilities where the use of such tropes carries the stigma of erasure and enforced invisibility of local history" (Schmidt, Mrozowski 2014).

The term "prehistoric", when applied to peoples:

- consigns their knowledge to a realm of culture
- frames that culture as primitive, at a stage of development before history can be said to begin
- serves to deny their existence as our contemporaries.

Beyond these issues, the way history treats its "others" has implications for their personhood. Linda Tuhiwai Smith reflects on the influence of German philosopher Hegel, who considered humankind as those who could "create" their own history, people capable of reflecting on themselves and their past—only they were seen as fully human. Others were regarded as non-human or prehistoric.

Historians, archaeologists, anthropologists and other cultural scholars in the past couple of decades have been producing critical scholarship on prehistory. Does the term "prehistory" have any usefulness today? If they conclude that the term has visited too much harm on Indigenous Peoples and its continued use is unacceptable, is discarding it enough? Schmidt and Mrozowski explain that the politics of knowledge and language are not simple in this case.

"This is more than a matter of political correctness, for when the prehistory trope is used and offends, then it must be recognized as a device that disenfranchises whole cultures and regions, writing them out of history. Simultaneously, we recognize that not all contexts are similar and that the use of the prehistory trope in Europe, for example, may have different and less negative implications … The problem arose, and continues, in those instances when Western-trained archaeologists look to the Indigenous populations of colonial-era Ireland, Africa, North America, or Australia as useful analogues for Palaeolithic or Neolithic Europeans. Our stance here is one of political action that seeks to change our language about how we re-represent histories that have been affected, truncated, and distorted through active use of tropes like prehistory. Truncated histories are not repaired or recuperated by the use of alternative tropes (protohistoric, ethnohistoric, contact, entanglements—all are mere substitutes while also acting as politically correct speech) … Complete avoidance of the term is not sufficient because active renunciation is required." (Schmidt, Mrozowski 2014)

Making connections

Language and voluntarily isolated tribes

This debate spills over into the question of how we describe the few remaining tribes around the world living in voluntary isolation. For example, in 2018 a missionary was killed in an attempt to contact the voluntarily isolated tribe on North Sentinel Island in the Indian Ocean. Some of the media coverage invoked the old, damaging tropes of lost tribes, Stone Age people and prehistoric humans. Chapter 5 discusses the topic of uncontacted tribes.

↑ **Figure 9.1** Bonda women on their way to a market in the eastern Indian state of Odisha

This section ends with the acknowledgement that the scope of history is not static. History has changed in response to the challenges and pressure described here, and through new technologies and interdisciplinary collaborations.

As a result, historical methods have evolved to deal with a wider range of sources, allowing new perspectives to enter into and enlarge the scope of inquiry. We explore this in the next section.

For discussion

Why is history an AOK?

Why, in TOK, does history qualify as an AOK when it is ordinarily a part of IB Diploma Programme group 3? Use the following questions as prompts for your discussion.

1. Is history an AOK because of the scope of its subject matter or because knowing history is of special importance to the individual?

2. Is it the methods of history that set it apart from the knowledge produced in the other AOKs?

3. Why does it matter that history is an AOK?

Discussing these questions will expose different perspectives and give you an opportunity to practise constructing your own informed answers.

II. PERSPECTIVES

> Our picture of Greece in the fifth century B.C. is defective not primarily because so many of the bits have been accidentally lost, but because it is, by and large, the picture formed by a tiny group of people in the city of Athens.
>
> (E.H. Carr quoted in H. Carr 2019)

The idea of perspectives takes on multiple meanings in history. There are the high-level perspectives—which we explore in every AOK—on what, in this case, history is and ought to be. On this topic, historians reflect on their observations and hopes for their own discipline. Then there are perspectives on how history as both a discipline and a body of knowledge has changed over time, perspectives that come from not only historians but also philosophers, theorists and critics who study the development of knowledge and ideas. Finally, there are perspectives on how historical knowledge is received and perceived more widely in society, and perhaps this shows us the great plurality of perspectives in this AOK. While few people would claim value in having a personal mathematics or science, many can and do insist on their personal and group histories. Some observers thus argue it is necessary to limit what is meant by history to knowledge produced by academic and professional historians. If so, we would have to account for the omissions and erasures that come with that claim, particularly in light of the role of literacy in history.

As newcomers to the discipline of history, students are often initiated with precisely

↑ **Figure 9.2** "A New Patriotic Song" from a collection of material relating to the fear of a French invasion (1803) British Library

the question we explored in section I: what is history and what do historians do? Typically students encounter two schools of thought, exemplified by two textbooks—Geoffrey Elton's *The Practice of History* and E.H. Carr's *What is History?* These texts are seen to typify the two traditional approaches to historiography.

> Historiography is the study of the methods that historians use; the writing of history.

Elton and Carr have not moved far from the required reading lists of history students for many decades, though several historians, such as Keith Jenkins (1995), have suggested that for various reasons this approach is "no longer good enough".

We explore the Elton-Carr debate in III.2, but should note first that both Elton and Carr were British historians, and it is important to consider how the issues of diversity and representation find expression in the historical community in your context.

In 2018 two reports commissioned by the Royal Historical Society (RHS) were published, one focusing on gender, and the other on racial and ethnic equality within the field. In the same year, Olivette Otele become the first ever female black professor of history in the UK (we repeat for emphasis: it was 2018). Follow the link below to hear why that is a point of concern for the discipline, through Otele's voice.

Box 9.2: Gender and ethnic diversity in the British historical profession

Linked here is a conversation with Otele and Sadiah Qureshi, who was involved with the RHS report.

 Search terms: Diversity in history HistoryExtra

Excerpts from their conversation and findings from the report are provided below, and raise significant questions for TOK.

- Only 11% of undergraduate students in the UK come from black, minority and ethnic backgrounds, as compared with 24% in undergraduate programmes overall. There are multiple reasons for this discrepancy. In some places, it has to do with the content of the history curriculum, which may not be designed to be relevant to a classroom of ethnically diverse students. But across the board, there is a concern about the diversity of history teachers. "There is this idea that who teaches you matters as much as what is taught", says Otele. It is a question of representation and relevance. Students need to see themselves in their teachers, and have teachers who speak about a history that matters to them.

- The RHS report found evidence of an attainment gap in terms of the number of students of colour who graduate with the highest distinction. "Students were very clear that the subject needs to be made more relevant to them … they are completely and utterly put off by the curriculum which they see as heavily dominated by Eurocentrism and whiteness in very, very damaging ways."

- Qureshi calls it "absolutely shocking" and "a national disgrace" that it took until 2018 for the first female black professor of history to be appointed in the UK, following Hakim Ali who in 2015 became the first black history professor. Qureshi argues that "for most students of history that have ever read this subject at university, they have never been taught by a black professor … or a professor of color". To understand why Qureshi emphasizes race here, over gender, consider that in the UK the first female professor of any subject was appointed 100 years ago, whereas the first black female professor of any subject was appointed only 20 years ago.

For discussion

The role of identity

This discussion focuses on the role of identity in the acquisition of historical knowledge. Think of arguments that support the statement about identity that follows, then think of arguments that contradict it. If you are working with a partner, one of you could present a case arguing "for" the statement

and the other "against". If you are in a group, split into two opposing teams for this. "Identity plays a different role in history as compared to the other AOKs."

1. The conversation between Olivette Otele and Sadiah Qureshi leaves us with the impression that diversity in history is worse than in other fields on average. Which factors affect whether a given discipline is better able to address issues of diversity?

2. Are the implications of a lack of diversity different for the various AOKs?

II.1 Diversity and histories

While issues of diversity and equity are important to all communities, professional historians being no exception, diversity has recursive implications for history as a body of knowledge. As section III will show, historians intentionally seek out diverse sources in constructing historical accounts. How then is the objectivity of history served by a lack of diversity among professional historians? To explore this question, we turn to the ideas of E.H. Carr, brought to us by his great-granddaughter Helen Carr, who traces the evolution of his thinking about objectivity. Carr was concerned with how a historian frequently draws not on objective fact but on their experience.

> *A History of Soviet Russia* was a bold attempt carefully and meticulously to collect all the facts available, and in doing so, [E.H. Carr] articulated an impressively objective approach to Russian history. … In the lengthy process of writing *A History of Soviet Russia* he … was initially optimistic; 'it is possible to maintain that objective truth exists', yet by 1950 he concluded: 'objectivity does not exist'. Nineteenth-century historians believed in objective history … Carr rejected this outdated approach, describing it as a 'preposterous fallacy'.
>
> (Carr 2019)

Carr was not alone in reflecting deeply about objectivity in the second half of the 20th century. After the First World War and Second World War there was particular interest in history and the forces that shape it, and a period of democratization of the practice of history. Whether or not historiographers agree with Carr, or the democratization of the discipline, they agree that these reconsiderations were prompted by the rise of social history and opened up the discipline to women and other formerly excluded groups. It also prompted an introspection of widespread historiographical assumptions about objectivity and neutral truths.

Follow the link to a short clip, entitled "A Brief Herstory", that recounts the humble and brave beginnings of the Lesbian Herstory Archives and its presence today. What can this teach us about grassroots efforts to diversify and contribute to history?

 Search terms: Lesbian Herstory Archives Vimeo

The Lesbian Herstory Archives are a milestone in the ongoing democratization of history and reveal the sense of social connectedness that arises when a community constructs its own narrative of its past.

It is not just us, in TOK, who dwell on these questions while historians get on with their work. The intellectual movement of post-modernism challenged history with deep questions and ushered in the opening of

history (singular, monolithic) to histories (plural). Consider the following questions for history that continue to shape the discipline through this process.

> Whose history gets told? In whose name? For what purpose? Post-modernism is about histories not told, retold, untold. History as it never was. Histories forgotten, hidden, invisible, considered unimportant, changed, eradicated. It's about the refusal to see history as linear, as leading straight up to today in some recognisable pattern—all set for us to make sense of. It's about chance. It's about power. It's about information.
>
> (Marshall 1992)

For discussion

Knowledge in history changing over time

Compare how knowledge in history changes over time as compared to how it changes in the natural sciences.

1. What happens to discarded knowledge?
2. What is the status of current knowledge?

II.2 Making history and thresholds of significance

Who makes history? We tend to hear this in the context of "(name of person) made history" and a lot of time this happens "today". States can make history by passing legislation, extraordinary athletes can do so by breaking records, groups of organized citizens can make history by disobeying authority and so on. In this common-sense view, history appears to be made by individual or collective action in the present. However, there are some implicit standards that govern when something goes from being one of many events in the past, to being significant enough to join the historical record.

What matters?

Find an example, perhaps an article or an event, that shows someone "making history". What criteria did you use to define this?

When you are ready, with a partner or in a small group, share your criteria.

1. What are significant similarities and differences?

2. If you share your ideas as a class, which things regularly emerge as markers of historical significance?

3. Draw on your implicit shared understanding to consider the following.

   (a) What does it mean for something to matter for history?

   (b) Which groups of people or kinds of events are less likely to qualify?

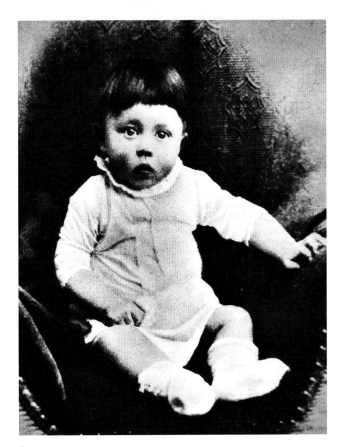

↑ **Figure 9.3** Adolf Hitler as a baby

Occasionally, we are given the opportunity to make history too, at least hypothetically in the context of thought experiments. For example, in 2015, the *New York Times* magazine ran a poll entitled: "Dear reader: Could you kill a baby Hitler?" A snapshot of the results on 23 October 2015 showed that 42% of respondents answered "yes", 30% answered "no" and 28% were not sure.

To take that discussion into the domain of TOK we need to explore the justifications behind the answers. It sounds like an ethics question but it is not quite so, rather it reveals how we believe that history is made: whether events are inevitable or contingent, and the importance of heroes, villains, monarchs and schemers. As Rebecca Onion puts it, answering the question about killing baby Hitler requires you to think deeply about: "your own beliefs about the nature of progress, the inherent contingency of events, and the influence of individuals—even very charismatic ones—on the flow of historical change" (Onion 2015).

These questions are fundamental to how we each think about history, and thought experiments about time travelling make them more accessible. "What if …?" questions are explored when discussing counterfactuals later in this chapter. And if you are still wondering about the ethics of killing baby Hitler, follow the link.

 Search terms: Atlantic Ethics of killing baby Hitler

A stricter definition of history sees it as made by historians when they study and write about past events. To study what we call "making history" in everyday language, historians consider the causes of historical events. Elton (who featured in section I) was deeply concerned with the question of human agency in history. He insisted that what drives history is the will, choices and actions of people, and not abstract forces, structures and patterns in society. These "abstractions" could be useful for describing a historical context, but not for explaining the causes of historical events. According to Elton, historians should want to explain the past and so they have a responsibility to recognize the impact of human activity and agency.

Elton focuses on human causes in history as opposed to structural causes. Consider, though, the argument that some individuals and groups are more likely to be recognized as drivers of history than others.

In *Decolonizing Methodologies* (1999), Linda Tuhiwai Smith explains that history, in Elton's

view, began with industrialization. Leaving aside the day-to-day lives of ordinary people, particularly women, and people who didn't belong to a certain class and race (in line with the historians of his time), he considered that history was made by those who helped build the modern state and brought about social change. The economists, philosophers, scientists and other successful entrepreneurs were the only rational individuals capable of shaping the new industrialized era.

Box 9.3: Changing markers of significance and correcting omissions

Malcolm Allbrook, Managing Director of the *Australian Dictionary of Biography* (ADB), explains the ADB's vision to include the biographies of "significant and representative" subjects from a "cross-section of Australian society". This collage of biographies was to tell the history of Australia and serve as a kind of source code of Australian identity.

↑ **Figure 9.4** Woollarawarre Bennelong (c. 1764–1813), a Wangal-born warrior and a peacemaker

In the first two volumes, published in 1966 and 1967, only eight out of the 1182 biographies were of Aboriginal people. In the next 15 or so years, the size of the ADB quadrupled. But only seven of the new entries were Aboriginal and Torres Strait Islander biographies. As of

2017, Aboriginal biographies consist of about 1.5% of all entries in the ADB. What are the implications of this for knowledge, ethics and inclusion?

To address this issue, Allbrook explains: "[a] working party made up of Aboriginal and Islander scholars from each state and territory is now preparing an Indigenous Australian Dictionary of Biography with nearly 200 new biographies" (Allbrook 2017).

These new entries will be added to the ADB but also published as a standalone Indigenous ADB. Commenting on the process, Allbrook says that: "because this is a largely community-driven process, it is likely that new markers of 'significance' will emerge, determined perhaps not so much by success or standing on national, state or local stages, as by what they brought to community and family life" (Allbrook 2017).

The omitted life stories of Aboriginal people are not the only concern with the ADB. Some colonists, implicated in atrocities against Aboriginal people, are described in very positive terms, including and especially regarding their supposed humanitarian actions towards Indigenous Peoples. Frank Bongiorno, who heads the history department at the university that produces the ADB, pointed out the following.

> "Inevitably when you've been running for 60 years, … the earliest work will sometimes be out of date, and especially so in relation to the Indigenous experience of dispossession and violence … [the ADB team] is decolonising a project whose origins lie in an era before most white Australians were prepared to face what they and their ancestors had done to Aboriginal people." (Bongiorno quoted in Daly 2019)

Decolonizing the ADB will require more than adding gender and ethnic diversity to the entry pool. The project of updating problematic existing entries is equally if not more important, but presents significant challenges (with interesting TOK implications) for the team. To find out more, follow the link to an article by Paul Daley.

 Search terms: Australian Dictionary of Biography history for the forgotten

The task of updating the ADB has clearly recognizable elements of historical revisionism. However, the anthropologist Mary Douglas (1986) has argued that 'history' is merely a reflection of the past, as seen through the lens of the present. Often, Douglas suggests, the process of revisionism says more about the present than it does about the past.

Perspectives on when and whether revisionism is necessary, suspect, valuable or futile are explored below.

II.3 International understanding and the revision of history textbooks

The years since the mid-20th century have been marked by the aftermath of war as well as profound global transformations. During this time the writing and teaching of history has been woven together with peace-building, nation-building and reconciliation efforts. Amid this backdrop, the role and approaches to historical knowledge have changed dramatically, especially in terms of its use for international understanding and educating for peace.

This has been both a scholarly as well as a political project, for the way we know the past has implications for the shared future. In the context of national school systems, school history textbooks have a wide and authoritative reach and are instruments of collective identity-building. Especially in public school systems, history textbooks define events of national pride, collective victimhood and historical relations of rivalry and hostility.

This chapter will have made clear that history textbooks inevitably select, omit, rearrange, interpret and simplify from the traces we have left of the past. When these textbooks are state-sanctioned in national school systems, their particular selections, omissions, arrangements, interpretations and simplifications become authoritative for most—not dissimilar to the "black boxes" we encounter in Chapter 7. Minority or oppressed groups within the state or other states may see these accounts as biased and manipulative. For these reasons, history textbooks have been at the centre of controversies—and educators, historians and politicians alike recognize their potential to promote peace, as well as perpetuate, or even provoke, conflict.

Therefore, there is much to be learned from looking closely at bilateral or multilateral textbook revision projects in conflict and post-conflict contexts, especially for peace- and friendship-building. Such projects are often conducted in the spirit of breaking down prejudice and inspiring mutual understanding between former or current hostiles or enemies. The teaching of history becomes a tool for international understanding and peaceful future relations.

Examples of this include powerful historical events such as the end of apartheid in South Africa and the work of the Truth and Reconciliation Commission; the respective break-ups of Yugoslavia and the Soviet Union; and the Franco-German history revision project ("Histoire-Geschichte", simply "History" written in both French and German). These examples set a blueprint for revision projects to tone down or eliminate historical hostility in each country's respective textbooks, to instead promote a narrative that supports peaceful coexistence. These efforts go back half a century. For instance, in 1950 a German newspaper referred to "detoxification squads" consisting of British and German historians and teachers who aimed to remove the "poisonous seeds sown by nationalistic hate campaigns in school textbooks" (Stöber quoted in Korostelina, Lässig 2013). French and Danish history teachers also eventually joined the project, to the point where the same newspaper followed up the project a year later with an article speculating whether there was going to be a "European" history textbook. Professor Georg Stöber writes:

> They were meeting … with the intention to review and discuss each other's national history textbooks in order to eliminate 'untrue accounts and deprecating descriptions of the other nation' and 'to prevent an immortalization of nationalistic tensions' or 'glorifications of war'.
>
> (Stöber quoted in Korostelina, Lässig 2013)

Indeed, the project almost exceeded revisionism to reach the further stage of a shared transnational textbook. It is one thing for nation states to challenge each other's narratives of history and cooperate in revising them; it is another thing entirely to transcend or cut across national divisions and have a common textbook.

Histoire-Geschichte is one such project, a shared history for both French and German students. It was proposed by the French-German Youth Parliament in 2003 and taken up by the German Department for Foreign Affairs and the French Ministry of Education, and finally launched in 2008 in the town of Peronne, the site of the bloodiest battles of the First World War.

Earlier projects of history textbook revision were championed by "internationally-minded" teachers. For a period, in the 1920s and 1930s, even the League of Nations, the predecessor of the United Nations, picked up the issue. These efforts focused on comparative analyses to identify and revise essential misrepresentations and misunderstandings of other nations.

For discussion

Perspectives and legitimacy

Consider the following extract from the 1937 League of Nations *Declaration Regarding the Teaching of History (Revision of School Text-Books)*, listing the principles for achieving international understanding.

1. "It is desirable that the attention of the competent authorities in every country, and of authors of school text-books, should be drawn to …

   a. … assigning as large a place as possible to the history of other nations;

   b. … giving prominence, in the teaching of world history, to facts calculated to bring about a realisation of the interdependence of nations.

2. It is desirable that every Government should endeavor to ascertain by what means, … especially in connection with the choice of school-books, … allegations and interpretations as might arouse unjust prejudices against other nations.

3. It is desirable that in every country a committee composed of members of the teaching profession, including history teachers, should be set up by the National Committee on Intellectual Co-Operation… ." (League of Nations 1937)

Discuss the following questions.

1. **(a)** Whose perspectives influence what historical facts are taught in schools? Consider the role of the governments, national history teachers' unions, international teachers' associations, domestic civic organizations, transnational non-governmental organizations and others.

   (b) How should this influence be checked and controlled?

2. What are the implications when:

   (a) experts from another state are allowed to influence how history is taught in a given national education system

   (b) experts from another state are not allowed to influence how history is taught and the state has a monopoly on what gets taught in the national history curriculum?

3. **(a)** In terms of the history curriculum, under what circumstances should the historian and history teachers' autonomy be limited?

   (b) Does the teaching of history require additional or different controls to the teaching of other subjects?

Over time, the scope of these projects has shifted from bilateral to regional and global efforts, with the result that their product is less about national "compromise narratives" which allow for aligned but separate histories, and more about a "common" shared history. What perspectives are gained or lost in a shared history textbook versus a national history textbook? Where do your history textbooks fit in this scheme?

How did the moral imperatives and standards for these projects arise? Or, as Simone Lässig asks, "Who initiated, inspired and carried out the projects? … what is the nature of the tension between *intervention* and *empowerment* with regard to history education reform …?" (Korostelina, Lässig 2013). Lässig uses the word "empowerment" here to describe local ownership of the outcomes of these projects, of the people whose history is being rewritten in those projects. The balance between local empowerment and external intervention ultimately influences whether the project will be "successful".

What would success look like? If the metric is whether it results in a textbook that is officially sanctioned and shared by two or more countries, then we have relatively few success stories, and Histoire-Geschichte is among them.

This becomes more complicated when revisionist projects are initiated, funded or supported by third parties, such as other international stakeholders and NGOs. For example, the Southeast European Joint History Project produced a set of "alternative educational materials", and one project in North East Asia resulted in textbooks that were not officially sanctioned but were used to complement national textbooks in China, South Korea and Japan.

For reflection

Common textbooks and "compromise narratives"

Private or independent schools often have the freedom to choose to use textbooks other than the approved state educational materials.

1. What are the advantages and disadvantages of this?

2. Have you encountered different accounts of "your" history?

3. Have you experienced or observed a clash between the historical narratives known to your parents or grandparents' generations versus the accounts taught to you today in national or international English education systems? How have you responded? Share and compare your answers in your class.

Making connections

History, objectivity and the knower

In Chapter 7 we encounter Thomas Nagel's description of objectivity as "the view from nowhere". To what extent is this the goal of international education systems in general, and of their history textbooks in particular? To what extent is this goal possible and desirable?

How has your acquisition of knowledge, in history and other AOKs, been shaped by the compromises that have been made to make knowledge objective or neutral?

Some of the contextual factors to consider are whether these projects are conducted in post-conflict or ongoing conflict theatres, and whether they spill over national boundaries. Additionally, an important factor is whether they emerge within post-colonial or present-day settler colonial states, such as India and Canada respectively.

> I used to think that the profession of history, unlike that of, say, nuclear physics, could at least do no harm. Now I know it can. ... We have a responsibility to historical facts in general, and for criticizing the politico-ideological abuse of history in particular.
>
> (Hobsbawm 1993)

Textbook revision projects require those involved to agree not merely on the facts of dates and places of events, but on the causes, significance and impact of events, and how these events construct the national narrative.

These examples reveal a political dimension to consensus and disagreement in history. Many projects are based on the idea of teaching history through multiple perspectives, with the objective being to give space to different voices, including conflicting views. This approach gained popularity in Western and Northern Europe in the 1970s, and moved the focus of historical knowledge from the content of textbooks—the "facts"—to the ability to evaluate multiple sources and perspectives. But is this approach to history appropriate on a global scale?

The extent to which "the use of multiple perspectives and controversy" is universally useful is an open question. Lässig describes this approach as necessarily a Western conception of historical instruction, and asks the following.

> Are there situations in which different source statements and historiographical interpretations simply place too high demands on pupils and teachers, in which both rather require a 'usable past' with a master narrative that provides direction ...?
>
> (Lässig in Korostelina, Lässig 2013)

Finally, the multiple-perspectives approach to disseminating historical knowledge will inevitably be complicated by issues of power and ideology. The US/USSR Textbook Study Project spanned over a decade from the 1980s and ultimately failed for political reasons. While many points of divergence in this case could have been be fixed by giving voice to the other's perspective, other issues, such as descriptions and explanations of the ideological dimensions of political and economic systems, proved irreconcilable. One of the reports on the project concluded: "Textbooks will continue to be written from the perspectives of each society. This need not impede accurate textbook treatment" (Mehlinger in Eklof 1993).

What is meant by "accurate" here, and in history as an AOK? Does it mean factually correct, balanced in terms of representation, fair in terms of description of different ideologies?

For reflection

Power imbalances in historial revision

We have discussed projects between stakeholders of relatively similar power—France and Germany, the United States and the USSR.

1. **(a)** What differences emerge when there is an imbalance of power between the parties?

   (b) What kinds of checks and balances can be put into place to safeguard against abuses of power in these cases?

III. METHODS AND TOOLS

> Historians, when practising their craft, must not be vulnerable to the chauvinism of their discipline, or of method, identity and ideology.
>
> (Guha 2019)

In doing history, what does the historian have access to? This question has for centuries shaped the methods and tools of historians who, whether by trial and error, or leaps of insight, have developed a practice that currently aims to find and evaluate sources, interpret the evidence, then reconstruct a truthful narrative of the past. Note that this view of history, in the preceding sentence, involves a composite of two knowledge claims: first, that the practice of history shapes its method; and second, that history is about discovering truths of the past. Neither should be taken for granted. What alternative claims exist? How would you evaluate these claims? This section will be your guide.

Students of history are well acquainted with the differences between the *past* (the set of events), the *knowable past* (the subset of events for which we have accessible records), and *history*, which we shall conceive of as a formalized narrative and interpretation of the knowable past. Interpretation, evaluation, objectivity, truth, access, fact and record are fundamental concepts within the practice and theory of history as an AOK, as well as within TOK. History is thus, perhaps more than any other AOK, closest in its practice to TOK, to the limited extent that such a comparison can be made.

III.1 What remains of the past?

A historical record is typically a written history in narrative form, although oral histories, photographs and film are increasingly accepted as part of the record. The record includes a huge variety of accounts, from intended factual documents to lyrical, metaphorical, mythical and artistic representations of the past. Until very recently, written language was the preserve of a powerful and privileged minority, among both those who sought to write history and those with an interest in reading it. What are the implications of this for the historical record?

Whatever was recorded, for whatever reason, in whatever form, we have only a small fraction of it left—traces floating through time. Historians must always ask: where do these traces come from? Who wrote them, or allowed them to reach us, or may have failed to stop them reaching us? As important as these traces are, historians must also consider the absence of traces, the parts of history that they cannot see. Historians therefore attempt to imagine (yes, you read that right) what they cannot see, what might be missing from the record, why it is missing, and what it could have shown them. Post-modern criticisms of history argue that this is impossible, and indeed that history is fundamentally problematic because it is based on subjective interpretations of traces of the past.

To this criticism, Gabrielle Spiegel, a historian and professor, and former President of the American Historical Association, has responded that: "if texts—documents, literary works, whatever—do not transparently reflect reality, but only other texts, then historical study can scarcely be distinguished from literary study, and the 'past' dissolves into literature" (Spiegel 1992). How have historians addressed this problem? This chapter has outlined a few such efforts. Democratizing the discipline by inviting a multiplicity of perspectives, for example from non-written sources, is one such example.

As noted in I.2, language and specifically literacy have played an eminent role given the discipline's reliance on the written record. Therefore, abilities to understand and translate language have restricted access to the historical record, among those who sought to contribute as well as those trying to gain knowledge from it.

The Victorian historian and philosopher, Thomas Carlyle, is attributed with the phrase: "[t]he history of the world is but the biography of great men", a cliché often satirized by contemporary social commentators, but also revealing of an important concern with historical knowledge: which individuals in the past have had both the interest and influence to have historical records written? How should we treat these records? Thus we see that the methods of evaluation and interpretation derive directly from the nature of the historical record.

Section II explored what historical knowledge can give to (and take away from) individuals, peoples and nations—especially in terms of power and identity. How do we recognize, find and grasp these traces of history? Who has access to history and who can control that access? The implications of access are profound for identity and power. Access can be blocked in obvious ways—confidential government files and secretive religious leaders that cinema goers are well acquainted with—as well as in more fundamental and structural ways. We have seen that the method and tools used in history (the ways in which it is recorded) can shape what counts as history, and who has the chance to record it.

For instance, only in the past few decades have oral histories been widely recognized, recorded and incorporated into historical records, even though Oral Traditions have been the primary means of intergenerational knowledge preservation and transfer for a vast number of peoples around the globe. What might be the implications of this for such communities, in terms of their representation and influence in economic, political and cultural life in a globalized world?

In her 1999 book, *Decolonizing Methodologie*s, Linda Tuhiwai Smith explains how many systems that value oral ways of approaching the world have been "reclassified as oral traditions rather than histories". This classification suggests that the stories and accounts which are an essential part of the fabric of these Indigenous communities and are embedded in the land, woven within people's names and genealogies and expressed through art and craft, do not constitute a valid method of acquiring or transmitting knowledge.

Making connections

Art, museums and ethics

Oral histories, along with generally labelled "material-cultural artefacts", have played an important role in carrying and communicating the knowledge systems of many peoples around the world, both for themselves and outsiders. For this reason, the modern practice of taking and storing such artefacts in museums in the large cities of advanced industrialized nations has significant implications for access to knowledge and ethics—whether it is historical, religious or artistic. This is how, for example, someone's battle shield ends up in the prehistoric or artistic exhibit of a museum, even when it belongs to a people or culture that is very much in the present. What are the implications of this practice, for history as well as other areas of knowledge? To what extent should we return these artefacts to their people, even if that means dismantling museums' collections? We explore this issue in more depth in Chapter 10, II.4.

Historians in the future may well have a very different problem, because present-day culture leaves such a vast material and digital footprint.

One argument within history is that its methods, and questions, are perennial: they apply to human life always and forever. Let's pursue this idea to see where it leads.

For reflection

Interpreting the historical record

Imagine you are a historian in 2120, trying to reconstruct the narrative of human life in 2020.

1. What records do you have of 2020?

2. Who made these records, why, and in what form?

3. What, and who, might be missing from these records?

4. How do the answers to questions 1–3 affect your interpretation of the record, and your narrative of human life in 2020?

III.2 The historian's role

> Study the historian before you begin to study the facts. The facts … are like fish on the fishmonger's slab. The historian collects them, takes them home and cooks and serves them.
>
> (Carr 1961)

Let's continue with the metaphor of traces of the past floating through time, and assume now that we have a historian willing and able to grasp them. The question before us is whether our historian can "see" these traces as they are—as objective remnants of the past—or whether the historian necessarily has a subjective interpretation. The keen observer will realize that there is another, more fundamental question: how can we discern between subjective and objective interpretations of the knowable past? How do we recognize objectivity and subjectivity when we see them?

Box 9.4: Does the past speak for itself?

The historian, journalist and diplomat E.H. Carr engaged with this subject intensely in his influential 1961 book *What is History*? Carr questioned what we call "historical facts", as explained by his great-granddaughter, Helen Carr (introduced in II.1).

"Facts can be changed or manipulated to benefit those relaying them, something we are acutely aware of today. During Carr's lifetime, Stalin's regime destroyed documents, altered evidence and distorted history ... It is the continued misrepresentation and misuse of fact, deliberate or accidental, that Carr interrogates in What is History? He encourages any student of history to be discerning: "What is a historical fact? This is a crucial question into which we must look a little more closely." (Carr 2019)

One of E.H. Carr's key points was that, because of the vast amount of information available to historians, and their subjective interpretation of the facts, they inevitably end up choosing which "facts" to make use of.

"What is a historical fact? ... According to the commonsense view, there are certain basic facts which are the same for all historians and which form, so to speak, the backbone of history—the fact, for example, that the Battle of Hastings was fought in 1066. But this view calls for two observations. In the first place, it is not with facts like these that the historian is primarily concerned. It is no doubt important to know that the great battle was fought in 1066 and not 1065 or 1067 ... . The historian must not get these things wrong. But when points of this kind are raised, I am reminded of Housman's remark that 'accuracy is a duty, not a virtue'. To praise a historian for his accuracy is like praising an architect for using well-seasoned timber. ... It is a necessary condition of his work, but not his essential function. ... It used to be said that facts speak for themselves. This is, of course, untrue. The facts speak only when the historian calls on them: it is he who decides to which facts to give the floor, and in what order or context. ... The only reason why we are interested to know that the battle was fought at Hastings in 1066 is that historians regard it as a major historical event. It is the historian who has decided for his own reasons that Caesar's crossing of that petty stream, the Rubicon, is a fact of history, whereas the crossings of the Rubicon by millions of other people before or since interests nobody at all. ... The historian is necessarily selective. The belief in a hard core of historical facts existing objectively and independently of the historian is a preposterous fallacy, but one which it is very hard to eradicate." (Carr 1990)

In Carr's view, it was very clear: the historian speaks for the past because the past cannot speak for itself. Carr thus advised his students to study the historian before studying their facts. The implication for historical knowledge was to examine the role of the interpreter and what might influence them. Carr was only one among many that grappled with these questions of truth and objectivity in history.

R.G. Collingwood was a pioneer of subjective historicism, arguing a few decades before Carr that historians "reconstruct" history based on a combination of the available record and an imagination of the thought processes of people in the past. Consider what his call to imagination means for neutrality, authenticity and truth in history.

For reflection

Three views on history

Carr did not go as far as Collingwood; his position is somewhere in the middle of a spectrum between the empirical approach espoused by Leopold von Ranke and the idealism of Collingwood. Ranke is famous for the saying that opened this chapter: "simply to show how it was"—arguing for an empirical history based on a set of "true facts". As we have seen, Carr's stance was that this was impossible: historians choose which facts are important and, further, the facts themselves could lead historians to change their views, in a sort of circular dance that he called "an unending dialogue between the past and present".

As a student of TOK, consider these questions.

1. How would you articulate the difference between the three views on history outlined above?

2. What are the differences in their implications for truth and objectivity in historical knowledge?

Carr's view, although midway between extremes, was still controversial and prompted a series of responses. In 1962, the esteemed philosopher and historian of ideas, Isaiah Berlin, reviewed Carr's work and criticized the central issues raised. Berlin argued that objectivity was obtainable if a historian used an appropriate method. But what would such a method look like? Elton offered his method in *The Practice of History* (1967), written largely in response to Carr's ideas. Elton re-emphasized the role of the historian as discoverer of truth, casting a net wide enough to gather empirical evidence and objectively analysing that evidence. This was a defence of the traditional empirical-scientific school of history associated with Ranke. Elton saw objectivity as recuperable, and truth as discoverable, provided the right method was used, which he described as a mirror of the scientific method: "historians must be committed to allowing interpretations of the past to emerge

from the evidence" (Elton quoted in Roberts 1998), like the dutiful scientist who does not allow their hypothesis or theories to influence their observations.

You may be wondering: what is the purpose of the historian, and history, according to Carr, if objectivity is impossible? His position was that the better historians choose the right facts, the important facts, to reach a close approximation to the truth. To do this they need to rise above their own context in history and comprehend what influences them—using a deeply self-aware analysis and judgment.

For discussion

History and truth

Think about the views of Elton and Carr.

1. Can you describe the difference in their views on historical facts?

2. How would they define truth in history?

3. How would they know whether their work had achieved truth in history?

4. To what extent do their views mirror the popular understanding of science?

5. How would Carr describe an ideal practice of history?

Leaving aside the issues of facts and truth, and interpretation and evaluation, what else makes for good history? There are a few generally agreed guidelines worth noting. If a large number of *independent* sources agree on a version of events, students of history should favour that version instead of other versions. On the matter of sources, a balance of primary and secondary sources should be sought, to provide eye-witness accounts as well as more-removed, and possibly less-sensational, big-picture perspectives. How do historians judge the independence of a source and detect vested interests? Students of history may be familiar with the "OPVL" method, which examines the origins, purposes, value and limitations of a source. Clearly, the person making judgments about these criteria is a key factor, and students would do well to remember Carr's advice to study the historian before you study their facts.

Making connections

History as art or science?

These contrasting views of the historian's role and method have had implications for how the discipline of history fits vis-à-vis the sciences and the arts. It may be obvious that the empirical traditionalists would firmly place history among the social sciences, claiming that historians, like social scientists, sought to fill gaps in their knowledge and reach generalizations that broadened their understanding of the subject. Carr and Collingwood agreed. Collingwood's limited definition of science as "any organized body of knowledge" (Collingwood *et al* 1999) was sufficiently vague to allow this—but made a clear differentiation between the natural sciences and history. Collingwood argued that scientists could know "real" things about the physical world in the present, whereas historians had to imagine the thoughts and motivations of actors in the past. Hugh Trevor-Roper, yet another late-20th century Oxford historian, took Collingwood's ideas further and argued that history should be understood as an art precisely because of this need for and reliance on imagination.

Part of the role of the historian is to overcome not just limitations in terms of available sources, but also in terms of their own and others' human fallibility. Hindsight bias affects history in particular; it refers to the tendency for people to perceive events that have already occurred as having been more predictable than they actually

were before the events took place. This has been shown to be true even when the events in question surprised people in real time. Another framing of this bias is that when people learn the outcome of events, they tend to overestimate their ability to have predicted it, or the extent to which it was inevitable. The study of hindsight bias and many other biases was pioneered by psychologists in the 1970s, and a large body of academic literature documents the existence and implications of these biases. Nick Chater, a professor of behavioural science, discusses some of the implications for history and historians.

> Hindsight bias raises a question about how we think about history. Looking back into the past, we often think we can understand how things really were—like what caused the 2008 financial crisis, the collapse of communism, or the first world war—because we know how things turned out. But now we know about hindsight bias we should be suspicious of this 'feeling of understanding'. The idea we can look back on history and understand it should be viewed with scepticism.
>
> (Chater 2015)

Psychologists have found that hindsight bias is due to three factors.

- Memory distortion, when you forget what you thought before an event and cannot look back without it being contaminated by your present opinions. For example, "I remember how bad things seemed when I visited communist Russia".

- People believe in the inevitability of events. For example, "communism was bound to collapse sooner or later".

- Foreseeability—the extent to which you think you can foresee things—is typically overstated. For example, "I always knew communism wouldn't last".

Chater recounts a study in which researchers describe an obscure battle in history, and ask two groups of people who was most likely to win based on the information given. However, the second group already knew who actually won the battle. While people in the first group on average could not tell, and had no idea who would win, those from the second group said it was obvious from the start who would win. "Yet the two groups had exactly the same information, except for this one fact: how it turned out" (Chater 2015).

For reflection

Overcoming the hindsight bias

1. What would be an example of how a historical account is affected by hindsight bias?

2. Refer to your example of hindsight bias.

    (a) To what extent are historians susceptible to this bias?

    (b) How might historians, through the use of the tools and methods in their discipline, control and overcome hindsight bias?

III.3 A very brief history of history

Historiography, as the study of the methods that historians use, is a useful entry point for students seeking to identify knowledge claims and issues within history as an AOK. For example, the historiography of colonialism reveals how historians have studied colonialism, including the different sources, methods, techniques and controversies, and can reveal what influenced historians in their work on colonialism.

This chapter has presented several of the views and contributions to historiography of British men, primarily at the universities of Oxford and Cambridge. It is worth noting the earlier contributions made by writers from other parts of the world, though this very brief history of history cannot do justice to the many diverse and important historical traditions around the world.

Different academic and cultural contexts have pursued different approaches to studying history, many of which have culminated in the practices of history we have today. The earliest histories on record are chronologies from Ancient Egypt and Mesopotamia, but the first narrative records by identifiable authors, written to inform future generations about events, come from China and Greece, emerging around the 5th century BCE. Herodotus is sometimes referred to as the founder of history and is among the first on record to attempt to judge between more and less reliable sources, and also to have produced written accounts of different cultures by travelling widely. His work attributed an important role to the gods in determining events. It was Thucydides, writing a few generations later, who established a more rationalistic approach by removing divine causality from his account of the war between Athens and Sparta, which set a precedent for future historians.

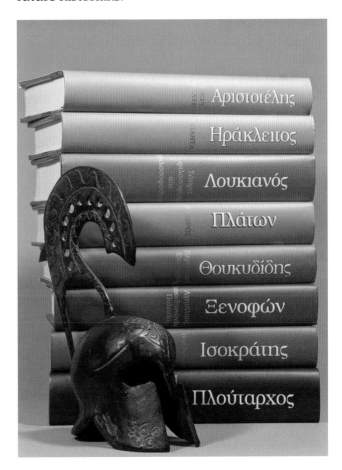

Early Christian and Islamic historiography both gave importance to written as opposed to oral sources, which had been preferred by classical historians in Greece and Rome. This set a precedent that would last millennia. Writing history was an important task among

Christian monks and clergy in the Middle Ages, who often recorded events year by year in chronicles. Early Islamic historical writings from the 7th century, on the other hand, had to contend with numerous conflicting narratives from competing sources about the Prophet Muhammad's life, and the writers developed methodologies such as Ilm al-Rijāl (the science of narration) to distinguish authentic hadiths, using both historic and religious knowledge.

The Arab historian and historiographer Ibn Khaldun, writing in the 14th century, is regarded by some as a pioneer of historiography and the philosophy of history, producing the first detailed studies and critiques of historical methods. His 1377 book, *Muqaddimah*, set out a framework for making observations of systematic bias in history. Like many historical works, the book contains elements that we know to be wrong today, as well as explicit racism, but has been nonetheless identified and praised as a seminal work. Franz Rosenthal, scholar and professor at Yale, has noted that Islamic scholars such as Khaldun "achieved a definite advance beyond previous historical writing in the sociological understanding of history and the systematisation of historiography" (Rosenthal 1952). More recently, Mark Zuckerberg included *Muqaddimah* as recommended reading in his 2015 year of books.

The famous Enlightenment-era philosopher Voltaire had a significant influence on the development of historiography, rejecting for instance supernatural forces and religious intolerance, and focusing less on kings, "great men" and wars. His approach would prove deeply influential to future historical writing. Edward Gibbon, a British historian writing a few years after Voltaire, would add to this style a heavy reliance on primary sources for his six-volume *History of the Decline and Fall of the Roman Empire*, published in 1776, that also influenced modern historians. Later the Annales school of history, perhaps directly inspired by Voltaire, was influential in pivoting the focus of French historical research towards long-term social histories, paying attention to economics, geography and sociology, rather than the traditional (and sensational) emphasis on war, politics and diplomacy practised by 19th and early-20th century historians. Yet this was not a definitive trend; Elton, as shown earlier, placed great emphasis on the role of individual agency in history, avoiding the emphasis on social trends.

Later in the 20th century saw a rise in the popularity of social history, in the tradition of the Annales. Although concerned with the experiences of ordinary people, social historians were less reliant on narrative, and more on social sciences and quantitative tools. This trend reversed to a degree towards the end of the 20th century, when narrative forms made a comeback.

Karl Marx inspired Marxist historiography that emphasized social and economic conditions, particularly class conflict and interactions, as determining historical outcomes. Marxist historiography was strikingly different in de-emphasizing the importance of human agendas and ideas. It was known as historical materialism because of the central role of material conditions in determining history. Marxist historians became known for writing "history from below", also called people's history, that consisted of narratives from the perspective of common people—particularly the poor, the oppressed and the nonconformists or outsiders, rather than leaders.

The more recent changes in the practice and theory of history have been driven by gender historians, post-colonial historians and post-modernists—with the latter questioning whether history can be truthful at all.

Review the overview

Look back through the brief overview of history above.

1. What has been the balance between direct and contextual causes of history?

2. How would you characterize the methods of, and perspectives in, this overview?

III.4 At the frontier of conventional historiography

As the following examples will show, history is not the isolated discipline that you might imagine it to be, written by lonely historians, ploughing through archives and sitting with their facts. Rather, history shares porous boundaries with other disciplines—psychology, economics, sociology, political science and geography—and exciting avenues of interdisciplinary research.

Such methodologies are deeply relevant to TOK because the separation of disciplines, including the broader separation of areas of knowledge, is contestable in the first place.

What remains of the past was explored in III.1. Here, in Box 9.5, we consider how Anne Kelly Knowles used advanced mapping and modelling, based on satellite imagery and military software, to simulate the Battle of Gettysburg and examine what may have caused General Lee and General Longstreet to make the decisions they did. This is an obvious example of how technology has both recast traditional historical questions and provided new tools to answer them. It has also brought new opportunities to bring disciplines together, such as historical geography, a rich and active discipline in its own right. Technology also has an increasing role in interactive transmission of historical knowledge, for example in virtual exhibitions that draw on psychology, cognitive science and history.

Box 9.5: The Battle of Gettysburg in 3D

Anne Kelly Knowles has used augmented historical geography to examine the disastrous Battle of Gettysburg during the American Civil War.

 Search terms: Smithsonian Battle of Gettysburg Robert E Lee

Particularly, Knowles used enhanced mapping aided by software used in the defence and video game industries to simulate what General Lee and General Longstreet would have seen during the battle. Knowles likens this to looking at the past through augmented 3D glasses. It reveals what may have caused the generals to make the decisions that resulted in thousands of casualties, questions that have captured Civil War historians ever since.

When considering General Lee's vantage point from the top of the Lutheran Seminary,

Knowles even factors in the extra inches of sightline afforded by Lee's boots. "We can't account for the haze and smoke of battle in GIS, though in theory you could with gaming software" she says (quoted in Horowitz 2012).

Historians have long debated Lee's decisions at Gettysburg.

> "How could such an exceptional commander, expert in reading terrain, fail to recognize the attack would be a disaster? The traditional explanation, favored in particular by Lee admirers, is that his underling, Gen. James Longstreet, failed to properly execute Lee's orders." (Horowitz 2012)

Knowles' analysis, based on modelling what both men could see, shows that Lee couldn't see what Longstreet was doing or what their enemy (the Union) was doing. Meanwhile, Longstreet saw what Lee could not: Union troops ready on the other side of open terrain that he had been ordered to march across. Instead of exposing his troops, Longstreet chose a much longer but shielded march before launching the assault. The delay allowed the Union officers to better line up their defence—and Knowles' mapping shows they had a much better view of the battlefield.

According to Knowles, this research helps vindicate Longstreet and reveals the difficulties Lee faced in overseeing the battle, but also raises questions rather than providing definitive answers.

> "What was the psychological effect on Lee of seeing all that carnage? He's been cool in command before, but he seems a bit unhinged on the night of the second day of battle, and the next day he orders [the disastrous] Pickett's Charge. Mapping what he could see helps us ask questions that haven't been asked much before." (Horowitz 2012)

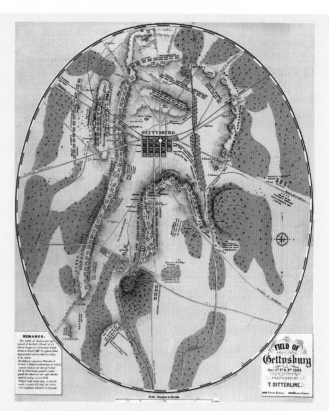

↑ **Figure 9.5** Map of the Battle of Gettysburg published in 1863. The Union Forces are shown in blue and the Confederate States Army in red.

Let's explore the vision of history as a full human science, applying quantitative and modelling techniques that process large sets of data to test hypotheses and yield generalized conclusions. This vision has come under attack repeatedly. The "historicist" idea that the study of the past can be used to shed light on contemporary issues or to predict events in the future has widely been judged illegitimate in historical circles. However, one example is explored below. Cliodynamics is an interdisciplinary program bridging history, sociology and political science with quantitative methods in an attempt to both understand the past and predict the future. As you read on, consider why this approach has not been embraced more enthusiastically by historians.

Case study

Using history to predict the future

 Search terms: Nature Human cycles History as science

Cliodynamics is named after Clio, the ancient Greek muse of history, and is the brainchild of Peter Turchin, who applied mathematical and scientific techniques to identify and model the social forces that, he says, shape history. But Cliodynamics is viewed with great scepticism by most historians, who have resisted the ideas that history operates on patterns, or that these patterns are knowable and can be used to predict the future. Instead, they see history "as a complex stew of chance, individual foibles and one-of-a-kind situations that no broad-brush 'science of history' will ever capture" (Spinney 2012).

Robert Darnton, a cultural historian at Harvard University stated: "After a century of grand theory, from Marxism and social Darwinism

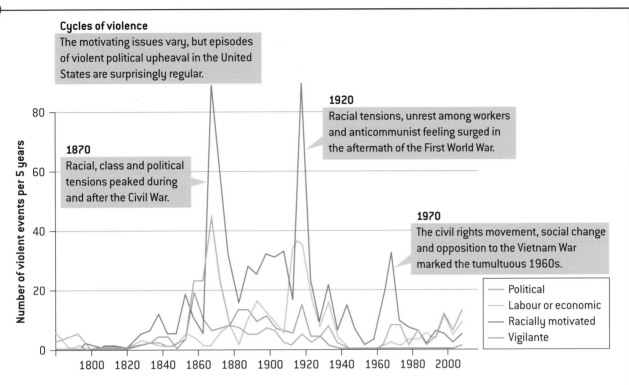

Cycles of violence
The motivating issues vary, but episodes of violent political upheaval in the United States are surprisingly regular.

1870
Racial, class and political tensions peaked during and after the Civil War.

1920
Racial tensions, unrest among workers and anticommunist feeling surged in the aftermath of the First World War.

1970
The civil rights movement, social change and opposition to the Vietnam War marked the tumultuous 1960s.

Legend:
— Political
— Labour or economic
— Racially motivated
— Vigilante

↑ **Figure 9.6** Pattern of violent events in the United States, 1800–2000

to structuralism and postmodernism, most historians have abandoned the belief in general laws" (quoted in Spinney 2012).

Yet, Turchin is determined to show that "history is not 'just one damn thing after another'" (quoted in Spinney 2012). His team states that new tools allow them to revisit the general laws, using simulations of individual interactions and massive databases of historical information. What is new is not their search for patterns—scholars have long correlated political instability with economic and demographic variables—but the scale of analysis, which spans centuries and plots millions of interactions. They focus on four parameters of long-term social trends: population numbers, social structure, state strength and political instability. Each is measured using several indicators. For example, social structure measures health inequality and wealth inequality.

This work complements research being done by other quantitative social scientists, such as Claudio Cioffi-Revilla, whose team uses computer models to understand the effects of climate change and drought in East Africa.

Seasonal migration patterns and ethnic alliances are considered by the team's models, and they hope eventually to predict flows of refugees and potential conflict hotspots. Cliodynamics could strengthen their model by providing patterns extracted from historical data.

Jack Goldstone, Director of the Center for Global Policy at George Mason University and a member of the Political Instability Task Force, funded by the CIA to forecast events outside the United States, also welcomes Cliodynamics but he cautions that it is useful only for looking at broad trends.

> For some aspects of history, a scientific or cliodynamic approach is suitable, natural and fruitful. [For example,] when we map the frequency versus magnitude of an event — deaths in various battles in a war, casualties in natural disasters, years to rebuild a state — we find that there is a consistent pattern of higher frequencies at low magnitudes, and lower frequencies at high magnitudes, that follows a precise mathematical formula.
>
> (Goldstone quoted in Spinney 2012)

It would be naive, though, to attempt to predict unique events based on such analyses.

The main weakness of predictions based on trends is the lack of historical data. Many records are destroyed or preserved by chance. Also, knowledge tends to accumulate around narrow subject areas. Daniel Szechi adds the following.

> We can tell you in great detail what the grain prices were in a few towns in southern England in the Middle Ages. But we can't tell you how most ordinary people lived their lives.
>
> (Szechi quoted in Spinney 2012)

Historians of the future may not have this problem. For now, Cliodynamics has made no major breakthroughs nor been abandoned as an area of study.

Isaiah Berlin made the following comments about pattern discovery in 1969.

> The notion that one can discover large patterns or regularities in the procession of historical events is naturally attractive to those who are impressed by the success of the natural sciences in classifying, correlating, and above all predicting. This they do in the service of an imaginary science; and, like the astrologers and soothsayers whom they have succeeded, cast up their eyes to the clouds, and speak in immense, unsubstantiated images and similes, in deeply misleading metaphors and allegories, and make use of hypnotic formulae with little regard for experience, or rational argument, or tests of proven reliability. Thereby they throw dust in their own eyes as well as in ours, obstruct our vision of the real world, and further confuse an already sufficiently bewildered public about the relations of morality to politics, and about the nature and methods of the natural sciences and historical studies alike.
>
> (Berlin 1969)

For reflection

Looking for patterns

Keep in mind the example of Cliodynamics as well as Isaiah Berlin's comments about pattern discovery.

1. To what extent does Berlin's warning apply today?

   (a) What has changed, and what has stayed the same, since he made the comments quoted above?

   (b) One could say that a lot has changed since 1969, but can we say that enough has changed? What criteria would you use to judge?

Technology and interdisciplinary investigation affect how we access and study traces of the past. How this changes the nature of historical knowledge, or the character of historical inquiry, remains an open question for us in TOK. Another open question, not because it is a new idea but because it touches on fundamental issues in history, is that of counterfactuals.

Counterfactuals are the "might-have-beens of history", a tool employed fondly by some historians (and derided as a "parlour game" by others) to explore the importance of historical incidents and individuals. Proponents of counterfactual history argue that it can clarify our understanding of cause and effect, and reduce the determinism that often creeps into historical narratives, with beneficial implications for historical knowledge. What if the Soviets had succumbed to the Nazis in the Second World War during Operation Barbarossa? The question could, one might argue, clarify the ability of the other Allied powers to win the war eventually.

A common criticism of counterfactual history is that it reinforces the exaggerated influence of kings and battles—of political, military and diplomatic events—the sensationalist histories eschewed by many modern historians. Choosing the "right" counterfactuals, in light of the methodological and ethical knowledge issues discussed in this chapter, could go some way to solving this. However, the practice of counterfactuals is entangled with the question of what is considered a historical event in the first place, which is why it interests us in TOK. The "What if… ?" question is only worth asking about events of causal significance that "made" history.

Counterfactuals give us a clue about what is considered of consequence to history. The kings-and-battles problem is not inherent to counterfactuals, but stems from the issue of thresholds of significance discussed in section II.

Some critics are unconvinced, arguing that counterfactuals are altogether a waste of time. In response to the public counterfactual discourse in the anniversary commemorations of the First World War, Richard Evans, professor of history at the University of Cambridge, said the following in 2014.

> This kind of fantasising is now all the rage, and threatens to overwhelm our perceptions of what really happened in the past, pushing aside our attempts to explain it in favour of a futile and misguided attempt to decide whether the decisions taken in August 1914 were right or wrong.
>
> (Evans 2014)

For discussion

What if … ?

1. Which factors influence the value of counterfactuals as historical knowledge?

2. What does a rigorous counterfactual practice look like?

3. What can we learn from a rigorous counterfactual practice?

4. Are some events too complex for counterfactual analysis?

5. If you concluded "yes" after discussing question 4: might the problem be overcome, and if so how?

IV. ETHICS

This chapter has already explored a number of ethical concerns within history as an AOK. These include the implications of knowledge issues, such as what counts as history, and who gets to read and write it, as well as the fundamental assumptions about the role of the historian and the nature of historical facts. This section examines ethical questions as they relate to knowledge in more detail. As other chapters show, TOK is not so much concerned with discerning right from wrong, as in exploring the knowledge issues involved in claims of right and wrong. Yet, the power that comes with history, and through history, ethically mandates the knower to consider their values and responsibilities in any exercise that deals with this AOK. An example might be to consider, in the frame of intellectual humility, what constitutes knowing enough about a given historical event or period to form or articulate an opinion about the cause and effect of that event or period. What are the implications, for example, of telling other people's stories, especially when problematic power dynamics are involved? The question is not dissimilar to the issue of appropriation we encounter in Chapter 5. Gregory Younging, author of *Elements of Indigenous Style: A Guide for Writing By and About Indigenous Peoples*, asserts that both the style and process with which we write about Indigenous Peoples contain politics that we must be sensitive to.

Within the practice and theory of history as an AOK, how do we know right from wrong? Let's start with a fundamental assumption about history itself: should it "be" something?

IV.1 Should history "be" something?

> How might we address a 'should' question in historiography? How do we decide what we 'ought' to research and communicate? ... Why question the assumptions people make about history making and the nature of history? Questioning assumptions can be, first, an ethical activity: that is, it may help us to better figure out what history should be, who should make it and how it might guide our actions now and in the future. It may even prompt us to wonder ... whether history making is unethical and ought to come to an end.
>
> (Hughes-Warrington 2015)

In recent decades, some historians have argued that history should embrace an ethical agenda to be a restitutive force, to do justice to those whose suffering has long been hidden.

> Restitutive means restoring rights, restoring to a previous state or compensating for loss or injury.

Part of this argument is based on the assertion, already encountered in this chapter, that an objective history is impossible, and so whatever history we "create" should be mobilized towards ethical ends. William Gallois notes that history's silence, or blindness, as he calls it, on this question so far has led it "to commit and perpetuate injustices towards its subjects".

> History ... has chosen to remain blind to the manner in which it constitutes knowledge and deaf to those who criticise the consequences which emanate from historical work and its logic.
>
> (Gallois 2012)

As an example of ethical historiography, Gallois cites Robert Young's *White Mythologies: History Writing and the West*, which criticizes modern historians for failing to comprehend how their work "underpinned western imperialism". Gallois calls upon history to "do justice to the colonised", as subaltern histories have sought to do and Mike Davis does in *Late Victorian Holocausts: El Niño Famines and the Making of the Third World*. Davis takes the task of restitutive history seriously, showing how the political, economic and intellectual power of colonialists came together in the exploitation of "natural disasters", going so far as to label these disasters genocide.

A restitutive history is also supported by Linda Tuhiwai Smith (1999) who notes that most historical accounts failed not only to do justice to subjugated peoples, but were essential (not just complicit) to the imperialist project. According to her, histories of imperialism emphasized a range of explanations, most famously as a system of securing economic expansion to new markets and resources, driven by the "needs" of Europeans. Some historians argued that beyond the economic, political and military ramifications, imperialism was an ideology, inspired by the Age of Enlightenment, which prompted a deep transformation of life in Europe on a cultural, intellectual and technical level. In this telling, "imperialism becomes an integral part of the development of the modern state, of science, of ideas and of the 'modern' human person".

Smith's point is that most histories of imperialism and colonialism do not do justice to the colonized peoples, as her examples above show. Young and Smith are among many who have argued for an ethical history. In recent decades there have been numerous efforts by feminist historians, post-colonial scholars and post-structuralist historians to critique and reimagine their field. For students this presents a relatively new challenge: we have long been taught that neutrality is a virtue, and to be alert to distortions of history. These critiques assert that neutrality is impossible, or simply not good enough.

Neutrality

Consider the issue of neutrality in history.

1. To what extent do historians have to ensure that history is neutral?

2. How could neutrality be achieved?

3. How would you weigh the case for neutrality against the case for an "ethical" and/or restitutive history?

Making connections

Historical art to uplift

Writing in *The Baffler* Adolf Reed describes the 2016 film *Birth of a Nation* as an example in this movement that prioritizes uplifting narratives, to correct for the wrongs of the past, over historical accuracy. Reed quotes Kenneth Warren as speculating that for Nate Parker, the director of the film: "the point of history is not so much to figure out what really happened but rather to enable reparative and redemptive mythmaking … history, for him, must remain narrow—a conduit for inspiration or therapy, for bequeathing legacies, or for purveying information or misinformation to the present—and not much more." (Warren quoted in Reed 2016)

History as activism

William Gallois said that "histories of disability have often conceived of themselves as being narratives of empowerment and modes of combating injustice. For many activist and support groups, the history of fields such as prosthesis, war wounds or thalidomide, is not solely about and for the past, but an engagement in political and ethical battles in our present" (Gallois quoted in Dunn, Faire 2012).

Consider the quotes on this page about the film *Birth of a Nation* and the histories of disability, then, discuss the following questions.

1. Is the primary role of history to be true to the past or to inform the present? Is there a difference?

2. Can serving the present be at odds with staying true to the past?

3. (a) To what extent would you agree that history should serve the needs of the present?

   (b) Who gets to decide what these needs are?

IV.2 Can history know itself?

Central to the position that history should strive to be something, is the assumption that history can know what it is; or, as E.H. Carr might have said, that the historians can rise above themselves. An ethical history presupposes a self-aware history. But consider the case presented below, of Victorian historians who thought they were exemplifying the best practices of neutrality but were, it turned out, unknowingly smuggling in their moral values. How can we know if we are doing any better? This question becomes especially relevant in the ideologically and politically charged environment of the current era, as Gallois explains.

> Empirical historians had long seen a central flaw in their nineteenth-century forebears' method as being their desire to promote certain moral and ideological causes in the course of the production of history. The classic example of this entanglement came in Whig histories of nineteenth-century Britain in which valorisations of parliamentary democracy and modern progress were also understood to be coded references to the moral superiority of the modern West and the place of Britain at the apex of this beneficent civilisation. It was, however, only the retrospective judgement of subsequent generations of historians which saw the Whigs cast in this light, for the Victorians themselves had viewed their practices as exemplifying the traditions of neutrality which emerged with the empirical method. If the Whigs were thus blinded as to the moral values they smuggled into their histories, were later historians any more self-aware, especially given the charged political environments of the twentieth century and the adoption of Marxist, conservative, feminist and other ideological positions and methods?
>
> (Gallois quoted in Dunn, Faire 2012)

IV.3 Judging the past by the standards of the present

History is filled with extraordinary figures who were considered great by the standards of their time, but whose greatness has not aged well. Prompted by the efforts of ethical historians, in the last few decades there have been a number of revised judgements that cast once-great historical figures into a negative light. That list of casualties, or reprehensible people, depending on your politics, includes Winston Churchill, Cecil Rhodes and many others on a long list of mostly white men. By contemporary standards these figures would be judged untenably racist or sexist—that is rarely open to question— but the debate raises some very important knowledge questions. What are the implications of judging people in the past by the present? How do we differentiate between individual and collective responsibility?

↑ **Figure 9.7** Following pressure by the "Rhodes Must Fall" movement, the Cecil Rhodes statue is removed at the University of Cape Town, South Africa, in 2015

Assumptions about the relationship between individuals and their social environment play a role in how we judge people in the past. We use the word "assumptions" because the human sciences are yet to reveal a clear answer to this question. If, for example, we assume that individuals have a significant degree of autonomy and independence, we may judge them more harshly despite the standards of their time. On the other hand, some argue that people are not entirely, or even mostly, free-thinkers, but rather deeply influenced by their social environment? The philosopher Julian Baggini has argued that the truth is somewhere in the middle. We are capable of thinking for ourselves, but we are also shaped by our environment in ways that we might not even consider.

In Baggini's view, two problematic ideas conspire together in historical judgment.

- The locus of moral responsibility is the individual.
- Individuals embedded in an immoral system can rise above that system.

How then should we judge individuals in the past? Is this view not in itself an argument in favour of a hopeless moral relativism? Baggini draws on Edith Hall's defence of Aristotle's misogyny as a way out: judge him not by contemporary standards, but ask whether his thinking would lead to the same prejudice today. This requires the sort of historical imagination encountered earlier in the chapter, for which few, if any, objective truths will guide us.

For discussion and reflection

How do we judge the past?

Read the article by Julian Baggini linked here.

 Search terms: "Why sexist and racist philosophers might still be admirable"

1. To what extent do you agree with Baggini's argument?

2. Does he resolve the moral relativism question?

3. What assumptions does he make about human nature, the past and our ability to know the past?

4. What are the risks and potential benefits of following his argument?

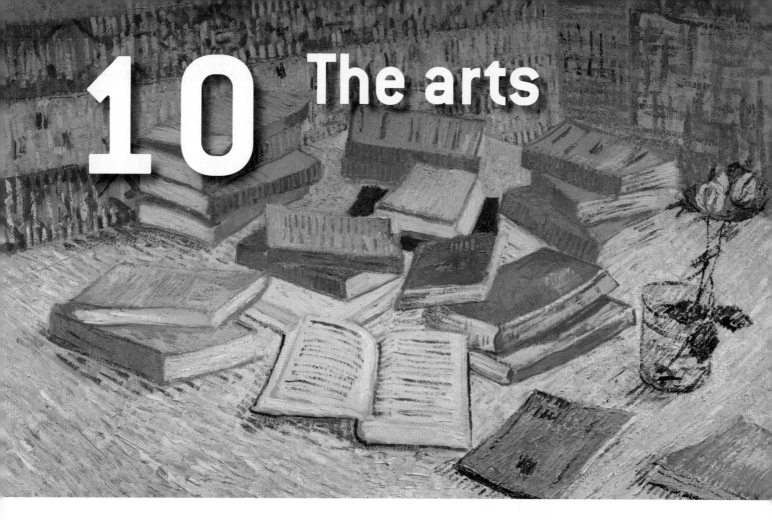

10 The arts

This chapter explores the human encounter with art, including the practices through which we produce it and the experience of being profoundly affected by it. We will examine the idea and workings of the art world, and the various roles of people and communities of knowers within it. At points where the arts intersect with culture, politics, religion, technology, language or science, we ask what gets included and excluded from the domain of art, and why.

In so doing, we critically reflect on who gets to decide what art is and is not, what makes for "good art", what it is worth, and how those decision-makers acquire and keep their power.

I. SCOPE

The history of art reveals that almost every time an art critic, historian or philosopher has come up with a definition of art, an artist or an entire art movement has challenged that definition, sometimes successfully. Let's consider the case of Marcel Duchamp; you may have heard about the urinal that shook the art world. *Fountain* was submitted to the Society of Independent Artists in New York for an exhibition in 1917. All artists paying $6 were told that they could exhibit their work and yet, of over 2000 submitted works,

Fountain was the only one rejected. The rejection provoked Duchamp's resignation from the Society, and a flurry of reactions.

Duchamp had submitted *Fountain* in secret, using the pseudonym "Richard Mutt". Passionately argued positions from both sides of the debate surfaced in response to what became known as "the Richard Mutt Case" and the art movement it belonged to, Dada. "'Fountain' may be a very useful object in its place, but its place is not an art exhibition, and it is by no definition, a work of art" wrote the committee (*New York Herald*, 14 April 1917). Critics of the decision questioned long-standing assumptions about what art is, how it is produced and how the way in which it is presented affects its status and value. *Fountain* posed many important questions, among them: in order to be considered artwork, must an object be produced with artistic intention, or can anything be re-contextualized and re-conceptualized as art?

Whatever we may think today about the artistic merit and value of *Fountain*, the events on the occasion of its centennial in 2017 testify to its profound influence. Given the ripples it sent through the art world, could one reasonably dismiss *Fountain* as a work of art?

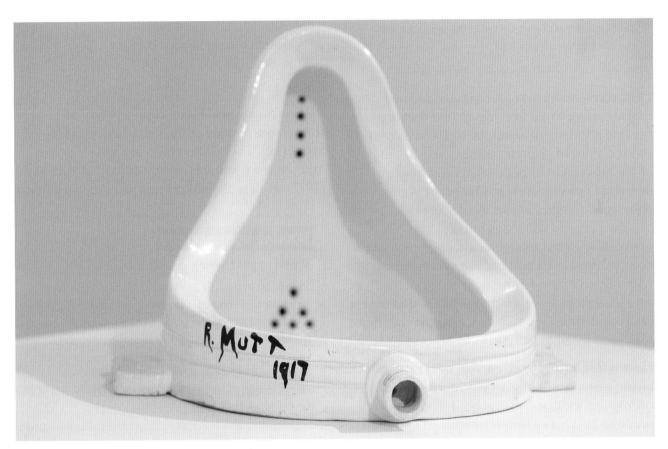

↑ **Figure 10.1** *Fountain* by Marcel Duchamp (1917)

For discussion

How to see "Readymades"

 Search terms: Duchamp Readymades MoMa YouTube

In the linked video, Museum of Modern Art curator Ann Temkin explains how Duchamp's "Readymades" challenged common beliefs: that art has to be beautiful, that being an artist requires skillful technique, or indeed that visual art needs to be seen.

1. Is the popularity of *Fountain* relevant in whether it is afforded artistic status?

2. We can speculate that had Duchamp, a respected artist, submitted the work in his own name it may have been exhibited. What would be the implications of this?

3. Is art unique in being able to evolve and expand over time to include things that were entirely outside or opposed to its definition?

Making connections

Art movements and paradigm shifts in science

Compare the historical development of the natural sciences with the changing boundaries of art over time. What can we say about the differences and similarities between new movements in art and paradigm shifts in science?

Consider to what extent knowledge is discarded, replaced or rendered obsolete in the historical development of the arts. How do these processes compare to the other AOKs?

> The most ground-breaking thing we did was address the public in a way that was non-elitist, equal, really looking into their eyes. There's one point at which I say something like, 'Question now what I'm saying, think about it, disagree if you want to'. That voice—companionable, a little conspiratorial—was the most important thing.
>
> (Berger quoted in Abbott 2012)

 Search terms: Berger Ways of seeing episode 1 YouTube

Once conventions were set aside, it seemed that anything could become art and that art became a statement about itself. The past century produced art of ordinary things, such as dance of the movement of pedestrians and music of everyday noise. It even produced art of the absence of things, such as blank canvases as visual art and silence as music, as in John Cage's *4'33"*. And while the intention may have been to liberate art and make it synonymous with life, so that we may "hear music in the everyday silences", the strange fact is that we can easily and cheaply purchase Cage's track called *4'33"* and listen to *that particular* silence.

How we as an audience engage with art can be out of sync with the art world's multiple, competing, evolving ideas about what art is or ought to be. Our experiences with art and the meanings we derive from it reveal questions and differences in how we engage with artistic knowledge and practices.

In his 1972 series *Ways of Seeing*, the artist and critic John Berger interrogates the elitism of art connoisseurship and the snobberies of high art culture. *Ways of Seeing* is an invitation to democratize our encounter with art, not just as consumers but as active and curious agents examining the production and reproduction of art, its presentation and its power to both shape and reflect the world.

Ways of Seeing also invites our scrutiny of formal evaluations of the value and meaning of artworks. "The relation between what we see and what we know is never settled", Berger says (1972). Follow the link to episode 1 to learn more.

Making connections

Digital ways of seeing

Broadcast in the 1970s, *Ways of Seeing* responded to a historical moment that saw great artworks reproduced as popular and readily available images in various media. Today's digital culture brings about new ways of accessing, producing and engaging with art. We explore whether new ways of seeing may be necessary in the digital age of art and culture, and what we can learn from Berger, in Chapter 4.

Despite the powerful 20th-century democratization of art, there are still institutions and conventions that maintain the boundaries of art in such a way that privileges certain practices, processes and traditions. A few examples of this boundary work are examined below.

I.1 Artists and artisans

Is there a difference between art and craft? It is not unusual for an art show or exhibition to specify "no craft or functional art". Even if you do not agree with this kind of cultural labelling, the blurring of this boundary requires active work, and one cannot simply ignore or wish the distinction away. First, let's consider the reasons behind this distinction and its implications for knowledge.

In this video, Laura Morelli traces the origins of the distinction between art and craft in the Western intellectual tradition.

 Search terms: Morelli art and craft TEDEd

Moreli's big claim is that the distinction between art and craft, more than anything essential or fundamental, is historically contingent. Cultural and art historians will evaluate the specific conditions that led to elevating certain types of creative work (and not others) to the dignity of art. What is of special interest to us in TOK is how defining art to the exclusion of craft, and the power to maintain this distinction, is a way to remove artistic status from, or reward it to,

specific communities. This had the effect, still felt today, of underpresented or absent perspectives from the body of knowledge and practices of art. For example, calling one site of knowledge production a "workshop" and another site a "studio" has implications for the status and value of the knowledge possessed by the people in that space, and the knowledge resulting from their work.

For reflection

Distinguishing between art and craft across cultures

Reflect on the implications of applying a distinction between art and craft cross-culturally. Some cultures maintain this boundary in different places, while others may not draw it at all.

1. Can we understand what is art and what is craft in different cultures?

2. What kind of knowledge is required to apply the distinction between art and craft across cultures?

3. What kind of claims are made about other cultures in the process of drawing this boundary between art and craft?

Box 10.1: Artwork, artisanry and women creatives

How has the status of women artists and traditionally feminine art forms changed over the past century? Peaking in 1910 in Europe, the Arts and Crafts movement was an aesthetic and labour response to the Industrial Revolution, spreading from the United Kingdom to North America, Japan and Australia. It raised the question of the quality of handmade versus mass-produced objects, and the value of traditional artisanry and craftsmanship versus mechanical manufacturing. It concerned objects of high artistic value that were nonetheless functional, and drew attention to ideas of design and aesthetics.

The movement valued the intimacy of work, as opposed to the alienation of people from work under industrialism, and elevated this particular form of creative work to the dignity of fine art.

All of this should have resulted in elevating the status of women creatives, but alas that was not to be. The role of women in the Arts and Crafts movement was ultimately a paradox; on the one hand, it invited women to produce and be paid for artistic handicrafts and homemade goods, but on the other, despite their significant involvement, women remained underrecognized, and the most celebrated and influential figures associated with the movement are men.

Several "her-stories" of the Arts and Crafts movement have been published in the last few decades to rectify the narrative of this particular episode in art history. The Arts and Craft movement had the potential to elevate women's artistic work. But what do we know about the status and prominence of women in art today? In 1971, art historian Linda Nochlin wrote an essay posing the question "Why Have There Been No Great Women Artists?" More than half a century after the Arts and Crafts movement, this was still a valid question. Art historians argue that it was the Feminist Art movement, starting in the 1960s, that really began to elevate the status of women artists, women's artwork, their creative knowledge and the female perspective in the art world.

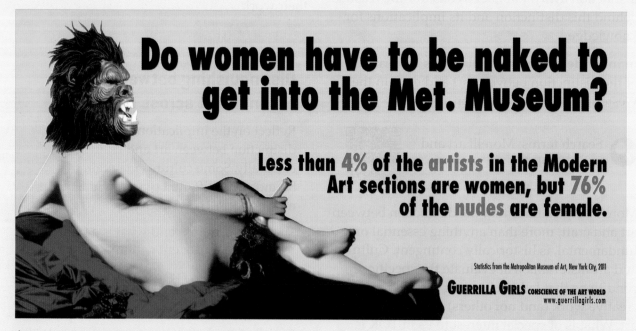

↑ Figure 10.2 The feminist activist art collective, Guerilla Girls, periodically tallies the number of women artists and female nudes on exhibition at the Metropolitan Museum in New York. This poster, *Do women have to be naked to get into the Met. Museum?*, is from 2012.

Feminist artists actively promoted the use of historically feminine materials, skills and artforms, thereby enriching and widening the perspective of the "fine arts". An example is Judy Chicago's significant and controversial 1979 installation *The Dinner Party*. Produced collaboratively over 5 years by over 400 artists, the installation consists of 39 seats at a dinner table, each place celebrating a famous woman from history. In addition, there are names of another 998 noteworthy women from history inscribed in gold on heritage floor tiles. Each table setting is unique, featuring forms of art such as china painting, pottery, embroidery, weaving and so on, and was meant to draw attention to the knowledge of these art forms, and their value as fine or high art, being exhibited in reputable art institutions. The installation has toured six continents and had over 15 million visitors.

But for all its success, and despite being hailed as a triumph for women artists and feminist art, *The Dinner Party* has also received criticism around questions of inclusion and representation of historical women figures. Which forms of art, and which women, were significant enough to be included? What is gained and lost by the presence or erasure of certain perspectives? These questions of representation, inclusion and significance, as well as the central question of what counts as knowledge, are woven throughout this book and will be important to engage with in your own TOK exhibition as part of the internal assessment. The choices you make will have implications. Consider the implications of Chicago's decisions for *The Dinner Party*.

↑ **Figure 10.3** *The Dinner Party* by Judy Chicago

The example above alerts us to the fact that erasing or blurring distinctions does not erase the underlying power relations; the powers have simply decided how far the boundary will shift and maintain it through various institutions and processes.

The TOK course itself is not outside the sphere of influence of the intellectual tradition that drew boundaries between art and craft, creative industries and cultural aesthetic practices. Making the arts a mandatory AOK signals the value and relevance of this body of knowledge and validates the importance of the knowledge community that produces it. However, the membership of potters, weavers, embroiderers and other craftspeople in this community is not uncomplicated or uncontroversial. This book, and the TOK course, does not have a chapter on craft: consider the implications and possible reasons for excluding the combined knowledge of craftspeople from the theory of knowledge.

For reflection

The "borderline" cases of art

Comic books, tattoos and advertisement are among the creative processes and products that have had their artistic status questioned. What factors influence whether these can be considered examples of art? Language also plays a role: for example, some tattoo *artists* go by that title, whereas others prefer to call themselves *tatooists*. To what extent would you maintain a boundary between art and other creative pursuits? How would you define this boundary?

I.2 Truth and knowledge in art: Two perspectives

Box 10.2 features an artwork of disputed status that allows important questions to be asked about the knowledge people gain from art.

Box 10.2: It is what it is, but is it art?

In 2009, Jeremy Deller acquired the rusty remains of a taxicab that had been destroyed in a suicide bomb in Baghdad two years previously. He towed it on a road trip across 14 cities from New York to Los Angeles, exhibiting it in public places, college campuses and eventually art museums. Accompanying him were Iraqi artist Esam Pasha and enlisted US soldier Jonathan Harvey. The art project, called *It Is What It Is: Conversations About Iraq*, aimed to create space for audiences to engage with the two experts. It was Deller's stated intention to present the project "neutrally" and keep the conversation open-ended. His project sparked much social engagement and many conversations, drawing a diverse audience. Yet, this project at the intersection of art and politics had a mixed reception among art critics and activists.

An art critic writing for the New York Times, Ken Johnson, praised the project's "sculptural presence" but chose not to call it art, using the term "artefact" instead. Johnson insisted on the project's educational value, its potential to raise consciousness and possible therapeutic virtues but maintained that calling it art would not be doing it justice, reminding viewers that by naming the project It Is What It Is, Jeremy Deller did not necessarily have such artistic pretentions but rather sought to prompt conversation.

While it was deemed by critics as too obvious to be art, activists argued that it was too vague to provoke any meaningful action. Art activist and curator Nato Thompson's view is as follows.

> "For many involved in the arts, an artwork must remain opaque enough to invite a proper amount of speculation and guesswork … An artwork easily open to interpretation provides a certain freedom from instrumentalization— from an agenda—and allows a viewer to experience speculation and consideration. In activism, though, clarity is celebrated, and a cogent message can reach a wide audience and can serve as a weapon. The two ends of this dynamic … have long proven irreconcilable." (Thompson 2015)

It Is What It Is: Conversations About Iraq invites us to consider what counts as art, the purpose and role of art for social change, and the tension between the clarity of activism and the ambiguity of art. Next we explore art's relationship to truth and accuracy.

For reflection

Art and truth

1. Are there some kinds of truths that:

   (a) we can know, and only know, through art?

   (b) we cannot know through art?

2. In producing artworks, how does an artist maintain "creative license" while honouring their commitment to the truth?

3. Does the pluralism of interpretations in art affect our ability to gain knowledge from it?

Practising skills: Exploring perspectives

A prescribed essay title from May 2011 included the claim: "Art is a lie that brings us nearer to the truth" (Pablo Picasso). Evaluate this claim in relation to a specific art form (for example, visual arts, literature or theatre).

Consider the various perspectives that exist within the arts.

1. What kind of arguments can you make in response to this claim, based on examples of different art forms?

2. How can you explain the diversity of perspectives on this claim within the arts?

3. (a) Based on your exploration of perspectives, what kind of conclusion can you draw in relation to this claim? Is there strong support for the claim, or strong rebuttal?

   (b) If your conclusion to (a) is that it depends on the art form, then what (more specifically) does it depend on?

"Ars Poetica #100: I Believe"

Poetry, I tell my students,
is idiosyncratic. Poetry

is where we are ourselves
(though Sterling Brown said

"Every 'I' is a dramatic 'I'"),
digging in the clam flats

for the shell that snaps,
emptying the proverbial pocketbook.

Poetry is what you find
in the dirt in the corner,

overhear on the bus, God
in the details, the only way

to get from here to there.
Poetry (and now my voice is rising)

is not all love, love, love,
and I'm sorry the dog died.

Poetry (here I hear myself loudest)
is the human voice,

and are we not of interest to each other?

Taken from *American Sublime*
(Alexander 2005)

I. Scope

 Search terms: Elizabeth Alexander Desire to know each other

Interviewed by Krista Tippett on the *Becoming Wise* podcast, Elizabeth Alexander explores the relationship between truth, power, language and knowledge in poetry.

> We crave truth tellers. We crave real truth … People sometimes ask me when they read poems that have an 'I' in them that seems to be autobiographical … Oh, did that really happen to you? Is that from you? What I try to explain is, even if I am drawing on personal experience, the truth of a poem is actually much deeper than whether or not something really happened. What matters is an undergirding truth that I think is the power of poetry. …
>
> I think that the truth of that poem is not about true things or things that happened, but rather in the question, are we not of interest to each other? … Are we human beings who are in community, do we call to each other? Do we heed each other? Do we want to know each other? To reach across what can be a huge void between human beings. I look at my children and I think, as deeply as I know you I do not know what's inside your heads. But I crave knowing them that deeply … And if we don't do that with language that's very, very, very precise—not prissy, but precise—then are we knowing each other truly?
>
> (Alexander quoted in Tippett 2016)

What does Alexander's poetry and reflection tell us about how art enlarges what is possible to think and know? This section opened with art that speaks to the question "what is art?" From Alexander, we have a poem about poetry. To what extent do we learn about art from art? In what ways is this self-referential knowledge— from art, about art—different from art that focuses on phenomena in the world?

For reflection

Description in poetry and science

Consider these words by Ursula Le Guin about the power of poetry and science to speak truths in different languages.

> "Poetry is the human language that can try to say what a tree or a rock or a river *is*, that is, to speak humanly *for it* … . A poem can do so by relating the quality of an individual human relationship to a thing, a rock or river or tree, or simply by describing the thing as truthfully as possible.
>
> Science describes accurately from outside, poetry describes accurately from inside … . We need the languages of both science and poetry to save us from merely stockpiling endless 'information' that fails to inform our ignorance or our responsibility." (Le Guin 2016)

Consider the meanings of accuracy and truth in the arts.

1. What would you say is the relationship between accuracy and truth in descriptions coming from art?

2. How does this differ from the relationship between accuracy and truth in science?

II. PERSPECTIVES

We have seen how conventions in art have been challenged from within, giving way to a pluralism of perspectives. In fact, the disciplines in art—across theatre, dance, visual arts, music and literature, to name a few large categories—are so richly varied that one might ask what unites them. Do disciplines in art diverge more than in other areas of knowledge? We turn now to explore the implications of pluralism in art. What knowledge issues arise from this pluralism of disciplines and the pluralism of tastes and judgments within each of them?

The following case study sheds light on the different knowledge claims about art made by people occupying roles of various contested artistic status. We encounter the issues of authorship and ownership that echo throughout the chapter. The messy business of how and why we value art, beyond the purposes of selling and buying it, is similarly fundamental to this AOK. Remember to consider what these have to do with knowledge. Maintaining a focus on knowledge when speaking about art can be difficult but fascinating. Consider what knowledge is gained from understanding the social, cultural and historical context in which a work is produced, shared or becomes prominent.

Case study

Han van Meegeren: artist, traitor and hero

In 1937, Abraham Bredius, famed art historian and expert on 17th-century master Johannes Vermeer, was approached to authenticate the painting shown in Figure 10.4. He published the following in the *Burlington Magazine*, the foremost art publication at the time.

> "It is a wonderful moment in the life of a lover of art when he finds himself suddenly confronted with a hitherto unknown painting by a great master, untouched, on the original canvas, and without any restoration, just as it left the painter's studio. And what a picture! … we have here—I am inclined to say—*the* masterpiece of Johannes Vermeer of Delft."
> (Bredius 1937)

↑ **Figure 10.4** *The Supper at Emmaus*

Paintings by Vermeer were rare—he produced only around 35 in all—and whenever a new one surfaced there was a frenetic race among interested buyers. Acting quickly, the Museum Boijmans van Beuningen in Rotterdam acquired this newly discovered masterpiece for a record sum. Many more art museums and collectors stayed on the market waiting for a Vermeer, among them self-proclaimed art expert and the second-most powerful man in Nazi Germany, Hermann Göring. Frank Wynne, author of *I Was Vermeer: The Rise and Fall of the Twentieth Century's Greatest Forger*, gives us the rest of this extraordinary story of the most riveting art controversy of the century. The story is also a rich source of knowledge issues and questions, as explored below.

"In May 1945, shortly after the liberation of Holland, two officers arrived at the studio of Han van Meegeren, then just a little-known Dutch painter and art dealer. The officers, from the Allied Art Commission, were responsible for repatriating works of art looted by the Nazis. They had come about a painting discovered among the collection of Hermann Göring: a hitherto unknown canvas by the great Johannes Vermeer … Since the Nazis had kept detailed records, it had been easy to trace the sale of the painting back to van Meegeren. Now, they wanted only the name of the original owner so that they might return his priceless masterpiece. When van Meegeren refused to name the owner, they arrested him and charged him with treason. If found guilty, he faced the death penalty.

The artist was entirely innocent of the charges against him, a fact he could easily have proved. But in doing so, he would have to confess to a series of crimes which he had plotted for decades and which, in five short years had earned him the equivalent of $60 million. Han van Meegeren was a forger.

He loathed modern art—he thought it childish and decadent, a passing fad for ugliness which would soon fade. For years he had eked out a living painting gloomy portraits of rich patrons in a faux-Rembrandt style and had winced as he heard his work ridiculed by his peers. A prominent critic reviewing van Meegeren's second solo exhibition wrote, 'A gifted technician who has made a sort of composite facsimile of the Renaissance school, he has every virtue except originality'." (Wynne 2006)

For reflection

Problems with originality

Wynne interchangeably refers to "originality" in relation to both artwork and artist. Consider the following questions about originality and knowledge in art.

1. What is the difference between originality as a virtue of the artist (one that van Meegeren was said not to possess) and as a quality of the artwork (not a copy or reproduction)?

2. Does originality affect the way we gain knowledge from art?

3. In which ways does the knowledge we gain from engaging with an original work differ from engaging with the work of an original artist?

"The time had come, van Meegeren felt, to revenge himself on his critics. He devised a plan to paint a perfect Vermeer—neither a copy, nor a pastiche, but an original work—and, when it had been authenticated by leading art experts, acquired by a major museum, exhibited and acclaimed, he would announce his hoax to the world.

His first step was concocting an ingenious mixture of pigments that 'would pass the five tests which any genuine 17th-century painting must pass'. Now he had only to paint a masterpiece.

The Supper at Emmaus was unlike any acknowledged Vermeer painting. Van Meegeren, true to his perversely moral scheme, painted it in his own style, adding only subtle allusions to works by the Dutch master, before signing it with the requisite flourish. He had it submitted to Abraham Bredius, the most eminent authority on Dutch baroque art of his day, and the critic took the bait ... .

Suddenly the world was at van Meegeren's feet. *The Supper at Emmaus* was bought by the prestigious Boijmans Gallery in Rotterdam for the equivalent of $6 million. More importantly for van Meegeren, it was advertised as the centrepiece, the crowning glory of the gallery's exhibition, 400 Years of European Art.

During the exhibition, van Meegeren would loudly proclaim the painting a forgery, a crude pastiche, and listen as the finest minds of his generation persuaded him that his painting was a genuine Vermeer. His triumph was now complete. He had only to do what he had promised himself: to stand up and claim the work for himself, thereby making fools of his critics. Instead, within a month, he was working on a new forgery." (Wynne 2006)

For discussion

Objectivity

Let's consider how objectivity complicates this story and the field of art more generally.

1. What does it mean to say that a piece of art is *objectively* good or *objectively* bad?

2. On what basis can objectivity be:
   (a) claimed
   (b) disputed?

3. Are there certain claims in art—about an artwork's origin, meaning, quality, value and so on—that can be objective, and others that cannot?

4. What are the implications of claiming that objectivity is impossible in art?

"In less than six years, van Meegeren would paint a further six 'Vermeers', earning the equivalent of $60 million. With money, came vice ... .

As van Meegeren's addictions to alcohol and morphine took hold, and the standard of his forgeries plummeted, still experts accepted them as genuine. He discovered that, regardless of how incompetent his painting, how crude his anatomy, how uncertain the provenance, the most erudite Vermeer critics were prepared to sanctify his work. His one mistake had been to allow one of his paintings to fall into enemy (Nazi Germany) hands.

No expert eye discovered van Meegeren's forgery. He was unmasked only because, after six weeks in prison, he cracked: 'Fools!' he roared at his jailers. 'You think I sold a priceless Vermeer to Göring? There was no Vermeer—I painted it myself.'

There was one thing van Meegeren had not counted on: no one believed his confession. It was one of the officers who naively suggested that if van Meegeren had painted Göring's Vermeer, he could paint a copy from memory. Van Meegeren arrogantly refused. 'To paint a copy is no proof of artistic talent. In all my career I have never painted a copy! But I shall paint you a new Vermeer. I shall paint you a masterpiece.'

And so, surrounded by reporters and court-appointed witnesses, and supplied with liberal quantities of alcohol and morphine, he worked for six weeks painting one final 'Vermeer', in a desperate attempt to prove himself guilty." (Wynne 2006)

For discussion

Disbelief, proof and evidence

In a pair or small group consider the following questions.

1. On what basis can van Meegeren's claims be doubted?

2. What would count as sufficient evidence of his claims?

3. Can it be proved that he was or was not telling the truth, and how?

"Having been denounced by the press as a traitor, a 'Dutch Nazi artist', van Meegeren was now a folk hero—the man who had swindled Göring. The Reichsmarschall was told that his beloved Vermeer was a forgery while awaiting execution in Nuremberg. According to a contemporary account: '[Göring] looked as if for the first time he had discovered there was evil in the world.'

In the wake of his confession and the scandal it caused, van Meegeren truly knew the fame he had craved. The trial, when it came, was a three-ring circus. Experts tripped over each other to exculpate themselves. Van Meegeren—more than the prosecuting counsel—was determined that he should be found guilty of committing these 'masterpieces', but even now, experts conspired against him, arguing that at least one of his forgeries might be genuine.

In the end, however, van Meegeren got his wish: on November 12, 1947 he was found guilty of obtaining money by deception and sentenced to one year's imprisonment.

But he would never serve a day of his sentence. While prosecution and defence wrangled to secure a full public pardon from the Queen, the forger—long a consummate hypochondriac—finally succumbed to angina. He was hospitalised on the day before he was scheduled to serve his sentence and died some weeks later.

Han van Meegeren's greatest gift to the art world is doubt. If forgers throughout the ages have taught us anything, it is to re-examine why we love what we love, to overcome our obsession with simple authenticity and appreciate the work for itself." (Wynne 2006)

In this video produced by Museum Boijmans, Hans Wessles offers a quick summary of the van Meergen affair, using news clips and footage from van Meegeren's trial.

 Search terms: "Van Meegeren's fake Vermeers" YouTube

↑ **Figure 10.5** A forgery of Dirck van Baburen's *The Procuress* by Han van Meegeren's

The van Meegeren case study illuminates some challenges of expertise in the arts, but nonetheless experts continue to play central roles in authenticating the origin or appraising the value of artworks. We turn now to consider what happens when experts disagree and who should have the last word on questions of art authenticity.

II.1 Expertise and aesthetic judgment

Art authentication can involve disagreements and controversy, and sometimes a good deal of drama, too. Processes by which knowledge communities settle disagreements and arrive at consensus are of interest to us in all AOKs, and in art they shed light on what counts as evidence, how expert opinions are evaluated, how trust and suspicion work, and whether certainty can be achieved.

For example, how would we verify whether a painting, newly surfaced on the art market, is an authentic and formerly unknown work of one of the great masters? Experts in the fields of art history and sometimes forensic science work to answer this question. In 2016, a drawing believed to be an original sketch by Leonardo da Vinci appeared in Paris. Within a few months,

consensus was forming around its authenticity and it was valued at 15 million euros. There are only about 20 original "Leonardos" in the world and so experts at the French Ministry of Culture declared that this rediscovered masterpiece was a national treasure. With that status came an export ban, to give French museums 30 months to raise money to match the asking price so that they could keep the drawing. To dig deeper into this riveting story, follow the link.

 Search terms: Charney Is it really a Leonardo?

The process of authenticating artworks is meticulous, and is influenced by the supposed artist and potential value of the work. Experts consider a range of variables and factors with practised judgment. The technique is analysed to determine whether an artwork is consistent with the time period and the artist's specific style.

Clues are found in the brushstrokes, ink blobs, shadows and any writing on the canvas. Sometimes authenticity is judged by small details. But imagine that an expert, or multiple experts, conclude that the ink on a drawing is pooling in a way that is unmistakably Leonardo. Is this sufficiently convincing, or would an art collector need to hear more to be convinced to spend $15 million? Who can disagree with expert aesthetic judgments? In art, questions of authenticity and value are often the exclusive domain of experts with highly specialized knowledge. It raises the question of whether non-experts are confined to making legitimate claims about matters of taste, and not matters of *fact*.

Art experts may have considerable training and experience, but even the best among them have been fooled by forgers. Partly, this is explained by their fallible human senses of perception; and partly by the high stakes incentives of big money, which pit art experts against expert forgers. Forensic science has been used to resolve disputes among art experts about the authenticity of an artwork. Forensic evidence may suggest the work is more recent than is claimed, through carbon dating or the compounds in the pigments. Forensic science can thus assist art experts, especially in *falsifying* claims to authenticity, as opposed to *verifying* them, as we discuss in Chapter 7. But forensic methods should not be considered foolproof.

In terms of discerning the particular technique, style or intent of an artist, scientific tools are not yet a substitute for the trained, if fallible, and experienced, if subjective, aesthetic judgments of art experts. In the art market, these judgments are the basis for decisions to spend millions of dollars every year.

Practising skills: Constructing arguments and analysing claims

Consider the question: to what extent is certainty possible in the arts?

1. What argument, in relation to art, can you construct to answer this question?

2. What evidence or examples can you offer in support of your argument?

3. Try to incorporate the van Meegeren example from the case study above into your evaluation, either as further support or as a counterexample. How does it fit into your analysis?

It may be tempting to tailor your evidence or present your examples in such a way that more directly supports your argument. Remember, however, that the world of knowledge is messy and complex, with many nuances and caveats, exceptions that prove the rule, examples that break the pattern and things that are not what they seem. It will strengthen your essay if you can invite compelling examples into your analysis, and especially if you can demonstrate nuanced awareness of their real-world complexity.

II.2 Art and access

Throughout this book we consider the judgments, decisions, structures and communities that influence access to knowledge. In the arts, how is access to artistic knowledge facilitated, enabled or obstructed? By looking at access in art, what would you conclude about whom knowledge in art is for?

Consider the *greatest* art piece or performance you have experienced. How was it made accessible to you? Was access easy and open, or afforded to the few? And what does that reveal about your ability to access "great" art? Is there something about knowledge in art that is about power and status? Is there something in it that is about privilege? This is a commonly invoked stereotype, but points towards an important concern about access to art, which has been affected in recent years by rising economic inequality.

For reflection and discussion

Superyacht art collections

 Search terms: Guardian
Mind my Picasso
superyacht art

Depending on what you know about billionaires and exclusive art collections, you might be surprised to learn that many famous works of fine art are housed on superyachts, the floating mansions of the extremely rich. Some of these artworks have made the news for surprising reasons, such as a Jean-Michel Basquiat painting that was damaged by breakfast cereal after an unnamed billionaire's children threw cornflakes at it "because they thought it was scary" (Mather-Lees quoted in Neate 2019). While we do not know exactly which painting it was, a Basquiat painting of a crazed skull-shaped face sold at auction for $110.5 million in 2017. The yachts' crew made the damage worse when they tried to wipe off the cornflakes.

According to Pandora Mather-Lees, an art historian and conservator, some of these superyachts have "better collections than some national museums", and the owners "want to show off their art collection when guests come on board" (Mather-Lees quoted in Neate 2019). However, yachts may be less secure than museums and, even if they are not, private collectors are free to do what they please with works of art. A painting by the modern artist Takashi Murakami, for example, was reportedly cut into three pieces on the request of its owner to make it fit next to the jet skis at the back of the yacht.

Sheikh Mansour bin Zayed al-Nahyan, owner of the UK's Manchester City Football Club (as of 2020) and Deputy Prime Minister of the United Arab Emirates, is known to have several hundred works of art on his $440 million superyacht Topaz.

1. To what extent should access to the cultural and artistic heritage of humanity be guaranteed for everyone?

2. What is lost when great artworks that are privately owned get damaged?

3. Who should be accountable for the loss, and to whom?

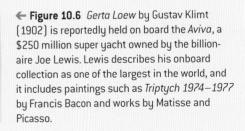

← **Figure 10.6** *Gerta Loew* by Gustav Klimt (1902) is reportedly held on board the *Aviva*, a $250 million super yacht owned by the billionaire Joe Lewis. Lewis describes his onboard collection as one of the largest in the world, and it includes paintings such as *Triptych 1974–1977* by Francis Bacon and works by Matisse and Picasso.

Ownership of art is a complex topic, and owners can perform a variety of roles including steward, protector, benefactor and investor of significant artworks. Part of that complexity is the issue of access to ownership, as it can be too expensive for people earning an average income to afford to own the kinds of prized artworks that trade at auction. Perhaps financial and technological innovations could partly solve this problem.

For reflection and discussion

Bitcoin art

 Search terms: CNN Business Innovate: Singapore Owing a Warhol

A Singapore-based start-up is using blockchain technology to enable individuals to buy "shares" in an artwork. This could allow artists to maintain partial ownership of their work, and enable smaller investors who would be unable to afford an entire work. The shares can be bought and sold by investors more easily, which may allow the market to realize the true value of a work more efficiently. Fractional ownership enables people to own parts of an artwork just like parts of corporations. While this opens up access to art ownership, it does not directly improve access to art in general. In fact, it may even reduce access to art, if the multiple owners cannot agree to display it publicly they may decide to store it in a secure, restricted area away from the public.

1. For the purpose of knowledge, what kind of access to art is more important—as an audience or as owners?

2. To whom should the benefits of the value of an artwork accrue?

3. Apart from using blockchains, how can artists retain partial ownership of their work?

↑ **Figure 10.7** *Portrait of an Artist (Pool with Two Figures)* by David Hockney broke records in 2018 when it sold for $90 million. None of the money from that sale went to Hockney, as he had sold the original in 1972 for $18,000.

We can access art in various ways, as an audience, as students, as owners and so on. A related concern is access to platforms for artists. Which art forms are considered art, and specifically good art, valued enough to be exhibited? Clues to the answer are found at the complicated intersection between the art world and the art market. Below, we consider the role of art institutions in deciding art status and art value, in the context of our present cultural moment, described by some as late stage capitalism.

Box 10.3: The artworld and the art market

How do you respond to the phenomenon of artwork that sells for millions of dollars? What criteria would you use to define the monetary value, and price tag, of art?

Arthur Danto, the philosopher and art critic, challenged aesthetics and art price valuations in his influential 1964 essay "The Artworld", which suggested an answer to the eternal question of "what is art". Andy Warhol had just created an exhibition of *Brillo Boxes*, which were replicas of ordinary supermarket cartons of soap, stacked high as if in a warehouse. Interested readers can look up Warhol's intentions and explanations of his exhibition. Here we are concerned with Danto's interrogation of this phenomena, of ordinary objects that could be conceived of as art. He concluded that "what in the end makes the difference between a Brillo box and a work of art consisting of a Brillo box is a certain theory of art" (Danto 1964). More specifically, Danto argued that art is what select artists, and art institutions, define as art. The philosopher George Dickie expanded upon this idea by defining supplementary artworld roles such as critic, teacher, director and curator, among others. But, as Dr Sarah Hegenbart argues, Dickie and Danto failed to account for the massive influence that the art market, and wealth, was asserting on the art world. Increasingly, key artworks are being seen as investments, raising eye-watering prices in specialist sales and sitting in the homes and bank vaults of the super-rich. This view of "art as investment" has the potential to redefine what art is and what it is for.

How do we decide on the "value" of an artwork when art institutions and experts value it differently from the market? What would it mean to label those art institutions that are trying to resist higher valuations as "conservative"? What would it mean to describe the art market as "commodified"?

In economic theory, the free market, in the absence of state intervention and market failures, arrives at the "right" price for a given good. If the art market appears to be failing in

that function, why might this be, and what alternatives for valuing art exist? Some observers have cautioned, for example, that expensive art is used to transfer money out of countries without paying tax, a practice known as money laundering. This is greatly facilitated by the anonymity of art work transactions and the inherent difficulties of valuing art as opposed to, for example, a house. Follow the link for one analysis by the *New York Times*.

 Search terms: Has art market unwitting partner in crime NYTimes

Hegenbart (2019) suggests that curators, being more removed from the "capitalist spectacle" of high art (as opposed to artists, dealers and art institutions), function as more neutral or objective gatekeepers, ensuring that works are displayed for artistic, rather than monetary, value. By virtue of their position as curators they may also be better placed to influence, rather than merely reflect, the financial and artistic values of their time.

For reflection

The art world as a knowledge community

1. What are some of the tensions between different members in the art world (audiences, artists, art critics, curators, art historians, art teachers and students, art dealers, gallery owners, art magazines,

digital art communities and so on) with regards to access to art?

2. Whose perspective has weight and should matter on the value of art? How would you decide?

3. What are the different responsibilities of different members of the art world with respect to knowledge?

II.3 Art as unspoken and unspeakable truths

Is art uniquely well placed to express the unspoken and unspeakable? Can it be thought of as a language that does what other languages cannot?

We have an abundance of artworks produced in the context of a problematic past. The painter and sculptor Titus Kaphar works at the intersection of art and history, reclaiming artworks into new narratives. In the linked TED talk, Kaphar paints over a replica of a 17th-century painting that invokes the racial dynamics of the time, to draw attention to elements that it intentionally downplays. Kaphar's art is an amendment to history; he does not erase or replace problematic historical narratives and representations, but invites us to look at them anew, paying attention to the margins, the overlooked characters, as a way of coming to terms with the unspoken truths of a past of slavery and racism.

 Search terms: Can art amend history? Kaphar TED

Think about how this reframing and shifting of attention in art could be done in your context. How should art speak to history, and what should it say? Below, we consider how art today is helping to lift the shadows cast by colonialism over centuries of African history, including art history.

The 2019 exhibition Caravans of Gold, Fragments in Time: Art, Culture and Exchange Across

Medieval Saharan Africa sought to reinstate West Africa's global legacy. West Africa was not "discovered" by colonists, as is frequently heard, but rather was a thriving, globally significant commercial centre in the medieval period, between the 8th and 16th centuries, connected through trade networks with other regions as far as China and the Alps.

This is a very different legacy from the one presented in most art and history museums even today. The arts of Africa are usually "positioned as having been discovered ... and folded into major Western art movements for the first time in the late 19th and early 20th centuries" (Sandy 2019). But the Caravans of Gold exhibition uses art history to shed light on "the story of the thriving African cities and empires that were foundational to the global medieval world" (Berzock quoted in Sandy 2019). Fragments of these ancient art works include Chinese porcelain found in Mali and a lost-wax cast made of Alpine copper found in Nigeria.

↑ **Figure 10.8a** Virgin and child, France, circa 1275–1300, made of African ivory

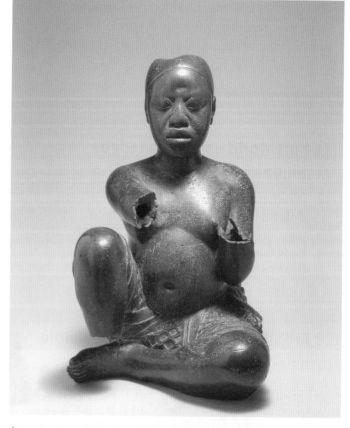

↑ **Figure 10.8b** Tada seated figure, Nigeria, late 13th–14th century, made of copper

In addition to its progressive role of illuminating unspoken truths about the past or present, art has also played subversive or transgressive roles, expressing the unspeakable loudly or hiding it in plain sight. From the French Decadent poets of the late 19th century, who rallied behind art to *"épater la bourgeoisie"*, that is, "shock the upper/middle classes", to the 1990s obscenity charges against hip-hop artists that reached the US Supreme Court, subversive art has a long history with no shortage of controversies. These transgressions have been met with appeals to freedom of expression and freedom of speech, as well as calls for censorship, often simultaneously from opposing sides of the political spectrum.

We encounter tricky intersections when subversive art touches religious belief or widely accepted societal norms. It can be seen as liberatory or dangerously disruptive, depending on one's perspective. Would you agree that we tend to celebrate subversive art in oppressive times, but condemn transgressive art in presumably progressive times? This is complicated by what may be a tendency to view the past, or geographically distant contexts— the elsewheres and elsewhens—as oppressive; whereas our present—our here and now, no matter where we are—is more frequently perceived as progressive.

For discussion

Labels in art

Before reading what the curators said about their collections, consider how a collective label such as "feminist art" may be similar to or different from "Renaissance art" or "Indigenous art".

1. Did the artists think of themselves as producing work in a particular genre, for a particular purpose or a specific audience?

2. If you think the answer to question 1 is "no", when do labels applied after a work is created meaningfully bring artists and artworks together

II.4 Patrimony, repatriation and redistribution of art

All sorts of strange things happen when the artworks and artefacts of another culture are "taken and protected", which could be a modern euphemism for "stolen and exhibited". It is complex enough when this is done in the name of cultural and aesthetic exchange involving an open dialogue, but many cases involve artworks or artefacts that have been stolen, misappropriated, misunderstood and misrepresented.

> Museums are home to millions of artworks and cultural artifacts. The Metropolitan Museum of Art alone holds two million objects. The Hermitage has three million. The British Museum eight million. Some of these objects have made their way to these institutions through unjust means. Some were stolen or plundered, others acquired through coerced or exploitative transactions. Should these injustices be rectified, and if so, how?
>
> (Matthes 2017)

> All of these things that belong to our people in Australia—they don't tell a story about the Queen of England, do they? No way. … They tell stories about the people that made them and used them—that's our people here in Australia. We don't have the Queen's crown jewels. And we don't want them. But what we do want is to get our things back from the British Museum. We want them back.
>
> (Murray quoted in Daly 2015)

Over the last few hundred years artwork from around the world, created by a multitude of cultures and peoples, has slowly been concentrated in a small number of primarily Western galleries, museums and private collections. The processes through which this has happened have been documented by cultural and art historians, and derive from major forces of the modern age such as colonialism and globalization.

The ethical issues relating to the appropriation, ownership and stewardship of artwork, as they relate to TOK, are discussed in section IV. Here we examine the implications of this concentration of artistic knowledge in the broader context of material cultural artefacts having been globally displaced. As knowledge is embedded in material culture and practice, our ability to stitch together coherent narratives in the arts (and in other AOKs) is improved by an understanding of the ownership, provenance and context of artwork, and much can be learned from placing and studying art in its historical and cultural context. The idea of ownership, transplanted onto art knowledge, feels like reducing cultural heritage to copyright. Yet, it deeply matters where art is from: let's consider the case of the Benin Bronzes.

Box 10.4: The Benin Bronzes

In 1897 the British Imperial Navy launched a punitive expedition against the Kingdom of Benin, completely destroying Benin City and looting the artwork of the Royal Palace. Among the loot were hundreds, and perhaps over a thousand, intricate bronze, brass and ivory sculptures that over the ensuing decades would become known as the Benin Bronzes. They were held in collections across Europe, raising the profile of African art. The resulting exposure of the Benin Bronzes tells us an interesting story, in the words of Professor Emmanuel Konde.

"Initially, the looted Benin art treasures were treated with some kind of curiosity. However, as the wonderful quality of the ivory carvings and bronzes became appreciated and this was reflected in ever-increasing prices they fetched in the art auction rooms of the world, the Foreign Office sold considerable quantities to defray the costs of the expedition.... The presence of Benin Bronzes in Europe and the United States exposed the high quality of workmanship expended on them. Familiarity with these works would eventually revolutionize western views of African art, and transform the designation of these from 'primitive' to just simply 'art'." (Konde 2014)

However, it was not as simple as that. For at the time, following several hundred years of slavery, "the African people as well as their art were held in abject contempt by the Europeans who stole them" (Konde 2014). Ernst Grosse confidently asserted in 1894, for example, that "[t]he sentiments of [African] primitive art are narrower and cruder, its material poorer, its forms simpler" (Grosse quoted in Bodrogi 1968). About prevailing attitudes and judgments towards African art, Carl Einstein observed the following.

"There is hardly any art that is approached by Europeans with so much distrust as that of Africa. They are disinclined to recognize it as art and regard the contrast between its products and the accustomed continental concepts with a contempt and scorn that have actually created a special terminology of rebuttal." (Einstein quoted in Bodrogi 1969)

It is quite easy to imagine the cognitive dissonance of European admirers of the Benin Bronzes. Konde offers two anecdotes as to how this dissonance was overcome. Initially the British soldiers, upon looting the bronzes and realizing their merit, "concocted the tale that the sculptures they had stolen must have been made by the Portuguese, the Egyptians, or the lost tribes of Israel" (Konde 2014). The changes brought on by the First World War, however, transformed (or coincided with)

a reassessment of African art. By 1926, the ethnologist Ernst Vatter would write: "… primitive art as well as the hitherto similarly neglected prehistoric and medieval European art constitute nowadays an integral part of art as a whole" (Vatter 1926). Note his use of the term "prehistoric", which, as outlined in Chapter 9, carries some problematic assumptions.

It only took 30 years for the Benin Bronzes to have a significant effect on the understanding of art in the European paradigm. Today the largest collection of Benin Bronzes is in London, with the vast majority held between England and Germany. Between 1951 and 1972, the British Museum sold over 30 "redundant" bronzes "back" to Nigeria, because they were duplicate specimens. In late 2018, the British Museum agreed to loan a selection of the bronzes temporarily to Nigeria.

II.4.1 Why has repatriation not happened?

There are hundreds of thousands of works of art such as the Benin Bronzes still held in colonial-era collections around the world, and their repatriation back to their "homeland" is an issue that has gathered momentum over the past five decades, with the independence of many formerly colonized nations. Apart from a few instances, particularly from museums based in the United States, this has not yet happened on any meaningful scale. One reason appears entirely practical—up to 85–90% of "classical and certain other types of artifacts on the market do not have a documented provenance" (Franzen 2013)—but museums and trustees may have a conflict of interest to investigate the provenance of works already in their collection. Even if the provenance can be traced, it may not be traceable to a contemporary national or cultural group.

Tess Davis, a lawyer with the Antiquities Coalition, praised the Cleveland Museum of Art for voluntarily returning the Hanuman statue, but argued that it should never have been allowed to enter the collection in the first place.

> The Hanuman first surfaced on the market while Cambodia was in the midst of a war and facing genocide. How could anyone not know this was stolen property? The only answer is that no one wanted to know.
>
> (Davis quoted in Tharoor 2015)

Collectors have historically claimed that a work belongs to them because they "found" it, "saved" it or were the first to recognize its value. Indeed, some objects acquire artistic status in the process of being collected and exhibited, while in other cases, functional objects (such as a table) can become culturally displaced works of art in a museum halfway around the world. The fact remains that objects, artworks and artefacts that have been stolen, acquired, or found and later exhibited are identified as being of value, even if they originally did not have artistic status "back home". Once this value is identified, if a claim to a work is made, why is it not honoured?

The United Nations convention of 1970 provides a framework for the legal export or repatriation of art and archeological materials discovered after that date, but for anything acquired before that, no meaningful multilateral cooperation exists. Museums and collectors have avoided repatriation by appeals to the idea of stewardship: even if the provenance of an artwork can be clearly traced to a contemporary people, nation or culture, they claim to be the best custodians of the work, whether that is due to their technological apparatus (for example, temperature and humidity controlled preservation systems), security, or social and political stability. What do you think about these claims?

> The ongoing destruction of ancient sites in the Middle East by the Islamic State has galvanised the case for the universal museum, with advocates such as Gary Vikan, the former Director of the Walters Art Museum in Baltimore, arguing that only institutions in the West can preserve the world's cultural heritage.
>
> (Tharoor 2015)

With growing and widespread recognition of the political, cultural and economic value of art, claimants to the ownership of an artwork, especially iconic art, have been very willing to make the required investments in protecting the work. Even where they cannot intervene, or choose not to, do other peoples, nations or organizations have a right to intervene?

Perhaps the most ideological argument against repatriation hinges on the idea of a universal collection, belonging to all of humankind, "that only by juxtaposition in global centres can we truly make sense of global art and the experience of being human" (Joy 2019). The argument is that even if colonial-era collections are an accident of history, they are still the best place, now, for us to understand and appreciate art in a pluralistic, cosmopolitan sense.

> Works of art have not adhered to modern political borders. They have always sought connection elsewhere to strange and wonderful things.
>
> (Tharoor 2015)

The sentiment is upheld by the headline "Museums have no borders, they have a network" on the website of the International Council of Museums, that seems to ignore issues of national and sovereign embeddedness. At any given time, the large museums display only a fraction of their collection, with the rest put in storage. As Charlotte Joy, lecturer of anthropology at Goldsmiths, University of London, puts it, "to date, the logic of the museum is not one of access and display but of acquisition and retention" (Joy 2019). It is possible to imagine an alternative: replicas could be sent to these global centres and the originals repatriated.

> The idea of the 'universal museum', for all its Enlightenment virtues and educational potential, is at its core a Western imperial project, and museums that acquired sacred objects in earlier times absolutely must rethink their display, their function and their narrative.
>
> (Farago 2015)

Box 10.5: What is cultural property? Who belongs to a culture?

Claims for repatriation can be difficult to reconcile if the ownership of the artwork or artefact in question is not traceable to a present-day owner. Is it possible for a work to belong to a culture? What would that mean in legal terms? Claims of cultural ownership have been used as the basis of nationalistic claims to artwork and artefacts.

However, "cultural property" refers to materials that, rather than belonging to a family, territory or state, belong instead to a cultural collectivity. This could be dispersed Indigenous Peoples for instance. As Janna Thompson puts it, cultural property can be understood as property that "plays an important role in the religious, cultural or political life of people of the collectivity" (Thompson 2003).

When an item of cultural property is very closely linked to the identity of an existing collectivity, it may be referred to as "cultural patrimony". According to James Cuno, this "is not something owned by a people, but something of them, a part of their defining collective identity" (Cuno 2001). The more important the item, the more likely it is to pass beyond the category of property.

However, who counts as a member of a cultural group? It might be pointless to argue about a culture owning property if the members of that culture cannot be identified. But this should not be used as an easy excuse to dismiss claims to patrimony. Kwame Anthony Appiah points out the following.

"When Nigerians claim a Nok sculpture as part of their patrimony, they are claiming for a nation whose boundaries are less than a century old, the works of a civilization more than two millennia ago, created by a people that no longer exists, and whose descendants we know nothing about." (Appiah 2006)

The corollary of this problem is how we can know, for instance, that an artwork or artefact was taken (or given) unjustly in the first place: who is allowed to give something on behalf of a cultural group? Is it their kings, leaders or elders? Is consensus required?

Legal systems of property rights may be challenged by these concepts, but progress is required, especially given the many cases where cultural continuity to a contemporary group—the "moral descendents"—is traceable.

II.4.2 Appropriation

Ownership, as an issue, is much more tangible than the issue of appropriation, which can have implications for the authenticity of a work, and the rewards accruing to it. In its technically legitimate form, appropriation is recognized as a means of artistically recontextualizing something borrowed to create a new work. There are at least two categories of dubious appropriation: the most obvious is the appropriation of economic or material value, as many such artworks can be invaluable. The Koh-i-Noor, for example, one of the largest diamonds in the world, was taken from Punjab in 1849 and subsequently worn by Queen Victoria in a brooch. It is currently part of the British Crown Jewels. Less obvious is the appropriation of cultural, artistic and/or historical narratives.

First, we have the appropriation of narratives, as told without the participation of contemporary groups to whom an artwork's provenance and/or significance can be traced. Over the last century, Indigenous Peoples' art has been interpreted, studied, exhibited

and appropriated innumerable times without their participation. Painfully, cultural work by Indigenous People was often "treated as natural history, to be filed away with rocks and bird carcasses, rather than treated as a vital culture in its own right" (Farago 2015). This is simultaneously an ethical as well as knowledge issue: to what extent can we understand the artworks, and more broadly the material and immaterial culture, without the active participation of the subject group? In light of what we have encountered in this chapter so far, would you say that this art can speak for itself, or be spoken for by outsiders?

> In Paris, for example, pre-Columbian sculptures have migrated over and over: from the Louvre and the Musée Guimet in the early-to-mid-19th Century, where they were exhibited as antiquities; to the ethnographic Trocadéro in the late 19th Century, where aesthetics were irrelevant; and now to the Musée du Quai Branly, which proudly calls itself an art museum.
>
> (Farago 2015)

There have been examples of progress: in the United States, the Association of Art Museum Directors, the main authority for US museums, instructs its members to work with Indigenous groups on display and interpretation. The Australian Museum in Sydney has been acknowledged for collaborating "with indigenous communities to improve its interpretive displays" (Farago 2015).

Art and cultural artefacts are said to contain encoded knowledge, from the context and culture of their creation. Sometimes the work is artistically inseparable from that context—consider, for example, props and artwork used in ritualistic performance, such as masks and costumes used in ceremonial dance. To what extent can these masks be comprehended by a foreign audience, without the context of the dance? How much context is enough for the transfer or sharing of knowledge to an artwork?

Some art forms are more prone to this predicament than others; film, for example, is perceived to be more readily transferable than religious iconography or fine art. It is the sharing or transfer of art across social, cultural or linguistic borders that generally causes this problem. Even in recent decades, attempts to understand or appreciate artwork out of its cultural context, for example art that has been geographically or temporally displaced, has carried the risk of trivializing, exoticizing or further othering the object and the subject culture to which it belongs.

Box 10.6: "You have our soul": Easter Island pleads with British for statue's return

Hoa Hakananai'a ("lost or stolen friend") is an eight-foot basalt statue that was taken from Easter Island in 1868, and has been kept at the British Museum ever since. In November 2018, the governor of Easter Island urged the museum to return it, saying its keepers have the "soul" of the Easter Island people.

Search terms: You have our soul Easter Island

Tarita Alarcón Rapu, Governor of Easter Island, recently asked the British Museum to lend the statue back to Easter Island temporarily.

> "And it is the right time to maybe send us back (the statue) for a while, so our sons can see it as I can see it. You have kept him for 150 years, just give us some months." (Rapu quoted in Holland 2018)

The British Museum released a statement to CNN that described a "warm, friendly and open conversation" with the Easter Island delegation, adding the following.

> "It was very helpful to gain a better understanding of Hoa Hakananani'a's significance for the people of Rapa Nui today … . The museum is keen to work collaboratively with partners and communities across the globe and welcomes discussions around future joint projects with Rapa Nui … . We believe that there is great value in presenting objects from across the world, alongside the stories of other cultures at the British Museum. The museum is one of the world's leading

lenders and the trustees will always consider loan requests subject to usual conditions." (Holland 2018)

Regarding the claim made by Tarita Rapu, that the statue is a part of her people's soul, consider the following questions.

1. **(a)** To what extent are you able to comprehend this claim?

   (b) What factors affect your ability to do so?

2. What do you make of the British Museum's response, that there is "great value in presenting objects from across the world alongside … other cultures at the British Museum?"

3. **(a)** Given your answers to questions 1 and 2, what would you suggest is the best place for the statue, in terms of knowledge and in terms of ethics?

   (b) What additional information would you need to more effectively answer this question?

II.4.3 The role of museums: Does all culture belong to all humankind?

Museums especially have long embraced the idea that "cultural products are contributions to the culture of all humankind" (Matthes 2017). The Hague Convention of 1954 includes the following declaration.

> "Damage to cultural property belonging to any people whatsoever means damage to the cultural heritage of all mankind, since each people makes its contribution to the culture of the world."
>
> (UNESCO 1954)

The 1982 UNESCO Convention argues similarly for artefacts from World Heritage sites.

> "Their value cannot be confined to one nation or to one people, but is there to be shared by every man, woman and child of the globe."
>
> (UNESCO 1982)

In addition, a 2016 declaration by the United Nations Human Rights Council suggests that access to universal human heritage is a human right.

> "Convinced that damage to cultural heritage, both tangible and intangible, of any people constitutes damage to the cultural heritage of humanity as a whole; Noting that the destruction of or damage to cultural heritage may have a detrimental and irreversible impact on the enjoyment of cultural rights, in particular the right of everyone to take part in cultural life, including the ability to access and enjoy cultural heritage."
>
> (UNHRC 2016)

These ideas have been used to argue in favour of foreign intervention to "protect" culture, and to support universal collections, against repatriation of cultural property.

There may be an inherent tension between individual and collective interests when it comes to cultural property, such as art. Janna Thompson wrote the following.

> If we think of art as being of value for individual development and to humankind as a whole, then distributional issues cannot be avoided.
>
> (Thompson 2004)

Who would be best placed to navigate this tension: museums or national governments? If we accept that museums might be custodians for public goods that belong to all of humanity, what can we say about the fact that most of them are in Western nations?

In the "Declaration of the Importance and Value of Universal Museums", the directors of leading museums including the Metropolitan Museum of Art, the Getty Museum, the Hermitage Museum and the British Museum write that "museums serve not just the citizens of one nation but the people of every nation" (quoted in Matthes 2017). Matthes writes that Western museums "have a long history of cultural marginalization" (Matthes 2017). For instance, he states that non-Western artworks have long been excluded to:

> anthropology museums as opposed to art museums, their designation as 'primitive' within the artworld context, and, despite these aspersions on their artistic status, the colonialist acquisition of many such objects.
>
> (Matthes 2017)

The mission and values of many leading museums—to serve for the collective good of humankind—seems at odds with their concentration in just one part of the world. A key consideration in the redistribution and repatriation of artistic works, argues Matthes, is how it can facilitate the recognition for marginalized groups.

Private collections also house vast quantities of knowledge away from public access. To what extent should governments intervene in private collections, and what would be some implications of this?

III. METHODS AND TOOLS

In this section we explore the methods of becoming and being an artist, and how knowledge is acquired and produced in the process. We also look at the role of tools and materials.

III.1 Method and art education

"Every child is an artist. The problem is how to remain an artist once we grow up." So goes the quote, often attributed to Pablo Picasso, but iterated on by many others to suggest that we all have an innate artistic ability, and that education is at best irrelevant to it.

And yet, going to art school and formally participating in the knowledge community of artists remains something of a stepping stone in the trajectory of many if not most artists. What is the purpose of an art education and the knowledge that is passed on and acquired through it?

Granted, an education in art looks different in the various disciplines—from theatre and literature, to film, dance and so on. And yet, these diverse art forms, studied in the context of modern university programmes, may perhaps be more similar than we recognize. What can we learn about how knowledge is transferred by looking at how art education has changed over time and the different forms it takes across cultures?

To explore this question we turn to Hindustani classical music from the northern regions of the Indian subcontinent. For close to 10 centuries, music knowledge was traditionally transferred in the context of the *guru–shishya parampara* system, where a student or disciple (*shishya*), acquires knowledge under the direct guidance of a trusted teacher or master (*guru*). The *guru–shishya* is defining as both a professional and personal relationship, marked by ceremony and an initiation into a community and lineage.

Through their *guru*, the *shishya* is connected to and belongs to a recognized and reputable musical lineage, called *gharana*, which grants them legitimacy as a performer.

In the *guru–shishya paramapara*, knowledge was transferred orally from one generation to the other, through the authoritative teaching of the *gurus*. The different *gharanas*—or lineages—developed and preserved diverse music knowledge and practices, and only shared them with trusted disciples. Attached to receiving this knowledge was a responsibility to eventually pass on what is learned, and to successfully carry the tradition forward. It was essential that the material was passed on precisely and remembered exactly. To this end, students participated in *talim*, or formal musical training, differentiated to each *shishya* based on their ability and their *guru's* vision for their musicianship. Students were also expected to take part in *riyaz*, a form of dedicated individual practice, demanding rigour and regularity. The specific qualities and responsibilities of both the *guru* and the *shishya* were embedded in a centuries-long intellectual tradition.

In the 20th century, with the influence of colonialism, globalization and a nation-building project in India, the role of the *guru–shishya parampara* as the primary method of transferring knowledge in Hindustani classical music began to shift. Changing social, political and economic circumstances gave rise to non-hereditary musicians and reformers who sought to modernize and democratize this music tradition and turn it into a matter of national interest and pride. Where we previously see an exclusive knowledge community propagated through Oral Tradition, individual instruction based on trust and authority, and a diversity of styles through the different *gharanas*, a new approach to transmitting and acquiring knowledge began to take shape. Among the reforms were a notational system, a standardized curriculum and teaching methodology, and new institutionalized conventions of theory and practice suitable for mass music education. Of these, notation—which allowed Hindustani music to be written down—was intended to raise it to the dignity of a "classical" music tradition, asserting its sophistication and complexity, and putting it on par with Western classical music. Hindustani musical texts could now travel further, independent of the one-on-one in-person oral transmission between *gurus* and *shishyas*.

A lot has been written about how these changes, combined with technological advancements and a global South Asian diaspora, affected the reach of this musical tradition. What do you imagine was gained, and what was lost, in terms of knowledge in the course of this transformation? Can some forms of knowledge only be transferred and shared in specific ways? And how did this allow more diverse knowers to have access to this knowledge?

For discussion

Learning to draw waves and the Buddha

Contrary to the quote we opened this section with, Hokusai Katsushika, the artist of the *Great Wave off Kanagawa*, the iconic Japanese woodblock print, wrote the following.

"From around the age of six, I had the habit of sketching from life. I became an artist, and from fifty on began producing works that won some reputation, but nothing I did before the age of seventy was worthy of attention."

To explore this idea of mastery, consider these two examples.

 Search terms:
Book of Tibetan Proportions
Public Domain Review

 Search terms:
Japanese book
of wave and ripple Public
Domain Review

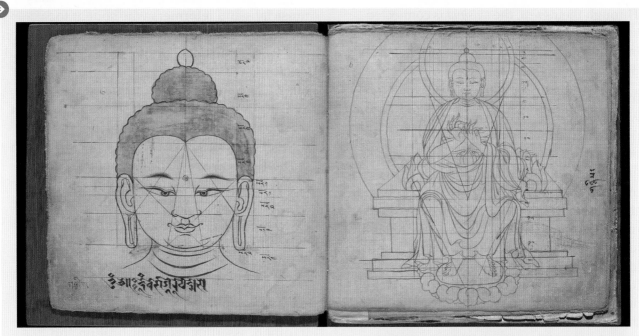

1. Is having knowledge of the arts necessary for being able to make great art?

2. In the arts, what is the relationship between mastery of skill and the quality of knowledge?

3. How does the role of convention influence knowledge in the arts?

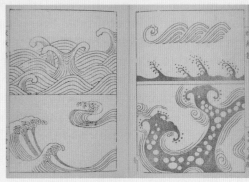

III.2 Method and art production

When one speaks of art production, one might imagine the art studio, the theatre company, the writer's desk—at least in the popular imagination of sites of art production. But how does art arise out of specific local contexts, and what is the relationship between art and place? How are globalization and other forces of modernity affecting traditions of artistic knowledge that have continued for centuries?

Let's consider two examples from South India. The first arose during the 10th-century dynasty of the Chola kings of Tanjore, and reveals how landscape, monarchy, religion and divinity came together to inspire a resurgence in traditional art. During this period, land features such as the hills, waterfalls and groves surrounding villages were animated with spiritual stories connecting them

to a pantheon of deities, many of whom had large stone idols made in their honour. Over time, these idols were replaced with smaller, portable bronze statues. Among the best-known examples of these are the Chola bronzes, sculptures made using the lost-wax casting technique, commissioned and produced by the Chola kings of Tanjore. The sculptures communicate with mudras, the hand and finger gestures of South Indian dance, and are widely described as deeply beautiful, communicating theological truths; they are also sometimes described as unabashedly sexual, their near-naked bodies symbolizing fecundity and eroticism. While the Chola bronzes can be seen as "art from above", an example of religious art produced through elite patronage, we also have *theyyam* from South India, a ritual dance tradition that is thousands of years old and predates Hinduism.

Theyyam combines theatrical, religious and lived culture in a performance that can transform space and the identity of the performer, who is said to be possessed by gods during the performance.

> Before it happens, I always get very tense, even though I have been doing this for 26 years now. It's not that I am nervous of the god coming. It's more the fear that he might refuse to come. It's the intensity of your devotion that determines the intensity of the possession. If you lose your feeling of devotion, if it even once becomes routine or unthinking, the gods may stop coming … . When the drums are playing and your make-up is finished, they hand you a mirror and you look at your face transformed into that of a god. Then it comes. It's as if there is a sudden explosion of light. A vista of complete brilliance opens up—it blinds the senses … . That light stays with you all the way during the performance. You become the deity. You lose all fear. Even your voice changes. The god comes alive and takes over. You are just the vehicle, the medium. In the trance, it is god who speaks, and all the acts are the acts of the god—feeling, thinking, speaking. The dancer is an ordinary man—but this being is divine. Only when the head-dress is removed does it end.
>
> (Das quoted in Dalrymple 2009)

Theyyams, or rather the human performers who are possessed, are Dalits, or untouchables—designated as so low a caste that higher-caste Hindus will not touch them. But because of the perceived strength and authenticity of their possession, *theyyams* are worshipped during the ritual season, from December to February, with even the highest-caste Hindus seeking their blessings and touching their feet. How does this example speak to the production of artistic knowledge?

Hari Das describes his experiences when he is not performing *theyyam*.

> For nine months a year, I work as a manual labourer. I build wells during the week, then at the weekend I work in Tellicherry Central Jail. As a warder … . I need to make a living. I am poor enough to be ready to do virtually anything if someone pays me a daily wage. It's not for pleasure—it's very dangerous work … . The inmates rule the jail. Many have got political

> backing. No one dares to mess with them … . I keep my head down. I never beat any prisoner, and just try to avoid being beaten up myself. We all just try to get through the day alive and intact.
>
> (Das quoted in Dalrymple 2009)

In his book *Nine Lives* (2009) William Dalrymple interviews Hari Das and describes *theyyam* as originating from a deeply casteist context where, even in the 20th century "lower-caste tenants were still regularly being murdered by their Nayar (high caste) landlords for failing to present sweets as tokens of their submission".

Today Dalits are still expected to show deference and respect, and to avoid physical contact or close proximity with higher castes. Dalrymple suggests this context clearly plays a role in the *theyyam* art form.

> These inequalities are the fertile soil from which Theyyam grew, and the dance form has always been a conscious and ritualised inversion of the usual structures of Keralan life: for it is not the pure and sanctified Brahmins into which the gods choose to incarnate, but the shunned and insulted Dalits … . The Theyyams take place not in Brahminical temples, but small shrines in the holy places and sacred groves of the countryside …
>
> (Dalrymple 2009)

In these two examples—the Chola bronzes and *theyyam*—the methods through which art is produced, and the knowledge involved in the process, does not seem *typical* for this AOK. We invite you to reflect on ideas about how art usually works, and the processes that produce it. Where do these ideas come from, and how are they maintained? Art can be, and often is, entangled with the domains of culture and religion, and even science. This entanglement influences the methods of art, and it may be the case that religious, scientific or cultural knowledge is essential in the process of producing art.

Where does the artist sit in the midst of all this? In the interview below, we speak to theatre artist Nandita Dinesh about the practices that inform the production of her work.

Voices: Interview with Nandita Dinesh

[Interviewer]: In your work making theatre in contexts of conflict, is there a particular 'method' or 'methodology' that you've found to be particularly useful?

[Dinesh]: The first thing to nuance here, is the term 'conflict'. While much of my work has occurred in active war zones (like Kashmir), I'm also curious about the potential/limitations of theatre in conflicts that are less easy to classify as 'war': the conflicts surrounding incarceration in the United States, for example, where a 'war-like' situation exists—although one is less likely to call the US a 'war zone'.

In these contexts of conflict, I often go in as an outsider: because I'm of a different gender, nationality, ethnicity, or social condition from that which is being experienced by the folks I work with. I say this because this 'outsider-ness'—and a constant critical engagement with the politics and ethics of that identity—have led to autoethnography being the primary tool that I use when creating theatre about/with/for/in conflicted contexts.

What this autoethnographic approach means, for me, is a constant [re]negotiation (in the processes of research, creation, and performance) of my own positioning—with all its biases and limitations.

[Interviewer]: What does this look like? Practically?

[Dinesh]: Practically, this means that all my works contain an explicit character called 'The Outsider': a character who emerges at different points in whatever I write/create in response to the conflict in question; a character who problematises the work, while also being part of it; a character who is semi-autobiographical, while also speaking to observed dynamics between 'host' and 'guest'.

So in a piece called *Chronicles from Kashmir* that was developed over six years with a theatre company in Srinagar, Kashmir, there are two 'Guides' who take the audience on their journey through the world of the performance. One of these 'Guides' is Kashmiri; the other is non-Kashmiri. And a central emphasis in the performance is how these two characters engage with each other, while they attempt to present different perspectives from Kashmir to the audience.

[Interviewer]: You've often used the term 'gray zones' to frame your work. Could you unpack that for us?

[Dinesh]: I'm borrowing the term from Primo Levi's *The Drowned and the Saved* where he speaks to the 'gray zones' of the Holocaust as being in the experiences of Jews who had to become complicit within the Nazi establishment to protect themselves and their families. Now Levi nuances his use of the term a lot more, but what stuck with me was the 'gray zone' as being an area in which the links between 'victim' and 'perpetrator' become harder to define … where someone/ some experience contains within it both qualities of 'victimhood' and 'perpetration'. Where simplistic binaries between 'good' and 'evil' are impossible … .

When approaching a conflict therefore, one of the first things that I embark on is a 'conflict mapping' of sorts. A process in which I try to understand the 'gray zones' that lie between/within mainstream depictions of that conflict—while never ignoring the reality that some voices are more powerful than others; some voices are more visible than others.

[Interviewer]: How do you dramatize 'gray zones' while also not simplistically saying that 'everyone is a victim'?

[Dinesh]: That is a question that I constantly deal with …

[Interviewer]: And how do you deal with that question?

[Dinesh]: One way I've been attempting to integrate this complexity in my work is through particular aesthetic choices.

For example, my works are most often staged in the 'promenade' i.e., audience members don't sit in one place and watch a performance on a stage. Instead, they walk between different, unconventional performance sites (kitchens, bathrooms, trees, passageways) and encounter different stories through movement. To me, this notion of moving the audience is an allegory for complexity … . To show the audience, experientially, that they need to 'work' to learn about the complexities of conflict. That they can't just sit in a comfortable chair and expect to be informed … that they need to move, to walk, to 'work', in order to better understand.

Another idea that I work with a lot is 'fragmentation'. Folks who are more accustomed to Realism expect a certain overarching narrative in a theatrical work. You know, the introduction, the rising action, the climax, the falling action, and all of that. In my work, I intentionally break apart that linearity—once again because I wonder if linear narratives facilitate a problematic outcome of something being seen as 'understandable' … while the trouble with conflict is that so many parts of it escape our understanding.

Finally, I work a lot with duration. *Chronicles from Kashmir* is a 24-hour long immersive experience where spectators and actors live together for a day … . Duration too, helps me unravel complexity in more evocative ways. To bring in narratives from the 'gray zones' while also taking the time to contextualize those voices within the larger fabric of the conflict that is being dealt with.

Nandita Dinesh is a 2002 IB graduate.

In this section we have explored significant material, personal and cultural practices that take place in the process of producing art, collectively referred to as "methods". Before we move on to examine the tools of art production more closely, take some time to examine this idea of methods, using the questions that follow.

For discussion

The role of methods in art

In pairs, small groups, or as a class consider the following questions.

1. To what extent is it necessary to follow a certain method in order to produce art?

2. How does following or not following the methods of art affect the quality of the artwork?

3. What kinds of knowledge are involved in artistic methods and how does the artist acquire them?

4. In which ways does method play a similar or different role in art as compared to science, history or mathematics?

III.3 Tools and instruments in art

The tools of art—pigments, brushes, but also stage sets, musical instruments and, recently, increasingly technological tools—participate in essential ways in knowledge in the arts. Knowing in arts is a deeply *material engagement*; it is not just about knowing how to use tools, but also how to work with materials. Artists shape and bake clay, chisel and polish stones, melt and mould metals, take and develop photographs, mix paints and apply them to different surfaces in order to produce art. Knowing in the arts is also an *embodied experience*—arguably to a greater extent than the other areas of knowledge. We might think of artistic knowledge as requiring our whole selves, and especially our bodies—to act, dance, sing or play instruments.

What kinds of knowledge might be unique to the arts as a result of its material and embodied nature? Are there any exceptions—among the different art forms—where tools and instruments play a lesser role? And how is the knowledge produced in the arts different from knowledge produced using different tools and methods in the other areas of knowledge?

Case study

Pigment feuds

Pigments can be deeply interesting, as we see in Kassia St Claire's *The Secret Lives of Color*. Many of us also take for granted that we can walk into an arts and crafts store to purchase a set of oil paints, even though that is a relatively new innovation.

And then there is Vantablack—one of the blackest blacks ever made. It absorbs almost all light—99.965% to be precise—so much so that some artists have described it as disturbing and confronting.

Created from carbon nanotubes, by accident in the laboratory of Surrey Nanosystems, an engineering and space science laboratory, Vantablack took the art world by storm. It was not widely available because the pigment had to be created under very specific laboratory conditions, using a reactor and highly trained staff.

Undeterred, artists flooded the company with enquiries. Among them was Anish Kapoor, a prominent contemporary artist, creator of Chicago's *Cloud Gate* sculpture (popularly known as "The Bean"), who ultimately purchased the rights to Vantablack for his exclusive use. Surrey Nanosystems, coming from the technology world, may have conceived of patents as a legitimate and obvious response to their innovation, and so the company patented the method and laboratory protocols for creating the pigment. This did not go down well with the art world.

Exclusive use of a technologically derived material is certainly not unheard of in the technology world; indeed, patents protect the incentives that propel research and development (R&D) in science, technology and industry. Without patents, the argument is, organizations would have no pay-off from pursuing costly R&D, and so no incentive to pursue it in the first place. But as Kapoor

and Surrey Nanosystems would find out, this was markedly different from the ethos and expectations of many artists.

New technologies and material possibilities have a long history of inspiring new art forms and movements. And that these innovations are sometimes, or even often, not freely and widely shared by their inventors is also not new. But something about Vantablack deeply upset many artists, perhaps none more so than Stuart Semple who, inspired by this episode, would go on to democratize pigments. He saw the Vantablack patent as elitist and immoral, limiting access to an art material that could advance art collectively. But Semple had been making his own pigments and not sharing them, and was struck by his own hypocrisy. And so, he made his pigment, the Pinkest Pink, available for purchase by other artists at a very cheap price. This was both an act of sharing as well as a performance, because every sale was made on the condition that the buyer was not Anish Kapoor, was not affiliated with him in any way, and would not allow Anish Kapoor access to the pigment.

Semple's performance went viral, shared or commented upon thousands of times on social media. Anish Kapoor somehow got his hands on the pigment and did a performance of his own, posting a picture on Instagram of his middle finger dripping in the Pinkest Pink. So commenced a massive feud. Semple along with a few others set out to create an alternative to Vantablack, spending years in R&D and collaborating with the make-up industry to create Black 3.0, not quite as black as Vantablack, but pretty close. It inspired another artist, Diemut Strebe, who alongside MIT scientists ultimately created a blacker black than Vantablack, a pigment that traps an astonishing 99.995% of light. Until a blacker black comes around, this one is available to any artist, including Anish Kapoor.

Within this example, consider how questions of context, access, values and incentives intersect in the production of artistic knowledge.

Technology can play the role of enhancing existing possibilities in the arts, as well as creating new forms of expression and production. To what extent is this presenting new challenges for knowledge in the arts? The debate, for example, about the artistic status of AI produced poetry and music is a relatively recent one, but the questions of authorship, originality, quality and value are concerns that have long been at the centre of discourse in the arts.

Let's explore an example of the interaction between artist and technology in digitally enhanced art production methods. Dan Tepfer's partner is a self-playing piano powered by an improvisational algorithm. Follow the link to find out how Tepfer has produced the algorithm and programmed a hybrid piano to co-create musical pieces with him in real time.

 Search terms: Improvisational algorithms digital player piano

What can we say about the artistic status of Tepfer's musical compositions? Consider how the involvement of the algorithm in this case changes or complicates your answer to the question. What if he had two algorithm-powered pianos playing with each other?

Making connections

Technology in the arts and mathematics

In Chapter 11 we encounter the example of non-surveyable proof, a computer-generated solution to a unsolved mathematical problem. There we ask the question: if the proof is too long or complex for humans to check it, can we confirm it and accept it as mathematical knowledge? Similarly here, if an algorithm composes a musical piece that a human cannot read or perform, to what extent can we call this an art piece? Comparing these two cases, consider what happens when technological advancements outpace our human abilities and what the implications of this are for knowledge.

IV. ETHICS

You may notice that many knowledge questions and claims in the arts are concerned with judgment: who decides something, and how they do that. These are important concerns throughout TOK and especially in the arts, because of the potentially transgressive and provocative nature of art that aims to change individual and collective attitudes. Around the world, ethical questions pertaining to art are being decided by someone, whether that is through the creation or exhibition of a given work or its censorship, for example. In seeking to understand the implications of these decisions, we can look to the implications of censorship and policing in art, and what this tells us about the power of art to influence preferences, value systems and moral judgments. At the outset of this section, consider to what extent artistic knowledge has influenced your personal moral values.

How far is too far in arts? In 1987 Andres Serrano submerged a crucifix in his urine. The photograph of the jar has been subsequently displayed as a work of art in various exhibitions around the world, but never with an explanation about the artist's intent, leaving individuals to interpret it as they would. It has been denounced by religious communities and political conservatives, with Serrano receiving threats for over two decades. The controversy raised familiar and perennial knowledge issues pertaining to the arts as an AOK.

 Search terms: Andres Serrano New York controversy

For discussion

Ethical questions in the creation of art

1. What criteria would you use for the censorship of art, and why?

2. Would you agree or disagree that Serrano failed to uphold his moral responsibility, as an artist, with this particular work of art?

3. Consider how we value art. Does it have to be morally good in order to be good art?

4. To what extent could you say that art as an AOK is better or worse off without works of art such as this one? How would you decide?

Andres Serrano has also worked on an exhibition about US President Donald Trump, spurring both interest and concern over his intentions. Serrano has stated: "I'm not interested in pointing fingers, because I think it's boring. I've seen a lot of artwork that's anti-Trump, and frankly it's not good, it's not interesting. I'd rather let the man speak for himself"(quoted in Stanley-Becker 2019).

Box 10.8: The power of art to influence ethics

On the tenth anniversary of the start of the First World War, Ernst Friedrich published *Krieg dem Kriege!* (*War Against War!*), an album of photographs sourced from German military and medical archives that were censored by the government during wartime. It has been referred to as a "Pacifist Bible", and starts with pictures of toy guns then proceeds into pictures of death, destruction, starvation, agony, mutilation and graves. The photographs' captions (in four languages) mock militarist ideology. The album was condemned by patriotic organizations but praised in anti-war, progressive, artistic and intellectual circles as something that would turn public sentiment against war. By 1930, *War Against War!* had been translated into many languages, and printed through 10 editions in Germany alone. And yet, within the decade the Second World War was underway.

40 000 „Stück" Totenschädel (bei Marville)

↑ **Figure 10.9** Image number 30 in Ernst Fridrich's photograph album *Krieg dem Kriege!* (*War Against War!*)

Within the arts as an AOK, ethical questions can arise at various points in the production, acquisition or dissemination of knowledge. In TOK, we seek to explore the claims and counterclaims in relation to ethics in the context of the production and dissemination of art.

These claims arise with respect to the intention, creation, presentation, impact and/or rewards of an artistic work. Think of these areas as "hotspots" around which ethical concerns in art tend to cluster.

Ethics hotspots in art

intention	creation	presentation	impact	rewards

- What was the artist's intention for the work, and why?
- How did the artist go about creating the work?
- How was the artistic work displayed, exhibited or introduced?
- What impact did the work have on the audience(s), and who is responsible for that impact?
- If there were rewards arising from the work, who benefited from them?

Table 10.1 contains examples of contemporary ethical issues with their corresponding TOK questions. Within TOK we are not so much concerned with arguing right from wrong, but rather in how we form judgment about right and wrong. Hopefully, our judgments about right and wrong are improved as a result.

Practising skills: Constructing claims and counterclaims

For each of the examples in Table 10.1, identify a real-life situation in art where a similar ethical issue finds expression. Next, relating to your example, formulate a set of claims and counterclaims in response to the knowledge questions provided.

Example ethical claim in art	Knowledge questions
"The artist's intent to confront the audience with inequality does not justify the paternalistic framing of people in poverty, even if the audience is moved to donate money to charity. The artist should be responsible for showing an uplifting narrative that reveals dignity in the face of hardship."	Can an artistic representation of a people ever be "neutral" or objective? If an aesthetic bias is inevitable, should we aim to regulate it, and if so, how, and who should do this? Is morality in the arts a matter of personal taste? What criteria should we use to find answers to the questions above, and do you think different people and cultures would agree on the criteria?
"The artist's intent to show us the beauty of Indigenous Peoples' dress exploits a power asymmetry, treats their culture as decorative, and perpetuates a romanticized and exoticized ideal that further distances the other. Good intentions do not absolve the artist of responsibility."	What are the implications of using an artistic impression as a source of knowledge about the subject? What other sources does it displace? How should we honour other people's rights to represent themselves while working for a home audience?
"Twenty years after a photograph was published in a magazine, we learn that the famous photographer did not follow local customs and norms in obtaining the iconic portrait, and did not ask the subject for permission, thereby offending the adults and scaring the child who was the subject of the photograph. We should denounce the work and demand the author and magazine apologize to the subject."	If we aim for ethical standards to improve over time, how should we apply contemporary standards to the past, when people "may not have known better"? What value is there in interrogating decisions taken in the past? If we say something was acceptable at the time, do we marginalize the people who thought it was not acceptable at the time, and so change history?
"The artistic work inspired an act of violence, and even though this was never the intent of the artist, she must be held partly responsible."	To what extent are artists responsible for the actions they inspire in their audience? How do we decide on the boundaries delineating how far artists are responsible for the impact of an artistic work?
"As an audience we generously rewarded the artist but have forgotten about the subject, who received no share of the financial rewards. The artist defended his actions by saying the person he used as a source of inspiration was barely known before but now enjoys wider recognition."	How do we know the difference between appropriation and inspiration, and what are the implications for this on the ownership of an artistic work?

↑ **Table 10.1** Examples of ethical claims and knowledge questions

Another issue deserving our attention is the extent to which we can separate an artwork from the artist. This question has gained importance in recent years with high-profile revelations about the crimes committed by artists, singers, actors and film-makers. Similar questions are asked in other disciplines—indeed, many influential philosophers and scientists were almost certainly racists, chauvinists or misogynists—but are artists and their art more inextricably linked? Do the crimes or unethical actions of an artist more deeply affect how we experience their artwork?

Some observers have argued that it is the badness in people that makes for good art, and that experiencing and learning from their art does not mean condoning or perpetuating their ideas, or rewarding them financially. (See, for example, Russell Smith's article "Good Art by Bad People" in the Canadian newspaper *The Globe and Mail*, 20 November 2016.)

IV.1 The role of the audience

In 2007 Guillermo Vargas exhibited *Exposition No 1*, a dog tied to a wall in the Codice Gallery in Nicaragua, with the words "You are what you read" behind it, while the Sandinista anthem was played backwards. Vargas later claimed the dog, named Natividad, eventually died of starvation and dehydration due to the exhibition. This caused widespread outrage but Vargas responded by questioning why no one in the audience had taken any action to feed or free Natividad. Vargas was playing with a familiar tension: was the artist responsible, or the audience? More to the TOK point, how would we go about asking that question?

For those who are interested, it is not clear whether Natividad actually perished—reportedly the gallery's director, Juanita Bermúdez, stated that the dog was treated well by Vargas and released the next day. Vargas has never confirmed or denied this, insisting that the real outcome—the audience's inaction and complicity—was clear.

IV.2 Censorship

Art has a significant and perhaps unique power to evoke, provoke, offend or inspire humanity towards some end. This quality of framing, cropping, distorting, interpreting, revealing or hiding reality towards some truth has made art influential and powerful and, therefore, a target for those who wish to control influence and power. The practice of censorship is commonly attributed to governments, but humankind at all levels has a long history of censorship, based on calls to moral propriety and righteousness, sensitivity and respect for others, social stability and the protection of vulnerable groups. Examples range from the peculiar—Queen Victoria's encounter with the naked, 6-metre high marble statue of *David* prompted the making of a proportionately accurate "fig leaf" to cover his nudity—to the systematic erasure of revolutionary icons such as *Tank Man*. A less obvious form of censorship is in deciding what is, and is not, art, because artistic status confers social and legal protections to a work.

For discussion

Censoring art

Examples of censorship in the arts abound and the reasons for censorship are similarly varied. In groups, discuss the following questions.

1. Think about who censors art.

   (a) How are they given this power?

   (b) What criteria do they use?

2. What are tacit, or informal, forms of censorship?

IV.2.1 Censorship as a response to transgression

Section II outlined how art can serve at the vanguard of humanity's social, political and moral evolution. With the advantage of hindsight, we can identify works of art that were transgressive—violating the social, political or moral boundaries of the time—to promote a progressive agenda. For example, artistic works from an exhibition, Art AIDS America, may have helped to foster progressive attitudes towards AIDS, and yet were condemned and/or censored in their time. This is an obvious and recurring theme in art that has become something of a cliché. Should we therefore conclude that censorship is wrong? Of course, the situation is much more complicated. The history of art is filled with works that offended and provoked outrage and yet failed to deliver any positive social change. If it is difficult to recall particular examples, it may be because we scarcely noticed them (or because they were quickly censored), but there are many instances of sexist, racist or religiously hateful work masquerading as art.

A big part of the problem of what to censor and what to permit, is the difficulty in rigorously defining art. This provides people with a convenient shortcut to censorship: "Oh, that's not art, that's [something else]". Should artists be able to challenge our conceptions of human sexuality or religious righteousness? Of course they should. Are there limits to how they can do this? Apparently, yes, in every society and nation that we know of. How are those limits arrived at, who decides them and what are the implications of such censorship? These are TOK questions.

We would be fooled by survival bias to conclude that art should not be censored because it changes the world for the better; we would also be foolish to fail to realize that some artists never get that chance, because of censorship. And without censorship, would art not lose some of its transgressive powers to provoke, question and incite? Part of the progressive power of art comes from the response to it—the impulse to outrage and censorship. Ultimately, how we strike that balance is a result of the forces and voices that put forward their case on either side.

IV.2.2 Censorship of the past

A peculiar subset within the topic of censorship is the censoring of art from the past. If history is anything to go by, our tolerance to art has increased with time; works that were censored in the past, perhaps because of their blasphemous or provocative tone, are more widely accepted today. However, there is a contemporary movement to censor works from the past. What does this suggest about popular conceptions of morality and progress in art? Is truth in art more contextual than truth in other AOKs?

IV.3 The ethics of aesthetics

Writing in 2001, the music critic Anthony Tommasini described the distinction between art and reality—art takes many forms and is not always easy to define, but it is always one step removed from reality. Well-known images of Vietnamese children running from a napalm attack or of the falling twin towers might be artistically-composed and captivating to view, but, Tommasini stresses, we must recognise them as truth rather than art. Would you agree with Tommasini's distinction between truth and art?

Conversely, the Tate Modern Museum of London lists photojournalism as a form of art while emphasizing its need to remain "honest and impartial". To what extent is that possible? As discussed in section II, there can be value in considering photojournalism as an art even though its status as a documentary medium is widely accepted. Documentary photographers, by invoking particular aesthetics and narratives, can have a significant impact in this realm, much like artists striving to create a certain mood in their work. Therefore, photojournalists comply with strict ethical guidelines that have evolved and continue to improve over time. Let's explore how the aesthetic decisions in photography can affect the meaning of a work, beginning with the particularly shocking images taken by Willoughby Wallace Hooper of the Madras famine of 1876–1888.

Case study

Imagin(in)g the Global South

 Search terms: Mukherjee Who was the photographer who took dehumanizing images Madras famine

 Search terms: The Conversation Images of suffering can bring about change

In 1876 the Sanitary Commissioner of Madras, Dr Cornish, had felt that a photographer might help rally the British public and political class to lend relief to the famine. If they could "see the living skeletons assembled at feeding houses", as he had, perhaps they could be moved to act (Cornish quoted in Digby 1878). Others in the region felt similarly.

> " I feel an irresistible longing to send you photographs of some of the living skeletons, of which there are evidently hundreds in the districts immediately surrounding Madras. Words convey a poor idea of the appearance of a human being for some days before he dies of starvation.
>
> (unnamed special correspondent, *Friend of India* newspaper, quoted in Digby 1876) "

The intentions of Cornish and the unnamed special correspondent were to help the afflicted inhabitants of their district. The photographer who answered their call was Willoughby Wallace Hooper, and his photographs crossed a line between photojournalism and perverse aesthetic, with accompanying captions such as "Forsaken" and "The Last of the Herd". A separate incident describes how Hooper, at the execution of a gangster, interrupted the firing squad at the last moment to adjust his camera's focus. Once he was satisfied he asked them to carry on.

"For photographs to accuse and possibly invoke a moral response, they must shock" wrote Judith Butler (2007).

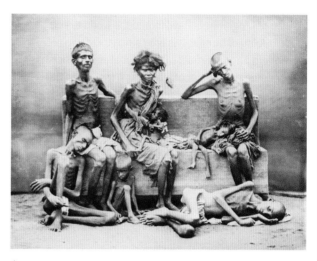

↑ **Figure 10.10** Photograph by Willoughby Wallace Hooper, from *The Graphic* magazine, 6 October 1877. The magazine featured images of the Madras famine in an exploitative aesthetic. This photograph was among the least disturbing of Hooper's images; others were deemed too hard-hitting for inclusion.

These photographs are from long ago but the ethical implications of aesthetic decisions have not gone away. Consider the linked article by Alison Dundes Rentein (2018). Rentein examines the power of visual media, particularly photography, in the politics of poverty, aid and human rights. The ethical issues surrounding the practice and impact of this genre of photography, sometimes called poverty-porn, have been thoroughly discussed in both academic and social discourse. The TOK issues within this area are still worth examining as they will drive dilemmas of the future.

One side of the debate is outlined by Jonathan Jones, writing in the UK newspaper the *Guardian*, that "mobilizing shame" through photographs can move people to contribute through philanthropy, activism and development assistance.

> The fact that people far away can see with visceral immediacy the facts of a crisis like the one now hitting the Horn of Africa is one of the most optimistic aspects of the modern world. Consciences are awakened by the camera. Don McCullin's pictures of Biafra in 1969 are moving examples of the way photographers have forced the world to see the reality of hunger. It is only since the dawn of modern photojournalism that global conscience has accepted the hunger of others as a responsibility.
>
> Before the camera it was almost incredibly easy to ignore famine. Victorian Britain ignored it in Ireland, so near and yet so far. Artists painted beautiful landscapes that rarely even hinted at the real lives of the rural poor. Only in paintings of apocalyptic horror such as Bruegel's 'Triumph of Death' do we glimpse the experience of famine in pre-modern art.
>
> A photograph can put suffering on the front of your paper while you eat breakfast.
>
> (Jones 2011)

↑ **Figure 10.11** This photo tells a different story from the one that comes out of the photographer's camera

> All these pictures overwhelmingly showed people as needing our pity—as passive victims. This was through a de-contextualised concentration on mid- and close-up shots emphasising body language and facial expressions. The photos seemed mainly to be taken from a high angle with no eye contact, thus reinforcing the viewer's sense of power compared with their apathy and hopelessness.
>
> (van der Gaag, Nash 1987)

However, the narrative of the Global South, beginning with Western literature in the 16th century and continuing through photographs well into the 21st century, has perpetuated inaccurate and disempowering stereotypes and fails to foreground important contextual factors. How many pictures of starving children in Africa simultaneously condemn the legacy of colonialism? Do modern photographs therefore continue to flatten the narrative, reducing the subjects of such photographs to objects of pity, without context or agency?

David Campbell, a professor of cultural and political geography, has raised questions about the "compassion fatigue" and damage caused by stereotypical mother-and-child photographs of poverty. He quotes the report "Image of Africa" published by Oxfam that studied the media representation of the Ethiopian famine:

Aesthetic decisions may sometimes appear inconsequential, but subtle signalling can still be powerful. For example, consider a 2010 article about rising food costs published in the UK newspaper the *Guardian*. The same article was presented with a different image in the printed and online editions. In the printed version, there was a starving young boy in the foreground against straws of grain in the sunset (Figure 10.12a). The online version uses an image of Somali men apparently rioting against high food prices (Figure 10.12b). The text is largely the same across both versions and can be accessed by following the link here. To what extent do the different images affect your understanding and/or response to the article?

 Search terms: Guardian 2010 Food prices rise UN report

Photojournalists and editors have been aware of this issue for a long time, and so there has been some improvement. In 2010, Doctors Without Borders/Médecins Sans Frontières (MSF) and VII Photo launched a project called Starved for Attention to rewrite the story of childhood malnutrition.

Search terms: Starved for attention documentary

"One of the things that was important about this project was trying to go beyond the obvious photos of malnutrition", said photographer Ron Haviv (quoted in Johnson 2009). That meant avoiding cliché images of starving children with distended stomachs, and documenting a more holistic and complex story. The resulting documentary was nominated for an Emmy Award.

Food prices to rise by up to 40% over next decade, UN report warns

Growing demand from emerging markets and for biofuel production will send prices soaring, according to the OECD and the UN Food and Agriculture Organisation

↑ **Figure 10.12b** The online article

Rising demand fuels fears of famine with food costs soaring over next decade

↑ **Figure 10.12a** The printed article

For discussion

National Geographic, Afghan Girl

 Search terms: Northrup Disturbing true story of the Afghan Girl YouTube

In the linked video, YouTube vlogger Tony Northrup examines the ethical issues involved in the famous photograph of Sharbat Gula, known as *Afghan Girl*, that appeared on the June 1985 cover of *National Geographic*. It is the most recognized photograph and one of the most famous covers in the history of the magazine.

Larger prints of the photograph have been sold for up to $178,900 at auctions.

In light of what we have encountered so far about the artistic and ethical implications of photography, consider the following.

"He poses her like an 80s glamour shot," Northrup says (2019), "shoulder tilted towards the camera, forehead forward a little bit, nice light to illuminate the eyes, and direct eye contact—something [that] she would never ever do". Northrup describes Sharbat Gula as a little Pashtun girl facing a Western man. "Photojournalism has been guilty of awful abuses through history, often exploiting the poor for profit and celebrity", he says (2019).

The episode witnesses a collision of two different photography communities and practices 35 years apart: YouTube vloggers and 1980s photojournalists. It also reveals some of the key difficulties in separating photojournalism from art.

Northrup's critique serves as an example of "call-out" culture and is presented as furthering an ethical cause. However, his critique is complicated because he stands to benefit from views on his YouTube channel. Northrup has thus been accused of doing a "hit piece" for commercial gain. The renowned photographer who took Sharbat Gula's portrait, Steve McCurry, is yet to personally respond but his foundation has responded to Northrup with corrections described in the video. The facts of the case may never be clearly established, and

Sharbat Gula herself has described mixed feelings about the photograph.

 Afghan Girl Follow-up: corrections sources & answers YouTube

In an April 2002 follow-up story by *National Geographic*, Sharbat Gula described feeling angry when the photograph was taken. In 2017 she told the Pakistani newspaper *The Express Tribune* that "the photo created more problems than benefits. It made me famous but also led to my imprisonment", but she also added "now I am very happy that it gave me honour and made me popular among people" (*The Express Tribune*, 19 January 2017).

How are individuals and communities online shaping artistic, journalistic and even ethical standards, and disrupting traditional platforms? What would make this desirable or undesirable? Is Northrup's critique legitimized by his large following of over 1.3 million people on YouTube? Is it less credible because he stands to gain from his YouTube channel?

Northrup's suggested ethical guidelines for photojournalists are nothing new—ethical codes exist in various forms for all professional photojournalist organizations—but his guidelines reach many more people precisely because of his presence on YouTube. They include the following.

- Don't bend cultures to your aesthetics … or stereotypes.
- Choose subjects based on their story, not looks.
- If a photo is … staged or posed, declare it.
- Proceeds from images of the poor should benefit the poor more than the photographer. (Northrup 2017)

To what extent are these ethical guidelines similar or different to, for example, the NPPA's code of ethics? (linked here).

 Search terms: NPPA Code of ethics

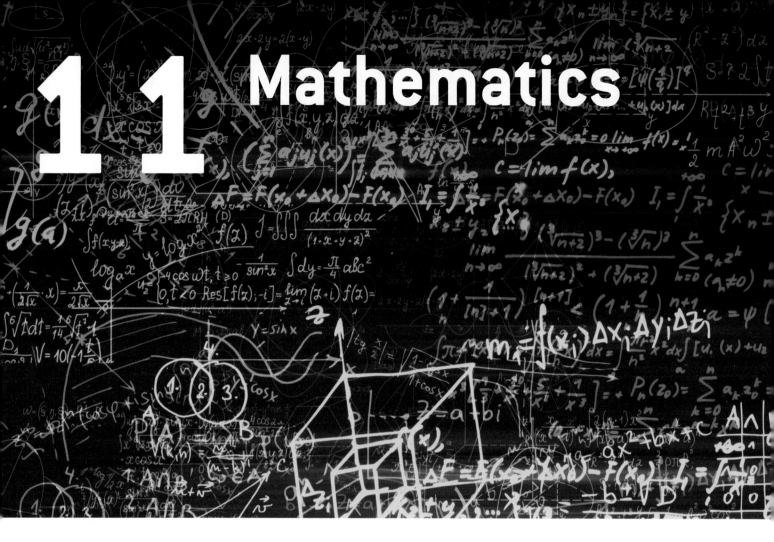

11 Mathematics

Among the AOKs, mathematics stands apart in important ways. It is said to be the language of the natural sciences, an important ally to the human sciences, and a self-contained discipline in its own right. Without mathematics, some of the other AOKs might be weakened, and yet mathematics would seem to do perfectly well by itself. Or would it? In this chapter, we explore what it means to know the universe mathematically, whether it has been discovered or created, and why it is thought of simultaneously as a language, practice and body of knowledge.

I. SCOPE

As with all the AOKs, the boundaries of mathematics are not definitively drawn. There is evidence of humans practising mathematics for as long as written records exist. In ancient Mesopotamia, algebra, arithmetic and geometry were used for various applications including taxation, astronomy and architecture as early as 3000 BCE. We still measure time and angles using the numeral system based on 60 (called the sexagesimal system) developed in Babylonian mathematics.

> [M]athematics might be the ultimate intellectual endeavour. … numeracy is one of the defining features of modernity … . Perhaps more than any other subject, mathematics is about the study of ideas.
>
> (Levy-Eichel 2018)

What is mathematics? Philosophers and historians often answer this question by referring to the contents and methods of mathematics.

Notably, mathematics carries an aura of authority because mathematical proofs are 100% certain and a supposed usefulness that justifies its privileged status in many education systems.

Where are the limits of mathematics? It is sometimes assumed that there are none—that it is a universal form of knowledge and feature of intelligent life. See the opening example in Chapter 4 about how mathematics was chosen as the common ground on which to communicate with any extraterrestrial intelligences.

One place to look for the limits of mathematics is in what it can describe, explain or predict. As the example of physics envy in Chapter 8 shows, mathematics may have been taken too far in the quest for rigour in the social sciences. In 1931 the mathematician Kurt Gödel published two incompleteness theorems that logically proved that any formal system of mathematics will contain truths that cannot be proven from within that system. Through mathematics, Gödel gave us the limitations of mathematics and sent powerful shockwaves through the discipline. Others have said that mathematics sets the benchmark for what we think of as truth, and is the oldest "scientific tool in Western thinking", with "perhaps the greatest scientific authority", as long as we do not think about Gödel's theorems! (Chiodo, Bursill-Hall 2018).

For discussion

The nature and limits of mathematics

1. Where would you outline the scope of mathematics? Consider what happens outside its scope—think of phenomena you would say are beyond mathematics.

2. What evidence is there to suggest that there are some things that we will never be able to describe or explain mathematically?

3. Is mathematical description more accurate, are mathematical explanations more true and are mathematical predictions more certain than those of other AOKs?

I.1 Becoming conversant in the language of the universe

Consider this statement written by Galileo Galilei (1564–1642).

> [The universe] cannot be read until we have learnt the language and become familiar with the characters in which it is written. It is written in mathematical language, and the letters are triangles, circles and other geometrical figures, without which means it is humanly impossible to comprehend a single word.
>
> (Galileo 1632)

Many philosophers have agreed with, built on or scrutinized his words. "The Unreasonable Effectiveness of Mathematics in the Natural Sciences", an essay written by theoretical physicist and mathematician Eugene Wigner, echoes Galileo's vision of mathematics. Wigner wrote that it is a "miracle" that mathematical concepts lead to "amazingly accurate descriptions" of physical phenomena (Wigner 1960). He identified the following three miraculous coincidences.

- Mathematics explains the structure of the universe.
- There is an apparent deep structure to the universe.
- Human beings are capable of this mathematics.

> The enormous usefulness of mathematics in the natural sciences is something bordering on the mysterious, and there is no rational explanation for it. It is difficult to avoid the impression that a miracle confronts us here.
>
> (Wigner 1960)

Is it really as miraculous as Wigner suggests—could there be no rational explanation? He was in the company of Albert Einstein (1922), who also wondered, "how can it be that mathematics, being after all a product of human thought which is independent of experience, is so admirably appropriate to the objects of reality?".

↑ **Figure 11.1** Statue of Galileo Galilei in Florence, Italy

the "purest" of pure mathematics for having no real world value. Such examples concern not just mathematics' effectiveness, but also the tension between defining what is applied and what is abstract mathematics. On the one hand, G.H. Hardy has said that pure mathematics is "more useful than applied", because it trains mathematical technique so well (Hardy 1940). On the other hand, we have Lobachevsky's argument that there is no such thing as "abstract" mathematics, because all mathematics will someday be applied to the real world (Lobachevsky quoted in dePillis 2002).

A well-known critique of Wigner's argument, by mathematician Richard Hamming (1980), provides four "partial explanations" to argue that the effectiveness of mathematics in the natural sciences is neither miraculous nor unreasonable.

- **We see what we look for:** "much of what we see comes from the glasses we put on" wrote Hamming (1980). The examples we find arise from the mathematical tools used, in a self-referential logic.

- **We create the kind of mathematics we look for:** for example, in efforts to understand physical forces, physicists first tried scalars, then vectors, and finally invented tensors. And Newton's theory of gravity was replaced by the newer, better model of general relativity. Instead of a miraculous effectiveness, we see here trial and error.

- **Mathematics and natural science address only a part of human existence, answering comparatively few problems:** ethics, aesthetics and political philosophy, for example, are certainly not effectively explained by mathematics. Chapter 8 explores how mathematics may have been taken too far in the human sciences.

- **Evolution has primed humans to think mathematically:** our mathematical ability is not a coincidence, we have survived because of it. This argument is one of survival bias.

As evidence for this unreasonable, even miraculous, effectiveness of mathematics, philosophers have given examples of abstract conjectures that somehow become useful in real-world applications. For example, complex numbers were long considered to be irrelevant and removed from material reality, but now seem necessary to quantum mechanics.

The law of gravitation is another example; originally conceived to explain falling bodies on Earth, it was extended on the basis of "very scanty observations" to describe the motion of planets, where it "proved accurate beyond all reasonable expectations" (Wigner 1960). In the 1970s developments in cryptography (which you might know as the mathematics behind WhatsApp encryption technology and cryptocurrencies) drew on number theory, and the fundamental theorem of arithmetic, which had been considered for 200 years to be among

> There is only one thing which is more unreasonable than the unreasonable effectiveness of mathematics in physics, and this is the unreasonable ineffectiveness of mathematics in biology.
>
> (Gelfand quoted in Borovik 2018)

> Mathematics is biology's next microscope, only better; biology is mathematics' next physics, only better.
>
> (Cohen 2004)

Most of the early examples of this "unreasonable effectiveness" were applications of mathematics in physics. As the mathematician Israel Gelfand quips above, it would be misguided to claim that mathematics has been miraculously effective in other sciences. That said, Gelfand became one of the pioneers of biomathematics. Towards the end of the 20th century biologists were systematically and extensively applying complex mathematics in a variety of fields. If you have the interest, do some research on stochastic modelling of enzyme dynamics, swarm intelligence and spatial modelling of neural networks.

For discussion

What is mathematics about?

1. If mathematics is the language in which nature expresses itself, is it better described as a method in the natural sciences rather than a body of knowledge in itself—and why?

2. When considering knowing mathematics:

   (a) What evidence suggests there is more to mathematics than method?

   (b) Is knowing mathematics knowing how to perform mathematical calculations, or is there more to this body of knowledge?

Thus far, our discussion has entertained the possibility that mathematics is the language of the universe; and that through it we gain insights into the structure of the universe. The counter to this claim, suggested by Hamming and others, is that mathematics is only our way of describing and understanding the universe, that there is nothing inherently mathematical about the universe, or universal about mathematics.

The physicist Derek Abbott (2013) has suggested that the supposed "unreasonable effectiveness" of mathematics is an illusion influenced by human timescales; that we live and die so quickly that the universe appears to be governed by mathematical laws but may not actually be so.

This discourse about mathematics' "unreasonable effectiveness" raises two related questions: whether mathematics is discovered or invented, and whether a numerical sense is biologically versus culturally endowed.

Practising skills: Constructing knowledge claims

Use this exercise to note your intuitions about mathematics. Write an ending to the following sentence: "Mathematical knowledge is different from other types of knowledge in that …."

If you do this exercise as a class, collect everyone's completed sentences and discuss the range of views and beliefs. Then organize the sentences into sets of claims and counterclaims.

II. PERSPECTIVES

II.1 Was mathematics discovered or invented?

> 317 is a prime, not because we think so, or because our minds are shaped in one way rather than another, but *because it is*, because mathematical reality is built that way.
>
> (Hardy quoted in Tarlach 2014)

Is Hardy's perspective shaped by his cultural context, or is it universal? Below we explore claims about the origins of mathematics. Does it exist in the world outside of human experience, or is it a product of the human mind? We will learn to recognize the assumptions that accompany these claims, and explore the implications of these different perspectives towards mathematics.

> … many physical systems have mathematical representations: the segmented arrangements in sunflowers, pine cones and pineapples (Fibonacci numbers); the curve of nautilus shells, elephant tusks and rams horns (logarithmic spiral); … atoms, stars and galaxies, which all now have powerful mathematical descriptors; even the cosmos as a whole, now represented by the equations of general relativity …? Why does the real world actualise maths at all? … Most physicists still explain this by some form of philosophical Platonism, which in its oldest form says that the universe is moulded by mathematical relationships which precede the material world.
>
> (Wertheim 2017)

Mathematical realism asserts that mathematics exists independently of the human mind, that it is discovered, and not created, by humans. Platonism, a form of realism, holds that the universe is composed of abstract and eternal "mathematical entities". This has been among the most debated topics in the philosophy of mathematics. If you are a mathematical realist, the unreasonable effectiveness of mathematics might not seem that unreasonable after all, because the universe is "mathematical".

On the other hand, anti-realist perspectives argue that mathematical entities do not exist, and that mathematics is a language humans have invented to talk about quantity, structure, space and change. The philosopher Hugh Lehman famously described mathematics as a "theoretical juice extractor" that is useful for squeezing meaning out of things, but has no content in itself.

Others argue that these anti-realist perspectives, such as nominalism, might be appealing but do not quite make sense because the truths which are revealed to us through mathematics in fact existed long before humans started to understand them or had a language with which to describe them.

One of the compelling anti-realist arguments is based on the question of why humans are able to "know" abstract mathematics in the first place. How would we know the difference between mathematics created by the human mind and mathematics independent of it? Within TOK we need not solve these riddles. But anyone measuring, calculating and modelling real-world phenomena mathematically should be aware of the claims and assumptions about the nature of reality they rest on.

Ultimately, why does any of this matter? The examples we look at next suggest that these perspectives influence attitudes in the mathematics community and, therefore, the production of mathematical knowledge. Our perspectives are shaped by, and in turn shape, the mathematical community around us, and how mathematics interacts with the wider world. Therefore, it is worth examining the value of having a diversity of perspectives in mathematics.

If mathematics is an invention, who gets credit for it, and why do we teach it as if it were universal? If it is discovered, has it been discovered independently, through different methods, by various cultures throughout history? How have different peoples differently discovered mathematics?

For discussion

Was symmetry there before we found it?

Philosopher and mathematician James Franklin invites us to consider whether there were entities of mathematical nature at a time before humans thought about mathematics and had a language with which to describe it. (Franklin 2014). He quickly suggests that indeed there were many such properties, and symmetry is among the better examples. The approximate bilateral symmetry of animals and the circular symmetry of trees have been used as examples for the way mathematics manifests in the world independent of humans.

In this video, mathematician Marcus du Sautoy explores symmetry not in the imagined world before humans, but in mid-13th century Islamic geometric art.

 Search terms: Sautoy Symmetry, reality's riddle

Sautoy takes us to the Alhambra in Granada in the south of Spain. Watch the video and consider the questions below.

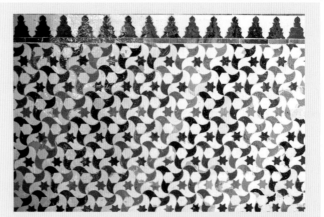

Today we know that the Moorish artists painted all 17 mathematically possible symmetries on the walls, ceilings and floors of the Alhambra. They did this six centuries before humans had proved that 17 is the maximum number of symmetries on a two-dimensional plane.

1. If two cultures arrive at a mathematical concept such as symmetry separately, using different methods, how does this affect your view of whether mathematics is discovered, as opposed to being invented?

2. What might be other explanations for the coincidence described in question 1?

3. Consider the patterns in the symmetries seen in the Alhambra.

    (a) In what sense are the patterns "real"?

    (b) What evidence is there for this?

Making connections

Knowledge in mathematics, art and religion

The example of Islamic geometrical art places mathematics at an intersection with AOK "The arts" and the theme "Knowledge and religion". How do artistic, religious and mathematical knowledge practices interact with one another in this example? What challenges or opportunities arise when they intersect?

II.2 Individuals and the mathematical community

The apparent timelessness of knowledge in mathematics may lead one to the assumption that mathematical knowledge is produced in a timeless way. In reality, the practice of mathematics is embedded in cultural contexts and has changed markedly over time.

In 18th-century Europe the idea of mathematics as the hidden language of the universe was widely accepted, and mathematicians fashioned themselves as "natural men" (Alexander 2010). Perspectives on mathematics shift, along with the norms and values of mathematical communities. Revealing this "hidden order" in the mathematical structure of reality may attract a particular kind of mathematician: someone able to grapple with abstract theories while grounded in the real world. These Enlightenment-era mathematicians were described as uncorrupted by the formalities, spectacles, rivalries and jealousies of society; and their contemporaries and biographers praised the "simplicity" and "purity" of their pursuit. These depictions, in turn, shaped social ideals and ideas about mathematics and mathematicians, with long-lasting effects.

In contrast, the perspective that mathematics is concerned with the relationships between abstract concepts may have attracted a very different personality. Historian of mathematics Amir Alexander examines how, at the beginning of the 19th century, the Enlightenment's "natural men" gave way to a new generation of mathematicians:

> mathematics ... was a wondrous alternative reality governed solely by the eternal laws of pure mathematics, unsullied by the crass realities of the world around us. Unlike their elders, the new mathematicians were not so much interested in acquiring new and useful results as they were focused on the internal architecture of mathematics itself, its interconnections, and the precise meaning of its statements. Mathematics, for them, was its own self-contained world and could be judged by mathematical standards alone.
>
> (Alexander 2010)

This perspective of mathematics, Alexander argues, has characterized the discipline since the beginning of the 19th century: it has "legitimized and allowed for a new type of mathematical knowledge: impractical, self-referential, irrelevant to worldly life, and judged only by its purity, its truth, and its beauty" (2010).

In TOK we often search for disagreements to shine a light on different perspectives. However, something about mathematics appears to make disagreements easier to resolve; we do not often hear of mathematical controversies. Could it be that mathematics has less scope for disagreement? Or that the practice of mathematics, or the community of mathematicians, is particularly effective in avoiding, silencing or resolving conflicting perspectives? Keep these questions in mind as you read through Box 11.1.

For discussion

The humans of mathematics

Many theorems and conjectures in mathematics carry the names of individuals.

1. Do individuals have an ability to make a disproportionate impact in the field of mathematics as compared to other disciplines?

2. How has the role and influence of individuals in mathematics changed over time?

3. Is the field of mathematics less or more collaborative compared to other disciplines?

4. Has mathematics been disproportionately shaped by particular cultures? If so, does it continue to be?

Box 11.1: A bitter dispute regarding human liberty and the infinitely small

Mathematical concepts can appear so stable, abstract and timeless that they seldom attract the attention of non-specialists or prompt social controversies. An important example to the contrary involves mathematical indivisibles, which were once at the heart of intellectual, political and religious life in 17th-century Europe. According to Alexander, the result of the controversy around them "helped open the way to a new and dynamic science, to religious toleration, and to political freedoms unknown in human history" (2014).

Why were mathematical indivisibles a matter of concern to political and religious authorities as well as to mathematicians and scientists? Let's first examine what we mean by an indivisible. Imagine a straight line that is composed of tiny little lines, so small that they cannot be divided. Perhaps you might have a billion little pieces on this line, in which case the size of each is 1 billionth of the big line. But dividing it into billions is arbitrary, you could divide it into two and then divide it into billions, in which case you would have two billion pieces. You could obviously divide the line in many different ways, and have different numbers of indivisibles. But could you arrive at an infinite number of indivisibles? It is a confounding question, because an infinite number of tiny pieces could be an infinitely long line. Could each little piece of the line have zero size? If so, how could they add up to a positive magnitude? This problem is more succinctly posed by Zeno's paradox.

Zeno's paradox and infinity

A tortoise challenges Achilles to a race, starting with a 10-metre head start. According to Zeno, logic dictates that Achilles can never catch up. By the time he has covered the 10 metres, the tortoise will have moved a tiny bit more, perhaps 4 centimetres. By the time Achilles covers those 4 centimetres, the tortoise will have advanced a little further, and so on, *ad infinitum*. Achilles is faced with an impossible

challenge: an infinite number of finite distances, thus an infinite number of times—which, argues Zeno, adds up to an infinite amount of time.

For a short video explanation of Zeno's paradox, visit this link.

 Search terms: Kelleher "What is Zeno's paradox?"

How do we reconcile this logic with our experience? Achilles obviously does catch up with the tortoise, but to solve the paradox we must know what is wrong with the argument, not just its conclusion.

If, as is widely believed, the problem lies in Zeno's claim that the sum of an infinite number of things is an infinite thing, then the solution is fairly straightforward: the calculus of convergent series shows us that the sum need not be infinite. Think about cutting a piece of string into infinitely small pieces of string: the sum of these is still finite, equivalent to the length of the original string.

↑ **Figure 11.2** Zeno's paradox asserted that Achilles could never catch up with the tortoise, because every time he got close, the tortoise moved a little further, in an infinite number of finite steps. An ancient Chinese paradox describes the same problem: "a one-foot stick, every day take away half of it, in a myriad ages it will not be exhausted" (Fraser 2017). The paradox is attributed to philosophers of the Mohism school between 500–200 BCE, around the same period that Zeno was active.

This set of problems has been known since at least the 6th century BCE. Nonetheless, classical mathematicians, with only few exceptions such as Archimedes, avoided the topic and its related techniques for about two millennia. Since the problems could not be explicated geometrically, they were outside the realm of "proper mathematics". The certainty provided by geometry was widely considered an ideal that all intellectual endeavours should strive for. Perhaps the ancient mathematicians did not want to ruin this reputation with paradoxes and riddles they could not solve. While other knowledge production efforts produced disputes, geometrical demonstration had for centuries built a base of seemingly incontestable knowledge.

> "It was not until the 1500s that a new generation of mathematicians rediscovered Archimedes's experiments with infinitesimals … Their boldness paid off, as the "method of indivisibles" revolutionized … early modern mathematics, making possible calculations of areas, volumes and slopes that were previously unattainable. … the method was formalized at the hands of Newton and Leibniz, and became the reliable algorithm that we call the "calculus," … the method of indivisibles, founded on the paradoxical doctrine of the infinitely small, became the foundation of all modern mathematics." (Alexander 2014)

In order for this new mathematics to come into being, the old order needed to shift, and there was resistance. By the mid-17th century, prominent intellectuals, and powerful political and religious figures from across Europe were organizing to invalidate infinitesimal techniques and eliminate this topic from the intellectual discourse.

"Why did the best minds of the early modern world fight so fiercely over the infinitely small? … The fight was over the face of the modern world. Two camps confronted each other over the infinitesimal. On the one side were ranged the forces of hierarchy and order—Jesuits, Hobbesians, French royal courtiers, and High Church Anglicans. They believed in a unified and fixed order in the world, both natural and human, and were fiercely opposed to infinitesimals. On the other side were comparative "liberalizers" such as Galileo, Wallis, and the Newtonians. They believed in a more pluralistic and flexible order, one that might accommodate a range of views and diverse centers of power, and championed infinitesimals and their use in mathematics." (Alexander 2014)

We leave this story about the clash over mathematics, Heaven and Earth here. Readers who are interested may wish to seek out Alexander's work to further explore how the "dangerous idea" of infinitesimals entered mathematics and prompted reflection about what it means to block and legitimize knowledge. Alexander makes claims about the effects of this clash on political and religious authority; claims that should be and are being evaluated by other historians.

For discussion

Mathematics on the public stage

During the dispute over indivisibles described above, mathematics enjoyed an unusually prominent place in public life. While that might be welcomed, the field of mathematics was also subject to external political pressures and religious influences. With this is mind, consider the following questions.

1. In mathematics, and other AOKs, is there a trade-off between the power of ideas and the autonomy of the field?

2. How does an overlap in subject matter between mathematics, politics and religion affect the practice of mathematics and the knowledge produced by it?

Infinitesimals show us what happens when the domains of knowledge, power and belief overlap. Chapter 2 explores the reasons why these domains have been kept separate. This chapter moves on to confront the difficulty of this separation, and to consider claims that mathematical knowledge is political and embedded in culture.

II.3 Is mathematics universal or culture-bound?

Since the early 1980s, the field of ethnomathematics has formed around explorations of the idea that mathematics is neither culture-free nor value-neutral. Researchers in this field hope to expand perspectives of mathematics to encompass the ideas of small-scale Indigenous societies that have been largely excluded from the practice and history of mathematics. For example, in one of the early ethnomathematics literature surveys, Marcia Ascher explores the mathematical traditions of a wide range of cultures and offers explanations of Navajo notions of space time, Warlpiri understanding of kinship relations, complex patterns in Malekula sand tracing and so on. We do not have the space to go over these examples in a way that befits their intellectual traditions. Instead we hope that you will take this as an invitation to explore the mathematics of other cultures. Below we offer ideas and questions to guide you in doing so.

For reflection

Mathematical ideas in different cultures

Many cultures do not isolate mathematics as a separate and specific activity or area of knowledge, and do not necessarily have something comparable to what we call mathematics. Mathematical ideas can be found in domains we would recognize as religious knowledge, art and design, games and stories, or navigation and orientation practices. How can we know when and whether other cultures are doing mathematics? Ethnomathematicians explore this question and the problems that arise from it. They take care to place mathematical ideas in the cultural contexts from which they arise, because isolating them can blind us to their depth.

Considering mathematical ideas that are embedded in cultures other than your own, reflect on the following questions.

1. What makes a culture's mathematical ideas mathematical? Is it that they conform to your understanding of mathematics and so you identify them as such, or is there something universal about them, or something else entirely?

2. How can we recognize and understand the mathematical ideas of other cultures if they do not have comparable formal mathematical practice?

 Search terms: Vijaya Nagarajan Kolam YouTube

The modern practice of mathematics has rarely acknowledged Indigenous mathematical traditions. One exception is the practice of kōlam. Kōlam, meaning "beauty" in the south Asian language Tamil, is the name of designs drawn in rice flour following a centuries-old tradition. Although kōlam patterns are a form of devotional art, they embody mathematical principles of symmetry and have been studied by mathematicians and computer scientists. Follow the link to find out more about this culturally embedded design tradition and how it has contributed to the field of mathematics from Vijaya R. Nagarajan, author of *Feeding a Thousand Souls: Women, Ritual and Ecology in India, an Exploration of the Kōlam.*

Examples of mathematics as artistic or religious practice, such as kōlam, draw attention to the possibility in mathematics of knowing by doing. This idea is explored further in III.5.

Is there a difference between understanding, doing and knowing mathematics? The writer Margaret Wertheim gives cross-cultural examples of mathematical know-how long before it was expressed as a formula. When reading the excerpt below, consider whether the people are doing mathematics. If mathematics is defined as something that has been or can be mathematically proven, the answer might have to be "no". To say "yes" would mean expanding the definition of mathematical knowledge and practice into the territories of cultural, religious and artistic traditions. Remember that this demarcation of knowledge into different territories (disciplines) is a relatively new, and far from universal, approach. What is lost and gained by doing so? Is there a case that mathematics transcends these boundaries more readily than other AOKs?

Wertheim writes that long before Europeans knew there were only 17 types of symmetry on a plane:

> … medieval mosaicists working with their hands using the Hasba method knew about them all. [They] also discovered aperiodic tiling, which is a way of filling a plane where the pattern never repeats. Western mathematicians discovered these tilings only in the 1960s, again after centuries of theorising that such patterns were impossible … .
>
> (Wertheim 2017)

Wertheim adds that African craftsman had discovered fractals centuries ago. "A wide variety of fractal patterns are incorporated into African textiles, hairstyling, metalwork, sculpture, painting and architecture" (Wertheim 2017). Follow the link to watch Ron Eglash's Ted Talk "The fractals at the heart of African designs".

 Search terms: Ron Eglash on African fractals

Mathematical practices can sometimes look strikingly different between cultures—but is all this cultural variation based on a universally shared mathematical ability? Early 20th-century theorists viewed Indigenous Peoples as incapable of sophisticated analytical thought or formal logical reasoning. Central to this prejudice was the question of whether all human minds and cultures are able to conceive of the concept of numbers. Over the past century, researchers have moved away from this line of thinking. Nevertheless, the question of numeracy remains complicated, as the case study below illustrates.

Making connections

Universality

The question of the universality of mathematical reasoning overlaps with the discussion about the universality of the human faculty of language in Chapter 4, and of the nature-nurture debate in Chapter 8. The assumptions made and the methods used to explore these questions in different disciplines meet in the case study below. As you read on, consider whether questions at the intersection of multiple disciplines benefit from or require an interdisciplinary approach.

Case study

Looking for numbers in the brain and in culture

To what extent is a number sense natural? The answer to this question has significant implications for how we think about human sameness and difference, and about the universality of mathematics. Further, *how* we answer this question reveals much about our understanding of human biology, cognition and evolution, and the scope and limitations of our knowledge in these areas, as well as the origins of special human capacities for music, art and language. This case study considers the arguments of neuroscientists and cognitive scientists, as presented by the writer Philip Ball. Many of his arguments are quoted below, but follow the link to read the full article.

 Search terms: Philip Ball "Why do humans have numbers?"

> Scientists have long claimed that our ability with numbers is indeed biologically evolved—that we can count because counting was a useful thing for our brains to be able to do … .
>
> (Ball 2017)

Indeed, other animals have demonstrated an ability to differentiate between small quantities of things. Perhaps it is a biological gift. But a number of cognitive scientists argue that this "number sense" is actually a product of culture. Ball sums up as follows.

> I'd argue that, while there's a biological grounding, language and cultural traits are necessary for the establishment of number itself'.
>
> (Ball 2017)

Many animals have a quantitative sense, for example being able to distinguish which bundle of food is bigger, and it appears innate to humans.

> Studies with newborns and infants show that, if you show them eight dots repeatedly and then change it to 16 dots, areas in the right parietal cortex of the brain respond to a change in numerosity. This response is very similar in adults.
>
> (Ansari quoted in Ball 2017)

This has led some researchers to theorize that a numerical sense is innate.

Others, such as Rafael Núñez, argue that the argument of a biologically endowed number sense is based on sketchy science: inaccurate understanding of biological evolution, over-emphasis on WEIRD population samples (as discussed in Chapter 8) and overinterpretation of results from trained animals. We must also note the difference between quantical and numerical cognition: quantical relates to how many apples there are in a basket, or how many dots on a board, whereas numerical cognition deals with symbols such as 3, 4 and 5.

> Just because a behaviour seems to derive from an innate capacity, that doesn't mean the behaviour is itself innate. … No non-human animal has yet been found able to distinguish 152 items from 153. Chimps can't do that, no matter how hard you train them, yet many children can tell you even by the age of five that the two numbers differ in the same way as do the equally abstract numbers 2 and 3: namely, by 1 … .
>
> (Núñez quoted in Ball 2017)

Other researchers do not accept that numerical cognition is a culturally derived ability. Neurobiologist Andreas Nieder, for example, argues that the brain is "predisposed to acquire a number system" that culture can further shape and refine. But without this biological capacity, humans would never have a number ability (Nieder quoted in Ball 2017).

In Chapter 8 we encounter the idea of natureculture, an argument that nature and culture are so tightly connected in ecological relationships that we are better off not separating them. If we accept Núñez's argument for the moment, that quantical cognition cannot evolve into numerical cognition without the influence of culture, what evidence do we have? Núñez suggests that many cultures around the world have no words or symbols for numbers larger than five or six. Instead, words equivalent to "many" are used.

> In the language of the Munduruku people of the Amazon, for example, *adesu* indicates 'several' whereas *ade* implies 'really lots'. These cultures live with what to us looks like imprecision: it really doesn't matter if, when the oranges are divided up, one person gets 152 and the other 153. And frankly, if we aren't so number-fixated, it really *doesn't* matter. So why bother having words to distinguish them?
>
> (Ball 2017)

Small differences between large numbers clearly matter for many technological and scientific applications. However, one argument is that humans' innate quantical sense is logarithmic: the difference between one and two is much greater than between five and six, and for most activities in the human era, this was sufficient.

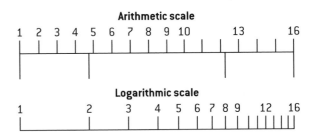

↑ **Figure 11.3** Arithmetic and logarithmic scales

II. Perspectives

The cognitive neuroscientist Stanislas Dehaene has suggested that while Western adults and children generally use an evenly spaced number line, the Munduruku use a logarithmic scale. The researchers speculate that children who learn to space numbers arithmetically must first overcome innate logarithmic intuitions. However, there is an inescapable irony in Western scientists attempting to precisely quantify the imprecise mapping of quantities by a small group of Indigenous People doing puzzles. The researchers have noted that the variability in their results is too great to allow for strong conclusions.

Thinking about outcomes from the replication crisis, to what extent would you generalize claims about humans having a logarithmic quantical sense?

> It's easy to read this as a 'primitive' way of reasoning, but anthropology has long dispelled such patronising prejudice … . You develop words and concepts for what truly matters to your society. From a practical perspective, one could argue that it's actually the somewhat homogeneous group of industrialised cultures that look odd, with their pedantic distinction between 1,000,002 and 1,000,003.
>
> (Ball 2017)

To further complicate matters, there is evidence that the two systems—quantical and numerical—are processed differently in the brain, and therefore appear to be uncorrelated. This challenges the idea that the quantical system evolved into a numerical system.

How does this matter for knowledge? The implications influence mathematics education, for example. Researchers at the Johns Hopkins University showed a correlation between 14-year-olds' ability to discriminate between exact numerical quantities (such as the number of dots in an image) and their test scores in mathematics all the way back to kindergarten (Halberda et al 2008). The correlation has been used to develop educational tools to assess and improve mathematical ability, for example in tests that ask children to quickly assess how many dots are on a page.

Could language be the origin of our numerical sense, and of mathematics? Did we begin counting when we could name numbers?

> Language in itself may be a necessary condition for number, but it is not sufficient for it … . All known human cultures have language, but by no means all have exact quantification in the form of number.
>
> (Núñez quoted in Ball 2017)

II.4 Diversity and many mathematics

The mathematician Morris Kline has written condescendingly that "compared with the accomplishments of their immediate successors, the Greeks, the mathematics of the Egyptians and Babylonians is the scrawling of children just learning to write as opposed to great literature" (Kline 1985).

The attitudes expressed in this quote have been strongly criticized and encouraged the decolonization effort in mathematics. Kline's comment echoes the same myths encountered elsewhere—in history and the human and natural sciences—that non-Western cultures and intellectual traditions lag behind.

Mathematics is a curious and challenging case in the wider movement for educational equity and decolonizing education. Energized debates have arisen in at least two areas. One is how the history of mathematics is told and taught. The second tackles the persistent belief that mathematics is neutral from the point of race, class and gender. This has been the site of significant debate and controversy, such as the #IStandWithRochelle movement in late 2017.

↑ **Figure 11.4** A section of the Rhind papyrus, a 5-metre-long Egyptian scroll dated 1550 BCE. The Rhind papyrus contains arithmetic and geometry, and specifically outlines a method for approximating the value of π to within 1% accuracy.

Professor of mathematics education, Rochelle Gutiérrez delivered a talk on "mathematx", referring to a mathematics reimagined in both of the following ways.

- It is aware of the current dominance of eurocentric ideas in the field.
- It actively seeks to incorporate Indigenous knowledges into the teaching and practice of mathematics.

Gutiérrez has a fundamentally political outlook on the field of mathematics. She maintains that in order for students and professionals to bring their full selves to their work and learning, they need to take steps towards "rehumanizing" mathematics. She explains these steps in a 10-minute segment (16:15–25:55) from the talk, at this link.

 Search terms: Gutiérrez: Rehumanizing mathematics: a vision for the future YouTube

When Gutiérrez's claims, such as "on many levels, mathematics itself operates as whiteness" (Gutiérrez 2018) were noticed online, she became a target of hate mail, threats, and racist and misogynist attacks. Academic colleagues and professional organizations responded by issuing statements condemning the attacks and expressing solidarity with Gutiérrez. The claim that mathematics is inevitably entangled with power and politics had provoked a strong reaction.

#IStandWithRochelle was embedded in the context of the United States, but we can generalize the question about why identity and mathematics appear entangled in this cultural moment. Stereotypes about certain genders, ethnicities and cultures being good or bad at mathematics are still widespread.

Depending on your background and location, the issue of identity in the practice and teaching of mathematics may not be urgent for you. But the assumptions of the neutrality of mathematical knowledge and practice is political. To what extent is the claim that mathematics is neutral a denial of its potential

II. Perspectives

to perpetuate inequality or injustice? Does the neutrality assumption limit our ability to address problems with mathematics and to improve it? We revisit this question in section IV. Ultimately, do educators have a responsibility to teach an anti-discriminatory mathematics education, rather than merely a non-discriminatory one?

For discussion

Decolonizing mathematics

 Search terms: Brodie The Conversation Decolonised mathematics

Follow the link to the article "Yes, Mathematics can be Decolonised. Here's How to Begin", by mathematics education professor Karin Brodie, where she offers the following thoughts.

"Mathematics has a problem with diversity. All over the world, black and women mathematicians remain rare. They simply don't take mathematics at higher academic levels as much as their white and male peers. … But maths should and does belong to everybody. Everybody deserves access to its beauty and its power—and everybody should be able to push back when the discipline is used to destroy and oppress." (Brodie 2016)

Brodie suggests that students' identities are important in teaching and learning mathematics. Consider her article and what we have covered so far in this section as you discuss the following questions.

1. What role does identity play in the acquisition and transfer of mathematical knowledge?

2. How is the role of identity that you identified in question 1 similar to or different from the role of identity in other AOKs?

The Fields Medal, established in 1924, has only been awarded to a woman once, in 2014. Her name is Mariyam Mirzakhani, and you can follow the link to learn more about her and her work.

 Search terms: Wired.com Mirzakhani Fields Medal

Claims that the profession and teaching of mathematics are gendered and racialized are still being debated. Meanwhile, teachers in mathematics classrooms find that students can feel supported when the diversity of mathematicians studied in the curriculum reflects the diversity in the classroom, and when they can see themselves reflected in it. The movie *Hidden Figures* (2016), which tells the story of African-American female mathematicians—or as they were called at the time, calculators—at NASA during the Space Race and the racial segregation era, was well received by popular culture.

↑ **Figure 11.5** Iranian-American mathematician Mariyam Mirzakhani, the only woman to be awarded the Fields Medal

III. METHODS AND TOOLS

III.1 Once proven: The eternal truth of mathematics

In TOK we regularly engage with the concepts of certainty, truth and objectivity. Mathematics, it is claimed, has a special relationship with these concepts, being able to achieve them through the pursuit of mathematical proof. A proof is true only if it is always true. This standard of rigour and certainty, arrived at through reasoning detached from empirical arguments, is often said to be a hallmark of mathematics.

Mathematical proofs are built using logical inferences from theorems, which are previously proven conjectures, and axioms, which are either self-evident or assumed statements used as the starting point. The obvious "weak spot", if there is one, in mathematical proof is in the axioms used.

For discussion

A closer look at axioms

1. Consid mathematical axioms.

    (a) On what basis can axioms be chosen?

    (b) Who chooses axioms, using what criteria?

2. Is all of mathematics predicated on our predecessors' choice of axioms?

3. If our predecessors had chosen a different set of axioms, would we have a different mathematics today?

4. Do mathematical realists and anti-realists have different answers to question 3?

5. **(a)** Do mathematicians have faith in axioms?

    (b) To what extent does faith play a role in mathematics?

If all the steps in the proof are logically sound, it becomes a theorem. Mathematical proof is different from the evidence-based proof in law, for example, in that once proven a theorem is conclusive and final. The mathematical community then checks the steps and judges the completeness, accuracy and originality of the proof. That last point is important: for all the rigour and certainty attributed to mathematical proofs, theorems are verified in a social process that is not infallible.

> When mathematicians prove theorems . . . . The correctness of the arguments is determined by the scrutiny of other mathematicians, in informal discussions, in lectures, or in journals … the means by which mathematical results are verified is essentially a social process and is thus fallible.
>
> … [T]he history of mathematics has many stories about false results that went undetected for a long time. In addition, … important theorems have required such long and complicated proofs that very few people have the time, energy and necessary background to check through them. And some proofs contain extensive computer code to, for example, check a lot of cases that would be infeasible to check by hand. How can mathematicians be sure that such proofs are reliable? To get around these problems, computer scientists and mathematicians began to develop the field of formal proof. A formal proof is one in which every logical inference has been checked all the way back to the fundamental axioms of mathematics. … [S]uch proofs are so long and cumbersome that it would be impossible to have them checked by human mathematicians. But now one can get "computer proof assistants" to do the checking.
>
> (American Mathematical Society 2008)

In this next section we examine how the use of computers is affecting mathematics.

Let's consider two contrasting claims about mathematical truth. The first, by Avigad (2018), asserts that "the truth of a mathematical statement does not rely on historical context or the circumstances of the speaker". On the other hand, Levy-Eichel argues that mathematics has no timeless standard, despite what many assume today, as the standard of rigour in mathematical proof has changed throughout history. The advent of computer proof assistants and automated theorem provers, as discussed below, has already begun to change what is meant by mathematical rigour and proof.

Practising skills: Evaluating claims

Consider the claim that consensus on a proof in mathematics forms uncontroversially.

1. What argument can you offer to support this claim?

2. How would you construct and support a counterclaim?

Consider how reaching consensus in mathematics compares to the process of reaching consensus in other AOKs.

3. What are significant similarities and differences between consensus in mathematics and in one other AOK of your choice?

4. What can you say about the sources of these similarities and differences?

For reflection

A mathematical "je ne sais quoi"

John von Neumann stated the following.

"The very concept of 'absolute' mathematical rigour is not immutable. The variability of the concept of rigour shows that something else besides mathematical abstraction must enter into the makeup of mathematics." (von Neumann 1947)

What could be this "something else" that von Neumann refers to?

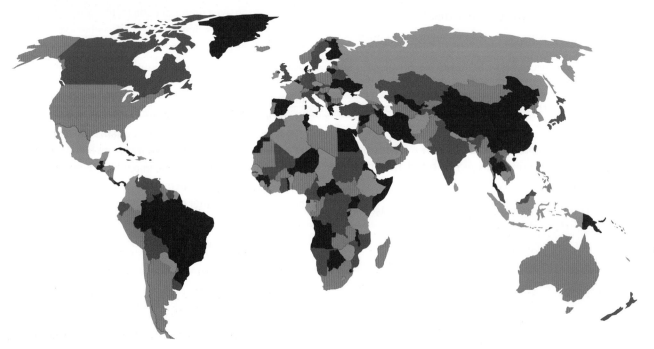

↑ **Figure 11.6** The four-colour theorem. The four-colour theorem states that only four colours are required on a map so that no two adjacent regions have the same colour. It was the first major theorem proved using computer assistance, in 1976 by Kenneth Appel and Wolfgang Hakenand, but was not accepted by all mathematicians as no individual human could check it. New forms of the proof (all of which have used computer assistance in some form) have been easier for humans to verify.

III.1.1 Mathematical proof in the digital age

How will advances in computing affect mathematics? To answer this question we need to have a grasp on what mathematics is, and more precisely, what mathematicians do, and how computational power fits with that. We mentioned that formal proofs can be particularly long, even impossible, for a mathematician to verify, so computer proof assistants have become useful.

Mathematicians have used computers not just to verify but to generate proofs for some time. The four-colour theorem completed in 1976 (Figure 11.6) was the first such proof. It was so complicated that no human being could verify it without having to trust the software. Another example is the 1998 proof of the Kepler conjecture, which contained over 3 gigabytes of data. "Proof by exhaustion" is a term given to proofs where a computer has checked all possible cases. Proofs of this nature are considered problematic because they can't be verified by a single person—some people disregard them on this basis, but others accept them.

Automated theorem provers (ATPs) are programs that can prove mathematical results logically using a set of axioms. ATPs can also run millions of simulations in mission-critical applications, such as in nuclear power plants, to ensure a system is working properly—a task that would prove extremely time-consuming for human beings. ATPs are changing how we see mathematics. Yet computers solve differently from humans, who look for graceful connections between possibilities. Computer proofs can be clumsy and awkward—as long as they find a proof, they have done their job.

Perhaps these are just the problems associated with a new technology; perhaps mathematicians and computer scientists may eventually be able to code ATPs to deliver beautiful proofs that reveal new insights to their human developers. Or perhaps not: whether software is capable of the feats of intuition and imagination that characterize the best examples of human mathematics is an open question. Regardless of whether ATPs will be able to match or exceed their human counterparts, the pursuit of developing them is deepening our understanding of what it means, and takes, to make a mathematical proof.

> "It is also possible to let computers loose to explore mathematics on their own, and in some cases they have come up with interesting conjectures that went unnoticed by mathematicians. We may be close to seeing how computers, rather than humans, would do mathematics.
>
> (American Mathematical Society 2008)"

A common fear is, of course, that once software is good enough at proving results, and in deciding which results to prove, human mathematicians will become irrelevant. How would you decide if this fear is misguided or valid?

III.1.2 Non-surveyable proof

> "Suppose some supercomputer … reported a proof … which was so long and complex that no mathematician could understand it beyond the most general terms. Could we have sufficient faith in computers to accept this result, or would we say that the empirical evidence for their reliability is not enough?
>
> (Tymoczko 1979)"

Thomas Tymoczko coined the term "non-surveyable proof" to describe proofs that are infeasible for a human mathematician to verify, such as the 1979 computer-assisted proof by Appel and Haken of the four-colour theorem. Tymoczko argued that mathematical proofs must meet three criteria.

- Convincingness: the proof can persuade a rational verifier of its conclusion.
- Surveyability: the proof is accessible for verification by humans.
- Formalizability: the proof uses only logical relationships between concepts.

Computer-assisted proofs were criticized as non-surveyable, requiring too many logical steps to be verifiable by humans. Tymoczko argued that such proofs were changing the nature of mathematical proof, replacing logical deduction with trust in an *empirical* computational process. Accepting the four-colour theorem, for instance, requires changing our understanding of "theorem" and "proof".

A non-surveyable or difficult-to-survey proof may be convincing and yet fail to enlighten the reader as to why it is true; serving not as a mathematical argument but as an observation, and this exposes mathematics to a much higher potential for error.

How do mathematicians decide whether a proof is surveyable or not? Paul Teller (1980) argues that this is contingent on time and place, on the abilities and tools of the community of mathematicians attempting to verify it. It is a social process contingent on the mathematical community. Surveyability may not be an inherent quality of a proof, but more a reflection of the mathematicians of the time.

Box 11.2: "In computers we trust?"

Follow the link to this article about Doron Zeilberger, a mathematician at Rutgers University.

 Search terms: Quanta Magazine In computers we trust?

Consider the following question.

1. Do you agree that computer programs should be credited as authors when they prove, or help prove, a mathematical theorem?

Hales is certainly not the last to have encountered this problem. Shinichi Mochizuki submitted a 500-page proof of the ABC conjecture in 2012, but as of 2020 no one has been able to verify whether it is correct.

2. For something to count as mathematical knowledge, should humans be able to understand it, or is proof by computer enough?

For reflection

Overcoming the limitations of mathematics

Refer to section I for a reminder of Gödel's incompleteness theorem, then consider these questions.

1. Do you think that in the future ATPs could overcome the theorem?

2. What would need to happen for ATPs to overcome the theorem?

Beyond mathematical proofs, technology is also allowing mathematicians to collaborate in real time on online platforms, solving-problems together and verifying their colleagues' work. But it is the potential of computer mathematicians, working alongside or for their human colleagues, that most excites many observers, and prompts particularly meaningful TOK questions.

For example, what are mathematical proofs for? There is value in both knowing that something is true as well as in how it was solved. The best proofs reveal deeper insights into mathematics, explaining "why" things are true. What would it mean to have proofs done by computer that no human being could understand? What would we lose and gain?

Making connections

Exploring the question of intent

Chapter 10 reports that artificial intelligence has already, in a very short period of time, succeeded in producing music and poetry that appeals to human tastes. In the arts the question of intent is inseparable from aesthetics and metaphysics—we cannot yet escape the doubt about whether software "intends" to make art. To what extent does this concern of intent apply in the case of ATPs producing "elegant" mathematics?

III.2 Beauty

> Why are numbers beautiful? It's like asking why is Beethoven's Ninth Symphony beautiful. If you don't see why, someone can't tell you. I know numbers are beautiful. If they aren't beautiful, nothing is.
>
> (Devlin 2000)

Philosophers of mathematics have sometimes commented that mathematical aesthetics are vaguely stated. What makes a proof beautiful, or elegant, especially in comparison to another that is also logically true? At the same time, to what extent is beauty any more or less tightly defined in the other AOKs, and should we expect mathematics to be different?

Mathematical beauty is subjective and mathematicians do not always agree, but many will know a beautiful proof or result when they see it. Nahin (2006) elaborates as follows.

> Like a Shakespearean sonnet that captures the very essence of love, or a painting that brings out the beauty of the human form that is far more than just skin deep, Euler's equation reaches down into the very depths of existence.
>
> (Nahin 2006)

Euler's formula ($e^{i\pi} + 1 = 0$) is cited as an example of deep mathematical beauty. Feynman (1977) called it "our jewel" and "the most remarkable formula in mathematics". It contains three of the basic arithmetic operations, each occurring exactly once, and links together five fundamental mathematical constants: 0, 1, π, e and i. e, π and i are complicated and seemingly unrelated numbers, so some mathematicians have remarked that it is "amazing that they are linked by this concise formula" (Percy quoted in Gallagher 2014).

Researchers in 2014 used functional magnetic resonance imaging (fMRI) to observe the activity in the brains of 15 mathematicians when they viewed mathematical formulae they had individually rated as beautiful, indifferent or ugly. The experiment showed that experiencing mathematical beauty correlates with emotional activity in the brain in the same way as the experience of beauty from other sources (Zeki *et al* 2014). Davis and Hersh have commented that an aesthetic sense is universal among practising mathematicians. But to what extent is mathematical beauty accessible only to mathematicians?

Deep beauty is said to refer to a result or method that contains unexpected insights into mathematical structures. Trivial theorems lack beauty, as do proofs or results derived in an obvious or repetitive way, or which apply only to special cases. Hardy (1940) suggested that beauty comes from the "inevitability", "unexpectedness" and "economy" of a work. He also argued that pure mathematics is inherently superior in beauty to applied mathematics because it cannot be used for common or violent human ambitions. Elegance and beauty have been ascribed to proofs that are unusually succinct, based on original insight, have an element of surprise, use a minimum of assumptions and can be generalized to solve similar problems.

The applications of mathematics to science, technology and engineering are widely discussed, but there is also a dimension of mathematics as joy, as art and as literature. Scheinerman, for example, has compiled "joyful, beautiful" theorems and proofs in *The Mathematics Lover's Companion* (2017), arrived at "through the sweat of intellectual play that, like the best poems, contain perfectly expressed truths about the world" (Levy-Eichel 2018).

For reflection

No truth without beauty, no beauty without truth?

Consider the role of beauty for the truth in mathematics as well as the arts.

"Mathematics, rightly viewed, possesses not only truth, but supreme beauty—a beauty cold and austere, like that of sculpture, without appeal to any part of our weaker nature, without the gorgeous trappings of painting or music, yet sublimely pure, and capable of a stern perfection such as only the greatest art can show. The true spirit of delight, the exaltation, the sense of being more than Man, which is the touchstone of the highest excellence, is to be found in mathematics as surely as poetry." (Russell 1919)

1. What role does beauty play in relation to truth in mathematics?

2. In the quote below, Bertrand Russell describes the "cold and austere" beauty of mathematics.

   (a) Do you agree with this description, and if so why?

   (b) If you do not agree with Russell's description, how would you describe mathematical beauty?

III.3 How should mathematics be taught and communicated?

In *A Mathematician's Lament* (2009) Paul Lockhart, a school teacher, expresses deep disappointment that mathematics is often taught in a way that fails to reveal the excitement, beauty and passion that drives mathematicians. Read the excerpt below to explore how beauty and aesthetic taste relate to the teaching and learning of mathematics. As you read, reflect on whether this has been a part of your own experience of learning mathematics.

> At no time are students let in on the secret that mathematics, like any literature, is created by human beings for their own amusement; that works of mathematics are subject to critical appraisal; that one can have and develop mathematical taste. A piece of mathematics is like a poem, and we can ask if it satisfies our aesthetic criteria: ... Is it simple and elegant? Does it get me closer to the heart of the matter? ...
>
> People ... think they do know what math is about—and are apparently under the gross misconception that mathematics is somehow useful to society! ... Mathematics is viewed by the culture as some sort of tool for science and technology. Everyone knows that poetry and music are for pure enjoyment and for uplifting and ennobling the human spirit ... but no, math is important.
>
> (Lockhart 2009)

Lockhart inspires questions relevant to us in TOK, such as to what extent does the process of learning mathematics leave space for learners to reach their own conclusions? The bar for contributions to the field of mathematics seems very high; indeed, for the overwhelming majority of learners the journey of mathematics ends well before they contribute or even encounter advances in the field. For the few who reach the frontier of mathematics, the knowledge produced there is seldom popularized or widely communicated.

Mathematics PhD theses are not usually the kind of content to go viral on the internet, but Piper Harron's came close to internet fame. Harron felt that mathematics was too important to go misunderstood or remain incomprehensible to most. Her doctoral thesis, entitled "The Equidistribution of Lattice Shapes of Rings of Integers of Cubic, Quartic, and Quintic Number Fields: An Artist's Rendering" is presented at different levels. The first level is a "layscape" with "laysplanations", using language appropriate and understandable to the layperson or student of mathematics. Next, Harron presents the "mathscape" and "mathsplanations", for the amateur mathematician or peers in the professional mathematics community. She invites readers to follow the arguments up to their mathematical threshold, and you can try to find yours by following the link.

 Search terms: Equidistance of lattice shapes Piper thesis

In principle, her full argument should be possible to grasp at either level, and the thesis is intended to be "approximately readable by approximately anyone" (Harron 2016).

In an interview published in *The Hindu* (Desikan 2016) Harron identifies the idea of the genius mathematician as one of the harmful myths perpetuated in the mathematics community, and calls for it to be discarded. "There's the idea that math is fixed, you get it or you don't; that there's a right way to think about things. … We need more different people in math. We need different ways of thinking in math" (Harron quoted in Desikan 2016).

Box 11.3 explores two conceptions of, and two possibilities regarding, the acquisition of mathematical knowledge.

Box 11.3: The "maths brain" and mathematical fluency

Mathematics is one of the areas of knowledge in which students commonly hold limiting beliefs about their ability. Teachers can challenge these beliefs or create and reinforce them. Below are two articles relevant to this issue of knowledge acquisition in mathematics.

Source 1, by professor of mathematics education Jo Boaler, explores how discoveries from neuroscience should reshape the teaching and learning of mathematics. Boaler approaches mathematics less as a matter of right answers and proven methods, and more as an exercise that achieves understanding through collaboration and creativity. Follow the link to read the article in full.

Source 1: Boaler, J. 2019. "Everyone Can Learn Mathematics to High Levels: the Evidence from Neuroscience that Should Change our Teaching" (American Mathematical Society Blogs)

 Search terms: AMS Boaler Everyone can learn mathematics to high levels

Source 2, by Barbara Oakley, presents a different but related vision of mathematics, one that moves away from understanding, whether arrived at creatively or through rote learning. Oakley instead explores the idea of fluency in mathematics, in line with the conception of mathematics as a language. Oakley believes that mathematics is a habit of mind, a pattern of thinking that is developed through sustained practice. In Oakley's view, mathematical knowledge is closer to know-how than to know-that. Follow the link to read the details.

Source 2: Oakley, B. 2016. "How I Rewired my Brain to Become Fluent in Math" (*Nautilus*, 15 September 2016)

 Search terms: Oakley How I rewired my brain Nautilus

What we think mathematics *is* affects how we teach and learn it. It affects what access and barriers to mathematics learning looks like, and what it means to fail and succeed in acquiring knowledge in this AOK.

III.4 In what ways can mathematics be known?

Knowing mathematics is commonly understood as the ability to reason through mathematical formulae and symbols. Is it possible to know mathematics in other ways, not as language or representation but as activity or performance—mathematics as know-how? Examples from ethnomathematics show that the mind is not our only channel into the realm of mathematics, but that it can be "known" through the whole body as an embodied practice, and even through the arrangement of other objects in the physical world. If we can do and find mathematics outside of the human mind, how far can we go looking for mathematics?

> Sea slugs do maths, electrons do maths, minerals do maths. Rainbows do an incredible mathematical performance … Next time you see a good rainbow, stop and take a look … classical geometric optics doesn't begin to capture its complexity. A stunning piece of mathematical performance is enacted by a peregrine falcon as it hurtles towards its prey; with its head held straight so it can fix one eye steadily on the quarry at a constant angle of 40 degrees, it swoops down at 200 mph in a perfect logarithmic spiral. Leonhard Euler's 18th-century formula, with its unique mathematical properties, is enacted here by a bird.
>
> (Wertheim 2017)

Follow the link to read the full article: "How to Play Mathematics".

 Search terms: Aeon There's more maths in slugs

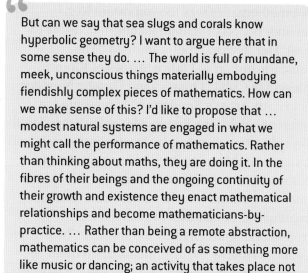

↑ **Figure 11.7** Sea slug

> But can we say that sea slugs and corals know hyperbolic geometry? I want to argue here that in some sense they do. … The world is full of mundane, meek, unconscious things materially embodying fiendishly complex pieces of mathematics. How can we make sense of this? I'd like to propose that … modest natural systems are engaged in what we might call the performance of mathematics. Rather than thinking about maths, they are doing it. In the fibres of their beings and the ongoing continuity of their growth and existence they enact mathematical relationships and become mathematicians-by-practice. … Rather than being a remote abstraction, mathematics can be conceived of as something more like music or dancing; an activity that takes place not so much in the writing down as in the playing out.
>
> (Wertheim 2017)

How do these creatures challenge what it means to "know" mathematics? Wertheim likens mathematics to music; the intersection of the two disciplines has a comprehensive discourse in itself, across many different cultural traditions. The ragas of Indian classical music, for example, traditionally passed down aurally from master to student, are recognized as inherently mathematical. The Sanskrit word *prastara* means the study of mathematically arranging ragas and rhythms into pleasing compositions.

For discussion

Language, reading and writing

1. What is the difference between treating mathematics as a language versus treating it as an activity?

2. (a) Do you have to know how to write mathematics to do mathematics?

   (b) To what extent is this the case in the other AOKs?

3. To what extent is playing music without being able to read music comparable to doing mathematics without being able to read mathematics?

Hyperbolic geometry was dismissed for hundreds of years as impossible, because it violates Euclid's axiom about parallel lines. It was also extremely difficult to visualize or model, even using computers. Daina Taimina began using crochet to construct tangible 3D models that made it easier to comprehend. If you are curious about tactile mathematics and hyperbolic crochet, you can follow the link to find out more.

 Search terms: Crocheting hyperbolic planes YouTube

With crochet models, ragas and sea slugs in mind, we should ask to what extent mathematics can be embodied knowledge. Wertheim describes it as a knowing that emerges from hands performing mathematics, a kind of embodied figuring—but would schools and teachers hesitate to use crochet in advanced mathematics classes? Do algebraic equations feel more or less valid as a teaching tool? Is that feeling derived from a particular cultural context?

III.5 Doing impossible mathematics

The shape shown in Figure 11.8 consists of 4 regular dodecagons and 12 decagons, with 28 little gaps in the shape of equilateral triangles. However, it is also an impossible shape, with polygons that will not meet at the edges. It should not be able to close, but it works because of very slight warping of the paper.

> ❝ The fudge factor that arises just from working in the real world with paper means that things that ought to be impossible actually aren't.
>
> (Kaplan quoted in Lamb 2017) ❞

This category of almost perfect mathematics is called near-miss mathematics. There is no precise definition of a near miss, but Craig Kaplan's belief is that the mathematical error is comparable to practical errors arising from using "real-world materials and your imperfect hands" (Kaplan quoted in Lamb 2017).

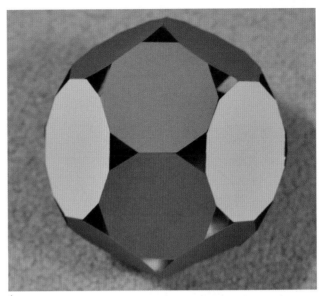

↑ **Figure 11.8** A mathematically impossible shape, made possible only because of imperceptible warping of the paper

Another example of near-miss mathematics is the missing-square puzzle (see Figure 11.9). Triangle A is cut into four pieces and arranged into triangle B, but suddenly a gap appears. How can this be? It is another near miss: the triangles are not actually triangles, as the hypotenuse is not a straight line—the gradient changes from 0.4 (blue hypotenuse) to 0.375 (red hypotenuse). To what extent do near misses diminish or add to our knowledge about mathematics? Is there value in practical, but impossible, mathematics that cannot be gained from abstract mathematics?

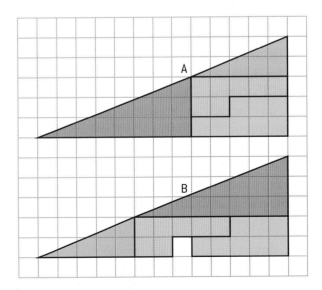

↑ **Figure 11.9** The missing-square puzzle

Box 11.4: D'oh! That time Homer Simpson nearly solved Fermat's last theorem

The writers of *The Simpsons* television series sometimes communicate with their mathematically-inclined viewers by casually dropping near misses into the background of scenes. In the episode "The Wizard of Evergreen Terrace", Homer Simpson writes out the equation

$$3987^{12} + 4365^{12} = 4472^{12}$$

which violates the theorem that $a^n + b^n = c^n$ has no integer solution if $n > 2$. Viewers who checked the equation on their calculators may have been shocked to find that Homer Simpson had disproved Fermat's last theorem! In fact, most calculators are not precise enough to show the left side of the equation:

$$3{,}987^{12} + 4{,}365^{12} = 4{,}472.00000000070576171875^{12}$$

which is a very near-miss. Fermat's last theorem is safe.

The writers of *The Simpsons* are known for including references to advanced mathematics in the show. Simon Singh, author of *Fermat's Enigma* (1998) and *The Simpsons and Their Mathematical Secrets* (2013), explains further in the linked video.

 Search terms: Homer's last theorem YouTube

Near-miss mathematics is more than a curiosity or basis for practical jokes. The reason pianos have 12 keys in an octave, for example, is due to a near miss. The two most important musical intervals are an octave (a frequency ratio of 2:1) and a fifth (a ratio of 3:2), but it is impossible to divide an octave in a way that ensures all the fifths will be perfect. It is mathematically impossible to reconcile the different frequencies (tones) of octaves and fifths. "But you can get very close by dividing the octave into 12 equal half-steps, seven of which give you a frequency ratio of 1.498. That's good enough for most people" (Lamb 2017).

Consider also the Ramanujan constant: $e^{\pi \sqrt{163}}$, which almost equals a whole number:

262,537,412,640,768,743.99999999999925. How do three irrational numbers combine to form a rational number? Could it be a clue to a deeper piece of mathematics? The mathematician John Baez, among others, thinks so.

Near misses have inspired practical applications as well as curiosity in mathematicians to look closer and dig deeper. They can serve as clues about what discoveries might be true, by being almost true. Mathematicians discover near misses through experimentation, play, real-world imperfections, and trial and error—words that are not typically associated with mathematical methods.

Practising skills: Exploring perspectives

Consider one or more of the statements below, drawn from past prescribed titles for the TOK essay. Based on what we have discussed so far or on your previous knowledge, what can you claim, argue or offer as an example from the perspective of mathematics in response?

"In knowledge there is always a trade-off between accuracy and simplicity." (IBO May 2016)

"Without the group to verify it, knowledge is not possible." (IBO November 2015)

"Technology both enables us to produce knowledge and limits the knowledge that is produced." (IBO November 2013)

IV. ETHICS

Ethics in mathematics is very commonly concerned with the ethical implications of applied mathematics in environmental science, economic policy, industry and technology. In her book *Weapons of Math Destruction*, mathematician Cathy O'Neil illustrates the dangers of our reliance on applications powered by mathematics. These applications, she explains, were programmed by "fallible human beings". Built with good intentions, the models have unavoidably inherited the prejudices and biases of their human creators and, as such, they perpetuate the injustices in our society. The programmes are so complex that, save for a few experts, their outputs are not questioned. At the same time, algorithms in "big data" and financial risk management have been identified as potential sources of privacy violations and economic instability.

Given the power and value of mathematical knowledge to these domains, an argument can be made that special ethical responsibilities fall on mathematicians.

Or should that responsibility rest with the scientists, technologists, economists and engineers responsible for applying mathematical knowledge to their respective domains? Where is the line of responsibility between mathematics and its application? For example, let's consider David Li, credited with the innovations that powered the collateralized debt obligations that played a starring role in the financial crisis of 2007–08. His work on

Gaussian copula was used to calculate financial risk by investment banks in the run-up to the 2007 crisis. The writer Felix Salmon described it as a "recipe for disaster" and "the formula that killed Wall Street" (Salmon 2009). Yet, even when admirers were singing his praises in 2005, well before the crisis, Li himself was cautioning about the limitations of his model, saying "The most dangerous part is when people believe everything coming out of it" (Li quoted in Whitehouse 2005). He would later explain that his formula "gains its popularity owing to its simplicity" but that there was "little theoretical justification" to it (Li quoted in Meissner 2008). The 2007–08 financial crisis was caused by many problems including government supervisory failures, fraud, moral hazard and predatory business practices. It presented an encyclopedia of ethical collapses. To focus the blame on Li would be as ridiculous as it is ignorant.

The issue of attributing ethical responsibility to mathematicians for applications of their work is deeply complicated. It may also have inspired some mathematicians to retreat into the supposed safety of pure mathematics, in the belief that such work is not relevant to the common, vulgar or violent interests of humankind.

G.H. Hardy rejoiced that pure mathematics was so far removed from human activities that it would stay "gentle and clean" (1940). He appeared to take pride in this aspect of his work, asserting that "I have never done anything 'useful'. No discovery of mine has made, or is likely to make, directly or indirectly, for good or ill, the least difference to the amenity of the world" (1940). Though Hardy was ultimately wrong about the lack of utility of purely mathematical research, as we saw in section I, he could not have known that at the time. Even today, some mathematicians continue to argue that pure mathematical research is removed from questions of ethics because it is neutral and harmless.

IV.1 Is pure mathematics ethically neutral?

> To the extent that an applied mathematician gets involved with a real-world activity, like geology or engineering, he has to deal with the ethical issues of that field, not because he's a mathematician, but because he's involved in that application.
>
> … [W]hat about pure mathematics? Mathematicians who merely prove theorems. Is there any ethical component comparable to what you find in other fields of science … ?
>
> In pure mathematics, when restricted just to research and not considering the rest of our professional life, the ethical component is very small … . I can't think of any other field of which you could say that. That's why people say pure mathematicians live in an ivory tower. One answer to this could be, "…There's no need for mathematicians to have a code of ethics, because what we do matters so little that we can do whatever we like". … But when I think about this attitude, I find it rather scary. Because it means that if we become totally immersed in research on pure mathematics, we can enter a mental state which is rather inhuman, rather totally cut off from humanity.
>
> (Hersh 1990)

Leaving aside the problems of demarcating applied and pure mathematics, Reuben Hersh's closing sentences reveal a mathematical concern not about mathematical knowledge itself, but about the recursive impact on mathematics, that is perhaps unique to the discipline: its potential irrelevance to, and detachment from humanity. A recent argument along the same lines was made by Paul Ernest. "There is significant collateral damage caused by learning mathematics … the nature of pure mathematics itself leads to styles of thinking that can be damaging when applied beyond mathematics to social and human issues" (Ernest 2018).

Recall Rochelle Gutiérrez's argument, from II.4, that we need to "rehumanize" mathematics towards diversity and inclusion. It is not dissimilar to Ernest's fears that "ethical neutrality" in the teaching of mathematics may support a "dehumanizing outlook" that trains students to separate their intellectual and emotional lives. This concern is shared by mathematics educators who work towards educational equity, as we discussed in section II. Ernest's specific recommendation is that philosophy and ethics are included in the teaching of mathematics at all levels.

Making connections

The myth of impartiality

Chapter 3 explores the sources of bias in machine learning and artificial intelligence, and the implications of this for the predictive power and application of that knowledge. A recurring tension is whether we can separate biases inherent to the algorithim versus biases in the data sets used to train the artificial intelligence.

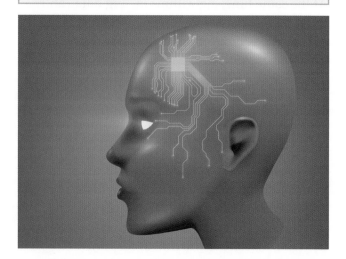

We have seen that the problem with the supposed neutrality of pure mathematics is that the line between pure and applied mathematics is imprecise and continuously shifting. This chapter

IV. Ethics

opened with Wigner's unreasonable effectiveness thesis, and examples of pure mathematical theorems that had no application for decades, or centuries, including complex numbers (now applied in quantum mechanics) and number theory (central to cryptography). Hardy's escape into pure mathematics in the 1940s was driven by his perception of the lack of usefulness of number theory or quantum mechanics. What can seem ethically neutral today may well be ethically problematic tomorrow. How then should we think of factors that affect the ethics of knowledge? Should we seek to untangle intent from implication and effect?

> Sophisticated mathematics is already ubiquitous in 21st century technology. Even the most ardent purists in number theory or algebra can no longer claim to 'just do the mathematics' and 'leave the implications to ethicists' as recent revelations about global mass surveillance have underscored the immediate social and political impact of their work. It is now evident that one can wield practically all branches of mathematics in ways that have profound social consequences, both for good and occasionally for ill, and that ethical questions can be raised everywhere in pure and applied mathematics. It seems that professional social responsibility and engagement in mathematics-specific ethical issues is unavoidable for mathematicians; we would suggest that those who deny this may be abdicating responsibility and power to others in the most dangerous way.
>
> (Chiodo, Bursill-Hall 2018)

Chiodo and Bursill-Hall add that many mathematicians are taught to believe that mathematics is ethically neutral, that any ethical issues lay with the user of the tools that they create. Yet many users of these tools will also deny social responsibility, claiming they are using only what was given to them, or that somebody else would inevitably use what exists towards their own ends. Behind many a pure mathematician, there is funding for the research—from a university, a government, a think-tank or a corporation. It is unlikely that all of these organizations are funding the pursuit for the sake of knowledge, elegance or beauty. Do mathematicians have a responsibility to comprehend, influence or challenge these agendas?

In the widely held Platonist view of mathematics, which sees mathematics as occupying an abstract or transcendental reality, ethical implications simply do not arise. However, Chiodo and Bursill-Hall argue that:

> no matter how Platonist they may be, it does not obviate their social and ethical responsibilities. Mathematics may well 'exist' in the sense of being a different kind or type of reality, but it is done (discovered, developed, studied, understood, used) by humans in our very material, social world and therefore exists for us in some sort of social matrix or social context.
>
> (Chiodo, Bursill-Hall 2018)

For discussion

Ethics, knowledge and truth

1. Intent is a fundamental concern within ethics.

   (a) Do good intentions, or the lack of bad intentions, absolve producers of mathematical knowledge from responsibility for the application of that knowledge?

   (b) What criteria might we use when considering intentions, and who would decide those criteria?

2. The statistician and hedge fund manager Nassim Taleb (quoted in a Royal Statistical Society report 2001) said: "[p]eople got very excited about the Gaussian copula because of its mathematical elegance, but the thing never worked … anything that relies on correlation is charlatanism". To what extent can we use statistical correlations to infer truths about reality?

3. More generally:

   (a) In mathematics is there a trade-off between accuracy and simplicity?

   (b) How is the relationship between accuracy and simplicity in mathematics similar to or different from the other AOKs?

IV.2 The trouble with statistics

An old adage, widely cited and often misattributed to Mark Twain, is "There are three kinds of lies: lies, damned lies, and statistics". This section takes a closer look at the implications of knowledge derived from statistics and the authority it carries.

Data dredging is one example of a statistical practice with murky ethics. It involves the speculative scanning of large data sets for correlations, without having a predefined hypothesis. Since a 95% confidence interval is usually used, meaning a 5% chance of finding a correlation between completely random variables, spurious yet statistically significant results are almost certainly found. One obvious solution is that any hypothesis found using data dredging must be tested against another data set not used in the original dredging.

Often, we may not see any reason to question correlations and statistical evidence. Most of the time, as non-experts, we may not have the skills to dig deeper, and must instead evaluate the credibility of experts to perform in the function of public intellectuals.

Simpson's paradox is a phenomenon in probability and statistics in which a trend that exists in several different data groups reverses or disappears when the groups are combined, due to a "lurking" variable (also called a confounding variable) that is not accounted for. This paradox reveals how correlations can be distorted by sampling errors, and the danger in making causal interpretations of correlations.

Consider the example shown in Table 11.1: the University of California, Berkeley 1973 admissions statistics.

	Men		Women	
	Applicants	Admitted	Applicants	Admitted
Total	8442	44%	4321	35%

↑ **Table 11.1** University of California, Berkeley: admissions 1973 (Bickel *et al* 1975)

Table 11.1 shows that men appear more likely than women to be admitted to the university, indicating an admissions bias. However, on analysing admissions rates by departments, the trend reverses, and it appears that more departments (A, B, D and E: see Table 11.2) had a bias in favour of admitting women. The pooled and corrected data showed a "small but statistically significant bias in favor of women" (Bickel *et al* 1975).

Department	Men		Women	
	Applicants	Admitted	Applicants	Admitted
A	*825*	66%	108	**82%**
B	*860*	63%	25	**68%**
C	325	**37%**	*593*	34%
D	417	33%	375	**35%**
E	191	**28%**	*393*	24%
F	373	6%	341	**7%**

↑ **Table 11.2** Date for different departments (Bickel *et al* 1975)

The paradox arises from the fact that men applied to departments such as engineering and chemistry that had fewer applicants and higher admission rates, whereas women applied to departments with a greater number of applicants and a lower rate of admission. Of course, the claim of a statistically significant bias in favour of women does not necessarily mean there was a practical bias in favour of women.

The paradox itself is explained in the TED-Ed video linked here.

 Search terms: Liddell How statistics can be misleading

The University of California Berkeley gender bias issue is explained in this linked video.

 Search terms: Are university admissions biased? Simpson's paradox part 2 YouTube

Box 11.5: Faulty statistics and the "prosecutor's fallacy"

Sally Clark was accused of having killed her first child at 11 weeks of age and her second child at 8 weeks of age. Sir Roy Meadow, a professor and consultant paediatrician, testified as an expert witness that the probability of two children in the same family dying from sudden infant death syndrome (SIDS, also called cot death) was approximately 1 in 73 million. This was a gross underestimate, arrived at by taking the probability of a single SIDS death (1 in 8,543) and squaring it, with the assumption that the probability of such deaths is uncorrelated between infants. However, that assumption was unjustified, and in fact the opposite would be true if a genetic predisposition to SIDS exists. Reporting on the incident, Ray Hill (2004) concluded that "after a first cot death the chances of a second become greatly increased", and also stated the following.

"When a cot death mother is accused of murder, the prosecution sometimes employs a tactic such as the following. If the parents are affluent, in a stable relationship and non-smoking, the prosecution will claim that the chances of the death being natural are greatly reduced, and by implication that the chances of the death being homicide are greatly increased. But this implication is totally false, because the very same factors which make a family low risk for cot death also make it low risk for murder." (Hill 2004)

The faulty mathematics did not stop there. Even if the 1-in-73 million assessment was accurate, this was not the probability of Clark's innocence, but rather an *a priori* probability that needed to be weighed against the *a priori* probabilities of the alternatives—all of them very unlikely—which were:

1. two successive SIDS deaths in the family

2. double homicide

3. other possibilities (such as one homicide and one SIDS).

It was an instance of the "prosecutor's fallacy". Crucially, probability estimates of outcomes 1 and 2 should have been compared in the statistical analysis of the prosecution. Clark was convicted in 1999. The Royal Statistical Society raised concerns about the decision, issuing a press release that stated the following.

"In the recent highly-publicised case of R v. Sally Clark, a medical expert witness drew on published studies to obtain a figure for the frequency of sudden infant death syndrome in families having some of the characteristics of the defendant's family. He went on to square this figure to obtain a value of 1 in 73 million for the frequency of two cases of SIDS in such a family.

This approach is, in general, statistically invalid. It would only be valid if SIDS cases arose independently within families, an assumption that would need to be justified empirically. Not only was no such empirical justification provided in the case, but there are very strong a priori reasons for supposing that the assumption will be false. There may well be unknown genetic or environmental factors that predispose families to SIDS, so that a second case within the family becomes much more likely.

The well-publicised figure of 1 in 73 million thus has no statistical basis … . The true frequency of families with two cases of SIDS may be very much less incriminating than the figure presented to the jury at trial. Aside from its invalidity, figures such as the 1 in 73 million are very easily misinterpreted. Some press reports at the time stated that this was the chance that the deaths of Sally Clark's two children were accidental. This (mis-)interpretation is a serious error of logic known as the Prosecutor's Fallacy. The jury needs to weigh up two competing explanations for the babies' deaths: SIDS or murder. Two deaths by SIDS or two murders are each quite unlikely, but one has apparently happened in this case. What matters is the relative likelihood of the deaths under each explanation, not just how unlikely they are under one explanation. …

The case of R v. Sally Clark is one example of a medical expert witness making a serious statistical error, one which may have had a profound effect on the outcome of the case.
Although many scientists have some familiarity with statistical methods, statistics remains a specialised area. The Society urges the Courts to ensure that statistical evidence is presented only by appropriately qualified statistical experts, as would be the case for any other form of expert evidence." (Royal Statistical Society 2001)

Clark's conviction was overturned in 2003 after evidence emerged that the pathologist who examined both babies had withheld evidence that one of them may have died from an infection.

After a review of hundreds of similar cases, another two women convicted of murdering their children had their convictions overturned. A third woman who had also been accused of murdering her three children was acquitted in June 2003. Roy Meadow had testified as an expert witness in each case, describing the unlikelihood of multiple cot deaths in a single family. He was removed from the medical register by the General Medical Council in 2005 for serious professional misconduct, but later reinstated.

Mathematics or, more specifically, statistics is used regularly in criminal legal cases. DNA evidence, and its related statistical interpretations, is regularly used both in criminal investigations and on television, where it is portrayed as fool-proof evidence. How should courts ensure that jurors are capable of understanding the mathematics, or that lawyers do not misuse mathematical arguments?

IV.3 Professional standards

To cope with the ethical challenges arising from the production or application of mathematical knowledge, a number of initiatives have formed relatively recently. In the aftermath of the Cambridge Analytica scandal, which we discuss at length in Chapters 2 and 3, two Cambridge University scholars, Maurice Chiodo and Piers Bursill-Hall, set up the Ethics in Mathematics (EiM) Project, which organized its first conference in 2018. "So far as we know, there is no university in the world that currently offers a wide-ranging specifically mathematical ethical training for mathematicians", they write (Chiodo, Bursill-Hall 2018). To fill this gap, they have designed and piloted a course called "Ethics for the working mathematician", a series of eight hour-long lectures. Follow the link to learn more about the issues it explores.

 Search terms: Lecture course: Ethics for the working mathematician Chiodo

> "Nobody can do this from outside the profession. Only mathematicians can talk to mathematicians about ethics … and we need to begin the process of forming a community: supporting each other, sharing knowledge, experiences, best practice, and a vision of what we can teach our students.
>
> (Chiodo, Bursill-Hall 2018)"

Professional mathematics organizations have published ethical guidelines and codes of conduct, but these typically focus on issues of academic practice. The case study below explores one issue of a professional controversy in mathematics. Although not particular to this AOK, what would become known as the Perelman affair acquired a distinctive dimension and raised an important question: to what extent are ethical issues in mathematics specific to the individuals involved, traceable to the culture of the mathematics community, or general issues of academic practice and malpractice? Consider this question as you read the case study.

Case study

Pure and simple

On 18 August 2006 the *New Yorker* magazine published an article (linked here) that tells a rare story of controversy in the international mathematics community. The controversy concerned the Poincaré conjecture, which although widely accepted to be true, remained unproven for over 100 years. It is one of seven Millennium Prize Problems selected by the Clay Mathematics Institute, proofs of which are each rewarded with a million-dollar prize.

 Search terms: The New Yorker Manifold destiny

In November 2002 Russian mathematician Grigori Perelman published the first piece of a three-part proof of the Poincaré conjecture. With each part the excitement among mathematicians grew that the Poincaré conjecture might finally be proven. Perelman was already widely recognized in the international mathematics community as an exceptionally gifted mathematician. He was also reclusive and by some accounts eccentric. Declining offers from coveted academic institutions, he returned to St Petersburg, moved back in with his mother, took up a position at a local institute, and threw himself at the Poincaré conjecture.

When his proof was complete, he limited publicity by only self-publishing it on the internet and going on a speaking tour of the United States. Beyond this, he believed that the work should speak for itself: "[i]f the proof is correct, then no other recognition is needed" (Perelman quoted in Nasser, Gruber 2006).

Perelman self-published the proof by submitting a pre-print to arXiv.org, which we examine in Chapter 7. It was risky for him to publish pre-prints; had there been an error or fault in his logic, anyone who could identify or fix it could claim the proof as their own. But this was not a concern for Perelman. "My reasoning was: if I made an error and someone used my work to construct a correct proof I would be pleased", he said in an interview for the *New York Times* magazine (Nasser, Gruber 2016). Once he had returned from his US tour, Perelman distanced himself from the process of verifying his proof out of the desire to avoid influencing it, to the point of not replying to e-mails. Meanwhile, some of the brightest minds in the field were busy with a formal explication of his work. It took them several years, working in teams, to closely examine and check the proof, which was both very brief and very complex.

In the summer of 2006, just as one group had completed a manuscript analysing Perelman's proof, a 328-page article by Huai-Dong Cao and Xi-Ping Zhu was published, taking up a whole issue of the *Asian Journal of Mathematics.* The article presented their work as "a crowning achievement" and the first complete and original proof of the Poincaré conjecture. Cao and Zhu recognized Perelman's work as a stepping stone but also alleged to gaps in his logic that their article filled.

In the ensuing months, a story unfolded showing that the article by Cao and Zhu had been rushed to publication, sidestepping the usual checks of the peer-review process. When one of the central arguments in their paper turned out to be identical to previous work by mathematicians Bruce Kleiner and John Lott, Cao and Zhu retracted their article and the journal issued a letter of apology. The involvement in this affair of Harvard mathematician Shing-Tung Yau, who was Cao and Zhu's mentor and editor-in-chief of the journal that published their article, has been the subject of much controversy. Was this a case of a powerful and established mathematician breaching protocol and using his influence to upstage an eccentric young mathematical genius? Or was it merely an unfortunate clash of egos and brilliant minds in a high-stakes race?

In a letter to the American Mathematical Society Joan Birman, an esteemed mathematician and professor, called the episode "a very public and very bad black mark" on the entire profession (Birman 2007). Another mathematician, Phillip Griffiths, commented that "politics, power, and control have no legitimate role in our community, and they threaten the integrity of our field" (quoted in Alexander, 2010).

The *New Yorker* magazine article details the story of why, instead of enjoying due recognition for his accomplishment, Perelman left the field of mathematics in protest over the profession's ethical standards and tolerance of dishonesty. He also rejected the prestigious Fields Medal, which was offered to him at a public ceremony that he did not attend in 2006. In 2010, Perelman was finally awarded the million-dollar Millennium Prize, which he also declined.

Russian mathematician Mikhail Gromov is quoted as saying about Perelman that "[t]o do great work, you have to have a pure mind. You can think only about the mathematics. Everything else is human weakness. Accepting prizes is showing weakness" (Gromov quoted in Nasser, Gruber 2006). In light of all the stereotypes, myths and prejudices that we seek to overturn, those words and Perelman's actions continue to ring poignantly as we close this chapter.

12 Assessment

TOK aims to enable students to engage with the complexity, ambiguity, uncertainty and contradictions in the world with a sense of wonder, and to make them feel empowered to pursue knowledge with agency. The objectives and value of TOK therefore extend beyond the two IB assessment tasks—creating an exhibition and writing an essay—although these present rich opportunities for you to synthesize your learning in TOK. As in your course work, in these two tasks you will explore knowledge questions, and in the process:

- develop and demonstrate your ability to construct arguments
- offer examples as evidence in support of your claims
- engage with different perspectives
- draw conclusions that are of consequence.

This chapter aims to help you meaningfully engage with and score well in TOK assessment. Given that the exploration of knowledge questions is central to both assessment tasks, this chapter begins with a closer look at what knowledge questions are and how to approach them.

Knowledge questions

How are knowledge questions different from "normal" questions? Knowledge questions are intended to do something specific: they do some of the work for you, by setting you up to discuss what we claim to know and how we come to know it. To achieve this, knowledge questions are phrased in a way that invites you to explore different perspectives on how we produce, acquire, disseminate or apply knowledge in the world. The knowledge questions exist to guide your exploration of knowledge and make sure that your discussion stays in the realm of TOK, and not ethics, politics, psychology or philosophy more generally.

The IB also suggests that knowledge questions have the characteristics shown in Figure 12.1.

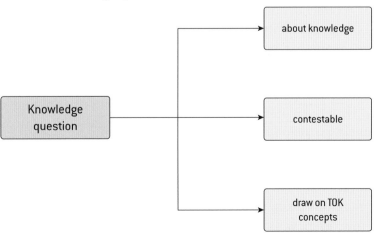

↑ **Figure 12.1** Characteristics of knowledge questions
Based on: *Theory of Knowledge Guide, First Assessment 2022* (IBO)

Knowledge questions are questions **about knowledge**—about how knowledge is produced, acquired, shared and used; what it is and what it is not; who has it and who does not; and who decides the answers to these questions. Instead of focusing on subject-specific content or specific examples, students focus on how knowledge is constructed and evaluated. In this sense, knowledge questions are distinct from many of the questions that students encounter in other subjects.

Knowledge questions are **contestable** in that there are a number of plausible answers to them. Dealing with these open contestable questions is a key feature of

TOK, although some students can find the lack of a single "right" answer slightly disorienting. In TOK discussions, it is perfectly conceivable that answers to a question may differ—what matters is that the analysis is thorough, accurate and effectively supported by examples and evidence.

Knowledge questions also **draw on TOK concepts** and terminology, rather than using subject-specific terminology or specific examples. Knowledge questions draw on central TOK concepts such as evidence, certainty, values and interpretation.

Adapted from: *Theory of Knowledge Guide, First Assessment 2022* (IBO)

This section examines knowledge questions in some detail because they are the basis for both the TOK exhibition and the TOK essay. They appear throughout this book and will have anchored many of your classroom discussions. Your learning is assessed through your ability to explore knowledge questions critically in relation to the areas of knowledge (AOKs) as well as the world around you.

Importantly, you do not have to worry about constructing your own knowledge questions because the IB provides them in the assessment tasks, so that you can focus on formulating the answers.

I. THE EXHIBITION

One of the two ways in which you will demonstrate your learning in TOK is by creating an exhibition. In a subject like TOK, which may sometimes strike you as abstract or conceptual, creating an exhibition is an opportunity to explore how knowledge manifests tangibly in objects around you.

What does this mean? The processes of knowing are bound up with the material world. We dance and make music, participate in online discussions, examine historical archives, grow and prepare food, take photographs, record field notes, perform experiments, tell and listen to stories, study religious texts, travel to new places, learn and practise new skills, and

investigate and live in ecological environments. Often these processes through which we come to know disappear from view, and all we are left with is a knowledge claim. The exhibition provides an opportunity for us to be reminded of the material practices and processes that enable us to make knowledge claims. It is also an opportunity to consider the material consequences of applying knowledge in the world. The exhibition encourages you to think of knowing as something we do with our whole selves and not just our intellect, and as a process that necessarily involves objects and materials, not just concepts and ideas.

What the task actually entails is outlined on the next page.

FIRST

As a starting point, you will choose one of the 35 prompts below to serve as the basis for your exhibition. The exhibition consists of only three objects, and all three need to be linked to the same prompt.

NEXT

You will explain why each object is included in the exhibition. You should include what your exhibition is about, the context each object comes from and its relationship with the prompt. You have 950 words for this, and a great deal of freedom about how to use them. Remember to state your selected prompt as the title and include images of your objects with your commentary all in a single file.

FINALLY

You will showcase your exhibition to an audience. This might be your TOK class or a community event.

I.1 TOK exhibition prompts

1. What counts as knowledge?

6. How does the way that we organize or classify knowledge affect what we know?

8. To what extent is certainty attainable?

9. Are some types of knowledge less open to interpretation than others?

10. What challenges are raised by the dissemination and/or communication of knowledge?

11. Can new knowledge change established values or beliefs?

24. How might the context in which knowledge is presented influence whether it is accepted or rejected?

30. What role does imagination play in producing knowledge about the world?

33. How is current knowledge shaped by its historical development?

34. In what ways do our values affect our acquisition of knowledge?

35. In what ways do values affect the production of knowledge?

Theory of Knowledge Guide,
First Assessment 2022 (IBO)

I.2 Curating a compelling TOK exhibition

Below are five steps to clarify how you can select and approach a prompt, curate objects and write the commentary.

Curating an exhibition draws on many of the questions asked in TOK, such as: who decides what is relevant and meaningful? In this task, *you* decide and have a responsibility to make informed decisions about how you explore these questions in the world. It is also a creative process that may be messy at times. We hope you will find joy in it: the uncertainty; the realization that you have too many ideas or none at all; the feeling of being stuck and also getting unstuck; moving towards clarity, and ultimately producing something to be proud of.

I.2.1 Choosing a prompt

How should you decide which prompt to choose? First, read and give some consideration to every one of the prompts. Maybe one of them stands out for you, or makes you think of an object or objects that align well with it. At first glance the prompts might all sound confusing, and you might have difficulty imagining how they relate to objects in the real world.

So, are some prompts easier than others? Some prompts may seem easier to address simply because of the way they are phrased. Consider, for example, prompt 23 "How important are material tools in the production or acquisition of knowledge?" Reading this may quickly call to mind the various objects in a scientific laboratory or an artist's studio. Prompt 25 "How can we distinguish between knowledge, belief and opinion?" might initially seem a lot more challenging. Remember, a 950-word write-up requires some depth of exploration. The prompts that are obviously about objects may not be the best choice. Once you begin developing your exhibition, your view may change. You may find that the objects and concepts that seemed like obvious choices are limiting your discussion at superficial level. We give further guidance about how to go into depth in your exhibition in 2. "Selecting objects".

What about deciding between prompts that sound *very* similar? If you think prompt 15 "What constraints are there on the pursuit of knowledge?" is interesting to explore from an ethical perspective, you might be conflicted when you read prompt 16 "Should some knowledge not be sought on ethical grounds?" A few prompts in the list sound alike. Keep developing your thoughts around a cluster of questions and gradually settle on one prompt that fits best. Remember that you need to justify the inclusion of each object in relation to the prompt, while at the same time avoiding repetition—all three objects should not have the exact same relationship to the prompt.

Look for a prompt that is wide enough to encompass your different objects, but not so narrow that all of your objects relate to it in the same way. Consider the following example.

Suppose you are interested in how knowledge changes over time. Both prompt 13 "How can we know that current knowledge is an improvement upon past knowledge?" and prompt 33 "How is current knowledge shaped by its historical development?" align with this interest. Whereas prompt 13 specifically asks about improvement over time, prompt 33 is a more open exploration of the relationship between past and current knowledge. As an example, let's look at developing this exhibition in the context of knowledge and technology, specifically about how imaging techniques have changed what we know about Pluto.

Let's suppose you settled on prompt 13. Two of our objects could be the low- and high-res photos of Pluto shown below. You should be careful to not just include other objects that make the same point—that more powerful technological tools allow us to improve our knowledge about phenomena in the world. Instead, to diversify your exhibition, consider, for example, how the design of the bicycle has changed over time and how we know whether or not this counts as an improvement.

↑ **Figure 12.2a** Pluto taken by the Faint Object Camera of the Hubble Space Telescope in 1994; the highest resolution image achieved from Earth.

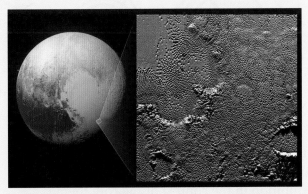

↑ **Figure 12.2b** Pluto taken by New Horizons 16 hours before closest approach in July 2015. This is the raw, compressed version seen by scientists shortly after midnight on 13 July. It demonstrates the dramatic improvement in imaging science content available from a flyby mission. The right-hand part is a close-up of the pits in the heart-shaped region of Pluto.

Including a new subject can sometimes lead you in a different direction from what you originally imagined. This can be exciting or it can be a dead-end, and you should explore a little further until you know. Let's say that after reading a bit more about the history of bicycle design, you want to explore the social, cultural and gendered dimensions of the development of the bicycle, as well as how what we know about Pluto today has been shaped and influenced by its former status as a planet and its subsequent demotion. In this case, a broader question such as prompt 33 might be more appropriate.

Still confused about where to start? The IB strongly encourages students to place their exhibition in the context of the core theme or one of the other themes. If you are having difficulty devising your exhibition, read the list of prompts again but this time with a particular theme in mind. You might find that you have more clarity, for example, on prompt 29 "Who owns knowledge?" when seen through the lens of knowledge and Indigenous societies—you may remember reading about cultural appropriation or stolen Indigenous artefacts in museums and private collections (discussed in Chapters 5 and 10). Alternatively, the same prompt considered in the context of knowledge and technology might remind you of open source software, creative commons licenses or digital remix culture.

I.2.2 Selecting objects

What can I use and how do I choose?

↑ **Figure 12.3** The cabinet of curiosities: Ferrante Imperato's museum in Naples, 1599

Objects play an important role in knowing—as the things that are known, the materials and tools through which we come to know things, or as results of the application of knowledge. Human-made objects are intertwined with the processes of knowing, and are therefore suitable to be included in the exhibition. Naturally occurring objects that relate to knowledge, such as celestial objects, clouds or rock formations can also be used. Given that the exhibition asks for objects, it is not appropriate to include living beings. Specific photographs of living beings may be used as long as it is the photograph, and not the being, that is being presented. We explore this nuance below.

Some objects may be too large to actually exhibit. Others may be privately owned or otherwise hard to access. In these cases an image of the object can be presented instead. Digital objects, such as a tweet or an Instagram post, are also suitable for the exhibition. It should be clear whether you are exhibiting an image in place of the physical object (such as a photograph of La Sagrada Familia in Barcelona) or the image itself (such as the 1984 photograph of Sharbat Gula by journalist Steve McCurry called *Afghan Girl*). Note: in the latter example, be clear that it is that particular photograph, featured on the *National Geographic* cover, a photograph that is iconic and potentially problematic, that is the object of the exhibition,

and not the person. In the case of La Sagrada Familia, your discussion should clearly focus on the basilica as the object in the exhibition, rather than the qualities and features of the image such as the lighting or perspective in the photograph.

What about objects you have created? These may be included as long as they are pre-existing; that is, they have not been specifically created for the purpose of this exhibition. Challenge yourself to find meaning in objects that already exist in the world and be curious about the incredible things that the rest of the world's humans have made, found and used. With this orientation you can discover objects more interesting than any you might have imagined. Margaret Mead describes this orientation as:

> the open-mindedness with which one must look and listen, record in astonishment and wonder, that which one would not have been able to guess.
>
> (Mead 1950)

For reflection

Selection and inclusion—why these objects and not others?

In making your selection of objects, be curious about the objects you include and exclude. To practise, consider prompt 1 "What counts as knowledge?"

1. As a class, brainstorm at least 10 objects you would include in an exhibition on this prompt.

2. Discuss as a class what your objects reveal about your biases and gaps.

   (a) What kinds of knowledge are underrepresented?

   (b) Why did these not readily come to mind?

3. Consider again the 10 objects your class has selected. Working on your own, select three that you would personally include. Compare your selection with that of a partner. Discuss where and how they differ. What were your reasons for including those specific objects and excluding the rest?

I.2.3 Linking your objects to the prompt

Representation

Recognizing that objects do not speak for themselves, how you represent them is essential in this task. Creating a successful TOK exhibition includes not only describing each object in its real-world context, but also connecting it to your chosen TOK prompt and justifying its inclusion in the exhibition. The better you contextualize your objects in a real-world setting, the more convincing will be your argument for why they have been included and how they respond to the prompt.

Avoid using generic objects or images that stand in for entire categories of things. Suppose you are exploring prompt 9 "Are some types of knowledge less open to interpretation than others?" and you wish to discuss the interpretation of religious texts. Your exhibition will not benefit from a stock image of bibles even if you have deep knowledge of biblical exegesis and can fully explain the magisterium of the Catholic Church or the Reformation principle of Sola Scriptura. Remember, the objects you present are not obstacles to be overcome just so that you can move on to what you wanted to write.

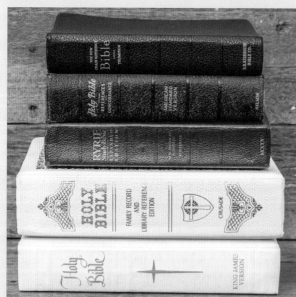

Try to choose and contextualize objects that perform specific functions in the world, and explain how this is the case. Consider, for example, the 2011 graphic novel *Sita's Ramayana*, which retells the Hindu epic from the perspective of the queen, repositioning the female character as the protagonist. This modern interpretation is itself inspired by a retelling of the *Ramayana* by the Bengali 16th-century poetess Chandrabati. *Sita's Ramayana* is further entangled in questions about whether the *Ramayana* can be considered a literary, historical or religious text, and what each of these would mean about its openness to interpretation.

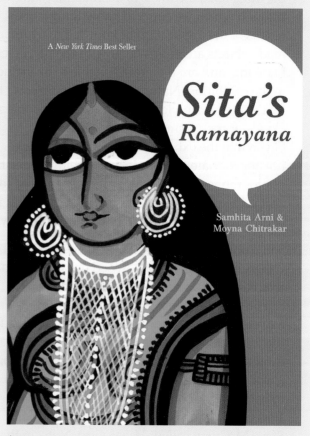

↑ **Figure 12.4** The front cover of *Sita's Ramayana* (2011)

A related pitfall to avoid is using objects to represent ideas symbolically. In exploring, for example, prompt 6 "How does the way that we organize or classify knowledge affect what we know?" you might offer an image of a broken mirror to symbolize the fragmentation of knowledge into separate disciplines. This would be a mistake.

It is tempting to engage with objects symbolically because we can attribute meaning to any object and gain approval. The exhibition is intended to engage with objects in their own right—with their origin stories, uniqueness, purpose and meanings beyond those you personally give them. With prompt 6 still in mind, consider Figure 12.5, an image of *The Siku Quanshu*, the 18th-century encyclopedia of Chinese knowledge. At 79,000 chapters and 800 million words, *The Siku Quanshu* is a compendium of a body of knowledge so large in volume that it has only been surpassed by Wikipedia, and that

has only happened recently. It is organized according to traditional classification into "4 Branches (部): (a) the Classics (經), (b) the Histories (史), (c) the Masters (子), and (d) the Anthologies (集)". This complex system developed over the course of 15 centuries and does not neatly map onto the domains of knowledge in Western thought. Including *The Siku Quanshu* in your exhibition allows you to engage with its specific historical and cultural meanings and make compelling connections to both the prompt and the world. You can explore how applying categories such as "literature" and "philosophy" to Chinese thought prior to the 18th century limits or distorts our understanding of them. Indeed, you can consider limitations and distortions that occur when we apply one way of organizing knowledge to an intellectual tradition that organizes knowledge differently.

↑ **Figure 12.5** *The Siku Quanshu*, the 18th-century encyclopedia of Chinese knowledge consisting of 79,000 chapters

In summary, the objects in your exhibition should meet these criteria.

- They should be specific, not generic.
- They should be pre-existing, not created for the purposes of your exhibition.
- They need to represent themselves, not abstract ideas.

In order to make your objects relevant to the prompt, you need a good understanding of their specific origins and histories. It is helpful to draw on objects you are already familiar with, or committed to finding out more about, in order to avoid misrepresentations, oversimplifications and generalizations. Working in this exhibition with objects contextualized in the real world keeps you accountable for the claims you make about them—how you describe them, what you claim about how they fit in the world and how you explain their relationship to the prompt.

Especially when referring to objects coming from material cultures you are not familiar with, you should be respectful of the knowledge traditions they are embedded in and the limitations of your own understanding. One of the prompts (14) even asks "Does some knowledge belong only to particular communities of knowers?" When selecting objects, consider what is your role and intention in having this object represented. Let the story of the Mataatua Wharenui, a carved Māori meeting house (figure 12.6), serve as a lesson. In the 1870s, it was disassembled and packed onto a steamship travelling from what is now known as New Zealand to the British Empire Exhibition in Sydney. The Mataatua was hauled on ships

and trains across multiple destinations in the Empire, and was even trimmed to fit inside museum buildings. It would be another 100 years before this meeting house ultimately returned home. On its first stop in Sydney, the Mataatua was reassembled with the intricate carvings facing the outside, in full view of the visitors, but also in full disregard of Māori protocol. By way of this transformation, the Mataatua went from being a culturally significant gathering site to being "an ethnological curiosity for strange people to look at the wrong way and in the wrong place" (Te Rūnanga o Ngāti Awa 1990). Don't be like the British Empire. In the exhibition the opportunity to represent objects is inseparable from the responsibility to do it well and accurately.

 Search terms: Mataatua Visitor Centre History

↑ **Figure 12.6** Mātaatua Wharenui in Sydney 1879. Notice how the entire structure has been reassembled so that the interior carvings are now on the exterior.

Being accountable for descriptions

Think back to the three objects you chose in the previous exercise, to represent prompt 1 "What counts as knowledge?" Reflecting on your selection, consider the following.

1. Do your objects contain any of the pitfalls and poor choices we discuss in this section?

2. Are you confident in your ability to offer an accurate and responsible description of each of the objects?

3. Why would you say that you have chosen interesting objects?

I.2.4 Creating meaning

As you work to establish the relationship between each of your objects and your prompt, keep in mind how the exhibition is shaping up as a whole. You add value not only by identifying, describing and linking three individual objects to the prompt, but also by selecting them such that they collectively present a nuanced understanding of the prompt.

For example, in creating an exhibition around prompt 4 "On what grounds might we doubt a claim?" it would be a good idea to select objects that highlight different causes for doubt.

Suppose one of the objects is Figure 12.7, a fake medieval miniature painting of Muslim scientists at work. These paintings are a curious phenomenon and they are done to various degrees of sophistication. Many similar paintings are for sale in Istanbul's historic Second Hand Book Market (Sahaflar Çarşısı), while many more circulate on the internet. A keen eye is often not enough to reveal them as modern forgeries, and at least some background knowledge in the history of science and technology or the history of art is necessary. Experience and expertise in these

↑ **Figure 12.7** Fake painting of Muslim scientists at work

fields can reveal the difference between fakes and the real thing. For example, there may be inconsistencies in the timelines of the spread of technologies, use of pigments that would not have been available at the time, or cultural inaccuracies such as garments that would not have been worn in the way depicted. So, the fake miniatures show us that inconsistencies, detectable by someone with experience and specialized knowledge, are good reasons to cast doubt on a claim about a painting's authenticity.

How might this object relate to your other two objects, say a screenshot of a deepfake video to illustrate the role and limitations of intuition in doubt, and a tweet by a politician included to show doubt as distrust towards the claims-maker? Can you make our understanding of doubt more refined by substituting one or both of these objects for a different one?

In thinking about your exhibition as a whole, consider how tensions between the objects and the different ways they relate to the prompt can contribute to a more thorough understanding of the concepts in the prompt. How can you, through an intentional selection of objects, offer a compelling exploration of doubt, to follow the example we started out with?

I.2.5 Writing it all up

Making your intentions visible

Even if you have gone through the process diligently, been intentional about your choice of objects and have a good sense about their relationship to the prompt, it is important that you articulate those decisions and intentions. You have 950 words to do this. The word allocation is generous enough for you to present some detail, and also difficult to fill if there is not much substance to your exhibition.

You might be wondering how to approach and structure this written component. How much space should you give to individual object descriptions versus discussing the prompt or the exhibition as a whole? The IB does not require a specific structure, and this gives you freedom in how you write about and present your work. The following guidance may help you.

- **Open with an exhibition rationale.** Why is the exhibition on this prompt significant? How will the exploration of this prompt through your selected objects help us better understand the concepts in the prompt? You need to be convinced of the rationale before you can write it convincingly. Include the rationale *only* if it adds value and allows you to open strongly. It does not have to be longer than a sentence or two. Keep in mind that this sets the tone for your exhibition and so it should not be trivial.

- **If you are placing your exhibition in the context of a theme, make this clear.** Explain why it might be particularly interesting, for example, to look at prompt 9 "Are some types of knowledge less open to interpretation than others?" through the lens of knowledge and religion.

- **Write significant descriptions of the objects.** Focus on what is of significance—which details about their origin, history of ownership and use, past and current location are relevant? Which are essential to contextualizing each object in its place in the world? Your objects should be simultaneously grounded in a real-world context and linked to your chosen prompt. Think of the objects' description and the justification for including them into the exhibition as two sides of the same coin.

- **Address "the big picture" of your exhibition.** Once you have described and linked each of your objects to the prompt, zoom out and consider the picture that emerges. To fail to do so would be a missed opportunity to extract meaning from the exhibition. Ideally, each of your objects will have a unique relationship to the prompt. By putting these three specific objects together, you should be able to say something unique about the prompt. What do your chosen objects, seen together, allow you to say about, for example, what counts as knowledge, or on what grounds we might doubt a claim? There may be tensions and contradictions between your objects; this is not something you need to hide or necessarily aim to resolve. Indeed, you may have even intentionally selected your objects to create these tensions. Highlighting them in relation to the prompt demonstrates that you have an understanding that knowledge manifests in the world in complex and messy ways. If done well, this can add depth and nuance to your exhibition.

Ultimately, the purpose of the written account is to *make your thinking visible* to anyone who is visiting your exhibition, even virtually, and who may not know you and your motivations.

The written explanation should convince them that you have not found these objects by chance, and that you have thought about and can articulate the reasons for including them in your exhibition. In doing this, you are demonstrating that you understand how TOK manifests in the world.

I.3 Assessment for the TOK exhibition

To determine how well you have done on the exhibition, your teacher will use the rubric below. As you develop your exhibition, consult it to ensure that you understand the demands of the task, and that you are meeting them.

Does the exhibition successfully show how TOK manifests in the world around us?					
Excellent 9–10	**Good 7–8**	**Satisfactory 5–6**	**Basic 3–4**	**Rudimentary 1–2**	**0**
The exhibition clearly identifies three objects and their specific real-world contexts. Links between each of the three objects and the selected internal assessment (IA) prompt are clearly made and well-explained. There is a strong justification of the particular contribution that each individual object makes to the exhibition. All, or nearly all, of the points are well-supported by appropriate evidence and explicit references to the selected IA prompt.	The exhibition identifies three objects and their real-world contexts. Links between each of the three objects and the selected IA prompt are explained, although this explanation may lack precision and clarity in parts. There is a justification of the contribution that each individual object makes to the exhibition. Many of the points are supported by appropriate evidence and references to the selected IA prompt.	The exhibition identifies three objects, although the real-world contexts of these objects may be vaguely or imprecisely stated. There is some explanation of the links between the three objects and the selected IA prompt. There is some justification for the inclusion of each object in the exhibition. Some of the points are supported by evidence and references to the selected IA prompt.	The exhibition identifies three objects, although the real-world contexts of the objects may be implied rather than explicitly stated. Basic links between the objects and the selected IA prompt are made, but the explanation of these links is unconvincing and/or unfocused. There is a superficial justification for the inclusion of each object in the exhibition. Reasons for the inclusion of the objects are offered, but these are not supported by appropriate evidence and/or lack relevance to the selected IA prompt. There may be significant repetition across the justifications of the different objects.	The exhibition presents three objects, but the real-world contexts of these objects are not stated, or the images presented may be highly generic images of types of object rather than being specific real-world objects. Links between the objects and the selected IA prompt are made, but these are minimal, tenuous or it is not clear what the student is trying to convey. There is very little justification offered for the inclusion of each object in the exhibition. The commentary on the objects is highly descriptive or consists only of unsupported assertions.	The response does not reach the standard described by the other levels or does not use one of the IA prompts provided.
Possible characteristics					
Convincing Lucid Precise	Focused Relevant Coherent	Adequate Competent Acceptable	Simplistic Limited Underdeveloped	Ineffective Descriptive Incoherent	

II. THE ESSAY

The other way you demonstrate your learning in TOK is by writing an essay, in response to one of six prescribed titles (PTs) issued by the IB each year. Unlike creating an exhibition, extended writing tasks are something you will be familiar with. And yet there are some differences between the TOK essay and other essays or long written tasks. An effective TOK essay is an exploration of TOK concepts and ideas, through the development and articulation of arguments, supported by real examples representing a diversity of perspectives, and consolidated into a conclusion that is of consequence. The essay is an opportunity to demonstrate that **knowledge matters** in the world, and has significant implications and consequences.

All PTs published by the IB will be in the form of *knowledge questions*, which we discussed earlier in this chapter. A worthy reminder here, however, is regarding the *contestability* of knowledge questions—they will by definition be open to a multiplicity of possible good answers. But to say that there is no right or wrong answer to a knowledge question is not the same as to say there are no *poor* answers to a knowledge question. The TOK essay task asks for an exploration of the knowledge question contained within the PT, but also asks for this to be done clearly and critically.

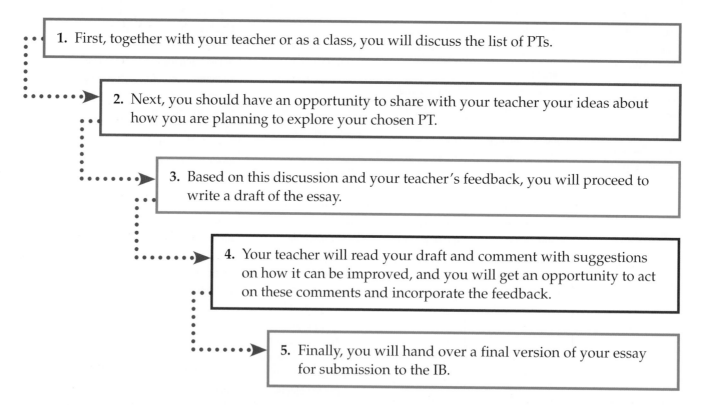

1. First, together with your teacher or as a class, you will discuss the list of PTs.

2. Next, you should have an opportunity to share with your teacher your ideas about how you are planning to explore your chosen PT.

3. Based on this discussion and your teacher's feedback, you will proceed to write a draft of the essay.

4. Your teacher will read your draft and comment with suggestions on how it can be improved, and you will get an opportunity to act on these comments and incorporate the feedback.

5. Finally, you will hand over a final version of your essay for submission to the IB.

In the following pages, we walk through different elements in the thinking and writing process for the essay and offer some essential guidance on moving through them while avoiding some of the most common pitfalls.

We address perhaps the biggest pitfall of all here at the start: you will notice that at no point in the process does it say "visit one of the many TOK help websites online" or "google your PT word for word". Whatever you do, do not let the internet be the first place you go to start thinking about your essay. There is a lot of material online specific to the TOK essay, designed to "help" with the task, and the advice you find there can be poor, misleading or outdated. Some websites even prey on students' insecurities and charge for their "service". If you have worked through this book, you know what you need to know to tackle the essay. Have confidence in that knowledge and in your ability to think independently. No website can give you that confidence. In fact, the model responses, templates and suggested examples take something away from you that is far more important: your unique, individual approach to the questions. Teachers have been warning students about this for years and we hope that you will trust us, and trust yourself. Provide yourself with time and space to think and reflect critically, honour your knowledge and experience—it is enough—and let the essay be a celebration of what you have learned in TOK.

Before we dive in, here is an overview of the requirements of the task.

- The essay has to be written on a **single PT** from the examination session that you are registered in. You may not write your own title or alter a PT in any way. Your essay should be a full and direct response to the PT, which should be clearly stated at the top of your essay.

- The word limit for the essay is **1600 words**. The examiner is not required to read anything over this word limit. An essay that is significantly under the word limit is self-penalizing and unlikely to be a fully developed response to the PT.

- There is no prescribed structure for the essay.

- The TOK essay is not primarily a research task. You are not expected to do a review of the literature or find out what everyone before you has said on the topic. That said, whenever you refer to someone else's words or ideas, you must cite the source. If you have questions or need further guidance about what and how to cite, ask your teacher.

- The essay should be **formatted** in a standard font (such as Arial) in 12 pt, and double spaced throughout. No cover page or other special formatting is necessary.

- No identifying information, such as your name or candidate number, should appear in the essay document. The script should be **anonymous** in order to support the impartiality of the marking.

II.1 Unpacking the PT

When you first see the list of PTs, much like the TOK exhibition prompts, they might strike you as very abstract and conceptual. Unpacking them—identifying the TOK concepts and key words—is something you will want to do for all PTs to some extent. This process will help you clarify your understanding of what each PT is asking and how you might approach answering it; also, which is the one you wish to explore further. However, endlessly unpacking PTs can turn into a form of procrastination.

We emphasize unpacking PTs here because this is the first step in ensuring a sustained discussion of knowledge in your essay. It helps you identify what it is that you should maintain focus on as you begin to write. Failure to do this can mean that you launch into your essay with an inaccurate interpretation of the demands of the question. The connection of your essay to the PT is one of the aspects that is assessed, and this needs to be clear to you in order to be clear in your writing. Let's practise unpacking one of the prescribed PTs.

Consider this PT from May 2016.

"To what extent do the concepts that we use shape the conclusions that we reach?"

A good place to start is to pay attention to the **requirements in the PT**. Some PTs will specify an AOK to be discussed, or the number of AOKs you must explore in the essay. Follow these requirements closely; your response must address the PT fully in order to be effective. If the PT calls for two AOKs, including a third and a fourth is seen as taking attention and words away from offering a deeper analysis of the two that were required. This particular PT leaves that open—you can technically discuss any number of AOKs, as long as you consider different perspectives.

The **key terms** that stand out are "concepts" and "conclusions". Having an understanding of these terms, and offering a discussion around them will be crucial to an effective response. This is where students sometimes turn to dictionary definitions. This is ineffective and strongly discouraged for a reason—unless you are specifically discussing the formation of definitions as a knowledge issue, it is mostly unhelpful to rely on and include dictionary definitions of key terms in your TOK essay. Instead consider what *concepts* look like in different AOKs, starting perhaps with the concepts you have encountered in your subjects. Are these concepts generally accepted, or disputed among practitioners in the AOK they belong to? What are the relationships between concepts and theories, schools of thought or ideologies? And what kind of conclusions do the different AOKs seek to reach? Are concepts necessary and useful for being able to reach conclusions in these AOKs? Think about questions like these early and you will be well placed to develop a strong essay.

Note also that this PT asks **a question of extent**; this type of question is common in PTs.

You can be given a statement or quote and asked about the extent to which you agree with it, or the extent to which this is the case in a number of AOKs. This specific PT asks about the extent of the influence of concepts on conclusions, and offers the term "shape" to describe that influence. You should evaluate the extent of the shaping influence of concepts on conclusions throughout your essay.

And then there is the word "we"—very easy to overlook, and yet critical to an effective response. In a PT, always look for the **knower or community of knowers** that is being referred to. Is it mathematicians, historians, experts, scientists, or is it—as is the case in this PT— an unspecified "we"? "We" should not be taken as an invitation to write an essay about a general group of unspecific knowers, as if such a group even existed. Instead, it should be seen as an opportunity to explore different knowers. For instance, does the influence of concepts on conclusions differ for experts versus non-experts? Is it more significant in one AOK as opposed to another?

It is important to flag that you must **make sure not to alter the PT** in the process of unpacking it, and to respond to it exactly as it was presented. Brainstorming a few questions in relation to the PT can be helpful to identify in which directions to take your response, but these questions must not displace the PT. In the case of this PT you might consider whether it is possible to reach different conclusions by using the same concepts, or the same conclusion by using different concepts. As you begin writing, always check that your discussion is related to what the PT is asking for and that you are giving adequate attention to all the key terms in the PT.

Following this sequence, try unpacking a few—or all—of the PTs in your session. If you are doing this for practice before they become available, try one of the PTs in the sections below, or a different one provided by your teacher.

Finally, unpacking the PT is something you do *both* as a step in the process of thinking about your essay and in the writing of your essay. An effective introduction will include your understanding of what the question is asking for as well as your plan for how you are going to approach and explore it. Meaningfully unpacking the prescribed title is a critical first step in structuring the argumentative arc of your response.

II.2 Articulating arguments and supporting them with examples

Once you have a good understanding of the prescribed title and what it asks for, it is time to articulate a few arguments in response, and start thinking about what kind of evidence you can offer in support. Note here that the way you advance your response in writing does not need to follow your thinking process—will you lead with your examples, or with your arguments? Either

is fine for the purposes of the TOK essay, and the structure of your essay should be able to adapt to the type of prescribed title you have chosen.

In fact, conforming your essay to a strict structure of claim-counterclaim or example-counterexample can lead to generalizations, arbitrary distinctions, misrepresentations and false dichotomies. Exploring a range of evidence, from within and across AOKs, allows you to offer some nuance and honour the complexity and messiness of knowledge in the real world. It is essential that your examples are grounded in the real world, that they refer to how actual practitioners and students of different disciplines gain and share knowledge. Hypothetical and speculative examples, as well as anecdotal ones that are impossible to verify, are therefore rarely effective. The kind of support you offer for your arguments should reflect what you have learned in this course about what makes for good evidence.

Consider how you might construct a response to this PT from May 2016.

"In knowledge there is always a trade-off between accuracy and simplicity." Evaluate this statement in relation to two areas of knowledge.

There is a lot in this PT that requires careful unpacking. For example, the title says "in knowledge", without identifying a specific process or context. You may choose to respond to this title by exploring how the trade-off between accuracy and simplicity manifests in the context of 1) the production and 2) the transfer of knowledge in two AOKs. Before we continue, it is important to note that when a PT calls for a discussion of the *production* of knowledge, then it is appropriate to focus specifically on the activities of specialists and experts in the AOKs.

In the first part of your essay you can explore the alleged inverse relationship between accuracy and simplicity in how knowledge is produced in two AOKs. Combinations of mathematical proof and natural laws, models of economic and biological processes, scientific and political theories, historical narratives and art performances can be invoked here to explore the accuracy and simplicity in knowledge production.

Here are some **pitfalls to avoid**.

- It is not uncommon for students to opportunistically choose AOKs that seem to give opposing answers to the question at hand. This can result in arguments that one thing happens in one AOK and exactly the opposite happens in the other. These arguments tend to be supported by oversimplified examples, that misrepresent the AOKs as monoliths.

- Another weak approach is to offer arguments both in favour and against the title, in both AOKs, effectively concluding nothing. This "both-sides-of-the-story" approach sounds as if you are doing TOK—but without evaluating the relative merits of the arguments in context, there is not much to say at the end.

- Another pitfall is to hang onto a strong word in the PT, such as "always", and argue that while there may be a trade-off between accuracy and simplicity, this is not *always* the case in your chosen AOKs. This approach can be limiting if you only offer a counterexample and leave it at that. However, if you can offer some discussion or analysis of the counterexample this approach may still be successful.

In the example of this prescribed title, you can **make a more nuanced argument**, such as that the relationship between accuracy and simplicity in one or both of your AOKs is best described as something other than a trade-off. You can then give examples of the specific conditions of the production of knowledge in your AOKs, and how they affect the relationship between accuracy and simplicity.

In the second part of the essay you may turn to the transfer of knowledge in the same two AOKs. Throughout this book we discuss examples of the distortions that arise when knowledge is simplified for the purpose of education—for example in the way it is presented in textbooks. You might recall examples from genetics (Chapter 7), history (Chapter 9) or economics (Chapter 8). You may argue that this trade-off is inevitable in order for the transfer of knowledge to work, and examine the effect—positive or negative—of sacrificing some degree of accuracy for simplicity.

II.3 Engaging with a diversity of perspectives and evaluating differences

In the TOK essay you will need to demonstrate awareness of multiple points of view, as well as an ability to evaluate them. These different points of view can come from various perspectives. On a big-picture level, there are the perspectives of the different AOKs—the arts, the human and natural sciences, history and mathematics. Within each AOK there are different fields or disciplines, and within each of the disciplines there are subdisciplines and schools of thought. Even within a single subdiscipline there can be a multiplicity of perspectives—claims made by a variety of claims-makers. For example, in the visual arts we can have the perspective of the artist, the art critic, the student of art, the curator, the art collector, the audience and so on.

Your awareness of different perspectives is reflected through the selection of points of view that you include in your essay. But more important than just having them represented is what you do with the different perspectives— what kind of analysis and evaluation can you offer? One thing that is often overlooked by students in such analyses is that the similarities among disciplines and AOKs are as interesting as the differences. When we encounter similarities between two academic fields, about what counts as evidence or what it means to give an explanation, it is important to pause and consider not only what makes AOKs different, but also how they are similar in the ways they produce, share and apply knowledge.

And whenever we focus on the differences, as we so often do in TOK, it is important to ask: where do these differences come from? How come reliability and accuracy take on different meanings in different AOKs? Does the legitimacy of experts come from different sources in different AOKs? It is not enough by way of TOK analysis to say that different things happen in mathematics and history because they are different AOKs; that is obvious. What can you say about the *source* of

their differences and, as we mentioned earlier, similarities? Even if it is difficult to articulate, it is still worth thinking about why it is that we have these different ways of coming to know about the world. Let's see what this looks like in practice.

Consider how you might engage with and evaluate different points of view in this PT from the May 2015 session.

"There is no reason why we cannot link facts and theories across disciplines and create a common groundwork of explanation." **To what extent do you agree with this statement?**

You might notice that the title contains the tricky word "we", and we discussed earlier why it is important and necessary to specify whom it is referring to. In this specific title, you can choose to answer the question with reference to, for example, 1) experts and researchers who produce knowledge, 2) teachers and communicators who disseminate knowledge, or 3) students and individuals who acquire and make sense of knowledge. Each of these groups of knowers, and subgroups, are likely to have different reasons for why we can or cannot "create a common groundwork of explanation". Notice how **in specifying the key term "we" you are inviting different perspectives** into your essay. This is an important step towards being able to draw

a meaningful conclusion; the better you do this the more convincing the outcome of your analysis will be. In what context and at what level are you going to explore the linking of facts and theories?

This PT in itself deals with multiple perspectives—the various points of view that exist across disciplines. Consider in which ways linking facts and theories across disciplines from the same AOK (economics, anthropology and psychology, for example) might differ from doing the same across history and mathematics. In your essay you should **demonstrate awareness of the similarities and differences between and within AOKs, as well as the source of those similarities and differences**. What might be the source? Consider what role having a similar set of methods and tools, or having a shared set of assumptions, plays in this PT.

The main pitfall you are going to want to avoid here is generalizing perspectives at the level of AOKs, uncritically presenting disciplines as monoliths; for example, "in the arts we see X, while in the sciences we see Y."

Something else to keep in mind is that in an essay a raft of rhetorical questions is not a substitute for analysis. Your analysis might raise more questions than it answers, but it must answer some.

II.4 Drawing conclusions that are of consequence

If you have done the work we talked about so far, by this point you should be well placed to

conclude your essay meaningfully. Below we discuss what that could look like.

The conclusions should leave the reader—and you—with a sense of having got somewhere at the end of your essay. In other words, we should not be back exactly where we started, having come full circle, to conclude that "it depends" or that it is true "to some extent". We knew that already, and 1600 words later, ideally we would know a bit more. By the time you need to present the conclusion, you should be able to say something about what it depends on, what the circumstances are, which factors affect it and why we should care about any of it.

And so, if you remember one thing about TOK essay conclusions, let it be this: **do not just give up the possibility of knowing**. Yes, we spend a lot of time and effort in TOK questioning the reliability and skill of those who produce knowledge; the legitimacy and trustworthiness of the institutions or persons who disseminate it; and our own ability to discern among multiple and often conflicting perspectives. So much so, it seems, that in the end students can be overwhelmed with the limitations and

challenges of knowing, with little to inspire confidence in knowledge. It can be tempting, from this standpoint, to conclude that since so much of knowledge is contestable, uncertain, incomplete and tentative that it is all relative, biased, unreliable and suspect. We hope that in your conclusion, and in what you take away from TOK, you can see both the difficulties of becoming knowledgeable and the achievement of having overcome them.

Like knowing, TOK is not easy, but it is not impossible either. It should certainly not be the kind of frustrating that makes it hard to appreciate why knowledge matters in the world. It matters too much to give it up.

Consider what you might conclude in response to this PT from May 2014.

"That which is accepted as knowledge today is sometimes discarded tomorrow." Consider knowledge issues raised by this statement in two areas of knowledge.

It has the word "sometimes"—and it would be easy, but also underwhelming, to flatly conclude on the basis of your extensive exploration that yes, sometimes this or that can be the case; the end. This title also has another tricky word, "tomorrow", that could well drag you into entirely speculative conclusions about what might happen to knowledge in different fields in the future. Hopefully you will have recognized both of these challenges with the title well in advance, and written an essay that discusses the second part of the prescribed title: the knowledge issues that arise from this statement in two AOKs.

A strong conclusion should demonstrate your ability to **extract meaning from the**

different perspectives you have explored. Consider: what have we learned from when and how knowledge has been discarded in the past? On what grounds was it discarded? What happens to discarded knowledge in your chosen AOKs? If there were significant or surprising similarities and differences between your AOKs—how can you explain these?

A strong conclusion also requires an **awareness of the implications** of the conclusion and the ability to **articulate a conclusion that is of consequence**. So, consider: what does the possibility of being discarded mean for the knowledge we have today and the confidence we have in it?

Note that we offer questions here to give you a sense of the kinds of ideas you can include in a conclusion. You can also offer some outstanding questions, but it is expected that you will attempt to answer them, and respond courageously—if provisionally—to the PT.

II.5 Assessment for the TOK essay

Your examiner will refer to the rubric below to evaluate your essay. You too can refer to it in the process of writing your essay to understand the criteria, self-assess and make sense of your teacher's feedback.

Does the student provide a clear, coherent and critical exploration of the essay title?					
Excellent 9–10	**Good 7–8**	**Satisfactory 5–6**	**Basic 3–4**	**Rudimentary 1–2**	**0**
The discussion has a sustained focus on the title and is linked effectively to areas of knowledge. Arguments are clear, coherent and effectively supported by specific examples. The implications of arguments are considered. There is clear awareness and evaluation of different points of view.	The discussion is focused on the title and is linked effectively to areas of knowledge. Arguments are clear, coherent and supported by examples. There is awareness and some evaluation of different points of view.	The discussion is focused on the title and is developed with some links to areas of knowledge. Arguments are offered and are supported by examples. There is some awareness of different points of view.	The discussion is connected to the title and makes superficial or limited links to areas of knowledge. The discussion is largely descriptive. Limited arguments are offered but they are unclear and are not supported by effective examples.	The discussion is weakly connected to the title. While there may be links to the areas of knowledge, any relevant points are descriptive or consist only of unsupported assertions.	The discussion does not reach the standard described by the other levels or is not a response to one of the prescribed titles for the correct assessment session.
Possible characteristics					
Insightful	Pertinent	Acceptable	Underdeveloped	Ineffective	
Convincing	Relevant	Mainstream	Basic	Descriptive	
Accomplished	Analytical	Adequate	Superficial	Incoherent	
Lucid	Organized	Competent	Limited	Formless	

Bibliography and further reading

Chapter 1

Baggini, J. 2017. "The Triage of Truth: Do Not Take Expert Opinion Lying Down". 2 October 2017. https://aeon.co/ideas/the-triage-of-truth-do-not-take-expert-opinion-lying-down

Campbell, T and Friesen, J. 2015. "Why People 'Fly from Facts'". 3 March 2015. www.scientificamerican.com/article/why-people-fly-from-facts/

Chakravartty, A. 2004. "Stance Relativism: Empiricism Versus Metaphysics". *Studies in History and Philosophy of Science*. Vol 35. Pp 173–184.

Clifford, WK. 1877. The Ethics of Belief. London, UK. Macmillan.

DeNicola, D. 2017. *Understanding Ignorance: The Surprising Impact of What We Don't Know*. Cambridge, MA, USA. The MIT Press.

DeNicola, D. 2018. "You Don't Have a Right to Believe Whatever You Want To". 14 May 2018. https://aeon.co/ideas/you-dont-have-a-right-to-believe-whatever-you-want-to

Dropp, K, Kertzer, J and Zeitoff, T. 2014. "The Less Americans Know About Ukraine's Location, the More They Want US to Intervene". 7 April 2014. www.washingtonpost.com/news/monkey-cage/wp/2014/04/07/the-less-americans-know-about-ukraines-location-the-more-they-want-u-s-to-intervene/

Firestein, S. 2012. *Ignorance: How it Drives Science*. New York, USA. Oxford University Press.

Fricker, M. 2007. *Epistemic Injustice: Power and the Ethics of Knowing*. New York, USA. Oxford University Press.

Ganeri, J. 2017. "The Tree of Knowledge is not an Apple or an Oak but a Banyan". 23 June 2017. https://aeon.co/ideas/the-tree-of-knowledge-is-not-an-apple-or-an-oak-but-a-banyan

Harman, G. 2000. "The Nonexistence of Character Traits". *Proceedings of the Aristotelian Society*. Vol 11. Pp 223–226.

Kappel, K. 2018. "There is No Middle Ground for Deep Disagreements about Facts". 15 October 2018. https://aeon.co/ideas/there-is-no-middle-ground-for-deep-disagreements-about-facts

Morris, E. 2010. "The Anosognosic's Dilemma: Something's Wrong but You'll Never Know What it is (Part 1)". 20 June 2010. https://opinionator.blogs.nytimes.com/2010/06/20/the-anosognosics-dilemma-1/

Sartre, JP. 1946. *Existentialism and Humanism*. Edition published 1973. London, UK. Methuen.

Chapter 2

Ahmed, M. 2018. "Chief's 'Hubris' Steered Cambridge Analytica to Data Scandal". 23 March 2018. www.ft.com/content/e4e95b6c-2dac-11e8-9b4b-bc4b9f08f381

Anderson, B and Horvath, B. 2017. "The Rise of the Weaponized AI Propaganda Machine". 12 February 2017. https://medium.com/join-scout/the-rise-of-the-weaponized-ai-propaganda-machine-86dac61668b

Arendt, H. 1951. *The Origins of Totalitarianism*. Berlin, Germany. Schocken Books.

Bakshy, E, Messing, S, and Adamic, LA. 2015. "Exposure to Ideologically Diverse News and Opinion on Facebook". *Science*. Vol 348, number 6239. Pp 1130–1132.

Boykoff, M and Boykoff, J. 2004. "Balance as Bias: Global Warming and the US Prestige Press". *Global Environmental Change*. Vol 14, number 2. Pp 125–136.

British Broadcasting Corporation. 2011. "BBC Trust Review of Impartiality and Accuracy of the BBC's Coverage of Science". July 2011. www.h2mw.eu/redactionmedicale/2011/08/BBC%20trust_science_impartiality.pdf

Cadwalladr, C. 2016. "Google, Democracy and the Truth about Internet Search". 4 December 2016. https://www.theguardian.com/technology/2016/dec/04/google-democracy-truth-internet-search-facebook

Cadwalladr, C. 2017. "Revealed: How US Billionaire Helped to Back Brexit". 26 Feb 2017. https://www.theguardian.com/politics/2017/feb/26/us-billionaire-mercer-helped-back-brexit?CMP=share_btn_link

Carrington, D. 2019. "Why the Guardian is Changing the Language it Uses about the Environment". 17 May 2019. www.theguardian.com/environment/2019/may/17/why-the-guardian-is-changing-the-language-it-uses-about-the-environment

Chan, E. 2016. "Donald Trump, Pepe the Frog, and White Supremacists: An Explainer". 12 September 2016. http://web.archive.org/web/20160913005409/https://www.hillaryclinton.com/feed/donald-trump-pepe-the-frog-and-white-supremacists-an-explainer/

Chen, A and Potenza, A. 2018. "Cambridge Analytica's Facebook Data Abuse Shouldn't Get Credit for Trump". 20 March 2018. www.theverge.com/2018/3/20/17138854/cambridge-analytica-facebook-data-trump-campaign-psychographic-microtargeting

Chomsky, N. 1998. *The Common Good*. Odonian Press. https://openlibrary.org/publishers/Odonian_Press

Confessore, N and Hakim, D. 2017. "Data Firm Says 'Secret Sauce' Aided Trump; Many Scoff". 6 March 2017. *New York Times*.

Cook, J *et al*. 2016. "Consensus on Consensus: A Synthesis of Consensus Estimates on Human-caused Global Warming". *Environmental Research Letters*. Vol 11, number 4. DOI:10.1088/1748-9326/11/4/048002.

Davis, M. 2001. *Late Victorian Holocausts*. New York, USA. Verso.

Dewey, C. 2016. "How Bernie Sanders Became the Lord of 'Dank Memes'". 23 February 2016. https://www.washingtonpost.com/news/the-intersect/wp/2016/02/23/how-bernie-sanders-became-the-lord-of-dank-memes/

Dubois, E and Blank, G. 2018. "The Echo Chamber is Overstated: The Moderating Effect of Political Interest and Diverse Media". *Information, Communication & Society*. Vol 21, number 5. Pp 729–745.

Economist. 2016. "Yes, I'd Lie To You". 10 September 2016. www.economist.com/briefing/2016/09/10/yes-id-lie-to-you

Eshelman, RS. 2014. "The Danger of Fair and Balanced". *Columbia Journalism Review*. 1 May 2014. https://archives.cjr.org/essay/the_danger_of_fair_and_balance.php

Financial Times. 2019. "India: The WhatsApp Election". www.ft.com/content/9fe88fba-6c0d-11e9-a9a5-351ee-aef6d84

Flaxman, S, Goel, S and Rao, JM. 2016. "Filter Bubbles, Echo Chambers, and Online News Consumption". *Public Opinion Quarterly*. Vol 80, number S1. P 298.

Garimella, K, De Francisci Morales, G, Gionis, A and Mathioudakis, M. 2018. "Political Discourse on Social Media: Echo Chambers, Gatekeepers, and the Price of Bipartisanship". In "WWW 2018: The 2018 Web Conference, April 23–27, 2018". New York, USA. ACM. https://arxiv.org/pdf/1801.01665.pdf

Gillett, G. 2017. "The Myth of Post-Truth Politics". 20 April 2017. https://georgegillett.com/2017/04/20/the-myth-of-post-truth-politics/

Guess, A, Nyhan, B and Reifler, J. 2018. "Selective Exposure to Misinformation: Evidence from the Consumption of Fake News During the 2016 US Presidential Campaign". European Research Council. P 1.

Hersh, ED. 2015. *Hacking the Electorate: How Campaigns Perceive Voters*. Cambridge, UK. Cambridge University Press.

Hosanagar, K. 2016. "Blame the Echo Chamber on Facebook. But Blame Yourself too". 25 November 2016. https://www.wired.com/2016/11/facebook-echo-chamber/

Kestler-D'Amours, J. 2017. "How to Fight Fake News in a Post Truth Environment". 24 April 2017. www.aljazeera.com/indepth/features/2017/03/fight-fake-news-post-truth-environment-170327162945897.html

Kosinski, M, Stillwell, D and Graepel, T. 2013. "Private Traits and Attributes are Predictable from Digital Records of Human Behavior". *Proceedings of the National Academy of Sciences of the United States of America*. Vol 110, number 15. Pp 5802–5805.

Le Guin, UK. 2004. *The Wave in the Mind*. Boston, MASS, USA. Shambhala Publications.

Lewandowsky, S, Pilditch, TD, Madsen, JK, Oreskes, N and Risbey JS. 2019. "Influence and Seepage: An Evidence-resistant Minority can Affect Public Opinion and Scientific Belief Formation". *Cognition*. Vol 188. Pp 124–139.

Mantzarlis, A. 2016. "No, We're Not in a 'Post-fact' Era". 21 July 2016. www.poynter.org/fact-checking/2016/no-were-not-in-a-post-fact-era/

Mayer, J. 2017. "The Reclusive Hedge-Fund Tycoon Behind the Trump Presidency". 17 March 2017. www.newyorker.com/magazine/2017/03/27/the-reclusive-hedge-fund-tycoon-behind-the-trump-presidency

Nagle, A. 2017. *Kill All Normies: Online Culture Wars from 4Chan and Tumblr to Trump and the Alt-Right*. Alresford, Hampshire, UK. Zero Books.

New Scientist. 2016. "Free Speech has met Social Media, with Revolutionary Results". 1 June 2016. www.newscientist.com/article/mg23030763-000-free-speech-has-met-social-media-with-revolutionary-results/

Nix, A. 2016. "How Big Data Got the Better of Donald Trump". 11 February 2016. www.campaignlive.co.uk/article/big-data-better-donald-trump/1383209

Nyhan, B. 2018. "Fake News and Bots may be Worrisome, but their Political Power is Overblown". 13 February 2018. www.nytimes.com/2018/02/13/upshot/fake-news-and-bots-may-be-worrisome-but-their-political-power-is-overblown.html

Obama, B. 2017. Transcript of Farewell Speech. 11 January 2011. http://time.com/4631007/president-obama-farewell-speech-transcript/

Pariser, E. 2011. *The Filter Bubble: What the Internet is Hiding From You*. New York, USA. Penguin Books.

Preston, P. 2012. "Broadcast News is Losing its Balance in the Post-truth Era". 9 September 2012. https://www.theguardian.com/media/2012/sep/09/post-truth-politics-us-broadcasting

Ressa, M. "War on Truth". 18 February 2019. www.aljazeera.com/programmes/witness/2019/02/maria-ressa-war-truth-190214144801371.html

Robson, D. 2018. "The Myth of the Online Echo Chamber". 17 April 2018. www.bbc.com/future/story/20180416-the-myth-of-the-online-echo-chamber

Scruton, R. 2017. "Post-truth? It's Pure Nonsense". 10 June 2017. www.spectator.co.uk/2017/06/post-truth-its-pure-nonsense/

Smith, LT. 1999. *Decolonizing Methodologies*. London, UK. Zed Books.

Stalder, F. 2019. "The Crisis of Epistemology and New Institutions of Learning" in *The New Alphabet*. https://www.hkw.de/mediathek/hkw/_default/assets/000/071/065/71065_download_the-new-alphabet-opening-days-pr_sxymtt.pdf

Tworek, H. 2017. "Cambridge Analytica, Trump, and the New Old Fear of Manipulating the Masses". 15 May 2017. www.niemanlab.org/2017/05/cambridge-analytica-trump-and-the-new-old-fear-of-manipulating-the-masses/

Vogel, KP and Parti, T. 2015. "Cruz Partners with Donor's 'Psychographic' Firm". Politico. 7 July 2015. www.politico.com/story/2015/07/ted-cruz-donor-for-data-119813#ixzz3zR4A2d8U

Vosoughi, S, Roy, D and Aral, S. 2018. "The Spread of True and False News Online". *Science*. Vol 359, number 6380. Pp 1146–1151.

Wakefield, J. 2018. "Cambridge Analytica: Can Targeted Online Ads Really Change a Voter's Behaviour?" 30 March 2018. https://www.bbc.com/news/technology-43489408

Weinberger, S. 2005. "You Can't Handle the Truth" 19 September 2005. https://slate.com/news-and-politics/2005/09/psy-ops-propaganda-goes-mainstream.html

Wood, P. 2016. "The British Data-crunchers Who Say They Helped Donald Trump to Win". 3 December 2016. www.spectator.co.uk/2016/12/the-british-data-crunchers-who-say-they-helped-donald-trump-to-win/

Wu, Y, Kosinski, M and Stillwell, D. 2015. "Computers Judge Personalities Better Than Humans". *Proceedings of the National Academy of Sciences of the United States of America*. Vol 112, number 4. Pp 1036–1040.

Young, T. 2016. "The Truth About 'Post-truth Politics'". 16 July 2016. https://www.spectator.co.uk/2016/07/the-truth-about-post-truth-politics/

Zannettou, S, Caulfield, T, De Cristofaro, E, Sirivianos, M, Stringhini, G and Blackburn, J. 2018. "Disinformation Warfare: Understanding State-Sponsored Trolls on Twitter and Their Influence on the Web". 4 March 2019. https://arxiv.org/abs/1801.09288

Chapter 3

Bolukbasi, T, Chang, KW, Zou, J, Saligrama, V and Kalai, A. 2016. "Man is to Computer Programmer as Woman is to Homemaker? Debiasing Word Embeddings". 21 July 2016. https://arxiv.org/abs/1607.06520

Bright, P. 2016 . "Tay, The Neo-Nazi Millennial Chatbot, Gets Autopsied". 26 March 2016. https://arstechnica.com/information-technology/2016/03/tay-the-neo-nazi-millennial-chatbot-gets-autopsied/

Buolamwini, J. 2018. "Gender Shades". http://gender-shades.org/

Caliskan, A, Bryson, JJ and Narayanan, A. 2017. "Semantics Derived Automatically from Language Corpora Contain Human-like Biases". *Science*. Vol 356, number 6334. Pp 183–186.

Dinkins, S. "Project al-Khwarizmi (PAK)". Date unknown. www.stephaniedinkins.com/project-al-khwarizmi.html

Hayes, D. 1977. *Rays of Hope: The Transition to a Post-Petroleum World*. New York, USA. WW Norton.

Jasanoff, S, Markle, GE, Peterson, JC, and Pinch, TJ (eds). 2001. *Handbook of Science and Technology Studies*. Thousand Oaks, CA, USA. Sage Publications.

Kosinski, M, Stillwell, D and Graepel, T. 2013. "Private Traits and Attributes are Predictable from Digital Records of Human Behavior". *Proceedings of the National Academy of Sciences of the United States of America*. Vol 110, number 15. Pp 5802–5805.

Lapowsky, I. 2018. "The Man Who Saw the Dangers of Cambridge Analytica Years Ago". 19 June 2018. www.wired.com/story/the-man-who-saw-the-dangers-of-cambridge-analytica/

Levitt, D. 2018. "In Search of an Ethics for the Age of Animation". 25 October 2018. www.publicseminar.org/2018/10/in-search-of-an-ethics-for-the-age-of-animation/

Matz, SC, Kosinski, M, Nave, G and Stillwell, D. 2017. *Proceedings of the National Academy of Sciences of the United States of America*. Volume 114, number 48. Pp 12714–12719.

Minard, J. 2014. "Internet Pioneer Brewster Kahle Has a Dream—Universal Access to All Knowledge". 28 August 2014. https://aeon.co/videos/internet-pioneer-brewster-kahle-has-a-dream-universal-access-to-all-knowledge

O'Neil, C. 2016. *"Weapons of Math Destruction: How Big Data Increases Inequality and Threatens Democracy"*. New York, USA. Penguin Random House.

Santamicone, M. 2019. "Is Artificial Intelligence Racist?". 2 April 2019. https://towardsdatascience.com/https-medium-com-mauriziosantamicone-is-artificial-intelligence-racist-66ea8f67c7de

Shane, S and Wakabayashi, D. 2018. "'The Business of War': Google Employees Protest Work for the Pentagon". 4 April 2018. www.nytimes.com/2018/04/04/technology/google-letter-ceo-pentagon-project.html

Sismondo, S. 2009. *An Introduction to Science and Technology Studies*. Chichester, UK. Wiley Blackwell.

Sontag, S. 2002. "Looking at War". 9 December 2002. www.newyorker.com/magazine/2002/12/09/looking-at-war

Thomas, R. 2018."Artificial Intelligence Needs All of us". 19 October 2018. https://www.youtube.com/watch?v=LqjP7O9SxOM&feature=youtu.be

Tippett, K. 2017. "Anil Dash: Tech's Moral Reckoning". 12 January 2017. https://onbeing.org/programs/anil-dash-techs-moral-reckoning-jan2017

Van Alstyne, M and Brynjolfsson, E. 1996. "Electronic Communities: Global Village or Cyberbalkans?" http://web.mit.edu/marshall/www/papers/CyberBalkans.pdf

Wajcman, J. 2001. "Feminist Theories of Technology" in Jasanoff, S, Markle, GE, Petersen, JC and Pinch, T (eds).

Handbook of Science and Technology Studies. Thousand Oaks, CA, USA. Sage Publications.

Wakefield, J. 2018. "Are You Scared Yet? Meet Norman, the Psychopathic AI". 2 June 2018. www.bbc.com/news/technology-44040008

Winner, L. 1980. "Do Artifacts Have Politics?". *Daedalus*. Vol 109, number 1. Pp. 121–136.

Wood, P. 2016. "The British Data-crunchers Who Say They Helped Donald Trump to Win". 3 December 2016. www.spectator.co.uk/2016/12/the-british-data-crunchers-who-say-they-helped-donald-trump-to-win/

Wu, Y, Kosinski, M and Stillwell, D. 2015. "Computers Judge Personalities Better than Humans". *Proceedings of the National Academy of Sciences of the United States of America*. Vol 112, number 4. Pp 1036–1040.

Chapter 4

Adichie, CM. 2017. *Dear Ijeawele, or a Feminist Manifesto in Fifteen Suggestions*. New York, USA. Knopf Publishing.

Belting, H. 2014. "Introduction for the English Reader" in *An Anthropology of Images: Picture, Medium, Body*. Princeton, NJ, USA. Princeton University Press

Boroditsy, L. 2009. "How Does our Language Shape the Way we Think?" 6 November 2009. www.edge.org/conversation/how-does-our-language-shape-the-way-we-think

Carrington, D. 2019. "Why the Guardian is Changing the Language it Uses about the Environment". 17 May 2019. www.theguardian.com/environment/2019/may/17/why-the-guardian-is-changing-the-language-it-uses-about-the-environment

Davis, W. 2003. "An Interview with Wade Davis". NPR/National Geographic Society. https://www.npr.org/programs/re/archivesdate/2003/may/mali/davisinterview.html

Davis-Young, K. 2017. "The College Student Who Decoded the Data Hidden in Inca Knots". 14 December 2017. www.atlasobscura.com/articles/khipus-inca-empire-harvard-university-colonialism

Gorenflo, LJ, Romaine, S, Mittermeier, RA and Waljker-Painemillla, K. 2012. "Co-occurring Linguistic and Biological Diversity". *Proceedings of the National Academy of Sciences of the United States of America*. May 2012, 201117511. www.pnas.org/content/early/2012/05/03/1117511109

Herman, JR. 1998. "Tao Te Ching: A Book about the Way and the Power of the Way" by Ursula K. Le Guin". *Journal of the American Academy of Religion*. Vol 66, number 3. Pp 686–689.

Jensen, E. 2019. "Reviewing NPR Language for Covering Abortion". 29 May 2019. www.npr.org/sections/publiceditor/2019/05/29/728069483/reviewing-nprs-language-for-covering-abortion

Klinkenborg, V. 2012. "Linking Twin Extinctions of Species and Languages". 17 July 2012. https://e360.yale.edu/features/linking_twin_extinctions_of_species_and_languages

Lakoff, G and Johnson, M. 1980. *Metaphors We Live By*. Chicago, IL, USA. University of Chicago Press.

Latronico, V. 2019. "Inside a Translator's Mind". *Das Neue Alphabet*. Berlin, Germany. Haus Der Kulturen Der Welt (HKW).

Lutz, W. 1996. *The New Doublespeak: Why No One Knows What Anyone is Saying Anymore*. New York, USA. HarperCollins.

McWhorter, J. 2016. "What's a Language Anyway? 19 January 2016. www.theatlantic.com/international/archive/2016/01/difference-between-language-dialect/424704/

Medrano, M and Urton, G. 2018. "The Inca's Knotty History". 26 July 2018. www.sapiens.org/technology/khipu-incas-knotty-history/

Norton, C and Hulme, M. 2019. *Geoforum*. "Telling One Story, or Many? An Ecolinguistic Analysis of Climate Change Stories in UK National Newspaper Editorials". *Geoforum*. Vol 104. Pp 114–136.

Patel, S. 2010. *Migritude*. Los Angeles, CA, USA. Kaya Press.

Popova, M. 2016. "A Small Dark Light: Ursula K. Le Guin on the Legacy of the Tao Te Ching and What It Continues to Teach Us About Personal and Political Power 2,500 Years Later". 21 October 2016. https://www.brainpickings.org/2016/10/21/lao-tzu-tao-te-ching-ursula-k-le-guin/

Rosenthal, J. 2016. "The Pioneer Plaque: Science as a Universal Language". 20 January 2016. www.planetary.org/blogs/guest-blogs/2016/0120-the-pioneer-plaque-science-as-a-universal-language.html

Stone, D. 2017. "Discovery May Help Decipher Ancient Inca String Code". 19 April 2017. www.nationalgeographic.com/news/2017/04/inca-khipus-code-discovery-peru/

Strochlic, N. 2018. "The Race to Save the World's Disappearing Languages". 16 April 2018. www.nationalgeographic.com/news/2018/04/saving-dying-disappearing-languages-wikitongues-culture/

Survival International. 2019. "Indigenous Languages Hold the Key to Understanding Who We Really Are". https://survivalinternational.org/articles/3567-indigenouslanguages

Tanu, D. 2017. *Growing Up in Transit: The Politics of Belonging at an International School*. New York, USA. Berghahn Books.

Thiong'o, N wa. 1986. *Decolonizing the Mind: The Politics of Language in African Literature*. London, UK. James Currey.

Chapter 5

Australian Human Rights and Equal Opportunities Commission/Aboriginal and Torres Strait Islander Social Justice Commissioner. 2002. "Human Rights and Equal Opportunity Commission, Submission G160". 13 May 2002. www.humanrights.gov.au/our-work/legal/protection-genetic-information-indigenous-peoples.

Alfred, GR. 1995. *Heeding the Voices of our Ancestors. Kahnawake Mohawk Politics and the Rise of Nationalism.* Toronto, Canada. Oxford University Press.

Anaya, SJ. 2004. *Indigenous Peoples in International Law* (second edition). Oxford, UK. Oxford University Press.

Antoine, A, Mason, R, Mason, R, Palahicky, S and Rodriguez de France, C. 2018. "Glossary of terms" in *Pulling Together: A Guide for Curriculum Developers. https://opentextbc.ca/indigenizationcurriculumdevelopers/back-matter/glossary/*

Artelle, KA, Zurba, M, Bhattacharyya, J, Chan, DE, Brown, K, Housty, J and Moola, F. 2019. "Supporting Resurgent Indigenous-led Governance: A Nascent Mechanism for Just and Effective Conservation". *Biological Conservation* Vol 240. https://doi.org/10.1016/j.biocon.2019.108284

Corry, S. 2014. Quoted in "Criticisms of Jimmy Nelson's 'Before They Pass Away'". Survival International. November 2014. www.survivalinternational.org/articles/3373-jimmy-nelson-before-they-pass-away

Davis, W. 2003. "Dreams from Endangered Cultures". February 2003. www.ted.com/talks/wade_davis_on_endangered_cultures

Emery, AR. 1997. *Guidelines for Environmental Assessments and Traditional Knowledge.* Unpublished. Ottawa, Canada. Centre for Traditional Knowledge.

Gammage, B. 2011. *The Biggest Estate on Earth: How the Aborigines Made Australia.* Crow's Nest, NSW, Australia. Allen & Unwin.

Hoover, E, Cook, K, Plain, R, Sanchez, K, Waghiyi, V, Miller, P, Dufault, R, Sislin, C and Carpenter DO. 2012. "Indigenous Peoples of North America: Environmental Exposures and Reproductive Justice". *Environmental Health Perspectives.* Vol 120, number 12. Pp 1645–1649.

Houde, N. 2007. "The Six Faces of Traditional Ecological Knowledge: Challenges and Opportunities for Canadian Co-Management Arrangements". *Ecology and Society.* Vol 12, number 2.

Huntington, HP and Mymrin, N. 1998."Traditional Ecological Knowledge of Beluga Whales". *Cultural Survival Quarterly Magazine.* September 1998. www.culturalsurvival.org/publications/cultural-survival-quarterly/traditional-ecological-knowledge-and-beluga-whales

Irwin, K. 1992. "Towards Theories of Maori Feminisms". In du Plessis, R (ed). *Feminist Voices: Women's Studies Texts for Aotearoa/New Zealand.* Auckland, New Zealand. Oxford University Press.

Kimmerer, RW. 2014. *Braiding Sweetgrass.* Minneapolis, MN, USA. Milkweed Editions.

Kopenawa, D. 2014. In "Criticisms of Jimmy Nelson's 'Before They Pass Away'". Survival International. November 2014. www.survivalinternational.org/articles/3373-jimmy-nelson-before-they-pass-away

Lagoutte, J. 2014. "Jimmy Nelson's Wrong: Tribal Peoples Aren't Passing Away, They Are Fighting Against Brutal Oppression". 12 November 2014. www.opendemocracy.net/en/opendemocracyuk/jimmy-nelsons-wrong-tribal-peoples-arent-passing-away-they-are-fighting-/openDemocracy

Le Guin, UK. 2004. "A War Without End" in *The Wave in the Mind.* Boston, MASS, USA. Shambhala Publications.

Le Guin, UK. 2016. *Late in the Day.* Oakland, CA, USA. PM Press.

Mazzocchi, F. 2006. "Western Science and Traditional Knowledge". *EMBO Reports.* Vol 7, number 5. Pp 463–466.

Mayor, F. 1997. Former Director General of UNESCO cited in Emery, AR. 1997. *Guidelines for Environmental Assessments and Traditional Knowledge.* Unpublished. Ottawa, Canada. Centre for Traditional Knowledge.

Merrill, J. 2014. "'Before They Pass Away': Endangered Communities Photographed 'like Kate Moss'". 28 September 2014. www.independent.co.uk/arts-entertainment/art/features/before-they-pass-away-endangered-communities-photographed-like-kate-moss-9757549.

Nelson, J. 2014. "Gorgeous Portraits of the World's Vanishing People". October 2014. https://www.ted.com/talks/jimmy_nelson_gorgeous_portraits_of_the_world_s_vanishing_people

Robbins, J. 2017. *The Wonder of Birds: What They Tell Us About Ourselves, the World, and a Better Future.* Spiegel and Grau, New York, USA.

Robbins, J. 2018. "Native Knowledge: What Ecologists Are Learning From Indigenous People". 26 April 2018. https://e360.yale.edu/features/native-knowledge-what-ecologists-are-learning-from-indigenous-people

Shiva, V. 1993. *Monocultures of the Mind: Perspectives on Biodiversity and Biotechnology.* London, UK. Palgrave Macmillan.

Slater, J and Gowen, A. 2018. "God, I Don't Want to Die,' U.S. Missionary Wrote Before he was Killed by Tribe on Indian Island". 22 November 2018. www.washingtonpost.com/world/2018/11/21/american-believed-dead-after-encounter-with-remote-indian-tribe-hostile-outsiders/

Smith, LT. 1999. *Decolonizing Methodologies: Research and Indigenous Peoples.* London, UK. Zed Books.

Sobrevila, C. 2008. "The Role of Indigenous Peoples in Biodiversity Conservation: The Natural but Often Forgotten Partners". Washington DC, USA. The World Bank.

Trask, HK. 1999. *From a Native Daughter: Colonialism and Sovereignty in Hawai'i*. Honolulu. University of Hawai'i Press.

University of British Columbia. 2009. First Nations Studies Program/Indigenous Foundation. https://indigenous-foundations.arts.ubc.ca/global_actions/

Wenda, B. 2014. Quoted in "Criticisms of Jimmy Nelson's 'Before They Pass Away'". Survival International. November 2014. www.survivalinternational.org/articles/3373-jimmy-nelson-before-they-pass-away

Wood, S. 2019. "How a Resurgence in Indigenous Governance is Leading to Better Conservation". 27 November 2019. https://thenarwhal.ca/how-a-resurgence-in-indigenous-governance-is-leading-to-better-conservation/

Yawanawá, N. 2014. Quoted in "Criticisms of Jimmy Nelson's 'Before They Pass Away'". Survival International. November 2014. www.survivalinternational.org/articles/3373-jimmy-nelson-before-they-pass-away

Younging, G. 2018. *Elements of Indigenous Style: A Guide for Writing by and About Indigenous Peoples*. Edmonton, Alberta, Canada. Brush Education.

Zaitchik, A. 2018. "How Conservation Became Colonialism". 16 July 2018. https://foreignpolicy.com/2018/07/16/how-conservation-became-colonialism-environment-indigenous-people-ecuador-mining/

Chapter 6

Aung San Suu Kyi. 1995. *Freedom from Fear and Other Writings*. Penguin. London, UK.

Anderson, W. 1990. *Green Man: The Archetype of Our Oneness with the Earth*. London, UK. HarperCollins.

Berger, PL. 1999. *The Desecularization of the World: Resurgent Religion and World Politics*. Ethics and Public Policy Centre/William B. Eerdmand Publishing Company. www.worldcat.org/wcpa/servlet/DCARead?standardNo=0802846912&standardNoType=1&excerpt=true

Bradley, J and Ruse, M. 2014. "The Evolution of the Science–Religion Debate". 26 June 2016. https://onbeing.org/programs/jim-bradley-michael-ruse-the-evolution-of-the-science-religion-debate/

Capra, F. 2010. *The Dao of Physics: An Exploration of the Parallels Between Modern Physics and Eastern Mysticism*. Boston, MA, USA. Shambhala Publications.

Chidester, D. 1987. *Patterns of Action: Religion and Ethics in a Comparative Perspective*. Belmont, CA, USA. Wadsworth.

Chidester, D. 2003. *Empire of Religion: Imperialism & Comparative Religion*. Chicago, IL, USA. University of Chicago Press.

Chitwood, K. 2019. "When Religion is Not Religion: Inside Religious Studies' Fight for Religious Literacy in the Public Sphere. 21 August 2019. www.religiousstudiesproject.com/2019/08/21/when-religion-is-not-religion/

Gandhi, M. 1927. *Autobiography or the Story of My Experiments with Truth*. Ahmedabad, India. Jitendra T Desai Navajivan Mudranalaya.

Glacken, C. 1967. *Traces on the Rhodian Shore: Nature and Culture in Western Thought from Ancient Times to the End of the Eighteenth Century*. Berkeley, CA, USA. University of California Press.

Goleman, D. 2004. *Destructive Emotions: A Scientific Dialogue with the Dalai Lama*. New York, USA. Bantam Dell.

Gopnik, A. 2015. *The Good Book: Writers Reflect on Favorite Bible Passages*. New York, USA. Simon & Schuster.

Harris, M. 1971. *Culture, Man, and Nature: An Introduction to General Anthropology*. New York, USA. Thomas Y Crowell.

Harrison, P. 2015. *The Territories of Science and Religion*. Chicago, IL, USA. University of Chicago Press.

Holmes, S. 1999. *The Young John Muir: An Environmental Biography*. Madison, WI, USA. University of Wisconsin Press.

Nash, RF. 1967. *Wilderness and the American Mind*. New Haven, CT, USA. Yale University Press.

Porritt, J. 1984. *Seeing Green: The Politics of Ecology Explained*. Oxford, UK. Wiley-Blackwell.

Sacks, J. 2003. *The Dignity of Difference: How to Avoid the Clash of Civilizations*. New York, USA. Continuum.

Safi, O. 2016. "The Spiritual is Political". 11 August 2016. https://onbeing.org/blog/the-spiritual-is-political/

Singer, P. 2010. *Practical Ethics*. New York, USA. Cambridge University Press.

Smith, JZ and Green, WS (eds). 1995. *The HarperCollins Dictionary of Religion*. New York, USA. HarperCollins.

Stoddard, B and Martin, C (eds). 2017. *Stereotyping Religion: Critiquing Clichés*. London, UK. Bloomsbury Publishing.

Suzuki, S. 2011. *Zen Mind, Beginner's Mind*. Boston, MA, USA. Shambhala Publications.

Sweeney, JG. 1989. "The Nude of Landscape Painting: Emblematic Personification in the Art of the Hudson River School". *Smithsonian Studies in American Art*. Vol 3, number 4. Pp 42–65.

Taylor, B (ed). 2005. *Encyclopedia of Religion and Nature*. New York, USA. Continuum.

Tippet, K. 2001. "Jean Bethke Elshtain, John Paul Lederach and Michael Orange Justice and a Just War". 9 November 2001. https://onbeing.org/programs/jean-bethke-elshtain-john-paul-lederach-and-michael-orange-justice-and-a-just-war/

Tippett, K. 2005. "Jelle De Boer and Ursula Goodenough The Morality of Nature". 7 April 2005. https://onbeing.org/programs/jelle-de-boer-and-ursula-goodenough-the-morality-of-nature/

Tippett, K. 2006a. "Peter Berger and Rosabeth Moss Kanter: Globalization and the Rise of Religion". 12 October 2006. https://onbeing.org/programs/peter-berger-and-rosabeth-moss-kanter-globalization-and-the-rise-of-religion/

Tippett, K. 2006b. "Leila Ahmed Muslim Women and Other Misunderstandings". 7 December 2006. https://onbeing.org/programs/leila-ahmed-muslim-women-and-other-misunderstandings/

Tippett, K. 2007. "Varadaraja V. Raman the Heart's Reason: Hinudism and Science". 22 November 2007. https://onbeing.org/programs/varadaraja-v-raman-the-hearts-reason-hinduism-and-science/

Tippett, K. 2009. "Robert Coles The Inner Lives of Children". 1 January 2009. https://onbeing.org/programs/robert-coles-the-inner-lives-of-children

Tippett, K. 2010. *Einstein's God: Conversations about Science and the Human Spirit. New York, USA. Penguin.*

Tippett, K. 2013 "Thupten Jinpa Translating the Dalai Lama". 21 February 2013. https://onbeing.org/programs/thupten-jinpa-translating-the-dalai-lama/

Tippett, K. 2014. "Reza Aslan Islam's Reformation". 20 November 2014. https://onbeing.org/programs/reza-aslan-islams-reformation/

Tippett, K. 2017. "Adam Gopnik Practicing Doubt, Redrawing Faith". 7 December 2017. https://onbeing.org/programs/adam-gopnik-practicing-doubt-redrawing-faith-dec2017/

Tippett, K. 2018. "Stephen Batchelor Wondrous Doubt". 1 March 2018. https://onbeing.org/programs/stephen-batchelor-wondrous-doubt-mar2018/

Wallace, A. 2003. *Buddhism and Science.* New York, USA. Columbia University Press.

Weinberg, S. 1999. "Address at the Conference on Cosmic Design, American Association for the Advancement of Science". April 1999. Washington DC, USA.

White, L. 1967. "The Historical Roots of Our Ecological Crisis". *Science.* Vol 155, number 3767. Pp 1203–1207.

Worster, D. 2008. *Passion for Nature.* Oxford, UK. Oxford University Press.

Chapter 7

Bohannon, J. 2013. "Who's Afraid of Peer Review?" Science. Vol 342, number 6154. Pp 60–65.

Brown, LM. 1978. "The Idea of the Neutrino". *Physics Today.* Vol 31, number 9. Pp 23–28.

Cohen, J. 1994. "The Duesberg Phenomenon". *Science.* Vol 2666, number 5191. Pp 1642–1644.

Collins HM. 1981. "Son of Seven Sexes: The Social Destruction of a Physical Phenomenon". *Social Studies of Science.* Vol 11, number 1. Pp 33–62.

Collins, HM and Pinch, T. 2012. *The Golem: What You Should Know About Science* (second edition). Cambridge, UK. Cambridge University Press.

Crick, F. 1995. *The Astonishing Hypothesis: The Scientific Search for the Soul.* New York, USA. Schribner.

Daston, L and Lunbeck, E (eds). 2011. *Histories of Scientific Observation.* Chicago, IL, USA. University of Chicago Press.

Deutsch, D. 1997. *The Fabric of Reality.* New York, USA. Penguin.

Elgin, CZ. 2017. *True Enough.* Cambridge, MA, USA. The MIT Press.

Enserink, M. 2010. "Elsevier to Editor: Change Controversial Journal or Resign". 8 March 2010. https://web.archive.org/web/20100312091113/http://news.sciencemag.org/scienceinsider/2010/03/elsevier-to-editor-change-contro.html

Epstein, S. 1996. *Impure Science.* Oakland, CA, USA. University of California Press.

Fox Keller, E. 1996. *Reflection on Gender and Science* (10th anniversary edition). New Haven, CT, USA. Yale University Press.

Goodall, J. 2000. *In the Shadow of Man.* New York, USA. First Mariner Books.

Hacking, I. 1983. *Representing and Intervening: Introductory Topics in the Philosophy of Natural Science.* Cambridge, UK. Cambridge University Press.

Hacking, I. 2012. "Foreword" in 50th Edition of Kuhn, T. *The Structure of Scientific Revolutions.* Chicago, IL, USA. University of Chicago Press.

Harding, SG (ed). 2011. *The Postcolonial Science and Technology Studies Reader.* Durham, NC, USA. Duke University Press.

Hopkin, M. 2005. "Chernobyl Ecosystems 'Remarkably Healthy'". *Nature.* 9 August 2005. https://www.nature.com/news/2005/050808/full/news050808-4.html

Horrobin, David F. 1975. "Ideas in Biomedical Science: Reasons for the Foundation of Medical Hypotheses". *Medical Hypotheses.* Vol 1, number 1. Pp 1–2.

Horst, M, Davies, SR and Irwin, A. 2017. *The Handbook of Science and Technology Studies* (fourth edition). Cambridge, MA. The MIT Press.

Horton, R. 1996. "Truth and Heresy about Aids". *The New York Review of Books.* 23 May 1996.

Kuhn, T. 1962. *The Structure of Scientific Revolutions*. Chicago, IL, USA. University of Chicago Press.

Lenzer, J. 2008. "AIDS 'Dissident' Seeks Redemption … and a Cure for Cancer". 15 May 2008. http://discovermagazine.com/2008/jun/15-aids-dissident-seeks-redemption-and-a-cure-for-cancer

Lewis, J. 2011. "Genetics and Genomics." In Reiss, M (ed). *Teaching Secondary Biology*. London, UK. Hodder Education.

Maxwell, G and Feigl, H (eds). 1962. *Minnesota Studies in the Philosophy of Science, Vol. III*. Minnesota, MN, USA. University of Minnesota Press.

Nattrass, N. 2009. "Still Crazy After All These Years: The Challenge of AIDS Denialism for Science". *AIDS and Behavior*. Vol 14, number 2. Pp 248–5.

Oppenheimer JR. 1947. *Physics in the Contemporary World*. Cambridge, MA, USA. MIT Press.

Planck, MKEL. 1968. *Scientific Autobiography and Other Papers*. Translated from German by Gaynor, F. Westport, CT, USA. Greenwood Press Publishers.

Paola, FA, Walker, R and Nixon, LL (eds). 2009. *Medical Ethics and Humanities*. Burlington, MS, USA. Jones & Bartlett Publishers.

Popper, KR. 1979. *Objective Knowledge. An Evolutionary Approach*. Oxford, UK. Oxford University Press.

Radick, G. 2016. "Teach students the biology of their time". *Nature*. Vol 553, number 7603.

Sargent, R. 1999. "Selected Philosophical Works". Indianapolis, IN, USA. Hackett Publishing.

Scharrer, L, Rupieper, Y, Stadtler, M and Bromme, R. 2017. "When Science Becomes too Easy: Science Popularization Inclines Laypeople to Underrate their Dependence on Experts". *Public Understanding of Science*. Vol 26, number 8. Pp 1003–1018.

Scientific American. 2007. "When Pariahs have Good Ideas". 1 May 2007. https://www.scientificamerican.com/article/when-pariahs-have-good-ideas/

Sismondo, S. 2010. *An Introduction to Science and Technology Studies*. Oxford, UK. Wiley Blackwell.

Snow, CP. 1959. *The Two Cultures and the Scientific Revolution*. Cambridge UK. Cambridge University Press.

Specter, M. 2007. "The Denialists". 5 March 2007. https://www.newyorker.com/magazine/2007/03/12/the-denialists

Sutton, C. 1992. *Spaceship Neutrino*. Cambridge University Press, Cambridge, UK.

Tenner, E. 2015. "The Original Natural Born Killers". 3 December 2015. http://nautil.us/issue/31/stress/the-original-natural-born-killers-rp

Than, K. 2015. "Estimated Social Cost of Climate Change not Accurate, Stanford Scientists say". 12 January 2015. https://news.stanford.edu/2015/01/12/emissions-social-costs-011215/

Ware, M and Mabe, M. 2015. *The STM Report: An Overview of Scientific and Scholarly Journal Publishing*. The Hague, Netherlands. International Association of Scientific, Technical and Medical Publishers.

Weldon, WFR. 1902. "Mendel's Laws of Alternative Inheritance in Peas" *Biometrica*. Vol 1, number 2. Pp 228–254.

Wulf, A. 2015. *The Invention of Nature: The Adventures of Alexander von Humboldt, the Lost Hero of Science*. London, UK. John Murray.

Chapter 8

Arendt, H. 2006. *Eichmann in Jerusalem: A Report on the Banality of Evil*. London, UK. Penguin Classics/Penguin Random House.

Baker, M. 2015. "Over Half of Psychology Studies Fail Reproducibility Test". 27 August 2015. https://www.nature.com/news/over-half-of-psychology-studies-fail-reproducibility-test-1.18248

Baker, M. 2016. "Psychology's Reproducibility Problem is Exaggerated—Say Psychologists". 3 March 2016. https://www.nature.com/news/psychology-s-reproducibility-problem-is-exaggerated-say-psychologists-1.19498

Blum, B. 2018. "The Lifespan of a Lie". 7 June 2018. https://medium.com/s/trustissues/the-lifespan-of-a-lie-d869212b1f62

Boulding, K. 1973. "*Energy Reorganization Act of 1973: Hearings, Ninety-third Congress, First Session, on H.R. 11510*". Washington, DC, USA. United States Congress.

Bourke, J. 2011. *What It Means to Be Human: Historical Reflections from 1791 to Present*. Berkeley CA, USA. Counterpoint Publishing.

Bourke, J. 2014. "This Won't Hurt a Bit: The Cultural History of Pain". *New Statesmen*. 19 June 2014. www.newstatesman.com/culture/2014/06/wont-hurt-bit-cultural-history-pain

Buchanan, M. 2007. *The Social Atom: Why the Rich Get Richer, Cheaters Get Caught, and Your Neighbor Usually Looks Like You*. New York, USA. Bloomsbury.

Chakrabarti, BK, Chakraborti, A, Chakravarty, SR and Chatterjee, A. 2013. *Econophysics of Income & Wealth Distributions*. Cambridge, UK. Cambridge University Press.

Chawla, DS. 2018. "Scientists Rarely Admit Mistakes. A New Project Wants to Change That". 7 February 2018. https://undark.org/2018/07/02/loss-of-confidence-project-replication-crisis/

Cole, HSD, Freeman, C, Jahoda, M, Pavitt, KLR (eds). 1973. *Models of Doom: A Critique of the Limits to Growth*. Bloomington, IN, USA. Universe Publishing.

Colvile, R. 2016. "Spot the WEIRDo". 20 July 2016. https://aeon.co/essays/american-undergrads-are-too-weird-to-stand-for-all-humanity

Coyle, D. 2014. *GDP: A Brief but Affectionate History*. Princeton, NJ, USA. Princeton University Press.

Davis, W. 2003. "Dreams from endangered cultures". www.ted.com/talks/wade_davis_on_endangered_cultures/transcript?language=en#t-1049427%20around%2017:25

Durkheim, E. 1895. *The Rules of Sociological Method*. 1982 edition published in New York, USA. Free Press/Simon & Schuster.

Economist. 2004. "The Pursuit of Happiness". 16 December 2004. https://www.economist.com/christmas-specials/2004/12/16/the-pursuit-of-happiness

Economist. 2016. Briefing: "The Trouble with GDP". 30 April 2016. https://www.economist.com/briefing/2016/04/30/the-trouble-with-gdp

Epstein, R. 2007. "The Myth of the Teen Brain". 1 June 2007. https://www.scientificamerican.com/article/the-myth-of-the-teen-brain-2007-06/

Fourcade, M, Ollion, E and Algan, Y. 2015. "The Superiority of Economists" in *Journal of Economic Perspectives*. Vol 29, number 1. Pp 89–114.

Fox, RG (ed). 1991. *Recapturing Anthropology: Working in the Present*. Sante Fe, NM, USA. School of American Research Press.

Gardiner, SM and Hartzell-Nichols, L. 2012. "Ethics and Global Climate Change". *Nature Education Knowledge* . Vol 3, number 5. P 5

Geertz, C. 1967. "Under the Mosquito Net". *The New York Review of Books*. 14 September 1967. https://www.nybooks.com/articles/1967/09/14/under-the-mosquito-net/

Gertner, J. 2010. "The Rise and Fall of the G.D.P." 13 May 2010. https://www.nytimes.com/2010/05/16/magazine/16GDP-t.html

Gieben, B and Hall, S (eds). 1993. *Formations of Modernity: Understanding Modern Societies—An Introduction*. Cambridge, UK. Polity Press.

Gilbert, D. 2007. *Stumbling on Happiness*. New York USA. Vintage.

Graeber, D. 2011. *Debt: The First 5000 Years*. Hoboken, NJ, USA. Melville House Publishing.

Gunter, J. 2013. "Circular Economy isn't Just Recycling Products; Repair and Reuse are Also Vital". 4 December 2013. https://www.theguardian.com/sustainable-business/circular-economy-recycling-repair-reuse

Hastrup, K. 1990. "The Ethnographic Present: A Reinvention". *Cultural Anthropology*. Vol 5. Pp 45-61.

Henrich, J, Heine, SJ and Norenzayan, A. 2010a. "Most People are Not WEIRD". *Nature*. Vol 466. P 29.

Henrich J, Heine SJ and Norenzaya, A. 2010b. "The Weirdest People in the World?". *Behavioral and Brain Sciences*. Vol 33, number 2–3. Pp 61–83.

Henrich J, Heine SJ and Norenzaya, A. 2015. "Beyond WEIRD: Towards a Broad-based Behavioral Science". *Behavioral and Brain Sciences*. Vol 33, number 2–3. Pp 111–35.

Humphrey, C. 1985. "Barter and Economic Disintegration". *Man*. Vol 20, number 1. Pp 48–72.

Hruschka, D. 2018. "You Can't Characterize Human Nature if Studies Overlook 85 Percent of People on Earth". 16 November 2018. https://theconversation.com/you-cant-characterize-human-nature-if-studies-overlook-85-percent-of-people-on-earth-106670

ICTA. 2018. "Manifesto to the European Union: 'Europe, It's Time to End the Growth Dependency'". 17 September 2018. https://ictaweb.uab.cat/noticies_news_detail.php?id=3484

Iggers, GG. 1959. "Further Remarks about Early Uses of the Term 'Social Science'". *Journal of the History of Ideas*. Vol 20, number 3. Pp 433–36.

Jaffe, A. 2015. "Addiction, Connection and the Rat Park Study". 14 August 2015. https://www.psychologytoday.com/intl/blog/all-about-addiction/201508/addiction-connection-and-the-rat-park-study

Kahn, J and Yardley, J. 2007. "Choking on Growth: As China Roars, Pollution Reaches Deadly Extremes". 26 August 2007. *The New York Times*.

Keller, H. 2018. "Universality Claim of Attachment Theory: Children's Socioemotional Development Across Cultures." *Proceedings of the National Academy of Sciences of the United States of America*. Vol 115, number 45. Pp 11414–11419.

Krugman, P. 2009. "How did Economists get it so Wrong?". *New York Times*. 2 September 2009. https://www.nytimes.com/2009/09/06/magazine/06Economic-t.html

Lomborg, B and Rubin, O. 2009. "The Dustbin of History: Limits to Growth". 9 November 2009. https://foreignpolicy.com/2009/11/09/the-dustbin-of-history-limits-to-growth/

MacBride, K. 2017. "This 38-year-old Study is Still Spreading Bad Ideas About Addiction". 5 September 2017. https://theoutline.com/post/2205/this-38-year-old-study-is-still-spreading-bad-ideas-about-addiction?zd=1&zi=yesiyxii

Malinowski, B. 1922. *Argonauts of the Western Pacific: An Account of Native Enterprise and Adventure in the Archipelagoes of Melanesian New Guinea*. London, UK. Routledge and Kegan Paul.

McCarthy, J . 2018. "The Birthplace of Gross National Happiness is Growing a Bit Cynical". 12 Feb 2018. https://www.npr.org/sections/parallels/2018/02/12/584481047/the-birthplace-of-gross-national happiness-is-growing-a-bit-cynical

Medin, D, Ojalehto B, Marin, A and Bang, M. 2017. "Systems of (Non-)diversity". *Nature Human Behaviour*. Vol 1. Pp 1–5.

Mesman, J, van IJzendoorn MH and Sagi-Schwartz A. 2008. "Cross-cultural Patterns of Attachment: Universal and Contextual Dimensions". In Cassidy, J and Shaver PR (eds). *Handbook of Attachment: Theory, Research, and Clinical Applications* (second edition). New York, USA. Guilford Press.

Pentland, A. "What is Social Physics?". Accessed 26 June 2019. www.endor.com/social-physics

Pinker, S. 2012. *The Better Angels of Our Nature: Why Violence Has Declined*. New York, USA. Random House.

Rad, MS, Martingano, AJ and Ginges, J. 2018. "Toward a Psychology of *Homo sapiens*: Making Psychological Science More Representative of the Human Population". *Proceedings of the National Academy of Sciences of the United States of America*. Vol 115, number 45. Pp 11401–11405.

Randall, K. 1999. *Economics: Case, Fair, Heather, Gartner. 1999. New York, USA. Prentice Hall*.

Rapley, J. 2018. "Few Things are as Dangerous as Economists with Physics Envy". 9 February 2018. https://aeon.co/ideas/few-things-are-as-dangerous-as-economists-with-physics-envy

Ricke, K, Drouet, L, Caldeira K and Tavoni, M. 2018. "Country-level Social Cost of Carbon". *Nature Climate Change*. Vol 8. Pp 895–900.

Romer, PM. 2015. "Mathiness in the Theory of Economic Growth". *American Economic Review*. Vol 105, number 5. Pp 89--93.

Roy, EA. 2019. "Grant Robertson: 'New Zealand's Prosperity is About Much More than GDP Growth'". 11 June 2019. https://www.theguardian.com/society/2019/jun/11/grant-robertson-new-zealand-prosperity-growth-wellbeing

Sen, A. 2010. See Fox, J. 2012. *Harvard Business Review*. "The Economics of Well-being". January-February 2012. *https://hbr.org/2012/01/the-economics-of-well-being*

Shankman, P. 2009. *The Trashing of Margaret Mead: Anatomy of an Anthropological Controversy*. Madison, WI, USA. University of Wisconsin Press.

Steinberg, L. 2006. "Risk taking in Adolescence: What Changes and Why?" *New York Academy of Sciences*. Vol 1021, number 1.

Thomson, W. 1883. "Electrical Units of Measurement". Lecture delivered at the Institution of Civil Engineers. 3 May 1883.

Time. 1969. "Behavior: Margaret Mead Today: Mother to the World". 21 March 1969. http://content.time.com/time/magazine/article/0,9171,839916,00.html

Wagner, G. 2004. "Fixing GDP: Green Accounting in the United States". 9 April 2004. https://web.archive.org/web/20070602190235/http://gwagner.com/writing/2004/04/fixing-gdp-green-accounting-in-united.html

Wagner, P. 2001. *A History and Theory of the Social Sciences: Not All That is Solid Melts Into Air*. London, UK. Sage.

Xiaohua, S. 2007. "Call for "Return to Green Accounting". 19 April 2007. www.chinadaily.com.cn/china/2007-04/19/content_853917.htm

Yong, E. 2018. "Psychology's Replication Crisis Is Running Out of Excuses" 19 November 2018. www.theatlantic.com/science/archive/2018/11/psychologys-replication-crisis-real/576223/

Chapter 9

Allbrook, M. 2017. "Indigenous Lives, the 'Cult of Forgetfulness' and the Australian Dictionary of Biography". 1 November 2015. http://theconversation.com/indigenous-lives-the-cult-of-forgetfulness-and-the-australian-dictionary-of-biography-86302

Baggini, J. 2018. "Why Sexist and Racist Philosophers Might Still be Admirable". 7 November 2018. https://aeon.co/ideas/why-sexist-and-racist-philosophers-might-still-be-admirable

Berlin, I. 1969. *Four Essays on Liberty*. Oxford, UK. Oxford University Press.

Carr, EH. 1961. *What is History?* London, UK. Penguin.

Carr, H. 2019. "History According to EH Carr". 8 May 2019. www.newstatesman.com/culture/books/2019/05/eh-carr-what-is-history-truth-subjectivity-facts

Chater, N. 2015. "Hindsight is Not So Wonderful After All Say Scientists" 22 January 2015. www.wbs.ac.uk/news/hindsight-is-not-so-wonderful-after-all-say-scientists/

Collingwood, RG, Dray, WH, van der Dussen, WJ. 1999. *The Principles of History and Other Writings in Philosophy of History*. New York, USA. Oxford University Press.

Daley, P. 2019. "Decolonising the Dictionary: Reclaiming Australian History for the Forgotten". 16 February 2019. www.theguardian.com/books/2019/feb/17/decolonising-the-dictionary-reclaiming-history-for-the-forgotten

Douglas, M. 1986. *How Institutions Think*. New York, USA. Syracuse University Press.

Dunn, S and Faire, L. 2012. *Research Methods for History*. Edinburgh, UK. Edinburgh University Press.

Eklof, B (ed). 1993. *School and Society in Tsarist and Soviet Russia*. London, UK. Palgrave Macmillan.

Elton, G. 1991. *Return to Essentials: Some Reflections on the Present State of Historical Study*. Cambridge, UK. Cambridge University Press.

Evans, R J. 2014. "'What If' is a waste of time" 13 March 2014. www.theguardian.com/books/2014/mar/13/counterfactual-history-what-if-waste-of-time

Gallois, W. 2012. "Ethics and Historical Research". In Dunn, S and Faire, L (eds). *Research Methods for History*. Edinburgh, UK. Edinburgh University Press.

Guha, R. 2019. "The Historian and Chauvinism." 8 March 2019. www.theindiaforum.in/article/historian-and-chauvinism

Horowitz, T. 2012. "Looking at the Battle of Gettysburg Through Robert E. Lee's Eyes". December 2012. www.smithsonianmag.com/history/looking-at-the-battle-of-gettysburg-through-robert-e-lees-eyes-136851113/

Hobsbawm, E. 1993. "The New Threat to History". *New York Review of Books*. 16 December 1993. www.nybooks.com/articles/1993/12/16/the-new-threat-to-history/

Hughes-Warrington, M. 2015. *Fifty Key Thinkers on History* (third edition). London, UK. Routledge.

Jenkins, K. 1995. *On What is History? From Carr and Elton to Rorty and White*. London, UK. Routledge.

Korostelina, KV and Lässig, S (eds). 2013. *History Education and Post-Conflict Reconciliation. Reconsidering Joint Textbook Projects*. Routledge. London, UK. Routledge.

LaCapra, D. 1985 *History and Criticism*. New York, USA. Cornell University Press.

Marshall, BK. 1992. *Teaching the Postmodern*. London, UK. Routledge.

Onion, R. 2015. "What If?". 8 December 2015. https://aeon.co/essays/what-if-historians-started-taking-the-what-if-seriously

Reed, A. 2019. "The Trouble with Uplift". 10 July 2019. https://thebaffler.com/salvos/the-trouble-with-uplift-reed

Roberts, G. 1998. "*Defender of the Faith: Geoffrey Elton and the Philosophy of History*". Chronicon 2. R1: 1–22. http://xml.ucc.ie/chronicon/elton.htm

Rosenthal, F. 1952. *A History of Muslim Historiography*. Leiden, Netherlands. Brill Publishers.

Royal Historical Society. 2018. *Race, Ethnicity and Equality in UK History: A Report and Resource for Change*. London, UK. The Royal Historical Society.

Schmidt, PR and Mrozowski, SA, (eds). 2014. *The Death of Prehistory*. Oxford, UK. Oxford University Press.

Smith, LT. 1999. *Decolonizing Methodologies: Research and Indigenous Peoples* (second edition). London, UK. Zed Books.

Spiegel, GM. 1992. "History and Post-Modernism". *Past and Present*. Vol 135, number 1. Pp 194–208.

Spinney, L. 2012. "Human Cycles: History as Science". *Nature News*. 1 August 2012. https://www.nature.com/news/human-cycles-history-as-science-1.11078

Chapter 10

Abbott, K. 2012. "How We Made: John Berger and Michael Dibb on 'Ways of Seeing'". 2 April 2012. www.theguardian.com/culture/2012/apr/02/how-we-made-ways-seeing

Alexander, E. 2005. *American Sublime: Poems*. Minneapolis. MN, USA. Graywolf Press.

Alexander, E. 2016. "The Desire to Know Each Other". 11 April 2016. https://onbeing.org/programs/desire-know-elizabeth-alexander-2/

Appiah, KA. 2006. *Cosmopolitanism*. New York, USA. WW Norton.

Berger, J. 1972. *Ways of Seeing*. London, UK. BBC/Penguin.

Bodrogi, T. 1968. *Art in Africa*. Budapest, Hungary. Kossuth Printing House.

Bredius, A. 1937. "A New Vermeer". *Burlington Magazine*. Vol 71. Pp 210–211.

Butler, J. 2007. "Torture and the Ethics of Photography". *Environment and Planning D: Society and Space*. Vol 25. Pp 951–966.

Cuno, J.2001. "Museums and the Acquisition of Antiquities". *Cardozo Arts & Entertainment Law Journal*. Vol 19, number 1. P 85.

Dalrymple, W. 2009. *Nine Lives: In Search of the Sacred in Modern India*. New York, USA. Vintage Books.

Daly, P. 2015. "Indigenous Leaders Fight for Return of Relics Featuring in Major New Exhibition". 14 February 2015. www.theguardian.com/australia-news/postcolonial-blog/2015/feb/14/it-taunts-us-spiritually-the-fight-for-indigenous-relics-spirited-off-to-the-uk

Danto, A. 1964. "The Artworld". *The Journal of Philosophy*. Vol. 61, number 19. Pp. 571–584.

Digby, W. 1878. *The Famine Campaign in Southern India (Madras and Bombay Presidencies and Province of Mysore) 1876–1878*. London, UK. Longmans.

Farago, J. 2015. "To Return or Not: Who should Own Indigenous Art?" 21 April 2015. www.bbc.com/culture/story/20150421-who-should-own-indigenous-art

Franzen, C. 2013. "Ill-gotten Gains: How Many Museums have Stolen Objects in their Collections?" 13 May 2013. www.theverge.com/2013/5/13/4326306/museum-artifacts-looted-repatriation

Gula, S. 2017. "Deported Afghan Girl says NatGeo Picture Caused More Pain than Gain". 19 January 2017. https://tribune.com.pk/story/1299147/deported-afghan-girl-says-natgeo-picture-caused-pain-gain/

Hegenbart, S. 2019. "Zombie Formalism: Or How Financial Values Pervade the Art" 31 July, 2019. https://aestheticsforbirds.com/2019/07/31/zombie-formalism-or-how-financial-values-pervade-the-arts/

Holland, C. 2018. "You Have Our Soul": Easter Island Pleads with British for Statue's Return". 22 November 2018. https://edition.cnn.com/style/article/easter-island-british-museum-moai-return/index.html

Johnson, K. 2009. "From China, Iraq and Beyond, but Is It Art?" 19 February 2009. www.nytimes.com/2009/02/20/arts/design/20new.html

Johnson, W. 2010. "In Focus: Starved for Attention".13 July 2010. www.newyorker.com/culture/photo-booth/in-focus-starved-for-attention

Joy, C. 2019. "Does Art Have A Homeland?". 6 March 2019. www.sapiens.org/culture/patrimony-heritage-art/

Konde, E. 2014. *The African Bronze Art Culture of the Bight of Benin and its Influence on Modern Art.* Albany State University. Albaby, GA, USA.

Le Guin, U. 2016. *Words are My Matter*. Easthampton, MA, USA. Small Beer Press.

Matthes, EH. 2017. "Repatriation and the Radical Redistribution of Art". *Ergo*. Vol 4, number 32. P 1.

Merryman, J H. 1986. "Two Ways of Thinking About Cultural Property". *The American Journal of International Law.* Vol 80, number 4. P 836.

Neate, R. 2019. "Mind my Picasso … Superyacht Owners Struggle to Protect Art". 2 February 2019. www.theguardian.com/news/2019/feb/02/cornflakes-on-the-basquiat-perils-of-superyacht-art

Ngozi Adichie, Chimamanda. 2006. "Our 'Africa' Lenses From the West, Big Labels but Little Context". 13 November 2006. www.washingtonpost.com/archive/opinions/2006/11/13/our-africa-lenses-span-classbank-headfrom-the-west-big-labels-but-little-contextspan/a9f-2cc39-88f7-4ea6-832c-0e80eba43557/

Omland, A. 2006. "The Ethics of the World Heritage Concept". In Scarre, C and Scarre, G (eds). *The Ethics of Archaeology: Philosophical Perspectives on Archaeological Practice* . P 247. Cambridge, UK. Cambridge University Press.

Picasso, P. Quoted in 1976. "Modern Living: Ozmosis in Central Park". *Time Magazine*. 4 October 1976. http://content.time.com/time/magazine/article/0,9171,918412,00.html

Sandy, NS. 2019 "Unpacking Medieval African Art's Profound Global Legacy". 21 January 2019. www.artsy.net/article/artsy-editorial-unpacking-medieval-african-arts-profound-global-legacy

Stanley-Becker, I. 2019. "He Dunked a Crucifix in his own Urine. His Next Artistic Subject: Donald Trump". 2 April 2019. www.washingtonpost.com/nation/2019/04/02/he-dunked-crucifix-his-own-urine-his-next-artistic-subject-donald-trump/

Tharoor, K. 2015. "Museums and Looted Art: The Ethical Dilemma of Preserving World Cultures". 29 June 2015. www.theguardian.com/culture/2015/jun/29/museums-looting-art-artefacts-world-culture

Thompson, J. 2003. "Cultural Property, Restitution and Value". *Journal of Applied Philosophy.* Vol 20, number 3. P 252.

Thompson, J. 2004. "Art, Property Rights, and the Interests of Humanity." *The Journal of Value Inquiry*. Vol 38, number 4. Pp 558–559.

Thompson, N. 2015. *Seeing Power: Art and Activism in the Twenty-First Century.* New York, USA. Melville House.

Tippett, K. 2016. "Elizabeth Alexander The Desire to Know Each Other". 11 April 2016. https://onbeing.org/programs/desire-know-elizabeth-alexander-2/

Tommasini, A. 2001. "Music: The Devil Made Him Do It".30 September 2001. www.nytimes.com/2001/09/30/arts/music-the-devil-made-him-do-it.html

Tribune News Desk. 2017. "Deported Afghan Girl says NatGeo Picture Caused More Pain than Gain".

19 January 2017. https://tribune.com.pk/story/1299147/deported-afghan-girl-says-natgeo-picture-caused-pain-gain/

van de Gaag, N and Nash, C. 1987. *Images of Africa: The UK Report. Oxford, UK. Oxfam.*

Vatter, E. 1926. *Religiöse der Naturvölker.* Frankfurt, Germany. Frankfurter Verlags-Anstalt.

Wynne, F. 2006. *I Was Vermeer: The Rise and Fall of the Twentieth-Century's Greatest Forger*. New York, USA. Bloomsbury Press.

Chapter 11

Abbott, D. 2013. "The Reasonable Ineffectiveness of Mathematics (Point of View),". *Proceedings of the IEEE*. Vol 101, number 10. Pp 2147–53.

Alexander, A. 2010. *Duel at Dawn: Heroes, Martyrs, and the Rise of Modern Mathematics*. Cambridge, MA, USA. Harvard University Press.

Alexander, A. 2014. *Infinitesimal*. London, UK. Oneworld Publications.

Ascher, M. 1991. *Ethnomathematics*: *A Multicultural View of Mathematical Ideas*. Boca Raton, FL, USA. CRC Press.

Avigad, J. 2018. "Principia". 28 September 2018. https://aeon.co/amp/essays/does-philosophy-still-need-mathematics-and-vice-versa

Ball, P. 2017. "How Natural is Numeracy?" Aeon. 26 October 2017. https://aeon.co/essays/why-do-humans-have-numbers-are-they-cultural-or-innate

Bickel, PJ, Hammel, EA and O'Connell, JW. 1975. "Sex Bias in Graduate Admissions: Data From Berkeley". *Science*. Vol 187, number 4175. Pp 398–404. doi:10.1126/science.187.4175.398. PMID 17835295.

Birman, J. 2007. "Mathematical Community Should Police Itself". *Notices of the American Mathematical Society*. Vol 54, number 1. P 6.

Borovik, A. 2018. "Unreasonable Ineffectiveness of Mathematics in Biology" 14 April 2018. https://micromath.wordpress.com/2018/04/14/unreasonable-ineffectiveness-of-mathematics-in-biology/

Boyer, CB. 1991. *A History of Mathematics* (second edition). New York, USA. Wiley.

Brodie, K. 2016. "Yes, Mathematics can be Decolonized. Here's How to Begin". 13 October 2016. https://theconversation.com/yes-mathematics-can-be-decolonised-heres-how-to-begin-65963

Brown, K. 2019. "Zeno and the Paradox of Motion". *Reflections on Relativity*. MathPages. https://mathpages.com/rr/s3-07/3-07.htm

Chiodo, M and Bursill-Hall, P. 2018. "Four Levels of Ethical Engagement Discussion" paper 18/1. Cambridge University Ethics in Mathematics Project. https://ethics.maths.cam.ac.uk/pub

Chiodo, M and Bursill-Hall, P. 2019. "Motivation of the Workshop". 5 April 2019. https://ethics.maths.cam.ac.uk/EiM2/

Cohen, JE. 2004. "Mathematics is Biology's Next Microscope, Only Better; Biology is Mathematics' Next Physics, Only Better". PLoS Biology. Vol 2, number 12. Pp 2017–23.

dePillis, J. 2002. *777 Mathematical Conversations*. Washington, DC, USA. Mathematical Association of America.

Desikan, S. 2016. "Math is Awesome, Math Culture is Terrible". Interview with Piper Harron. 23 August 2016. https://www.thehindu.com/thread/arts-culture-society/article9022211.ece

Devlin, K. 2000. *The Math Gene: How Mathematical Thinking Evolved And Why Numbers Are Like Gossip*. New York, USA. Basic Books.

Eglash, R. 1999. *African Fractals: Modern Computing and Indigenous Design*. Piscataway, NJ, USA. Rutgers University Press.

Einstein, A. 1922. *Geometry and Experience*. London, UK. Methuen & Co.

Ernest, P (ed). 2018. *The Philosophy of Mathematics Education Today*. ICME-13 Monographs. Cham, Switzerland. Springer. https://doi.org/10.1007/978-3-319-77760-3_12

Feynman, RP. 1977. *The Feynman Lectures on Physics, vol. I*. Boston, MA, USA. Addison-Wesley.

Franklin, J. 1991. "Ethics of Mathematics". *The Mathematical Intelligencer*. Vol 13, number 1.

Franklin. J. 2014. "The Mathematical World". 7 April 2014. https://aeon.co/essays/aristotle-was-right-about-mathematics-after-all

Fraser, C. 2017. "School of Names". *The Stanford Encyclopedia of Philosophy* (Spring 2017 edition). Zalta, EN (ed). https://plato.stanford.edu/archives/spr2017/entries/school-names/

Freiberger, M and Thomas, R. 2015."The Future of Proof". 10 April 2015. https://plus.maths.org/content/future-proof

Galileo, G. 1632. *Opere Il Saggiatore* (*The Assayer*). https://www.loc.gov/item/29030462. P 171.

Gallagher, J. 2014. "Mathematics: Why the Brain Sees Maths as Beauty". 13 February 2014. Institute of Mathematics and its Applications. https://www.bbc.com/news/science-environment-26151062

Gutierrez, R. 2018. "Political Conocimiento for Teaching Mathematics: Why Teachers Need it and How to Develop it". In Kastberg, SE, Tyminski, AM, Lischka, AE and Sanchez, WB (eds). *Building Support for Scholarly Practices in Mathematics Methods*. Charlotte, NC, USA. Information Age Publishing.

Halberda, J, Mazzocco, MM and Feigenson, L. 2008. "Individual differences in non-verbal number acuity correlate with maths achievement". *Nature*. Vol 455. Pp 665—668.

Hamming, R. 1980. "The Unreasonable Effectiveness of Mathematics". *The American Mathematical Monthly*. Vol 87, number 2. Pp 81–90.

Hardy, GH. 2004. Originally published 1940. *A Mathematician's Apology*. Cambridge, UK. Cambridge University Press.

Harron, P. 2016. "The Equidistribution of Lattice Shapes of Rings of Integers of Cubic, Quartic, and Quintic Number Fields: An Artist's Rendering". *Proceedings of the American Mathematical Society*.

Hersh, R. 1990. "Mathematics and Ethics". *The Mathematical Intelligencer*. Vol 12, number 3. P 22.

Hill, R. 2004. "Multiple Sudden Infant Deaths—Coincidence or Beyond Coincidence?" *Paediatric and Perinatal Epidemiology*. Vol 18. Pp 320–326.

Joseph, GG. 2011. *The Crest of the Peacock: Non-European Roots of Mathematics*. Princeton, NJ, USA. Princeton University Press.

Kline, M. 1985. *Mathematics for the Nonmathematician*. New York, USA. Dover Publications.

Kline, M. 1990. *Mathematical Thought from Ancient to Modern Times*. New York, USA. Oxford University Press.

Lamb, E. 2017. "The Impossible Mathematics of the Real World". 8 June 2017. http://nautil.us/issue/49/the-absurd/the-impossible-mathematics-of-the-real-world

Lehman, H. 1974. "Is Mathematics a Theoretical Juice Extractor?" *Philosophical Forum*. Vol 6, number 2. P 237.

Levy-Eichel, M. 2018. "Mathematics as Thought". 11 October 2018. https://aeon.co/essays/the-secret-intellectual-history-of-mathematics

Lockhart, P. 2009. *A Mathematician's Lament*. New York, USA. Bellevue Literary Press.

Martin, G. 1956. *Mathematics Magic and Magic*. New York, USA. Dover Publications.

Meissner, G (ed). 2008. *The Definitive Guide to CDOs*. London, UK. Risk Books.

Nagarajan, VR. 2019. *Feeding a Thousand Souls: Women, Ritual and Ecology in India, an Exploration of the Kōlam*. Oxford, UK. Oxford University Press.

Nahin, PJ. 2006. *Dr. Euler's Fabulous Formula: Cures Many Mathematical Ills*. Princeton NJ, USA. Princeton University Press.

Nassar, S and Gruber, D. 2006. "Manifold Destiny". *The New Yorker*. 28 August 2006. Retrieved from https://www.newyorker.com/magazine/2006/08/28/manifold-destiny

Notices of the American Mathematical Society. 2008. "Computers Effective In Verifying Mathematical Proofs". 6 November 2008.

O'Neil, C. 2016. *Weapons of Math Destruction: How Big Data Increases Inequality and Threatens Democracy*. New York, USA. Crown Publishing, Penguin Random House.

Royal Statistical Society. 2001. "Royal Statistical Society Concerned by Issues Raised in Sally Clark Case" 23 October 2001. https://www.rss.org.uk/Images/PDF/influencing-change/2017/SallyClarkRSSstatement2001.pdf

Russell, B. 1919. *Mysticism and Logic: And Other Essays*. London, UK. Longman.

Salmon, F. 2009. "Recipe for Disaster: The Formula that Killed Wall Street". 23 Feb 2009. https://www.wired.com/2009/02/wp-quant/

Singh, S. 1998. *Fermat's Enigma: The Epic Quest to Solve the World's Greatest Mathematical Problem*. New York, USA. Random House.

Singh, S. 2013. *The Simpsons and Their Mathematical Secrets*. New York, USA. Bloomsbury.

Teller, P. 1980. "Computer Proof". *The Journal of Philosophy*. Vol 77, number 12. Pp 797–803.

Tymoczko, T. 1979. "The Four-Color Problem and its Mathematical Significance". *The Journal of Philosophy*. Vol 76, number 2. Pp 57–83.

von Neumann, J. 1947. *Works of the Mind Volume I Number 1*. Chicago. IL, USA. University of Chicago Press.

Wertheim, M. 2017. "How to Play Mathematics". 7 February 2017. https://aeon.co/essays/theres-more-maths-in-slugs-and-corals-than-we-can-think-of

Whitehouse, M. 2005. "How a Formula Ignited Markets That Burned Some Big Investors". 12 September 2005. *The Wall Street Journal*. https://www.wsj.com/articles/SB112649094075137685

Wigner, E. 1960. "The Unreasonable Effectiveness of Mathematics in the Natural Sciences". *Communications in Pure and Applied Mathematics*. Vol 13. Pp 1–14.

Wolchover, N. 2013. "In Computers We Trust?" 22 February 2017. https://www.quantamagazine.org/in-computers-we-trust-20130222/

Zeki S, Romaya JP, Benincasa, DMT and Atiyah, MF. 2014. "The Experience of Mathematical Beauty and its Neural Correlates". *Frontiers in Human Neuroscience*. https://doi.org/10.3389/fnhum.2014.00068

Chapter 12

Mead, M. 1950. *Sex and Temperament in Three Primitive Societies*. First published 1935. London UK. Routledge and Kegan Paul.